TRANSFORMERS
WINDBLADE

Licensed By:

Facebook: **facebook.com/idwpublishing**
Twitter: **@idwpublishing**
YouTube: **youtube.com/idwpublishing**
Tumblr: **tumblr.idwpublishing.com**
Instagram: **instagram.com/idwpublishing**

COVER ART BY
SARA PITRE-DUROCHER

COLLECTION EDITS BY
JUSTIN EISINGER
AND ALONZO SIMON

COLLECTION DESIGN BY
JEFF POWELL

PUBLISHER
TED ADAMS

ISBN: 978-1-68405-224-0   21 20 19 18   1 2 3 4

Originally published as THE TRANSFORMERS: WINDBLADE issues #1–4,
and THE TRANSFORMERS: WINDBLADE VOLUME 2 issues #1–7.

Ted Adams, CEO & Publisher
Greg Goldstein, President & COO
Robbie Robbins, EVP/Sr. Graphic Artist
Chris Ryall, Chief Creative Officer
David Hedgecock, Editor-in-Chief
Laurie Windrow, Senior VP of Sales & Marketing
Matthew Ruzicka, CPA, Chief Financial Officer
Lorelei Bunjes, VP of Digital Services
Jerry Bennington, VP of New Product Development

Special thanks to Ben Montano, David Erwin,
Josh Feldman, Ed Lane, Beth Artale, and
Michael Kelly for their invaluable assistance.

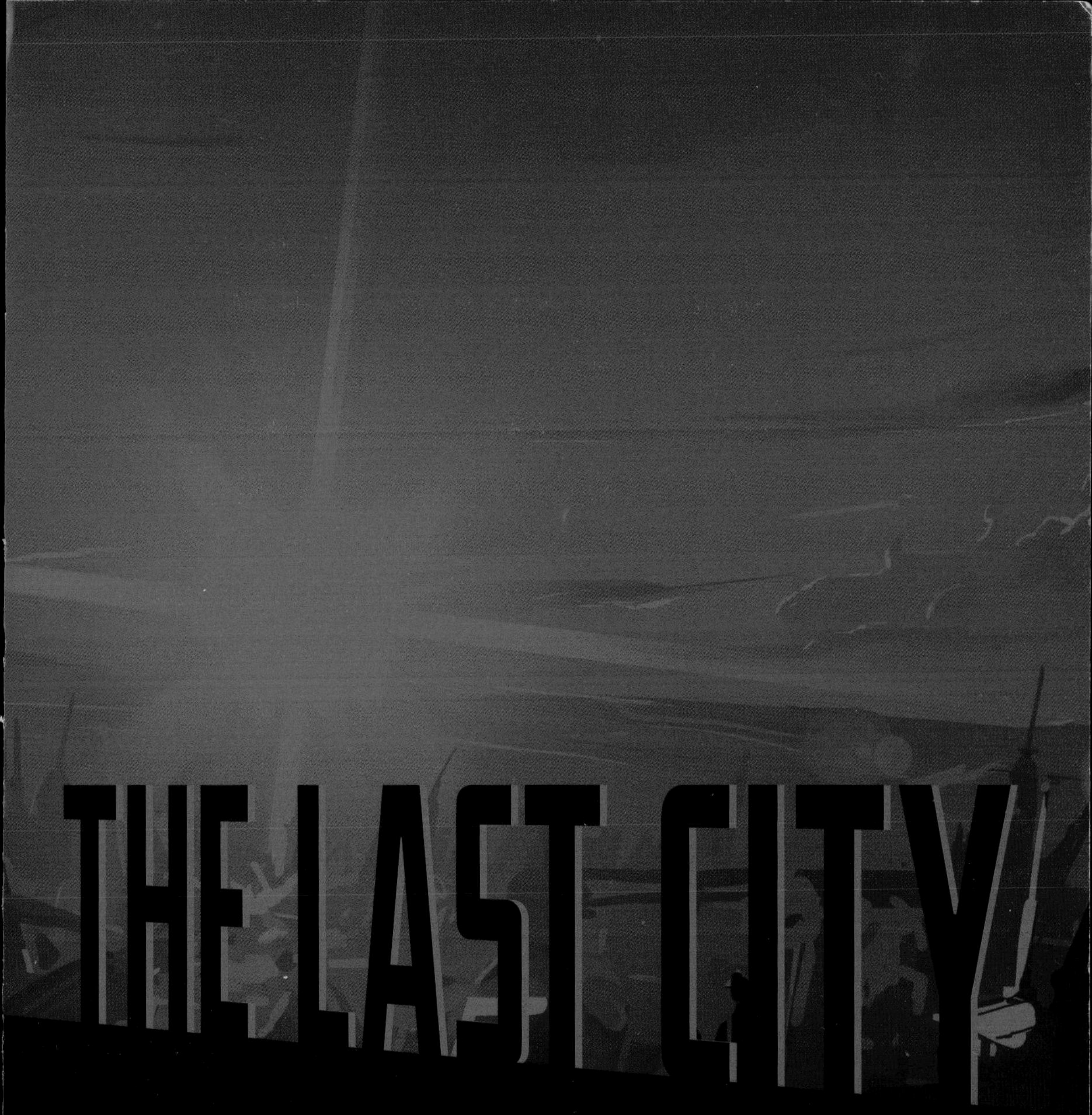

THE LAST CITY

WRITTEN BY
MAIRGHREAD SCOTT

ART BY
SARAH STONE (PT. 1–5),
LIVIO RAMONDELLI (PT. 6),
MARCELO FERREIRA (PT. 7),
CORIN HOWELL (PT. 7–11), AND
SARA PITRE-DUROCHER (PT. 12)

ADDITIONAL INKS BY
CORIN HOWELL (PT. 7),
BRIAN SHEARER (PT. 7), AND
JOHN WYCOUGH (PT. 7)

COLORS BY
YAMAISHI (PT. 7 & 12),
THOMAS DEER (PT. 7–11), AND
JOHN-PAUL BOVE (PT. 11)

LETTERS BY
CHRIS MOWRY AND
TOM B. LONG

SERIES EDITS BY
JOHN BARBER AND
CARLOS GUZMAN

ART BY **CASEY W. COLLER**
COLORS BY **JOANA LAFUENTE**

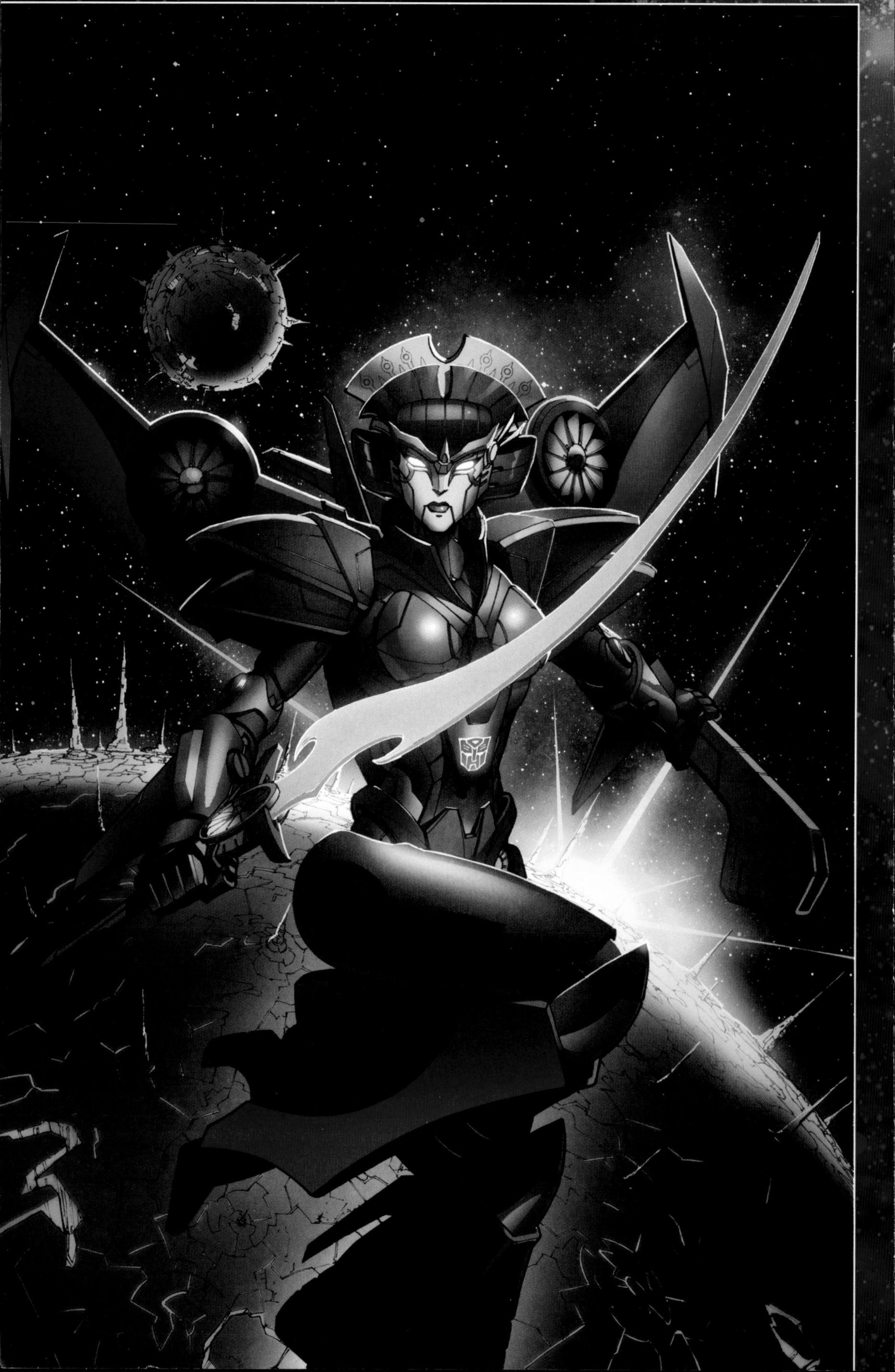

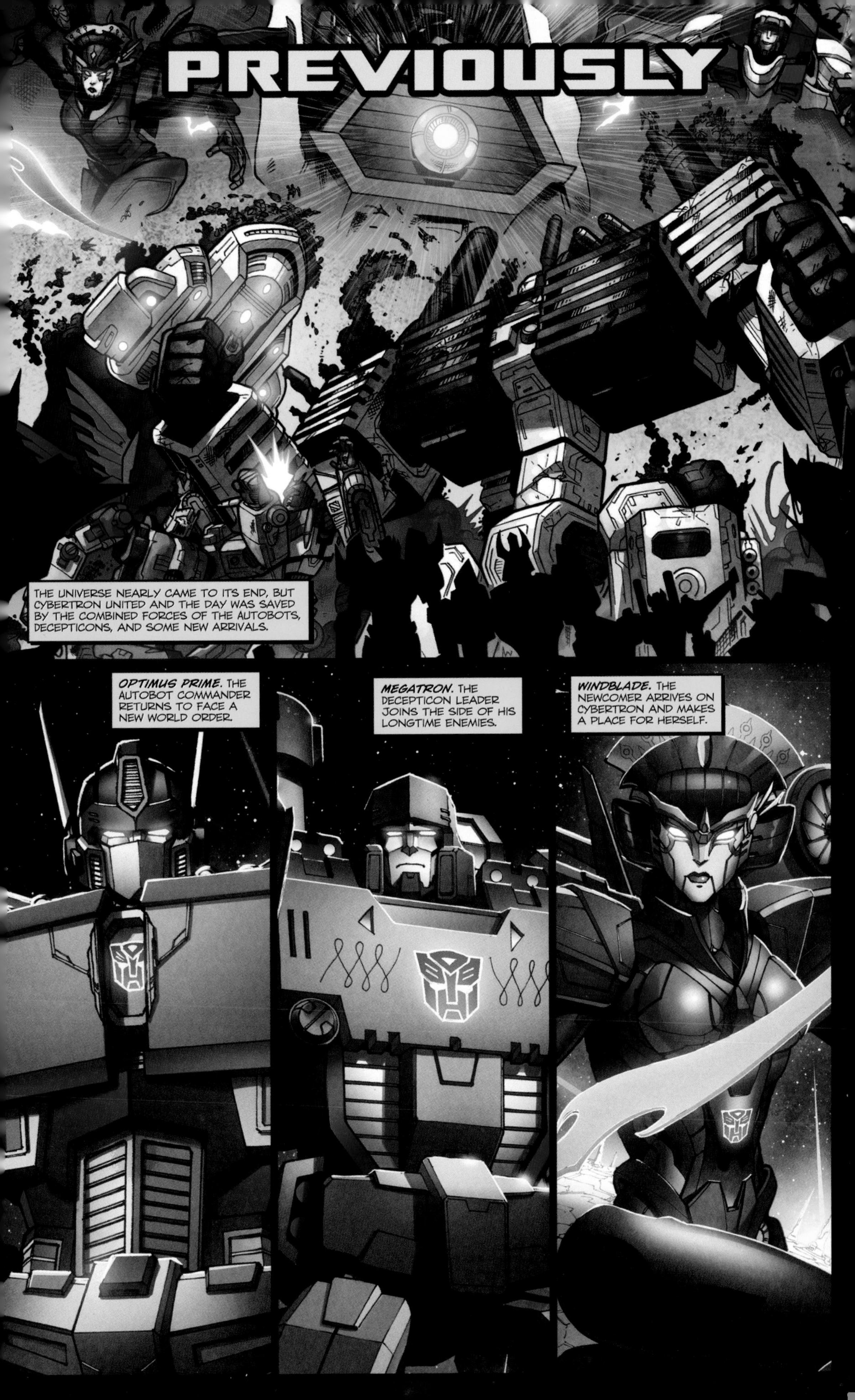
PREVIOUSLY
THE UNIVERSE NEARLY CAME TO ITS END, BUT CYBERTRON UNITED AND THE DAY WAS SAVED BY THE COMBINED FORCES OF THE AUTOBOTS, DECEPTICONS, AND SOME NEW ARRIVALS.
OPTIMUS PRIME. THE AUTOBOT COMMANDER RETURNS TO FACE A NEW WORLD ORDER.
MEGATRON. THE DECEPTICON LEADER JOINS THE SIDE OF HIS LONGTIME ENEMIES.
WINDBLADE. THE NEWCOMER ARRIVES ON CYBERTRON AND MAKES A PLACE FOR HERSELF.

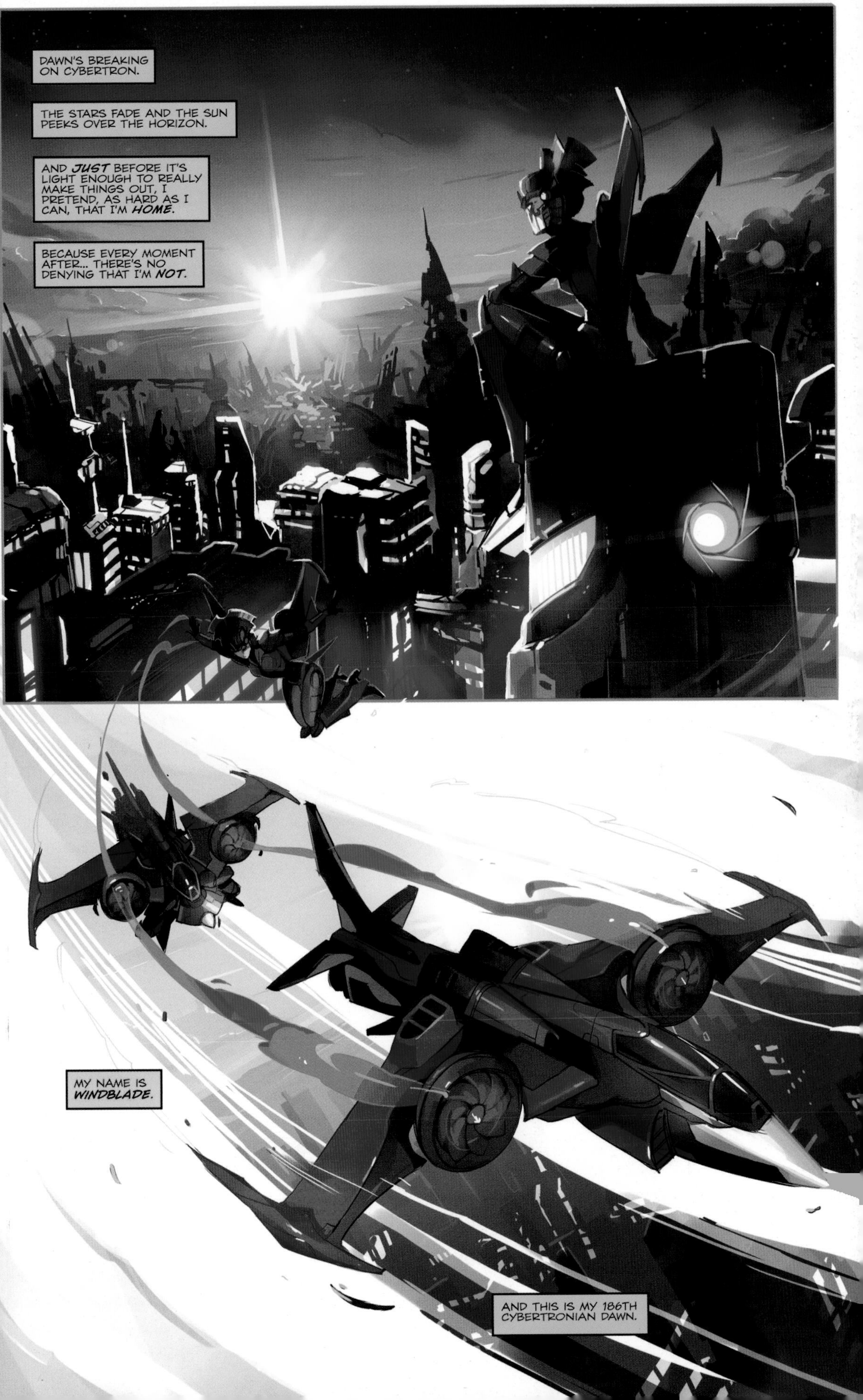
DAWN'S BREAKING ON CYBERTRON.
THE STARS FADE AND THE SUN PEEKS OVER THE HORIZON.
AND JUST BEFORE IT'S LIGHT ENOUGH TO REALLY MAKE THINGS OUT, I PRETEND, AS HARD AS I CAN, THAT I'M HOME.
BECAUSE EVERY MOMENT AFTER... THERE'S NO DENYING THAT I'M NOT.
MY NAME IS WINDBLADE.
AND THIS IS MY 186TH CYBERTRONIAN DAWN.

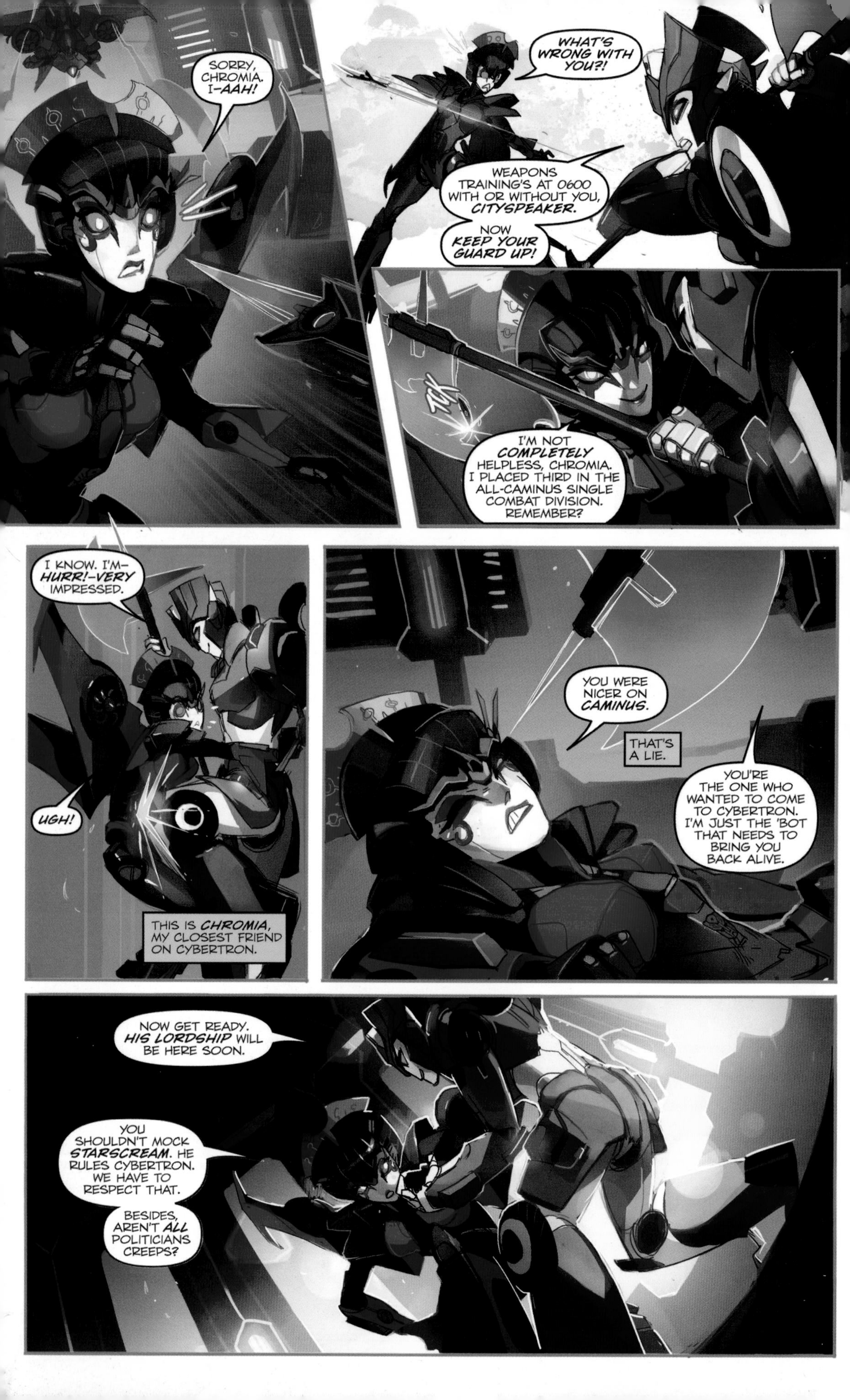
SORRY, CHROMIA. I-AAH!
WHAT'S WRONG WITH YOU?!
WEAPONS TRAINING'S AT 0600 WITH OR WITHOUT YOU, CITYSPEAKER.
NOW KEEP YOUR GUARD UP!
TCK
I'M NOT COMPLETELY HELPLESS, CHROMIA. I PLACED THIRD IN THE ALL-CAMINUS SINGLE COMBAT DIVISION. REMEMBER?
I KNOW. I'M-HURR!-VERY IMPRESSED.
UGH!
THIS IS CHROMIA, MY CLOSEST FRIEND ON CYBERTRON.
YOU WERE NICER ON CAMINUS.
THAT'S A LIE.
YOU'RE THE ONE WHO WANTED TO COME TO CYBERTRON. I'M JUST THE 'BOT THAT NEEDS TO BRING YOU BACK ALIVE.
NOW GET READY. HIS LORDSHIP WILL BE HERE SOON.
YOU SHOULDN'T MOCK STARSCREAM. HE RULES CYBERTRON. WE HAVE TO RESPECT THAT.
BESIDES, AREN'T ALL POLITICIANS CREEPS?

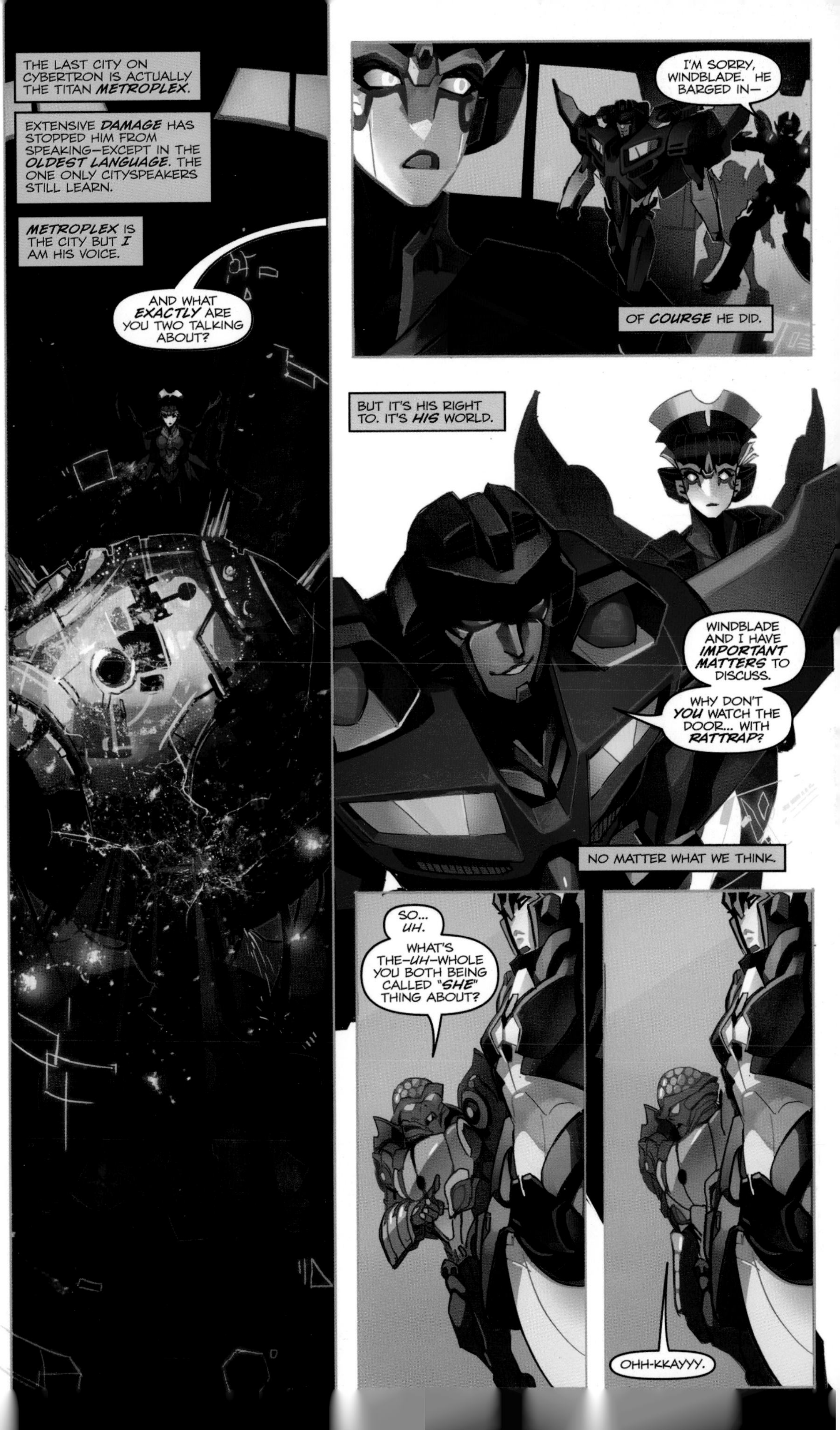
THE LAST CITY ON CYBERTRON IS ACTUALLY THE TITAN METROPLEX.
EXTENSIVE DAMAGE HAS STOPPED HIM FROM SPEAKING—EXCEPT IN THE OLDEST LANGUAGE. THE ONE ONLY CITYSPEAKERS STILL LEARN.
METROPLEX IS THE CITY BUT I AM HIS VOICE.
AND WHAT EXACTLY ARE YOU TWO TALKING ABOUT?
I'M SORRY, WINDBLADE. HE BARGED IN—
OF COURSE HE DID.
BUT IT'S HIS RIGHT TO. IT'S HIS WORLD.
WINDBLADE AND I HAVE IMPORTANT MATTERS TO DISCUSS.
WHY DON'T YOU WATCH THE DOOR... WITH RATTRAP?
NO MATTER WHAT WE THINK.
SO... UH.
WHAT'S THE-UH-WHOLE YOU BOTH BEING CALLED "SHE" THING ABOUT?
OHH-KKAYYY.

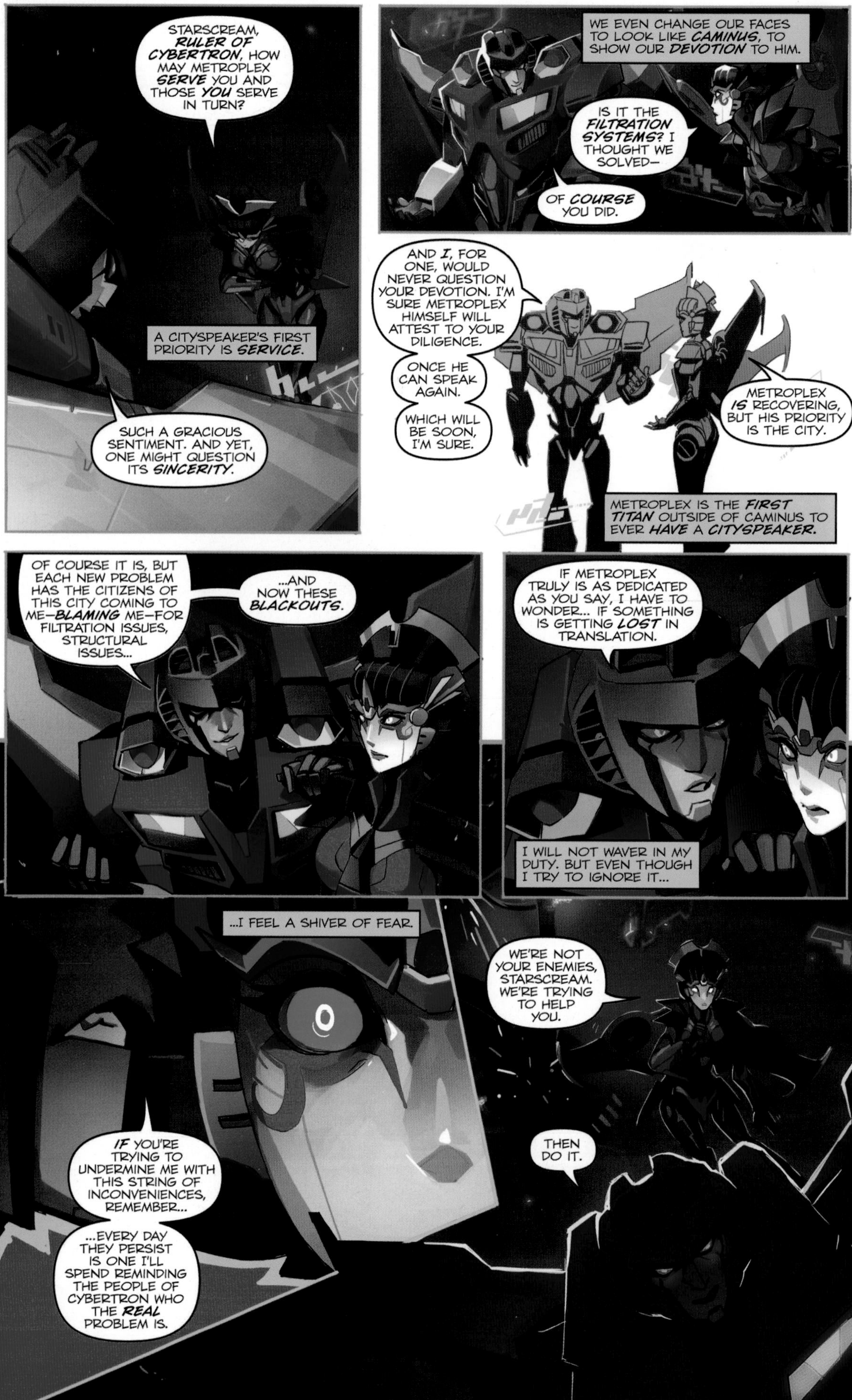
STARSCREAM, RULER OF CYBERTRON, HOW MAY METROPLEX SERVE YOU AND THOSE YOU SERVE IN TURN?
A CITYSPEAKER'S FIRST PRIORITY IS SERVICE.
SUCH A GRACIOUS SENTIMENT. AND YET, ONE MIGHT QUESTION ITS SINCERITY.
WE EVEN CHANGE OUR FACES TO LOOK LIKE CAMINUS, TO SHOW OUR DEVOTION TO HIM.
IS IT THE FILTRATION SYSTEMS? I THOUGHT WE SOLVED—
OF COURSE YOU DID.
AND I, FOR ONE, WOULD NEVER QUESTION YOUR DEVOTION. I'M SURE METROPLEX HIMSELF WILL ATTEST TO YOUR DILIGENCE.
ONCE HE CAN SPEAK AGAIN.
WHICH WILL BE SOON, I'M SURE.
METROPLEX IS RECOVERING, BUT HIS PRIORITY IS THE CITY.
METROPLEX IS THE FIRST TITAN OUTSIDE OF CAMINUS TO EVER HAVE A CITYSPEAKER.
OF COURSE IT IS, BUT EACH NEW PROBLEM HAS THE CITIZENS OF THIS CITY COMING TO ME—BLAMING ME—FOR FILTRATION ISSUES, STRUCTURAL ISSUES...
...AND NOW THESE BLACKOUTS.
IF METROPLEX TRULY IS AS DEDICATED AS YOU SAY, I HAVE TO WONDER... IF SOMETHING IS GETTING LOST IN TRANSLATION.
I WILL NOT WAVER IN MY DUTY. BUT EVEN THOUGH I TRY TO IGNORE IT...
...I FEEL A SHIVER OF FEAR.
WE'RE NOT YOUR ENEMIES, STARSCREAM. WE'RE TRYING TO HELP YOU.
THEN DO IT.
IF YOU'RE TRYING TO UNDERMINE ME WITH THIS STRING OF INCONVENIENCES, REMEMBER...
...EVERY DAY THEY PERSIST IS ONE I'LL SPEND REMINDING THE PEOPLE OF CYBERTRON WHO THE REAL PROBLEM IS.

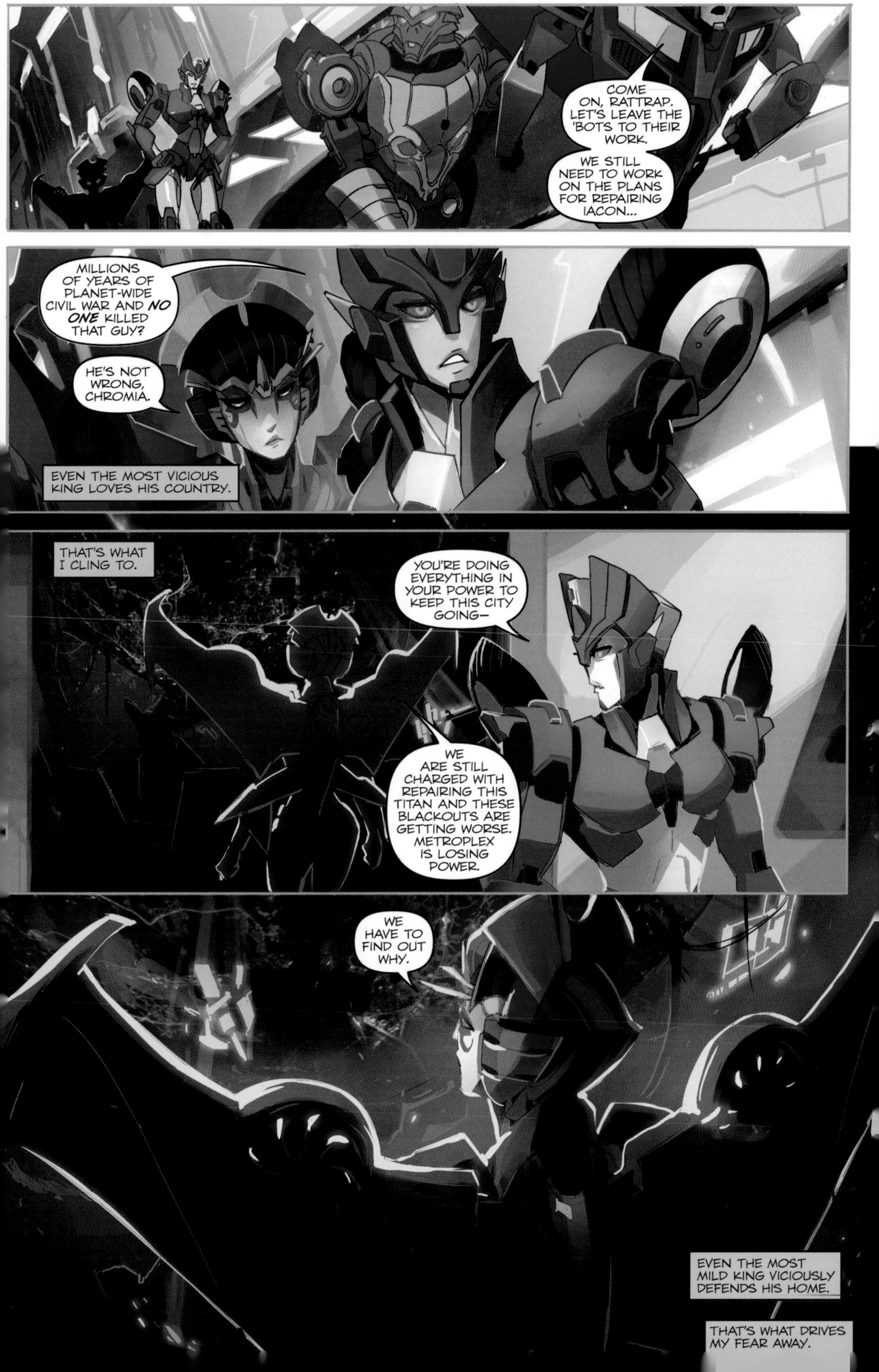
COME ON, RATTRAP. LET'S LEAVE THE 'BOTS TO THEIR WORK.
WE STILL NEED TO WORK ON THE PLANS FOR REPAIRING IACON...
MILLIONS OF YEARS OF PLANET-WIDE CIVIL WAR AND NO ONE KILLED THAT GUY?
HE'S NOT WRONG, CHROMIA.
EVEN THE MOST VICIOUS KING LOVES HIS COUNTRY.
THAT'S WHAT I CLING TO.
YOU'RE DOING EVERYTHING IN YOUR POWER TO KEEP THIS CITY GOING—
WE ARE STILL CHARGED WITH REPAIRING THIS TITAN AND THESE BLACKOUTS ARE GETTING WORSE. METROPLEX IS LOSING POWER.
WE HAVE TO FIND OUT WHY.
EVEN THE MOST MILD KING VICIOUSLY DEFENDS HIS HOME.
THAT'S WHAT DRIVES MY FEAR AWAY.

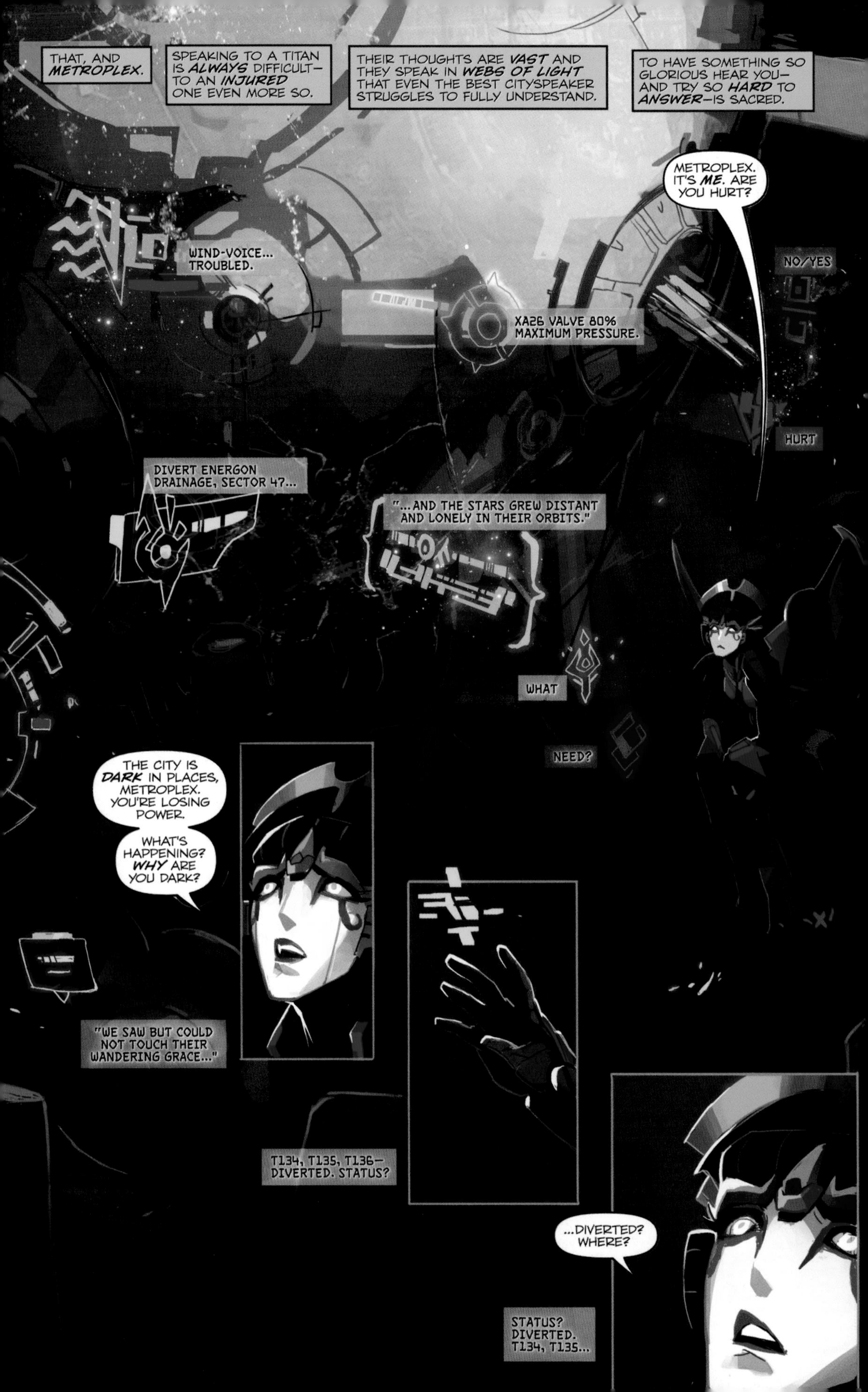

THAT, AND METROPLEX.
SPEAKING TO A TITAN IS ALWAYS DIFFICULT—TO AN INJURED ONE EVEN MORE SO.
THEIR THOUGHTS ARE VAST AND THEY SPEAK IN WEBS OF LIGHT THAT EVEN THE BEST CITYSPEAKER STRUGGLES TO FULLY UNDERSTAND.
TO HAVE SOMETHING SO GLORIOUS HEAR YOU—AND TRY SO HARD TO ANSWER—IS SACRED.
METROPLEX. IT'S ME. ARE YOU HURT?
WIND-VOICE... TROUBLED.
XA26 VALVE 80% MAXIMUM PRESSURE.
NO/YES
HURT
DIVERT ENERGON DRAINAGE, SECTOR 47...
"...AND THE STARS GREW DISTANT AND LONELY IN THEIR ORBITS."
WHAT
NEED?
THE CITY IS DARK IN PLACES, METROPLEX. YOU'RE LOSING POWER.
WHAT'S HAPPENING? WHY ARE YOU DARK?
"WE SAW BUT COULD NOT TOUCH THEIR WANDERING GRACE..."
T134, T135, T136—DIVERTED. STATUS?
...DIVERTED? WHERE?
STATUS? DIVERTED. T134, T135...

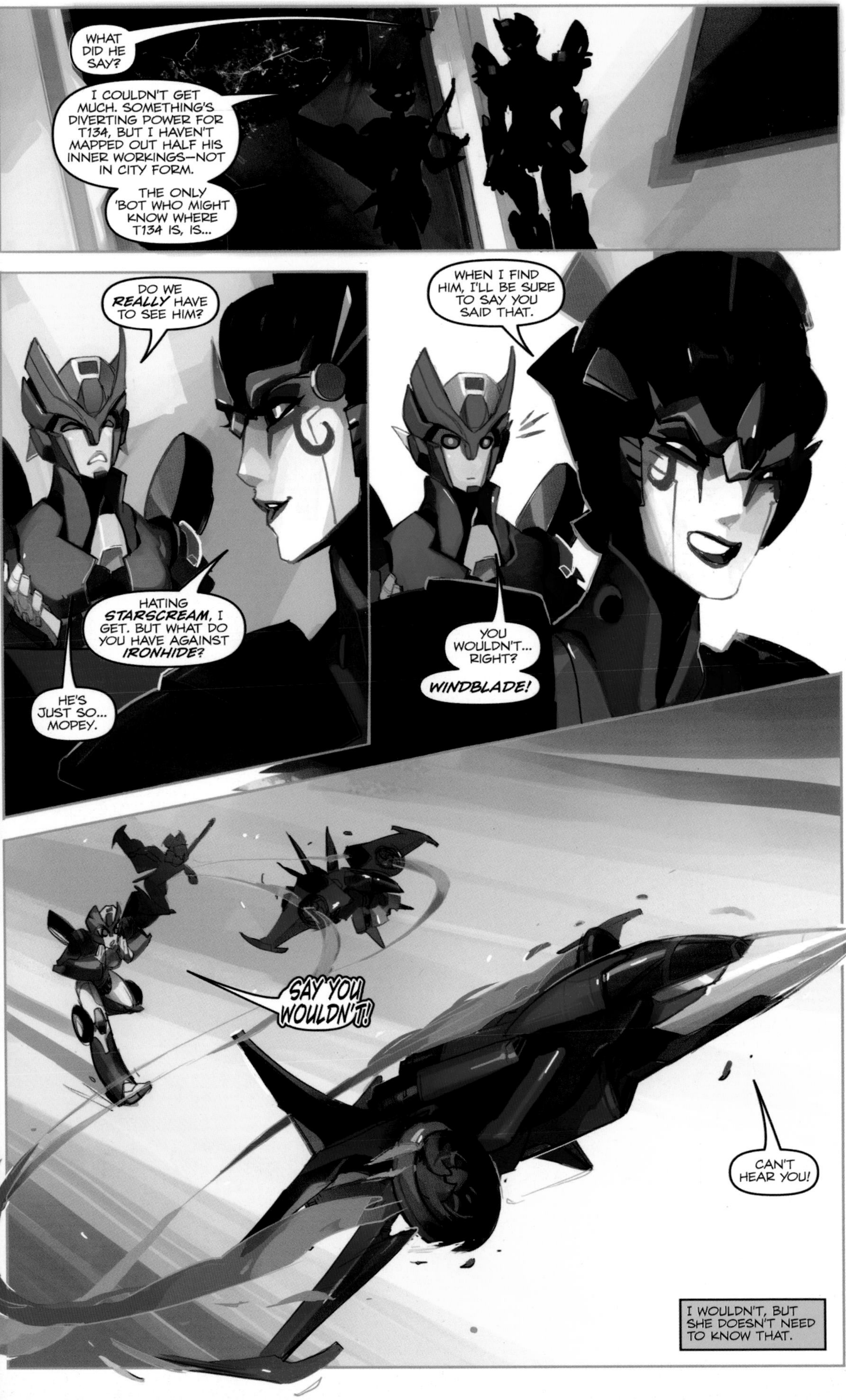
WHAT DID HE SAY?
I COULDN'T GET MUCH. SOMETHING'S DIVERTING POWER FOR T134, BUT I HAVEN'T MAPPED OUT HALF HIS INNER WORKINGS—NOT IN CITY FORM.
THE ONLY 'BOT WHO MIGHT KNOW WHERE T134 IS, IS...
DO WE *REALLY* HAVE TO SEE HIM?
HATING *STARSCREAM*, I GET. BUT WHAT DO YOU HAVE AGAINST *IRONHIDE*?
HE'S JUST SO... MOPEY.
WHEN I FIND HIM, I'LL BE SURE TO SAY YOU SAID THAT.
YOU WOULDN'T... RIGHT?
WINDBLADE!
SAY YOU WOULDN'T!
CAN'T HEAR YOU!
I WOULDN'T, BUT SHE DOESN'T NEED TO KNOW THAT.

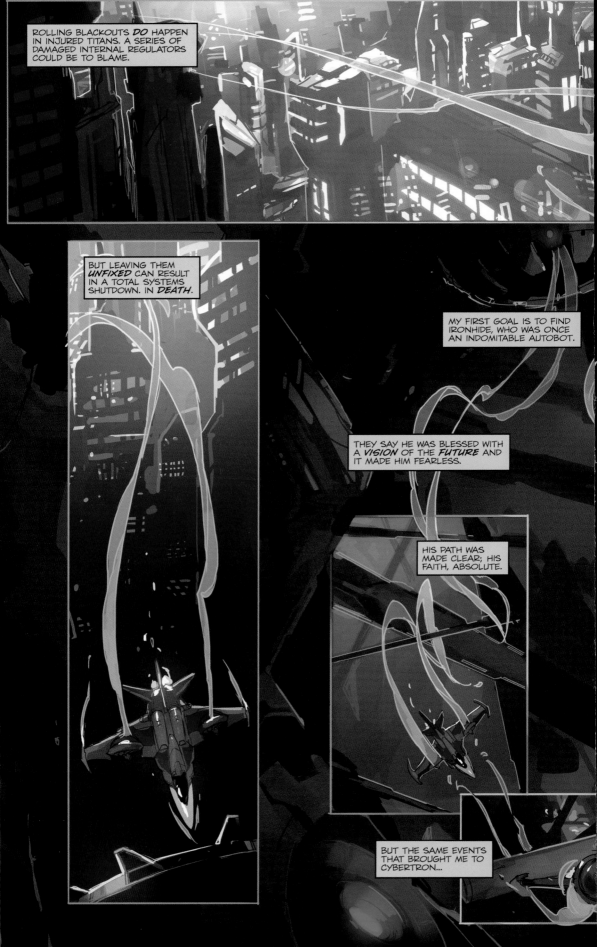

ROLLING BLACKOUTS *DO* HAPPEN IN INJURED TITANS. A SERIES OF DAMAGED INTERNAL REGULATORS COULD BE TO BLAME.

BUT LEAVING THEM *UNFIXED* CAN RESULT IN A TOTAL SYSTEMS SHUTDOWN. IN *DEATH*.

MY FIRST GOAL IS TO FIND IRONHIDE, WHO WAS ONCE AN INDOMITABLE AUTOBOT.

THEY SAY HE WAS BLESSED WITH A *VISION* OF THE *FUTURE* AND IT MADE HIM FEARLESS.

HIS PATH WAS MADE CLEAR; HIS FAITH, ABSOLUTE.

BUT THE SAME EVENTS THAT BROUGHT ME TO CYBERTRON...

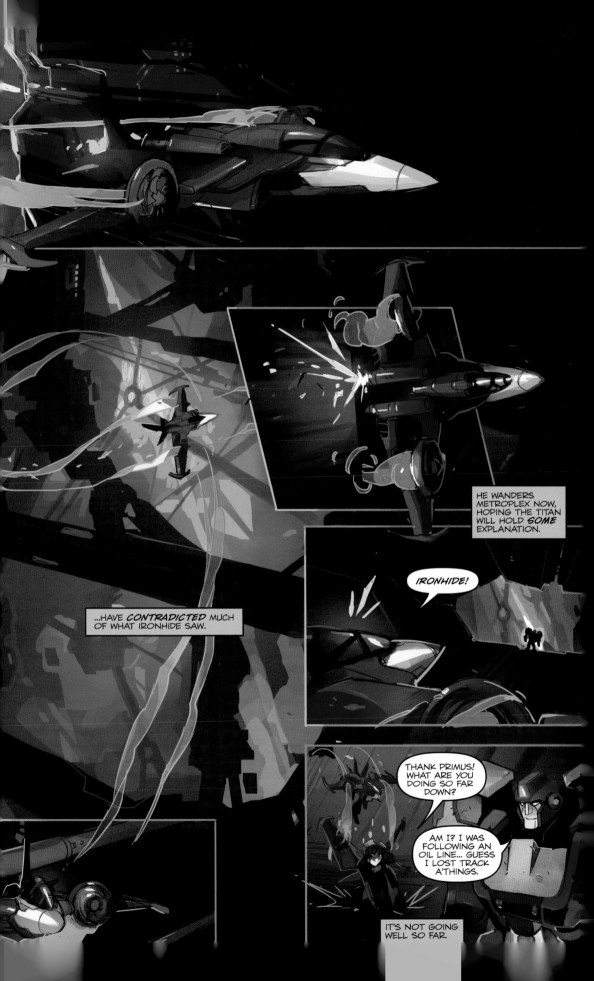

HE WANDERS METROPLEX NOW, HOPING THE TITAN WILL HOLD **SOME** EXPLANATION.

...HAVE **CONTRADICTED** MUCH OF WHAT IRONHIDE SAW.

IRONHIDE!

THANK PRIMUS! WHAT ARE YOU DOING SO FAR DOWN?

AM I? I WAS FOLLOWING AN OIL LINE... GUESS I LOST TRACK A'THINGS.

IT'S NOT GOING WELL SO FAR.

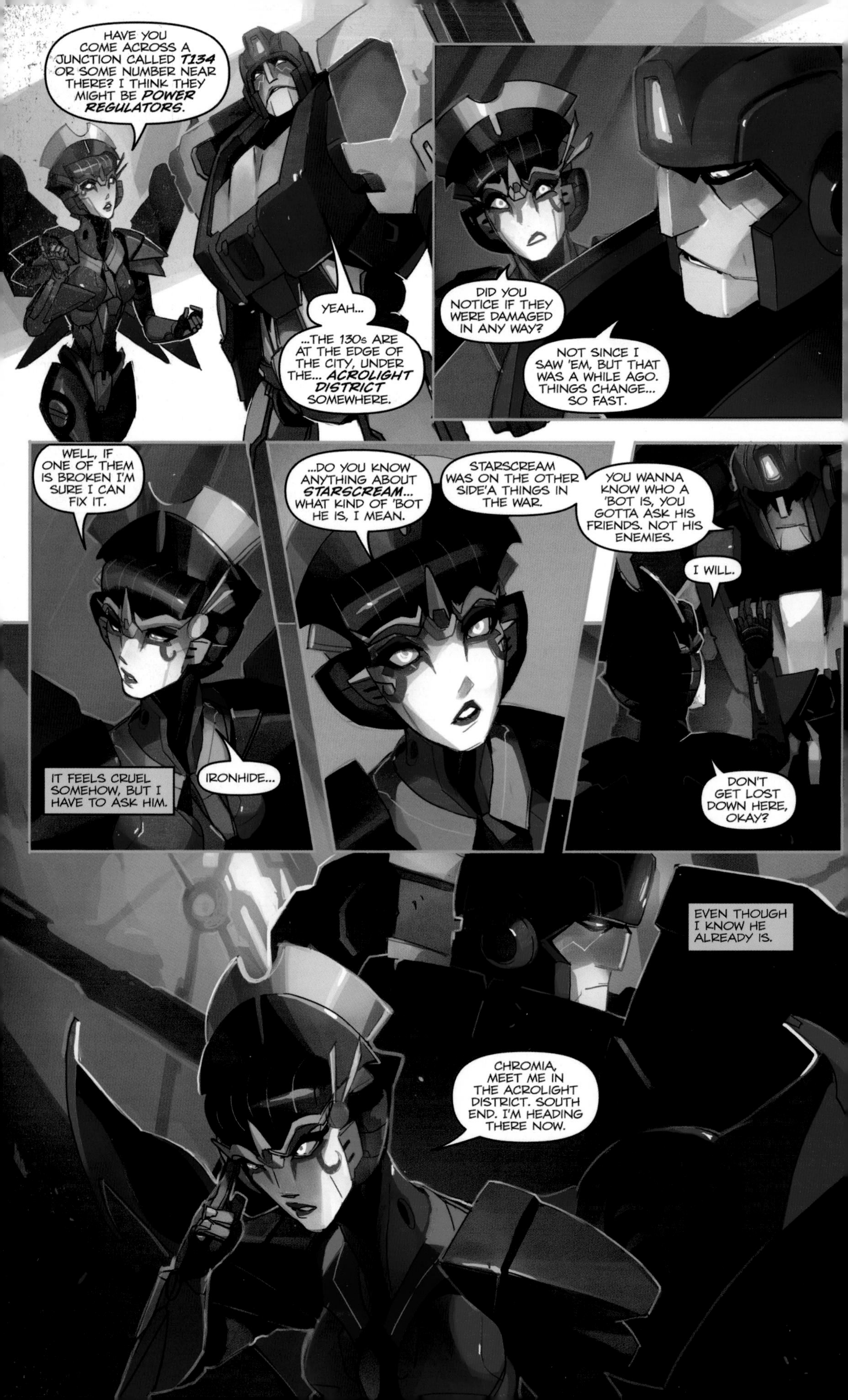
HAVE YOU COME ACROSS A JUNCTION CALLED T134 OR SOME NUMBER NEAR THERE? I THINK THEY MIGHT BE POWER REGULATORS.
YEAH...
...THE 130s ARE AT THE EDGE OF THE CITY, UNDER THE... ACROLIGHT DISTRICT SOMEWHERE.
DID YOU NOTICE IF THEY WERE DAMAGED IN ANY WAY?
NOT SINCE I SAW 'EM, BUT THAT WAS A WHILE AGO. THINGS CHANGE... SO FAST.
WELL, IF ONE OF THEM IS BROKEN I'M SURE I CAN FIX IT.
IT FEELS CRUEL SOMEHOW, BUT I HAVE TO ASK HIM.
IRONHIDE...
...DO YOU KNOW ANYTHING ABOUT STARSCREAM... WHAT KIND OF 'BOT HE IS, I MEAN.
STARSCREAM WAS ON THE OTHER SIDE'A THINGS IN THE WAR.
YOU WANNA KNOW WHO A 'BOT IS, YOU GOTTA ASK HIS FRIENDS. NOT HIS ENEMIES.
I WILL.
DON'T GET LOST DOWN HERE, OKAY?
EVEN THOUGH I KNOW HE ALREADY IS.
CHROMIA, MEET ME IN THE ACROLIGHT DISTRICT. SOUTH END. I'M HEADING THERE NOW.

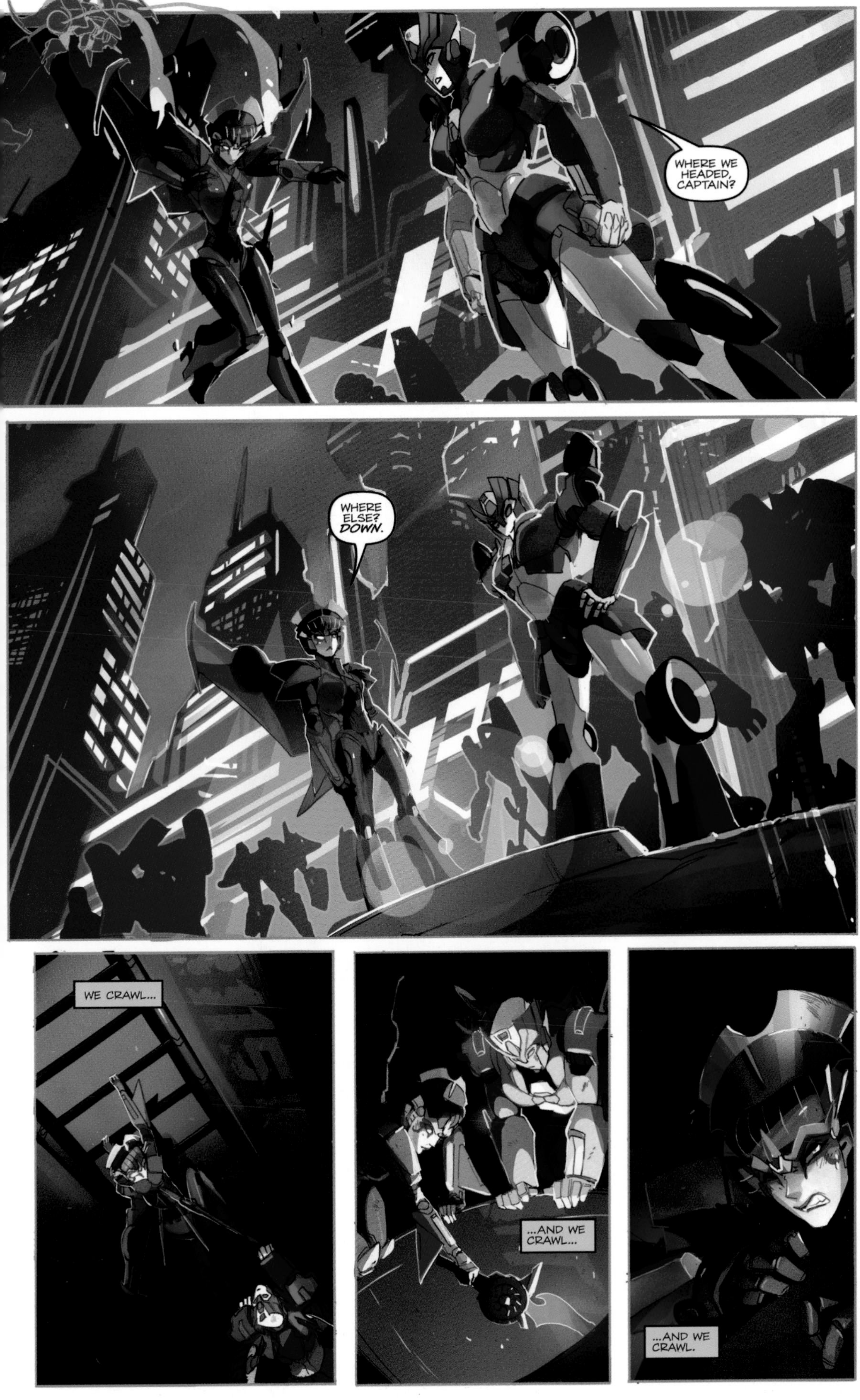
WHERE WE HEADED, CAPTAIN?
WHERE ELSE? DOWN.
WE CRAWL...
...AND WE CRAWL...
...AND WE CRAWL.

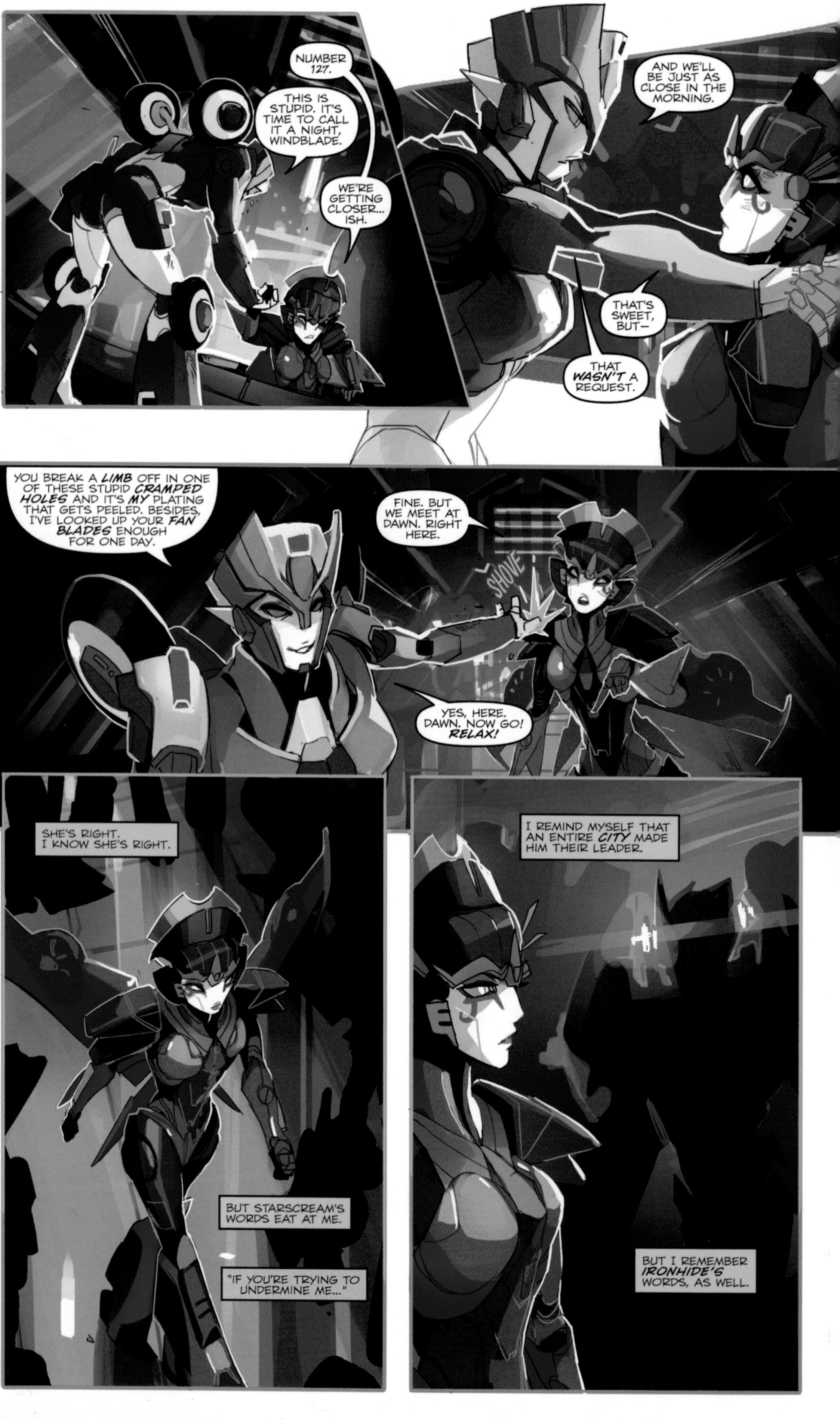
NUMBER 127.
THIS IS STUPID. IT'S TIME TO CALL IT A NIGHT, WINDBLADE.
WE'RE GETTING CLOSER... ISH.
AND WE'LL BE JUST AS CLOSE IN THE MORNING.
THAT'S SWEET, BUT—
THAT *WASN'T* A REQUEST.
YOU BREAK A *LIMB* OFF IN ONE OF THESE STUPID *CRAMPED HOLES* AND IT'S *MY* PLATING THAT GETS PEELED. BESIDES, I'VE LOOKED UP YOUR *FAN BLADES* ENOUGH FOR ONE DAY.
FINE. BUT WE MEET AT DAWN. RIGHT HERE.
SHOVE
YES, HERE. DAWN. NOW GO! *RELAX!*
SHE'S RIGHT. I KNOW SHE'S RIGHT.
BUT STARSCREAM'S WORDS EAT AT ME.
"IF YOU'RE TRYING TO UNDERMINE ME..."
I REMIND MYSELF THAT AN ENTIRE *CITY* MADE HIM THEIR LEADER.
BUT I REMEMBER *IRONHIDE'S* WORDS, AS WELL.

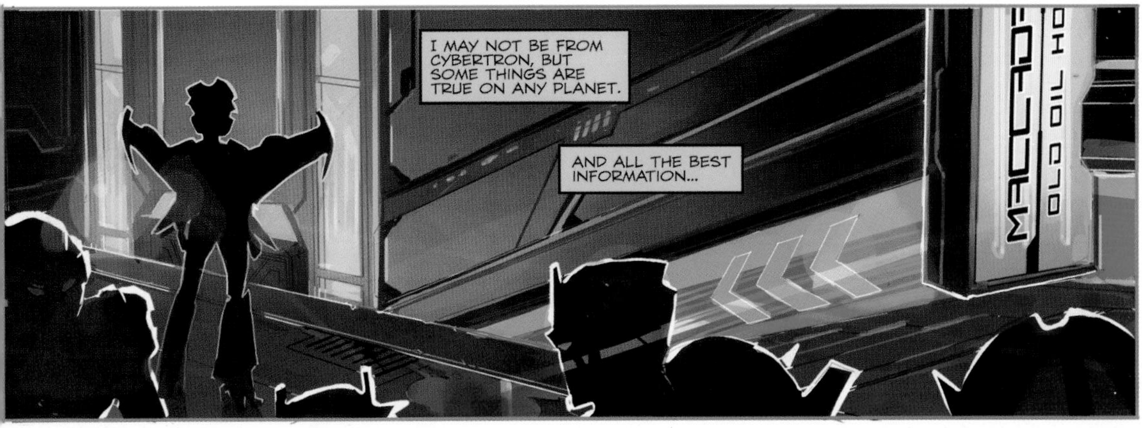
I MAY NOT BE FROM CYBERTRON, BUT SOME THINGS ARE TRUE ON ANY PLANET.
AND ALL THE BEST INFORMATION...
MACCADAM'S OLD OIL HO

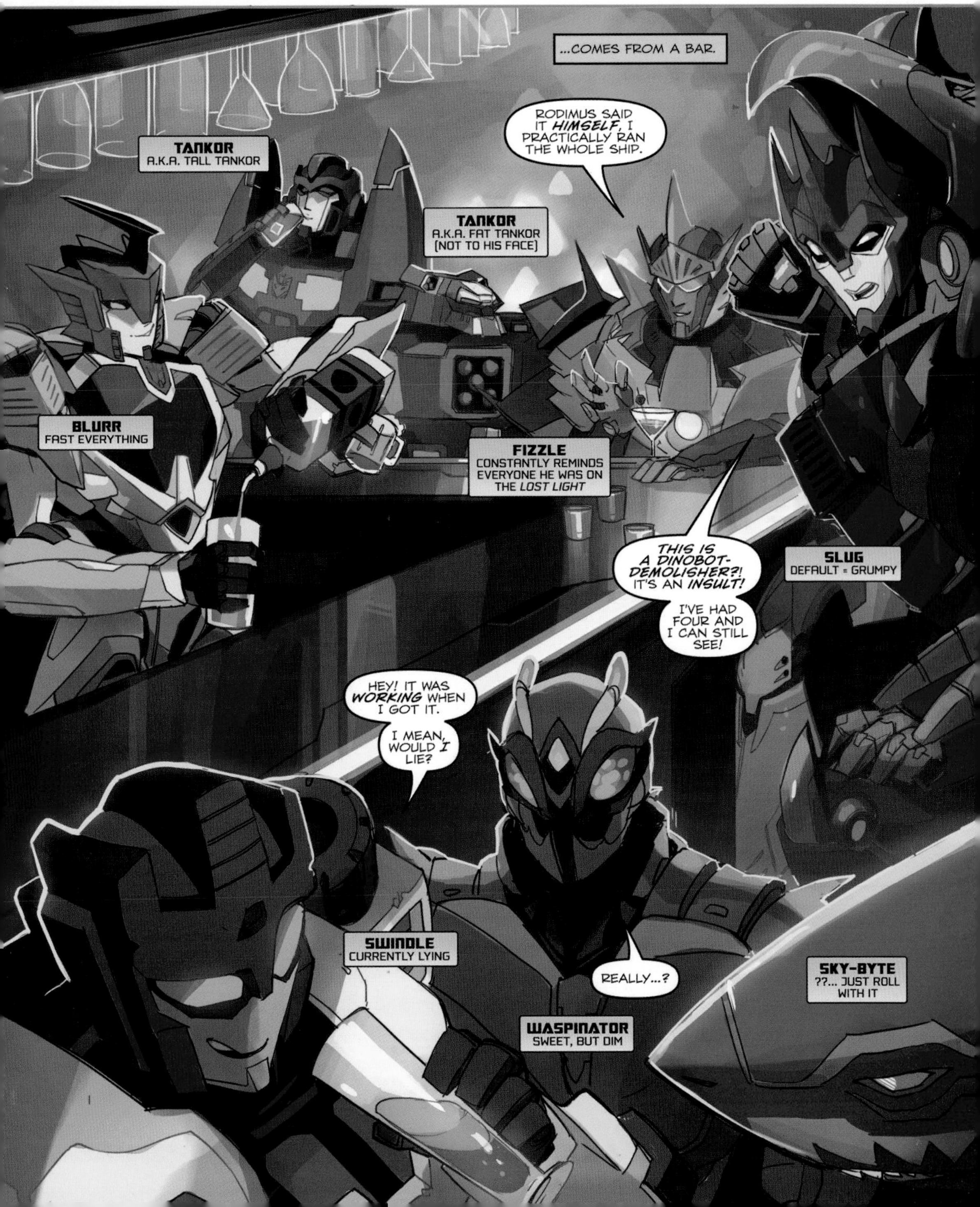
...COMES FROM A BAR.
TANKOR
A.K.A. TALL TANKOR
RODIMUS SAID IT HIMSELF, I PRACTICALLY RAN THE WHOLE SHIP.
TANKOR
A.K.A. FAT TANKOR (NOT TO HIS FACE)
BLURR
FAST EVERYTHING
FIZZLE
CONSTANTLY REMINDS EVERYONE HE WAS ON THE LOST LIGHT
THIS IS A DINOBOT-DEMOLISHER?! IT'S AN INSULT!
I'VE HAD FOUR AND I CAN STILL SEE!
SLUG
DEFAULT = GRUMPY
HEY! IT WAS WORKING WHEN I GOT IT.
I MEAN, WOULD I LIE?
SWINDLE
CURRENTLY LYING
REALLY...?
WASPINATOR
SWEET, BUT DIM
SKY-BYTE
??... JUST ROLL WITH IT

WELL, BEEN A LONG TIME SINCE WE'VE HAD ONE OF OUR *ESTEEMED GUESTS* VISIT *MACCADAM'S OLD OIL HOUSE.*

WINGBLADE, RIGHT?

WINDBLADE, ACTUA—

WINDBLADE! *OF COURSE!* I'M *BLURR,* THE OWNER AND PROPRIETOR. FIRST ROUND'S ON THE HOUSE FOR THE 'BOT KEEPING *METROPLEX* GOING. CERTAINLY MADE REBUILDING—*AGAIN*—A LOT EASIER.

ALTHOUGH IF YOU CAN PUT A WORD IN WITH THE *BIG GUY,* WE'VE GOT A LITTLE BIT OF A STORAGE PROBLEM—*AND THESE BLACKOUTS AREN'T—*

HIT THE BRAKES, CHATTER-BOT! IT'S A *CONVERSATION,* NOT A RACE.

WHAT CAN I GET YOU?

WHATEVER *HE'S* HAVING.

UNIVERSAL TRUISM #2: OLD SOLDIERS *LOVE* TELLING WAR STORIES.

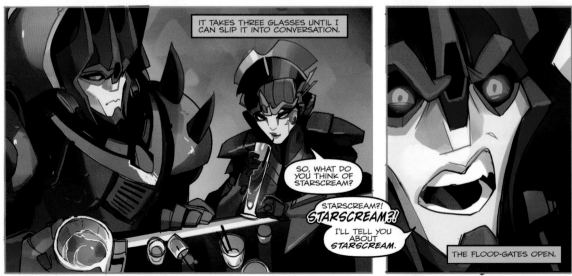

IT TAKES THREE GLASSES UNTIL I CAN SLIP IT INTO CONVERSATION.

SO, WHAT DO YOU THINK OF STARSCREAM?

STARSCREAM?! *STARSCREAM?!* I'LL TELL YOU ABOUT *STARSCREAM.*

THE FLOOD-GATES OPEN.

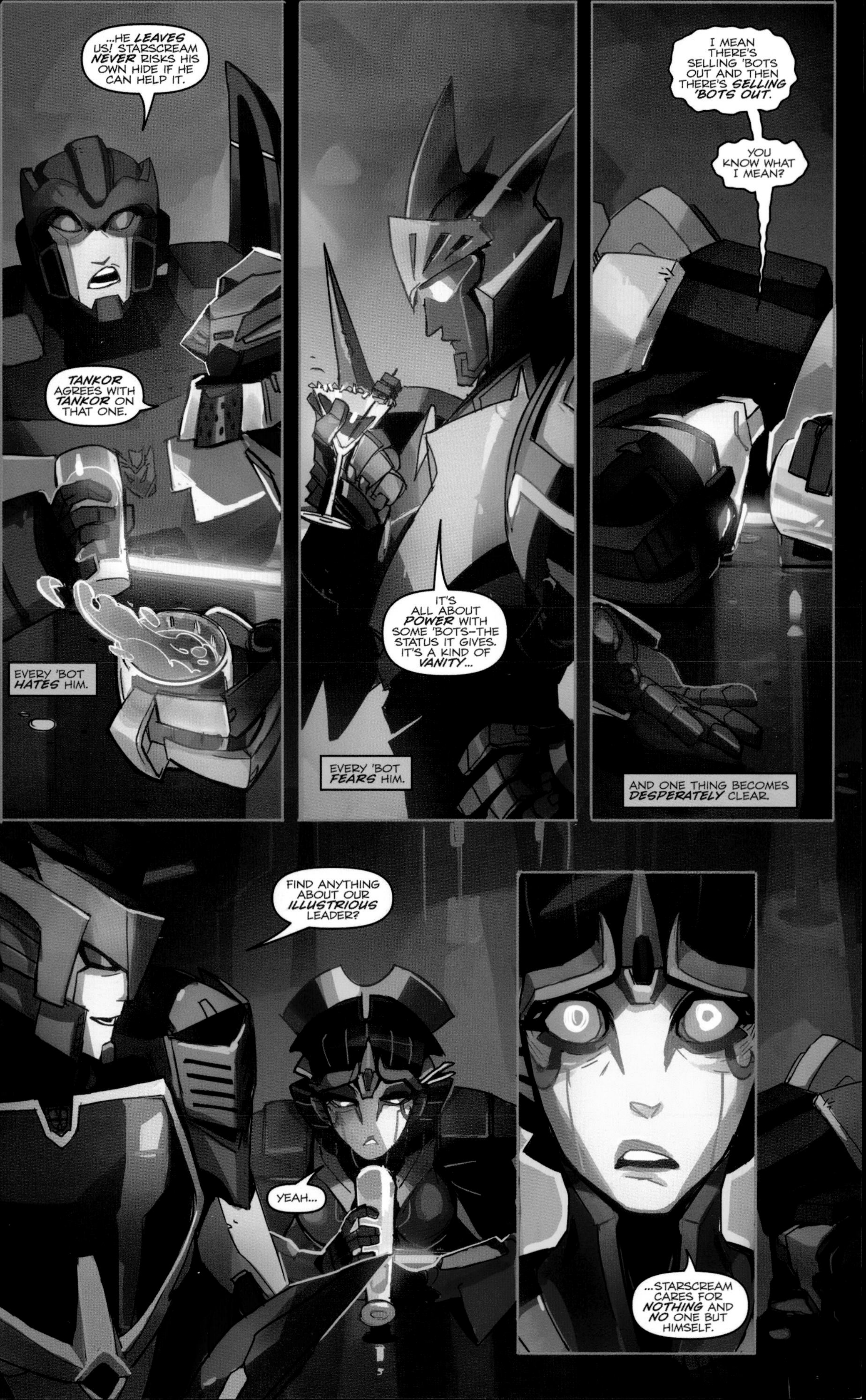
...HE LEAVES US! STARSCREAM NEVER RISKS HIS OWN HIDE IF HE CAN HELP IT.
TANKOR AGREES WITH TANKOR ON THAT ONE.
EVERY 'BOT HATES HIM.
IT'S ALL ABOUT POWER WITH SOME 'BOTS–THE STATUS IT GIVES. IT'S A KIND OF VANITY...
EVERY 'BOT FEARS HIM.
I MEAN THERE'S SELLING 'BOTS OUT AND THEN THERE'S SELLING 'BOTS OUT.
YOU KNOW WHAT I MEAN?
AND ONE THING BECOMES DESPERATELY CLEAR.
FIND ANYTHING ABOUT OUR ILLUSTRIOUS LEADER?
YEAH...
...STARSCREAM CARES FOR NOTHING AND NO ONE BUT HIMSELF.

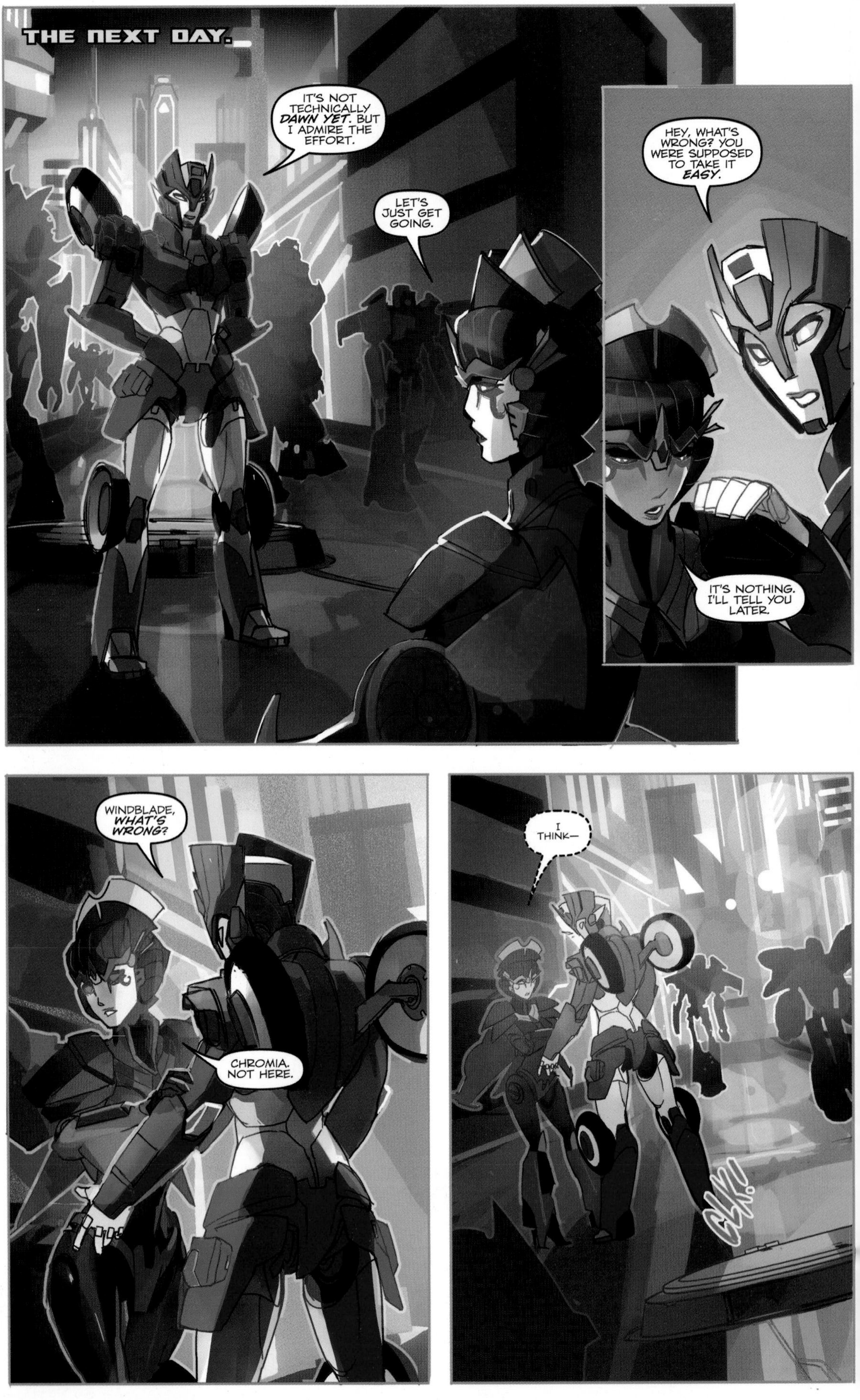
THE NEXT DAY.
IT'S NOT TECHNICALLY *DAWN YET*. BUT I ADMIRE THE EFFORT.
LET'S JUST GET GOING.
HEY, WHAT'S WRONG? YOU WERE SUPPOSED TO TAKE IT *EASY*.
IT'S NOTHING. I'LL TELL YOU LATER.
WINDBLADE, *WHAT'S WRONG?*
CHROMIA. NOT HERE.
I THINK—
CLK!

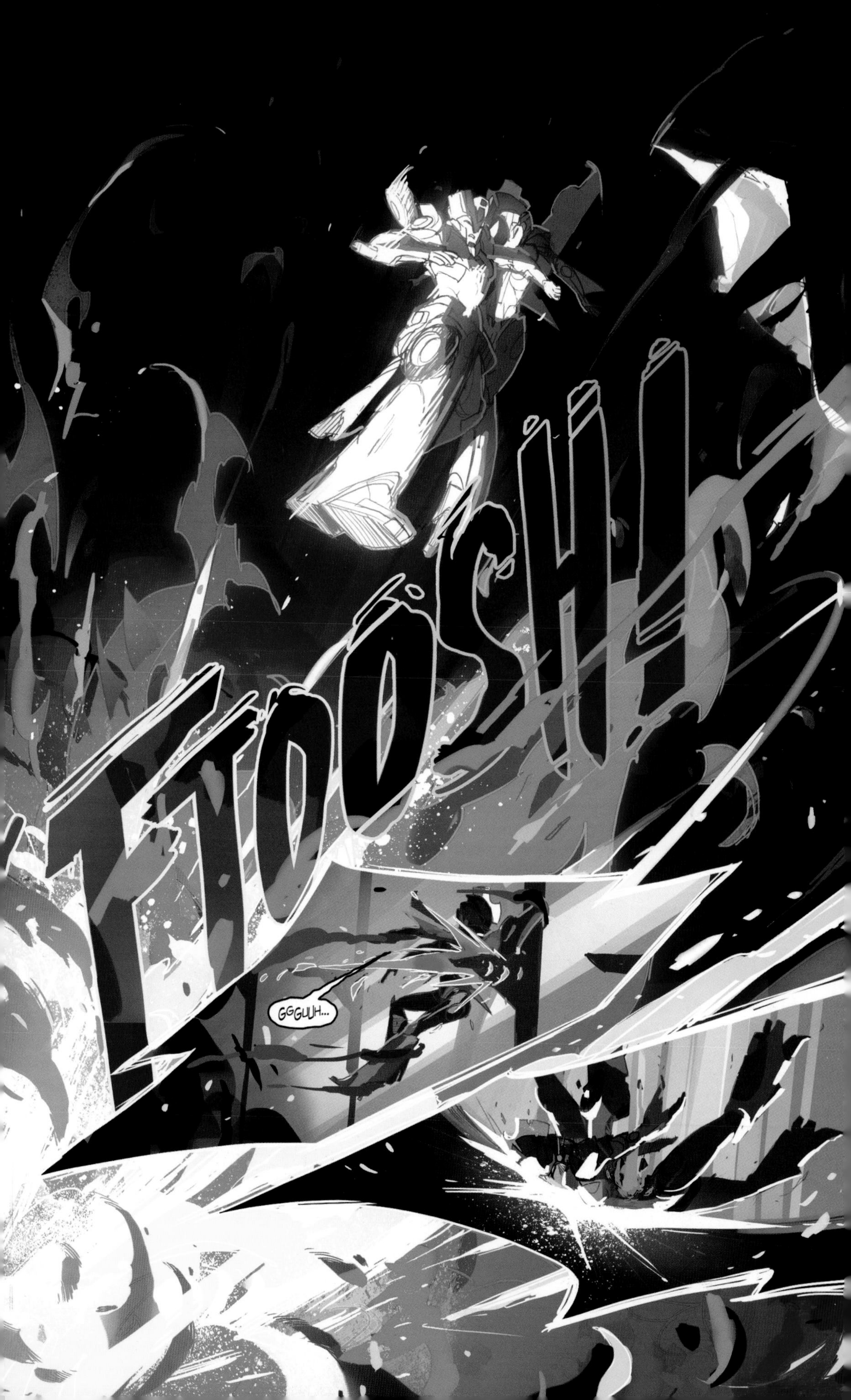
TOOSHH
GGGUUH...

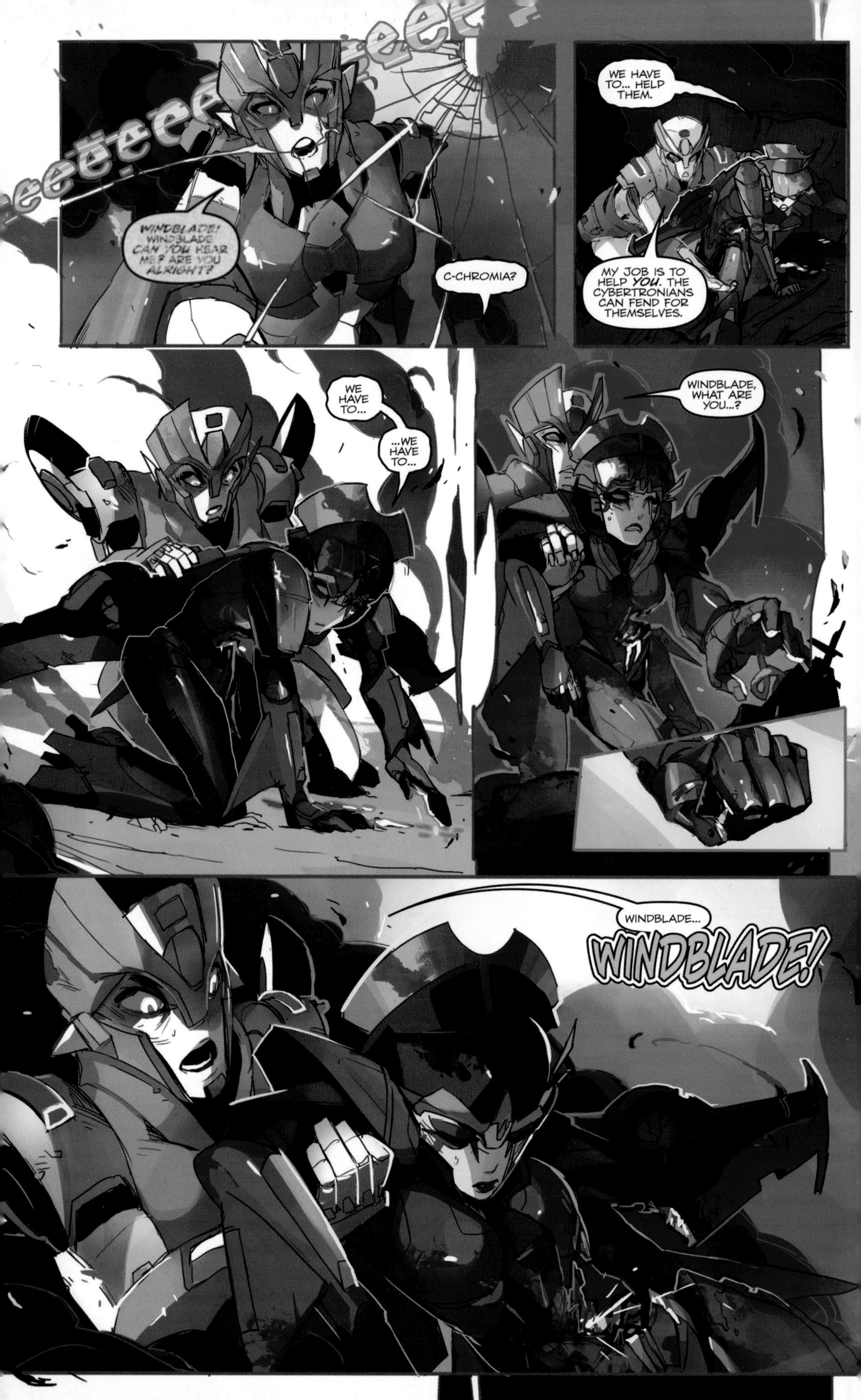
WINDBLADE! WINDBLADE CAN YOU HEAR ME? ARE YOU ALRIGHT?
C-CHROMIA?
WE HAVE TO... HELP THEM.
MY JOB IS TO HELP *YOU*. THE CYBERTRONIANS CAN FEND FOR THEMSELVES.
WE HAVE TO...
...WE HAVE TO...
WINDBLADE, WHAT ARE YOU...?
WINDBLADE...
WINDBLADE!

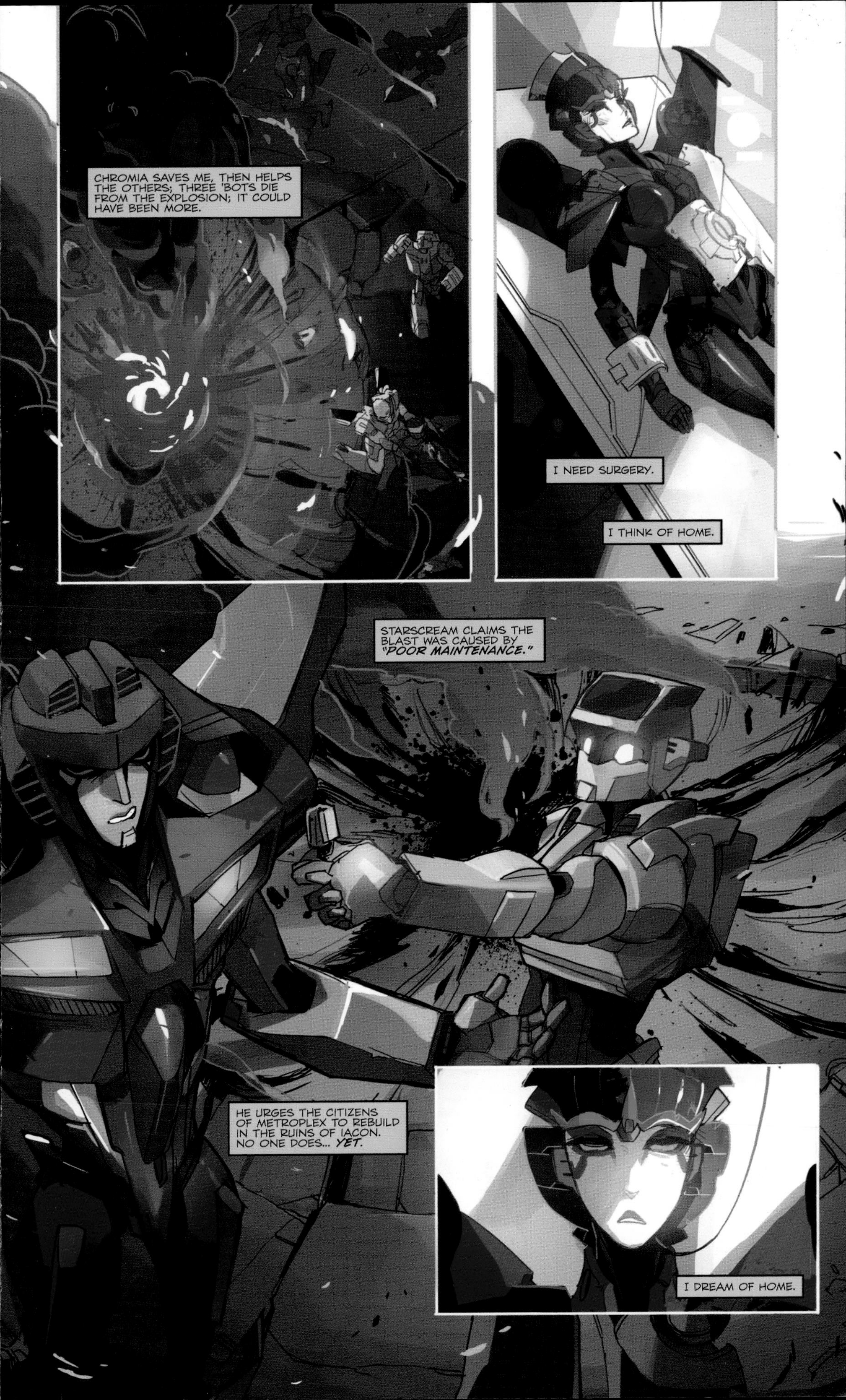

CHROMIA SAVES ME, THEN HELPS THE OTHERS; THREE 'BOTS DIE FROM THE EXPLOSION; IT COULD HAVE BEEN MORE.
I NEED SURGERY.
I THINK OF HOME.
STARSCREAM CLAIMS THE BLAST WAS CAUSED BY "POOR MAINTENANCE."
HE URGES THE CITIZENS OF METROPLEX TO REBUILD IN THE RUINS OF IACON. NO ONE DOES... YET.
I DREAM OF HOME.

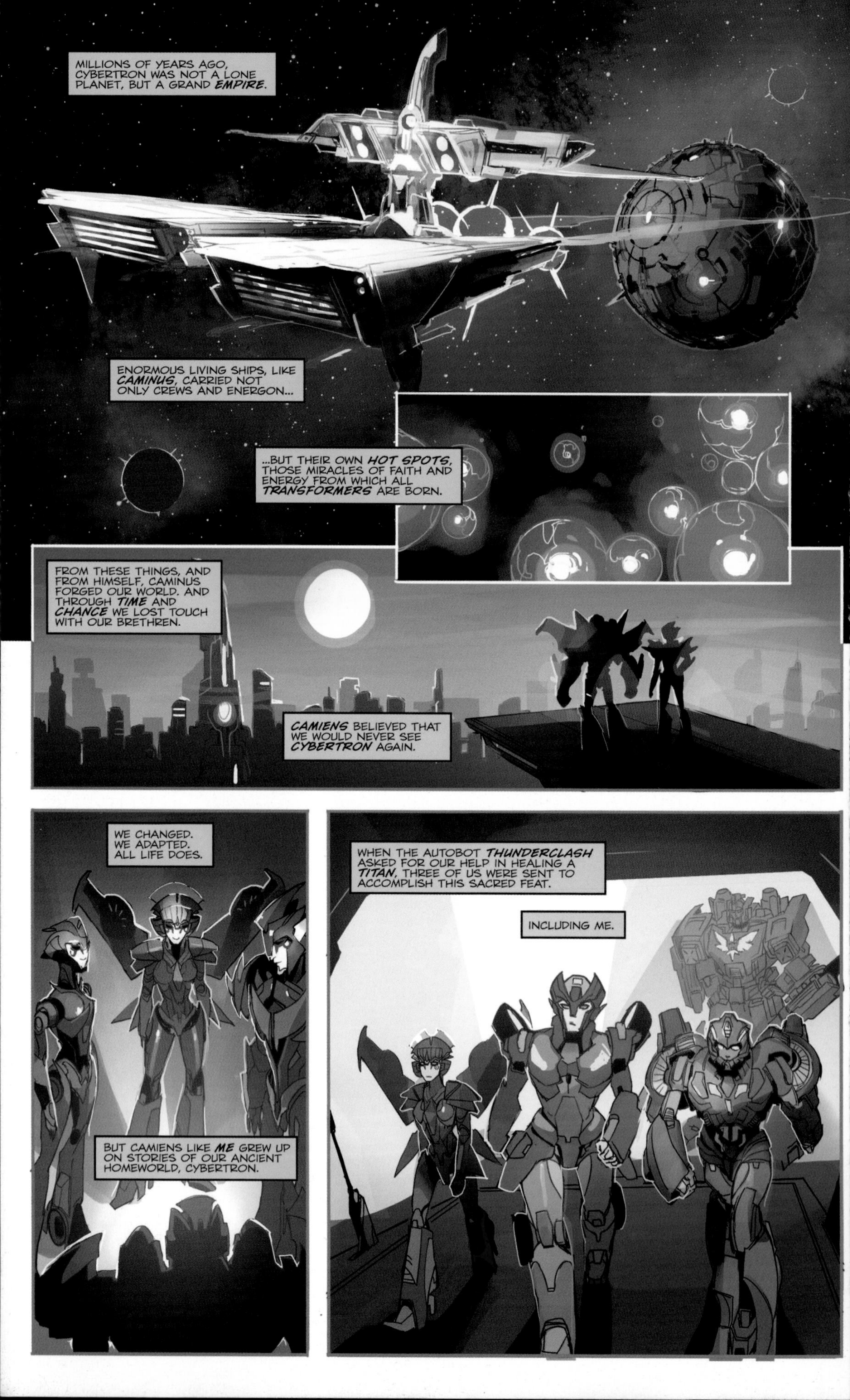
MILLIONS OF YEARS AGO, CYBERTRON WAS NOT A LONE PLANET, BUT A GRAND EMPIRE.
ENORMOUS LIVING SHIPS, LIKE CAMINUS, CARRIED NOT ONLY CREWS AND ENERGON...
...BUT THEIR OWN HOT SPOTS, THOSE MIRACLES OF FAITH AND ENERGY FROM WHICH ALL TRANSFORMERS ARE BORN.
FROM THESE THINGS, AND FROM HIMSELF, CAMINUS FORGED OUR WORLD. AND THROUGH TIME AND CHANCE WE LOST TOUCH WITH OUR BRETHREN.
CAMIENS BELIEVED THAT WE WOULD NEVER SEE CYBERTRON AGAIN.
WE CHANGED. WE ADAPTED. ALL LIFE DOES.
BUT CAMIENS LIKE ME GREW UP ON STORIES OF OUR ANCIENT HOMEWORLD, CYBERTRON.
WHEN THE AUTOBOT THUNDERCLASH ASKED FOR OUR HELP IN HEALING A TITAN, THREE OF US WERE SENT TO ACCOMPLISH THIS SACRED FEAT.
INCLUDING ME.

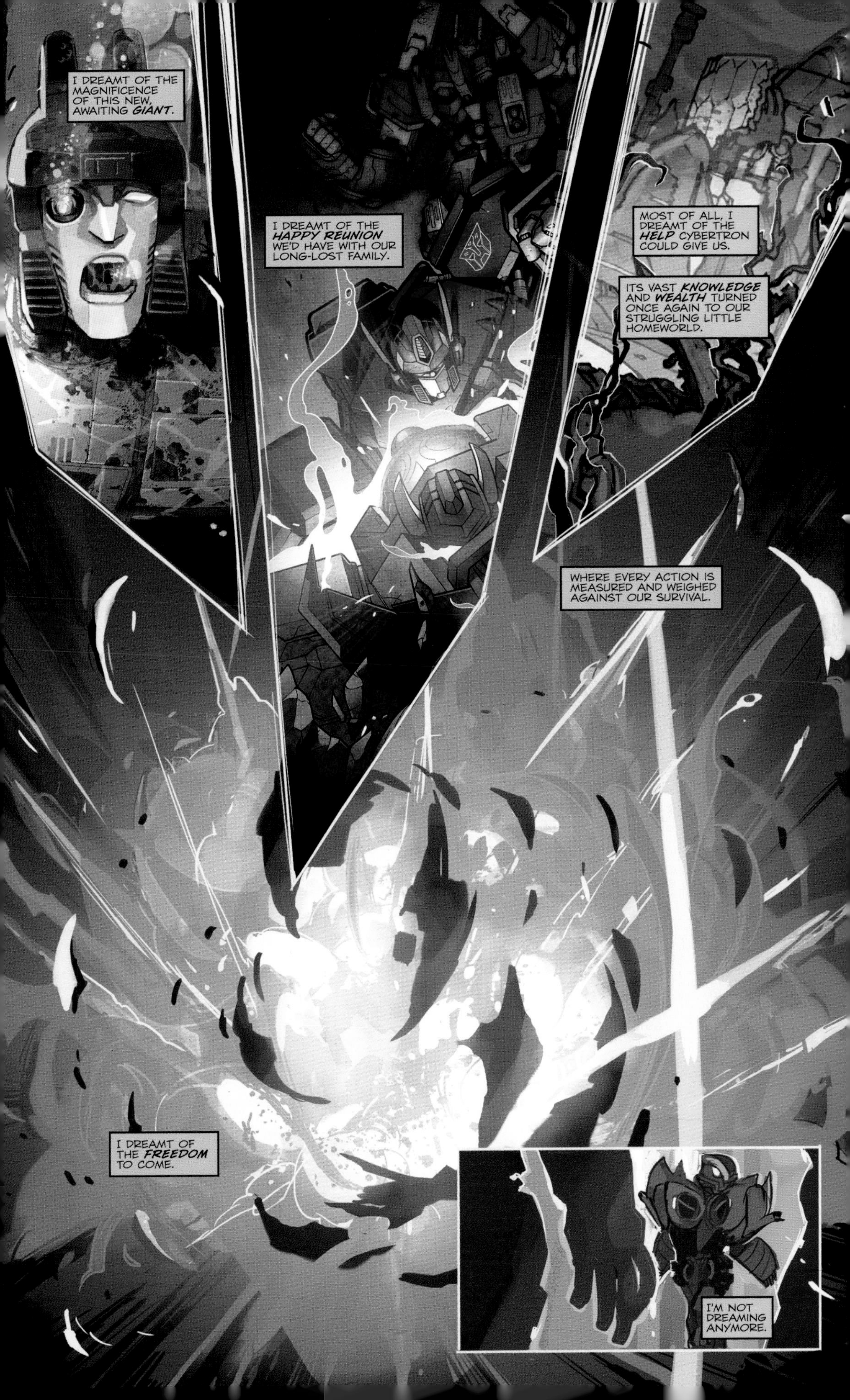
I DREAMT OF THE MAGNIFICENCE OF THIS NEW, AWAITING GIANT.
I DREAMT OF THE HAPPY REUNION WE'D HAVE WITH OUR LONG-LOST FAMILY.
MOST OF ALL, I DREAMT OF THE HELP CYBERTRON COULD GIVE US.
ITS VAST KNOWLEDGE AND WEALTH TURNED ONCE AGAIN TO OUR STRUGGLING LITTLE HOMEWORLD.
WHERE EVERY ACTION IS MEASURED AND WEIGHED AGAINST OUR SURVIVAL.
I DREAMT OF THE FREEDOM TO COME.
I'M NOT DREAMING ANYMORE.

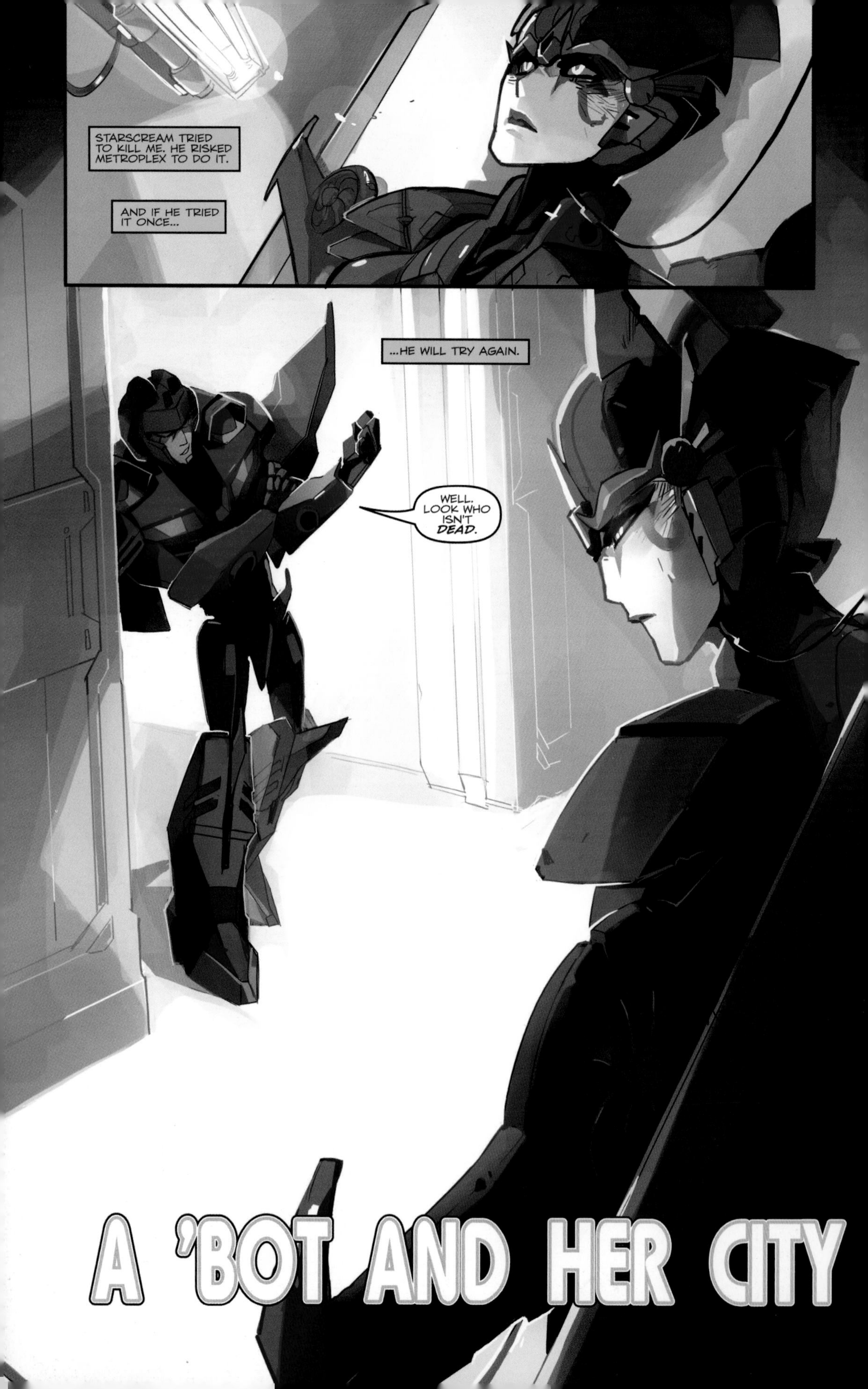
STARSCREAM TRIED TO KILL ME. HE RISKED METROPLEX TO DO IT.
AND IF HE TRIED IT ONCE...
...HE WILL TRY AGAIN.
WELL. LOOK WHO ISN'T DEAD.
A 'BOT AND HER CITY

ART BY **SARAH STONE**

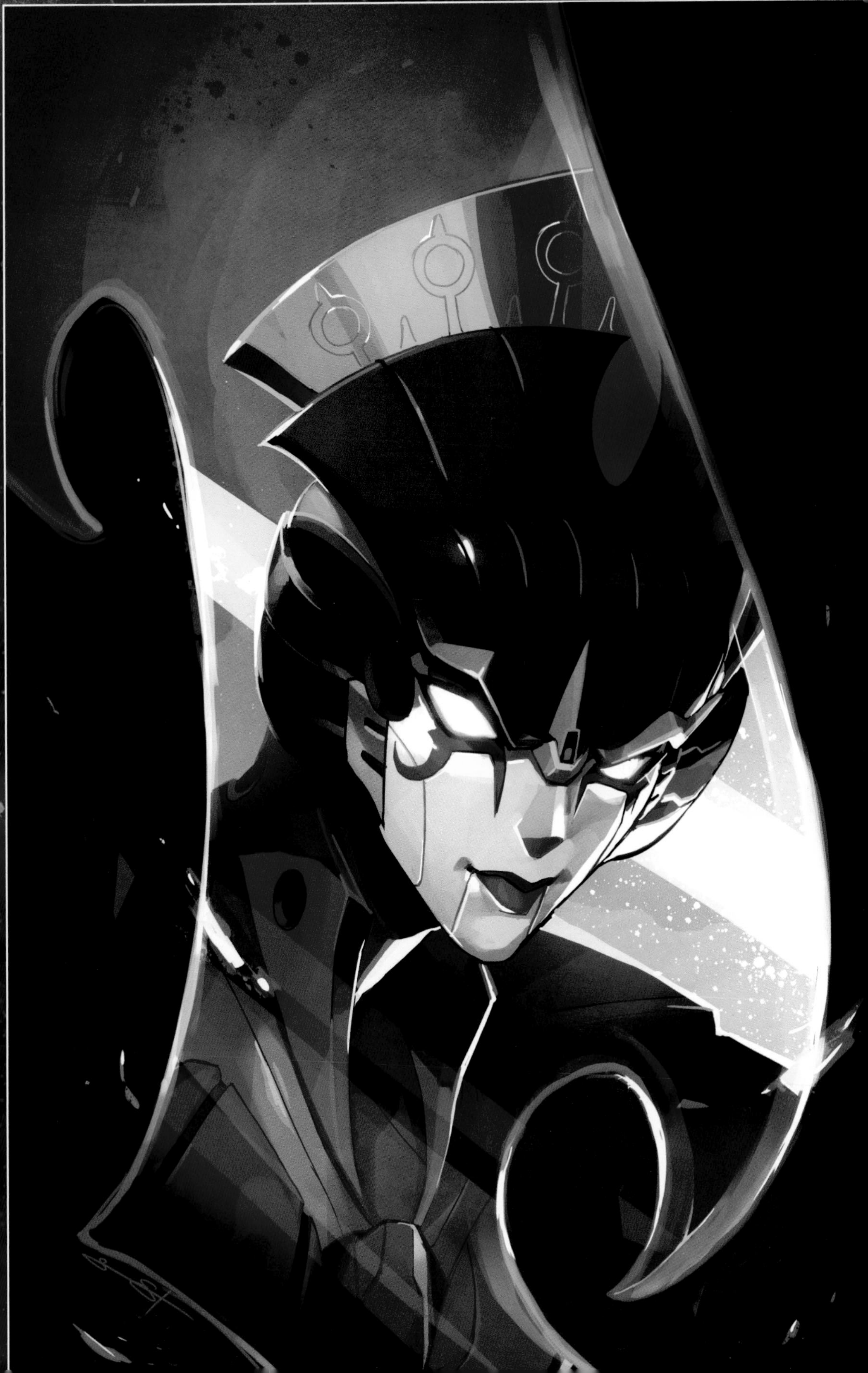

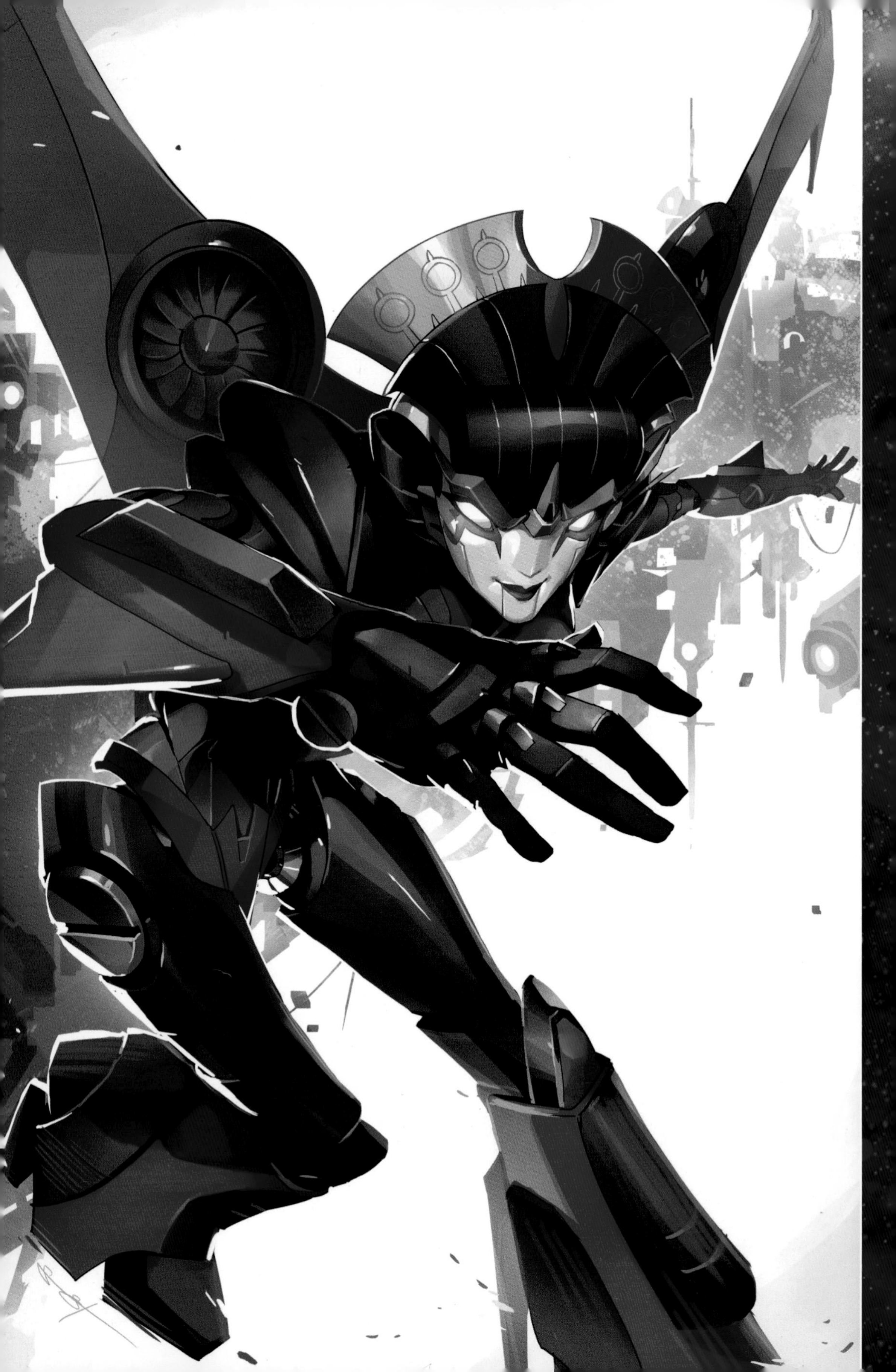

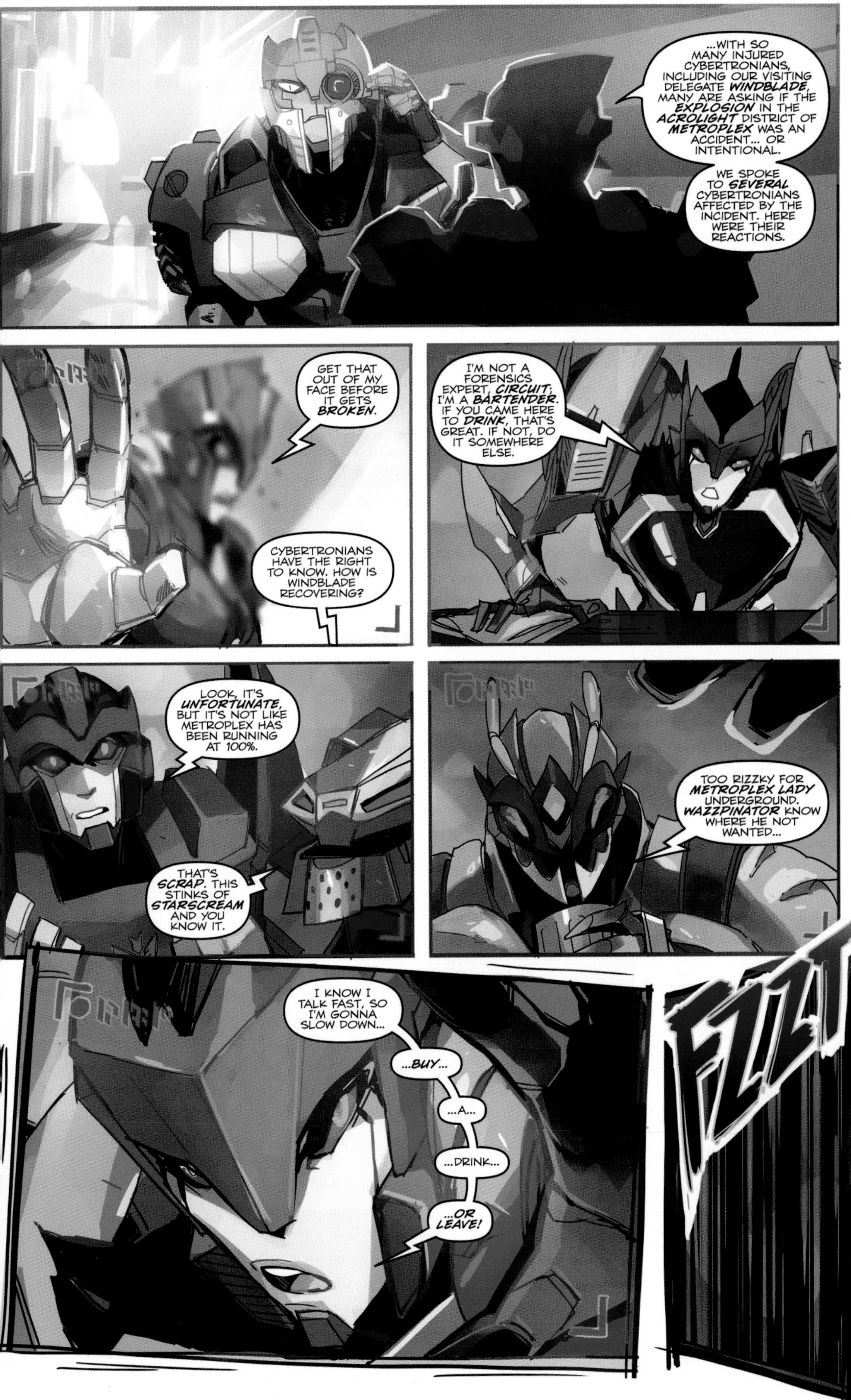
...WITH SO MANY INJURED CYBERTRONIANS, INCLUDING OUR VISITING DELEGATE WINDBLADE, MANY ARE ASKING IF THE EXPLOSION IN THE ACROLIGHT DISTRICT OF METROPLEX WAS AN ACCIDENT... OR INTENTIONAL.
WE SPOKE TO SEVERAL CYBERTRONIANS AFFECTED BY THE INCIDENT. HERE WERE THEIR REACTIONS.
GET THAT OUT OF MY FACE BEFORE IT GETS BROKEN.
CYBERTRONIANS HAVE THE RIGHT TO KNOW. HOW IS WINDBLADE RECOVERING?
I'M NOT A FORENSICS EXPERT, CIRCUIT; I'M A BARTENDER. IF YOU CAME HERE TO DRINK, THAT'S GREAT. IF NOT, DO IT SOMEWHERE ELSE.
LOOK, IT'S UNFORTUNATE, BUT IT'S NOT LIKE METROPLEX HAS BEEN RUNNING AT 100%.
THAT'S SCRAP. THIS STINKS OF STARSCREAM AND YOU KNOW IT.
TOO RIZZKY FOR METROPLEX LADY UNDERGROUND. WAZZPINATOR KNOW WHERE HE NOT WANTED...
I KNOW I TALK FAST, SO I'M GONNA SLOW DOWN...
...BUY...
...A...
...DRINK...
...OR LEAVE!
FZZZT

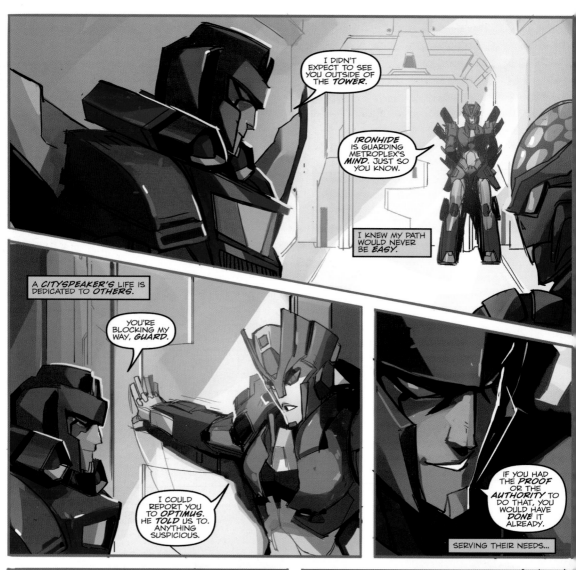

I DIDN'T EXPECT TO SEE YOU OUTSIDE OF THE *TOWER*.

IRONHIDE IS GUARDING METROPLEX'S *MIND*. JUST SO YOU KNOW.

I KNEW MY PATH WOULD NEVER BE *EASY*.

A *CITYSPEAKER'S* LIFE IS DEDICATED TO *OTHERS*.

YOU'RE BLOCKING MY WAY, *GUARD*.

I COULD REPORT YOU TO *OPTIMUS*. HE *TOLD* US TO. ANYTHING SUSPICIOUS.

IF YOU HAD THE *PROOF* OR THE *AUTHORITY* TO DO THAT, YOU WOULD HAVE *DONE* IT ALREADY.

SERVING THEIR NEEDS...

WELL. LOOK WHO ISN'T DEAD.

...PUTTING *THEIR* LIVES ABOVE YOUR OWN.

SLAM!

AW, SCRAP.

TWO DAYS AGO, SOMEONE NEARLY KILLED ME...

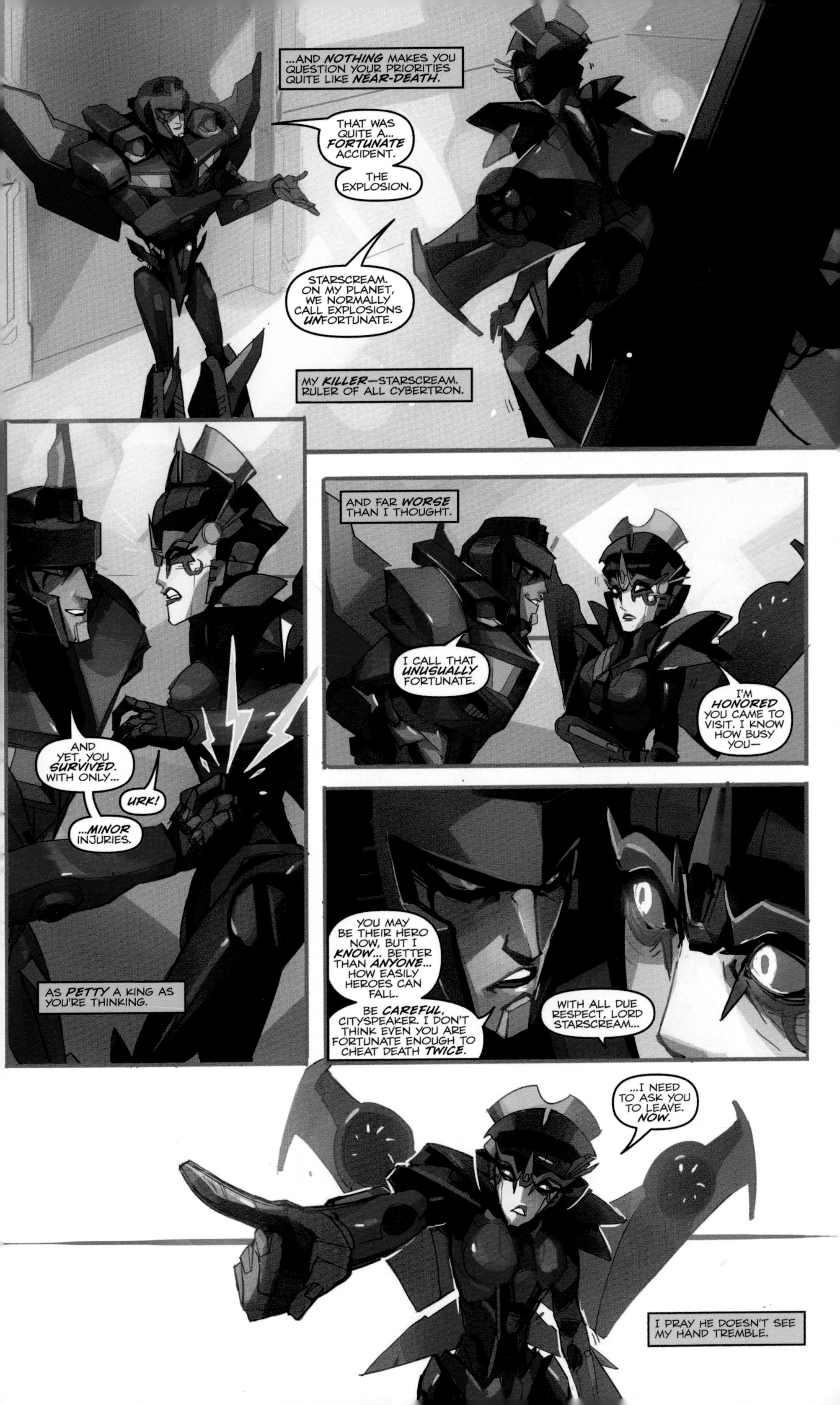
...AND NOTHING MAKES YOU QUESTION YOUR PRIORITIES QUITE LIKE NEAR-DEATH.
THAT WAS QUITE A... FORTUNATE ACCIDENT.
THE EXPLOSION.
STARSCREAM. ON MY PLANET, WE NORMALLY CALL EXPLOSIONS UNFORTUNATE.
MY KILLER—STARSCREAM. RULER OF ALL CYBERTRON.
AND YET, YOU SURVIVED. WITH ONLY...
URK!
...MINOR INJURIES.
AS PETTY A KING AS YOU'RE THINKING.
AND FAR WORSE THAN I THOUGHT.
I CALL THAT UNUSUALLY FORTUNATE.
I'M HONORED YOU CAME TO VISIT. I KNOW HOW BUSY YOU—
YOU MAY BE THEIR HERO NOW, BUT I KNOW... BETTER THAN ANYONE... HOW EASILY HEROES CAN FALL.
BE CAREFUL, CITYSPEAKER. I DON'T THINK EVEN YOU ARE FORTUNATE ENOUGH TO CHEAT DEATH TWICE.
WITH ALL DUE RESPECT, LORD STARSCREAM...
...I NEED TO ASK YOU TO LEAVE. NOW.
I PRAY HE DOESN'T SEE MY HAND TREMBLE.

RATTRAP, IT'S TIME TO GO.

GOOD TALK, BOSS?

I THINK WE SAID WHAT WAS NEEDED.

WHAT'S WRONG?

NOTHING.

YOU'RE AN AWFUL LIAR.

SHE'S *RIGHT*.

WHAT DID HE SAY?

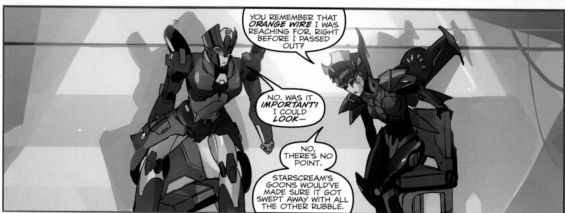

YOU REMEMBER THAT *ORANGE WIRE* I WAS REACHING FOR, RIGHT BEFORE I PASSED OUT?

NO. WAS IT *IMPORTANT*? I COULD *LOOK—*

NO, THERE'S NO POINT. STARSCREAM'S GOONS WOULD'VE MADE SURE IT GOT SWEPT AWAY WITH ALL THE OTHER RUBBLE.

WHY WOULD ANYONE CARE ABOUT A PIECE OF WIRE?

BECAUSE IT WAS PART OF AN *IGNITER CAPSULE!*

ARE YOU SAYING...?

I SAW *RATTRAP* THERE, YOU KNOW. RIGHT BEFORE IT HAPPENED. I—

AND THAT'S WHEN I REALIZE WE'RE BEING *FILMED.*

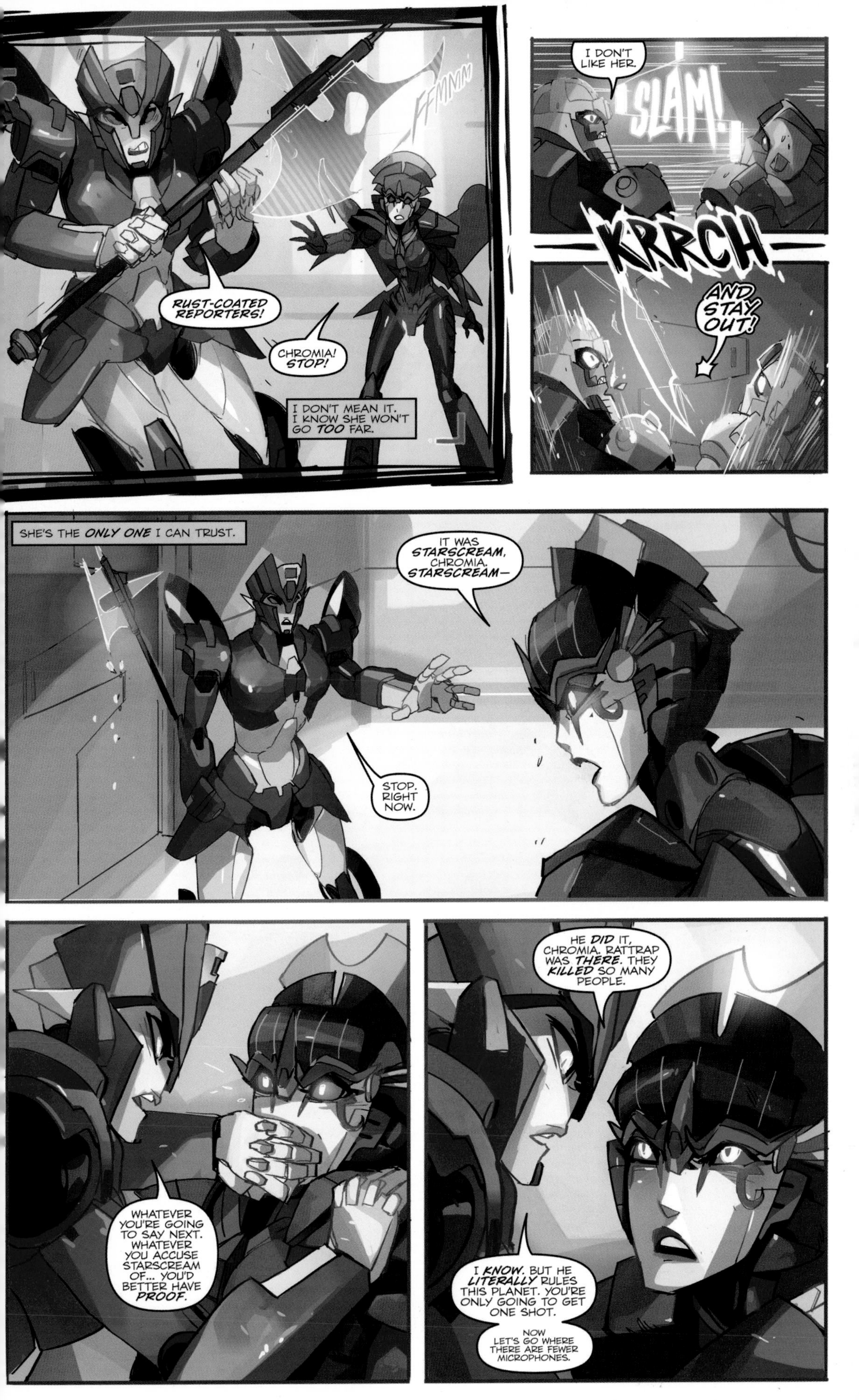
FFMMM
RUST-COATED REPORTERS!
CHROMIA! STOP!
I DON'T MEAN IT. I KNOW SHE WON'T GO TOO FAR.
I DON'T LIKE HER.
SLAM!
KRRCH
AND STAY OUT!
SHE'S THE ONLY ONE I CAN TRUST.
IT WAS STARSCREAM, CHROMIA. STARSCREAM—
STOP. RIGHT NOW.
WHATEVER YOU'RE GOING TO SAY NEXT. WHATEVER YOU ACCUSE STARSCREAM OF... YOU'D BETTER HAVE PROOF.
HE DID IT, CHROMIA. RATTRAP WAS THERE. THEY KILLED SO MANY PEOPLE.
I KNOW. BUT HE LITERALLY RULES THIS PLANET. YOU'RE ONLY GOING TO GET ONE SHOT.
NOW LET'S GO WHERE THERE ARE FEWER MICROPHONES.

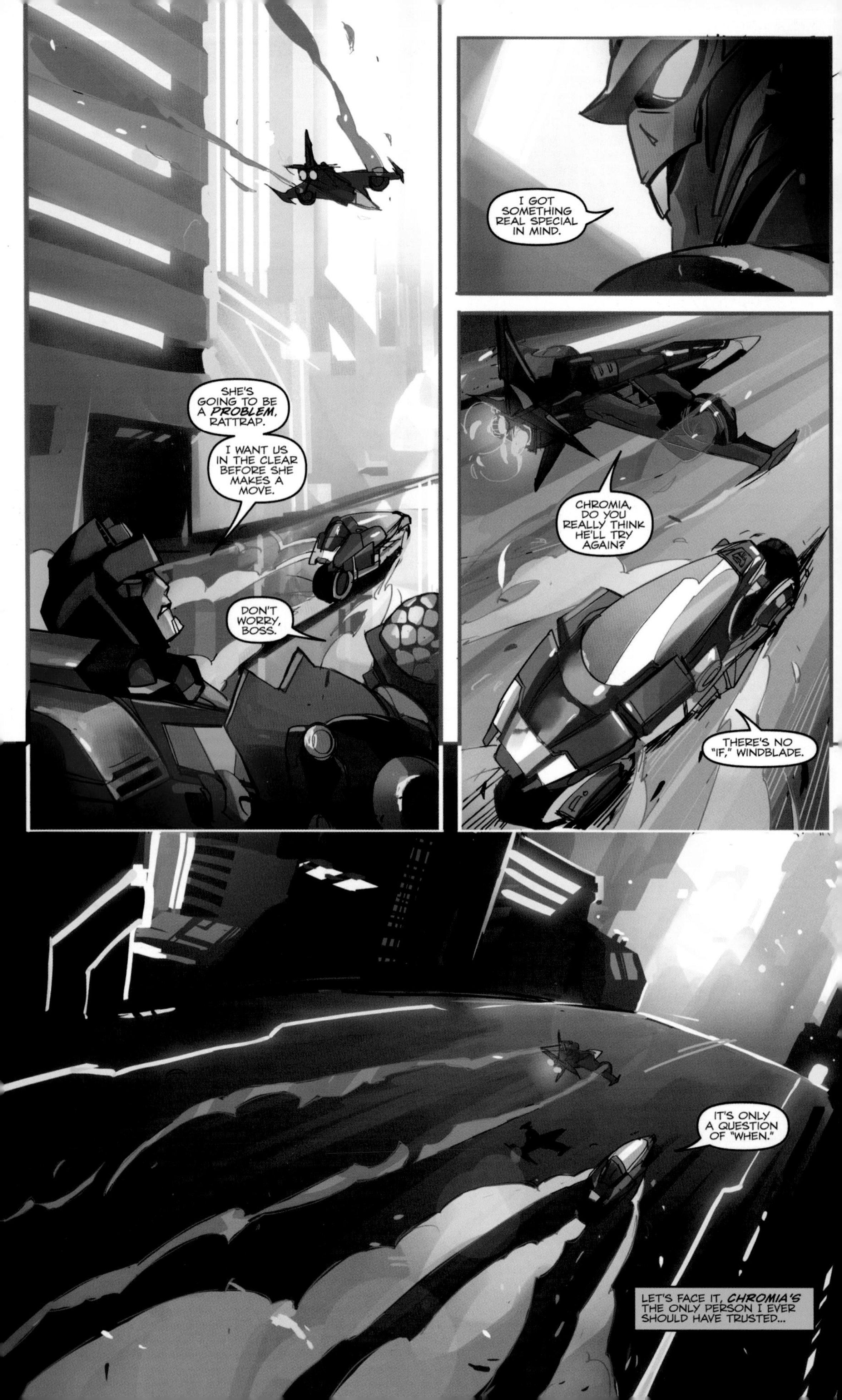
I GOT SOMETHING REAL SPECIAL IN MIND.
SHE'S GOING TO BE A PROBLEM, RATTRAP.
I WANT US IN THE CLEAR BEFORE SHE MAKES A MOVE.
DON'T WORRY, BOSS.
CHROMIA, DO YOU REALLY THINK HE'LL TRY AGAIN?
THERE'S NO "IF," WINDBLADE.
IT'S ONLY A QUESTION OF "WHEN."
LET'S FACE IT, CHROMIA'S THE ONLY PERSON I EVER SHOULD HAVE TRUSTED...

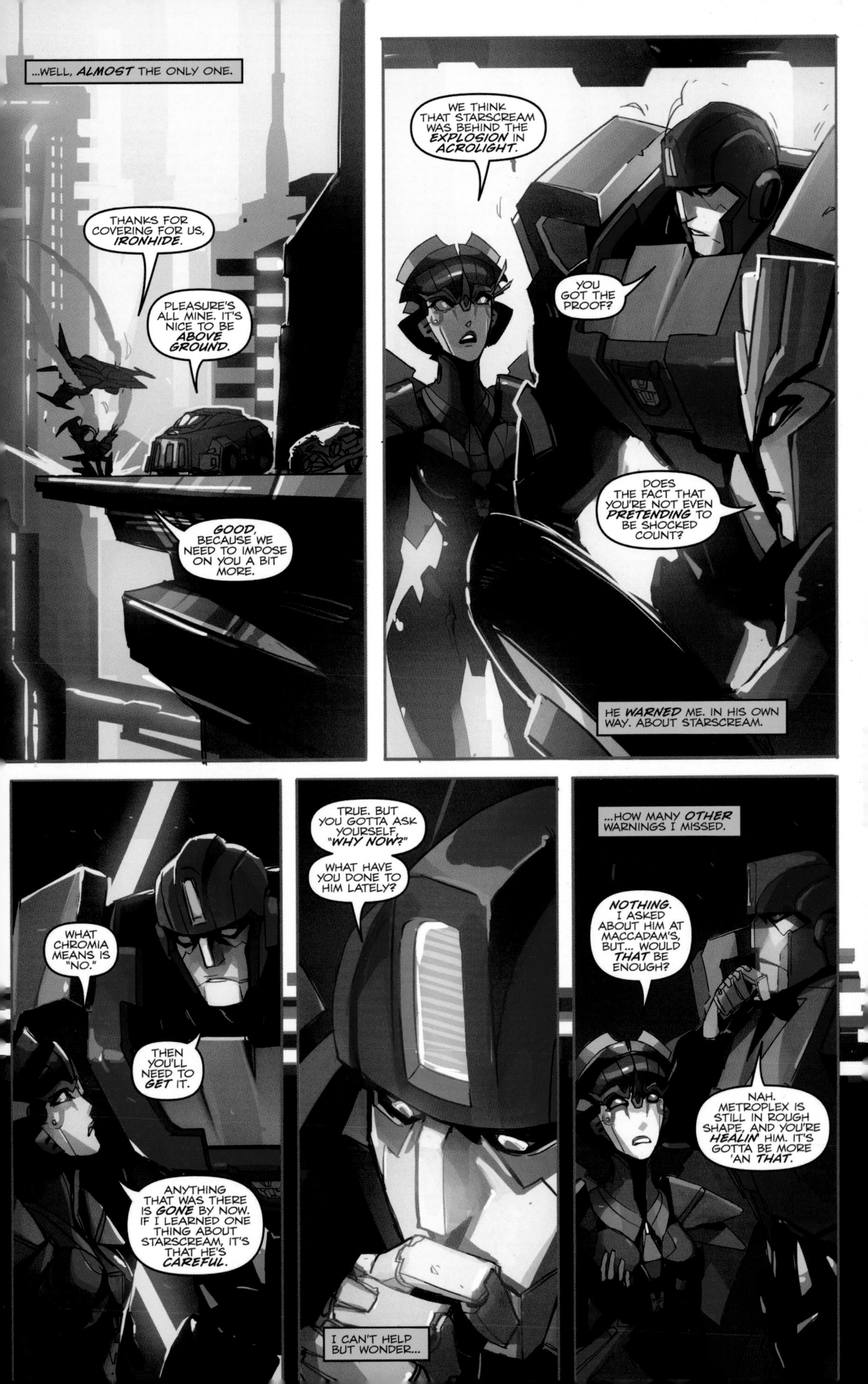
...WELL, ALMOST THE ONLY ONE.
THANKS FOR COVERING FOR US, IRONHIDE.
PLEASURE'S ALL MINE. IT'S NICE TO BE ABOVE GROUND.
GOOD, BECAUSE WE NEED TO IMPOSE ON YOU A BIT MORE.
WE THINK THAT STARSCREAM WAS BEHIND THE EXPLOSION IN ACROLIGHT.
YOU GOT THE PROOF?
DOES THE FACT THAT YOU'RE NOT EVEN PRETENDING TO BE SHOCKED COUNT?
HE WARNED ME. IN HIS OWN WAY. ABOUT STARSCREAM.
WHAT CHROMIA MEANS IS "NO."
THEN YOU'LL NEED TO GET IT.
ANYTHING THAT WAS THERE IS GONE BY NOW. IF I LEARNED ONE THING ABOUT STARSCREAM, IT'S THAT HE'S CAREFUL.
TRUE. BUT YOU GOTTA ASK YOURSELF, "WHY NOW?"
WHAT HAVE YOU DONE TO HIM LATELY?
I CAN'T HELP BUT WONDER...
...HOW MANY OTHER WARNINGS I MISSED.
NOTHING. I ASKED ABOUT HIM AT MACCADAM'S, BUT... WOULD THAT BE ENOUGH?
NAH. METROPLEX IS STILL IN ROUGH SHAPE, AND YOU'RE HEALIN' HIM. IT'S GOTTA BE MORE 'AN THAT.

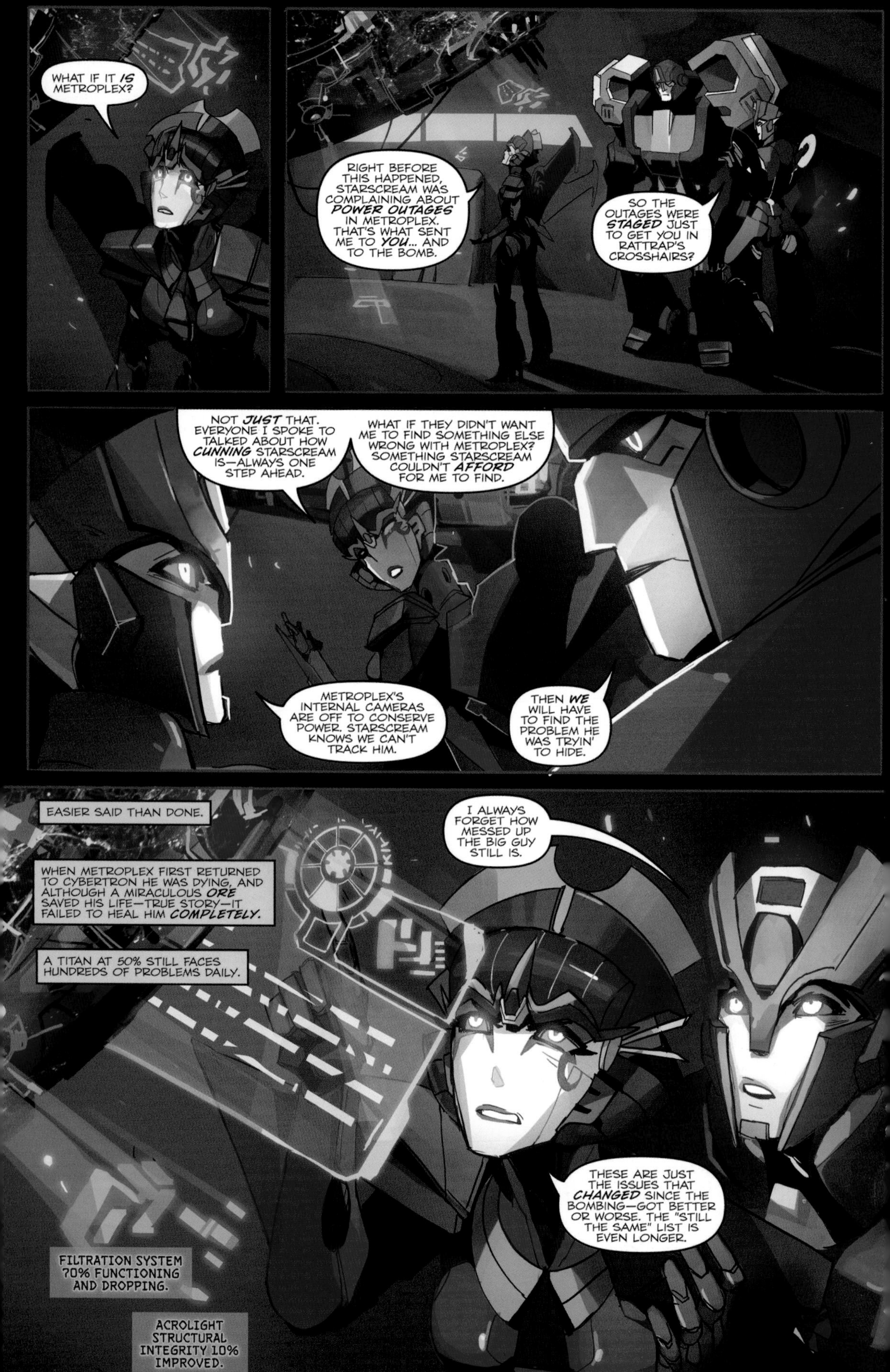
WHAT IF IT IS METROPLEX?
RIGHT BEFORE THIS HAPPENED, STARSCREAM WAS COMPLAINING ABOUT POWER OUTAGES IN METROPLEX. THAT'S WHAT SENT ME TO YOU... AND TO THE BOMB.
SO THE OUTAGES WERE STAGED JUST TO GET YOU IN RATTRAP'S CROSSHAIRS?
NOT JUST THAT. EVERYONE I SPOKE TO TALKED ABOUT HOW CUNNING STARSCREAM IS—ALWAYS ONE STEP AHEAD.
WHAT IF THEY DIDN'T WANT ME TO FIND SOMETHING ELSE WRONG WITH METROPLEX? SOMETHING STARSCREAM COULDN'T AFFORD FOR ME TO FIND.
METROPLEX'S INTERNAL CAMERAS ARE OFF TO CONSERVE POWER. STARSCREAM KNOWS WE CAN'T TRACK HIM.
THEN WE WILL HAVE TO FIND THE PROBLEM HE WAS TRYIN' TO HIDE.
EASIER SAID THAN DONE.
I ALWAYS FORGET HOW MESSED UP THE BIG GUY STILL IS.
WHEN METROPLEX FIRST RETURNED TO CYBERTRON HE WAS DYING, AND ALTHOUGH A MIRACULOUS ORE SAVED HIS LIFE—TRUE STORY—IT FAILED TO HEAL HIM COMPLETELY.
A TITAN AT 50% STILL FACES HUNDREDS OF PROBLEMS DAILY.
THESE ARE JUST THE ISSUES THAT CHANGED SINCE THE BOMBING—GOT BETTER OR WORSE. THE "STILL THE SAME" LIST IS EVEN LONGER.
FILTRATION SYSTEM 70% FUNCTIONING AND DROPPING.
ACROLIGHT STRUCTURAL INTEGRITY 10% IMPROVED.

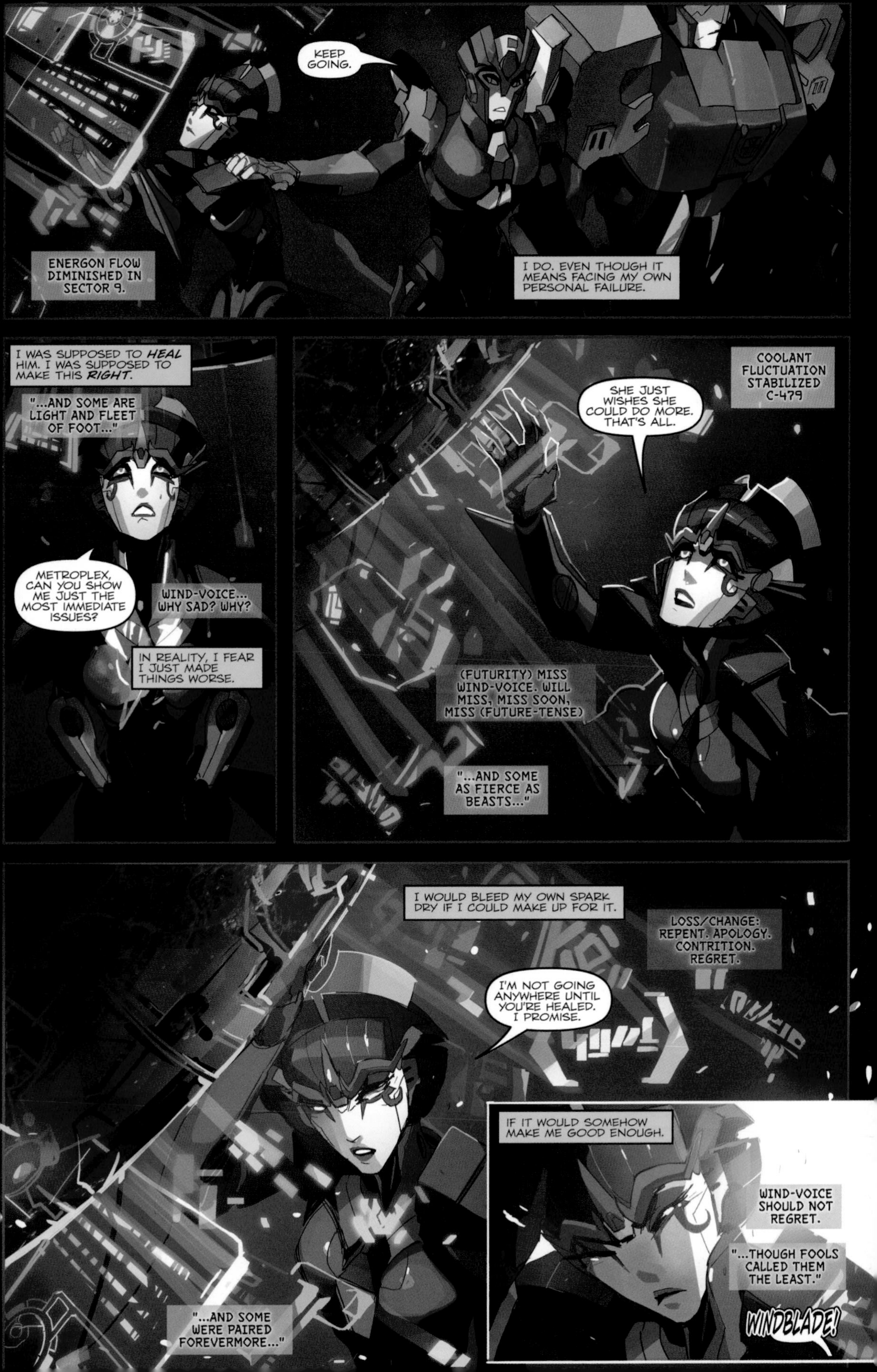
KEEP GOING.
ENERGON FLOW DIMINISHED IN SECTOR 9.
I DO. EVEN THOUGH IT MEANS FACING MY OWN PERSONAL FAILURE.
I WAS SUPPOSED TO HEAL HIM. I WAS SUPPOSED TO MAKE THIS RIGHT.
"...AND SOME ARE LIGHT AND FLEET OF FOOT..."
METROPLEX, CAN YOU SHOW ME JUST THE MOST IMMEDIATE ISSUES?
WIND-VOICE... WHY SAD? WHY?
IN REALITY, I FEAR I JUST MADE THINGS WORSE.
COOLANT FLUCTUATION STABILIZED C-479
SHE JUST WISHES SHE COULD DO MORE. THAT'S ALL.
(FUTURITY) MISS WIND-VOICE. WILL MISS, MISS SOON, MISS (FUTURE-TENSE)
"...AND SOME AS FIERCE AS BEASTS..."
I WOULD BLEED MY OWN SPARK DRY IF I COULD MAKE UP FOR IT.
LOSS/CHANGE: REPENT. APOLOGY. CONTRITION. REGRET.
I'M NOT GOING ANYWHERE UNTIL YOU'RE HEALED. I PROMISE.
"...AND SOME WERE PAIRED FOREVERMORE..."
IF IT WOULD SOMEHOW MAKE ME GOOD ENOUGH.
WIND-VOICE SHOULD NOT REGRET.
"...THOUGH FOOLS CALLED THEM THE LEAST."
WINDBLADE!

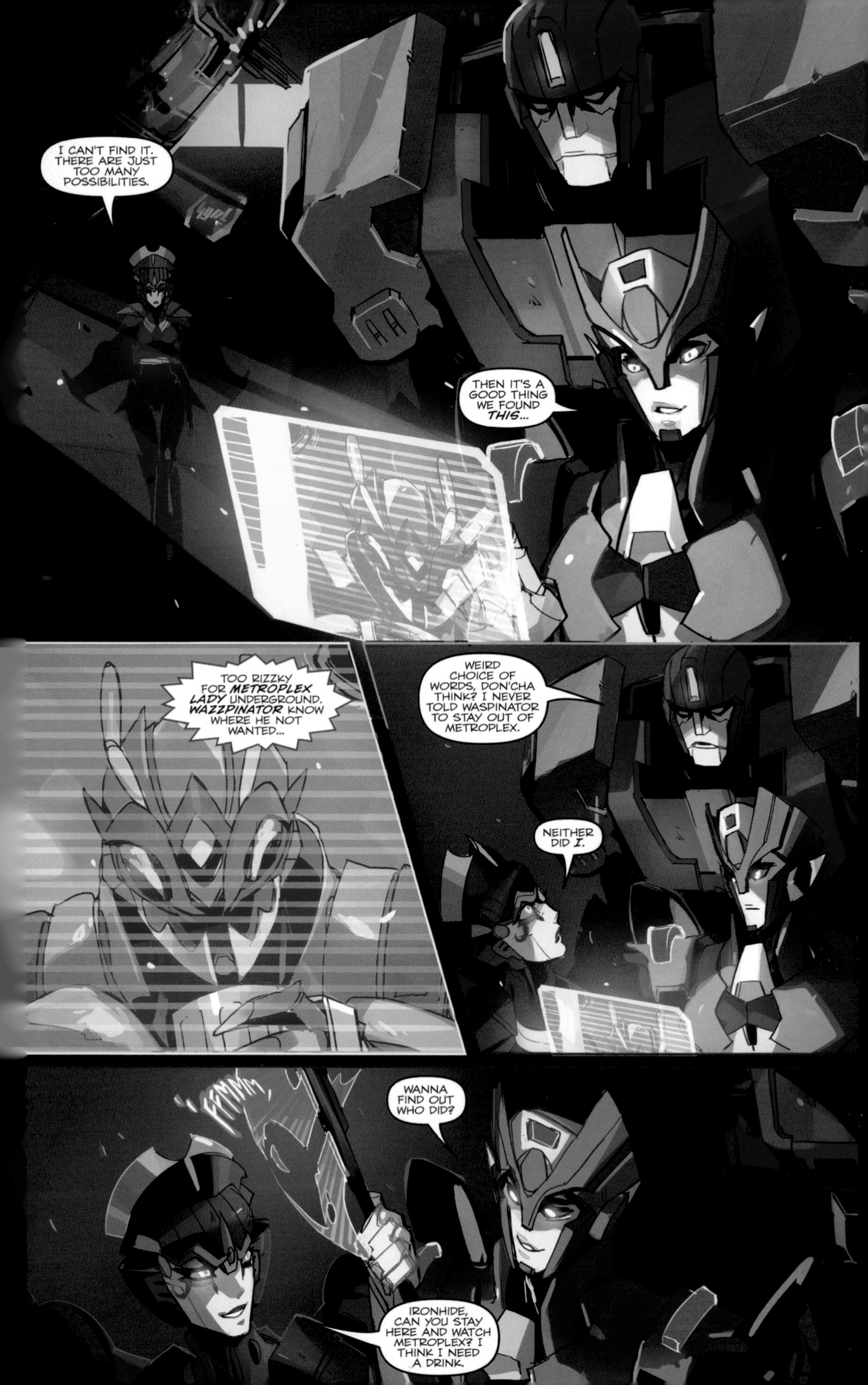
I CAN'T FIND IT. THERE ARE JUST TOO MANY POSSIBILITIES.
THEN IT'S A GOOD THING WE FOUND *THIS*...
TOO RIZZKY FOR **METROPLEX LADY** UNDERGROUND. **WAZZPINATOR** KNOW WHERE HE NOT WANTED...
WEIRD CHOICE OF WORDS, DON'CHA THINK? I NEVER TOLD WASPINATOR TO STAY OUT OF METROPLEX.
NEITHER DID *I*.
WANNA FIND OUT WHO DID?
IRONHIDE, CAN YOU STAY HERE AND WATCH METROPLEX? I THINK I NEED A DRINK.

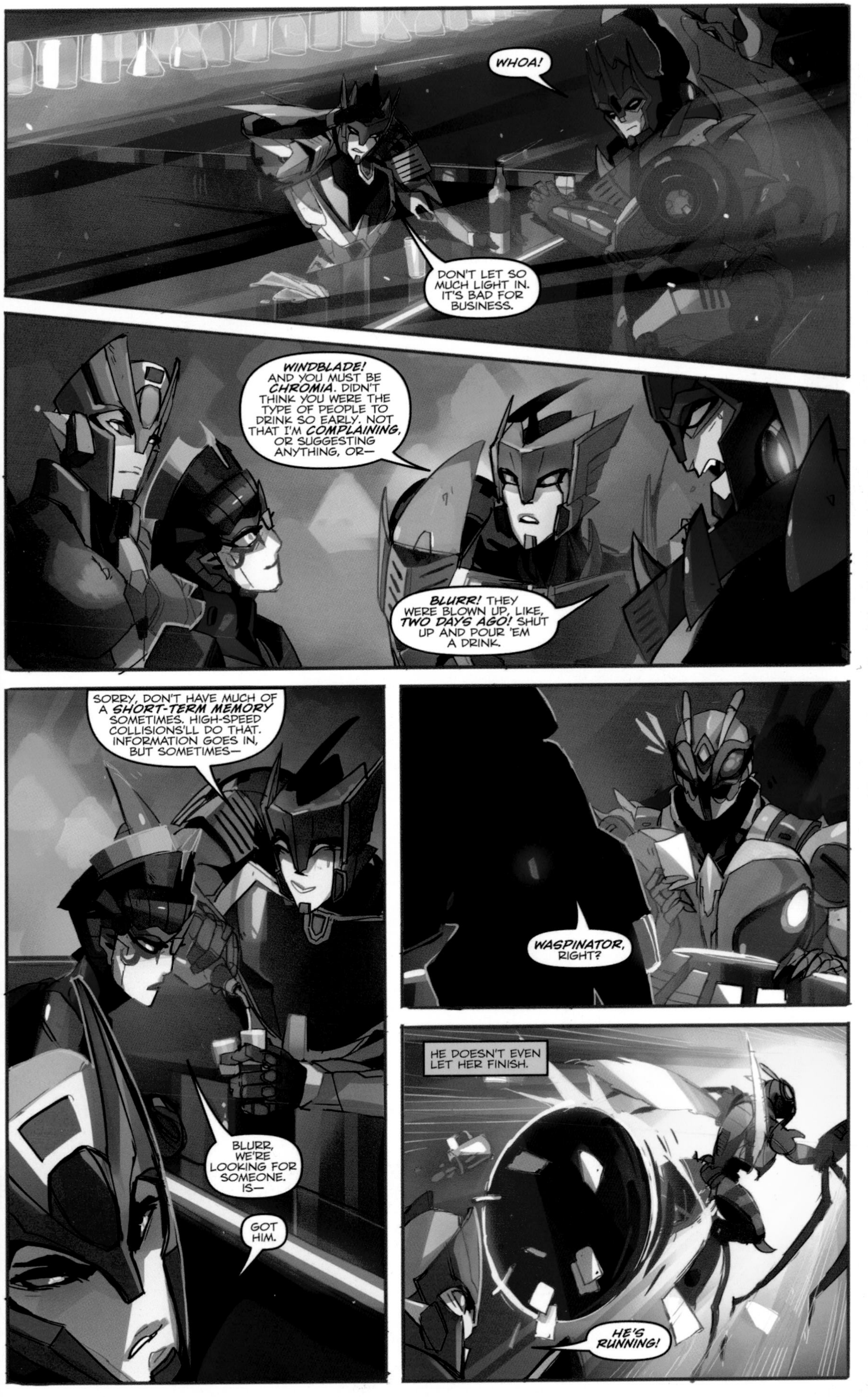
WHOA!
DON'T LET SO MUCH LIGHT IN. IT'S BAD FOR BUSINESS.
WINDBLADE! AND YOU MUST BE CHROMIA. DIDN'T THINK YOU WERE THE TYPE OF PEOPLE TO DRINK SO EARLY. NOT THAT I'M COMPLAINING, OR SUGGESTING ANYTHING, OR—
BLURR! THEY WERE BLOWN UP, LIKE, TWO DAYS AGO! SHUT UP AND POUR 'EM A DRINK.
SORRY, DON'T HAVE MUCH OF A SHORT-TERM MEMORY SOMETIMES. HIGH-SPEED COLLISIONS'LL DO THAT. INFORMATION GOES IN, BUT SOMETIMES—
BLURR, WE'RE LOOKING FOR SOMEONE. IS—
GOT HIM.
WASPINATOR, RIGHT?
HE DOESN'T EVEN LET HER FINISH.
HE'S RUNNING!

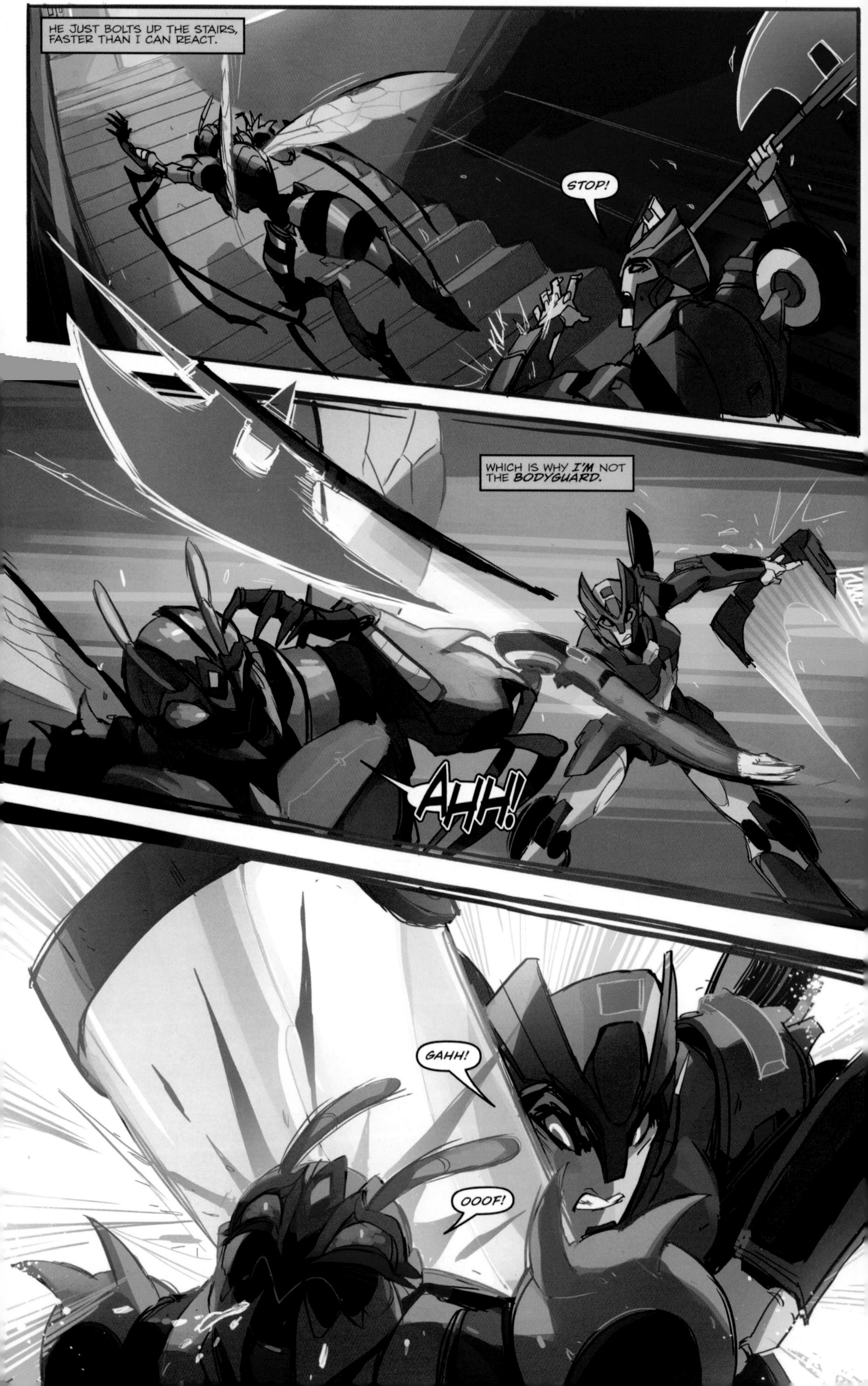
HE JUST BOLTS UP THE STAIRS, FASTER THAN I CAN REACT.
STOP!
WHICH IS WHY I'M NOT THE BODYGUARD.
AHH!
GAHH!
OOOF!

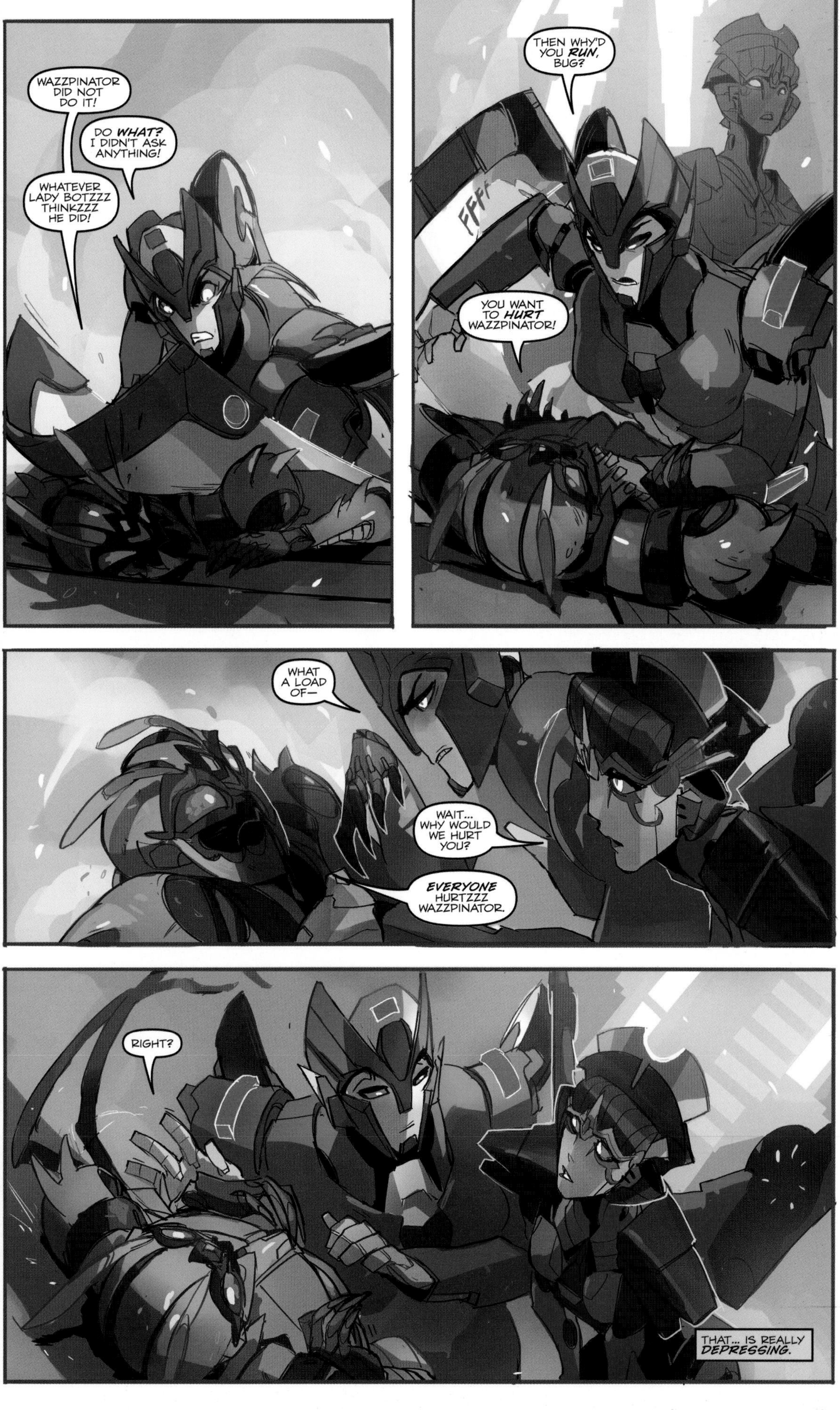
WAZZPINATOR DID NOT DO IT!
DO WHAT? I DIDN'T ASK ANYTHING!
WHATEVER LADY BOTZZZ THINKZZZ HE DID!
THEN WHY'D YOU RUN, BUG?
FFF
YOU WANT TO HURT WAZZPINATOR!
WHAT A LOAD OF—
WAIT... WHY WOULD WE HURT YOU?
EVERYONE HURTZZZ WAZZPINATOR.
RIGHT?
THAT... IS REALLY DEPRESSING.

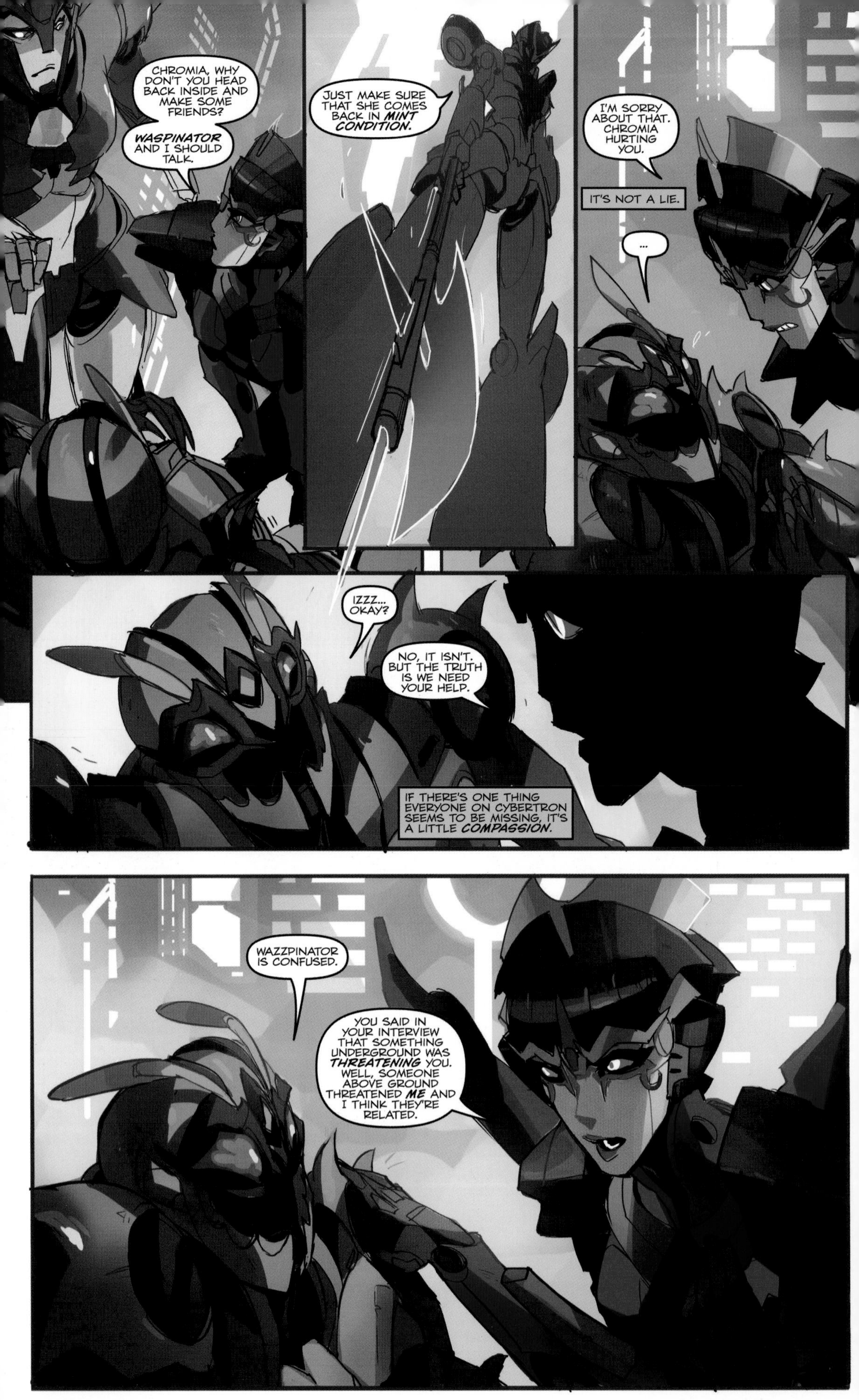
CHROMIA, WHY DON'T YOU HEAD BACK INSIDE AND MAKE SOME FRIENDS?
WASPINATOR AND I SHOULD TALK.
JUST MAKE SURE THAT SHE COMES BACK IN MINT CONDITION.
I'M SORRY ABOUT THAT. CHROMIA HURTING YOU.
IT'S NOT A LIE.
...
IZZZ... OKAY?
NO, IT ISN'T. BUT THE TRUTH IS WE NEED YOUR HELP.
IF THERE'S ONE THING EVERYONE ON CYBERTRON SEEMS TO BE MISSING, IT'S A LITTLE COMPASSION.
WAZZPINATOR IS CONFUSED.
YOU SAID IN YOUR INTERVIEW THAT SOMETHING UNDERGROUND WAS THREATENING YOU. WELL, SOMEONE ABOVE GROUND THREATENED ME AND I THINK THEY'RE RELATED.

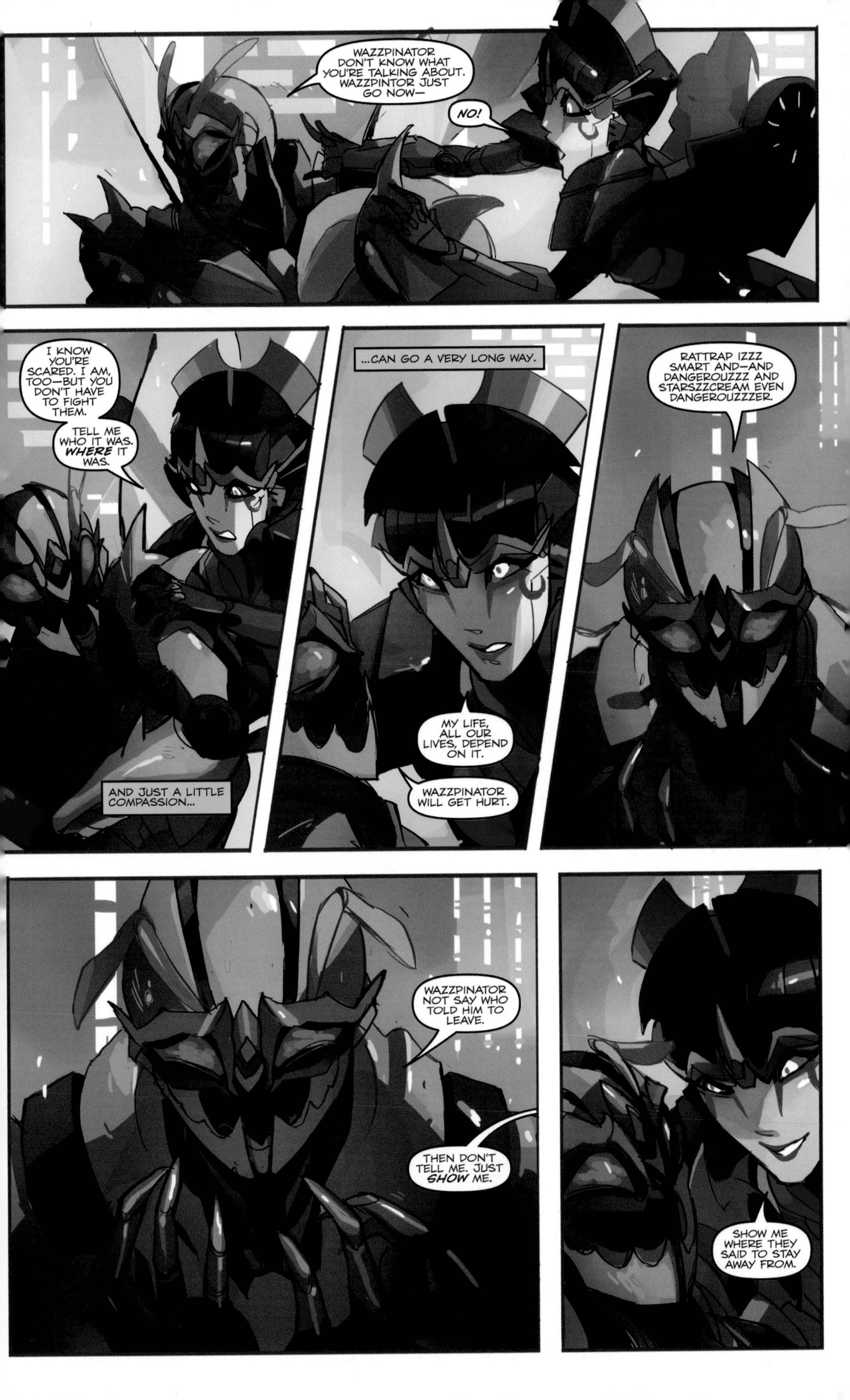
WAZZPINATOR DON'T KNOW WHAT YOU'RE TALKING ABOUT. WAZZPINTOR JUST GO NOW—
NO!
I KNOW YOU'RE SCARED. I AM, TOO—BUT YOU DON'T HAVE TO FIGHT THEM.
TELL ME WHO IT WAS. WHERE IT WAS.
AND JUST A LITTLE COMPASSION...
...CAN GO A VERY LONG WAY.
MY LIFE, ALL OUR LIVES, DEPEND ON IT.
WAZZPINATOR WILL GET HURT.
RATTRAP IZZZ SMART AND—AND DANGEROUZZZ AND STARSZZCREAM EVEN DANGEROUZZZER.
WAZZPINATOR NOT SAY WHO TOLD HIM TO LEAVE.
THEN DON'T TELL ME. JUST SHOW ME.
SHOW ME WHERE THEY SAID TO STAY AWAY FROM.

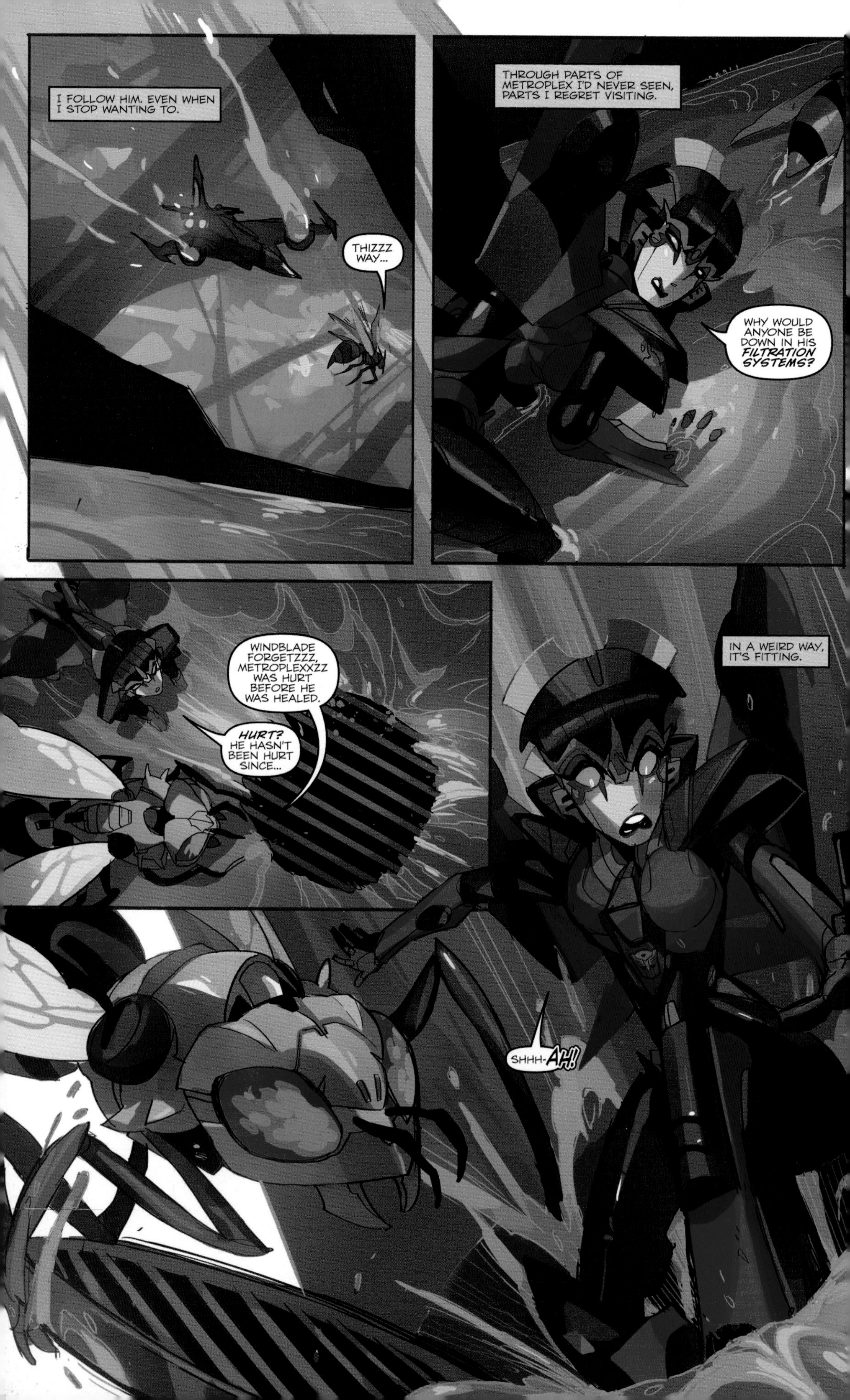
I FOLLOW HIM. EVEN WHEN I STOP WANTING TO.
THIZZZ WAY...
THROUGH PARTS OF METROPLEX I'D NEVER SEEN, PARTS I REGRET VISITING.
WHY WOULD ANYONE BE DOWN IN HIS FILTRATION SYSTEMS?
WINDBLADE FORGETZZZ, METROPLEXXZZ WAS HURT BEFORE HE WAS HEALED.
HURT? HE HASN'T BEEN HURT SINCE...
IN A WEIRD WAY, IT'S FITTING.
SHHH-AH!

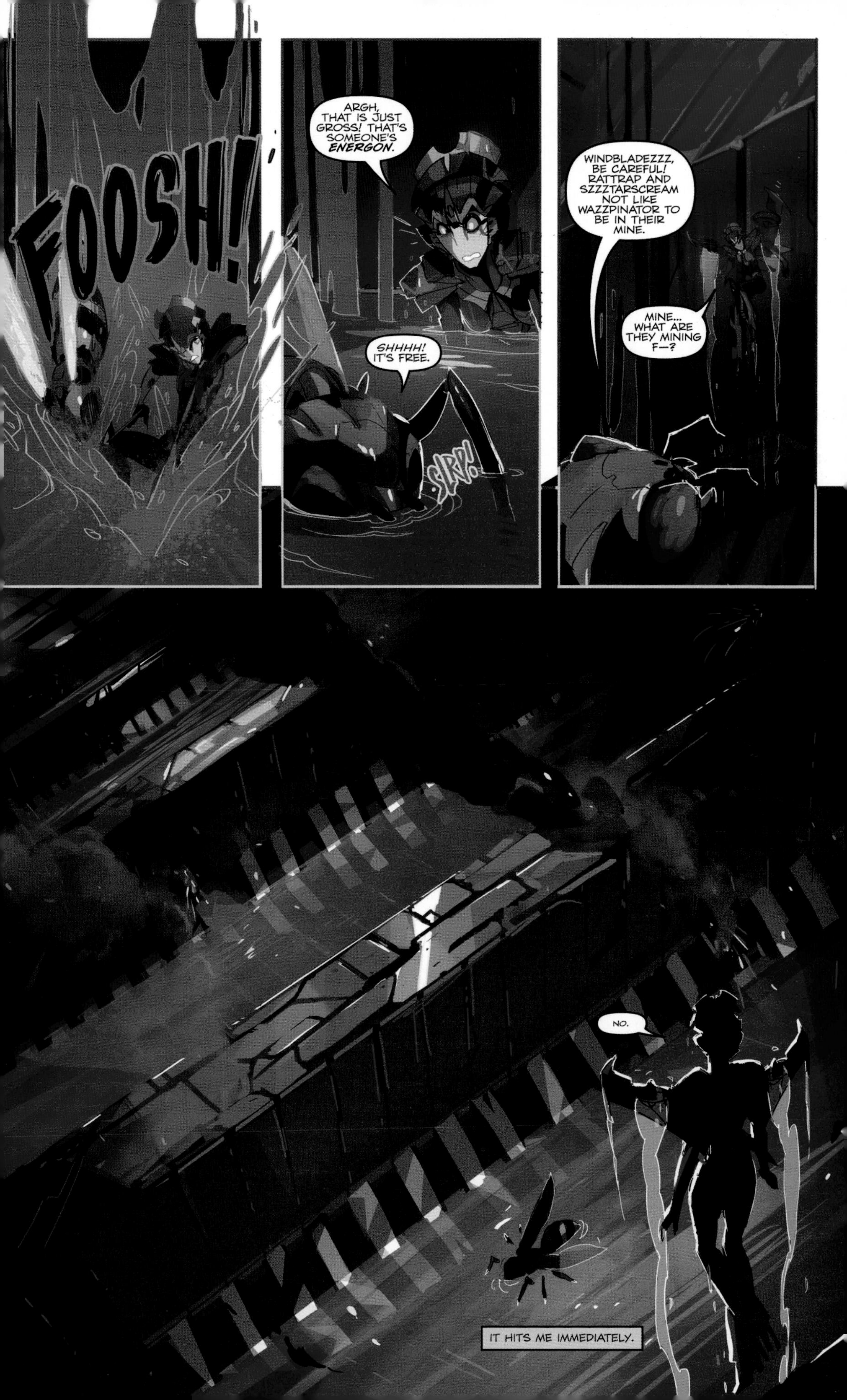
FOOSH!!
ARGH, THAT IS JUST GROSS! THAT'S SOMEONE'S ENERGON.
SHHHH! IT'S FREE.
SLRP!
WINDBLADEZZZ, BE CAREFUL! RATTRAP AND SZZZTARSCREAM NOT LIKE WAZZPINATOR TO BE IN THEIR MINE.
MINE... WHAT ARE THEY MINING F—?
NO.
IT HITS ME IMMEDIATELY.

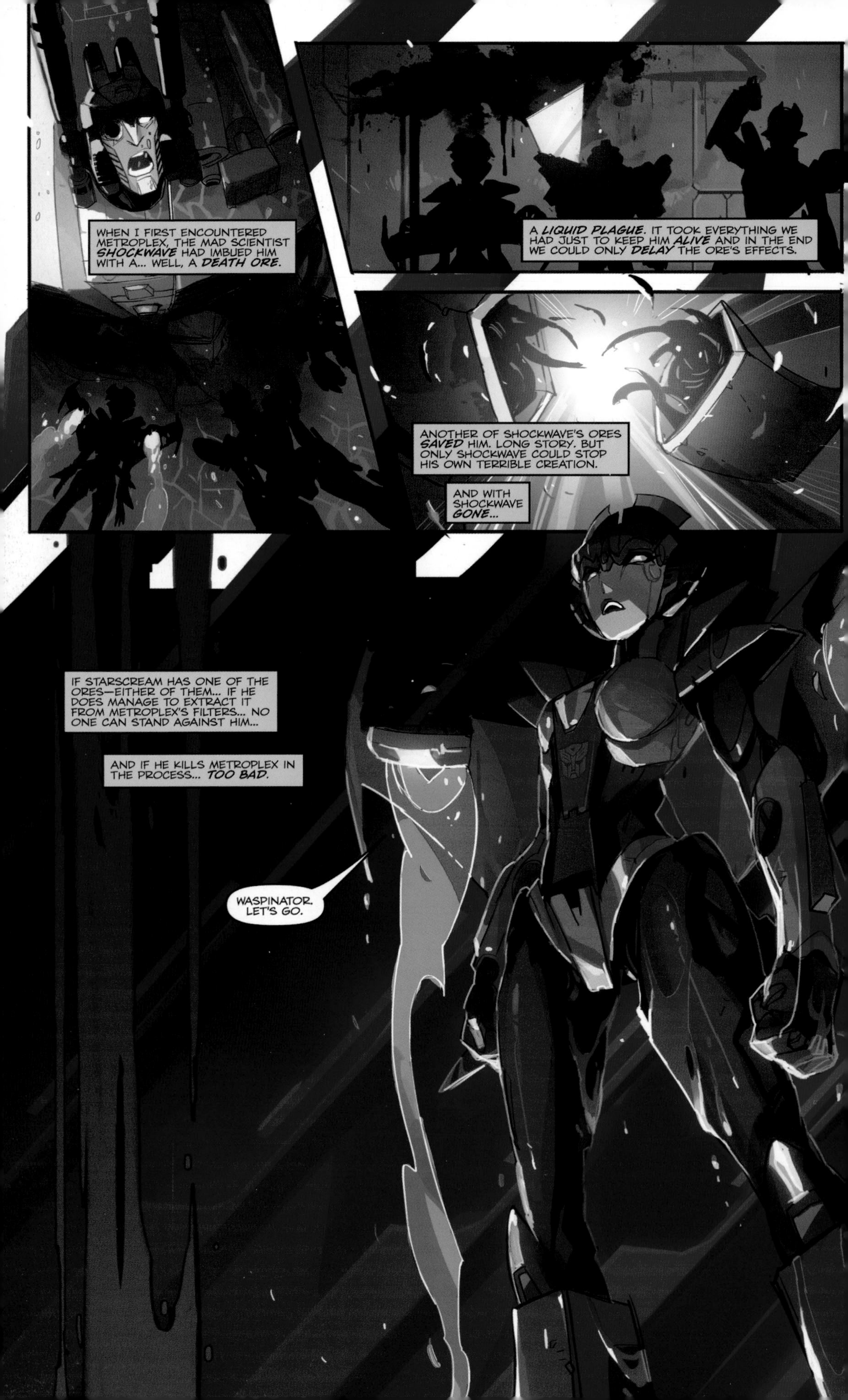

WHEN I FIRST ENCOUNTERED METROPLEX, THE MAD SCIENTIST SHOCKWAVE HAD IMBUED HIM WITH A... WELL, A DEATH ORE.
A LIQUID PLAGUE. IT TOOK EVERYTHING WE HAD JUST TO KEEP HIM ALIVE AND IN THE END WE COULD ONLY DELAY THE ORE'S EFFECTS.
ANOTHER OF SHOCKWAVE'S ORES SAVED HIM. LONG STORY. BUT ONLY SHOCKWAVE COULD STOP HIS OWN TERRIBLE CREATION.
AND WITH SHOCKWAVE GONE...
IF STARSCREAM HAS ONE OF THE ORES—EITHER OF THEM... IF HE DOES MANAGE TO EXTRACT IT FROM METROPLEX'S FILTERS... NO ONE CAN STAND AGAINST HIM...
AND IF HE KILLS METROPLEX IN THE PROCESS... TOO BAD.
WASPINATOR. LET'S GO.

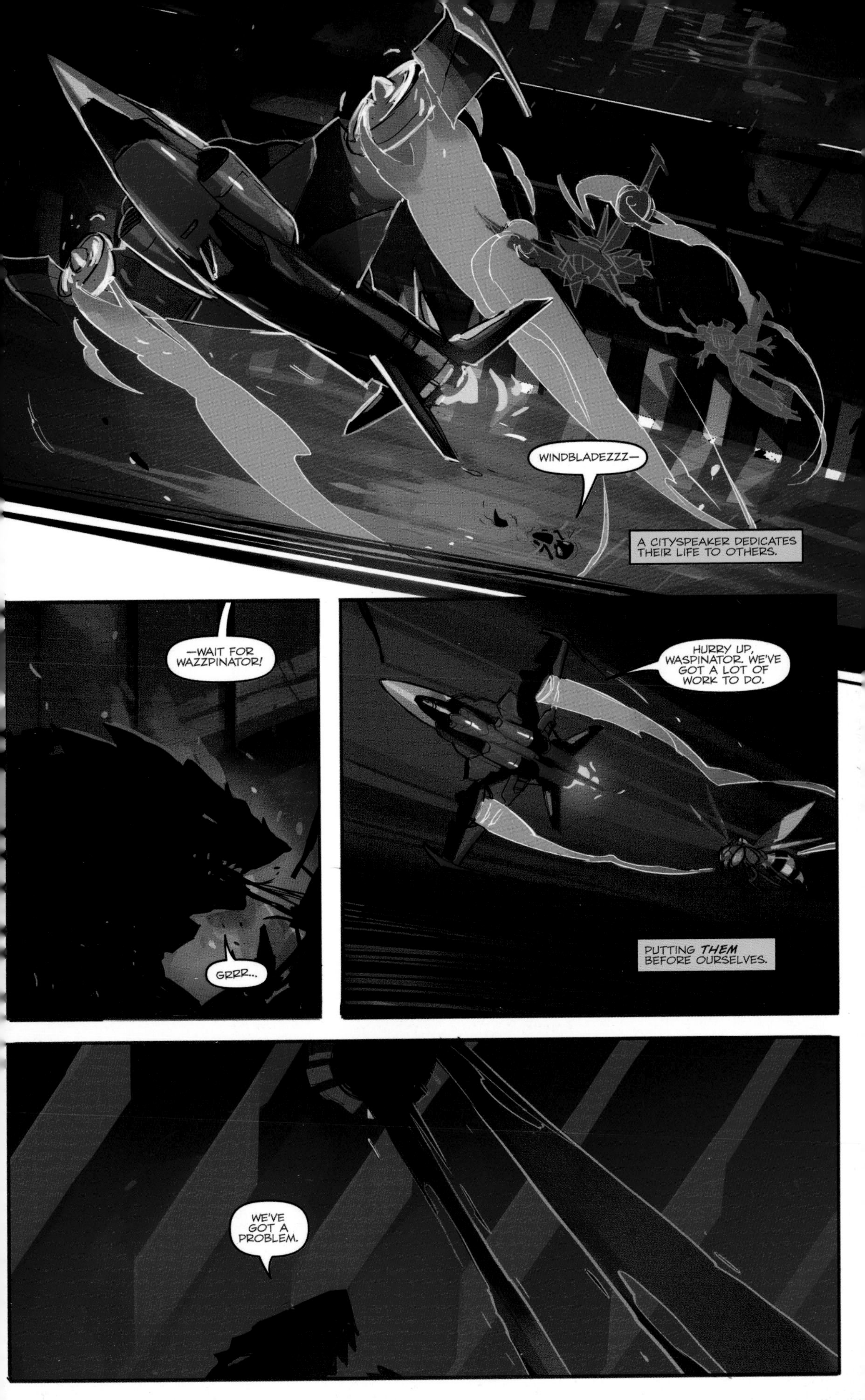
WINDBLADEZZZ—
A CITYSPEAKER DEDICATES THEIR LIFE TO OTHERS.
—WAIT FOR WAZZPINATOR!
GRRR...
HURRY UP, WASPINATOR. WE'VE GOT A LOT OF WORK TO DO.
PUTTING THEM BEFORE OURSELVES.
WE'VE GOT A PROBLEM.

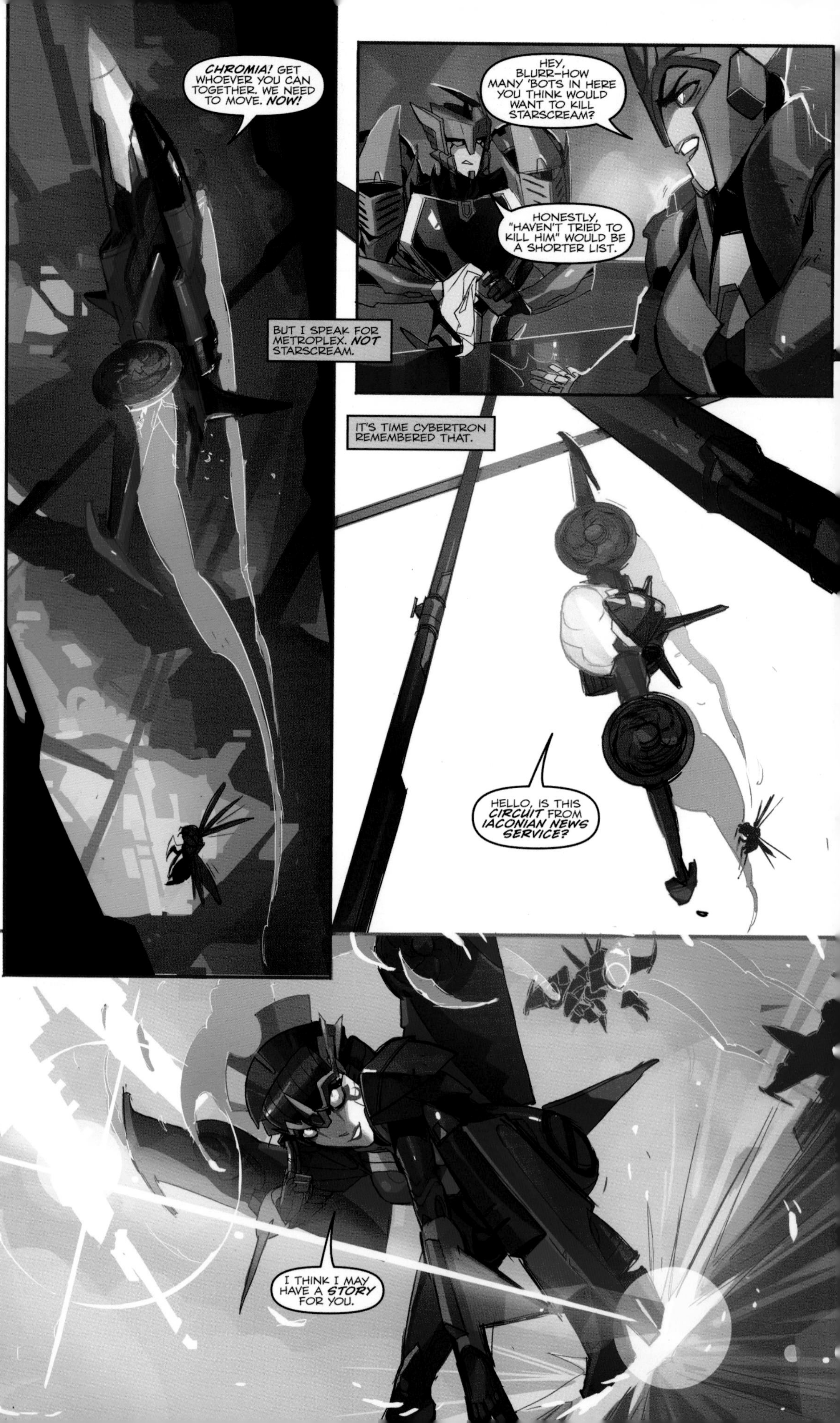
CHROMIA! GET WHOEVER YOU CAN TOGETHER. WE NEED TO MOVE. NOW!
HEY, BLURR—HOW MANY 'BOTS IN HERE YOU THINK WOULD WANT TO KILL STARSCREAM?
HONESTLY, "HAVEN'T TRIED TO KILL HIM" WOULD BE A SHORTER LIST.
BUT I SPEAK FOR METROPLEX. NOT STARSCREAM.
IT'S TIME CYBERTRON REMEMBERED THAT.
HELLO, IS THIS CIRCUIT FROM IACONIAN NEWS SERVICE?
I THINK I MAY HAVE A STORY FOR YOU.

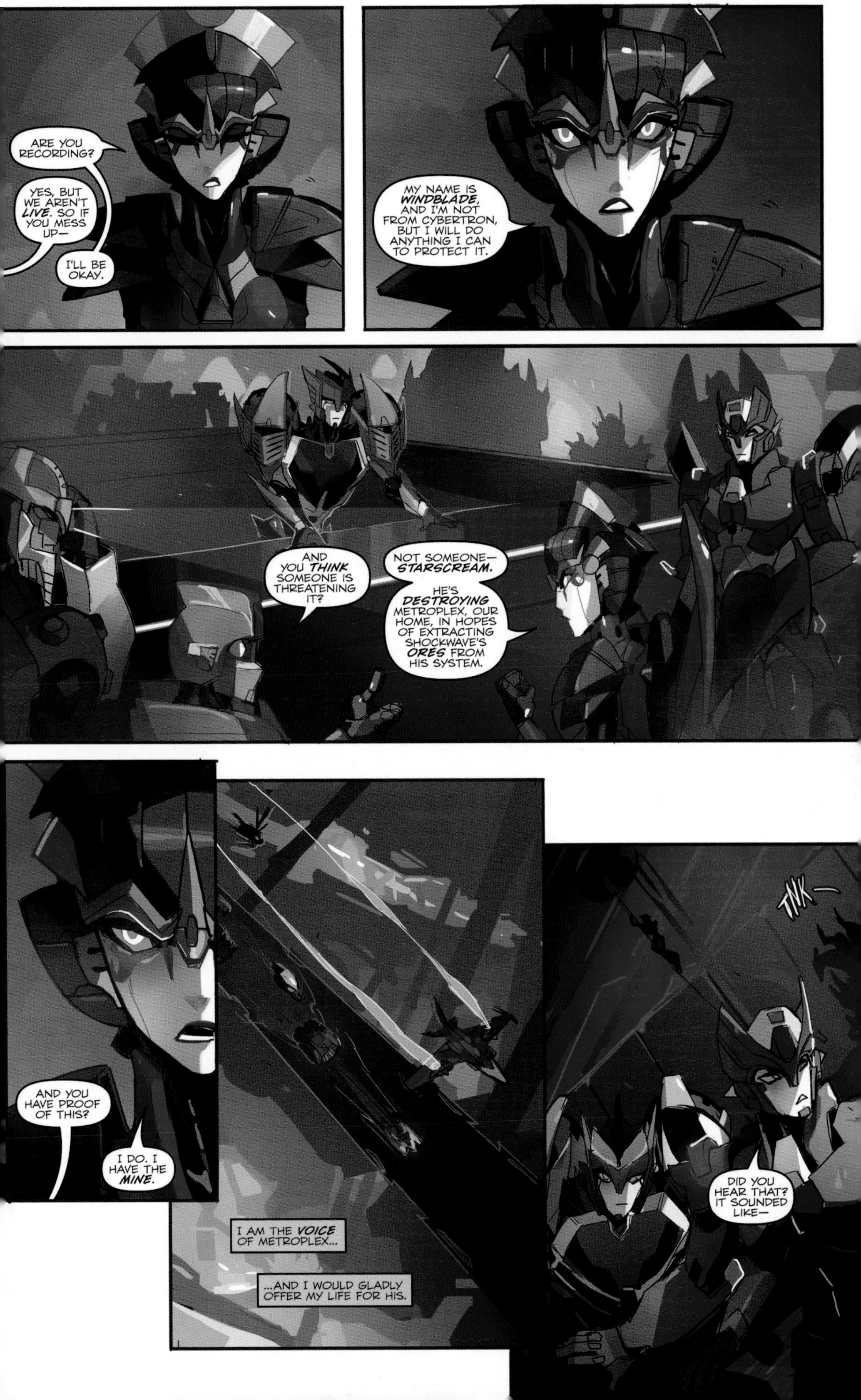
ARE YOU RECORDING?
YES, BUT WE AREN'T LIVE. SO IF YOU MESS UP—
I'LL BE OKAY.
MY NAME IS WINDBLADE, AND I'M NOT FROM CYBERTRON, BUT I WILL DO ANYTHING I CAN TO PROTECT IT.
AND YOU THINK SOMEONE IS THREATENING IT?
NOT SOMEONE— STARSCREAM.
HE'S DESTROYING METROPLEX, OUR HOME, IN HOPES OF EXTRACTING SHOCKWAVE'S ORES FROM HIS SYSTEM.
AND YOU HAVE PROOF OF THIS?
I DO. I HAVE THE MINE.
I AM THE VOICE OF METROPLEX...
...AND I WOULD GLADLY OFFER MY LIFE FOR HIS.
TNK—
DID YOU HEAR THAT? IT SOUNDED LIKE—

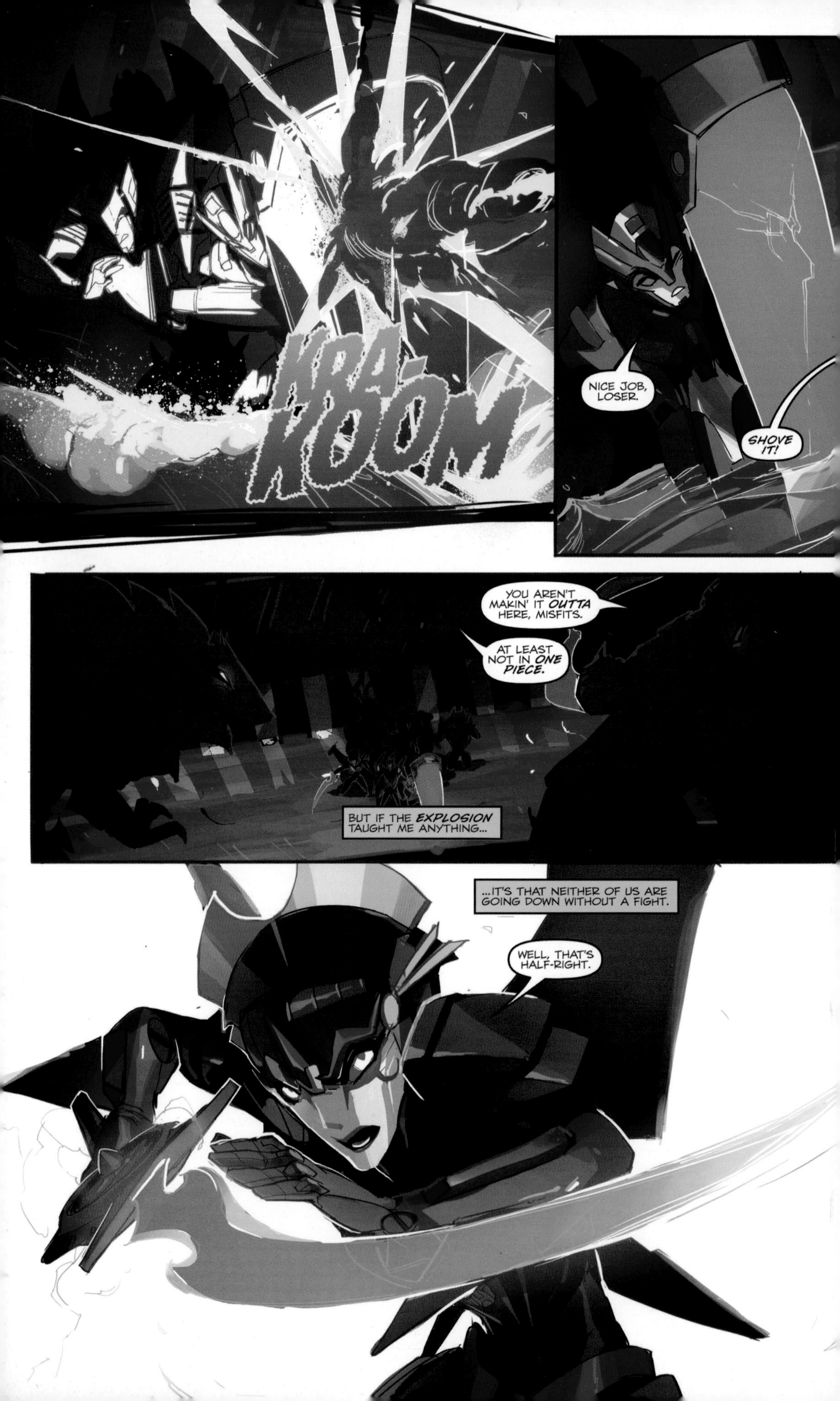
KRA-KOOOM
NICE JOB, LOSER.
SHOVE IT!
YOU AREN'T MAKIN' IT OUTTA HERE, MISFITS.
AT LEAST NOT IN ONE PIECE.
BUT IF THE EXPLOSION TAUGHT ME ANYTHING...
...IT'S THAT NEITHER OF US ARE GOING DOWN WITHOUT A FIGHT.
WELL, THAT'S HALF-RIGHT.

ART BY **ALEX MILNE**
COLORS BY **PRISCILLA TRAMONTANO**

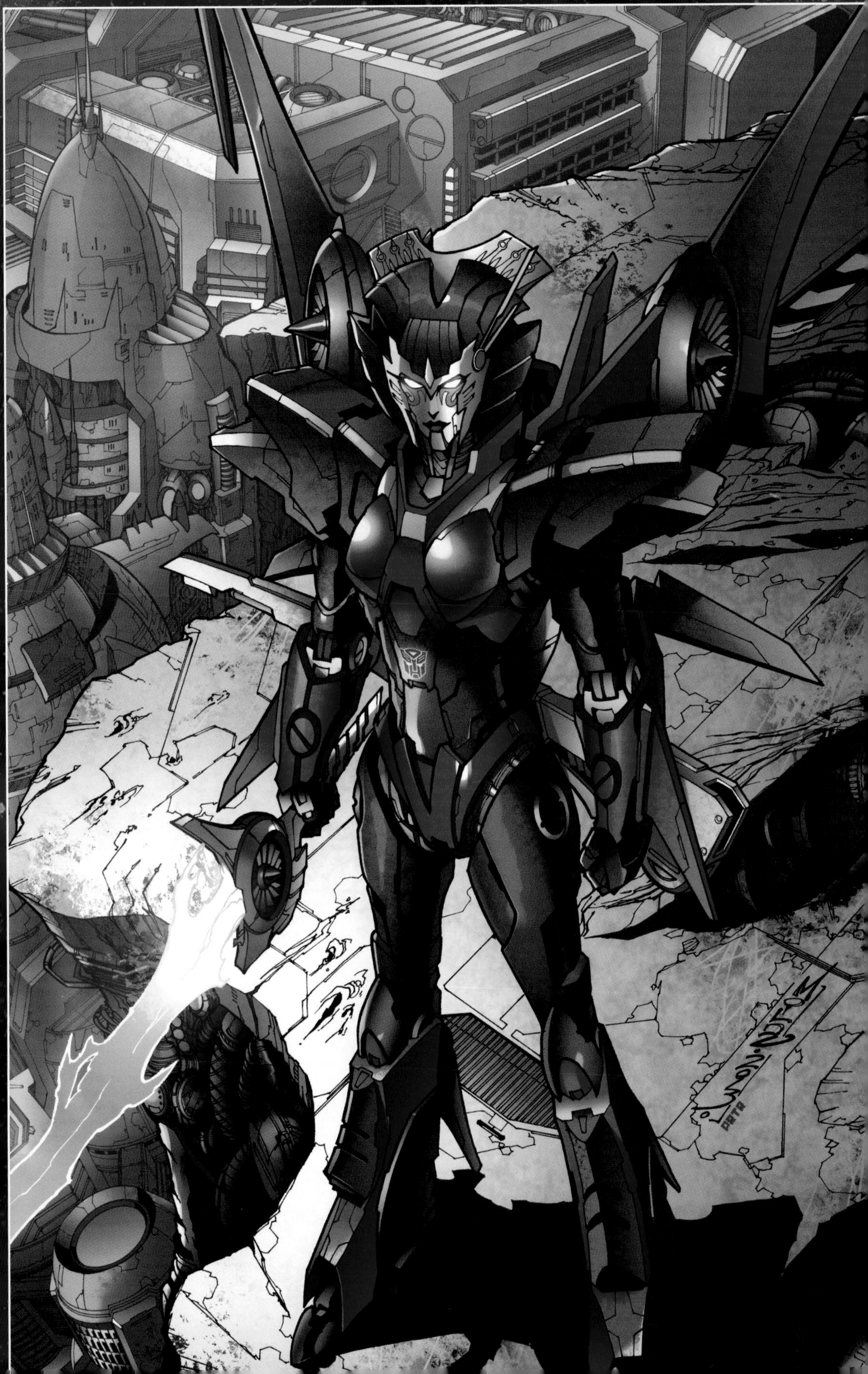

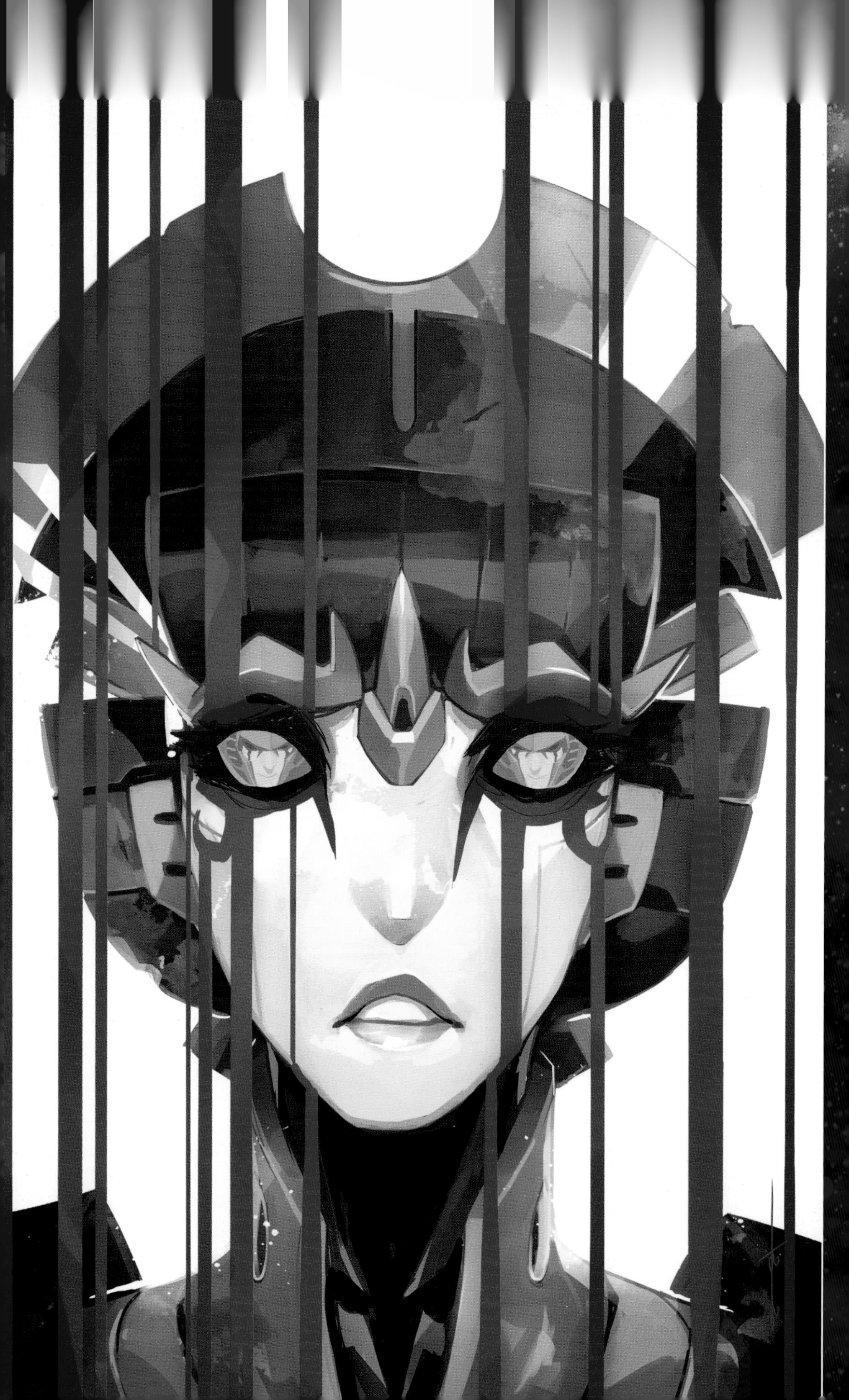

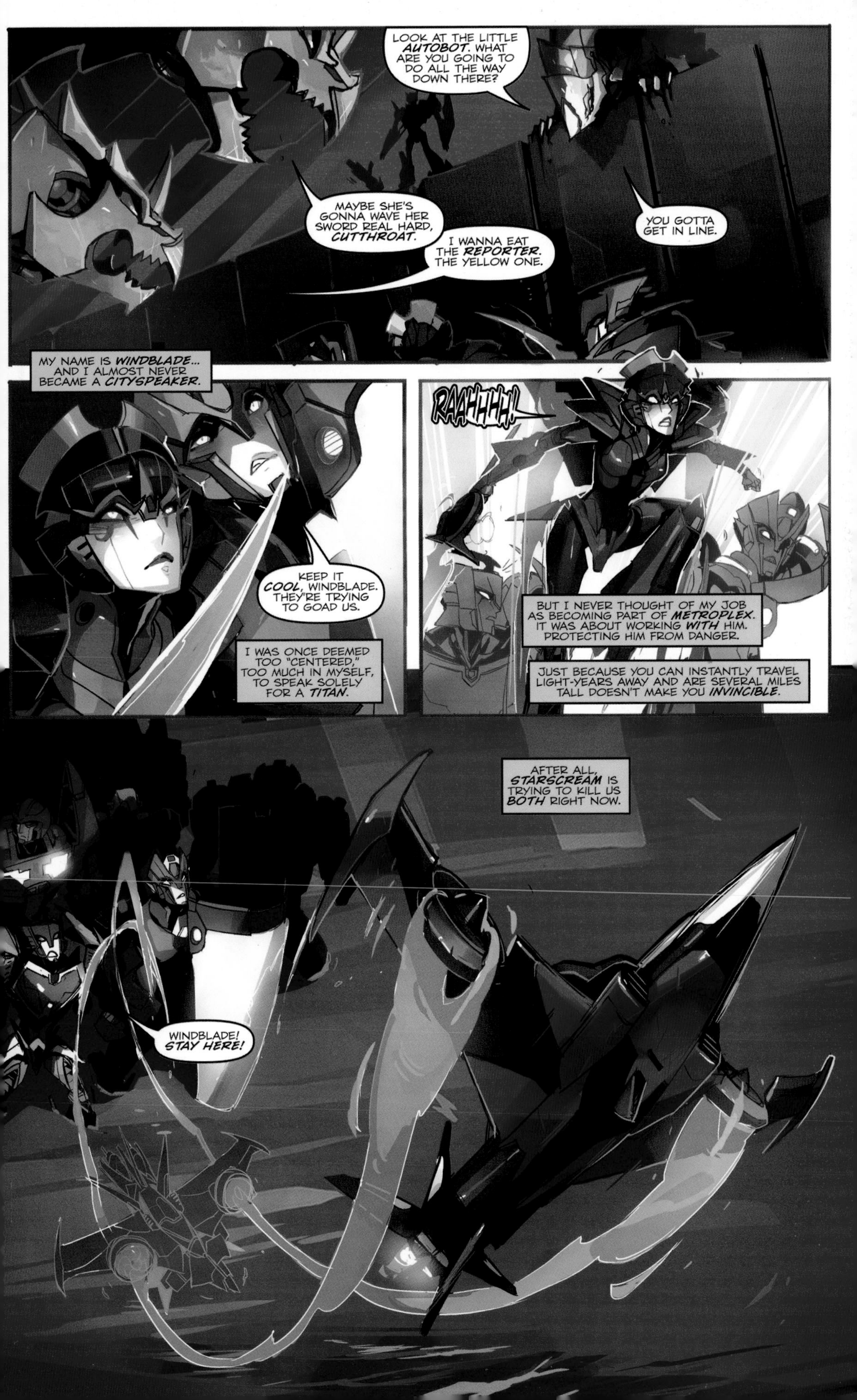
LOOK AT THE LITTLE AUTOBOT. WHAT ARE YOU GOING TO DO ALL THE WAY DOWN THERE?
MAYBE SHE'S GONNA WAVE HER SWORD REAL HARD, CUTTHROAT.
I WANNA EAT THE REPORTER. THE YELLOW ONE.
YOU GOTTA GET IN LINE.
MY NAME IS WINDBLADE... AND I ALMOST NEVER BECAME A CITYSPEAKER.
KEEP IT COOL, WINDBLADE. THEY'RE TRYING TO GOAD US.
I WAS ONCE DEEMED TOO "CENTERED," TOO MUCH IN MYSELF, TO SPEAK SOLELY FOR A TITAN.
RAAHHHH!
BUT I NEVER THOUGHT OF MY JOB AS BECOMING PART OF METROPLEX. IT WAS ABOUT WORKING WITH HIM. PROTECTING HIM FROM DANGER.
JUST BECAUSE YOU CAN INSTANTLY TRAVEL LIGHT-YEARS AWAY AND ARE SEVERAL MILES TALL DOESN'T MAKE YOU INVINCIBLE.
AFTER ALL, STARSCREAM IS TRYING TO KILL US BOTH RIGHT NOW.
WINDBLADE! STAY HERE!

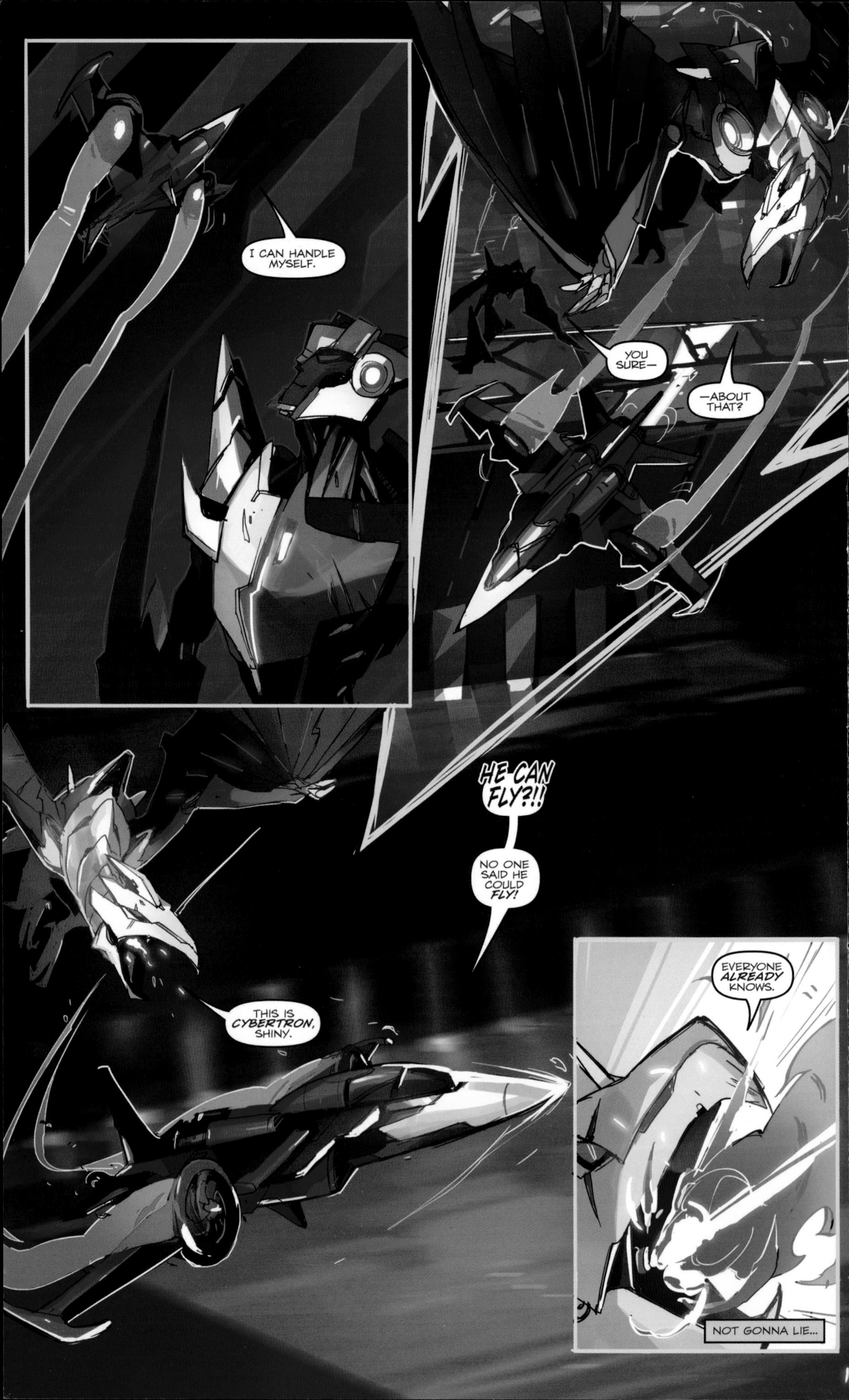
I CAN HANDLE MYSELF.
YOU SURE—
—ABOUT THAT?
HE CAN FLY?!!
NO ONE SAID HE COULD *FLY!*
THIS IS *CYBERTRON,* SHINY.
EVERYONE *ALREADY* KNOWS.
NOT GONNA LIE...

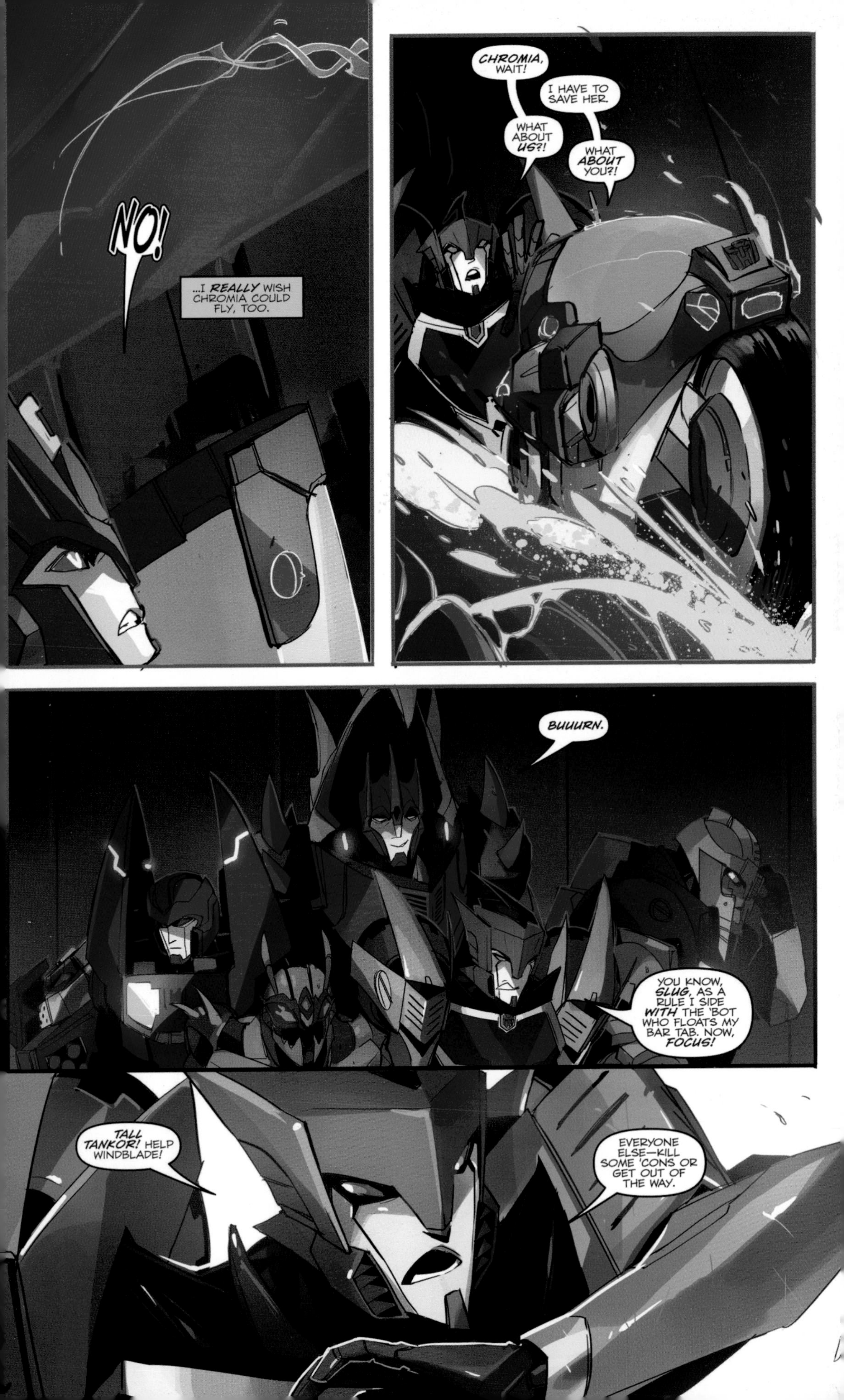
NO!
...I REALLY WISH CHROMIA COULD FLY, TOO.
CHROMIA, WAIT!
I HAVE TO SAVE HER.
WHAT ABOUT US?!
WHAT ABOUT YOU?!
BUUURN.
YOU KNOW, SLUG, AS A RULE I SIDE WITH THE 'BOT WHO FLOATS MY BAR TAB. NOW, FOCUS!
TALL TANKOR! HELP WINDBLADE!
EVERYONE ELSE—KILL SOME 'CONS OR GET OUT OF THE WAY.

GAH!

WE DON'T GENERALLY USE RANGED WEAPONS ON *CAMINUS.* THEY'RE DEEMED TOO *WASTEFUL.*

MISS WITH A GUN AND WHATEVER YOU SHOT IS *GONE.*

KEEP FILMING! COME ON!

NO OFFENSE, *CIRCUIT.* BUT GET YOUR HANDS *OFF MY HEAD!*

LONGTOOTH! HOLD THE SHOT!

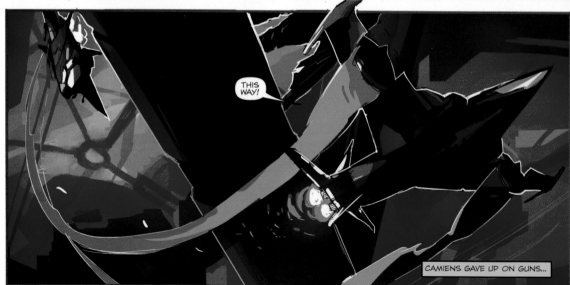

THIS WAY!

CAMIENS GAVE UP ON GUNS...

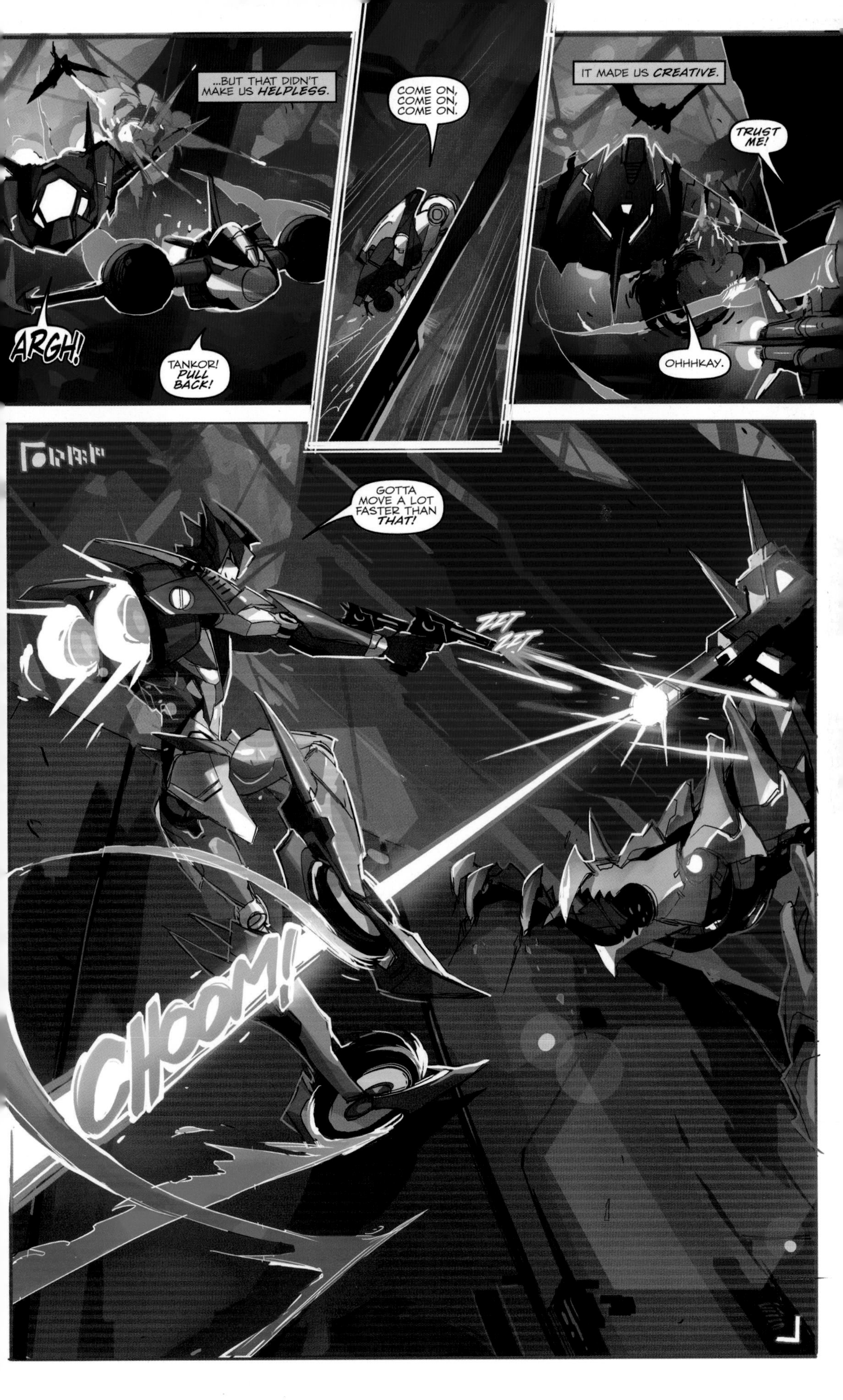
...BUT THAT DIDN'T MAKE US HELPLESS.
ARGH!
TANKOR! PULL BACK!
COME ON, COME ON, COME ON.
IT MADE US CREATIVE.
TRUST ME!
OHHHKAY.
GOTTA MOVE A LOT FASTER THAN THAT!
CHOOM!

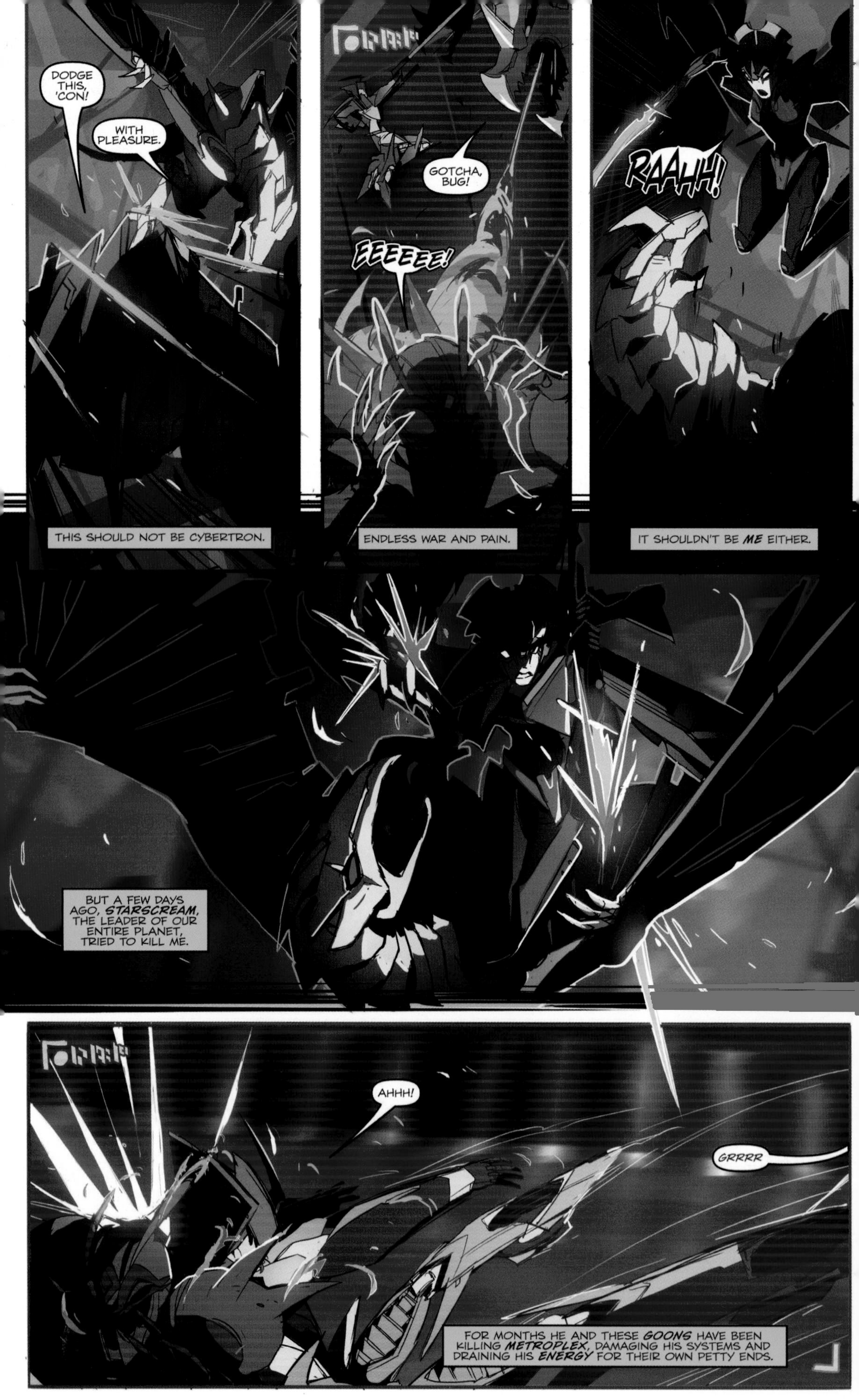
DODGE THIS, 'CON!
WITH PLEASURE.
THIS SHOULD NOT BE CYBERTRON.
GOTCHA, BUG!
EEEEEE!
ENDLESS WAR AND PAIN.
RAAHH!
IT SHOULDN'T BE ME EITHER.
BUT A FEW DAYS AGO, STARSCREAM, THE LEADER OF OUR ENTIRE PLANET, TRIED TO KILL ME.
AHHH!
GRRRR
FOR MONTHS HE AND THESE GOONS HAVE BEEN KILLING METROPLEX, DAMAGING HIS SYSTEMS AND DRAINING HIS ENERGY FOR THEIR OWN PETTY ENDS.

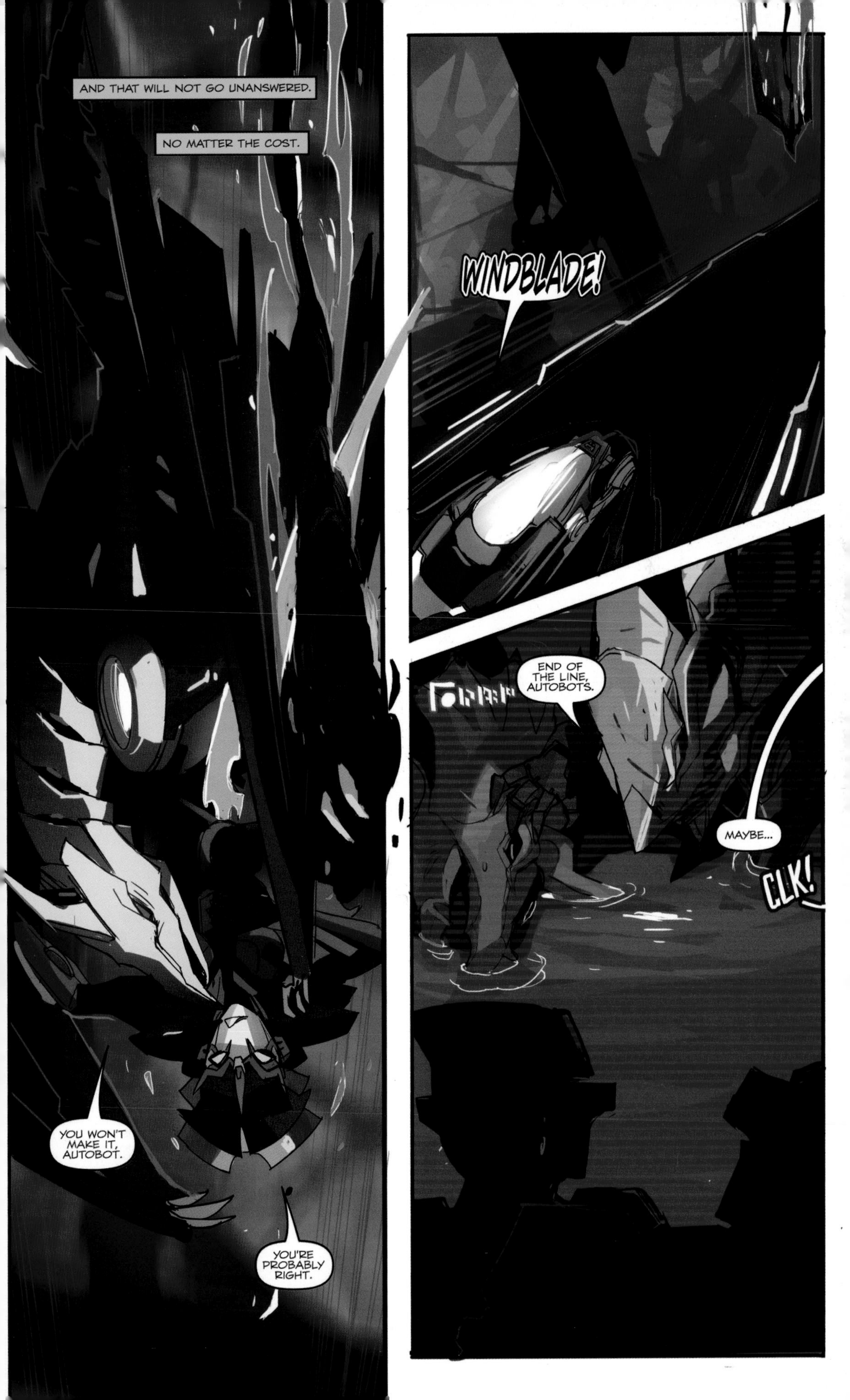
AND THAT WILL NOT GO UNANSWERED.
NO MATTER THE COST.
YOU WON'T MAKE IT, AUTOBOT.
YOU'RE PROBABLY RIGHT.
WINDBLADE!
END OF THE LINE, AUTOBOTS.
MAYBE...
CLK!

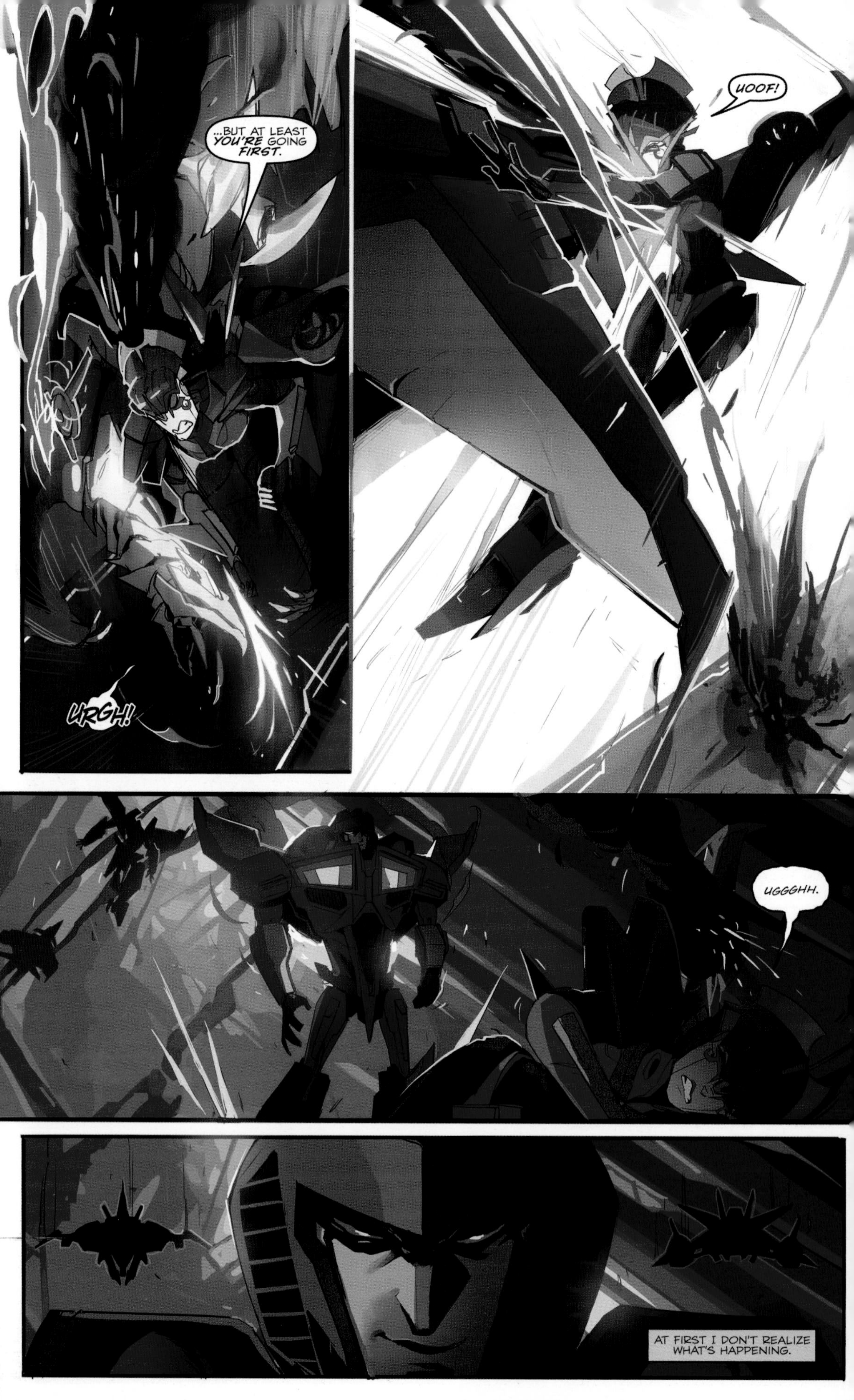
...BUT AT LEAST YOU'RE GOING FIRST.
URGH!
UOOF!
UGGGHH.
AT FIRST I DON'T REALIZE WHAT'S HAPPENING.

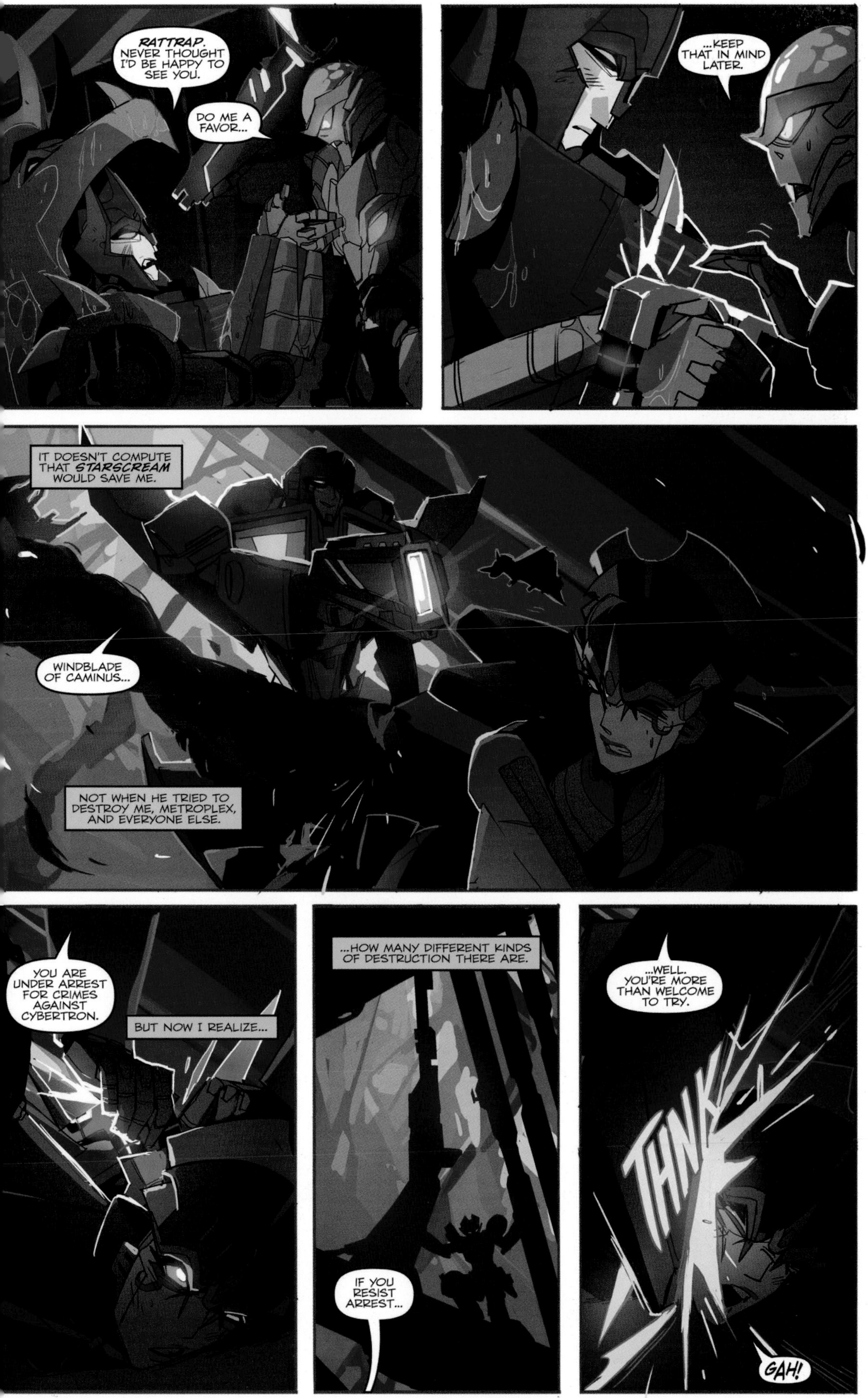

RATTRAP. NEVER THOUGHT I'D BE HAPPY TO SEE YOU.
DO ME A FAVOR...
...KEEP THAT IN MIND LATER.
IT DOESN'T COMPUTE THAT STARSCREAM WOULD SAVE ME.
WINDBLADE OF CAMINUS...
NOT WHEN HE TRIED TO DESTROY ME, METROPLEX, AND EVERYONE ELSE.
YOU ARE UNDER ARREST FOR CRIMES AGAINST CYBERTRON.
BUT NOW I REALIZE...
...HOW MANY DIFFERENT KINDS OF DESTRUCTION THERE ARE.
IF YOU RESIST ARREST...
...WELL. YOU'RE MORE THAN WELCOME TO TRY.
THNK
GAH!

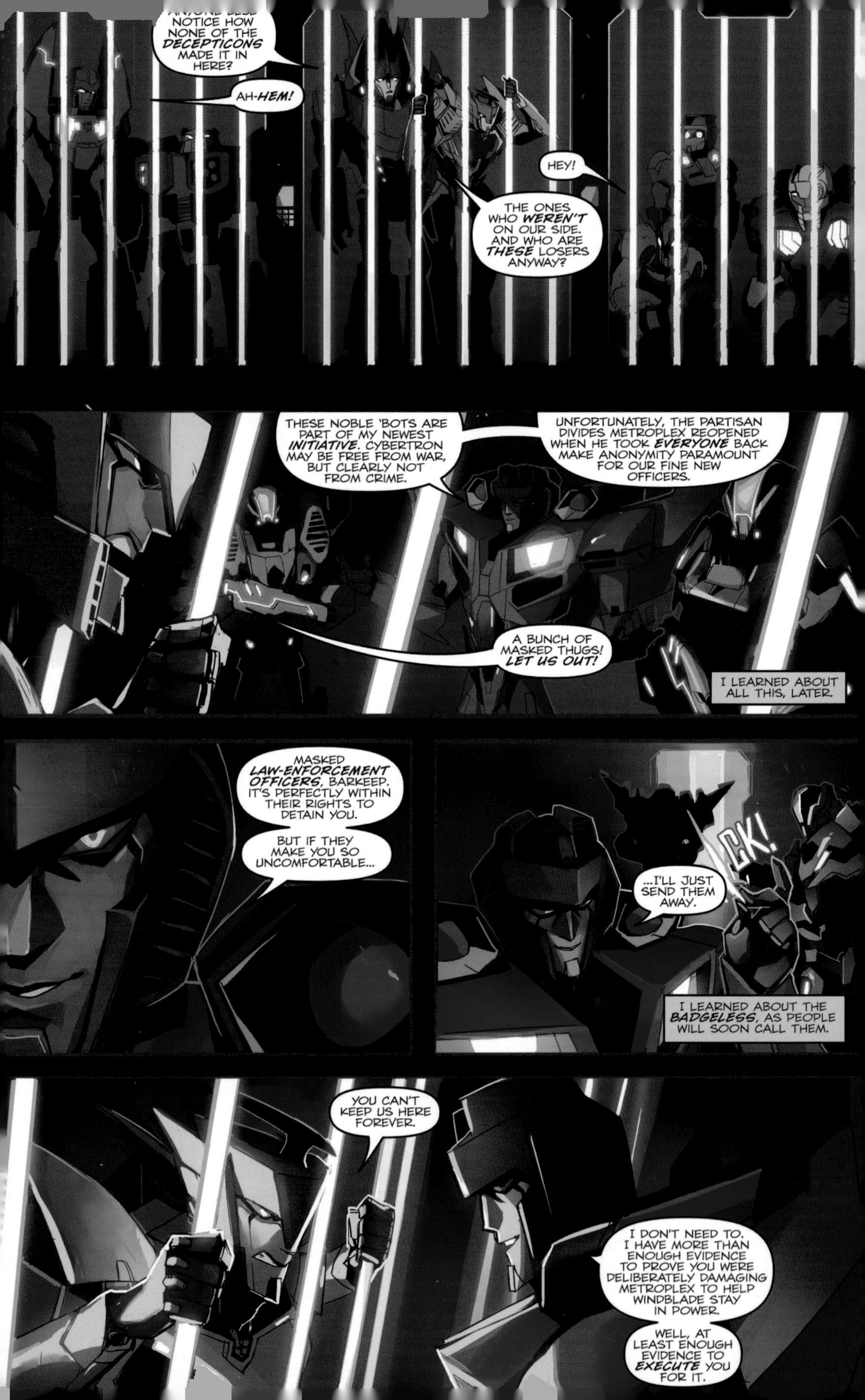
NOTICE HOW NONE OF THE DECEPTICONS MADE IT IN HERE?
AH-HEM!
HEY!
THE ONES WHO WEREN'T ON OUR SIDE. AND WHO ARE THESE LOSERS ANYWAY?
THESE NOBLE 'BOTS ARE PART OF MY NEWEST INITIATIVE. CYBERTRON MAY BE FREE FROM WAR, BUT CLEARLY NOT FROM CRIME.
UNFORTUNATELY, THE PARTISAN DIVIDES METROPLEX REOPENED WHEN HE TOOK EVERYONE BACK MAKE ANONYMITY PARAMOUNT FOR OUR FINE NEW OFFICERS.
A BUNCH OF MASKED THUGS! LET US OUT!
I LEARNED ABOUT ALL THIS, LATER.
MASKED LAW-ENFORCEMENT OFFICERS, BARKEEP. IT'S PERFECTLY WITHIN THEIR RIGHTS TO DETAIN YOU.
BUT IF THEY MAKE YOU SO UNCOMFORTABLE...
...I'LL JUST SEND THEM AWAY.
CK!
I LEARNED ABOUT THE BADGELESS, AS PEOPLE WILL SOON CALL THEM.
YOU CAN'T KEEP US HERE FOREVER.
I DON'T NEED TO. I HAVE MORE THAN ENOUGH EVIDENCE TO PROVE YOU WERE DELIBERATELY DAMAGING METROPLEX TO HELP WINDBLADE STAY IN POWER.
WELL, AT LEAST ENOUGH EVIDENCE TO EXECUTE YOU FOR IT.

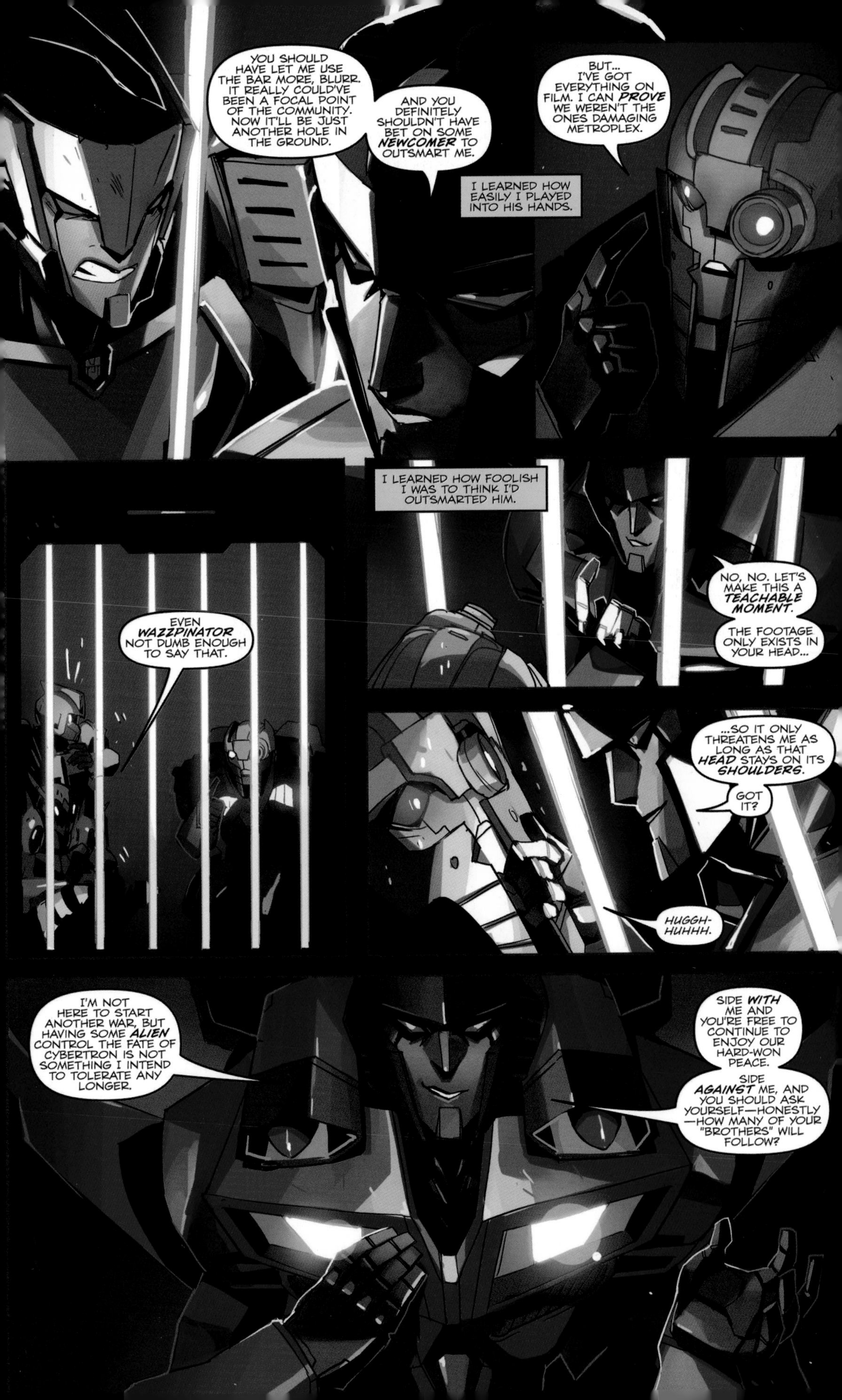
YOU SHOULD HAVE LET ME USE THE BAR MORE, BLURR. IT REALLY COULD'VE BEEN A FOCAL POINT OF THE COMMUNITY. NOW IT'LL BE JUST ANOTHER HOLE IN THE GROUND.
AND YOU DEFINITELY SHOULDN'T HAVE BET ON SOME NEWCOMER TO OUTSMART ME.
I LEARNED HOW EASILY I PLAYED INTO HIS HANDS.
BUT... I'VE GOT EVERYTHING ON FILM. I CAN PROVE WE WEREN'T THE ONES DAMAGING METROPLEX.
EVEN WAZZPINATOR NOT DUMB ENOUGH TO SAY THAT.
I LEARNED HOW FOOLISH I WAS TO THINK I'D OUTSMARTED HIM.
NO, NO. LET'S MAKE THIS A TEACHABLE MOMENT.
THE FOOTAGE ONLY EXISTS IN YOUR HEAD...
...SO IT ONLY THREATENS ME AS LONG AS THAT HEAD STAYS ON ITS SHOULDERS.
GOT IT?
HUGGH-HUHHH.
I'M NOT HERE TO START ANOTHER WAR, BUT HAVING SOME ALIEN CONTROL THE FATE OF CYBERTRON IS NOT SOMETHING I INTEND TO TOLERATE ANY LONGER.
SIDE WITH ME AND YOU'RE FREE TO CONTINUE TO ENJOY OUR HARD-WON PEACE.
SIDE AGAINST ME, AND YOU SHOULD ASK YOURSELF—HONESTLY—HOW MANY OF YOUR "BROTHERS" WILL FOLLOW?

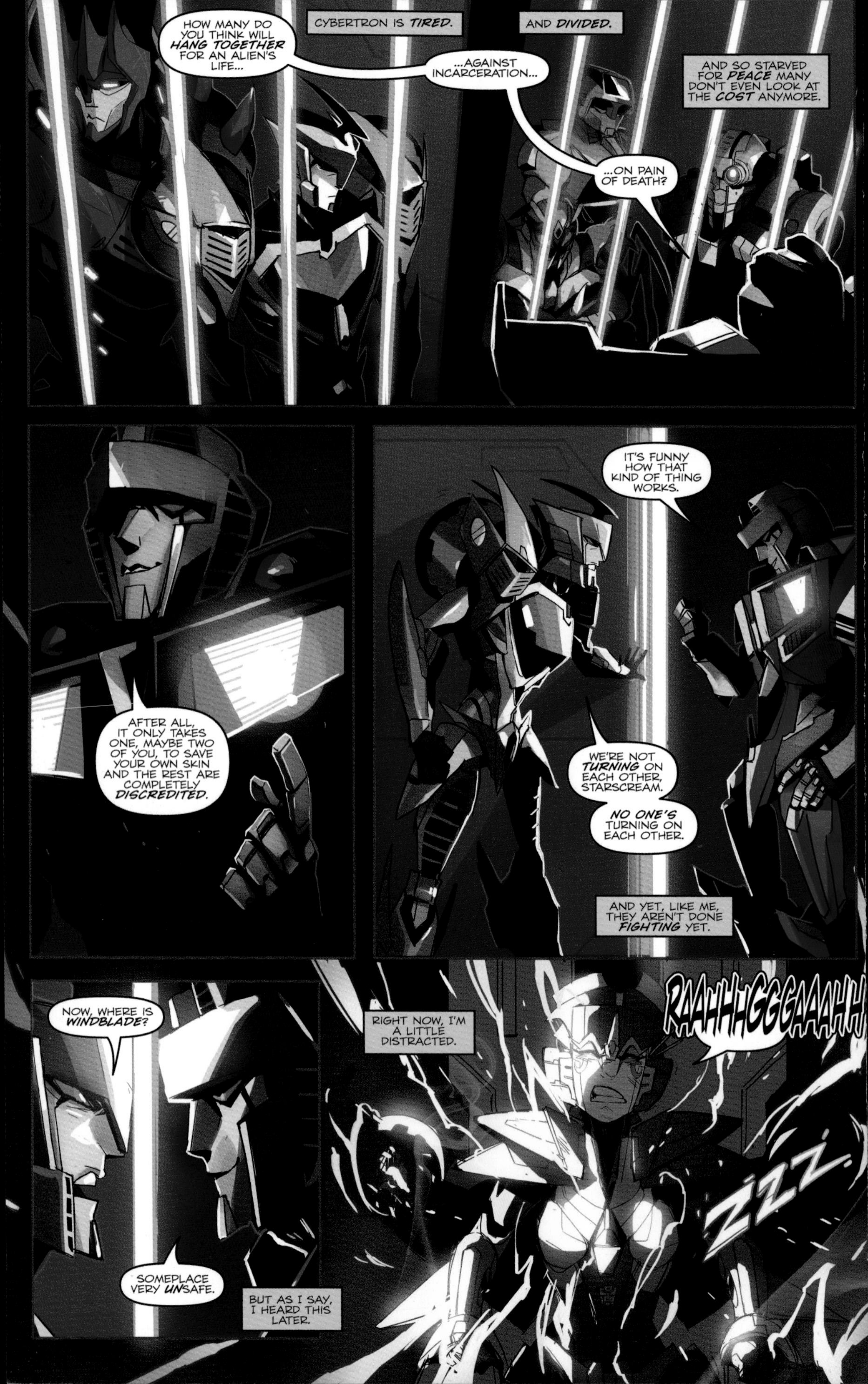
HOW MANY DO YOU THINK WILL HANG TOGETHER FOR AN ALIEN'S LIFE...
CYBERTRON IS TIRED.
AND DIVIDED.
...AGAINST INCARCERATION...
...ON PAIN OF DEATH?
AND SO STARVED FOR PEACE MANY DON'T EVEN LOOK AT THE COST ANYMORE.
AFTER ALL, IT ONLY TAKES ONE, MAYBE TWO OF YOU, TO SAVE YOUR OWN SKIN AND THE REST ARE COMPLETELY DISCREDITED.
IT'S FUNNY HOW THAT KIND OF THING WORKS.
WE'RE NOT TURNING ON EACH OTHER, STARSCREAM.
NO ONE'S TURNING ON EACH OTHER.
AND YET, LIKE ME, THEY AREN'T DONE FIGHTING YET.
NOW, WHERE IS WINDBLADE?
SOMEPLACE VERY UNSAFE.
BUT AS I SAY, I HEARD THIS LATER.
RIGHT NOW, I'M A LITTLE DISTRACTED.
RAAHHHGGGAAAHH
ZZZ

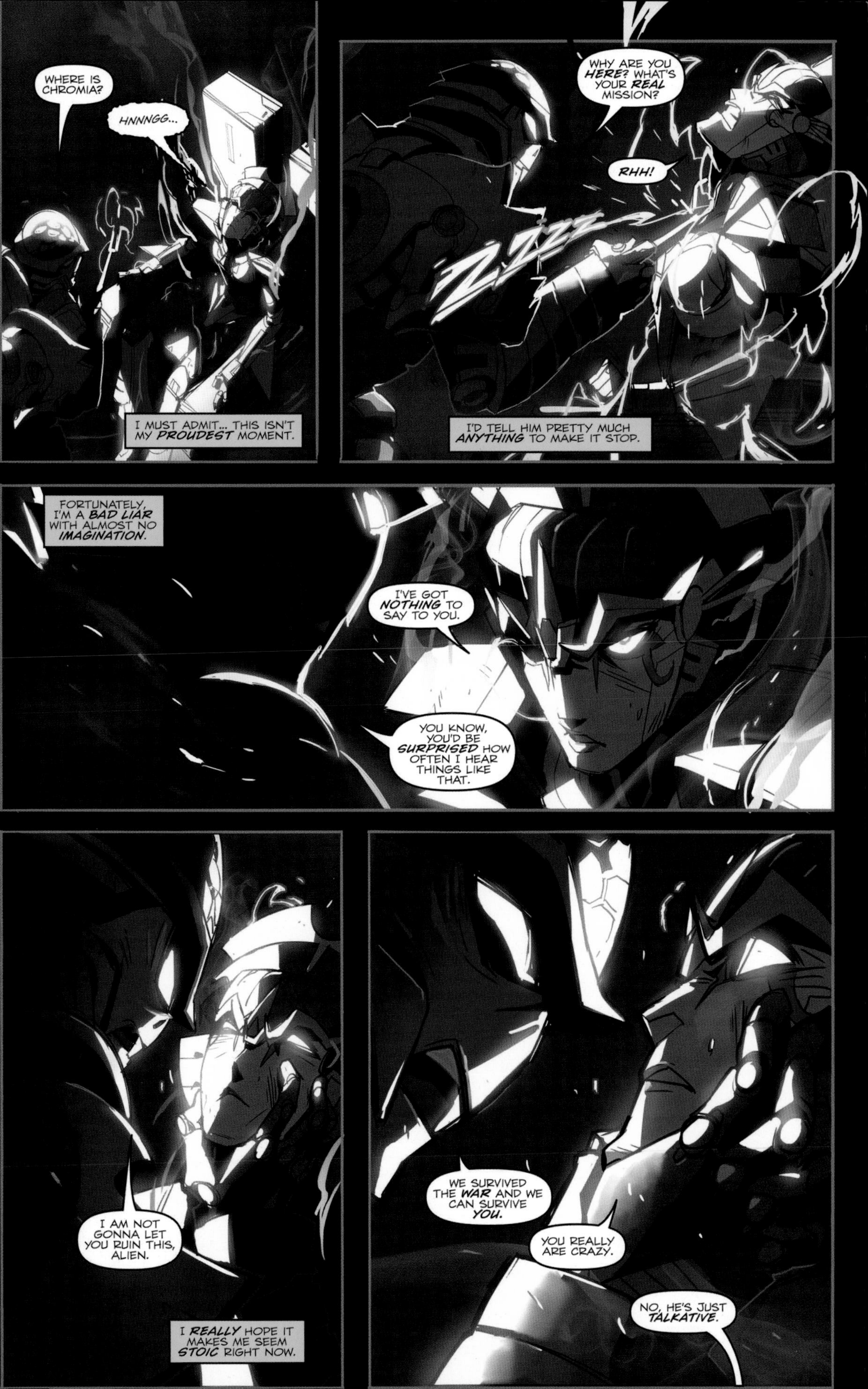
WHERE IS CHROMIA?
HNNNGG...
I MUST ADMIT... THIS ISN'T MY PROUDEST MOMENT.
WHY ARE YOU HERE? WHAT'S YOUR REAL MISSION?
RHH!
ZZZZ
I'D TELL HIM PRETTY MUCH ANYTHING TO MAKE IT STOP.
FORTUNATELY, I'M A BAD LIAR WITH ALMOST NO IMAGINATION.
I'VE GOT NOTHING TO SAY TO YOU.
YOU KNOW, YOU'D BE SURPRISED HOW OFTEN I HEAR THINGS LIKE THAT.
I AM NOT GONNA LET YOU RUIN THIS, ALIEN.
I REALLY HOPE IT MAKES ME SEEM STOIC RIGHT NOW.
WE SURVIVED THE WAR AND WE CAN SURVIVE YOU.
YOU REALLY ARE CRAZY.
NO, HE'S JUST TALKATIVE.

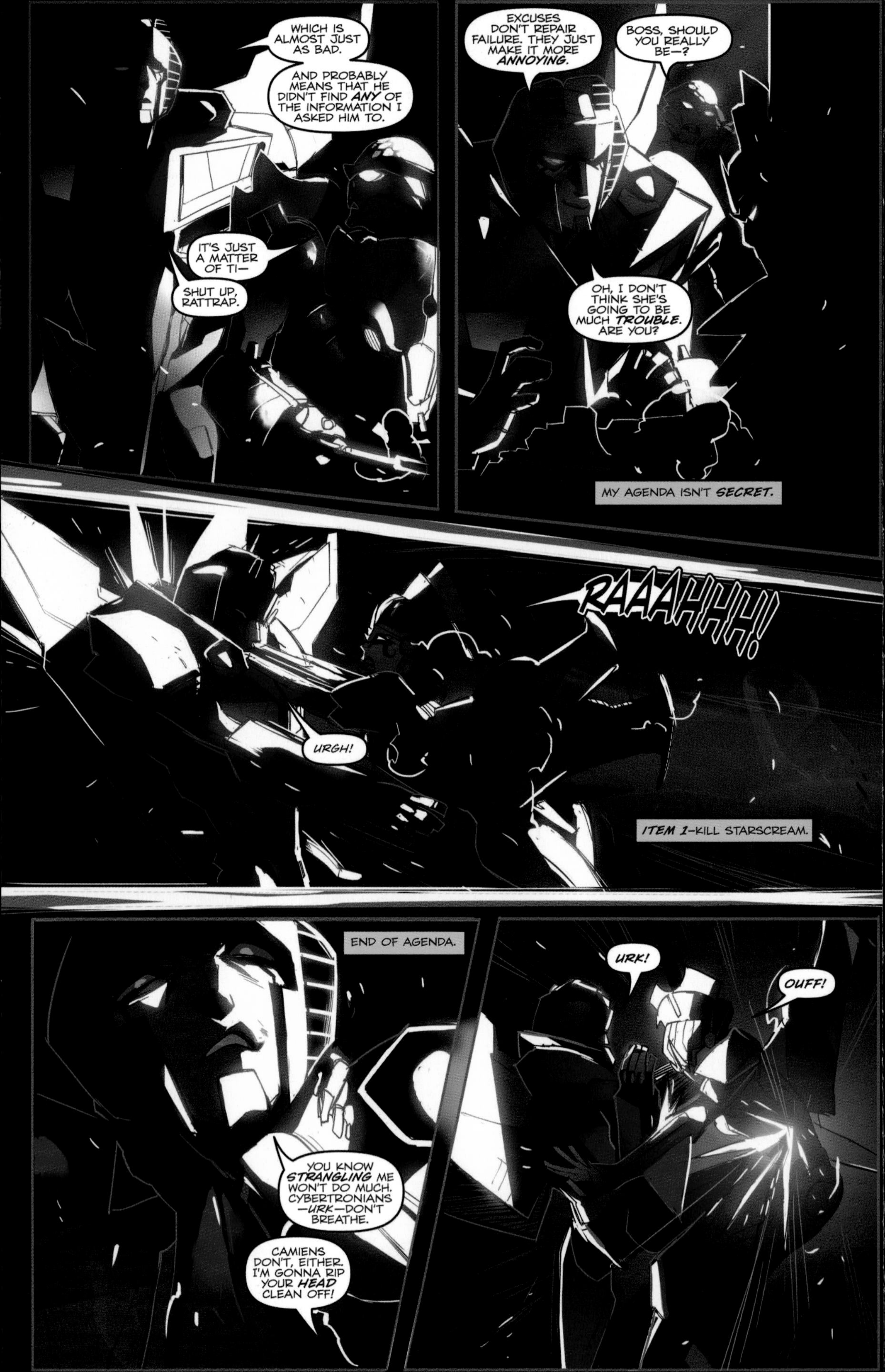
WHICH IS ALMOST JUST AS BAD.
AND PROBABLY MEANS THAT HE DIDN'T FIND ANY OF THE INFORMATION I ASKED HIM TO.
IT'S JUST A MATTER OF TI—
SHUT UP, RATTRAP.
EXCUSES DON'T REPAIR FAILURE. THEY JUST MAKE IT MORE ANNOYING.
BOSS, SHOULD YOU REALLY BE—?
OH, I DON'T THINK SHE'S GOING TO BE MUCH TROUBLE. ARE YOU?
MY AGENDA ISN'T SECRET.
RAAAHHH!
URGH!
ITEM 1—KILL STARSCREAM.
END OF AGENDA.
YOU KNOW STRANGLING ME WON'T DO MUCH. CYBERTRONIANS —URK—DON'T BREATHE.
CAMIENS DON'T, EITHER. I'M GONNA RIP YOUR HEAD CLEAN OFF!
URK!
OUFF!

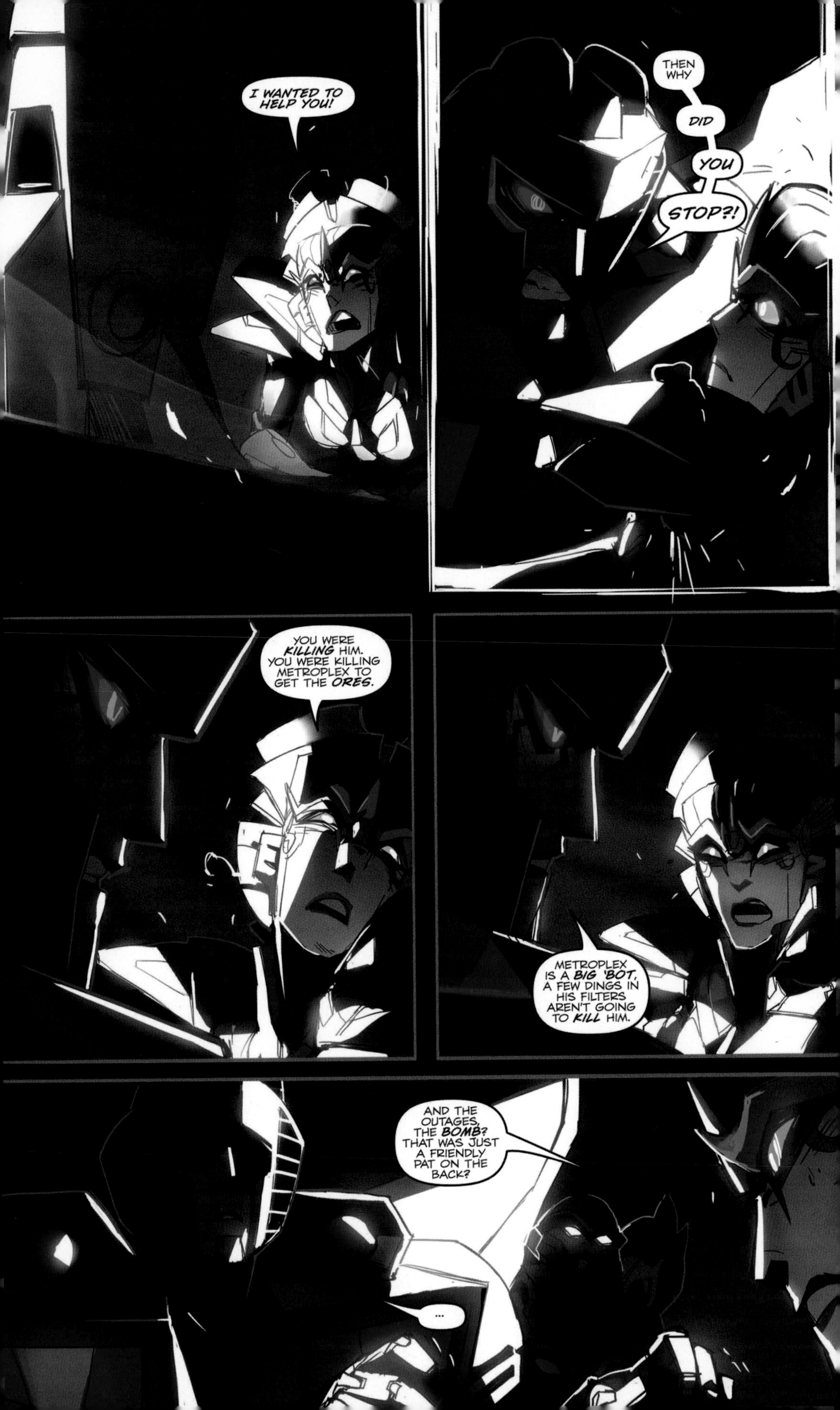
I WANTED TO HELP YOU!
THEN WHY
DID
YOU
STOP?!
YOU WERE KILLING HIM. YOU WERE KILLING METROPLEX TO GET THE ORES.
METROPLEX IS A BIG 'BOT, A FEW DINGS IN HIS FILTERS AREN'T GOING TO KILL HIM.
AND THE OUTAGES, THE BOMB? THAT WAS JUST A FRIENDLY PAT ON THE BACK?
...

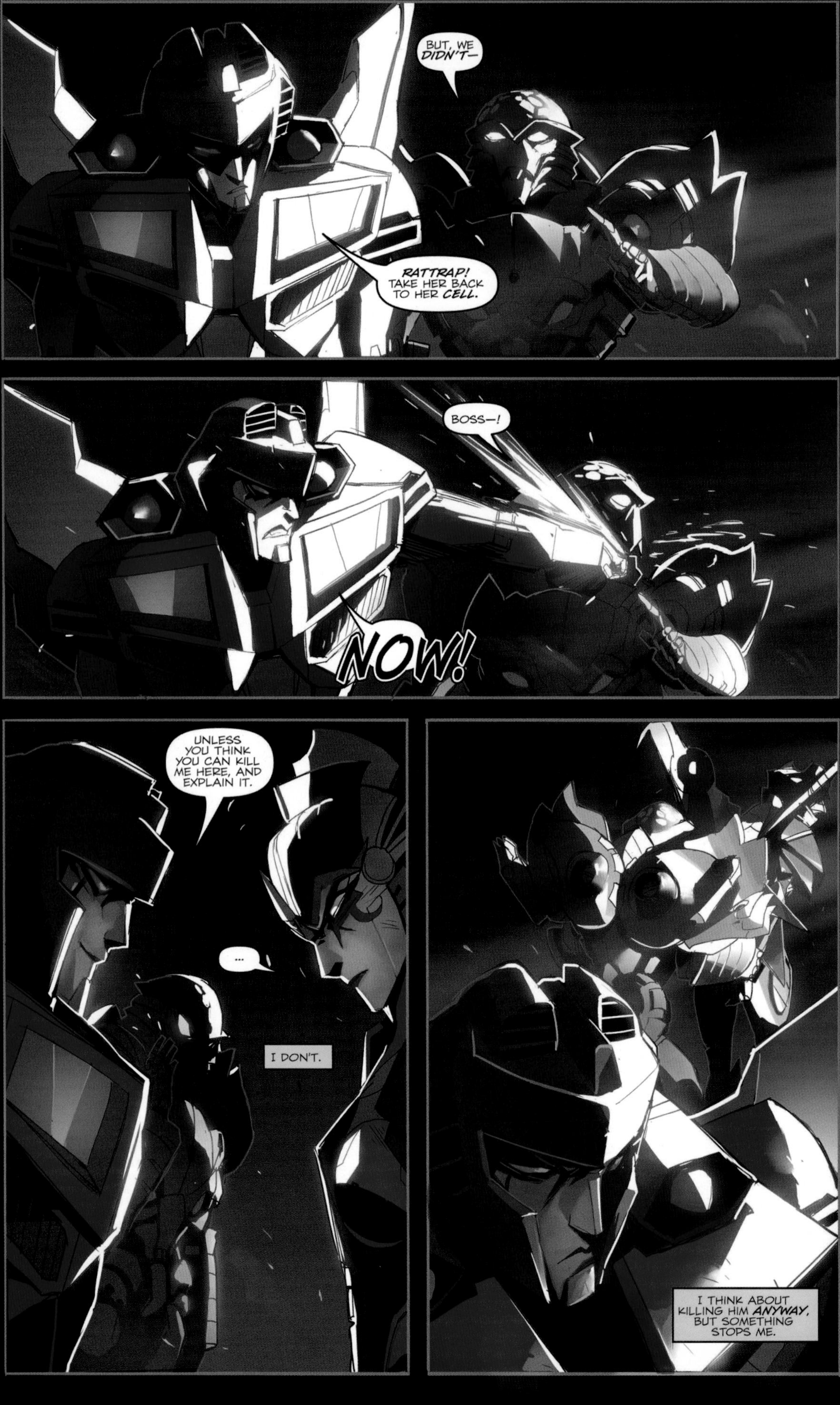

BUT, WE DIDN'T—
RATTRAP! TAKE HER BACK TO HER CELL.
BOSS—!
NOW!
UNLESS YOU THINK YOU CAN KILL ME HERE, AND EXPLAIN IT.
...
I DON'T.
I THINK ABOUT KILLING HIM ANYWAY, BUT SOMETHING STOPS ME.

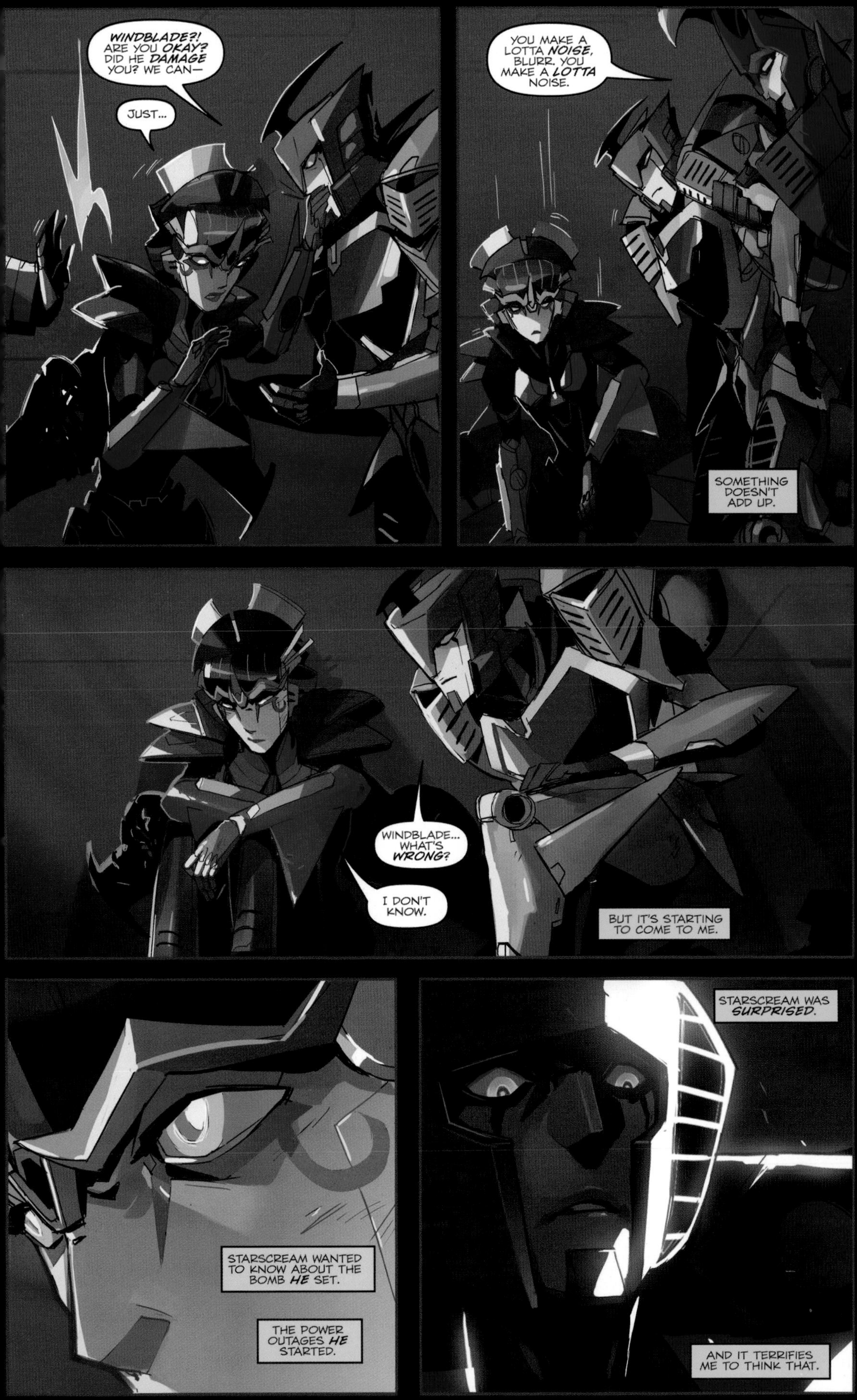
WINDBLADE?! ARE YOU OKAY? DID HE DAMAGE YOU? WE CAN—
JUST...
YOU MAKE A LOTTA NOISE, BLURR. YOU MAKE A LOTTA NOISE.
SOMETHING DOESN'T ADD UP.
WINDBLADE... WHAT'S WRONG?
I DON'T KNOW.
BUT IT'S STARTING TO COME TO ME.
STARSCREAM WANTED TO KNOW ABOUT THE BOMB HE SET.
THE POWER OUTAGES HE STARTED.
STARSCREAM WAS SURPRISED.
AND IT TERRIFIES ME TO THINK THAT.

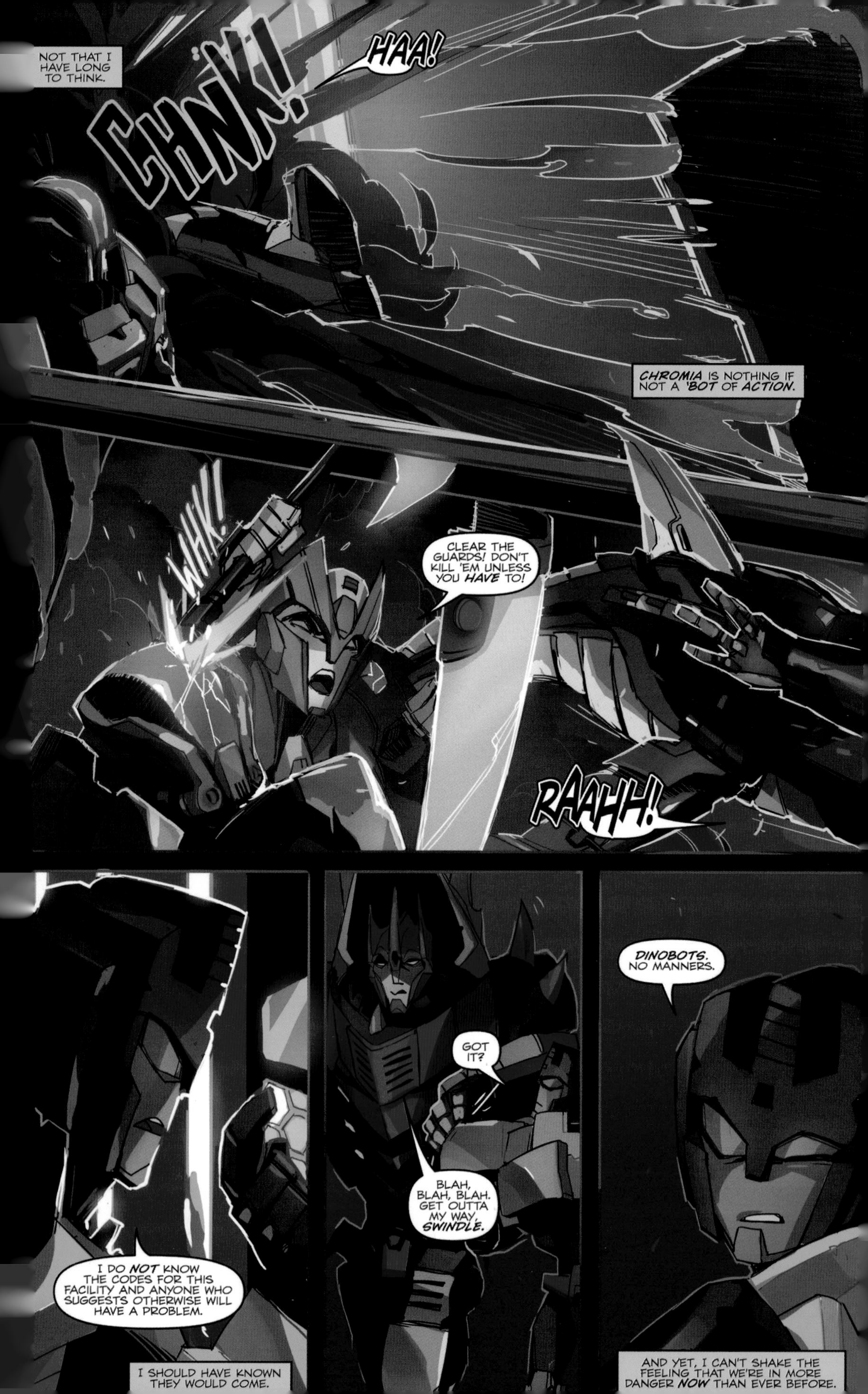
NOT THAT I HAVE LONG TO THINK.
HAA!
CHNK!
CHROMIA IS NOTHING IF NOT A 'BOT OF ACTION.
WHK!
CLEAR THE GUARDS! DON'T KILL 'EM UNLESS YOU HAVE TO!
RAAHH!
I DO NOT KNOW THE CODES FOR THIS FACILITY AND ANYONE WHO SUGGESTS OTHERWISE WILL HAVE A PROBLEM.
I SHOULD HAVE KNOWN THEY WOULD COME.
GOT IT?
BLAH, BLAH, BLAH. GET OUTTA MY WAY, SWINDLE.
DINOBOTS. NO MANNERS.
AND YET, I CAN'T SHAKE THE FEELING THAT WE'RE IN MORE DANGER NOW THAN EVER BEFORE.

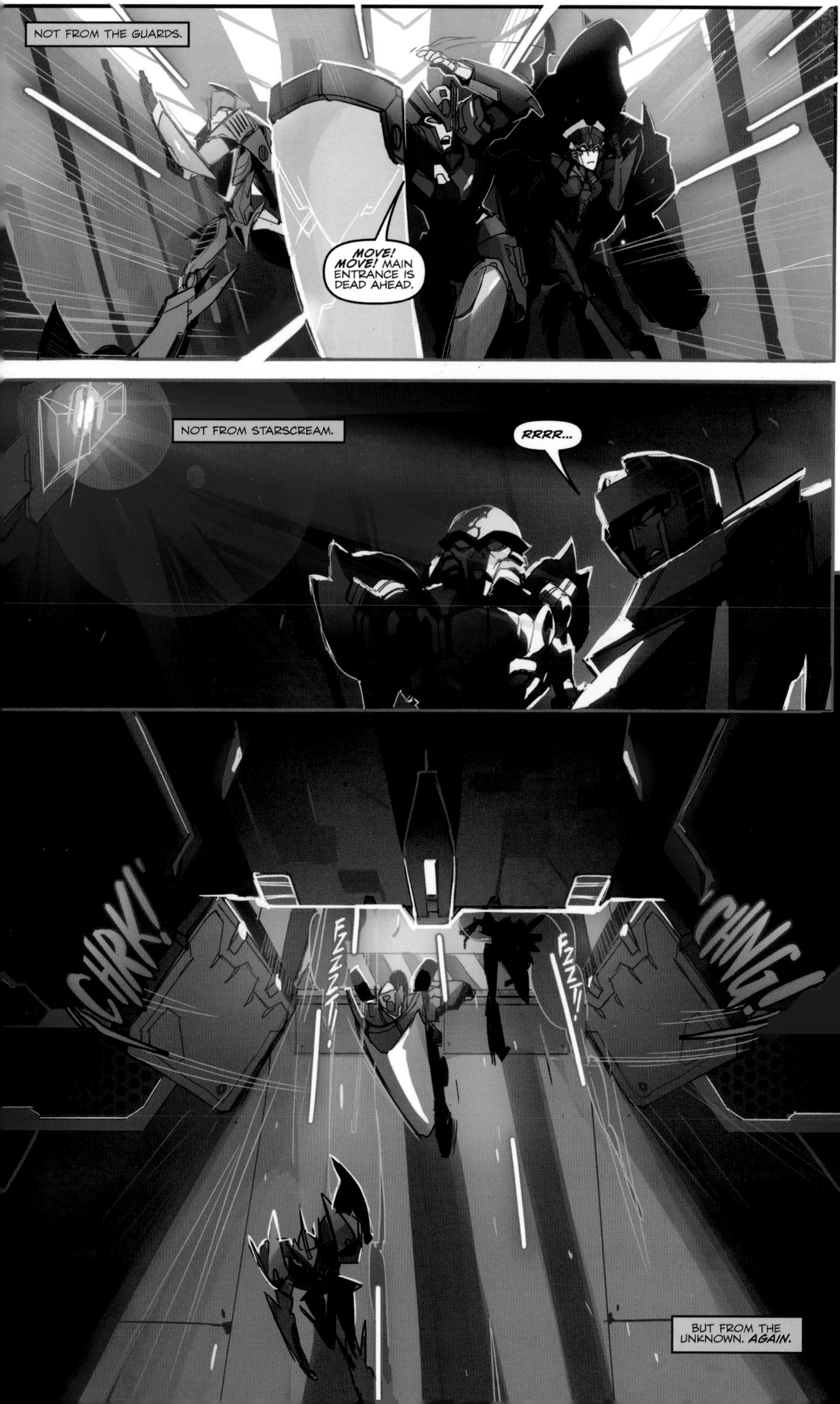
NOT FROM THE GUARDS.
MOVE! MOVE! MAIN ENTRANCE IS DEAD AHEAD.
NOT FROM STARSCREAM.
RRRR...
CHRK!
FZZZT!!
FZZZT!!
CHNG!!
BUT FROM THE UNKNOWN. AGAIN.

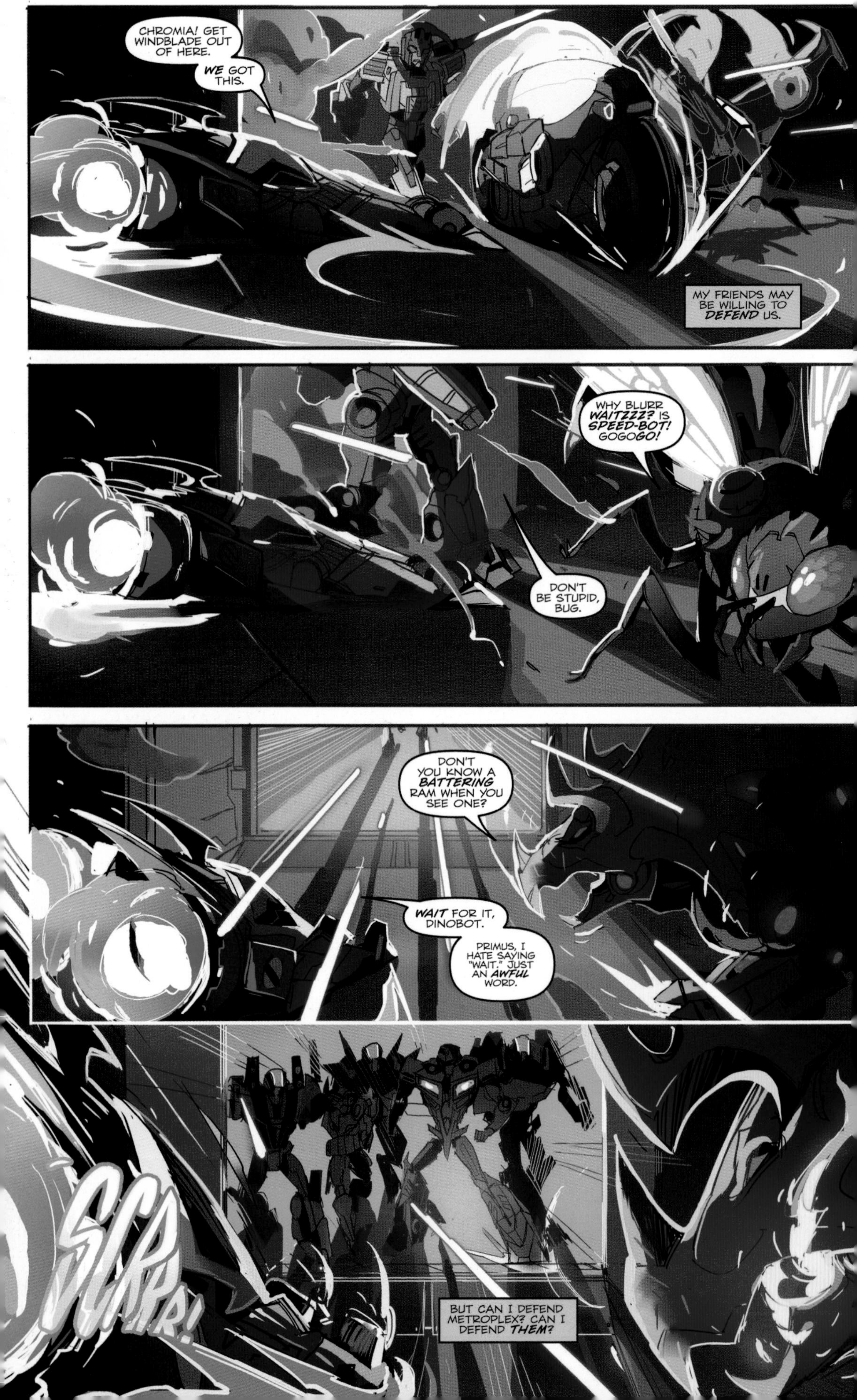
CHROMIA! GET WINDBLADE OUT OF HERE.
WE GOT THIS.
MY FRIENDS MAY BE WILLING TO DEFEND US.
WHY BLURR WAITZZZ? IS SPEED-BOT! GOGOGO!
DON'T BE STUPID, BUG.
DON'T YOU KNOW A BATTERING RAM WHEN YOU SEE ONE?
WAIT FOR IT, DINOBOT.
PRIMUS, I HATE SAYING "WAIT." JUST AN AWFUL WORD.
SCRR!
BUT CAN I DEFEND METROPLEX? CAN I DEFEND THEM?

KKRNCHH!

WE HAVE TO GET TO METROPLEX'S *BRAIN!* IT'S THE SAFEST PLACE.

WE CAN *STILL* STOP STARSCREAM.

IT ISN'T HIM, CHROMIA.

WHAT?!

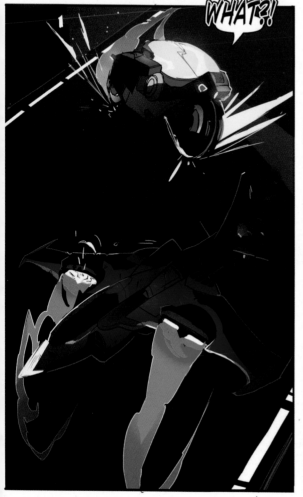

THE SABOTAGE, THE BOMB. IT *WASN'T* STARSCREAM.

WE SAW THE *FILTER DAMAGE,* WINDBLADE.

BUT SOMEONE *ELSE* IS CAUSING THE *REST* OF IT.

SOMEONE IS PULLING *POWER* FROM METROPLEX. THE ONLY QUESTION LEFT...

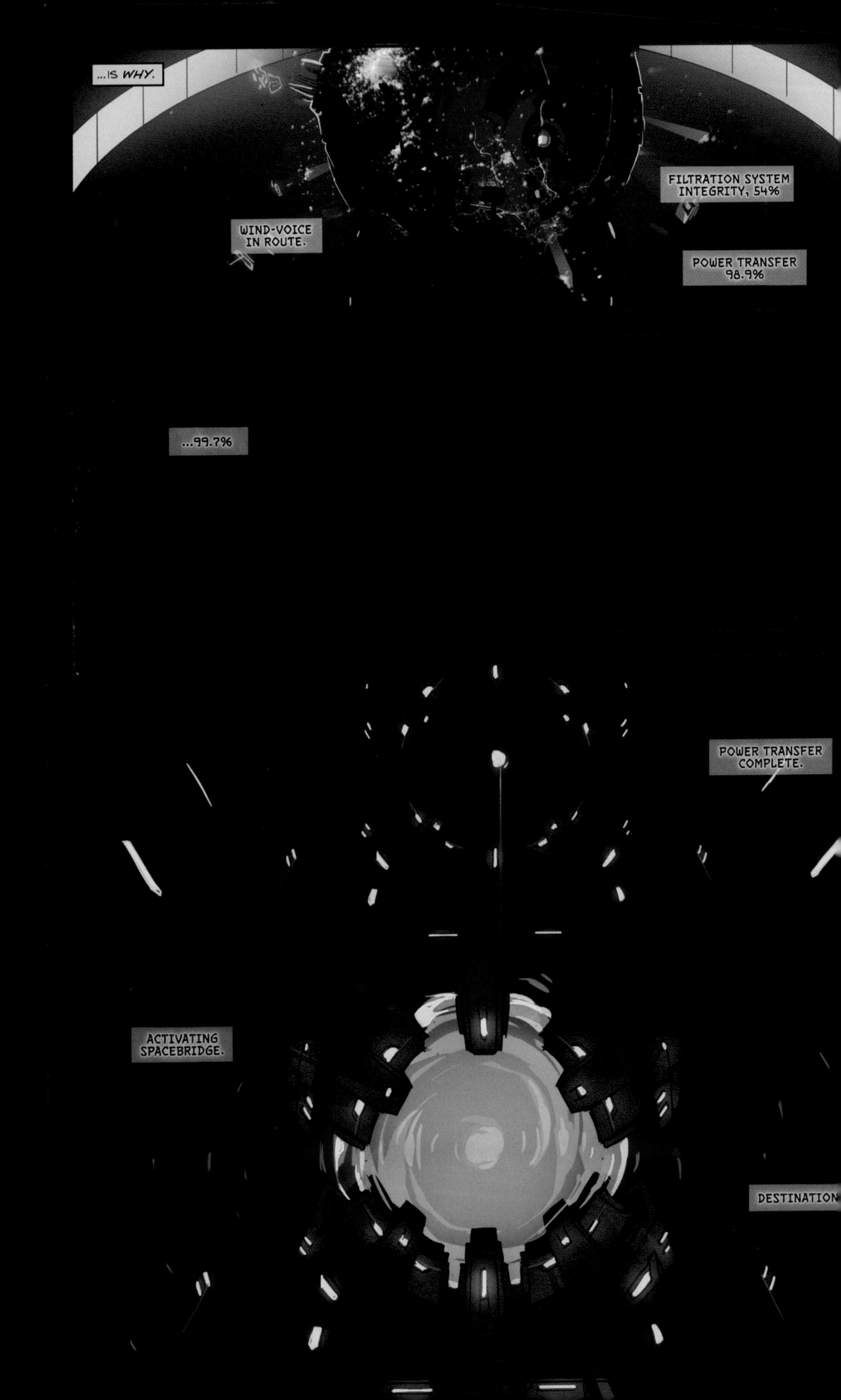
...IS WHY.
FILTRATION SYSTEM INTEGRITY, 54%
WIND-VOICE IN ROUTE.
POWER TRANSFER 98.9%
...99.7%
POWER TRANSFER COMPLETE.
ACTIVATING SPACEBRIDGE.
DESTINATION

ART BY **ALEX MILNE**
COLORS BY **JOANA LAFUENTE**

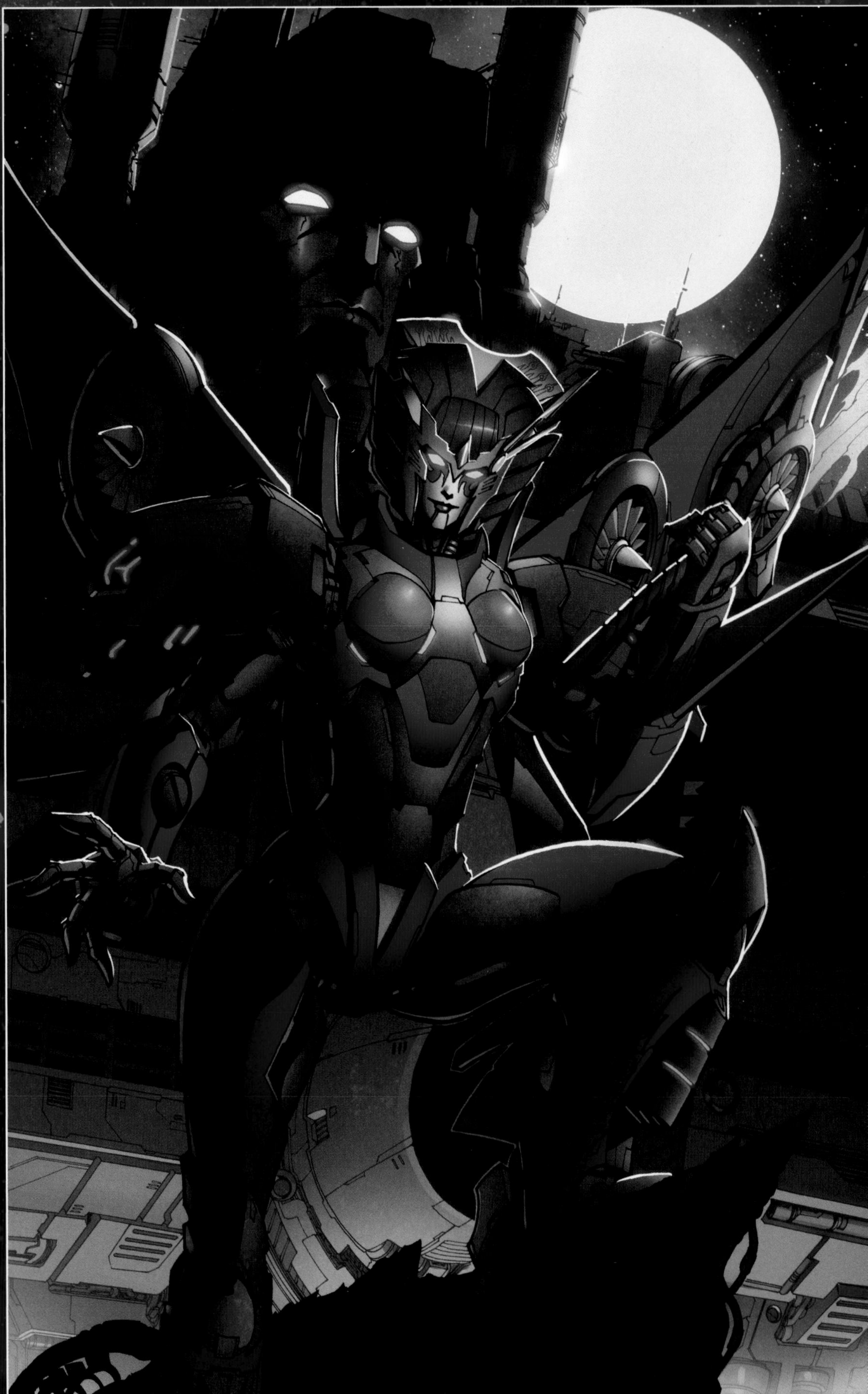

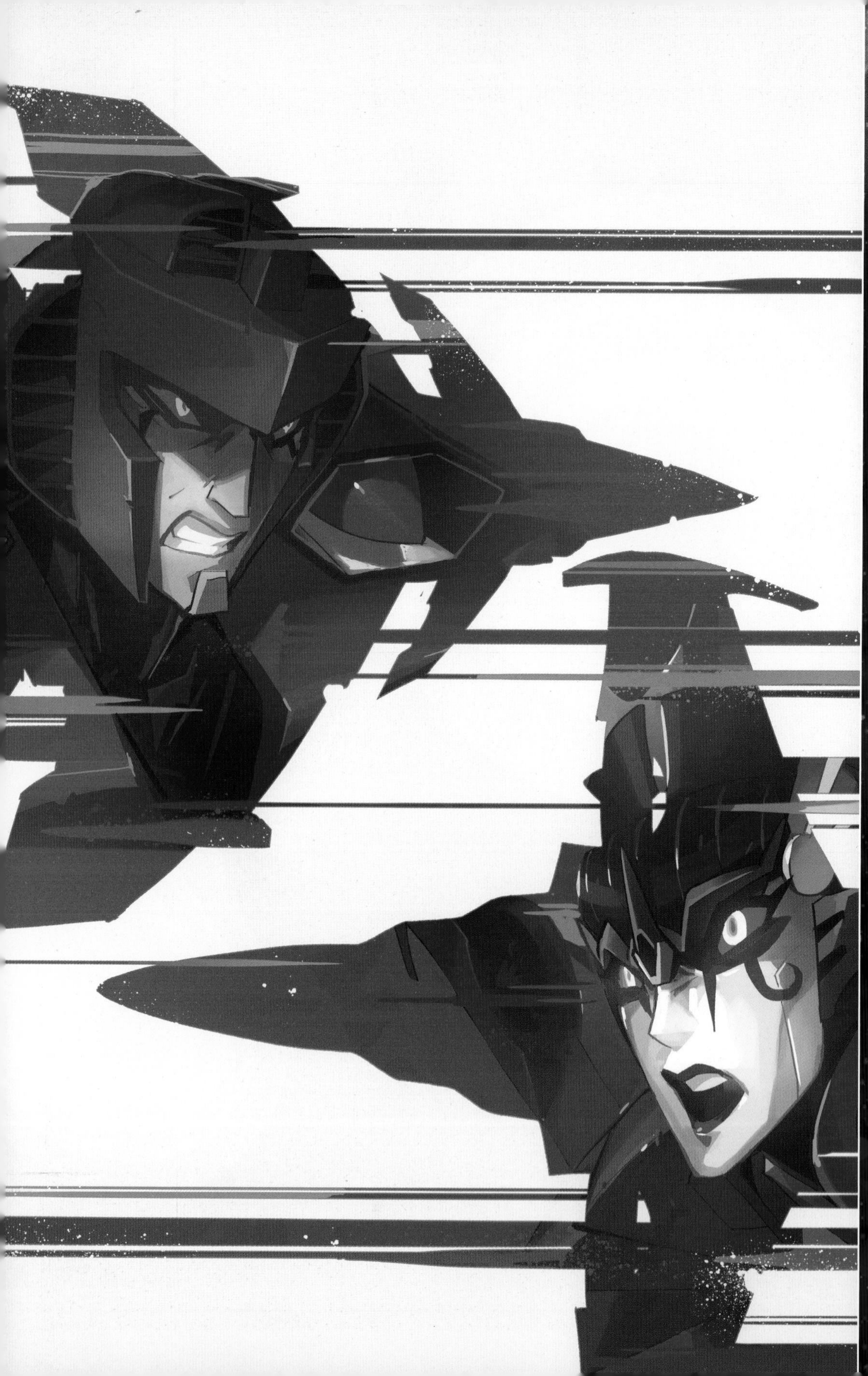

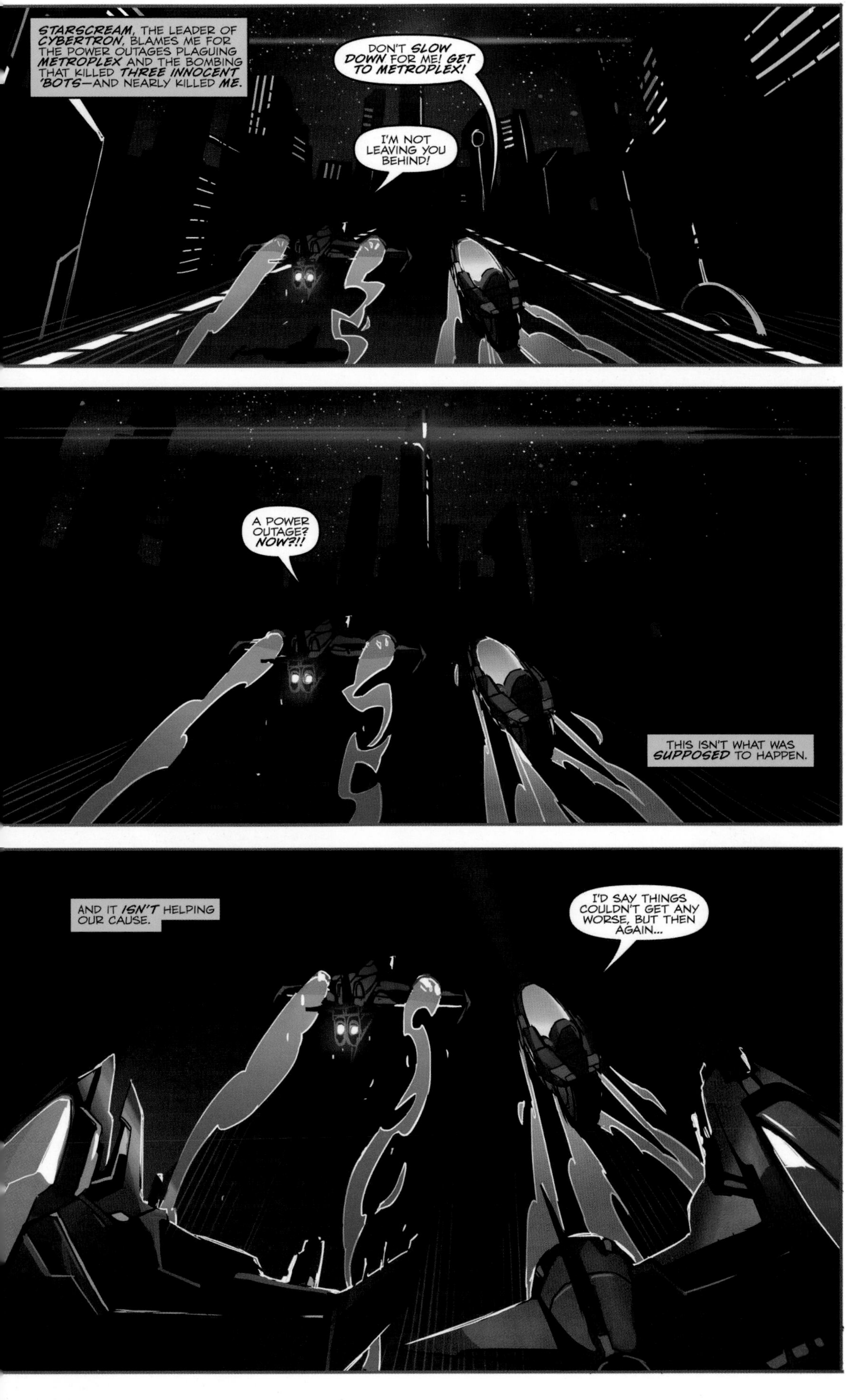
STARSCREAM, THE LEADER OF CYBERTRON, BLAMES ME FOR THE POWER OUTAGES PLAGUING METROPLEX AND THE BOMBING THAT KILLED THREE INNOCENT 'BOTS—AND NEARLY KILLED ME.
DON'T SLOW DOWN FOR ME! GET TO METROPLEX!
I'M NOT LEAVING YOU BEHIND!
A POWER OUTAGE? NOW?!!
THIS ISN'T WHAT WAS SUPPOSED TO HAPPEN.
AND IT ISN'T HELPING OUR CAUSE.
I'D SAY THINGS COULDN'T GET ANY WORSE, BUT THEN AGAIN...

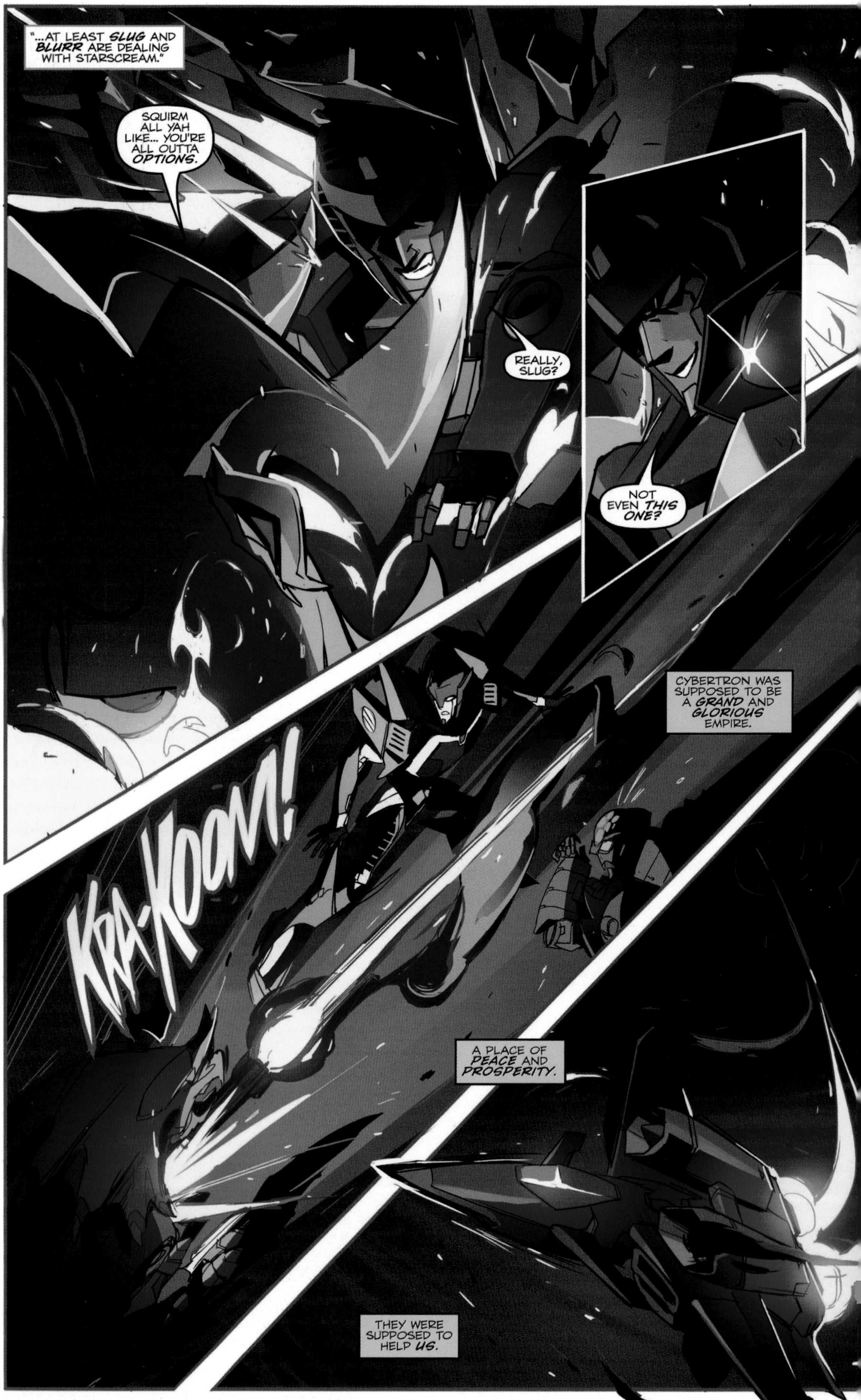
"...AT LEAST SLUG AND BLURR ARE DEALING WITH STARSCREAM."
SQUIRM ALL YAH LIKE... YOU'RE ALL OUTTA OPTIONS.
REALLY, SLUG?
NOT EVEN THIS ONE?
CYBERTRON WAS SUPPOSED TO BE A GRAND AND GLORIOUS EMPIRE.
KRA-KOOM!
A PLACE OF PEACE AND PROSPERITY.
THEY WERE SUPPOSED TO HELP US.

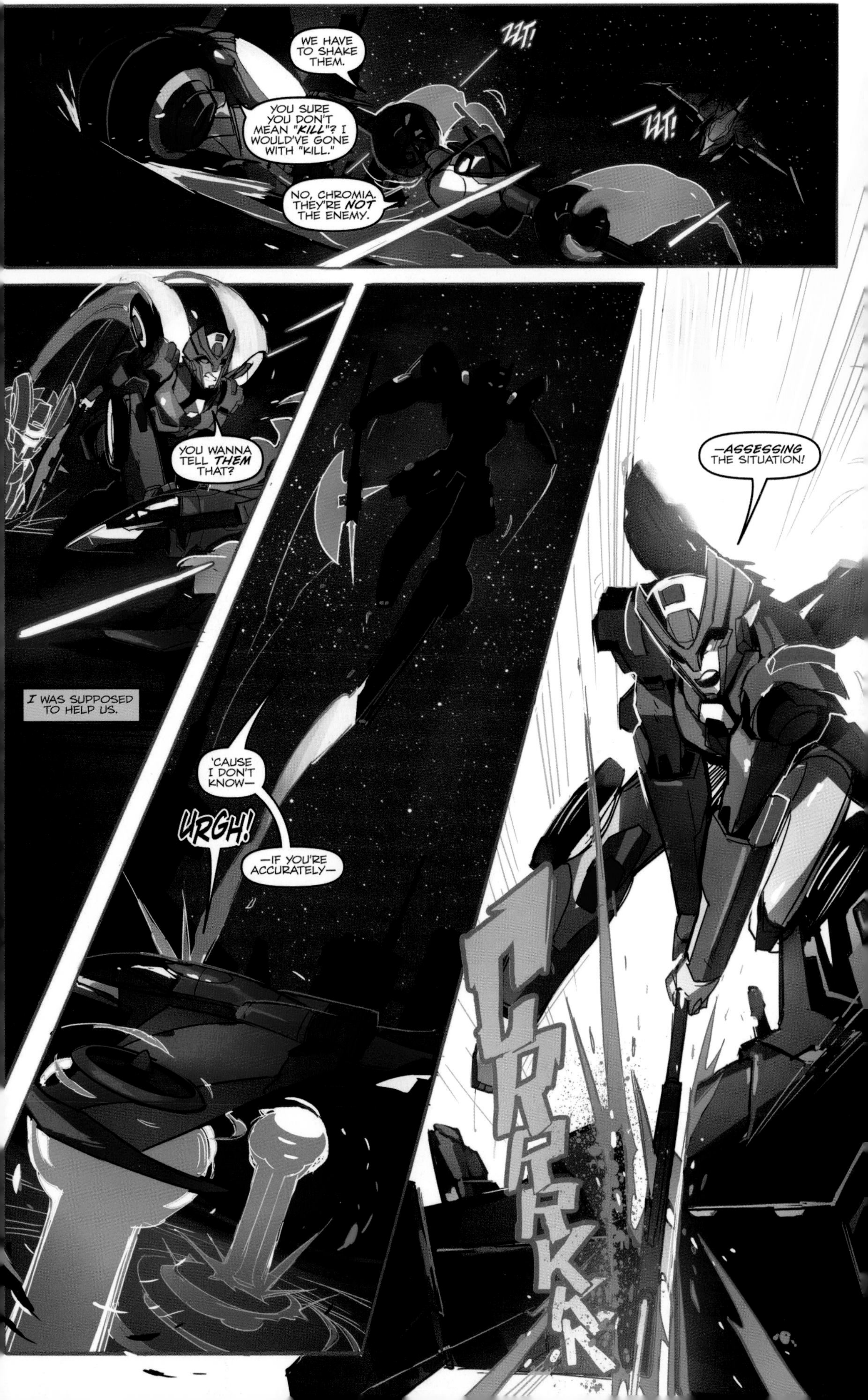
WE HAVE TO SHAKE THEM.
ZZT!
ZZT!
YOU SURE YOU DON'T MEAN "KILL"? I WOULD'VE GONE WITH "KILL."
NO, CHROMIA. THEY'RE NOT THE ENEMY.
YOU WANNA TELL THEM THAT?
I WAS SUPPOSED TO HELP US.
'CAUSE I DON'T KNOW—
URGH!
—IF YOU'RE ACCURATELY—
—ASSESSING THE SITUATION!
CLRRKKK

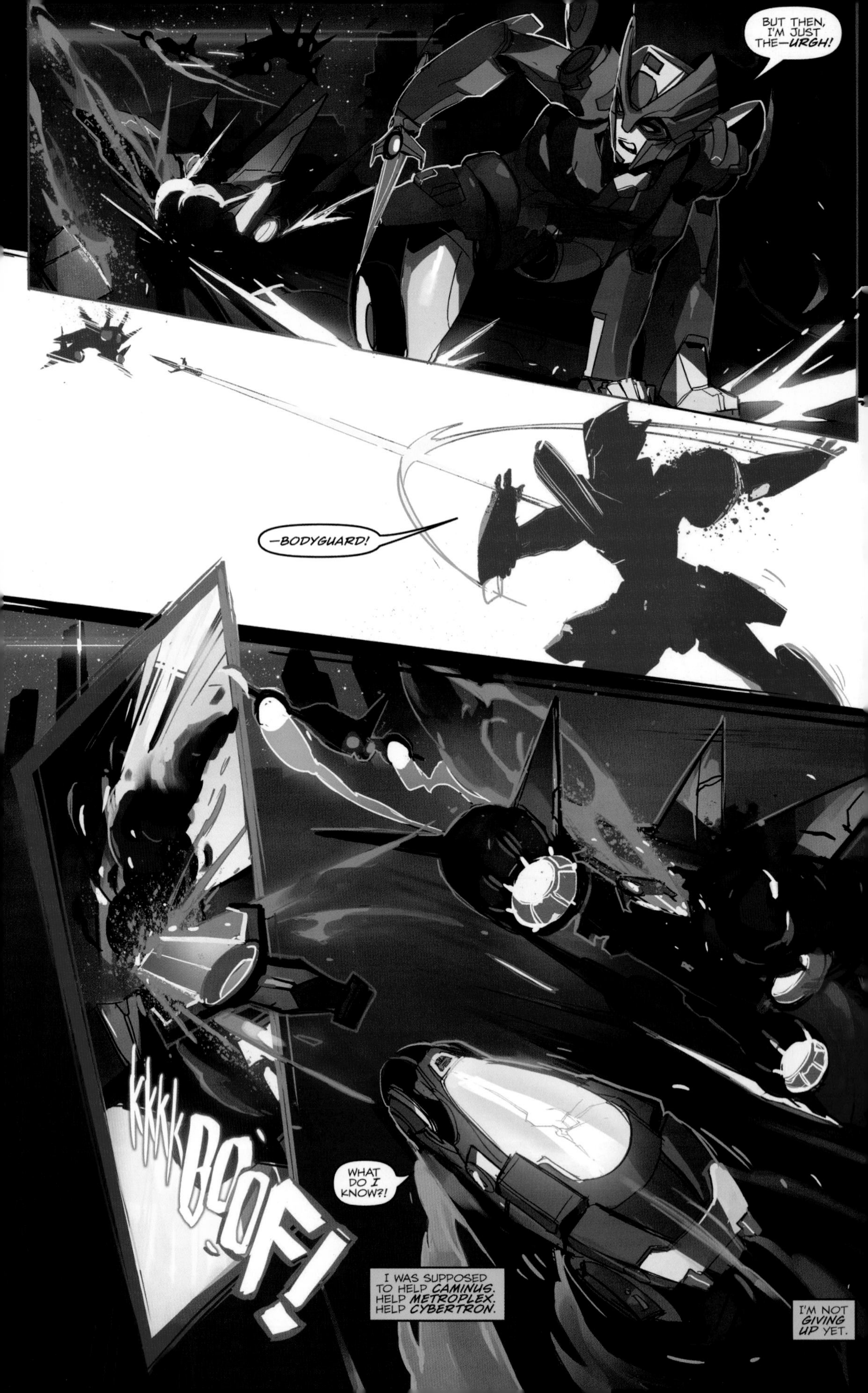
BUT THEN, I'M JUST THE—*URGH!*
—*BODYGUARD!*
KKKK-BOOF!
WHAT DO *I* KNOW?!
I WAS SUPPOSED TO HELP *CAMINUS*. HELP *METROPLEX*. HELP *CYBERTRON*.
I'M NOT *GIVING UP* YET.

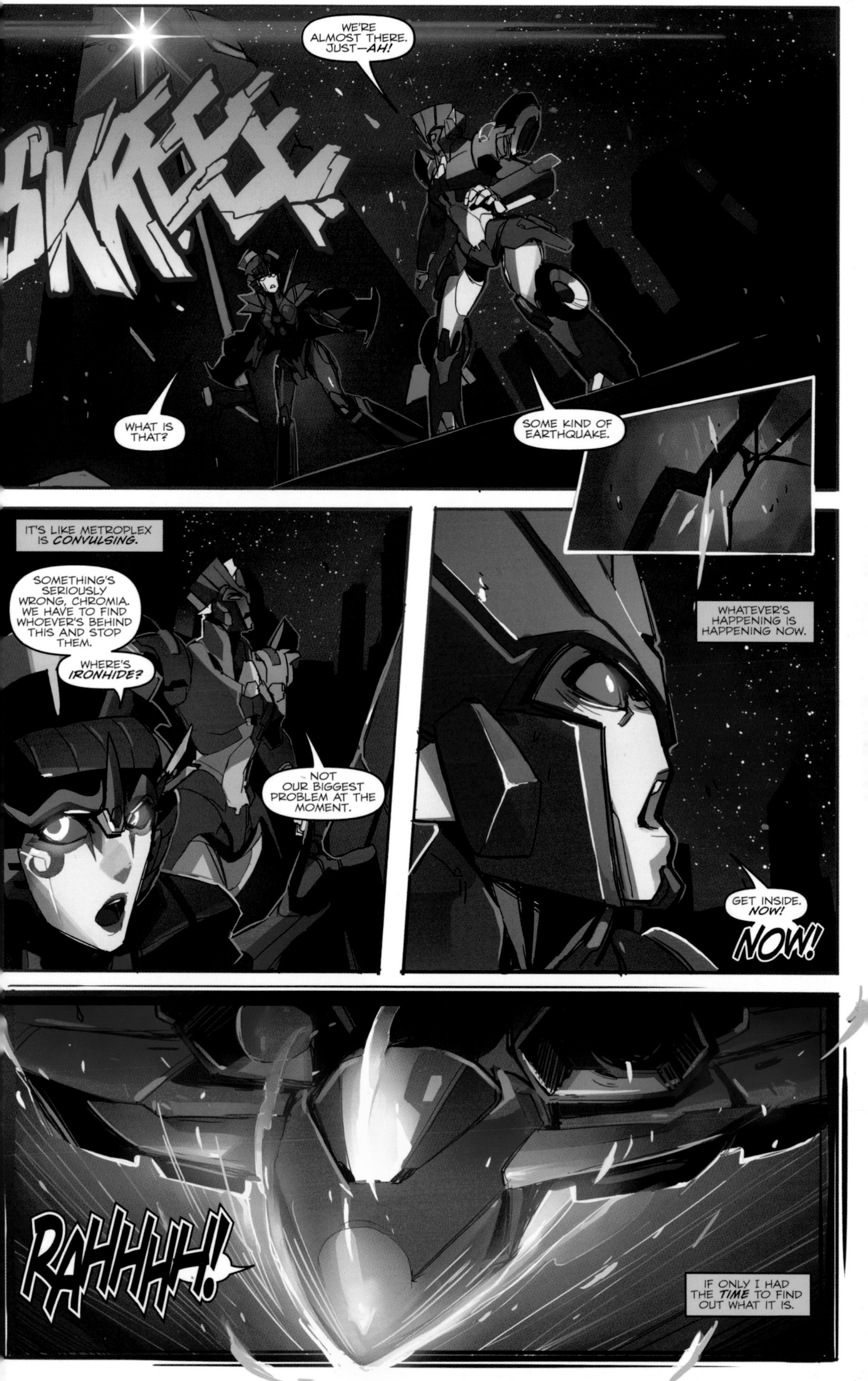
WE'RE ALMOST THERE. JUST—AH!
SKREEEE
WHAT IS THAT?
SOME KIND OF EARTHQUAKE.
IT'S LIKE METROPLEX IS CONVULSING.
SOMETHING'S SERIOUSLY WRONG, CHROMIA. WE HAVE TO FIND WHOEVER'S BEHIND THIS AND STOP THEM.
WHERE'S IRONHIDE?
NOT OUR BIGGEST PROBLEM AT THE MOMENT.
WHATEVER'S HAPPENING IS HAPPENING NOW.
GET INSIDE. NOW!
NOW!
RAHHHH!
IF ONLY I HAD THE TIME TO FIND OUT WHAT IT IS.

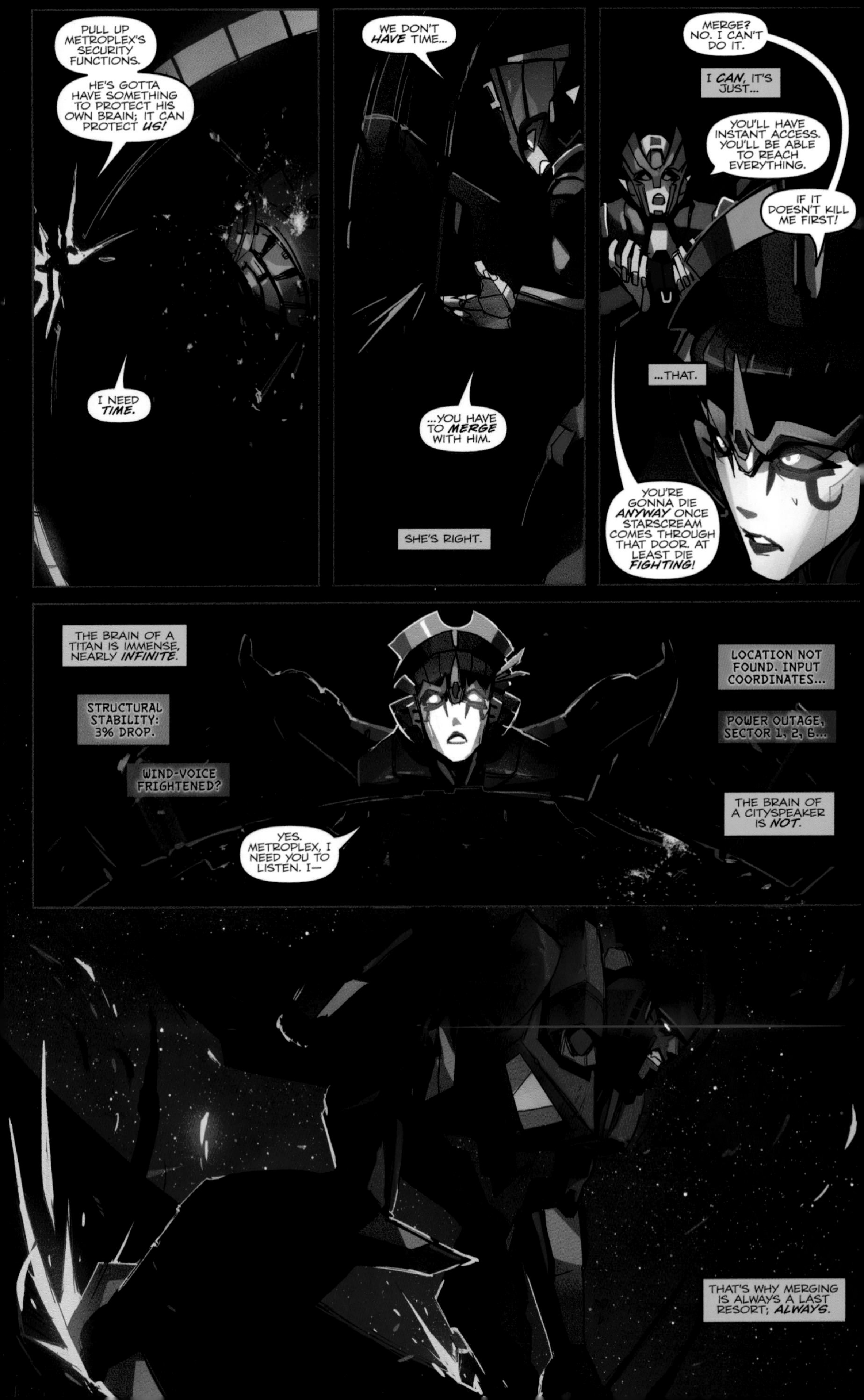
PULL UP METROPLEX'S SECURITY FUNCTIONS.
HE'S GOTTA HAVE SOMETHING TO PROTECT HIS OWN BRAIN; IT CAN PROTECT *US!*
I NEED *TIME.*
WE DON'T *HAVE* TIME...
...YOU HAVE TO *MERGE* WITH HIM.
SHE'S RIGHT.
MERGE? NO. I CAN'T DO IT.
I *CAN,* IT'S JUST...
YOU'LL HAVE INSTANT ACCESS. YOU'LL BE ABLE TO REACH EVERYTHING.
IF IT DOESN'T KILL ME FIRST!
...THAT.
YOU'RE GONNA DIE *ANYWAY* ONCE STARSCREAM COMES THROUGH THAT DOOR. AT LEAST DIE *FIGHTING!*
THE BRAIN OF A TITAN IS IMMENSE, NEARLY *INFINITE.*
STRUCTURAL STABILITY: 3% DROP.
WIND-VOICE FRIGHTENED?
YES. METROPLEX, I NEED YOU TO LISTEN. I—
LOCATION NOT FOUND. INPUT COORDINATES...
POWER OUTAGE, SECTOR 1, 2, 6...
THE BRAIN OF A CITYSPEAKER IS *NOT.*
THAT'S WHY MERGING IS ALWAYS A LAST RESORT; *ALWAYS.*

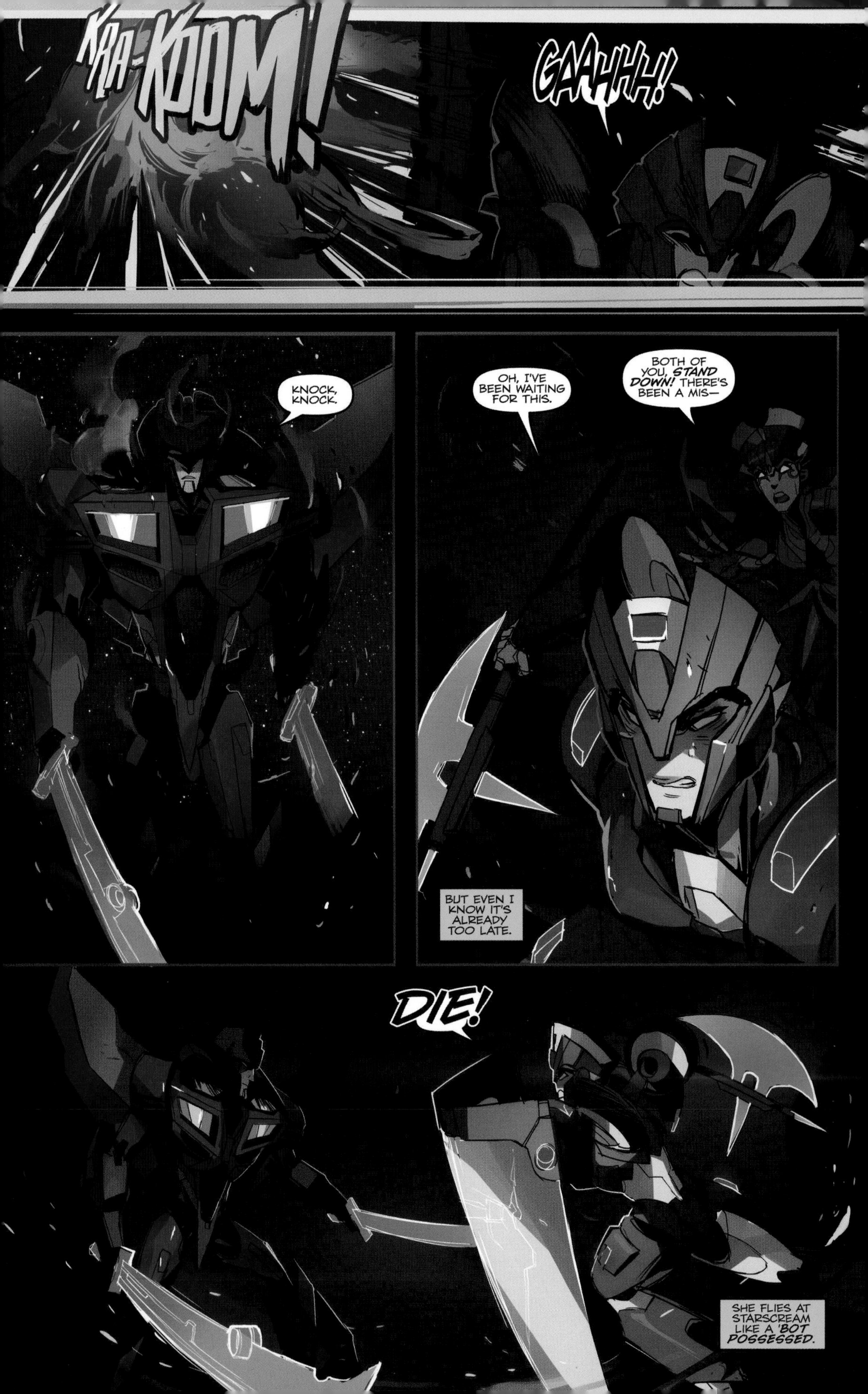
KRA-KOOM!!
GAAHHH!
KNOCK, KNOCK.
OH, I'VE BEEN WAITING FOR THIS.
BOTH OF YOU, STAND DOWN! THERE'S BEEN A MIS—
BUT EVEN I KNOW IT'S ALREADY TOO LATE.
DIE!
SHE FLIES AT STARSCREAM LIKE A 'BOT POSSESSED.

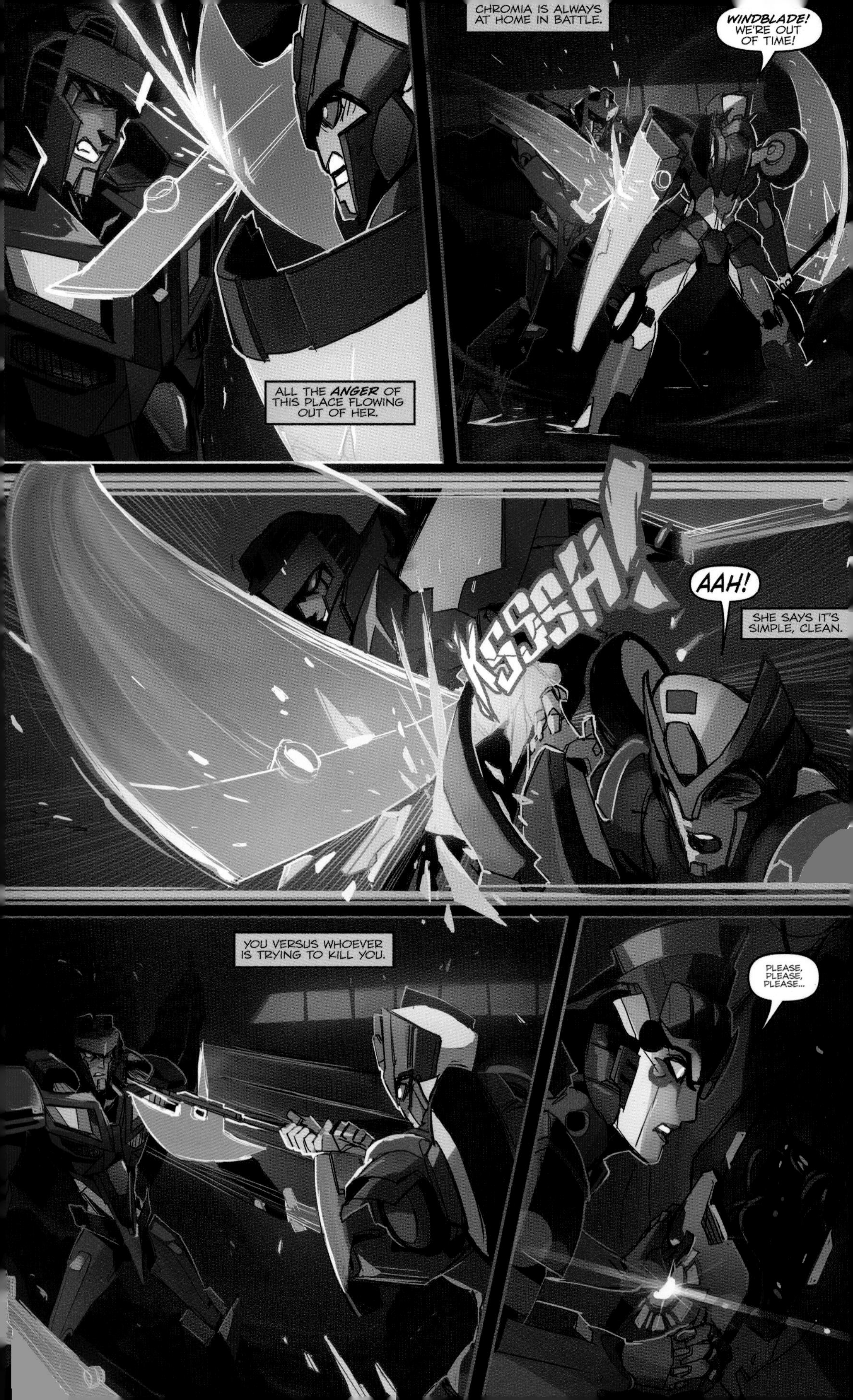

CHROMIA IS ALWAYS AT HOME IN BATTLE.
ALL THE ANGER OF THIS PLACE FLOWING OUT OF HER.
WINDBLADE! WE'RE OUT OF TIME!
KSSSH!
AAH!
SHE SAYS IT'S SIMPLE, CLEAN.
YOU VERSUS WHOEVER IS TRYING TO KILL YOU.
PLEASE, PLEASE, PLEASE...

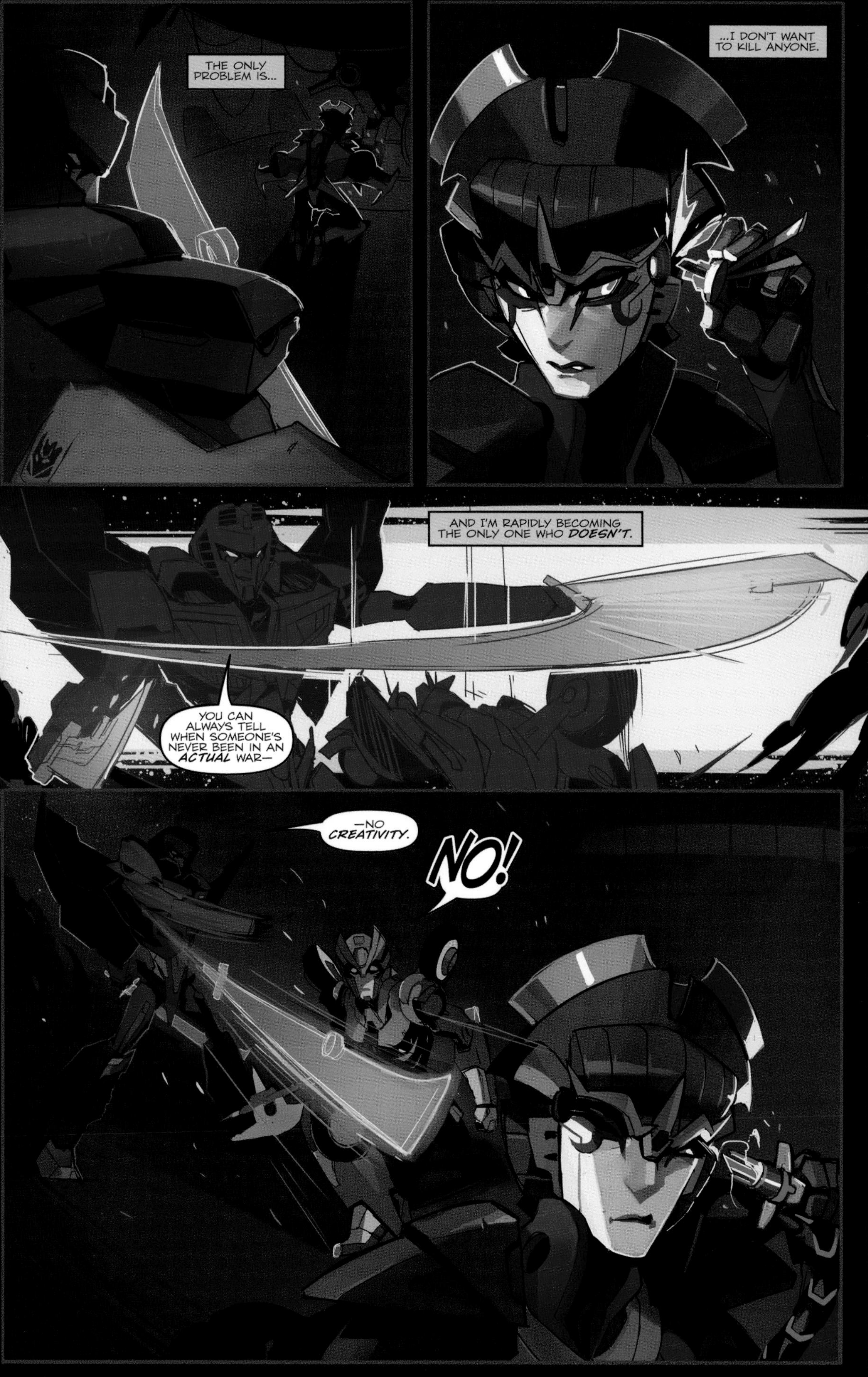
THE ONLY PROBLEM IS...
...I DON'T WANT TO KILL ANYONE.
AND I'M RAPIDLY BECOMING THE ONLY ONE WHO *DOESN'T*.
YOU CAN ALWAYS TELL WHEN SOMEONE'S NEVER BEEN IN AN *ACTUAL* WAR—
—NO *CREATIVITY*.
NO!

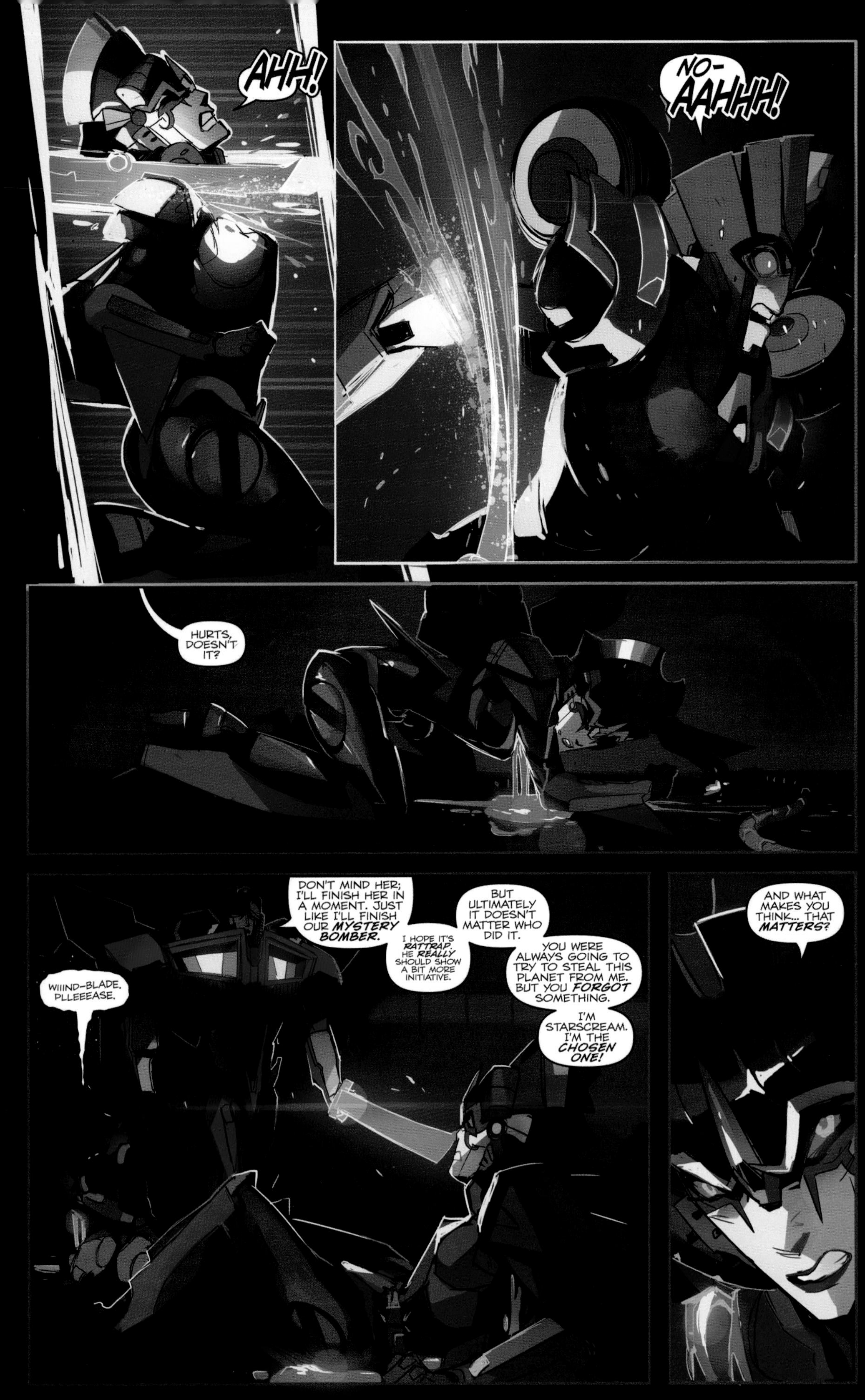
AHH!
NO-AAHHH!
HURTS, DOESN'T IT?
WIIIND-BLADE. PLLEEEASE.
DON'T MIND HER; I'LL FINISH HER IN A MOMENT. JUST LIKE I'LL FINISH OUR **MYSTERY BOMBER.**
I HOPE IT'S ***RATTRAP.*** HE ***REALLY*** SHOULD SHOW A BIT MORE INITIATIVE.
BUT ULTIMATELY IT DOESN'T MATTER WHO DID IT.
YOU WERE ALWAYS GOING TO TRY TO STEAL THIS PLANET FROM ME. BUT YOU ***FORGOT*** SOMETHING.
I'M STARSCREAM. I'M THE ***CHOSEN ONE!***
AND WHAT MAKES YOU THINK... THAT ***MATTERS?***

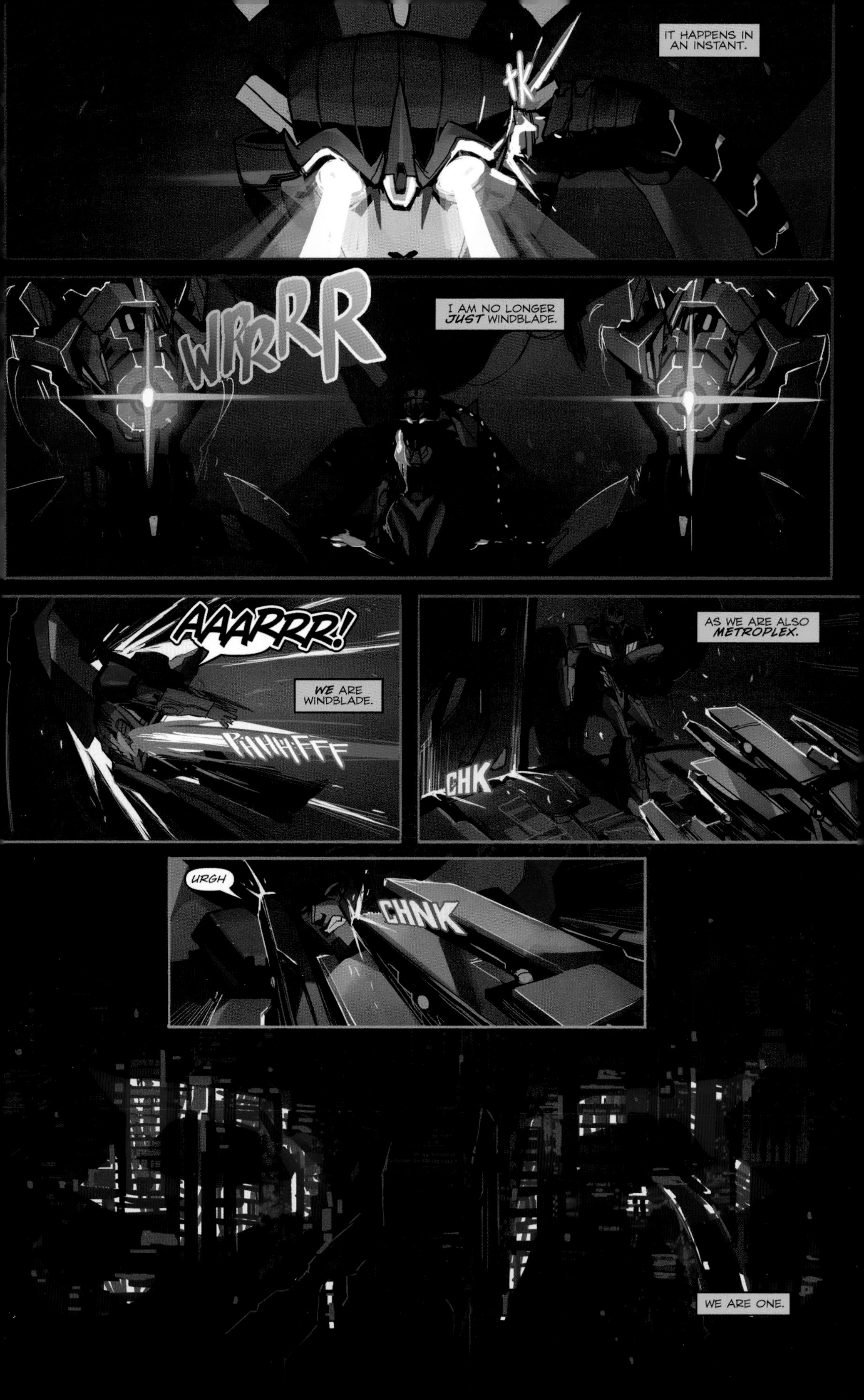
IT HAPPENS IN AN INSTANT.
TK
WRRRR
I AM NO LONGER JUST WINDBLADE.
AAARRR!
WE ARE WINDBLADE.
PHHHFFF
AS WE ARE ALSO METROPLEX.
CHK
URGH
CHNK
WE ARE ONE.

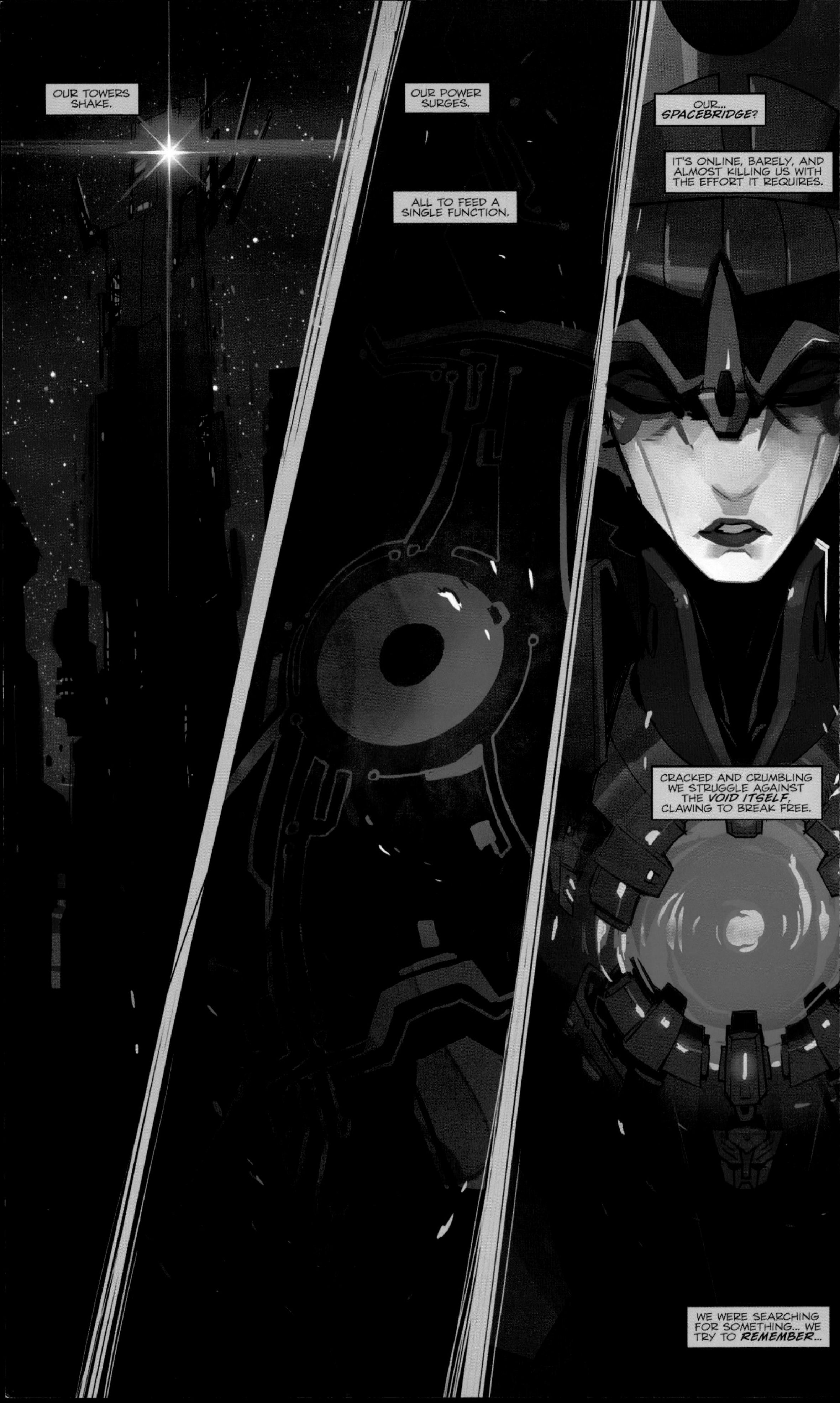
OUR TOWERS SHAKE.
OUR POWER SURGES.
ALL TO FEED A SINGLE FUNCTION.
OUR... SPACEBRIDGE?
IT'S ONLINE, BARELY, AND ALMOST KILLING US WITH THE EFFORT IT REQUIRES.
CRACKED AND CRUMBLING WE STRUGGLE AGAINST THE VOID ITSELF, CLAWING TO BREAK FREE.
WE WERE SEARCHING FOR SOMETHING... WE TRY TO REMEMBER...

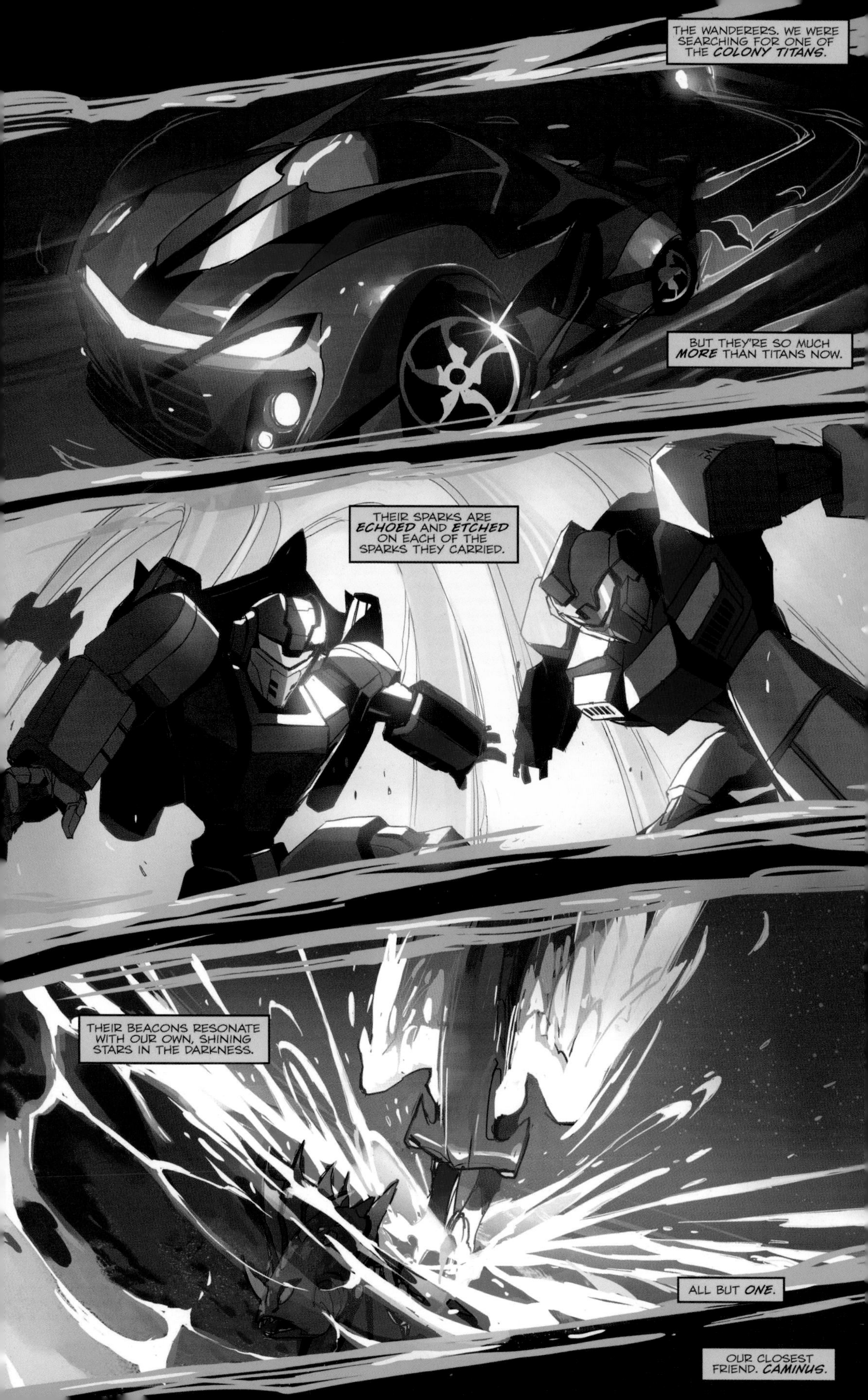
THE WANDERERS. WE WERE SEARCHING FOR ONE OF THE *COLONY TITANS*.
BUT THEY'RE SO MUCH *MORE* THAN TITANS NOW.
THEIR SPARKS ARE *ECHOED* AND *ETCHED* ON EACH OF THE SPARKS THEY CARRIED.
THEIR BEACONS RESONATE WITH OUR OWN, SHINING STARS IN THE DARKNESS.
ALL BUT *ONE*.
OUR CLOSEST FRIEND. *CAMINUS*.

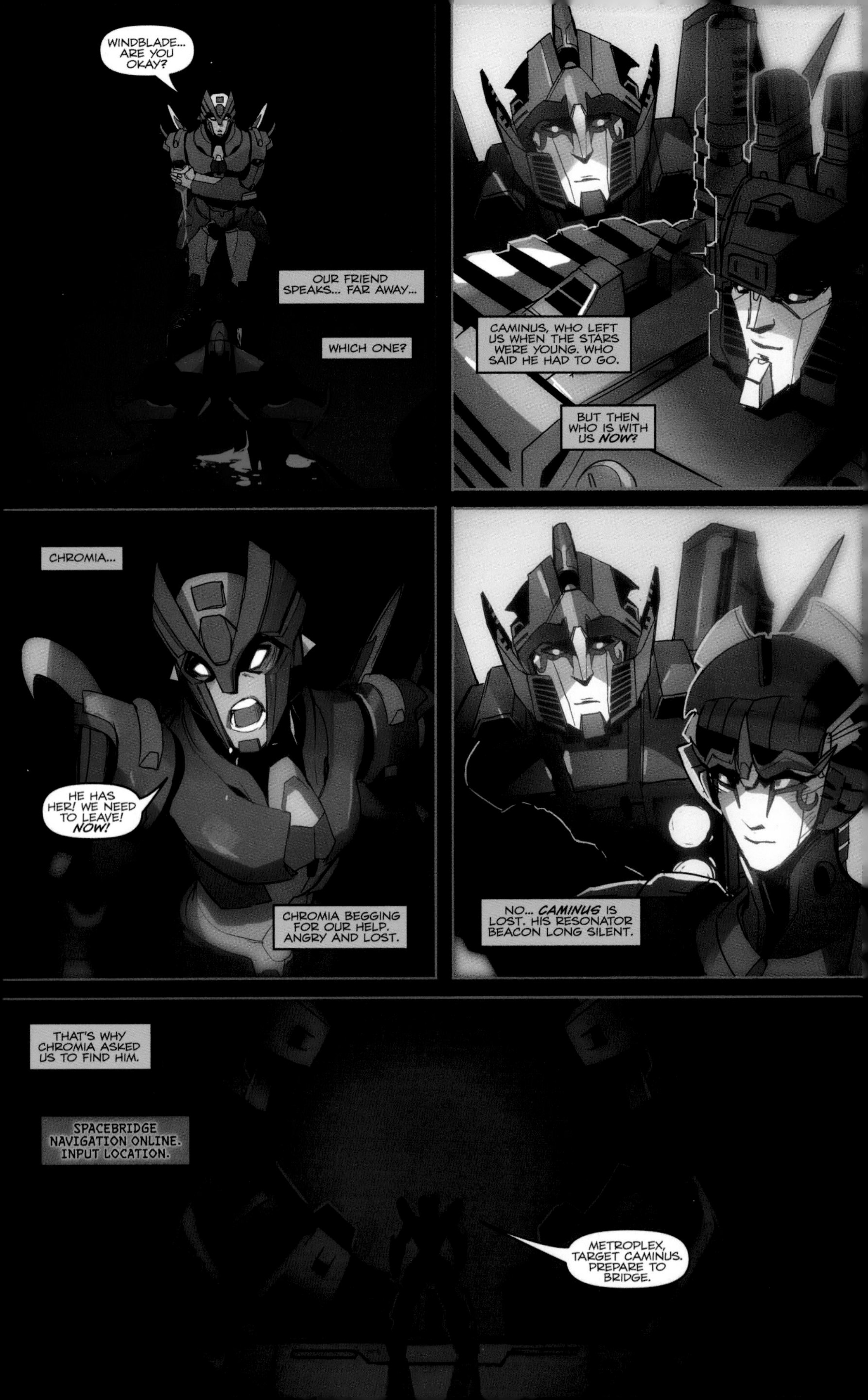
WINDBLADE... ARE YOU OKAY?
OUR FRIEND SPEAKS... FAR AWAY...
WHICH ONE?
CAMINUS, WHO LEFT US WHEN THE STARS WERE YOUNG. WHO SAID HE HAD TO GO.
BUT THEN WHO IS WITH US *NOW?*
CHROMIA...
HE HAS HER! WE NEED TO LEAVE! *NOW!*
CHROMIA BEGGING FOR OUR HELP. ANGRY AND LOST.
NO... *CAMINUS* IS LOST. HIS RESONATOR BEACON LONG SILENT.
THAT'S WHY CHROMIA ASKED US TO FIND HIM.
SPACEBRIDGE NAVIGATION ONLINE. INPUT LOCATION.
METROPLEX, TARGET CAMINUS. PREPARE TO BRIDGE.

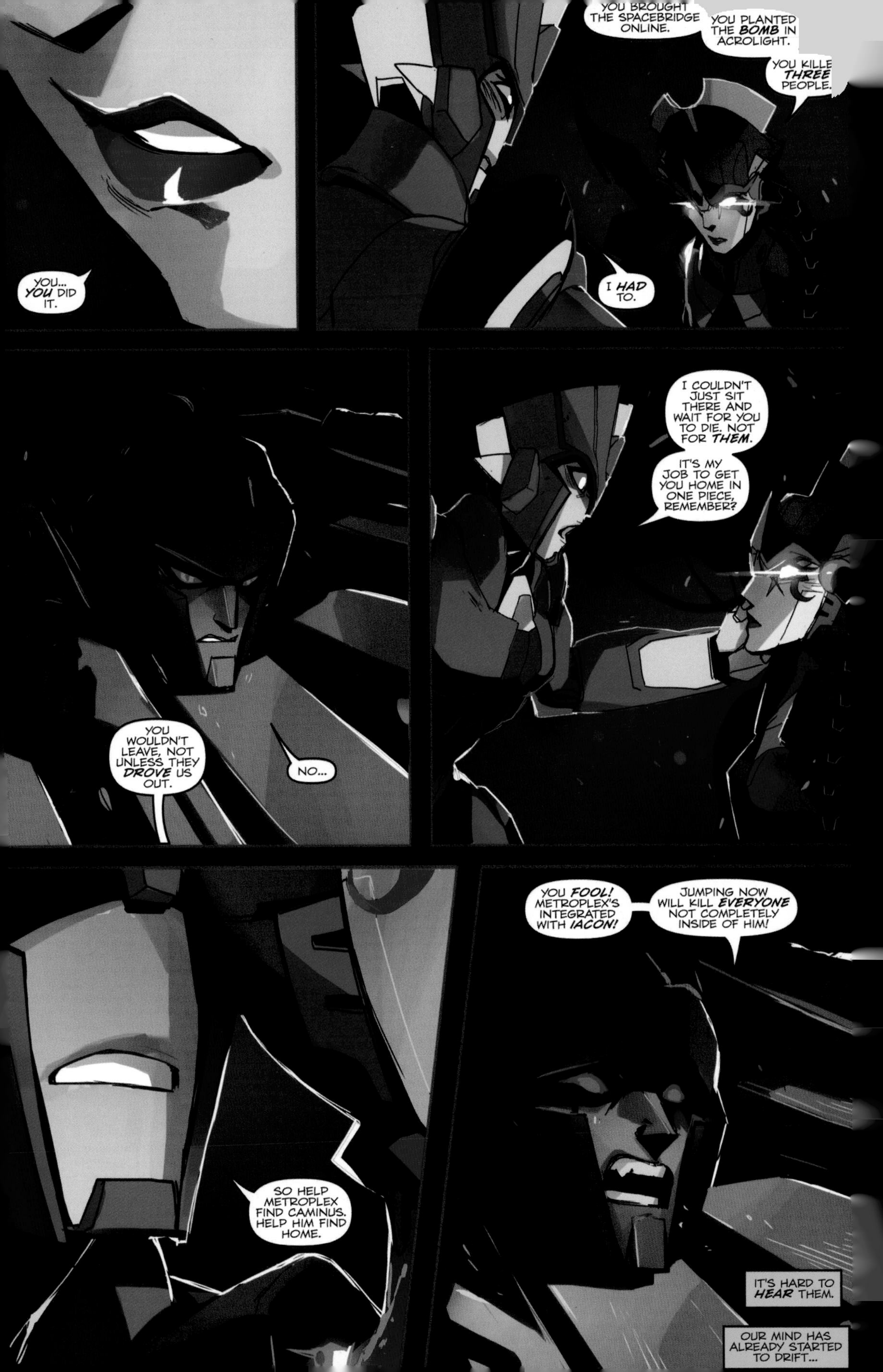

YOU... YOU DID IT.
YOU BROUGHT THE SPACEBRIDGE ONLINE.
YOU PLANTED THE BOMB IN ACROLIGHT.
YOU KILLE THREE PEOPLE.
I HAD TO.
YOU WOULDN'T LEAVE, NOT UNLESS THEY DROVE US OUT.
NO...
I COULDN'T JUST SIT THERE AND WAIT FOR YOU TO DIE. NOT FOR THEM.
IT'S MY JOB TO GET YOU HOME IN ONE PIECE, REMEMBER?
SO HELP METROPLEX FIND CAMINUS. HELP HIM FIND HOME.
YOU FOOL! METROPLEX'S INTEGRATED WITH IACON!
JUMPING NOW WILL KILL EVERYONE NOT COMPLETELY INSIDE OF HIM!
IT'S HARD TO HEAR THEM.
OUR MIND HAS ALREADY STARTED TO DRIFT...

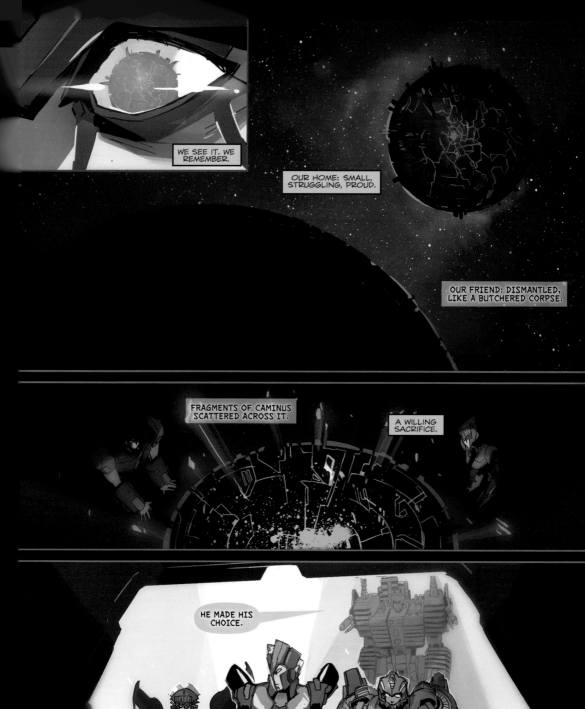

WE SEE IT. WE REMEMBER.

OUR HOME: SMALL, STRUGGLING, PROUD.

OUR FRIEND: DISMANTLED, LIKE A BUTCHERED CORPSE.

FRAGMENTS OF CAMINUS SCATTERED ACROSS IT.

A WILLING SACRIFICE.

HE MADE HIS CHOICE.

SHE MADE HERS.

WINDBLADE, TAKE US HOME.

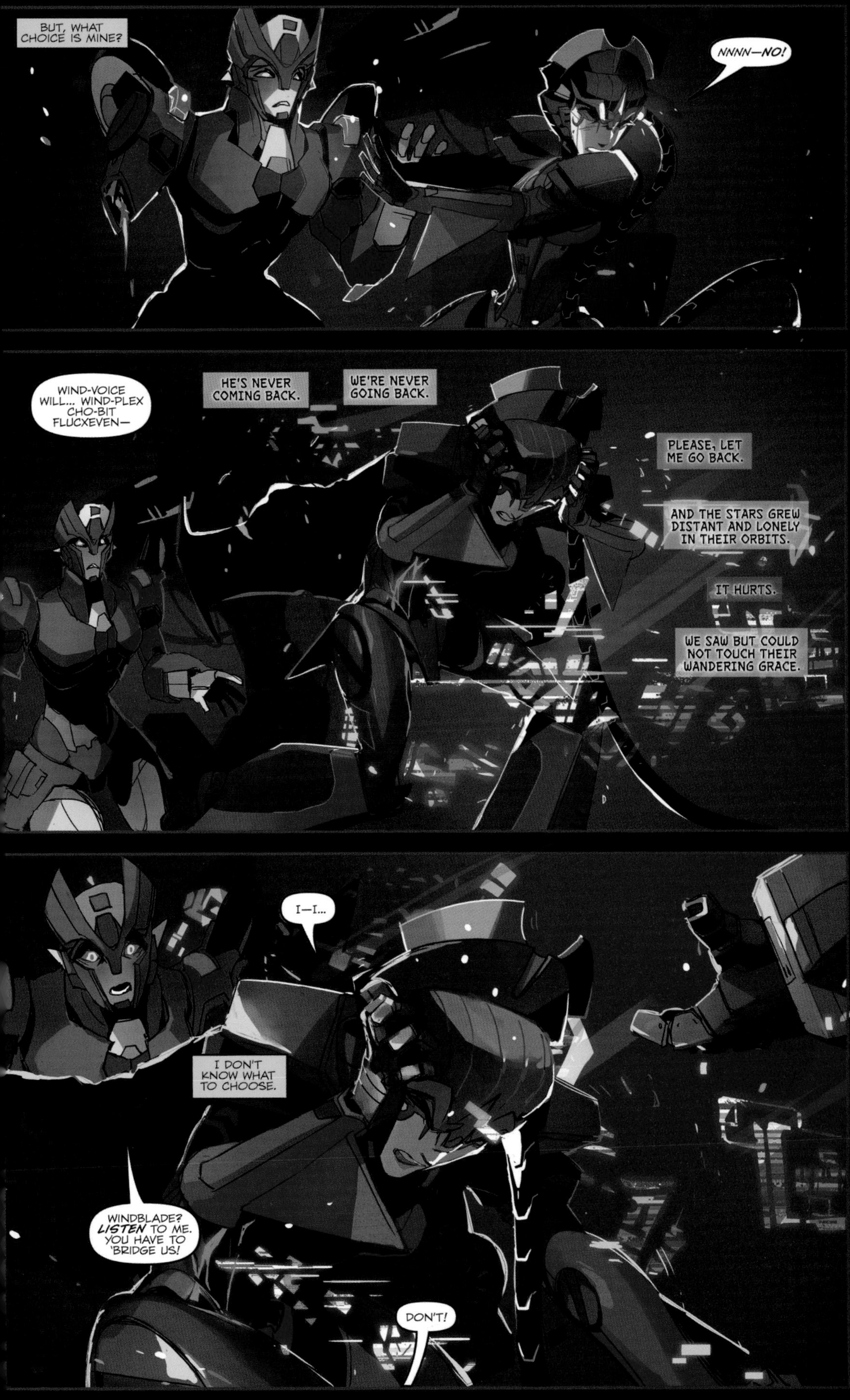
BUT, WHAT CHOICE IS MINE?
NNNN—NO!
WIND-VOICE WILL... WIND-PLEX CHO-BIT FLUCXEVEN—
HE'S NEVER COMING BACK.
WE'RE NEVER GOING BACK.
PLEASE, LET ME GO BACK.
AND THE STARS GREW DISTANT AND LONELY IN THEIR ORBITS.
IT HURTS.
WE SAW BUT COULD NOT TOUCH THEIR WANDERING GRACE.
I—I...
I DON'T KNOW WHAT TO CHOOSE.
WINDBLADE? LISTEN TO ME. YOU HAVE TO 'BRIDGE US!
DON'T!

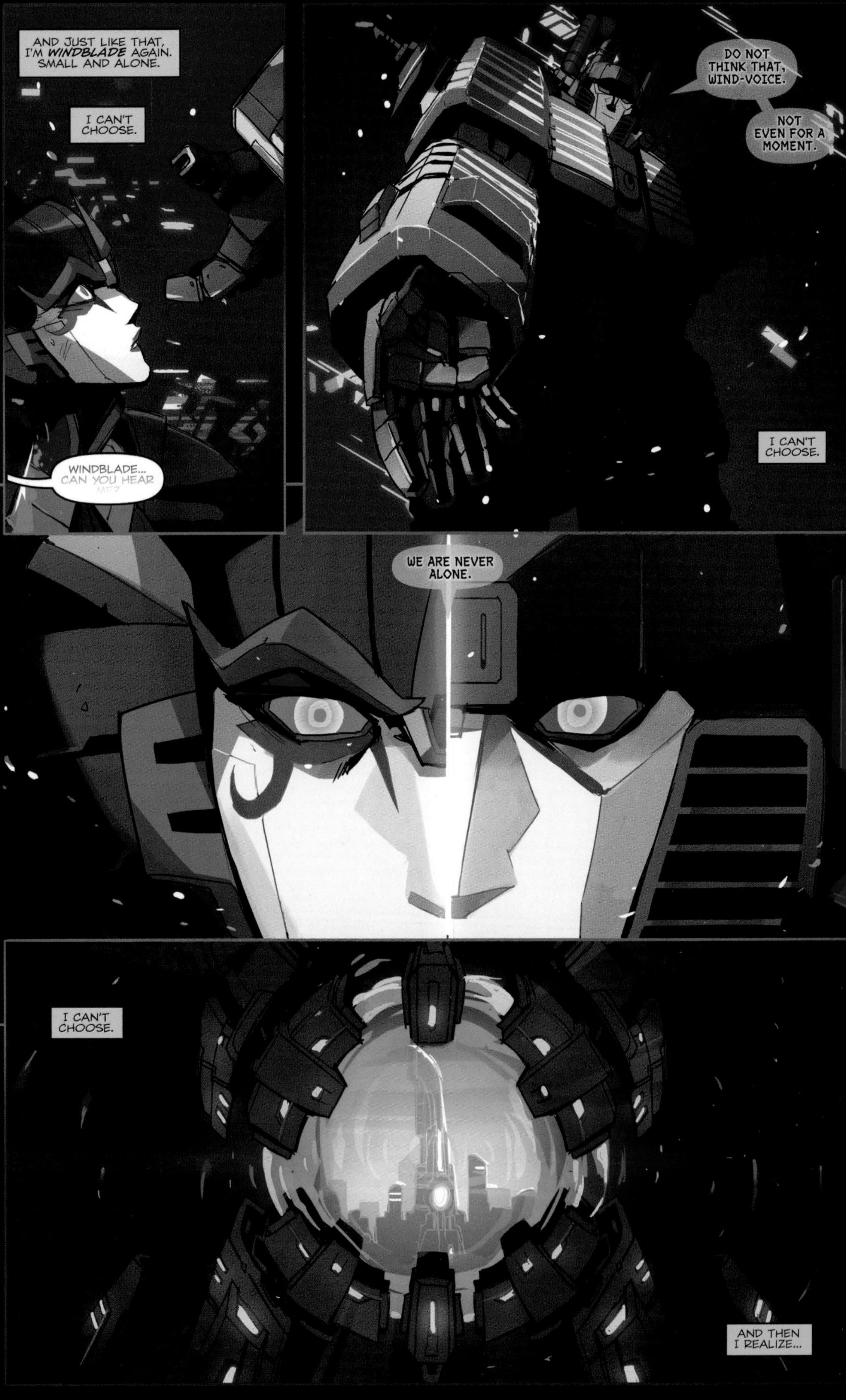
AND JUST LIKE THAT, I'M *WINDBLADE* AGAIN. SMALL AND ALONE.
I CAN'T CHOOSE.
WINDBLADE... CAN YOU HEAR ME?
DO NOT THINK THAT, WIND-VOICE.
NOT EVEN FOR A MOMENT.
I CAN'T CHOOSE.
WE ARE NEVER ALONE.
I CAN'T CHOOSE.
AND THEN I REALIZE...

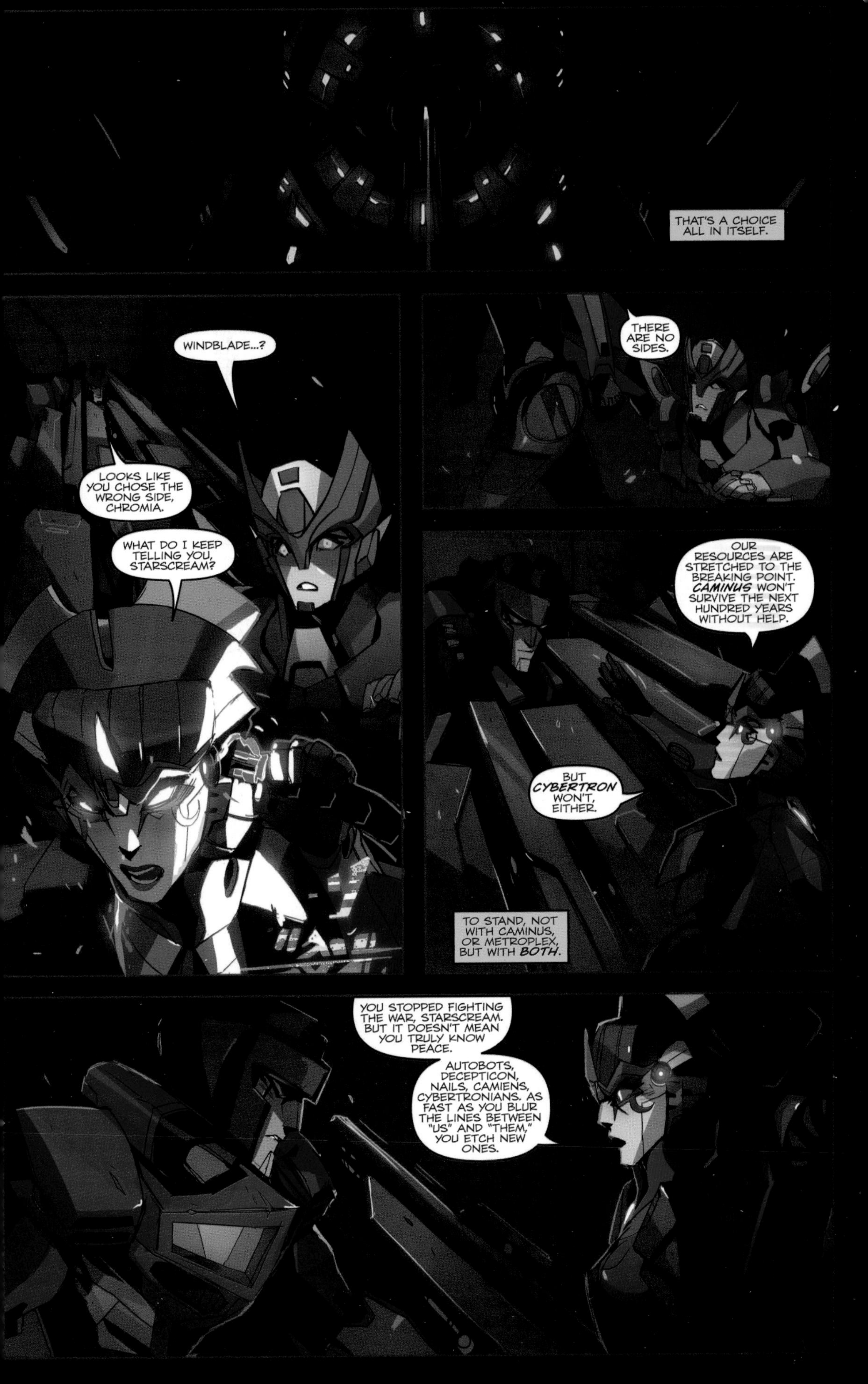
THAT'S A CHOICE ALL IN ITSELF.
WINDBLADE...?
LOOKS LIKE YOU CHOSE THE WRONG SIDE, CHROMIA.
WHAT DO I KEEP TELLING YOU, STARSCREAM?
THERE ARE NO SIDES.
OUR RESOURCES ARE STRETCHED TO THE BREAKING POINT. CAMINUS WON'T SURVIVE THE NEXT HUNDRED YEARS WITHOUT HELP.
BUT CYBERTRON WON'T, EITHER.
TO STAND, NOT WITH CAMINUS, OR METROPLEX, BUT WITH BOTH.
YOU STOPPED FIGHTING THE WAR, STARSCREAM. BUT IT DOESN'T MEAN YOU TRULY KNOW PEACE.
AUTOBOTS, DECEPTICON, NAILS, CAMIENS, CYBERTRONIANS. AS FAST AS YOU BLUR THE LINES BETWEEN "US" AND "THEM," YOU ETCH NEW ONES.

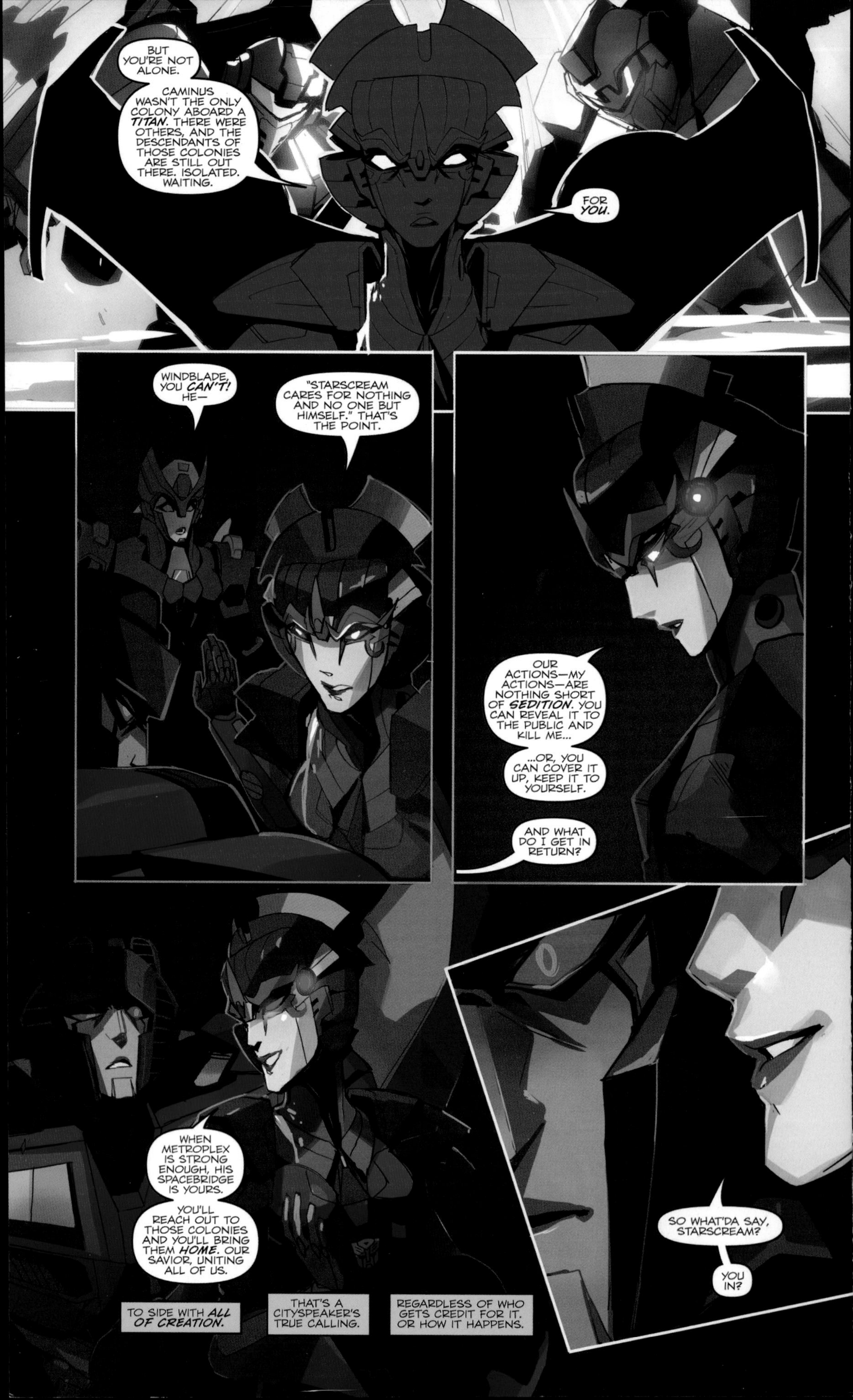
BUT YOU'RE NOT ALONE.
CAMINUS WASN'T THE ONLY COLONY ABOARD A *TITAN*. THERE WERE OTHERS, AND THE DESCENDANTS OF THOSE COLONIES ARE STILL OUT THERE. ISOLATED. WAITING.
FOR *YOU*.
WINDBLADE, YOU *CAN'T!* HE—
"STARSCREAM CARES FOR NOTHING AND NO ONE BUT HIMSELF." THAT'S THE POINT.
OUR ACTIONS—MY ACTIONS—ARE NOTHING SHORT OF *SEDITION*. YOU CAN REVEAL IT TO THE PUBLIC AND KILL ME...
...OR, YOU CAN COVER IT UP, KEEP IT TO YOURSELF.
AND WHAT DO I GET IN RETURN?
WHEN METROPLEX IS STRONG ENOUGH, HIS SPACEBRIDGE IS YOURS.
YOU'LL REACH OUT TO THOSE COLONIES AND YOU'LL BRING THEM *HOME*. OUR SAVIOR, UNITING ALL OF US.
TO SIDE WITH *ALL OF CREATION*.
THAT'S A CITYSPEAKER'S TRUE CALLING.
REGARDLESS OF WHO GETS CREDIT FOR IT. OR HOW IT HAPPENS.
SO WHAT'DA SAY, STARSCREAM?
YOU IN?

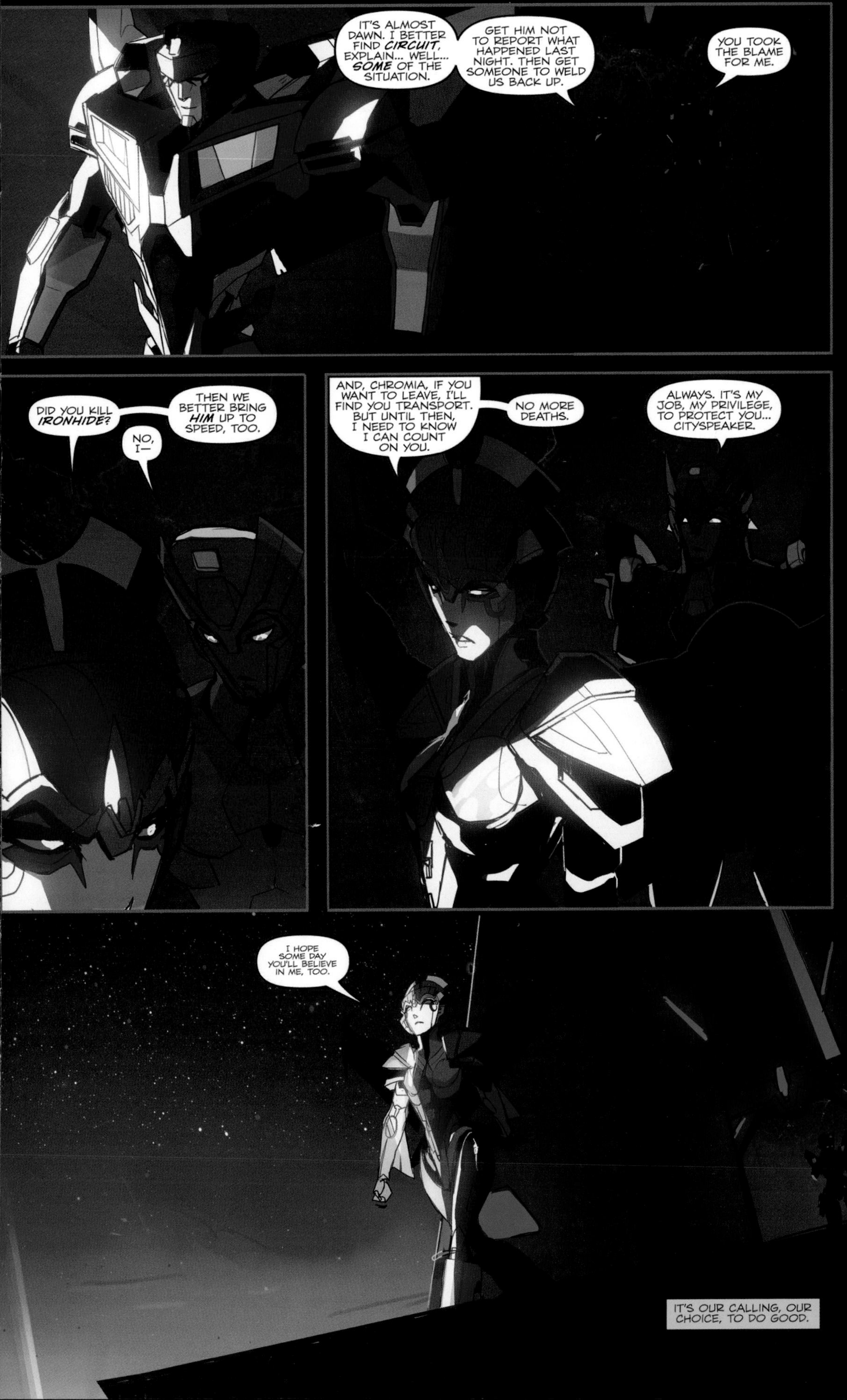
IT'S ALMOST DAWN. I BETTER FIND CIRCUIT, EXPLAIN... WELL... SOME OF THE SITUATION.
GET HIM NOT TO REPORT WHAT HAPPENED LAST NIGHT. THEN GET SOMEONE TO WELD US BACK UP.
YOU TOOK THE BLAME FOR ME.
DID YOU KILL IRONHIDE?
NO, I—
THEN WE BETTER BRING HIM UP TO SPEED, TOO.
AND, CHROMIA, IF YOU WANT TO LEAVE, I'LL FIND YOU TRANSPORT. BUT UNTIL THEN, I NEED TO KNOW I CAN COUNT ON YOU.
NO MORE DEATHS.
ALWAYS. IT'S MY JOB, MY PRIVILEGE, TO PROTECT YOU... CITYSPEAKER.
I HOPE SOME DAY YOU'LL BELIEVE IN ME, TOO.
IT'S OUR CALLING, OUR CHOICE, TO DO GOOD.

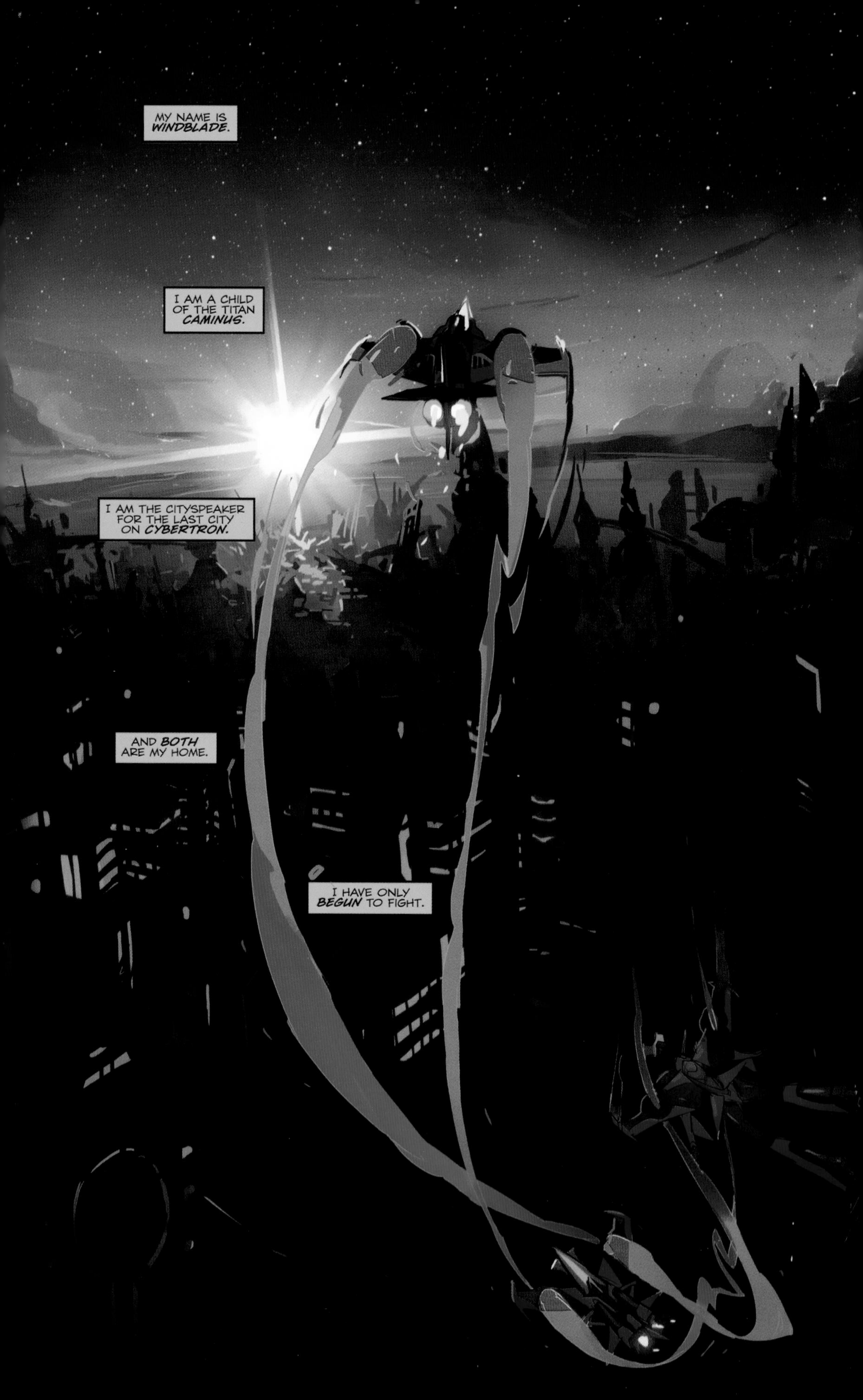
MY NAME IS *WINDBLADE*.
I AM A CHILD OF THE TITAN *CAMINUS*.
I AM THE CITYSPEAKER FOR THE LAST CITY ON *CYBERTRON*.
AND *BOTH* ARE MY HOME.
I HAVE ONLY *BEGUN* TO FIGHT.

ART BY **PHIL JIMENEZ**
COLORS BY **ROMULO FAJARDO, JR.**

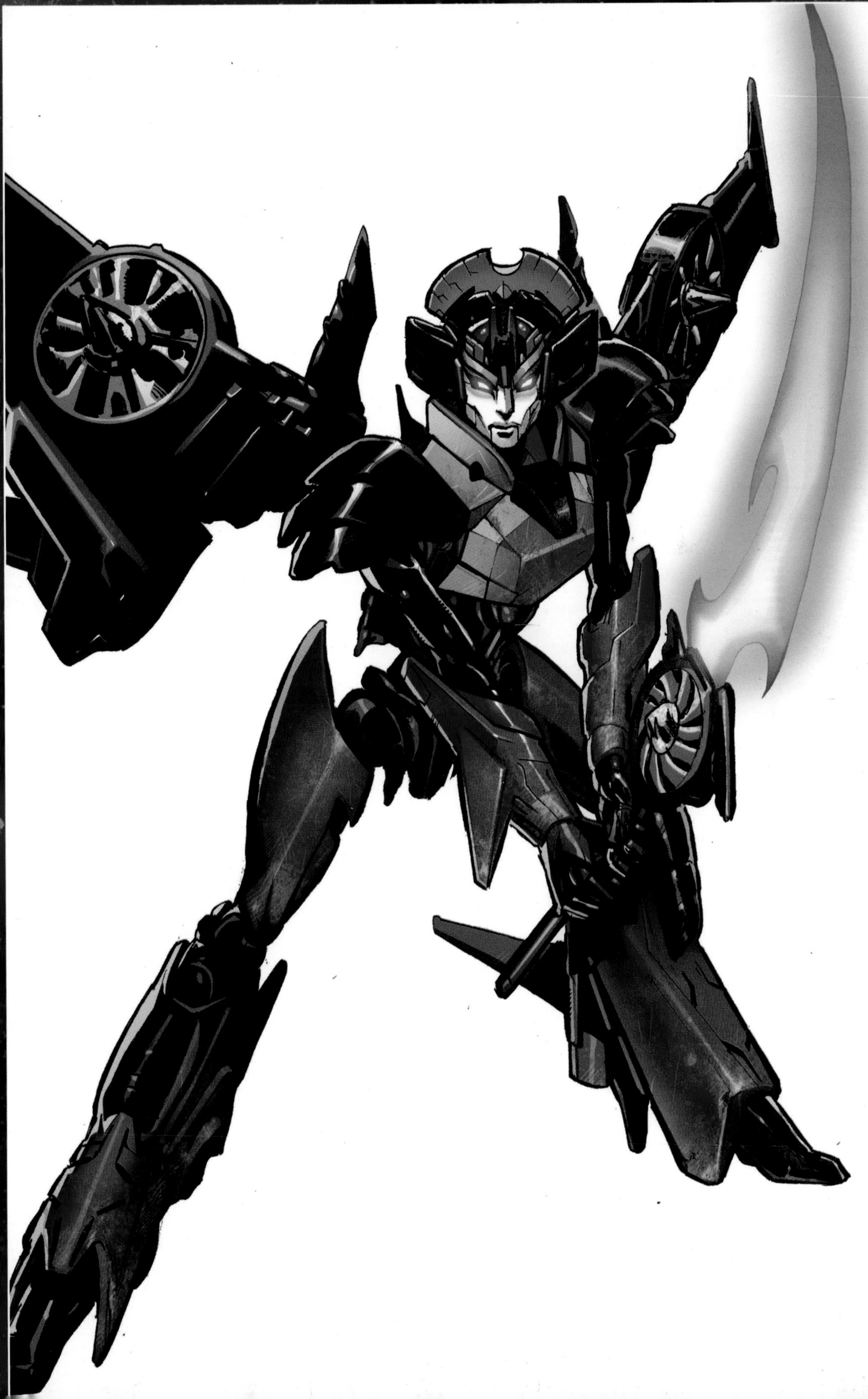

ART BY **CASEY W. COLLER**
COLORS BY **JOANA LAFUENTE**

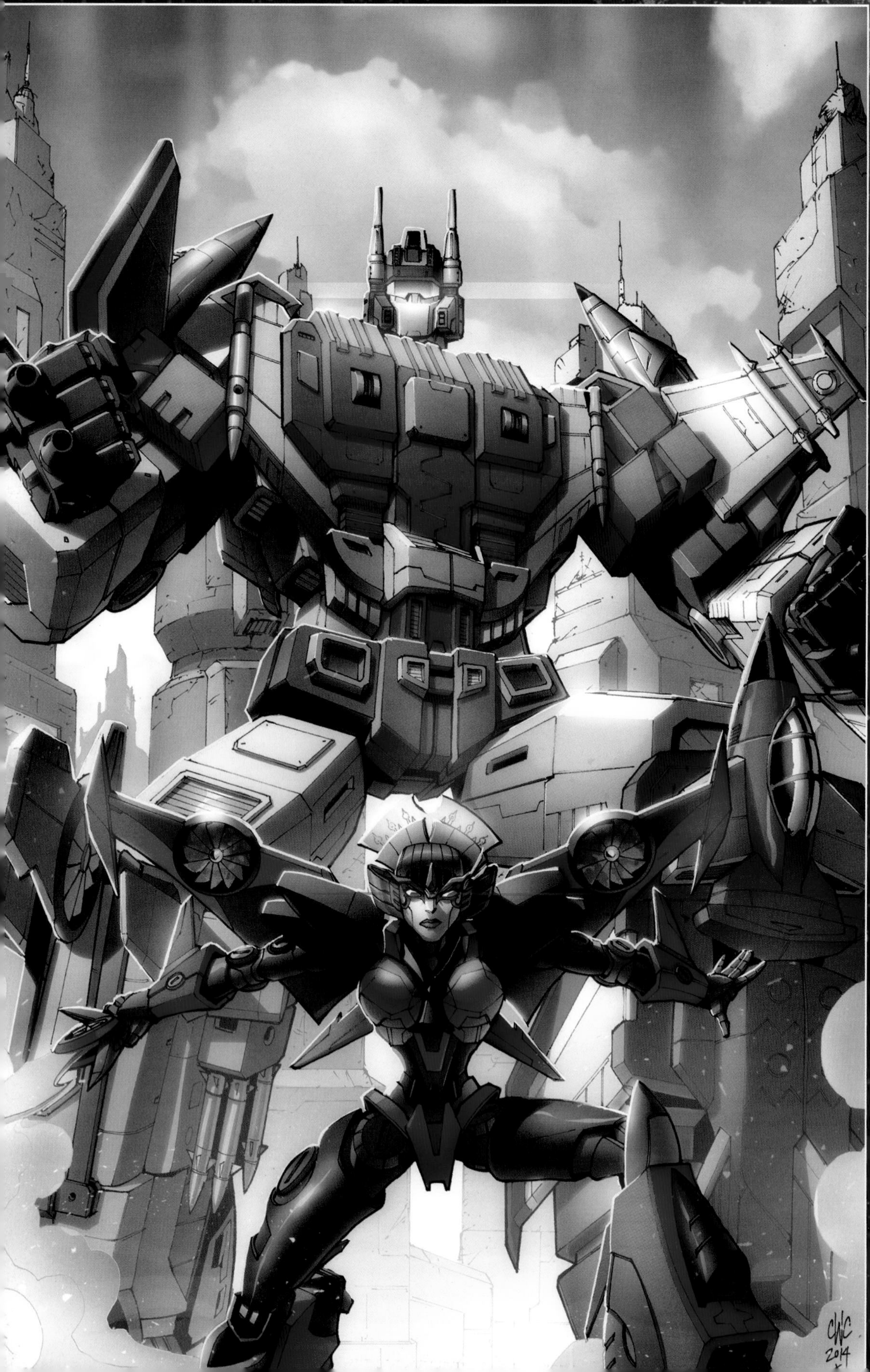

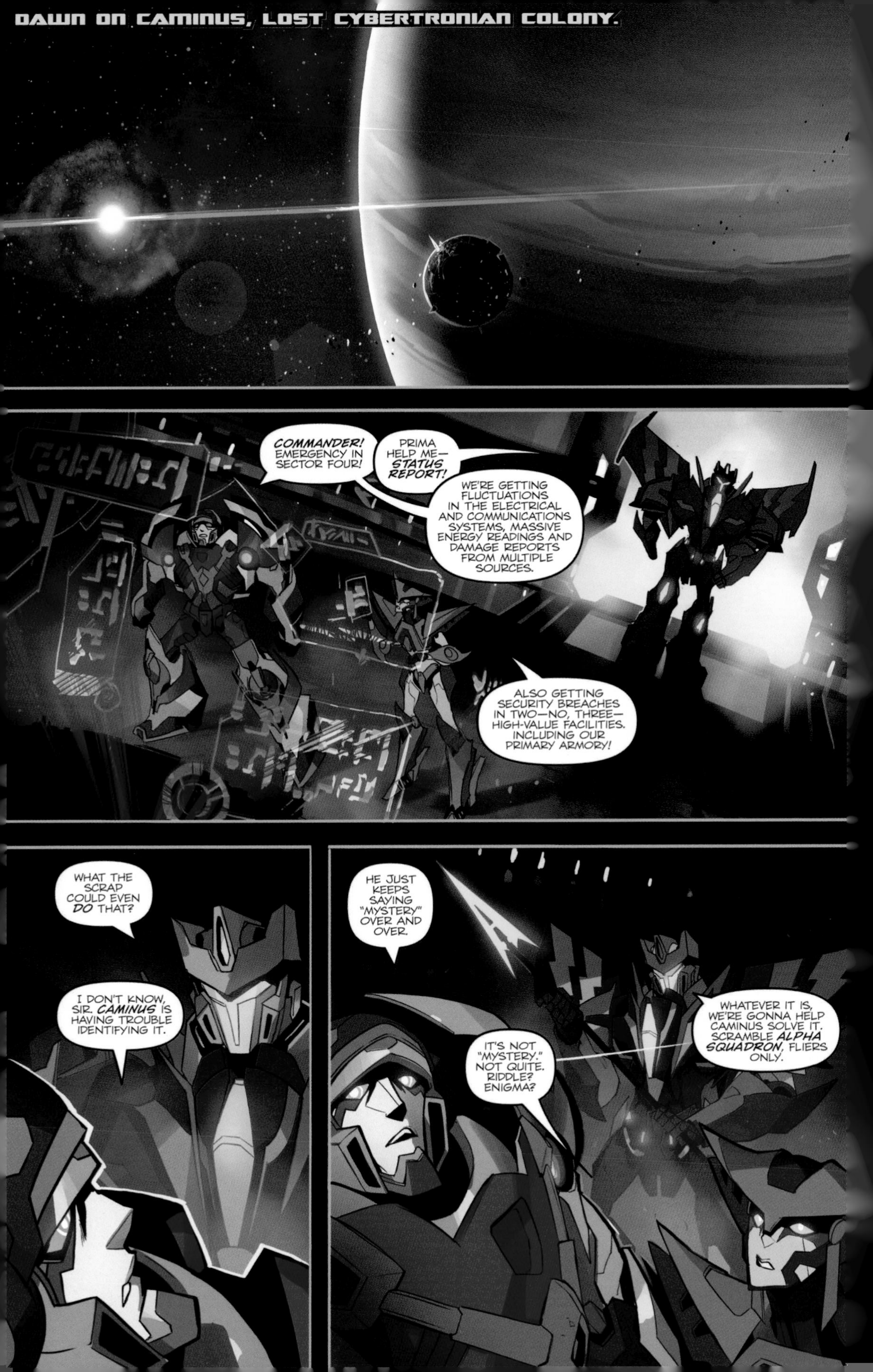
DAWN ON CAMINUS, LOST CYBERTRONIAN COLONY.
COMMANDER! EMERGENCY IN SECTOR FOUR!
PRIMA HELP ME— STATUS REPORT!
WE'RE GETTING FLUCTUATIONS IN THE ELECTRICAL AND COMMUNICATIONS SYSTEMS, MASSIVE ENERGY READINGS AND DAMAGE REPORTS FROM MULTIPLE SOURCES.
ALSO GETTING SECURITY BREACHES IN TWO—NO, THREE—HIGH-VALUE FACILITIES. INCLUDING OUR PRIMARY ARMORY!
WHAT THE SCRAP COULD EVEN DO THAT?
I DON'T KNOW, SIR. CAMINUS IS HAVING TROUBLE IDENTIFYING IT.
HE JUST KEEPS SAYING "MYSTERY" OVER AND OVER.
IT'S NOT "MYSTERY." NOT QUITE. RIDDLE? ENIGMA?
WHATEVER IT IS, WE'RE GONNA HELP CAMINUS SOLVE IT. SCRAMBLE ALPHA SQUADRON, FLIERS ONLY.

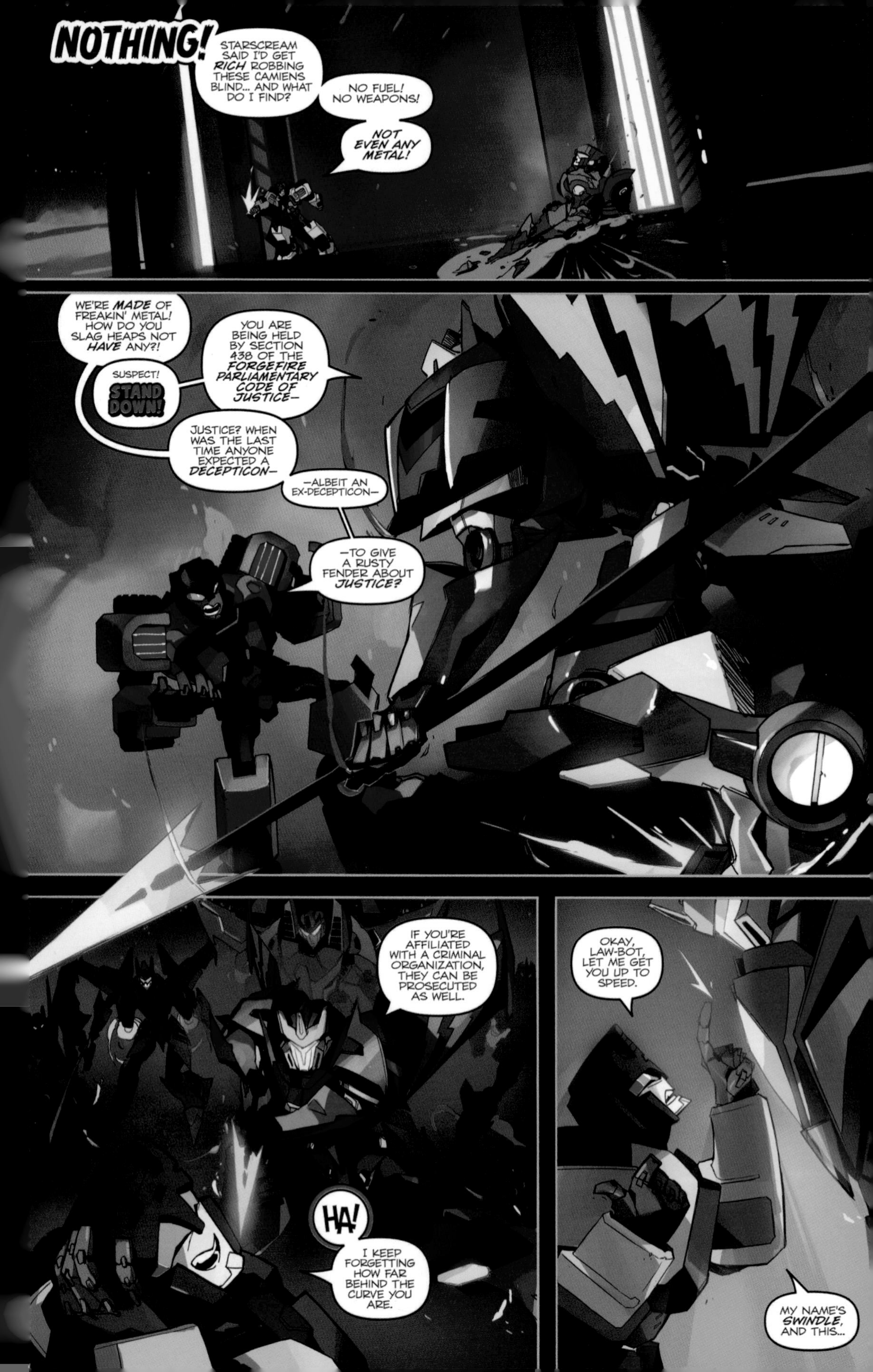
NOTHING!
STARSCREAM SAID I'D GET RICH ROBBING THESE CAMIENS BLIND... AND WHAT DO I FIND?
NO FUEL! NO WEAPONS!
NOT EVEN ANY METAL!
WE'RE MADE OF FREAKIN' METAL! HOW DO YOU SLAG HEAPS NOT HAVE ANY?!
SUSPECT!
STAND DOWN!
YOU ARE BEING HELD BY SECTION 438 OF THE FORGEFIRE PARLIAMENTARY CODE OF JUSTICE–
JUSTICE? WHEN WAS THE LAST TIME ANYONE EXPECTED A DECEPTICON–
–ALBEIT AN EX-DECEPTICON–
–TO GIVE A RUSTY FENDER ABOUT JUSTICE?
IF YOU'RE AFFILIATED WITH A CRIMINAL ORGANIZATION, THEY CAN BE PROSECUTED AS WELL.
HA!
I KEEP FORGETTING HOW FAR BEHIND THE CURVE YOU ARE.
OKAY, LAW-BOT, LET ME GET YOU UP TO SPEED.
MY NAME'S SWINDLE, AND THIS...

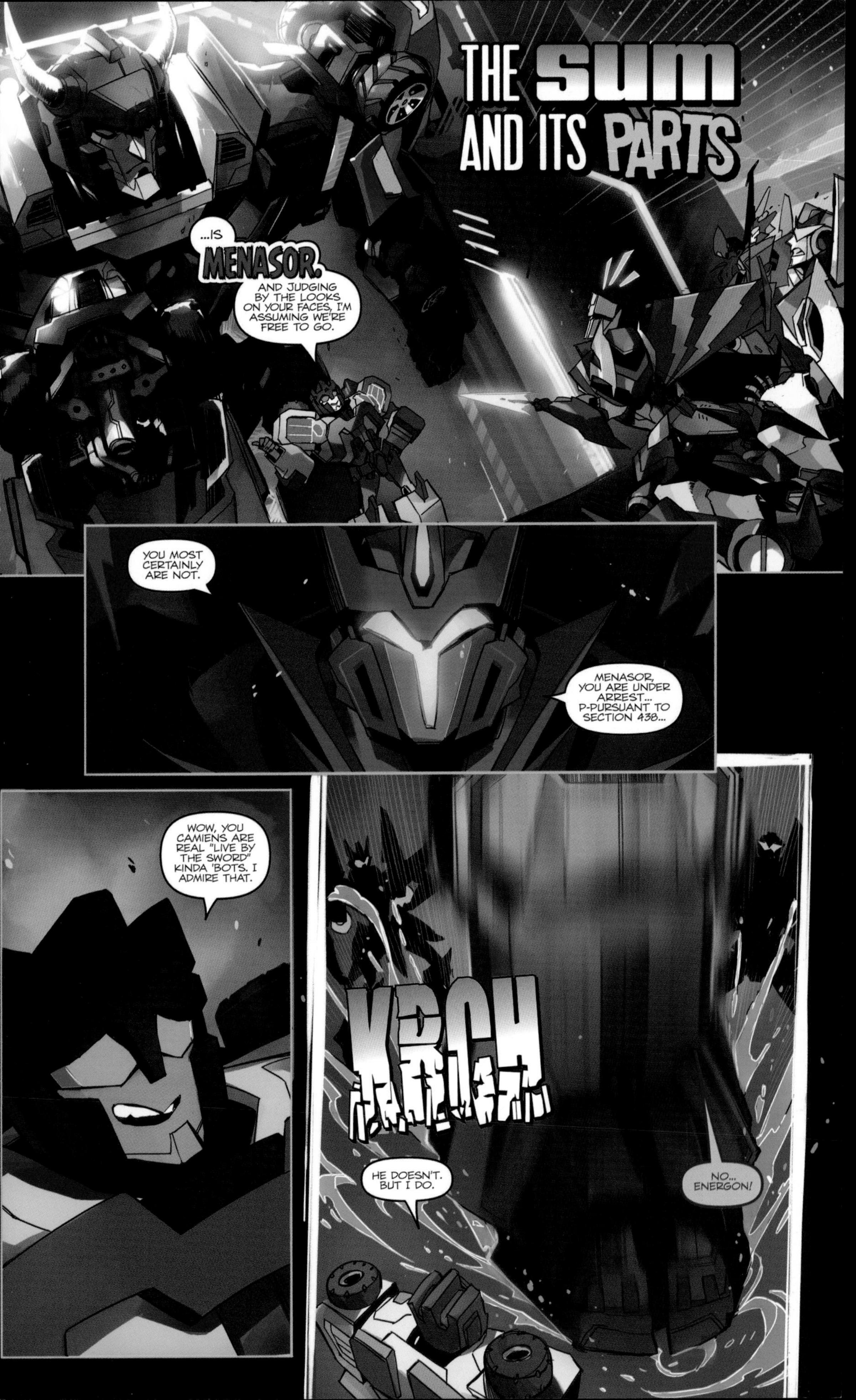
THE SUM AND ITS PARTS
...IS MENASOR.
AND JUDGING BY THE LOOKS ON YOUR FACES, I'M ASSUMING WE'RE FREE TO GO.
YOU MOST CERTAINLY ARE NOT.
MENASOR, YOU ARE UNDER ARREST... P-PURSUANT TO SECTION 438...
WOW, YOU CAMIENS ARE REAL "LIVE BY THE SWORD" KINDA 'BOTS. I ADMIRE THAT.
KRCH
HE DOESN'T. BUT I DO.
NO... ENERGON!

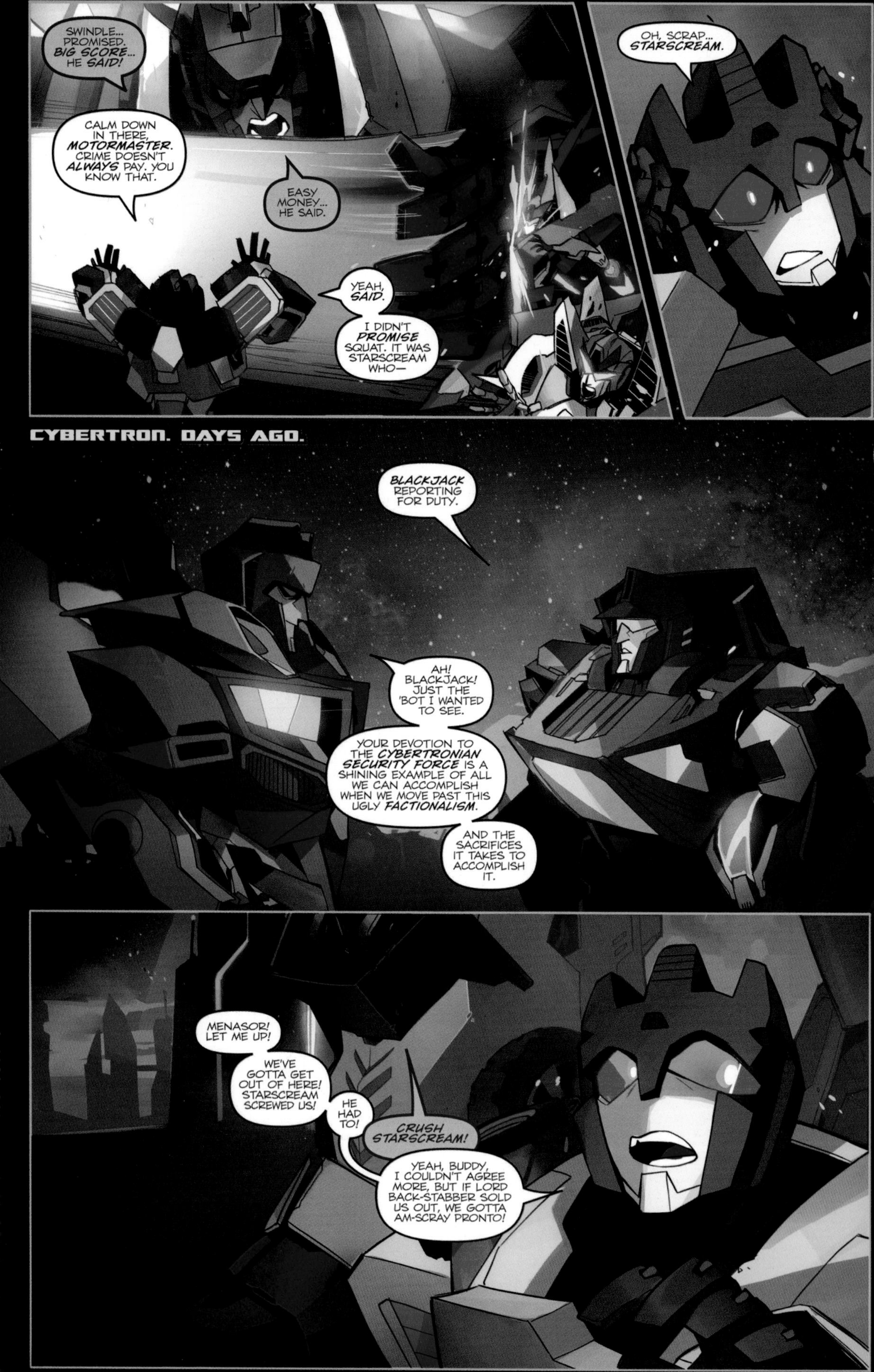
SWINDLE... PROMISED. BIG SCORE... HE SAID!
CALM DOWN IN THERE, MOTORMASTER. CRIME DOESN'T ALWAYS PAY. YOU KNOW THAT.
EASY MONEY... HE SAID.
YEAH, SAID.
I DIDN'T PROMISE SQUAT. IT WAS STARSCREAM WHO—
OH, SCRAP... STARSCREAM.
CYBERTRON. DAYS AGO.
BLACKJACK REPORTING FOR DUTY.
AH! BLACKJACK! JUST THE 'BOT I WANTED TO SEE.
YOUR DEVOTION TO THE CYBERTRONIAN SECURITY FORCE IS A SHINING EXAMPLE OF ALL WE CAN ACCOMPLISH WHEN WE MOVE PAST THIS UGLY FACTIONALISM.
AND THE SACRIFICES IT TAKES TO ACCOMPLISH IT.
MENASOR! LET ME UP!
WE'VE GOTTA GET OUT OF HERE! STARSCREAM SCREWED US!
HE HAD TO!
CRUSH STARSCREAM!
YEAH, BUDDY, I COULDN'T AGREE MORE, BUT IF LORD BACK-STABBER SOLD US OUT, WE GOTTA AM-SCRAY PRONTO!

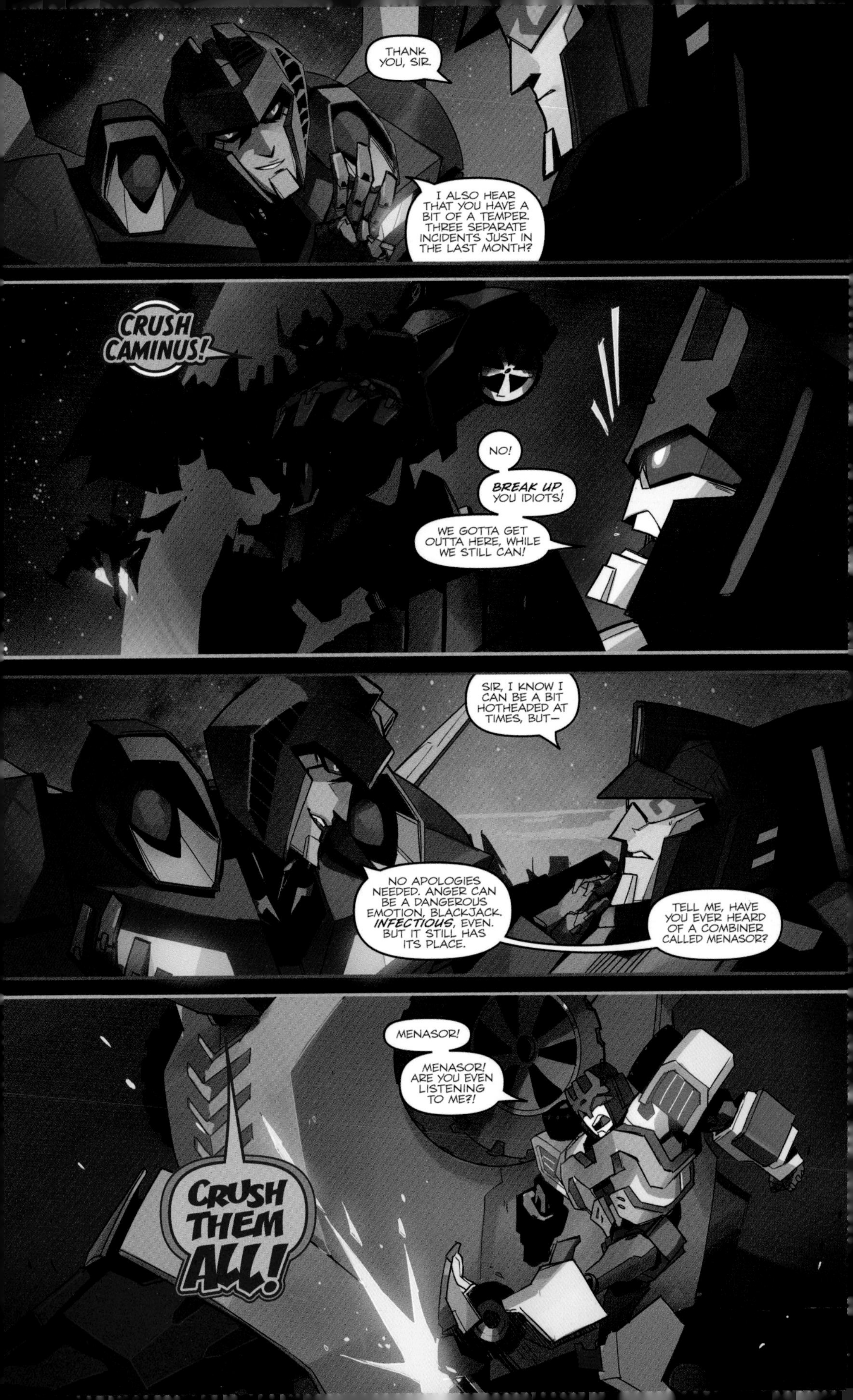

THANK YOU, SIR.
I ALSO HEAR THAT YOU HAVE A BIT OF A TEMPER. THREE SEPARATE INCIDENTS JUST IN THE LAST MONTH?
CRUSH CAMINUS!
NO!
BREAK UP, YOU IDIOTS!
WE GOTTA GET OUTTA HERE, WHILE WE STILL CAN!
SIR, I KNOW I CAN BE A BIT HOTHEADED AT TIMES, BUT—
NO APOLOGIES NEEDED. ANGER CAN BE A DANGEROUS EMOTION, BLACKJACK. INFECTIOUS, EVEN. BUT IT STILL HAS ITS PLACE.
TELL ME, HAVE YOU EVER HEARD OF A COMBINER CALLED MENASOR?
MENASOR!
MENASOR! ARE YOU EVEN LISTENING TO ME?!
CRUSH THEM ALL!

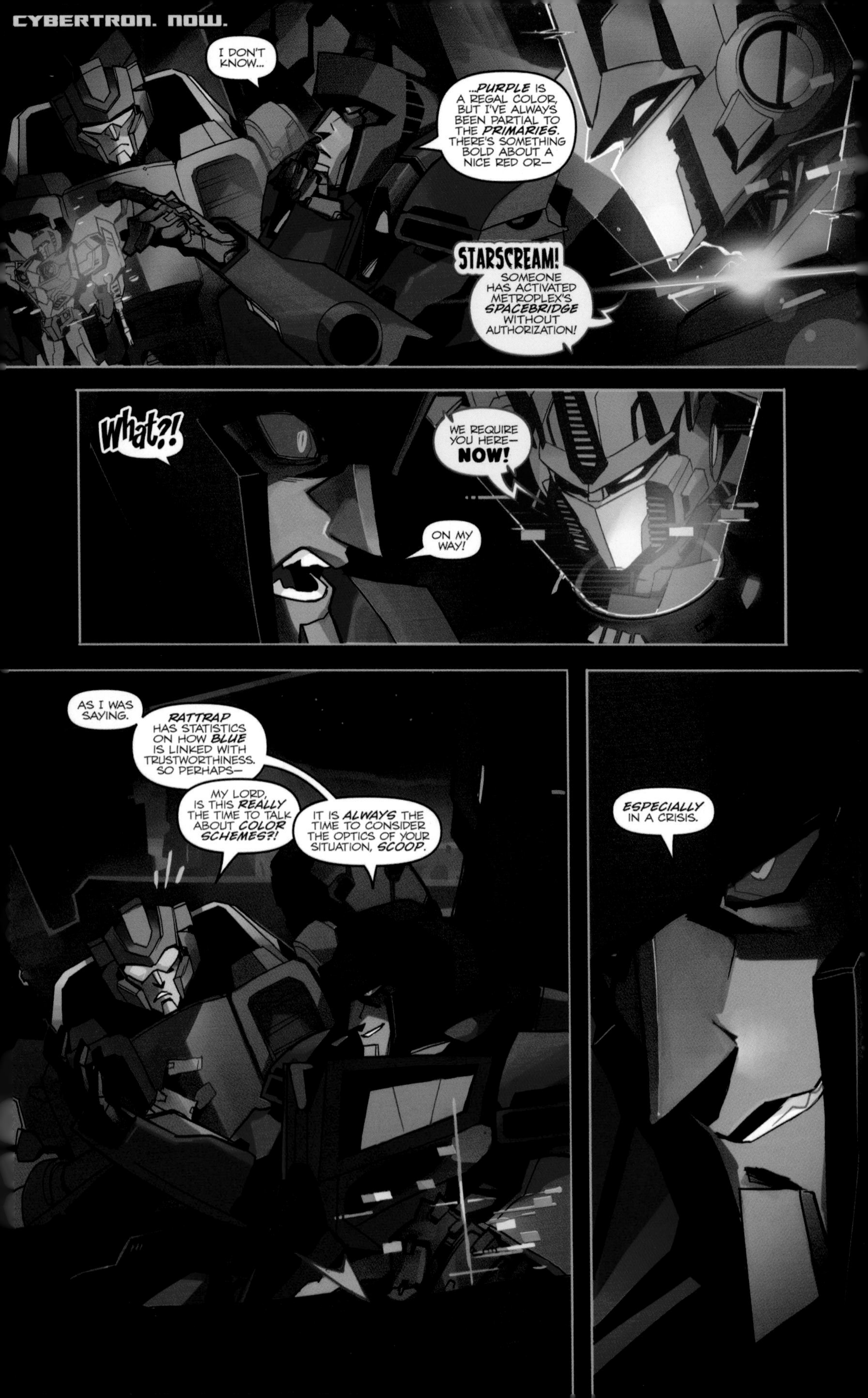
CYBERTRON. NOW.
I DON'T KNOW...
...PURPLE IS A REGAL COLOR, BUT I'VE ALWAYS BEEN PARTIAL TO THE PRIMARIES. THERE'S SOMETHING BOLD ABOUT A NICE RED OR—
STARSCREAM!
SOMEONE HAS ACTIVATED METROPLEX'S SPACEBRIDGE WITHOUT AUTHORIZATION!
WHAT?!
WE REQUIRE YOU HERE— NOW!
ON MY WAY!
AS I WAS SAYING.
RATTRAP HAS STATISTICS ON HOW BLUE IS LINKED WITH TRUSTWORTHINESS. SO PERHAPS—
MY LORD, IS THIS REALLY THE TIME TO TALK ABOUT COLOR SCHEMES?!
IT IS ALWAYS THE TIME TO CONSIDER THE OPTICS OF YOUR SITUATION, SCOOP.
ESPECIALLY IN A CRISIS.

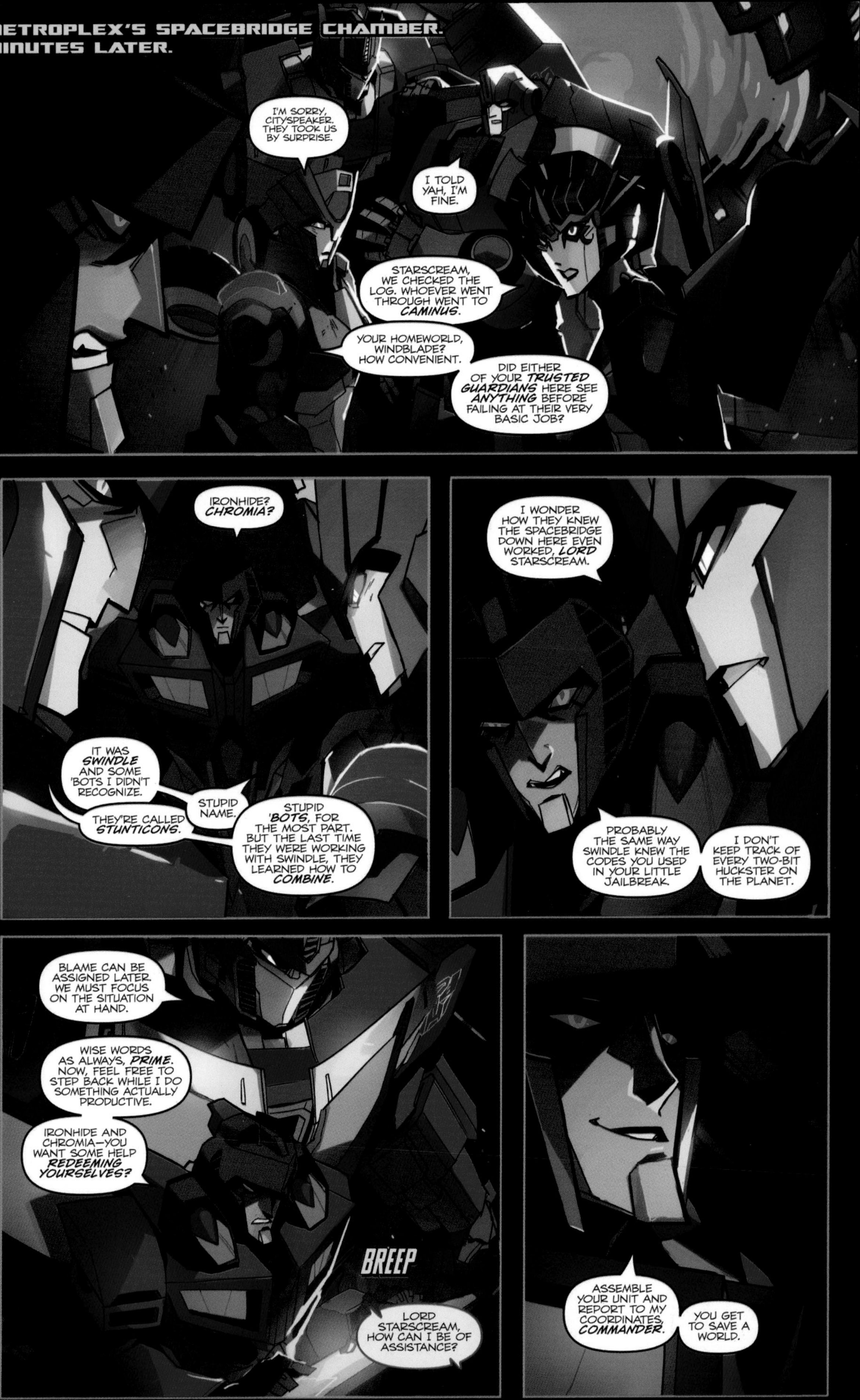

ETROPLEX'S SPACEBRIDGE CHAMBER.
INUTES LATER.
I'M SORRY, CITYSPEAKER. THEY TOOK US BY SURPRISE.
I TOLD YAH, I'M FINE.
STARSCREAM, WE CHECKED THE LOG. WHOEVER WENT THROUGH WENT TO CAMINUS.
YOUR HOMEWORLD, WINDBLADE? HOW CONVENIENT.
DID EITHER OF YOUR TRUSTED GUARDIANS HERE SEE ANYTHING BEFORE FAILING AT THEIR VERY BASIC JOB?
IRONHIDE? CHROMIA?
IT WAS SWINDLE AND SOME 'BOTS I DIDN'T RECOGNIZE.
THEY'RE CALLED STUNTICONS.
STUPID NAME.
STUPID 'BOTS, FOR THE MOST PART. BUT THE LAST TIME THEY WERE WORKING WITH SWINDLE, THEY LEARNED HOW TO COMBINE.
I WONDER HOW THEY KNEW THE SPACEBRIDGE DOWN HERE EVEN WORKED, LORD STARSCREAM.
PROBABLY THE SAME WAY SWINDLE KNEW THE CODES YOU USED IN YOUR LITTLE JAILBREAK.
I DON'T KEEP TRACK OF EVERY TWO-BIT HUCKSTER ON THE PLANET.
BLAME CAN BE ASSIGNED LATER. WE MUST FOCUS ON THE SITUATION AT HAND.
WISE WORDS AS ALWAYS, PRIME. NOW, FEEL FREE TO STEP BACK WHILE I DO SOMETHING ACTUALLY PRODUCTIVE.
IRONHIDE AND CHROMIA—YOU WANT SOME HELP REDEEMING YOURSELVES?
BREEP
LORD STARSCREAM, HOW CAN I BE OF ASSISTANCE?
ASSEMBLE YOUR UNIT AND REPORT TO MY COORDINATES, COMMANDER.
YOU GET TO SAVE A WORLD.

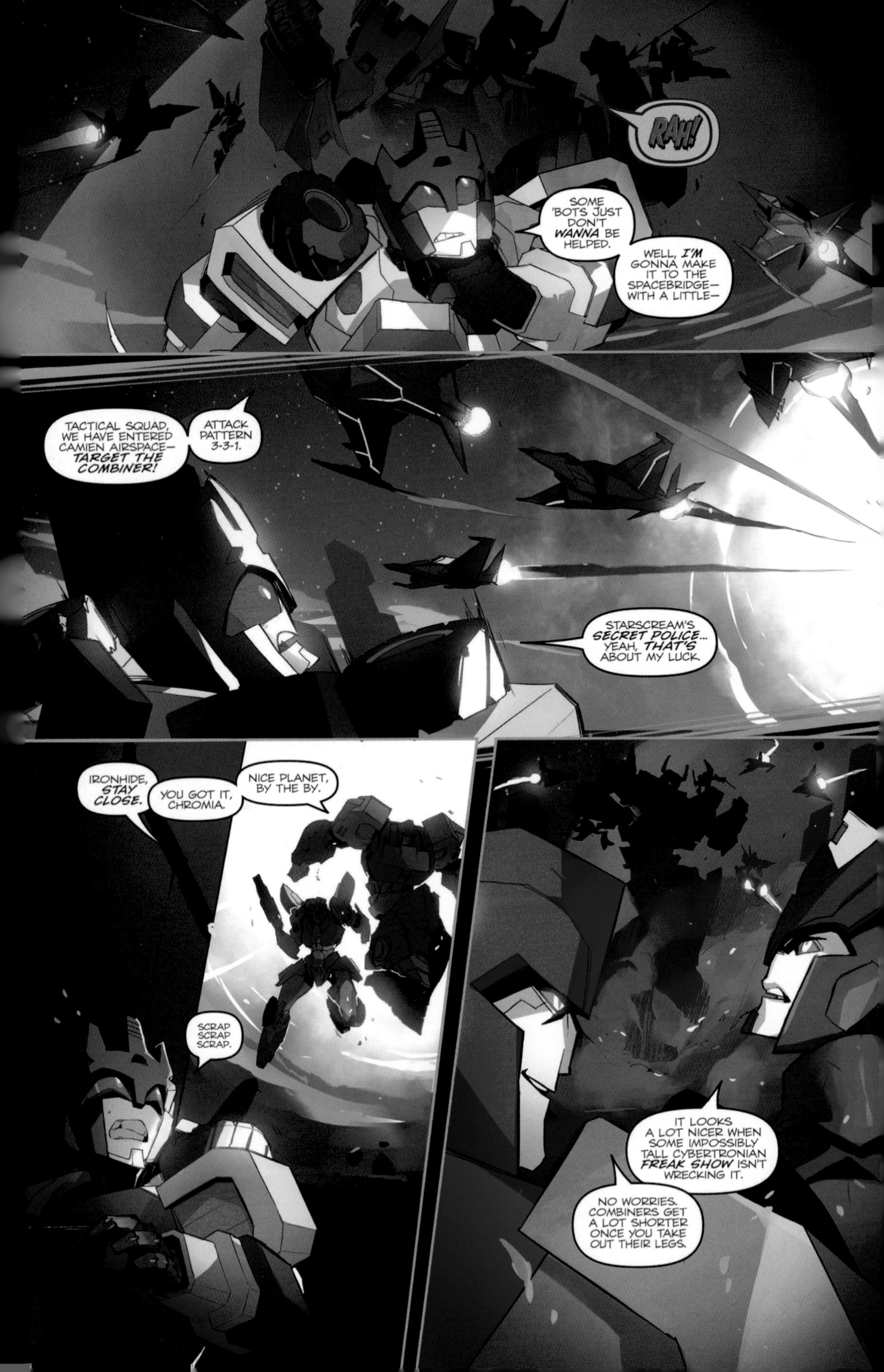
RAH!
SOME 'BOTS JUST DON'T WANNA BE HELPED.
WELL, I'M GONNA MAKE IT TO THE SPACEBRIDGE— WITH A LITTLE—
TACTICAL SQUAD, WE HAVE ENTERED CAMIEN AIRSPACE— TARGET THE COMBINER!
ATTACK PATTERN 3-3-1.
STARSCREAM'S SECRET POLICE... YEAH, THAT'S ABOUT MY LUCK.
IRONHIDE, STAY CLOSE.
YOU GOT IT, CHROMIA.
NICE PLANET, BY THE BY.
SCRAP SCRAP SCRAP.
IT LOOKS A LOT NICER WHEN SOME IMPOSSIBLY TALL CYBERTRONIAN FREAK SHOW ISN'T WRECKING IT.
NO WORRIES. COMBINERS GET A LOT SHORTER ONCE YOU TAKE OUT THEIR LEGS.

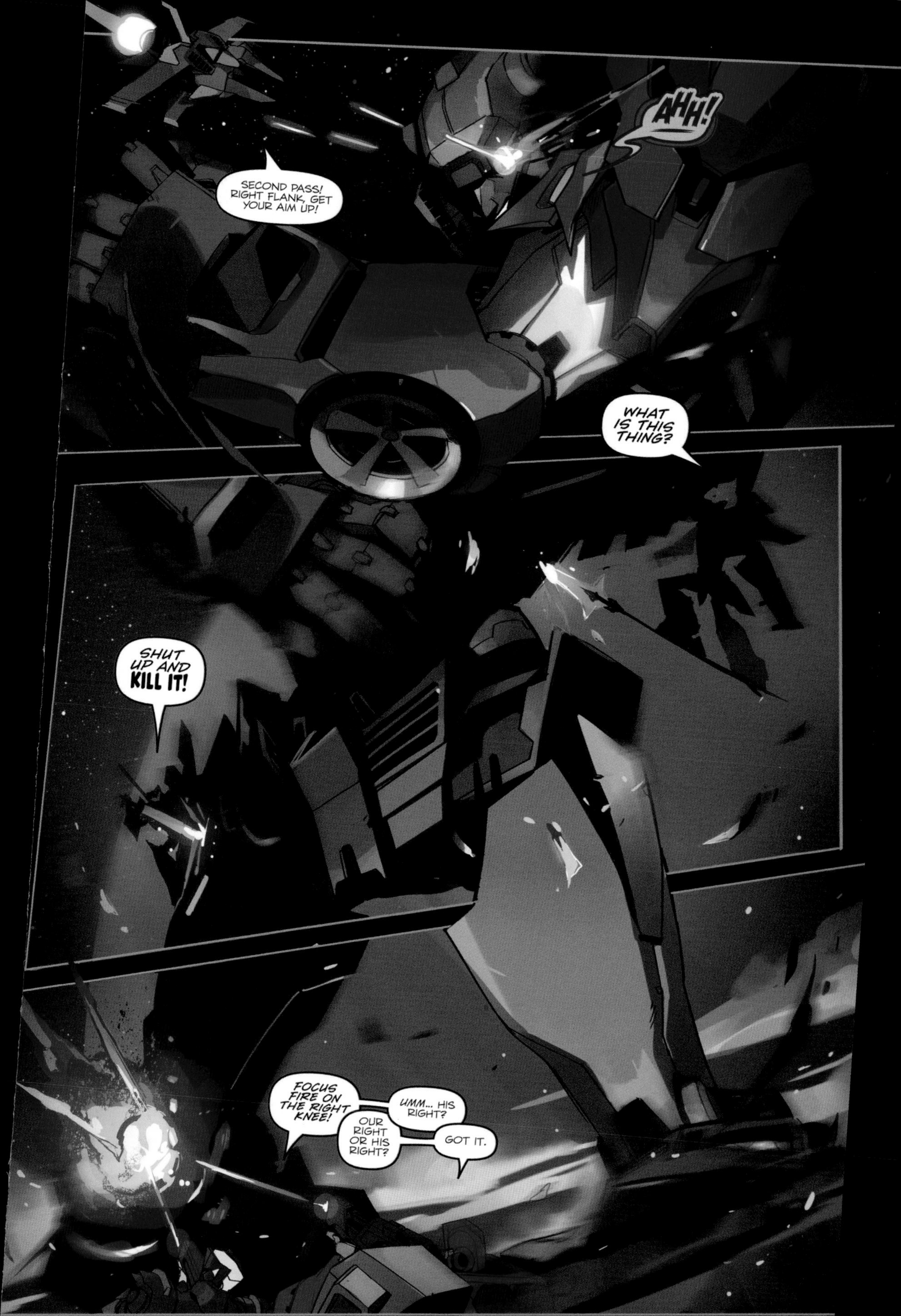
SECOND PASS! RIGHT FLANK, GET YOUR AIM UP!
AHH!
WHAT IS THIS THING?
SHUT UP AND KILL IT!
FOCUS FIRE ON THE RIGHT KNEE!
OUR RIGHT OR HIS RIGHT?
UMM... HIS RIGHT?
GOT IT.

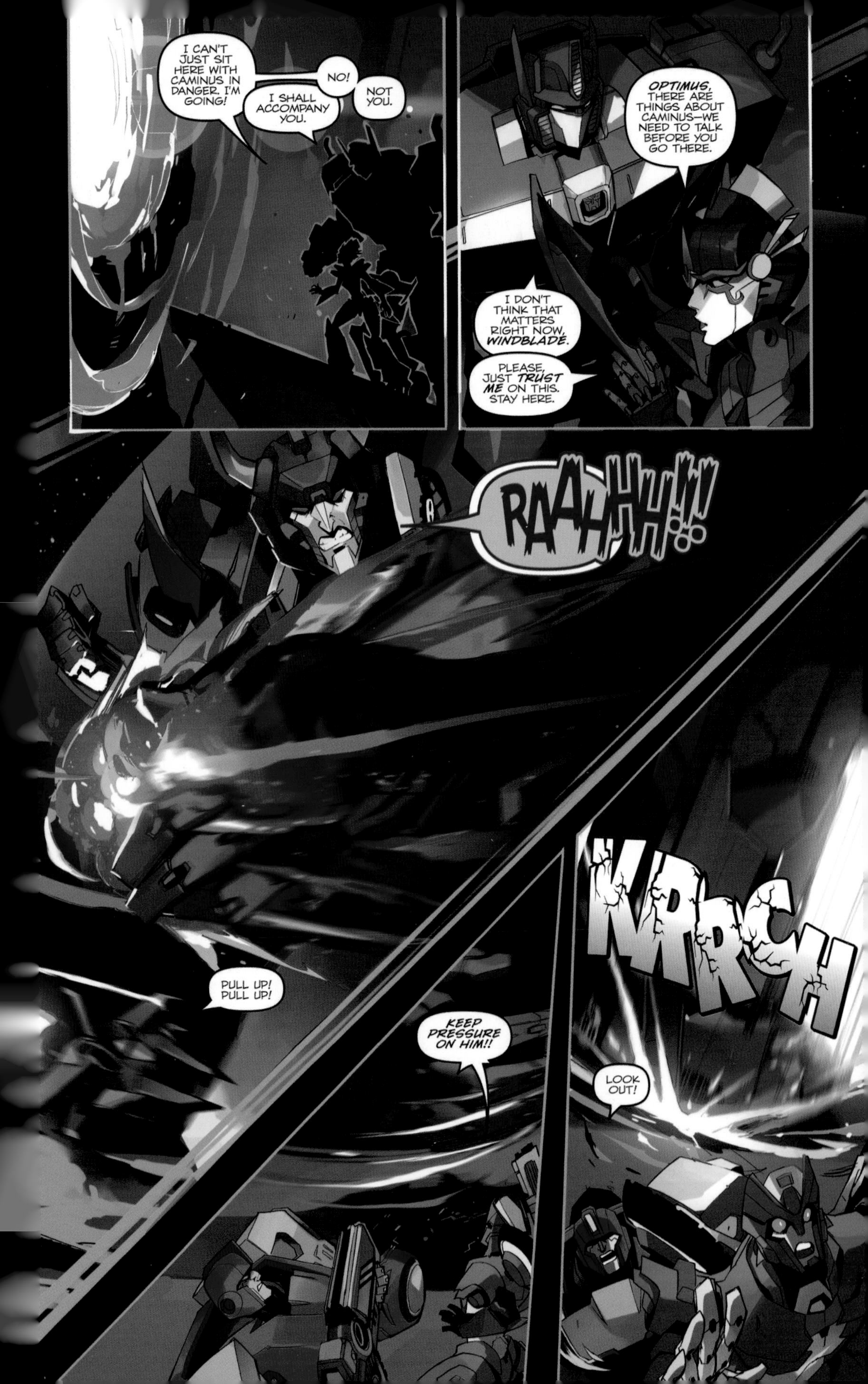

I CAN'T JUST SIT HERE WITH CAMINUS IN DANGER. I'M GOING!
NO!
I SHALL ACCOMPANY YOU.
NOT YOU.
OPTIMUS, THERE ARE THINGS ABOUT CAMINUS—WE NEED TO TALK BEFORE YOU GO THERE.
I DON'T THINK THAT MATTERS RIGHT NOW, WINDBLADE.
PLEASE, JUST TRUST ME ON THIS. STAY HERE.
RAAHHH!!!
PULL UP! PULL UP!
KEEP PRESSURE ON HIM!!
KRRCH
LOOK OUT!

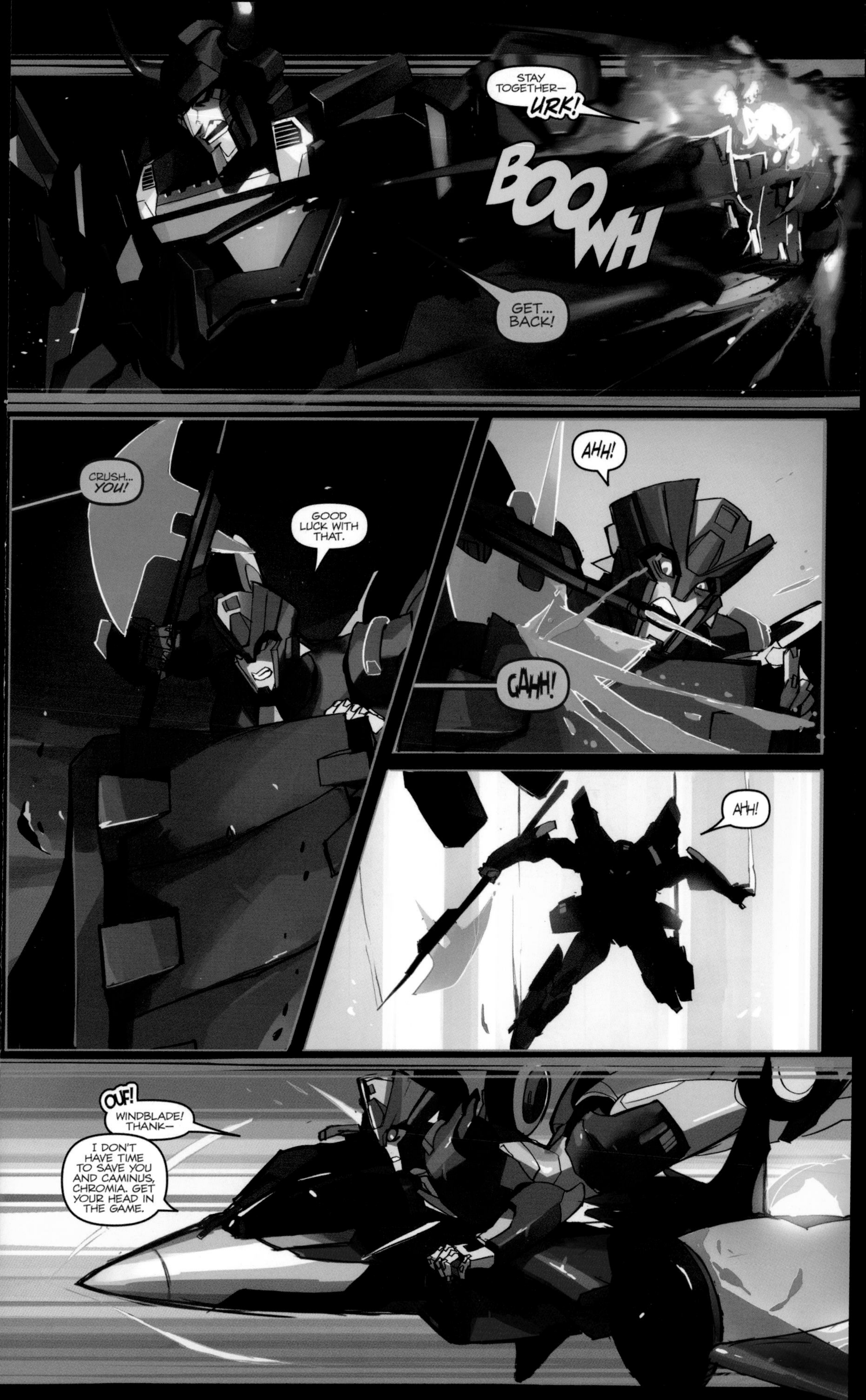
STAY TOGETHER—
URK!
BOOWH
GET... BACK!
CRUSH... YOU!
GOOD LUCK WITH THAT.
AHH!
GAHH!
AHH!
OUF!
WINDBLADE! THANK—
I DON'T HAVE TIME TO SAVE YOU AND CAMINUS, CHROMIA. GET YOUR HEAD IN THE GAME.

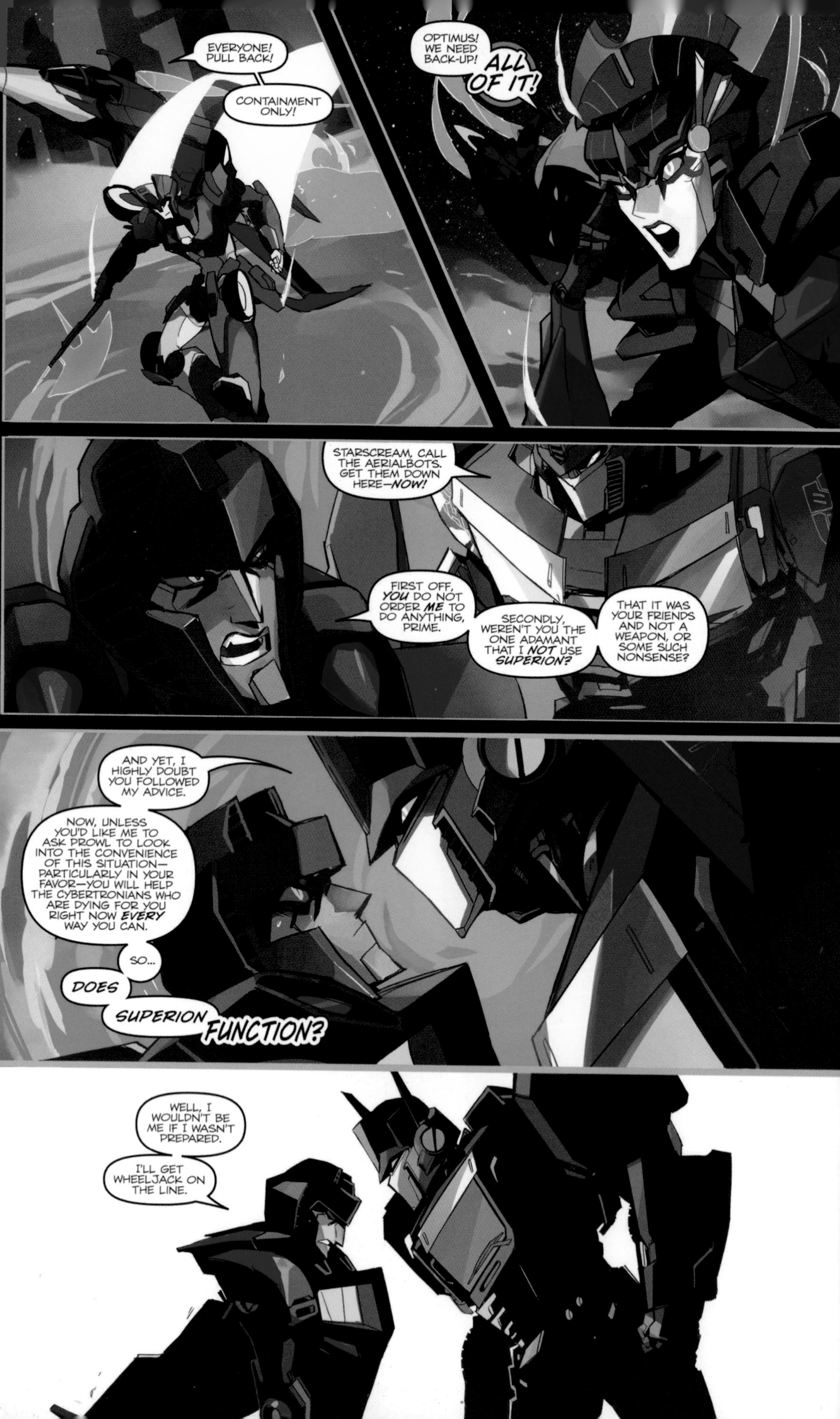

EVERYONE! PULL BACK!
CONTAINMENT ONLY!
OPTIMUS! WE NEED BACK-UP!
ALL OF IT!
STARSCREAM, CALL THE AERIALBOTS. GET THEM DOWN HERE—NOW!
FIRST OFF, YOU DO NOT ORDER ME TO DO ANYTHING, PRIME.
SECONDLY, WEREN'T YOU THE ONE ADAMANT THAT I NOT USE SUPERION?
THAT IT WAS YOUR FRIENDS AND NOT A WEAPON, OR SOME SUCH NONSENSE?
AND YET, I HIGHLY DOUBT YOU FOLLOWED MY ADVICE.
NOW, UNLESS YOU'D LIKE ME TO ASK PROWL TO LOOK INTO THE CONVENIENCE OF THIS SITUATION—PARTICULARLY IN YOUR FAVOR—YOU WILL HELP THE CYBERTRONIANS WHO ARE DYING FOR YOU RIGHT NOW EVERY WAY YOU CAN.
SO...
DOES
SUPERION
FUNCTION?
WELL, I WOULDN'T BE ME IF I WASN'T PREPARED.
I'LL GET WHEELJACK ON THE LINE.

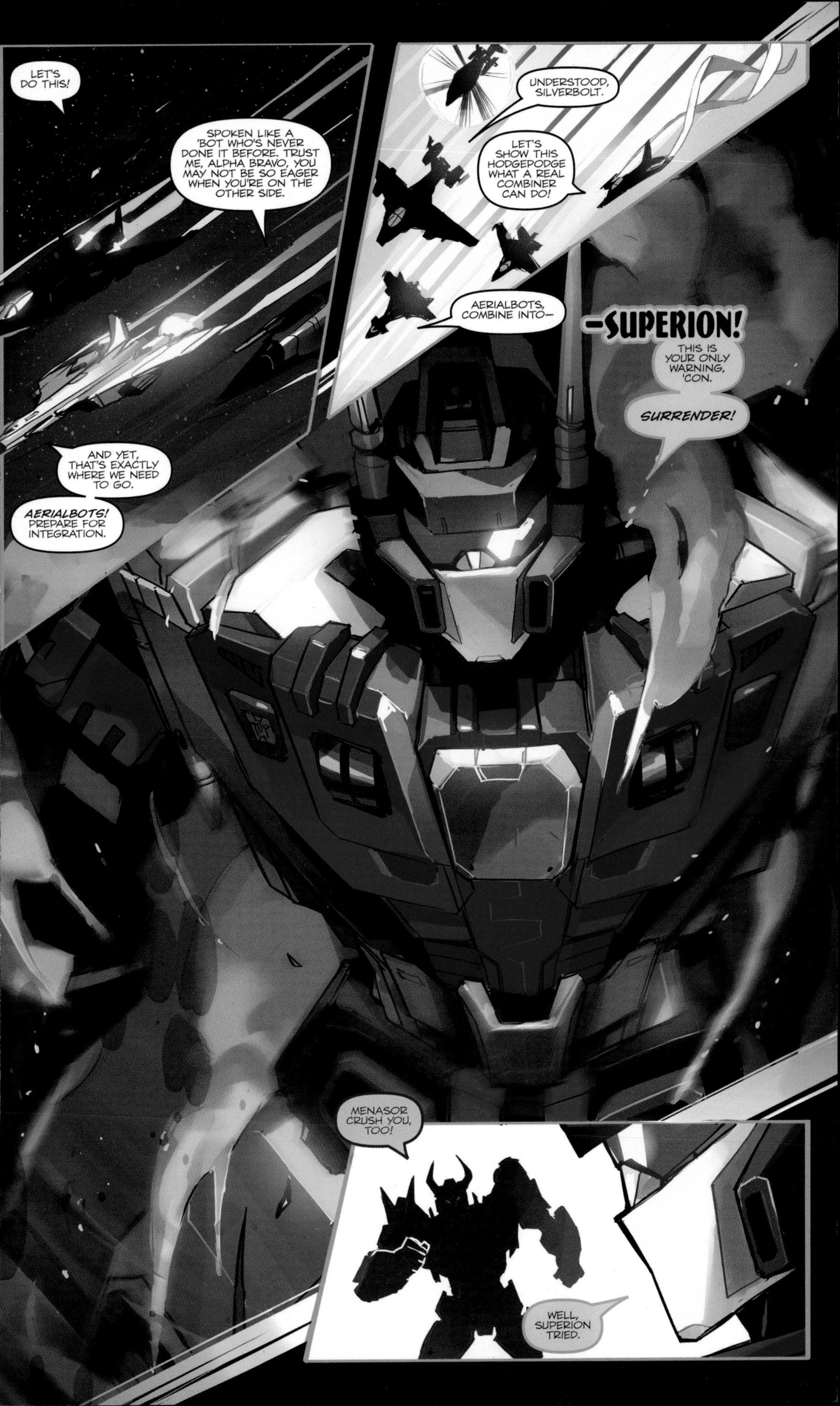

LET'S DO THIS!
SPOKEN LIKE A 'BOT WHO'S NEVER DONE IT BEFORE. TRUST ME, ALPHA BRAVO, YOU MAY NOT BE SO EAGER WHEN YOU'RE ON THE OTHER SIDE.
AND YET, THAT'S EXACTLY WHERE WE NEED TO GO.
AERIALBOTS! PREPARE FOR INTEGRATION.
UNDERSTOOD, SILVERBOLT.
LET'S SHOW THIS HODGEPODGE WHAT A REAL COMBINER CAN DO!
AERIALBOTS, COMBINE INTO—
—SUPERION!
THIS IS YOUR ONLY WARNING, 'CON.
SURRENDER!
MENASOR CRUSH YOU, TOO!
WELL, SUPERION TRIED.

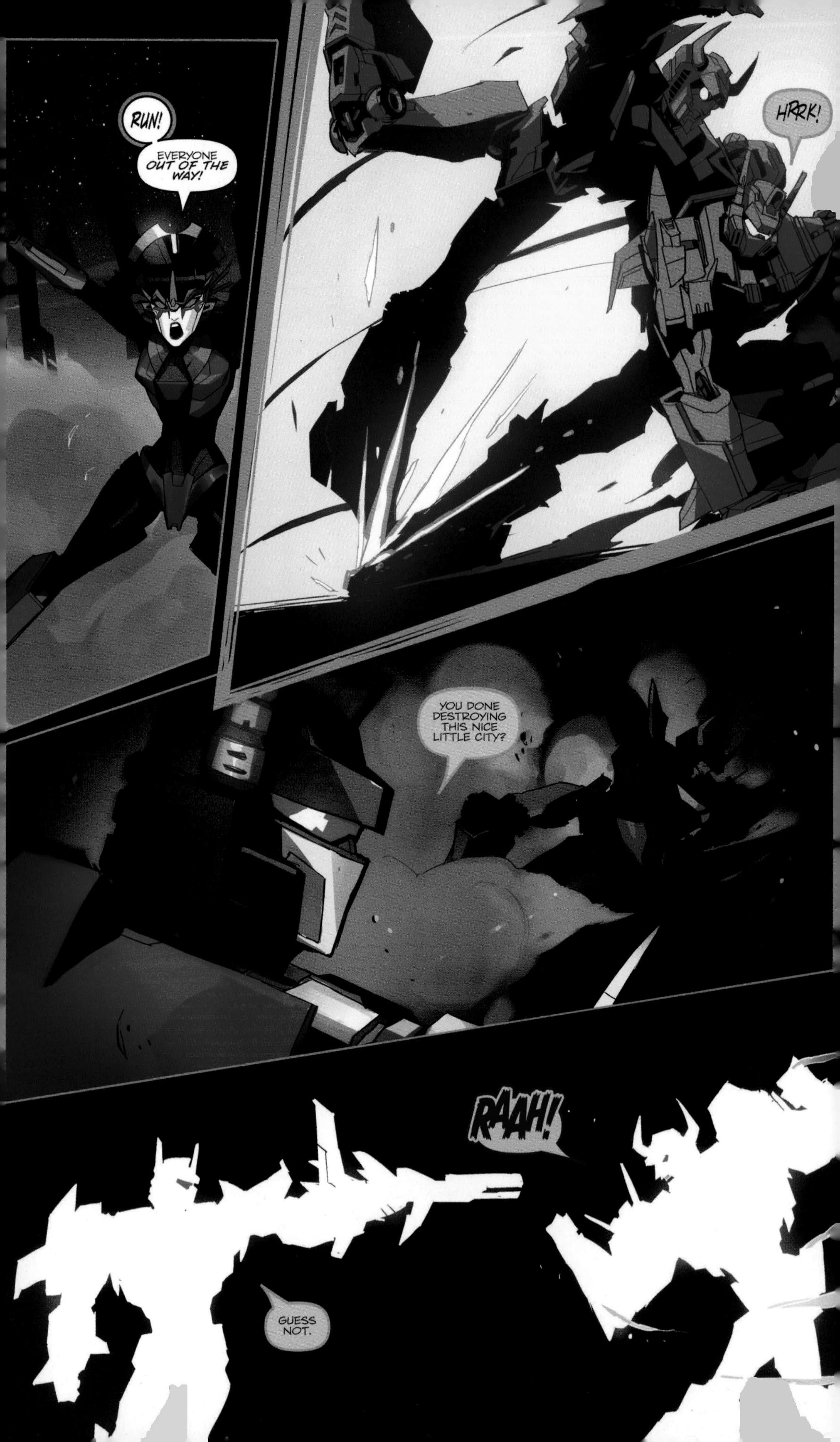
RUN!
EVERYONE OUT OF THE WAY!
HRRK!
YOU DONE DESTROYING THIS NICE LITTLE CITY?
RAAH!
GUESS NOT.

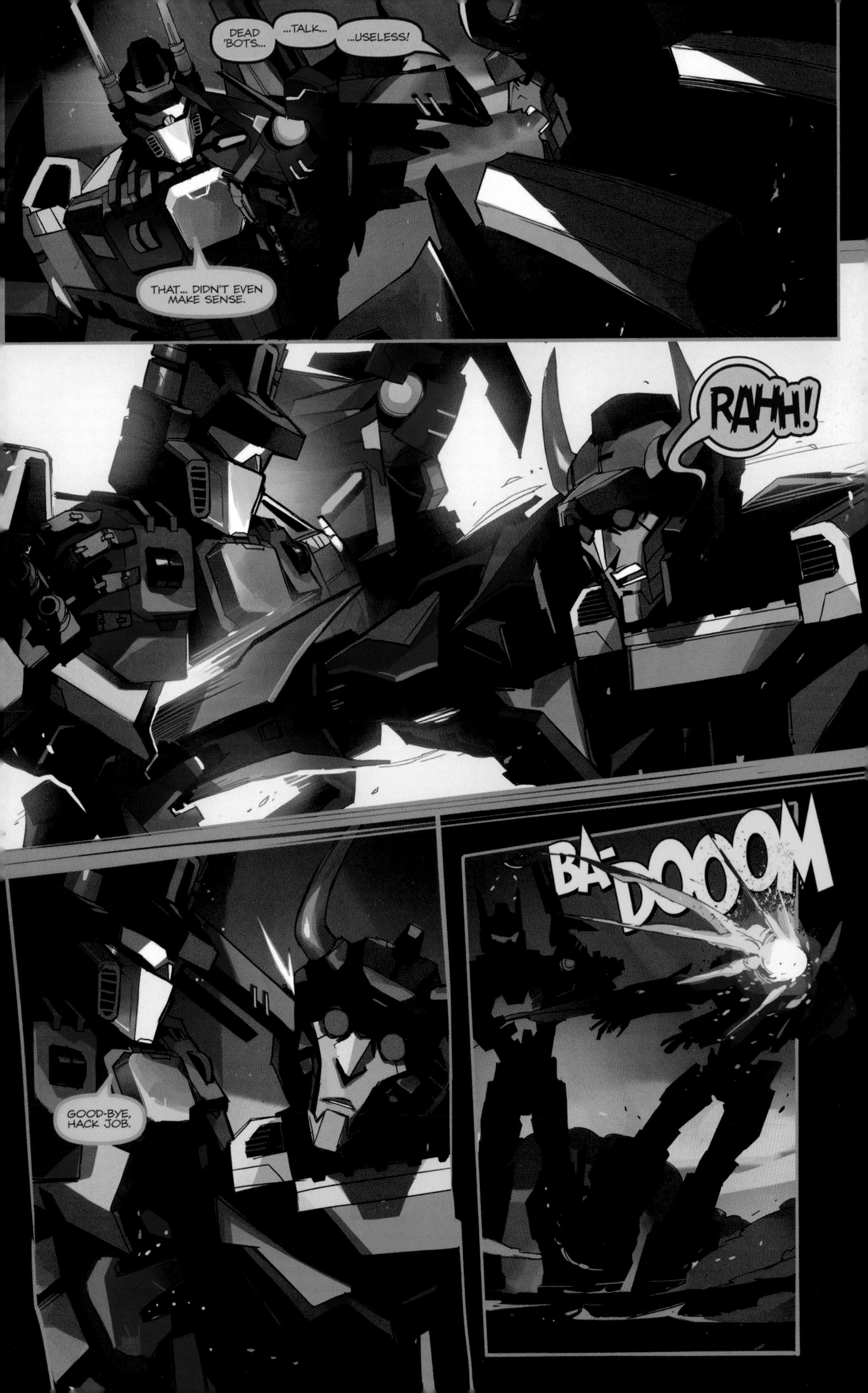
DEAD 'BOTS...
...TALK...
...USELESS!
THAT... DIDN'T EVEN MAKE SENSE.
RAHH!
GOOD-BYE, HACK JOB.
BA-DOOOM

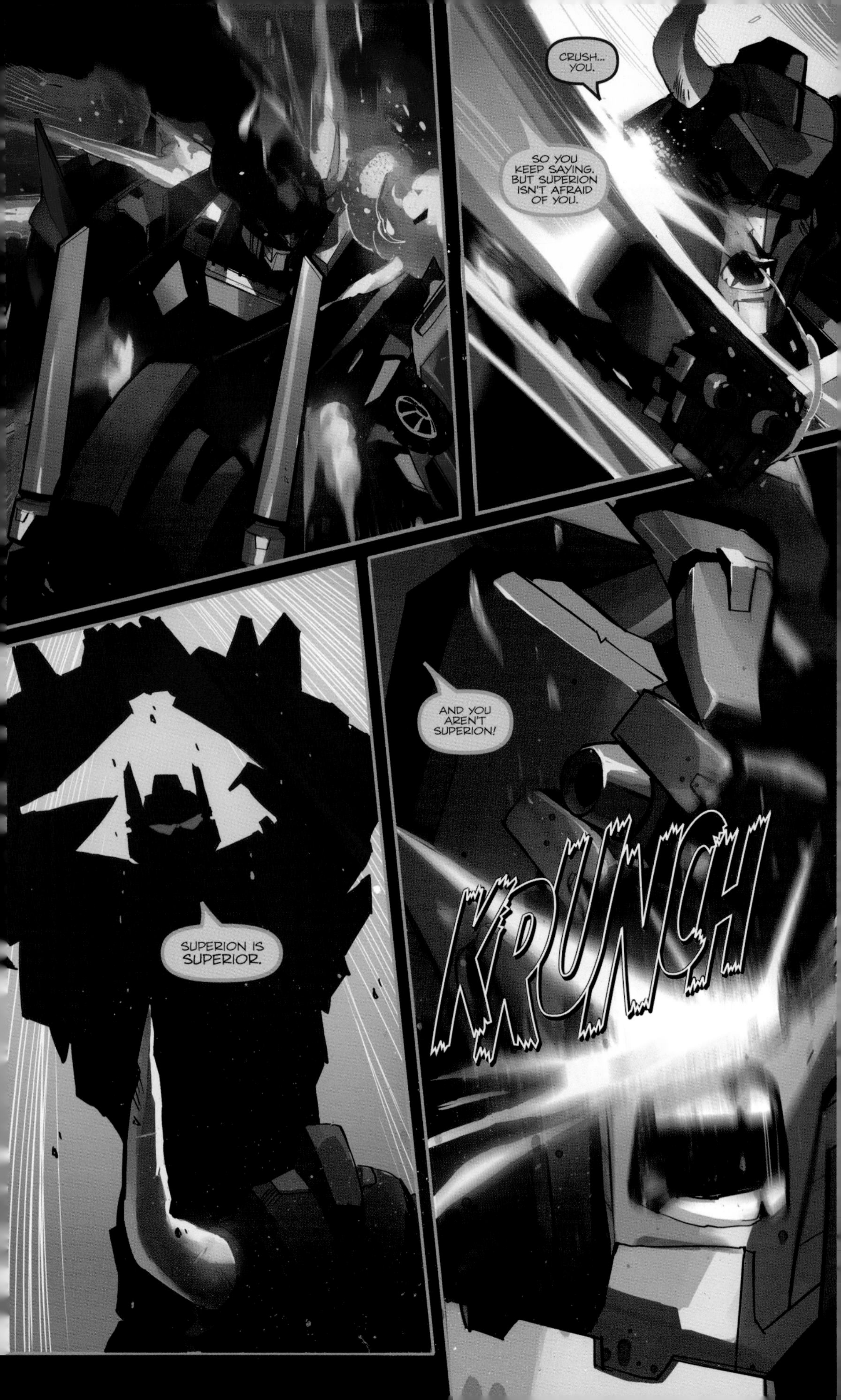
CRUSH... YOU.
SO YOU KEEP SAYING. BUT SUPERION ISN'T AFRAID OF YOU.
SUPERION IS SUPERIOR.
AND YOU AREN'T SUPERION!
KRUNCH

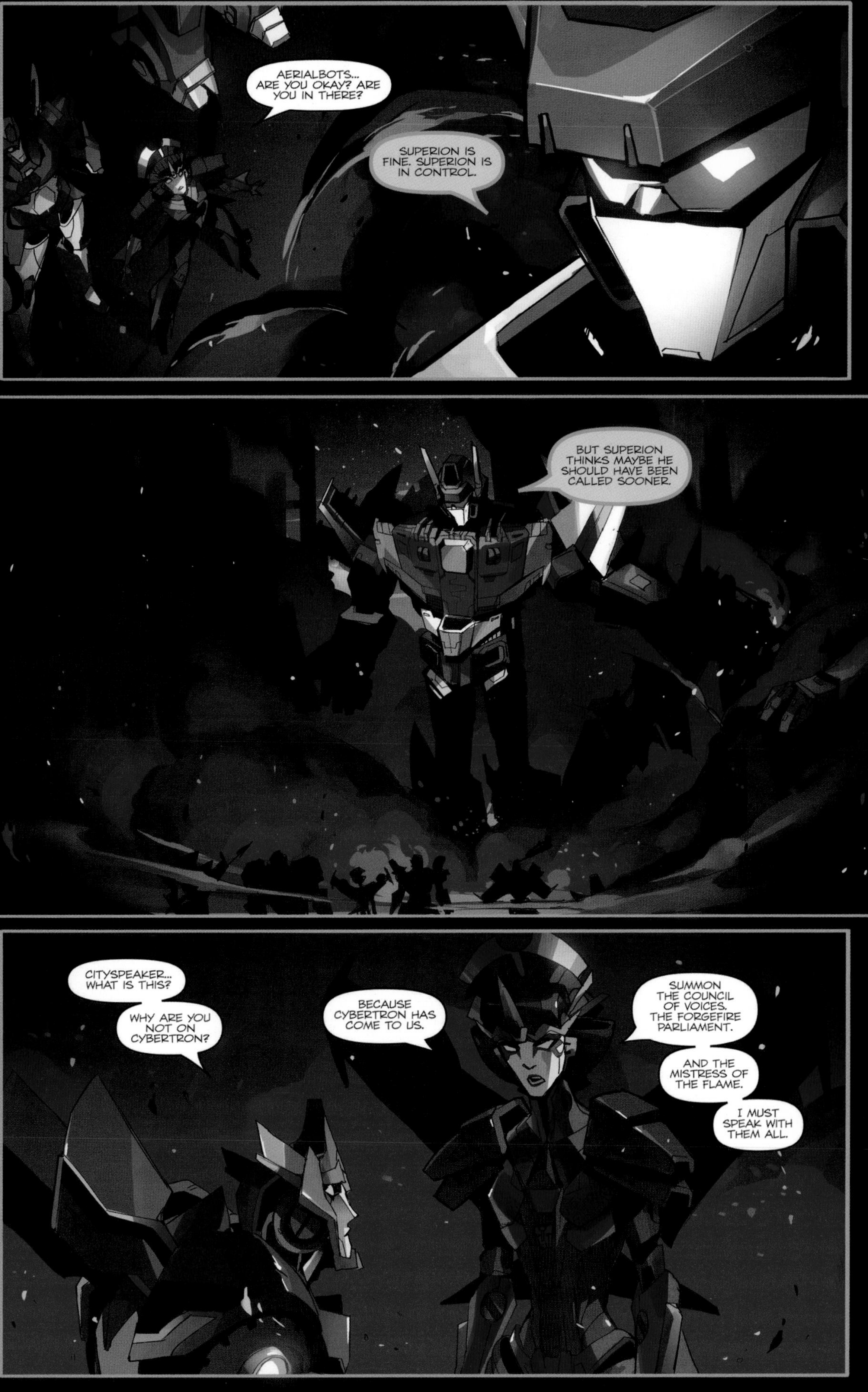
AERIALBOTS... ARE YOU OKAY? ARE YOU IN THERE?
SUPERION IS FINE. SUPERION IS IN CONTROL.
BUT SUPERION THINKS MAYBE HE SHOULD HAVE BEEN CALLED SOONER.
CITYSPEAKER... WHAT IS THIS?
WHY ARE YOU NOT ON CYBERTRON?
BECAUSE CYBERTRON HAS COME TO US.
SUMMON THE COUNCIL OF VOICES. THE FORGEFIRE PARLIAMENT.
AND THE MISTRESS OF THE FLAME.
I MUST SPEAK WITH THEM ALL.

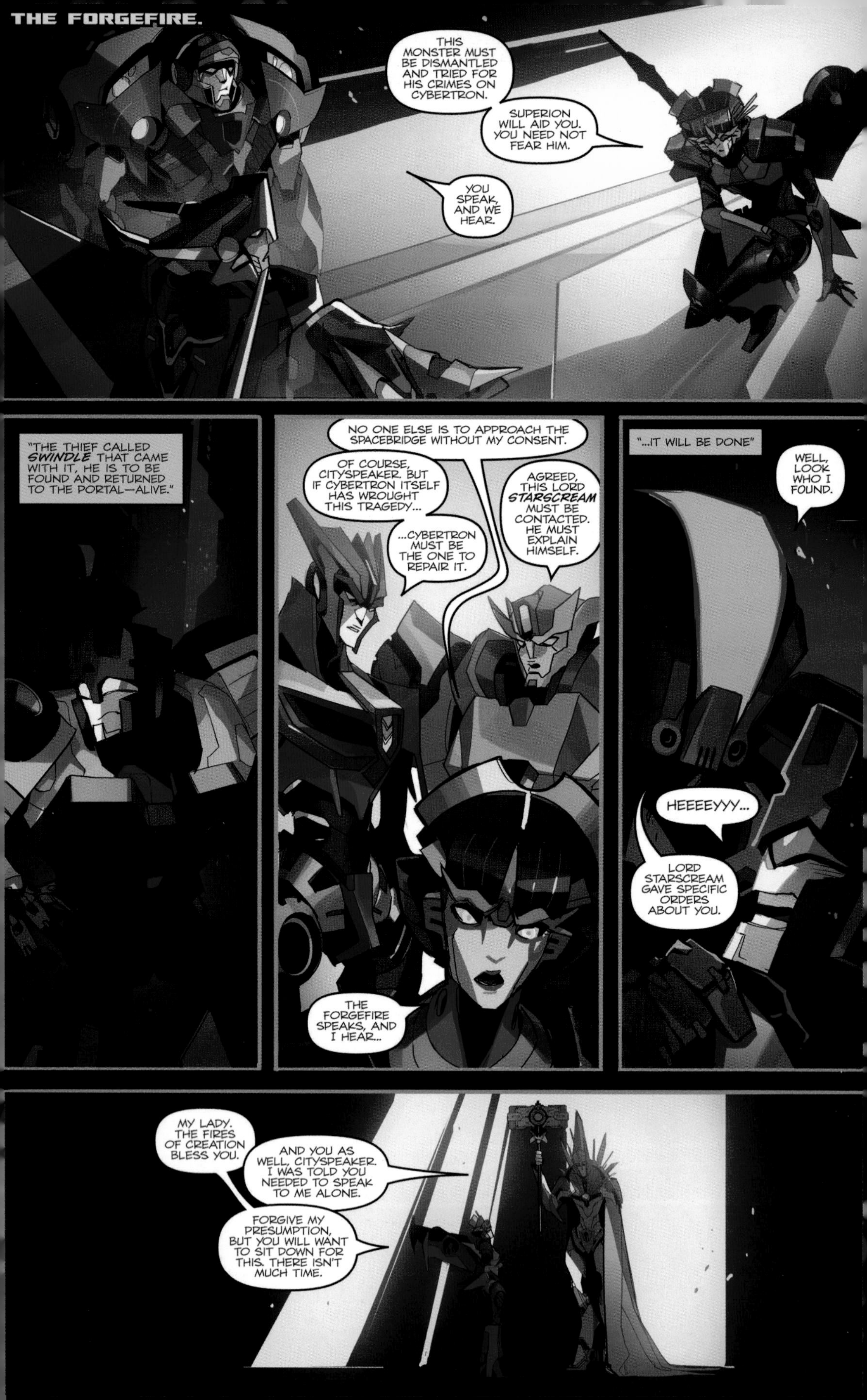
THE FORGEFIRE.
THIS MONSTER MUST BE DISMANTLED AND TRIED FOR HIS CRIMES ON CYBERTRON.
SUPERION WILL AID YOU. YOU NEED NOT FEAR HIM.
YOU SPEAK, AND WE HEAR.
"THE THIEF CALLED SWINDLE THAT CAME WITH IT, HE IS TO BE FOUND AND RETURNED TO THE PORTAL—ALIVE."
NO ONE ELSE IS TO APPROACH THE SPACEBRIDGE WITHOUT MY CONSENT.
OF COURSE, CITYSPEAKER. BUT IF CYBERTRON ITSELF HAS WROUGHT THIS TRAGEDY...
...CYBERTRON MUST BE THE ONE TO REPAIR IT.
AGREED, THIS LORD STARSCREAM MUST BE CONTACTED. HE MUST EXPLAIN HIMSELF.
THE FORGEFIRE SPEAKS, AND I HEAR...
"...IT WILL BE DONE"
WELL, LOOK WHO I FOUND.
HEEEEYYY...
LORD STARSCREAM GAVE SPECIFIC ORDERS ABOUT YOU.
MY LADY. THE FIRES OF CREATION BLESS YOU.
AND YOU AS WELL, CITYSPEAKER. I WAS TOLD YOU NEEDED TO SPEAK TO ME ALONE.
FORGIVE MY PRESUMPTION, BUT YOU WILL WANT TO SIT DOWN FOR THIS. THERE ISN'T MUCH TIME.

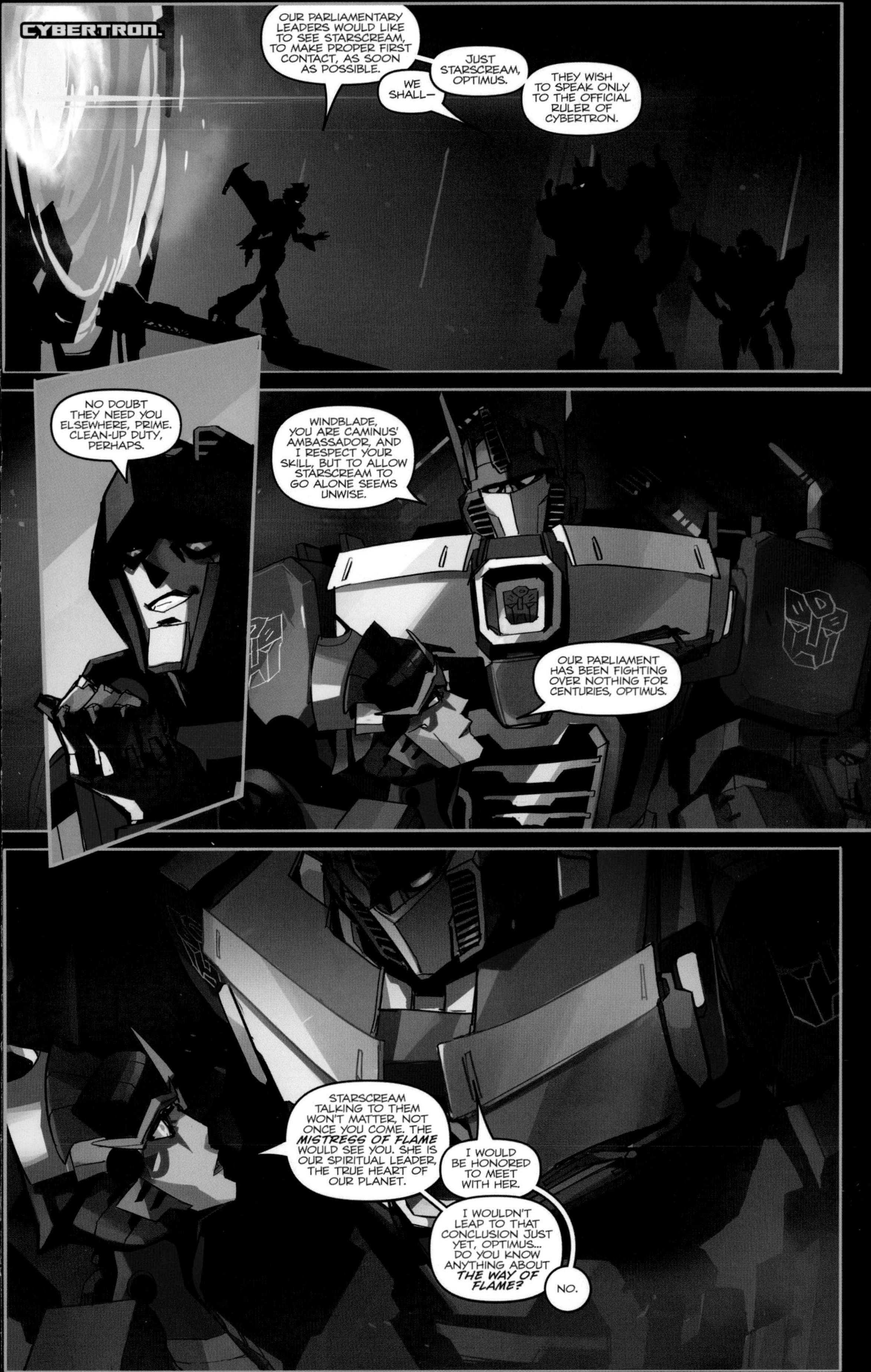
CYBERTRON.
OUR PARLIAMENTARY LEADERS WOULD LIKE TO SEE STARSCREAM, TO MAKE PROPER FIRST CONTACT, AS SOON AS POSSIBLE.
WE SHALL—
JUST STARSCREAM, OPTIMUS.
THEY WISH TO SPEAK ONLY TO THE OFFICIAL RULER OF CYBERTRON.
NO DOUBT THEY NEED YOU ELSEWHERE, PRIME. CLEAN-UP DUTY, PERHAPS.
WINDBLADE, YOU ARE CAMINUS' AMBASSADOR, AND I RESPECT YOUR SKILL, BUT TO ALLOW STARSCREAM TO GO ALONE SEEMS UNWISE.
OUR PARLIAMENT HAS BEEN FIGHTING OVER NOTHING FOR CENTURIES, OPTIMUS.
STARSCREAM TALKING TO THEM WON'T MATTER, NOT ONCE YOU COME. THE ***MISTRESS OF FLAME*** WOULD SEE YOU. SHE IS OUR SPIRITUAL LEADER, THE TRUE HEART OF OUR PLANET.
I WOULD BE HONORED TO MEET WITH HER.
I WOULDN'T LEAP TO THAT CONCLUSION JUST YET, OPTIMUS... DO YOU KNOW ANYTHING ABOUT ***THE WAY OF FLAME?***
NO.

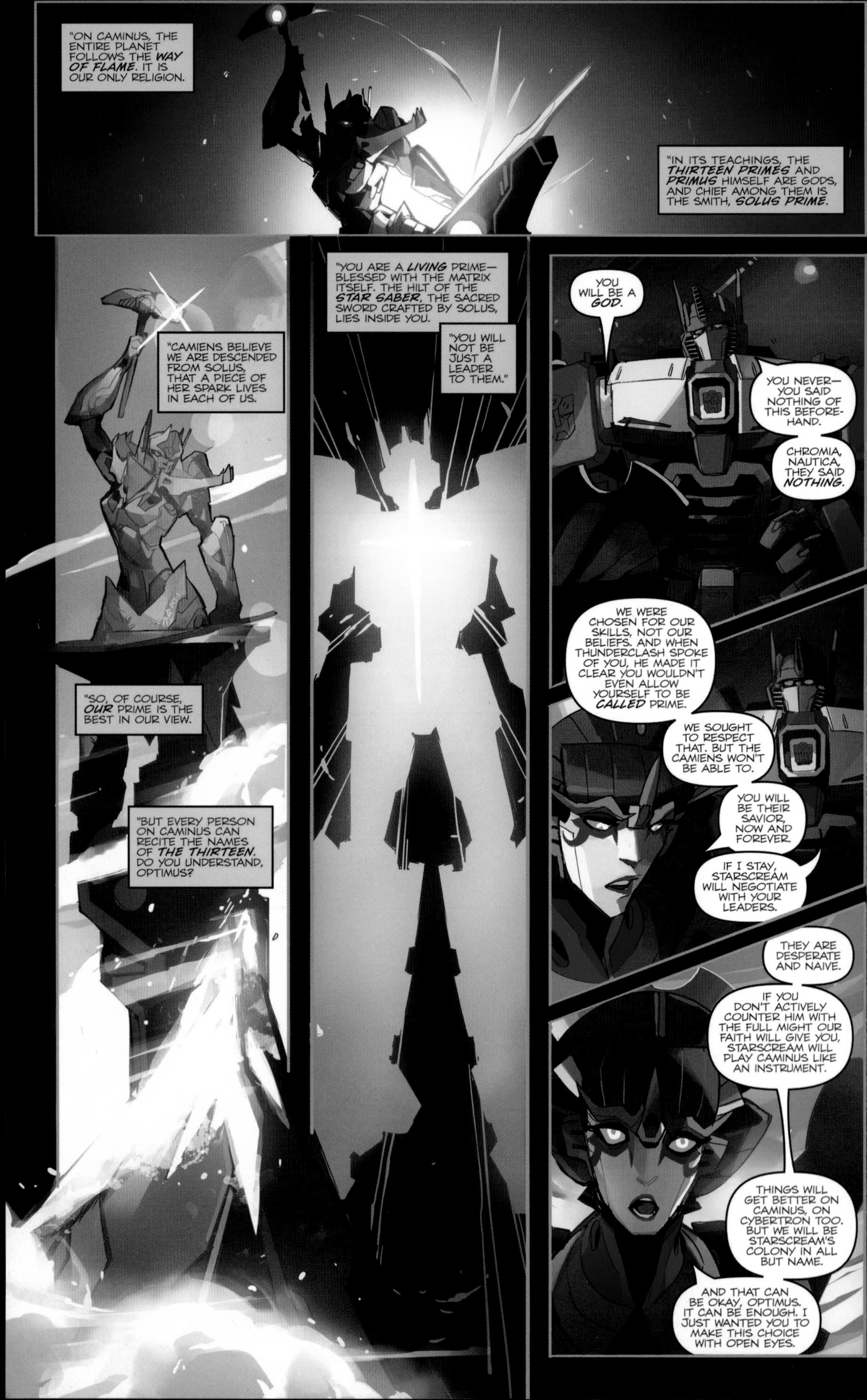
"ON CAMINUS, THE ENTIRE PLANET FOLLOWS THE WAY OF FLAME. IT IS OUR ONLY RELIGION.
"IN ITS TEACHINGS, THE THIRTEEN PRIMES AND PRIMUS HIMSELF ARE GODS, AND CHIEF AMONG THEM IS THE SMITH, SOLUS PRIME.
"CAMIENS BELIEVE WE ARE DESCENDED FROM SOLUS, THAT A PIECE OF HER SPARK LIVES IN EACH OF US.
"SO, OF COURSE, OUR PRIME IS THE BEST IN OUR VIEW.
"BUT EVERY PERSON ON CAMINUS CAN RECITE THE NAMES OF THE THIRTEEN. DO YOU UNDERSTAND, OPTIMUS?
"YOU ARE A LIVING PRIME— BLESSED WITH THE MATRIX ITSELF. THE HILT OF THE STAR SABER, THE SACRED SWORD CRAFTED BY SOLUS, LIES INSIDE YOU.
"YOU WILL NOT BE JUST A LEADER TO THEM."
YOU WILL BE A GOD.
YOU NEVER— YOU SAID NOTHING OF THIS BEFOREHAND.
CHROMIA, NAUTICA, THEY SAID NOTHING.
WE WERE CHOSEN FOR OUR SKILLS, NOT OUR BELIEFS. AND WHEN THUNDERCLASH SPOKE OF YOU, HE MADE IT CLEAR YOU WOULDN'T EVEN ALLOW YOURSELF TO BE CALLED PRIME.
WE SOUGHT TO RESPECT THAT. BUT THE CAMIENS WON'T BE ABLE TO.
YOU WILL BE THEIR SAVIOR, NOW AND FOREVER.
IF I STAY, STARSCREAM WILL NEGOTIATE WITH YOUR LEADERS.
THEY ARE DESPERATE AND NAIVE.
IF YOU DON'T ACTIVELY COUNTER HIM WITH THE FULL MIGHT OUR FAITH WILL GIVE YOU, STARSCREAM WILL PLAY CAMINUS LIKE AN INSTRUMENT.
THINGS WILL GET BETTER ON CAMINUS, ON CYBERTRON TOO. BUT WE WILL BE STARSCREAM'S COLONY IN ALL BUT NAME.
AND THAT CAN BE OKAY, OPTIMUS. IT CAN BE ENOUGH. I JUST WANTED YOU TO MAKE THIS CHOICE WITH OPEN EYES.

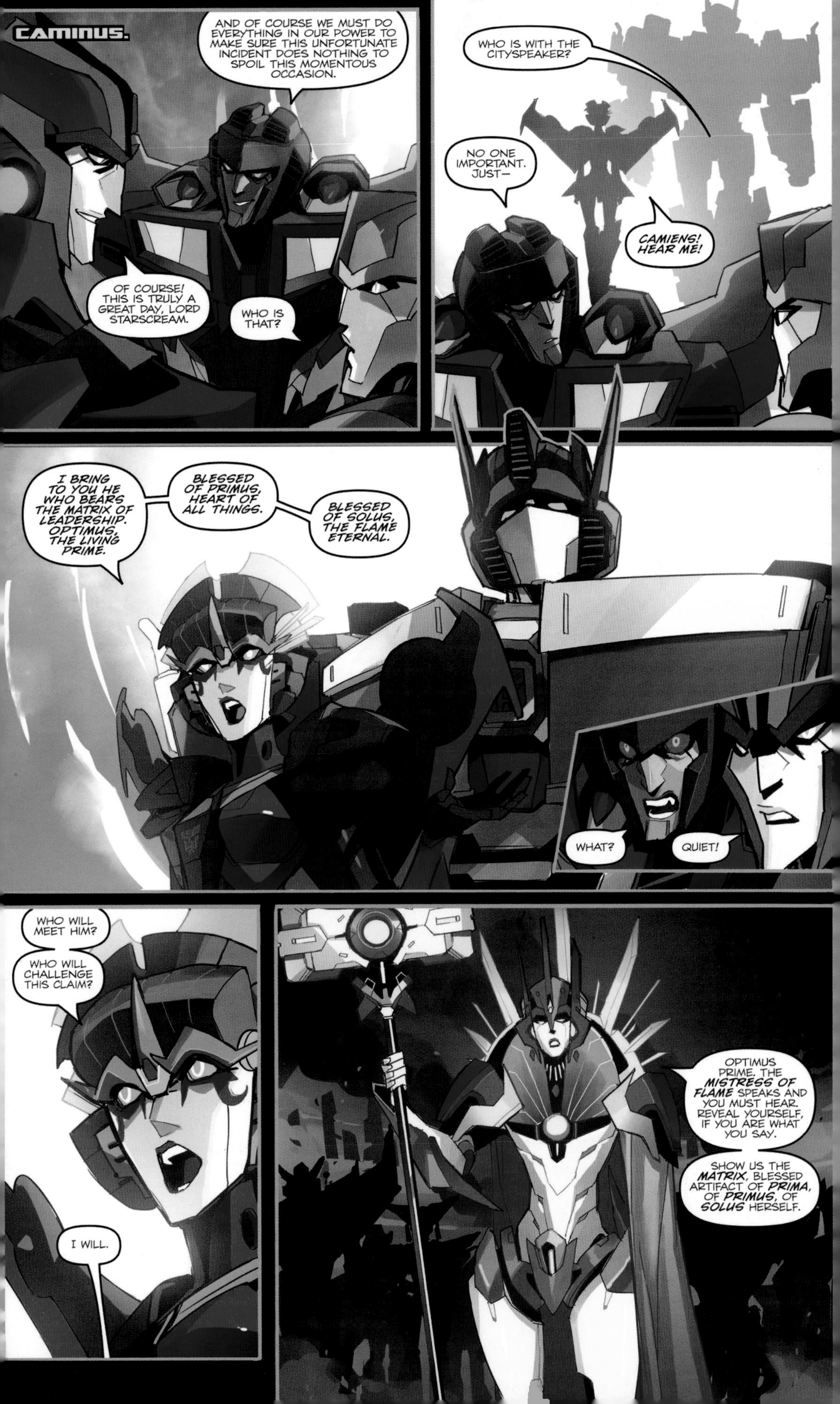
CAMINUS.
AND OF COURSE WE MUST DO EVERYTHING IN OUR POWER TO MAKE SURE THIS UNFORTUNATE INCIDENT DOES NOTHING TO SPOIL THIS MOMENTOUS OCCASION.
OF COURSE! THIS IS TRULY A GREAT DAY, LORD STARSCREAM.
WHO IS THAT?
WHO IS WITH THE CITYSPEAKER?
NO ONE IMPORTANT. JUST—
CAMIENS! HEAR ME!
I BRING TO YOU HE WHO BEARS THE MATRIX OF LEADERSHIP. OPTIMUS, THE LIVING PRIME.
BLESSED OF PRIMUS, HEART OF ALL THINGS.
BLESSED OF SOLUS, THE FLAME ETERNAL.
WHAT?
QUIET!
WHO WILL MEET HIM?
WHO WILL CHALLENGE THIS CLAIM?
I WILL.
OPTIMUS PRIME. THE MISTRESS OF FLAME SPEAKS AND YOU MUST HEAR. REVEAL YOURSELF, IF YOU ARE WHAT YOU SAY.
SHOW US THE MATRIX, BLESSED ARTIFACT OF PRIMA, OF PRIMUS, OF SOLUS HERSELF.

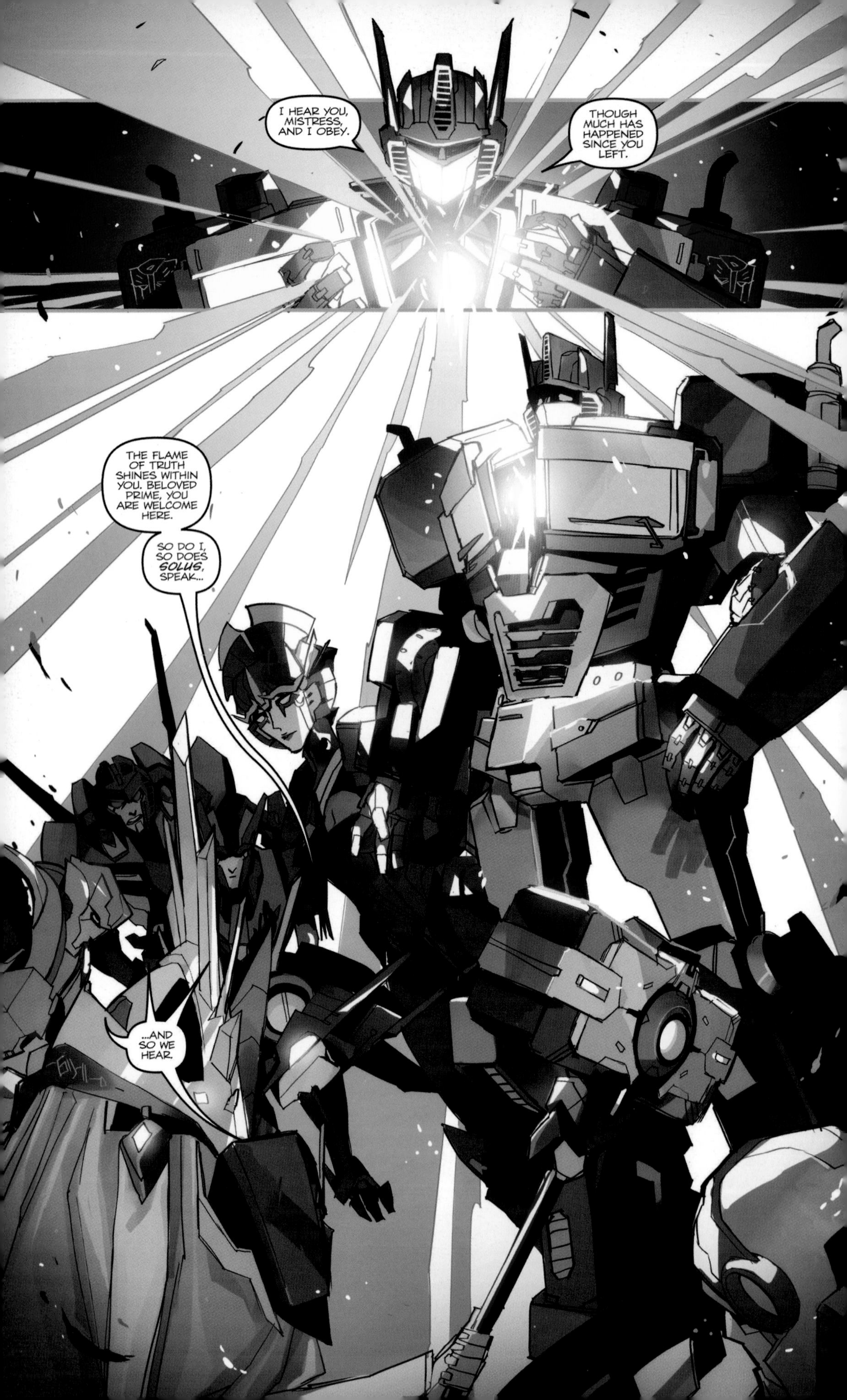
I HEAR YOU, MISTRESS, AND I OBEY.
THOUGH MUCH HAS HAPPENED SINCE YOU LEFT.
THE FLAME OF TRUTH SHINES WITHIN YOU. BELOVED PRIME, YOU ARE WELCOME HERE.
SO DO I, SO DOES SOLUS, SPEAK...
...AND SO WE HEAR.

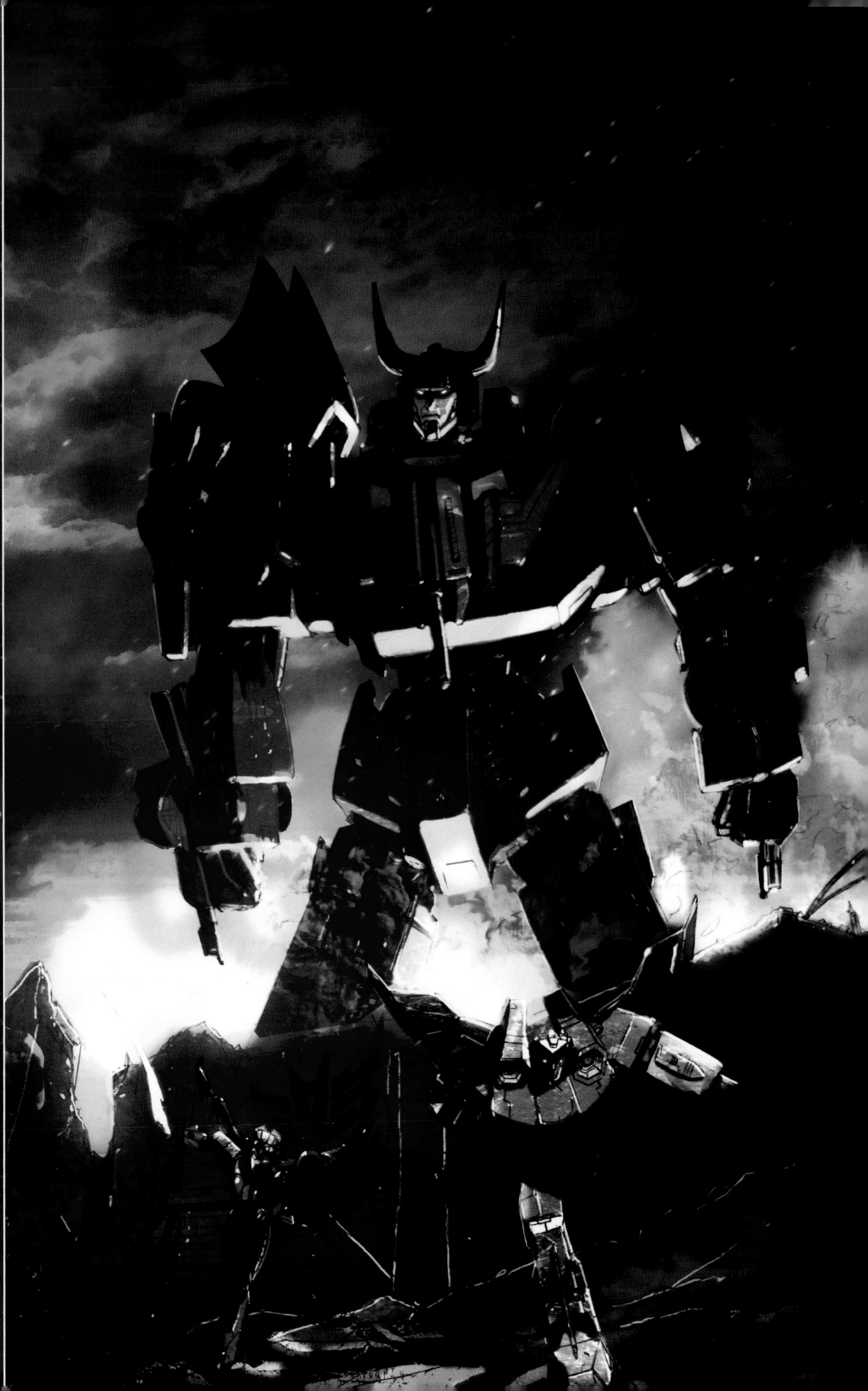

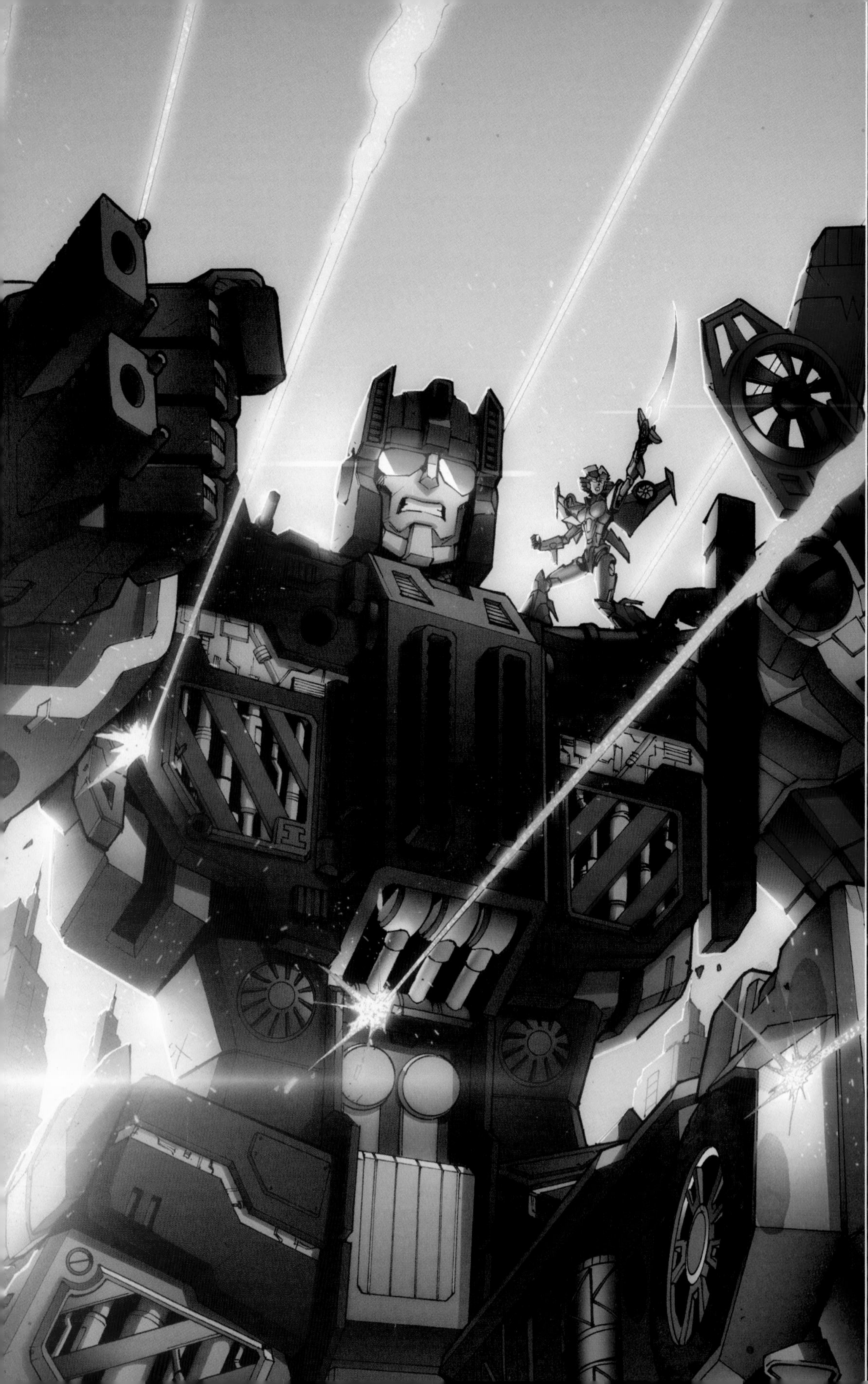

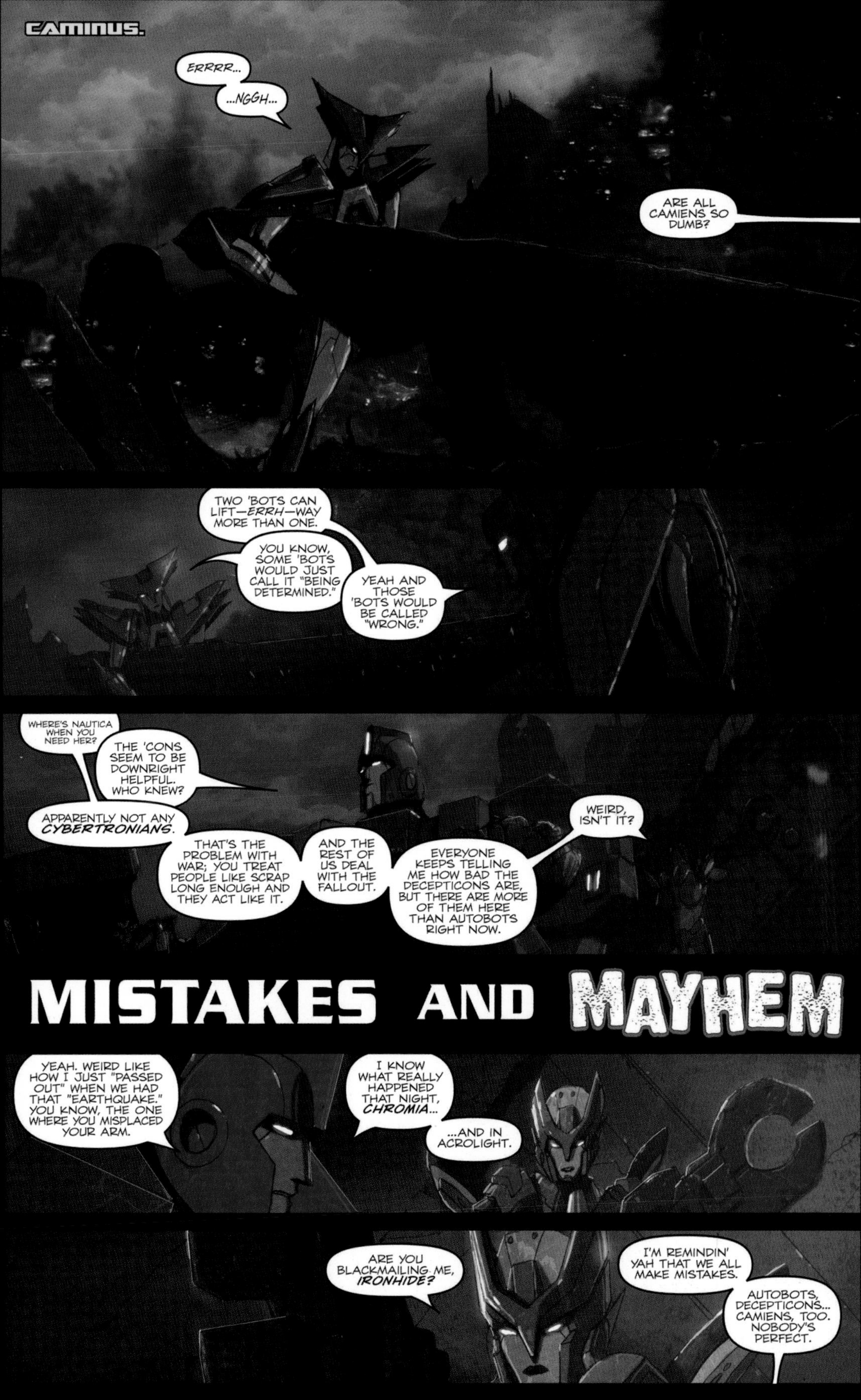
CAMINUS.
ERRRR...
...NGGH...
ARE ALL CAMIENS SO DUMB?
TWO 'BOTS CAN LIFT—ERRH—WAY MORE THAN ONE.
YOU KNOW, SOME 'BOTS WOULD JUST CALL IT "BEING DETERMINED."
YEAH AND THOSE 'BOTS WOULD BE CALLED "WRONG."
WHERE'S NAUTICA WHEN YOU NEED HER?
THE 'CONS SEEM TO BE DOWNRIGHT HELPFUL. WHO KNEW?
APPARENTLY NOT ANY CYBERTRONIANS.
THAT'S THE PROBLEM WITH WAR; YOU TREAT PEOPLE LIKE SCRAP LONG ENOUGH AND THEY ACT LIKE IT.
AND THE REST OF US DEAL WITH THE FALLOUT.
WEIRD, ISN'T IT?
EVERYONE KEEPS TELLING ME HOW BAD THE DECEPTICONS ARE, BUT THERE ARE MORE OF THEM HERE THAN AUTOBOTS RIGHT NOW.
MISTAKES AND MAYHEM
YEAH. WEIRD LIKE HOW I JUST "PASSED OUT" WHEN WE HAD THAT "EARTHQUAKE." YOU KNOW, THE ONE WHERE YOU MISPLACED YOUR ARM.
I KNOW WHAT REALLY HAPPENED THAT NIGHT, CHROMIA...
...AND IN ACROLIGHT.
ARE YOU BLACKMAILING ME, IRONHIDE?
I'M REMINDIN' YAH THAT WE ALL MAKE MISTAKES.
AUTOBOTS, DECEPTICONS... CAMIENS, TOO. NOBODY'S PERFECT.

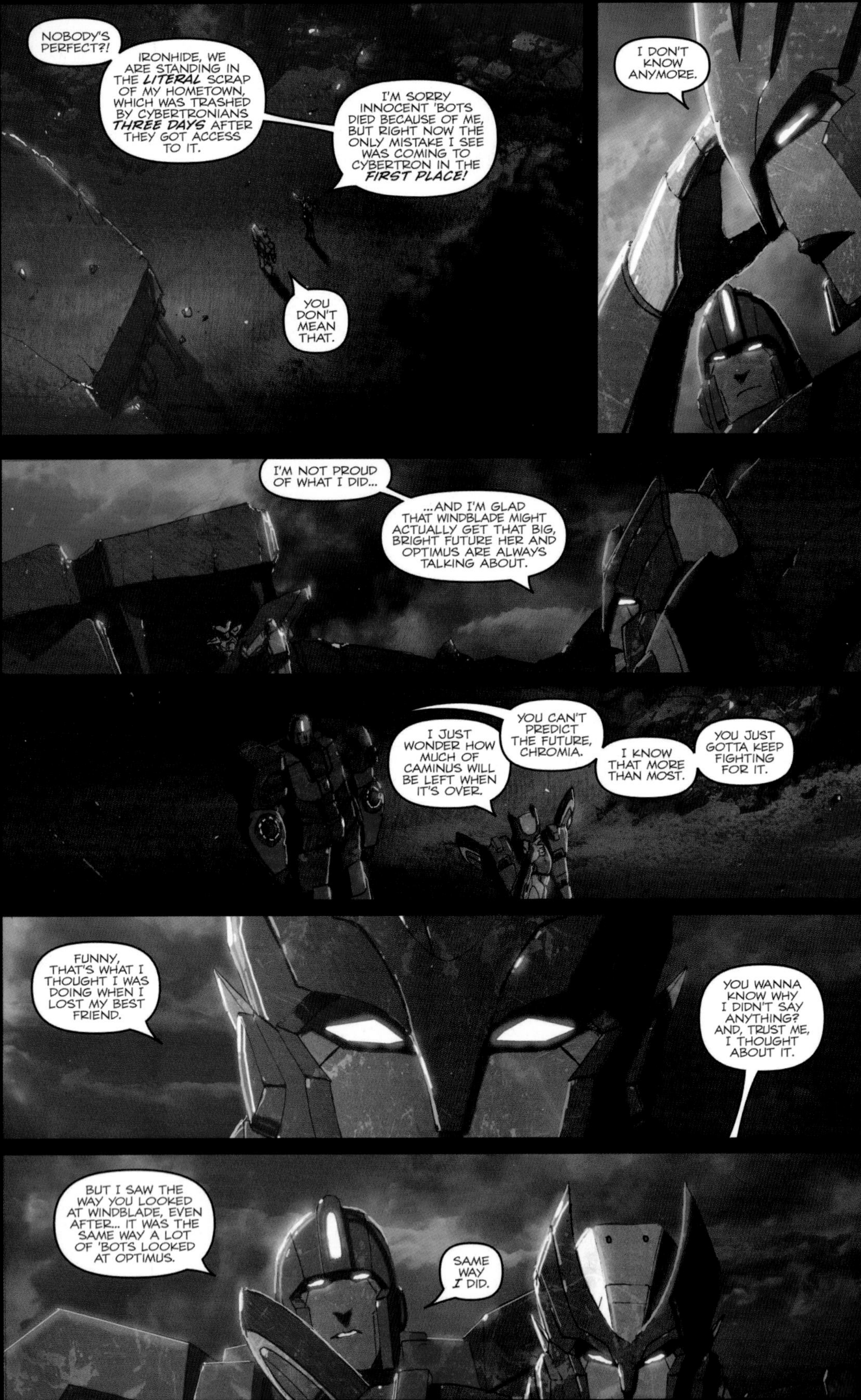

NOBODY'S PERFECT?!
IRONHIDE, WE ARE STANDING IN THE LITERAL SCRAP OF MY HOMETOWN, WHICH WAS TRASHED BY CYBERTRONIANS THREE DAYS AFTER THEY GOT ACCESS TO IT.
I'M SORRY INNOCENT 'BOTS DIED BECAUSE OF ME, BUT RIGHT NOW THE ONLY MISTAKE I SEE WAS COMING TO CYBERTRON IN THE FIRST PLACE!
YOU DON'T MEAN THAT.
I DON'T KNOW ANYMORE.
I'M NOT PROUD OF WHAT I DID...
...AND I'M GLAD THAT WINDBLADE MIGHT ACTUALLY GET THAT BIG, BRIGHT FUTURE HER AND OPTIMUS ARE ALWAYS TALKING ABOUT.
I JUST WONDER HOW MUCH OF CAMINUS WILL BE LEFT WHEN IT'S OVER.
YOU CAN'T PREDICT THE FUTURE, CHROMIA.
I KNOW THAT MORE THAN MOST.
YOU JUST GOTTA KEEP FIGHTING FOR IT.
FUNNY, THAT'S WHAT I THOUGHT I WAS DOING WHEN I LOST MY BEST FRIEND.
YOU WANNA KNOW WHY I DIDN'T SAY ANYTHING? AND, TRUST ME, I THOUGHT ABOUT IT.
BUT I SAW THE WAY YOU LOOKED AT WINDBLADE, EVEN AFTER... IT WAS THE SAME WAY A LOT OF 'BOTS LOOKED AT OPTIMUS.
SAME WAY I DID.

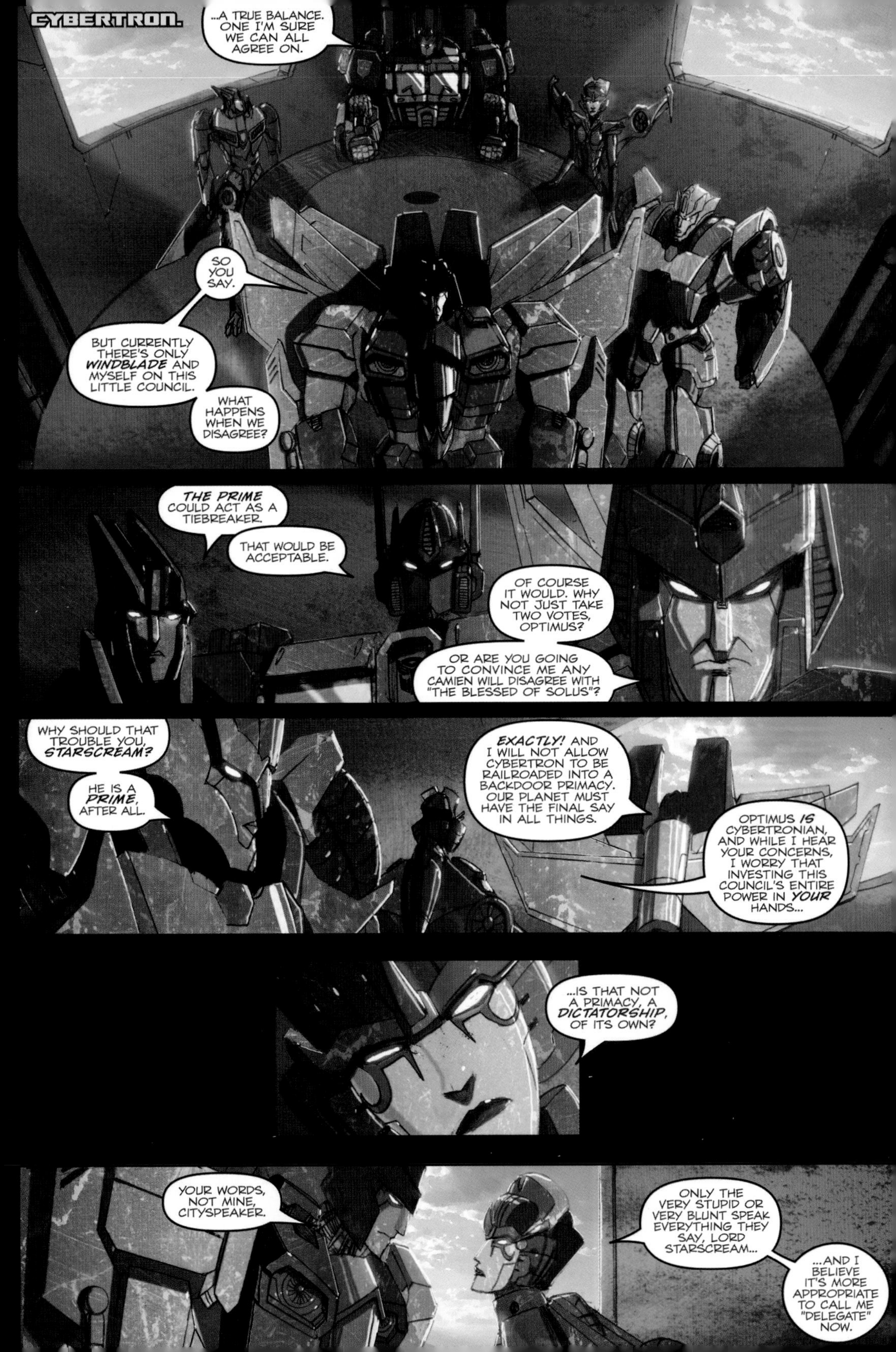
CYBERTRON.
...A TRUE BALANCE. ONE I'M SURE WE CAN ALL AGREE ON.
SO YOU SAY.
BUT CURRENTLY THERE'S ONLY WINDBLADE AND MYSELF ON THIS LITTLE COUNCIL.
WHAT HAPPENS WHEN WE DISAGREE?
THE PRIME COULD ACT AS A TIEBREAKER.
THAT WOULD BE ACCEPTABLE.
OF COURSE IT WOULD. WHY NOT JUST TAKE TWO VOTES, OPTIMUS?
OR ARE YOU GOING TO CONVINCE ME ANY CAMIEN WILL DISAGREE WITH "THE BLESSED OF SOLUS"?
WHY SHOULD THAT TROUBLE YOU, STARSCREAM?
HE IS A PRIME, AFTER ALL.
EXACTLY! AND I WILL NOT ALLOW CYBERTRON TO BE RAILROADED INTO A BACKDOOR PRIMACY. OUR PLANET MUST HAVE THE FINAL SAY IN ALL THINGS.
OPTIMUS IS CYBERTRONIAN, AND WHILE I HEAR YOUR CONCERNS, I WORRY THAT INVESTING THIS COUNCIL'S ENTIRE POWER IN YOUR HANDS...
...IS THAT NOT A PRIMACY, A DICTATORSHIP, OF ITS OWN?
YOUR WORDS, NOT MINE, CITYSPEAKER.
ONLY THE VERY STUPID OR VERY BLUNT SPEAK EVERYTHING THEY SAY, LORD STARSCREAM...
...AND I BELIEVE IT'S MORE APPROPRIATE TO CALL ME "DELEGATE" NOW.

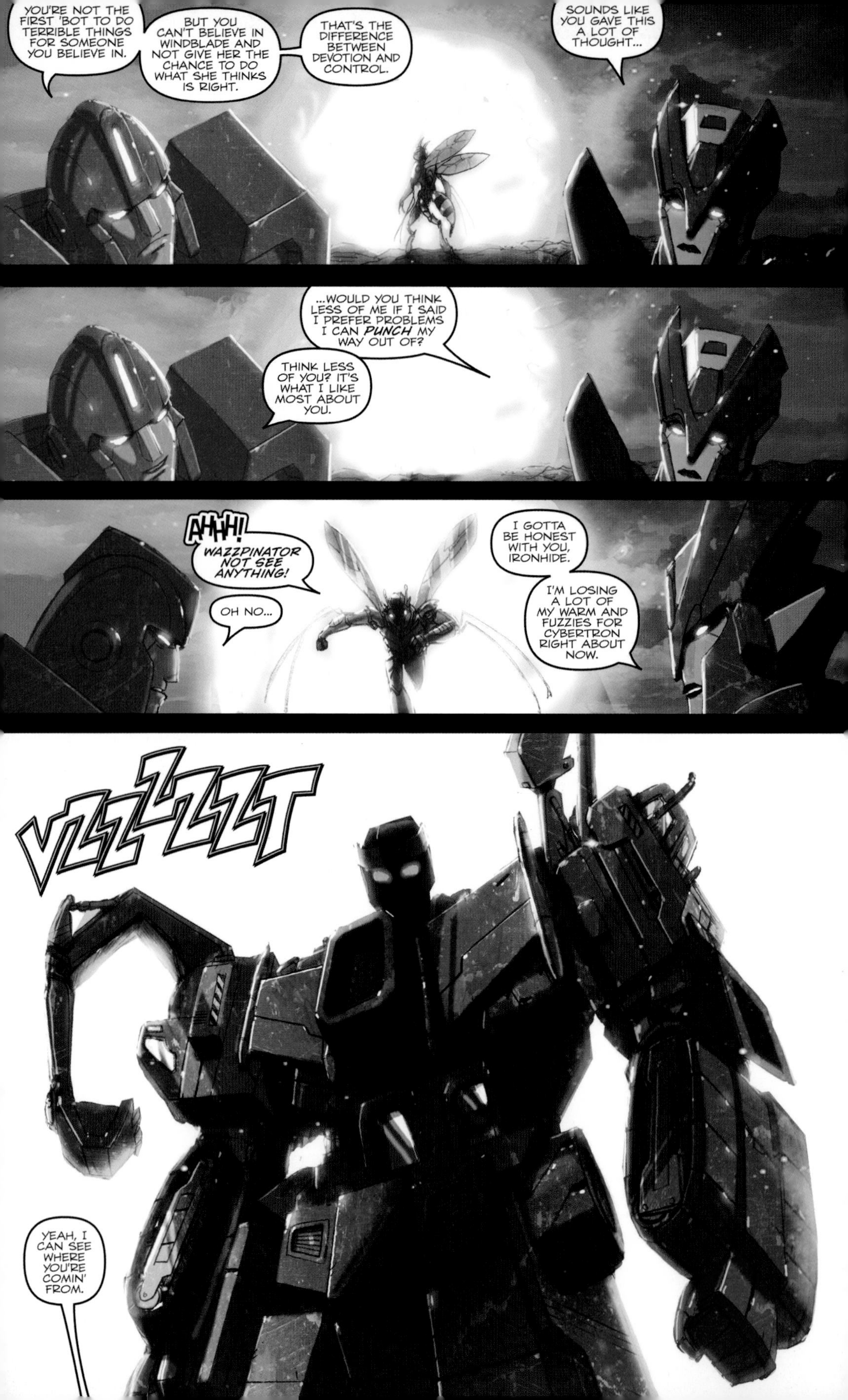
YOU'RE NOT THE FIRST 'BOT TO DO TERRIBLE THINGS FOR SOMEONE YOU BELIEVE IN.
BUT YOU CAN'T BELIEVE IN WINDBLADE AND NOT GIVE HER THE CHANCE TO DO WHAT SHE THINKS IS RIGHT.
THAT'S THE DIFFERENCE BETWEEN DEVOTION AND CONTROL.
SOUNDS LIKE YOU GAVE THIS A LOT OF THOUGHT...
...WOULD YOU THINK LESS OF ME IF I SAID I PREFER PROBLEMS I CAN *PUNCH* MY WAY OUT OF?
THINK LESS OF YOU? IT'S WHAT I LIKE MOST ABOUT YOU.
AHHH! *WAZZPINATOR NOT SEE ANYTHING!*
OH NO...
I GOTTA BE HONEST WITH YOU, IRONHIDE.
I'M LOSING A LOT OF MY WARM AND FUZZIES FOR CYBERTRON RIGHT ABOUT NOW.
VZZZZZT
YEAH, I CAN SEE WHERE YOU'RE COMIN' FROM.

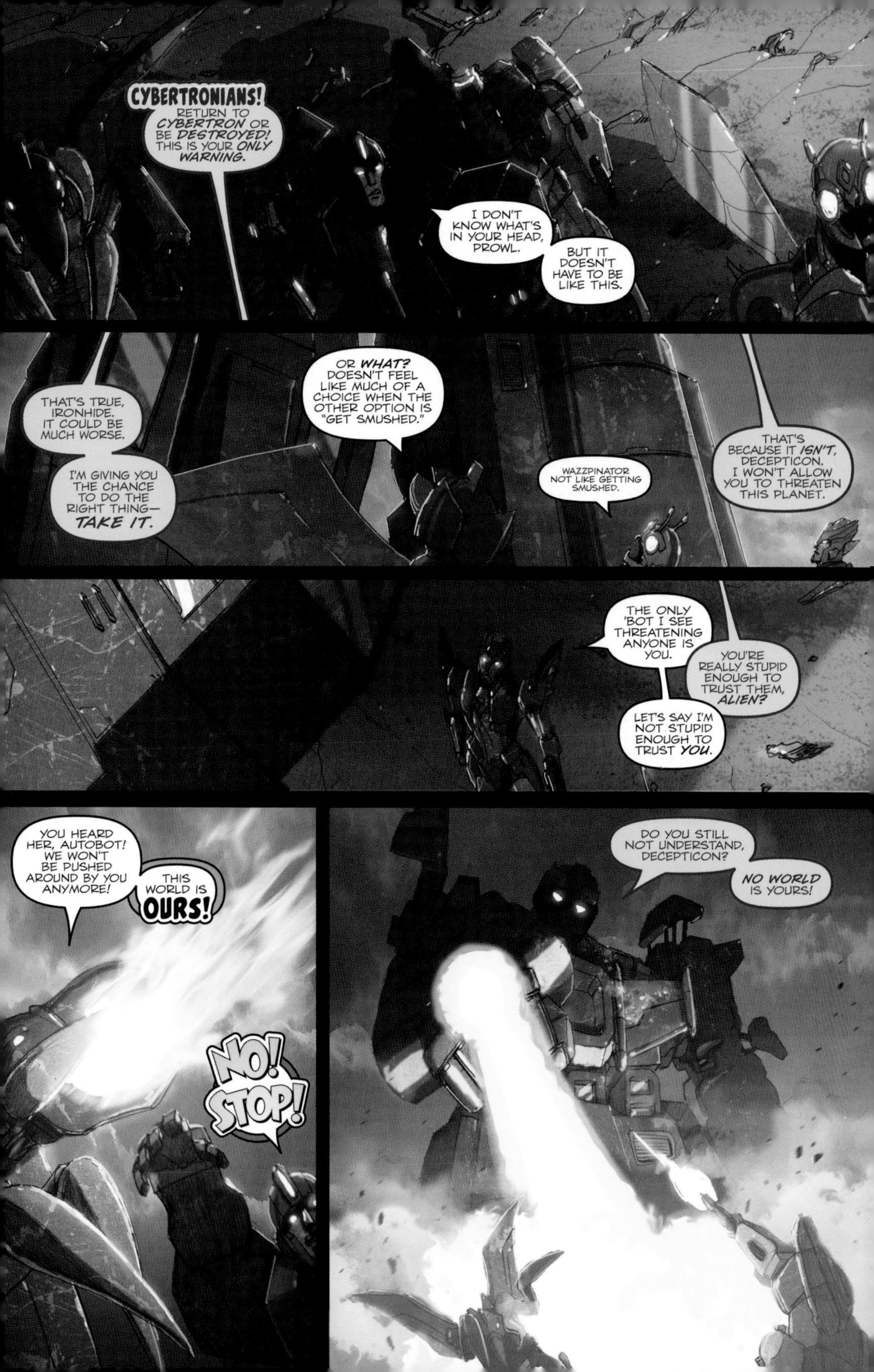
CYBERTRONIANS!
RETURN TO CYBERTRON OR BE DESTROYED! THIS IS YOUR ONLY WARNING.
I DON'T KNOW WHAT'S IN YOUR HEAD, PROWL.
BUT IT DOESN'T HAVE TO BE LIKE THIS.
THAT'S TRUE, IRONHIDE. IT COULD BE MUCH WORSE.
I'M GIVING YOU THE CHANCE TO DO THE RIGHT THING— TAKE IT.
OR WHAT? DOESN'T FEEL LIKE MUCH OF A CHOICE WHEN THE OTHER OPTION IS "GET SMUSHED."
WAZZPINATOR NOT LIKE GETTING SMUSHED.
THAT'S BECAUSE IT ISN'T, DECEPTICON. I WON'T ALLOW YOU TO THREATEN THIS PLANET.
THE ONLY 'BOT I SEE THREATENING ANYONE IS YOU.
YOU'RE REALLY STUPID ENOUGH TO TRUST THEM, ALIEN?
LET'S SAY I'M NOT STUPID ENOUGH TO TRUST YOU.
YOU HEARD HER, AUTOBOT! WE WON'T BE PUSHED AROUND BY YOU ANYMORE!
THIS WORLD IS OURS!
NO! STOP!
DO YOU STILL NOT UNDERSTAND, DECEPTICON?
NO WORLD IS YOURS!

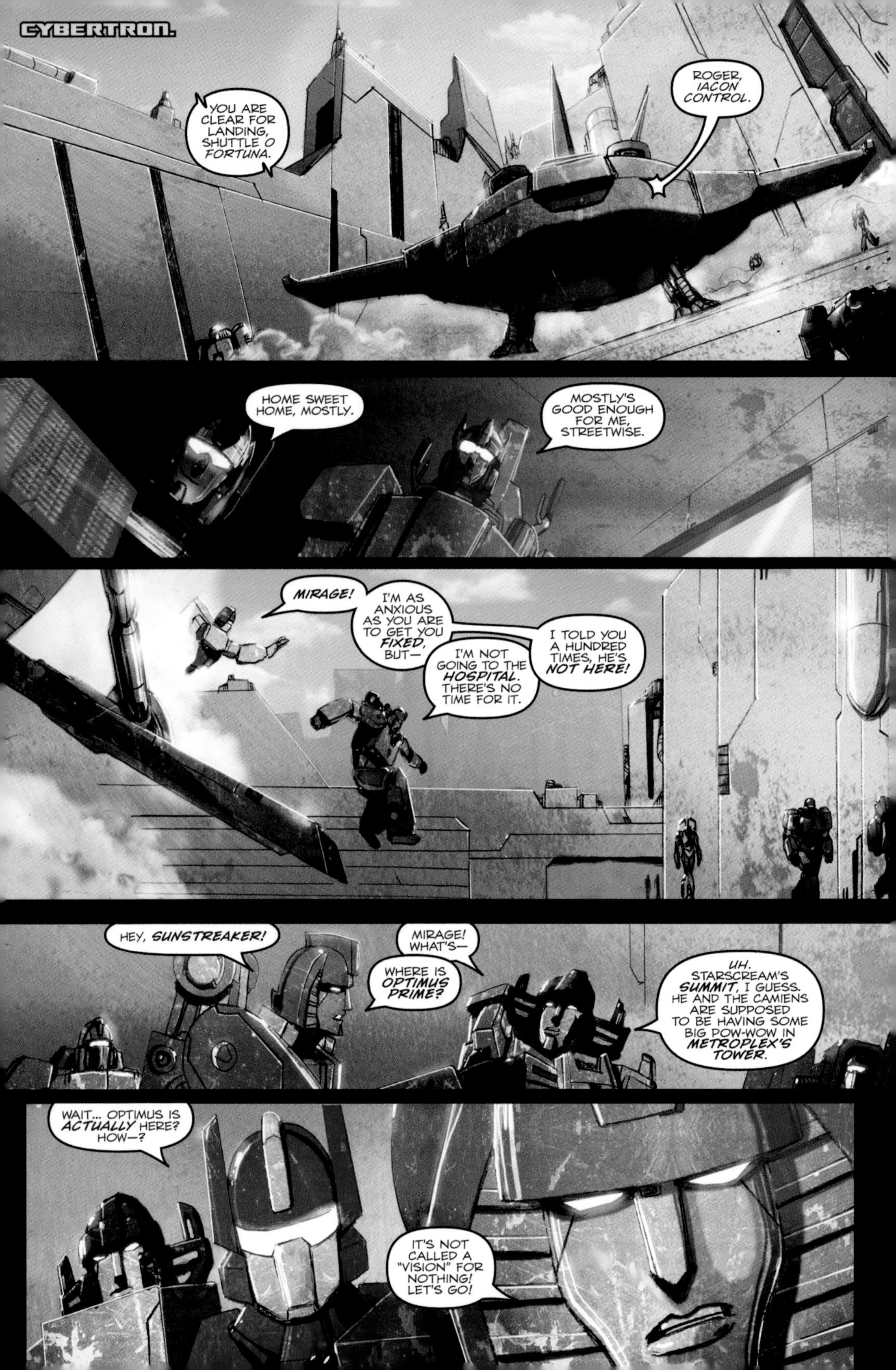

CYBERTRON.
YOU ARE CLEAR FOR LANDING, SHUTTLE O FORTUNA.
ROGER, IACON CONTROL.
HOME SWEET HOME, MOSTLY.
MOSTLY'S GOOD ENOUGH FOR ME, STREETWISE.
MIRAGE!
I'M AS ANXIOUS AS YOU ARE TO GET YOU FIXED, BUT—
I TOLD YOU A HUNDRED TIMES, HE'S NOT HERE!
I'M NOT GOING TO THE HOSPITAL. THERE'S NO TIME FOR IT.
HEY, SUNSTREAKER!
MIRAGE! WHAT'S—
WHERE IS OPTIMUS PRIME?
UH. STARSCREAM'S SUMMIT, I GUESS. HE AND THE CAMIENS ARE SUPPOSED TO BE HAVING SOME BIG POW-WOW IN METROPLEX'S TOWER.
WAIT... OPTIMUS IS ACTUALLY HERE? HOW—?
IT'S NOT CALLED A "VISION" FOR NOTHING! LET'S GO!

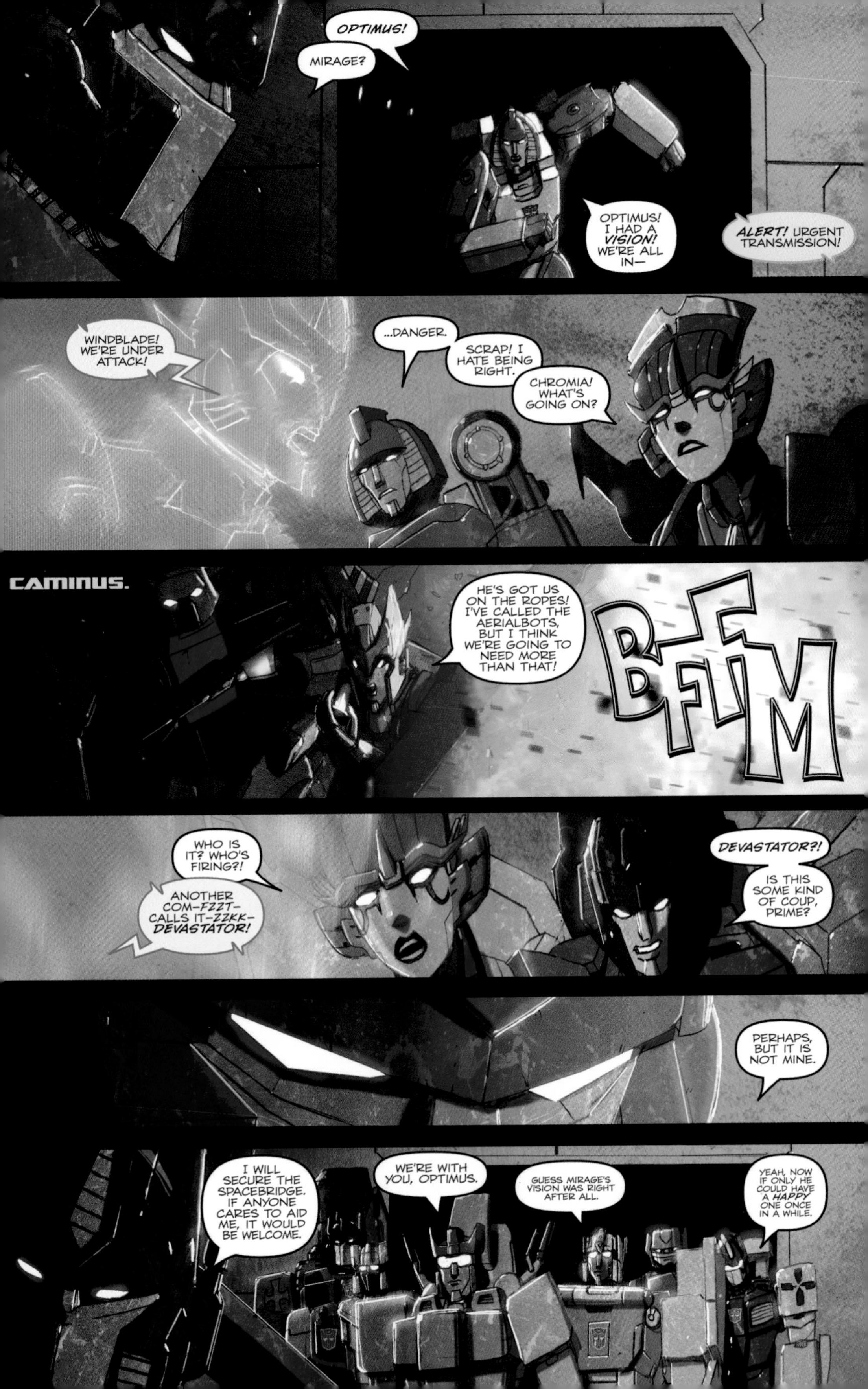
OPTIMUS!
MIRAGE?
OPTIMUS! I HAD A VISION! WE'RE ALL IN—
ALERT! URGENT TRANSMISSION!
WINDBLADE! WE'RE UNDER ATTACK!
...DANGER.
SCRAP! I HATE BEING RIGHT.
CHROMIA! WHAT'S GOING ON?
CAMINUS.
HE'S GOT US ON THE ROPES! I'VE CALLED THE AERIALBOTS, BUT I THINK WE'RE GOING TO NEED MORE THAN THAT!
BFFUM
WHO IS IT? WHO'S FIRING?!
ANOTHER COM–FZZT– CALLS IT–ZZKK– DEVASTATOR!
DEVASTATOR?!
IS THIS SOME KIND OF COUP, PRIME?
PERHAPS, BUT IT IS NOT MINE.
I WILL SECURE THE SPACEBRIDGE. IF ANYONE CARES TO AID ME, IT WOULD BE WELCOME.
WE'RE WITH YOU, OPTIMUS.
GUESS MIRAGE'S VISION WAS RIGHT AFTER ALL.
YEAH, NOW IF ONLY HE COULD HAVE A HAPPY ONE ONCE IN A WHILE.

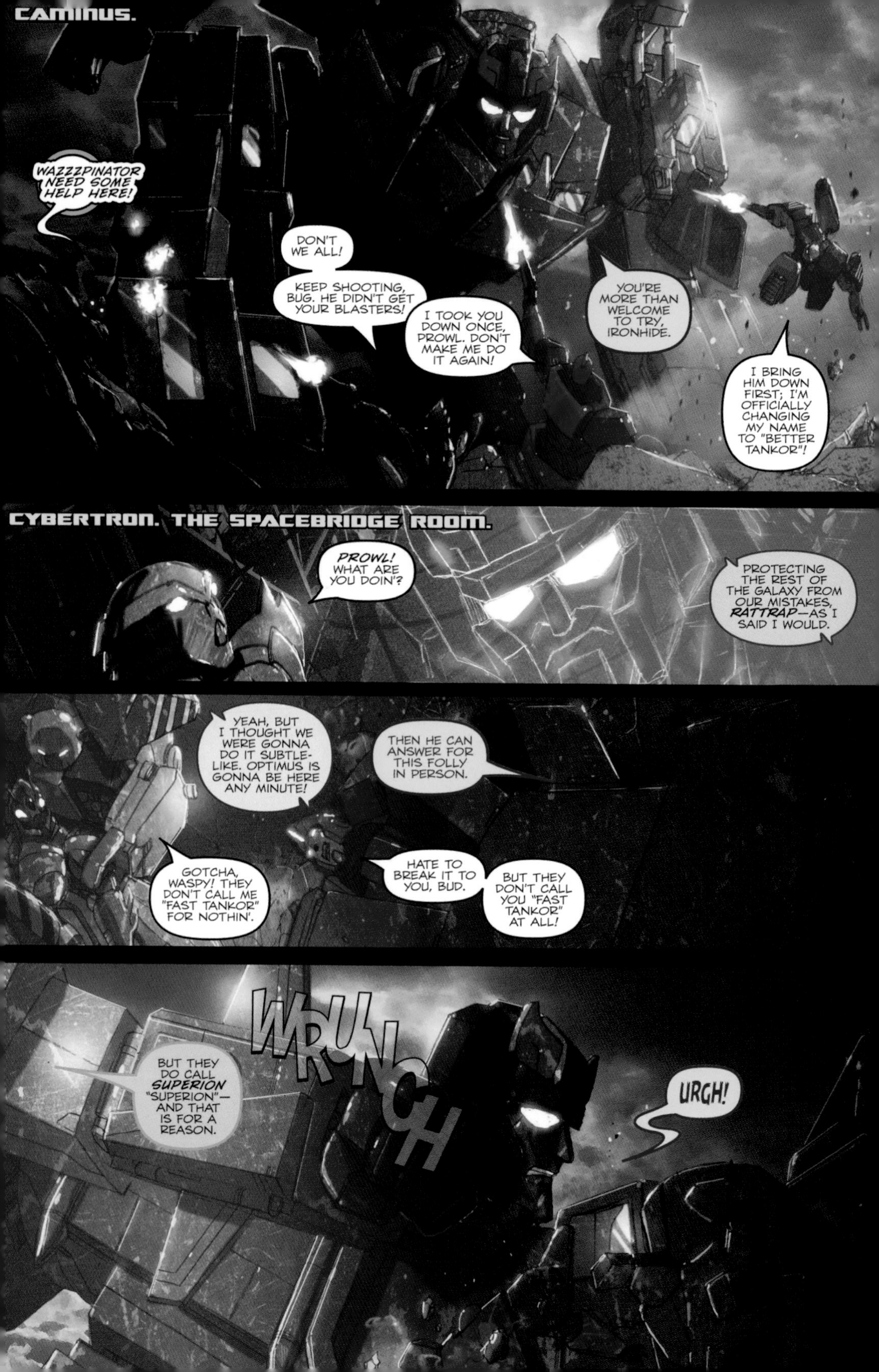
CAMINUS.
WAZZZPINATOR NEED SOME HELP HERE!
DON'T WE ALL!
KEEP SHOOTING, BUG. HE DIDN'T GET YOUR BLASTERS!
I TOOK YOU DOWN ONCE, PROWL. DON'T MAKE ME DO IT AGAIN!
YOU'RE MORE THAN WELCOME TO TRY, IRONHIDE.
I BRING HIM DOWN FIRST; I'M OFFICIALLY CHANGING MY NAME TO "BETTER TANKOR"!
CYBERTRON. THE SPACEBRIDGE ROOM.
PROWL! WHAT ARE YOU DOIN'?
PROTECTING THE REST OF THE GALAXY FROM OUR MISTAKES, RATTRAP—AS I SAID I WOULD.
YEAH, BUT I THOUGHT WE WERE GONNA DO IT SUBTLE-LIKE. OPTIMUS IS GONNA BE HERE ANY MINUTE!
THEN HE CAN ANSWER FOR THIS FOLLY IN PERSON.
GOTCHA, WASPY! THEY DON'T CALL ME "FAST TANKOR" FOR NOTHIN'.
HATE TO BREAK IT TO YOU, BUD.
BUT THEY DON'T CALL YOU "FAST TANKOR" AT ALL!
WRUNCH
BUT THEY DO CALL SUPERION "SUPERION"—AND THAT IS FOR A REASON.
URGH!

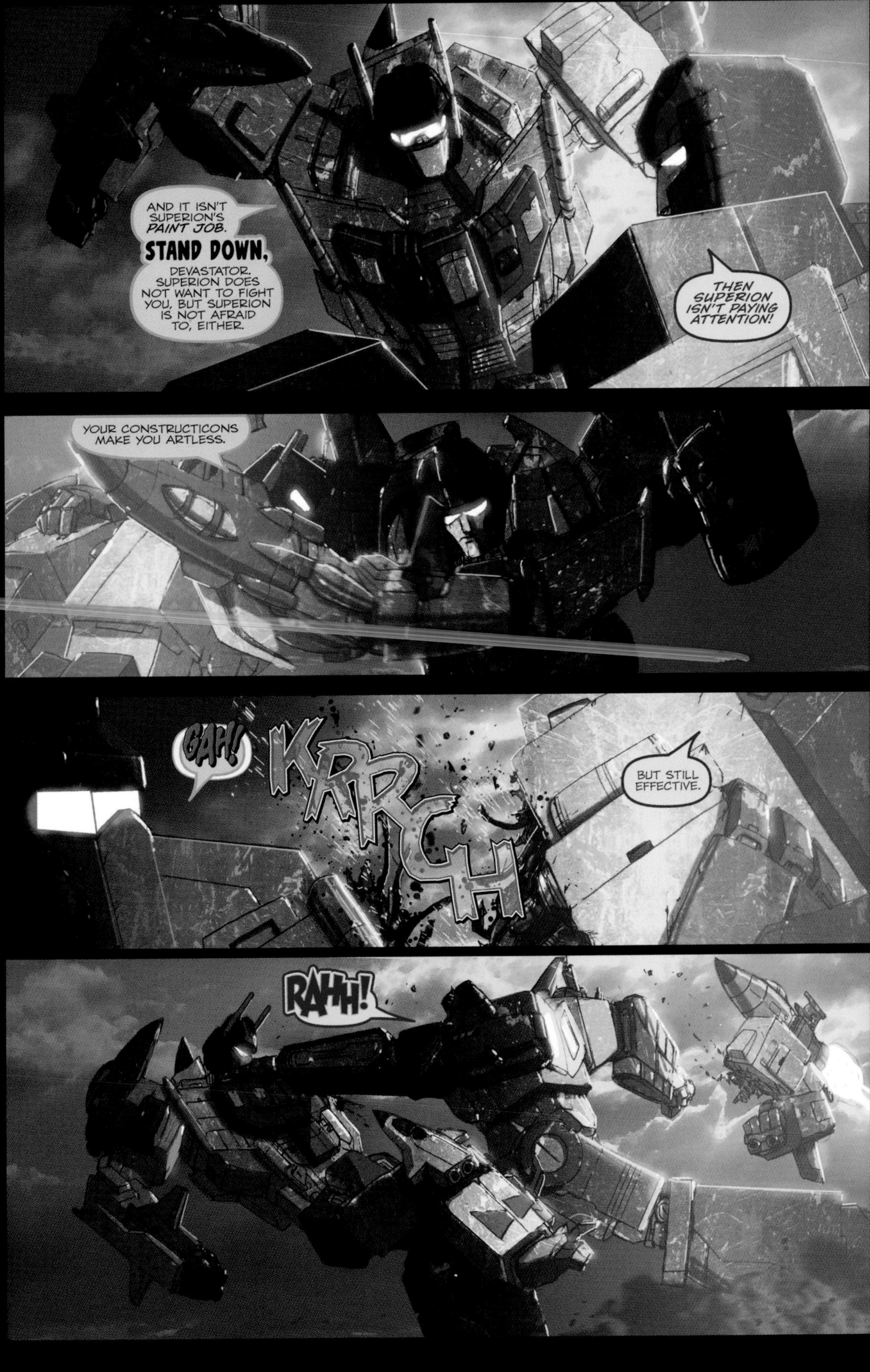
AND IT ISN'T SUPERION'S PAINT JOB.
STAND DOWN,
DEVASTATOR. SUPERION DOES NOT WANT TO FIGHT YOU, BUT SUPERION IS NOT AFRAID TO, EITHER.
THEN SUPERION ISN'T PAYING ATTENTION!
YOUR CONSTRUCTICONS MAKE YOU ARTLESS.
GAH!
KRRCH
BUT STILL EFFECTIVE.
RAHH!

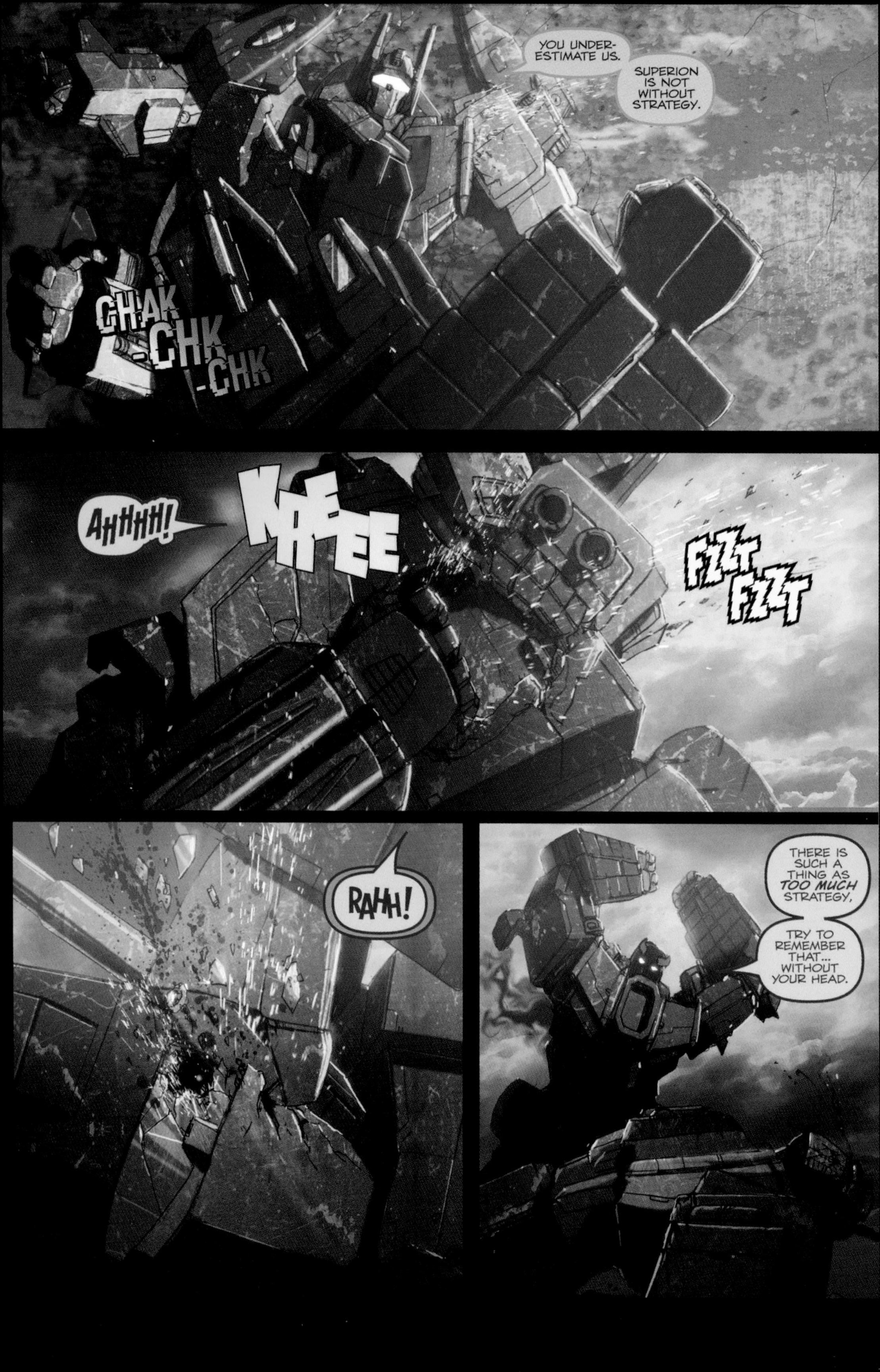
YOU UNDER-ESTIMATE US.
SUPERION IS NOT WITHOUT STRATEGY.
CHAK -CHK -CHK
AHHHH!
FZZT FZZT
RAHH!
THERE IS SUCH A THING AS *TOO MUCH* STRATEGY,
TRY TO REMEMBER THAT... WITHOUT YOUR HEAD.

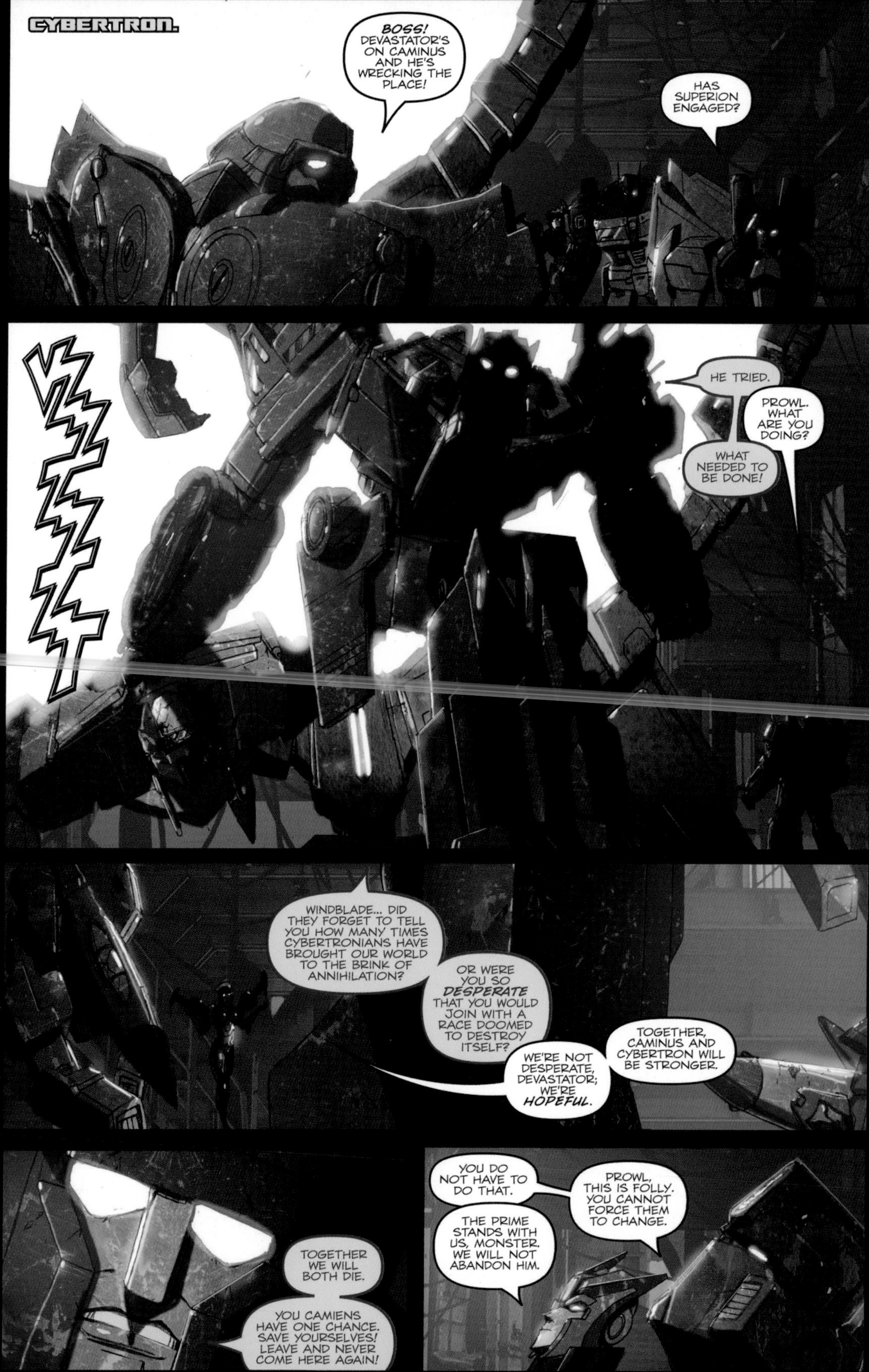
CYBERTRON.
BOSS! DEVASTATOR'S ON CAMINUS AND HE'S WRECKING THE PLACE!
HAS SUPERION ENGAGED?
VZZZZZT
HE TRIED.
PROWL. WHAT ARE YOU DOING?
WHAT NEEDED TO BE DONE!
WINDBLADE... DID THEY FORGET TO TELL YOU HOW MANY TIMES CYBERTRONIANS HAVE BROUGHT OUR WORLD TO THE BRINK OF ANNIHILATION?
OR WERE YOU SO DESPERATE THAT YOU WOULD JOIN WITH A RACE DOOMED TO DESTROY ITSELF?
WE'RE NOT DESPERATE, DEVASTATOR; WE'RE HOPEFUL.
TOGETHER, CAMINUS AND CYBERTRON WILL BE STRONGER.
TOGETHER WE WILL BOTH DIE.
YOU CAMIENS HAVE ONE CHANCE. SAVE YOURSELVES! LEAVE AND NEVER COME HERE AGAIN!
YOU DO NOT HAVE TO DO THAT.
PROWL, THIS IS FOLLY. YOU CANNOT FORCE THEM TO CHANGE.
THE PRIME STANDS WITH US, MONSTER. WE WILL NOT ABANDON HIM.

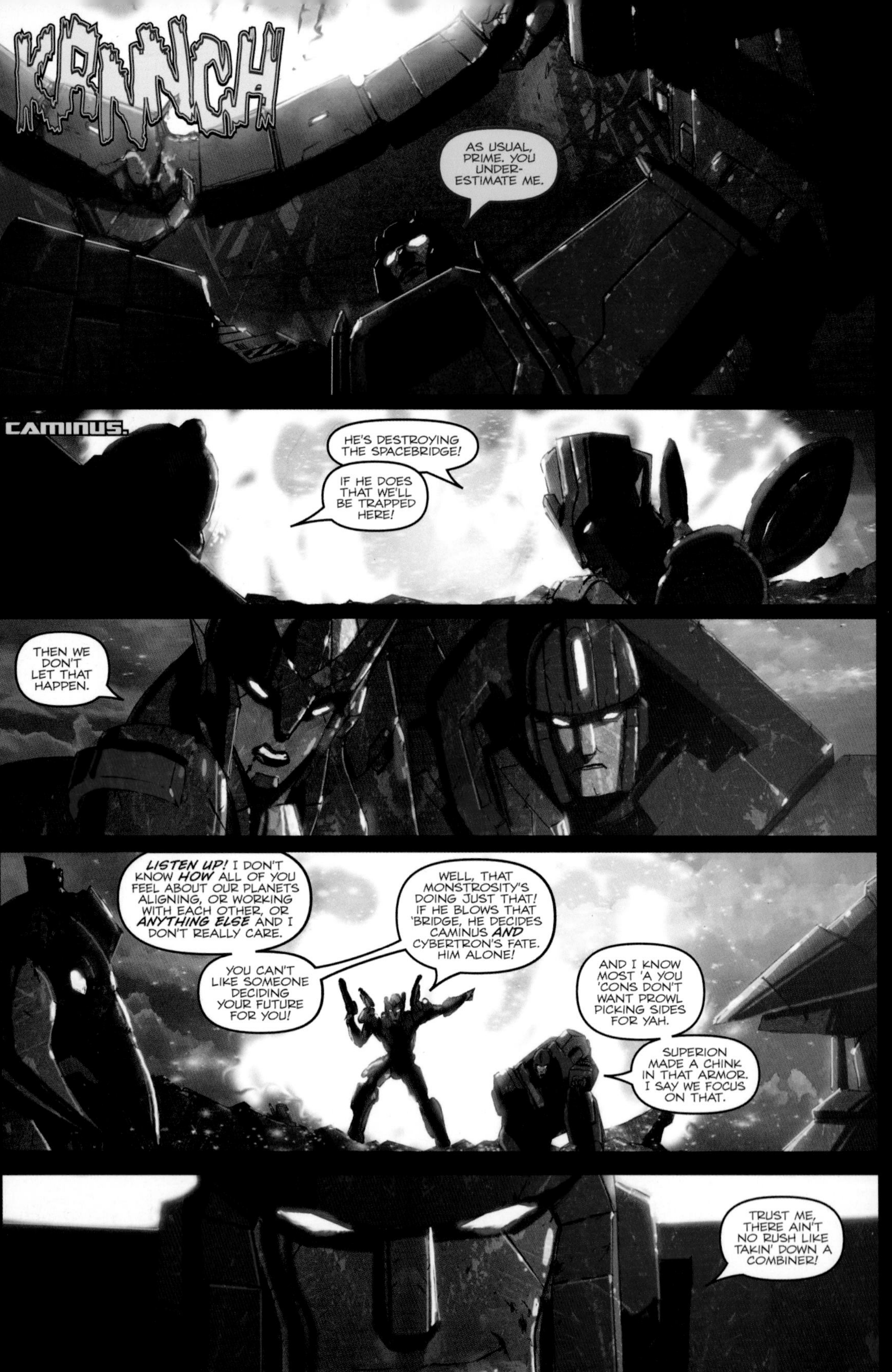
KRNNCH
AS USUAL, PRIME. YOU UNDER-ESTIMATE ME.
CAMINUS.
HE'S DESTROYING THE SPACEBRIDGE!
IF HE DOES THAT WE'LL BE TRAPPED HERE!
THEN WE DON'T LET THAT HAPPEN.
LISTEN UP! I DON'T KNOW HOW ALL OF YOU FEEL ABOUT OUR PLANETS ALIGNING, OR WORKING WITH EACH OTHER, OR ANYTHING ELSE AND I DON'T REALLY CARE.
YOU CAN'T LIKE SOMEONE DECIDING YOUR FUTURE FOR YOU!
WELL, THAT MONSTROSITY'S DOING JUST THAT! IF HE BLOWS THAT 'BRIDGE, HE DECIDES CAMINUS AND CYBERTRON'S FATE. HIM ALONE!
AND I KNOW MOST 'A YOU 'CONS DON'T WANT PROWL PICKING SIDES FOR YAH.
SUPERION MADE A CHINK IN THAT ARMOR. I SAY WE FOCUS ON THAT.
TRUST ME, THERE AIN'T NO RUSH LIKE TAKIN' DOWN A COMBINER!

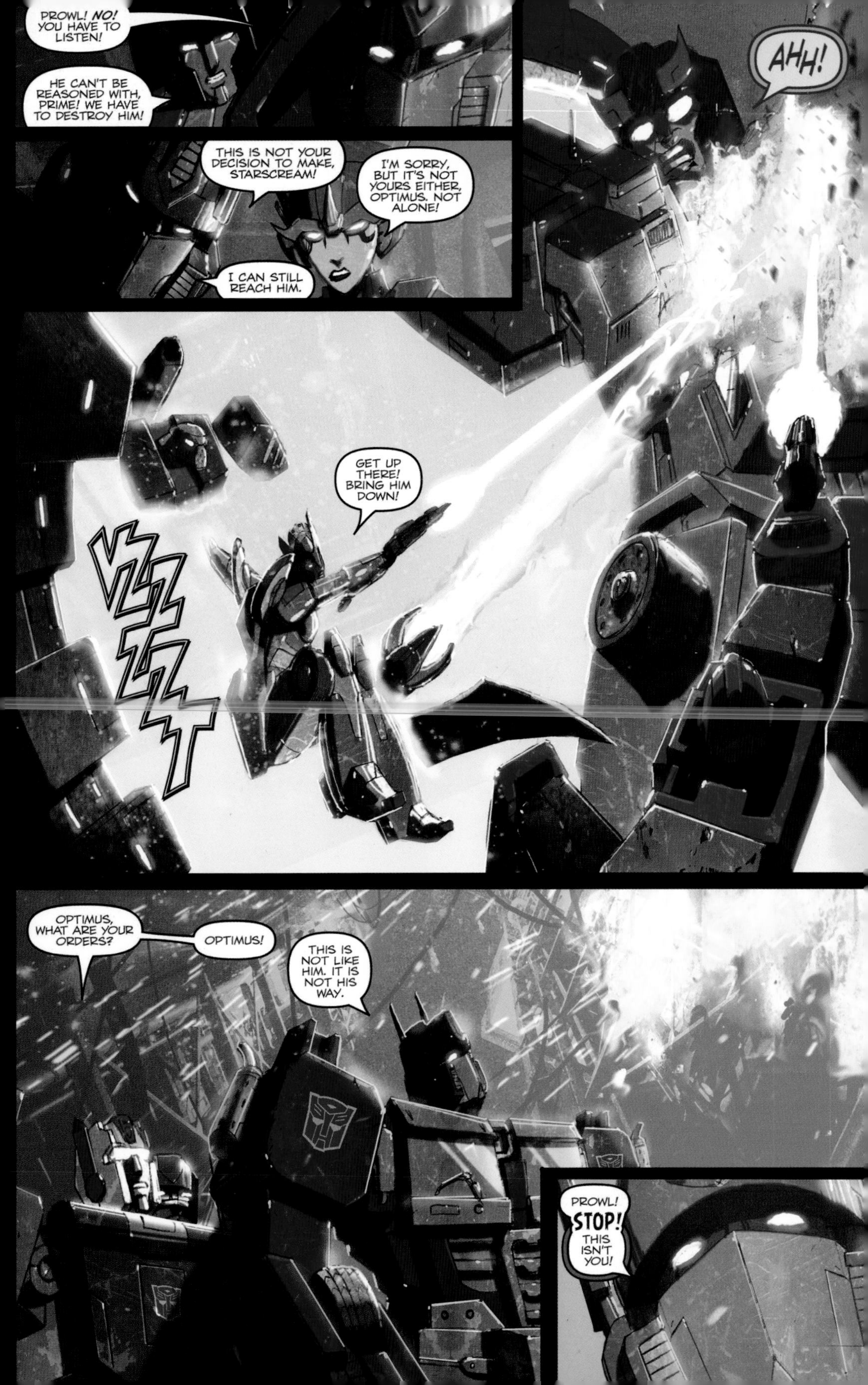
PROWL! NO! YOU HAVE TO LISTEN!
HE CAN'T BE REASONED WITH, PRIME! WE HAVE TO DESTROY HIM!
AHH!
THIS IS NOT YOUR DECISION TO MAKE, STARSCREAM!
I'M SORRY, BUT IT'S NOT YOURS EITHER, OPTIMUS. NOT ALONE!
I CAN STILL REACH HIM.
GET UP THERE! BRING HIM DOWN!
VZZZT
OPTIMUS, WHAT ARE YOUR ORDERS?
OPTIMUS!
THIS IS NOT LIKE HIM. IT IS NOT HIS WAY.
PROWL! STOP! THIS ISN'T YOU!

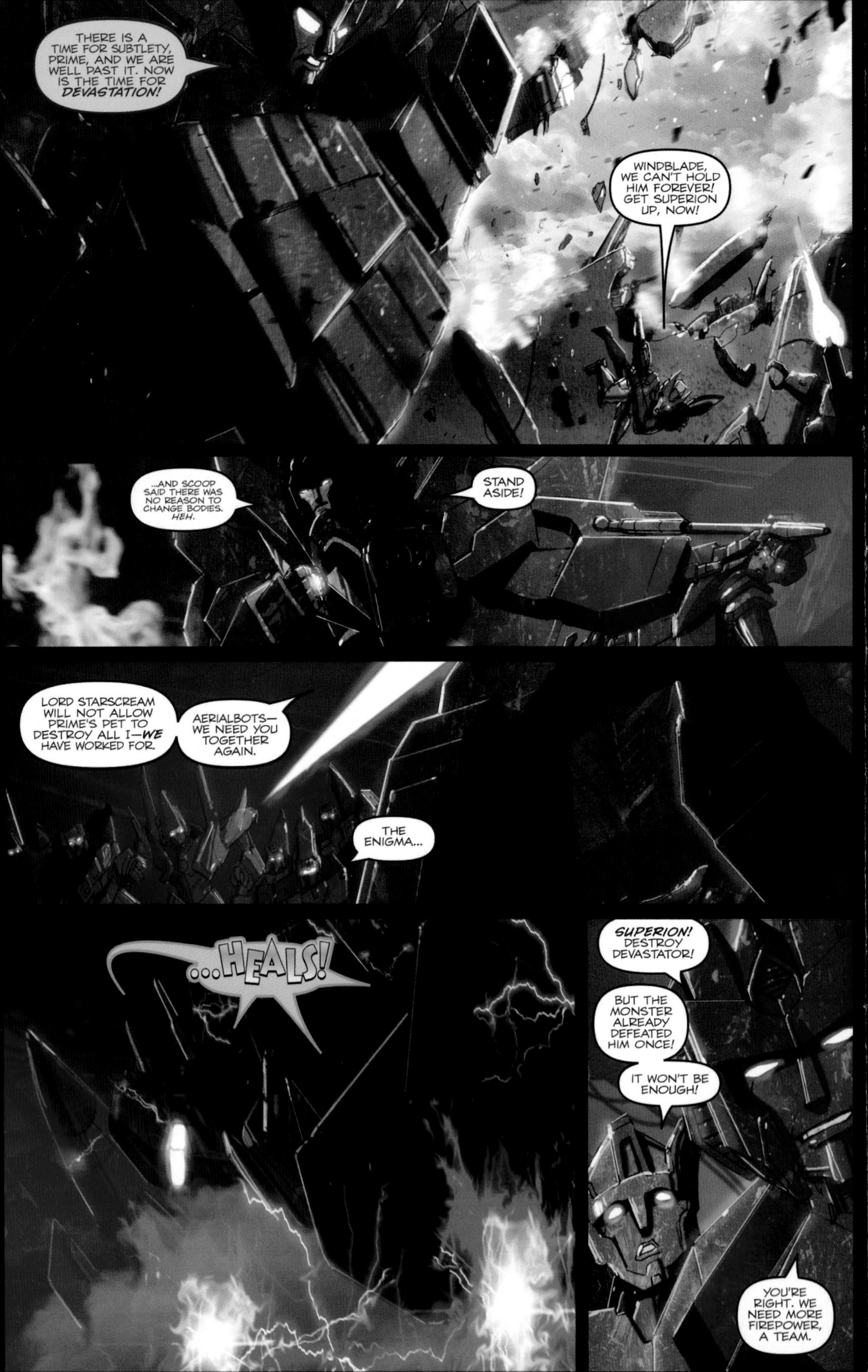
THERE IS A TIME FOR SUBTLETY, PRIME, AND WE ARE WELL PAST IT. NOW IS THE TIME FOR DEVASTATION!
WINDBLADE, WE CAN'T HOLD HIM FOREVER! GET SUPERION UP, NOW!
...AND SCOOP SAID THERE WAS NO REASON TO CHANGE BODIES. HEH.
STAND ASIDE!
LORD STARSCREAM WILL NOT ALLOW PRIME'S PET TO DESTROY ALL I—WE HAVE WORKED FOR.
AERIALBOTS— WE NEED YOU TOGETHER AGAIN.
THE ENIGMA...
...HEALS!
SUPERION! DESTROY DEVASTATOR!
BUT THE MONSTER ALREADY DEFEATED HIM ONCE!
IT WON'T BE ENOUGH!
YOU'RE RIGHT. WE NEED MORE FIREPOWER, A TEAM.

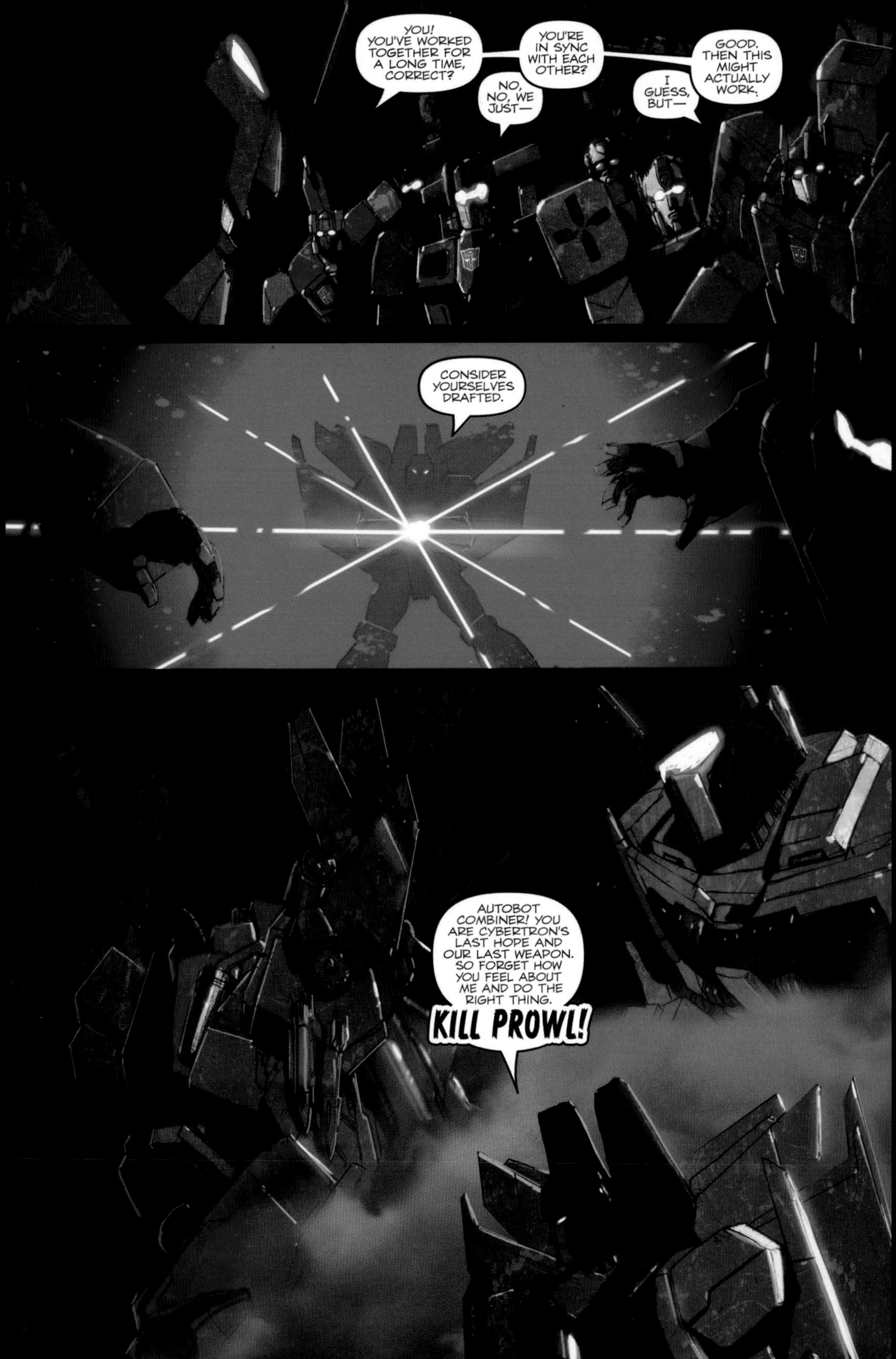
YOU! YOU'VE WORKED TOGETHER FOR A LONG TIME, CORRECT?
NO, NO, WE JUST—
YOU'RE IN SYNC WITH EACH OTHER?
I GUESS, BUT—
GOOD. THEN THIS MIGHT ACTUALLY WORK.
CONSIDER YOURSELVES DRAFTED.
AUTOBOT COMBINER! YOU ARE CYBERTRON'S LAST HOPE AND OUR LAST WEAPON. SO FORGET HOW YOU FEEL ABOUT ME AND DO THE RIGHT THING.
KILL PROWL!

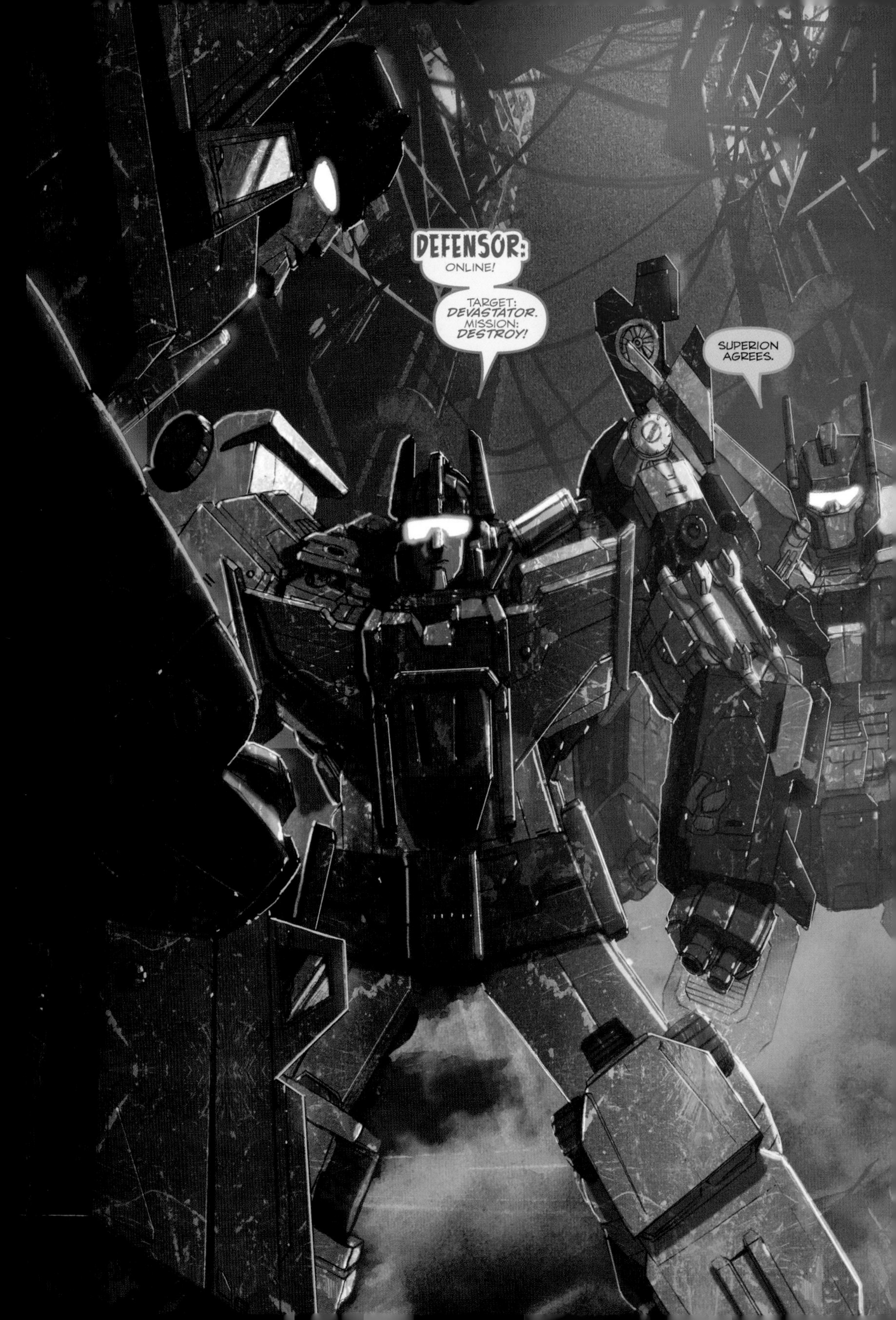
DEFENSOR:
ONLINE!
TARGET: DEVASTATOR. MISSION: DESTROY!
SUPERION AGREES.

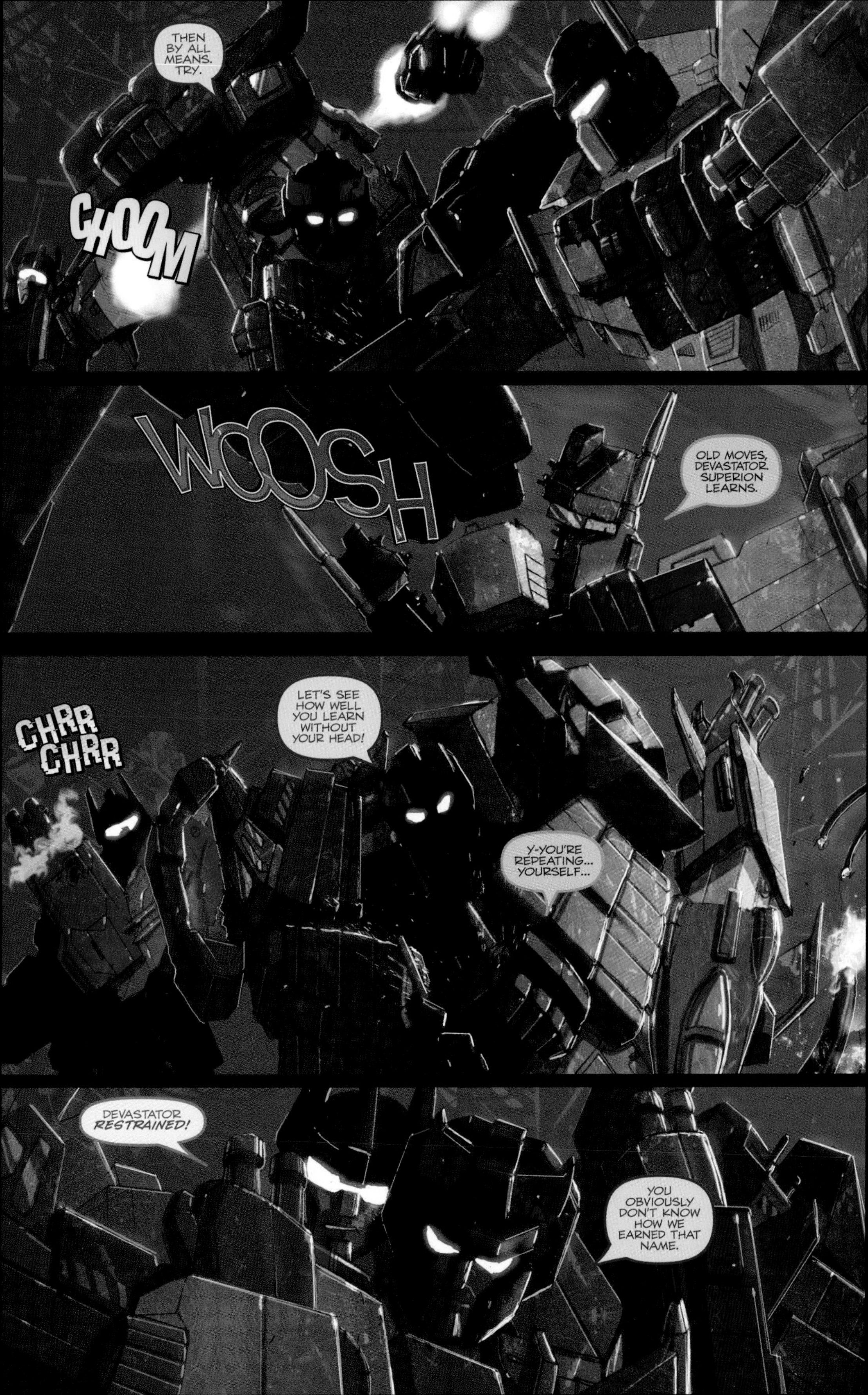
THEN BY ALL MEANS. TRY.
CHOOM
WOOSH
OLD MOVES, DEVASTATOR. SUPERION LEARNS.
CHRR CHRR
LET'S SEE HOW WELL YOU LEARN WITHOUT YOUR HEAD!
Y-YOU'RE REPEATING... YOURSELF...
DEVASTATOR RESTRAINED!
YOU OBVIOUSLY DON'T KNOW HOW WE EARNED THAT NAME.

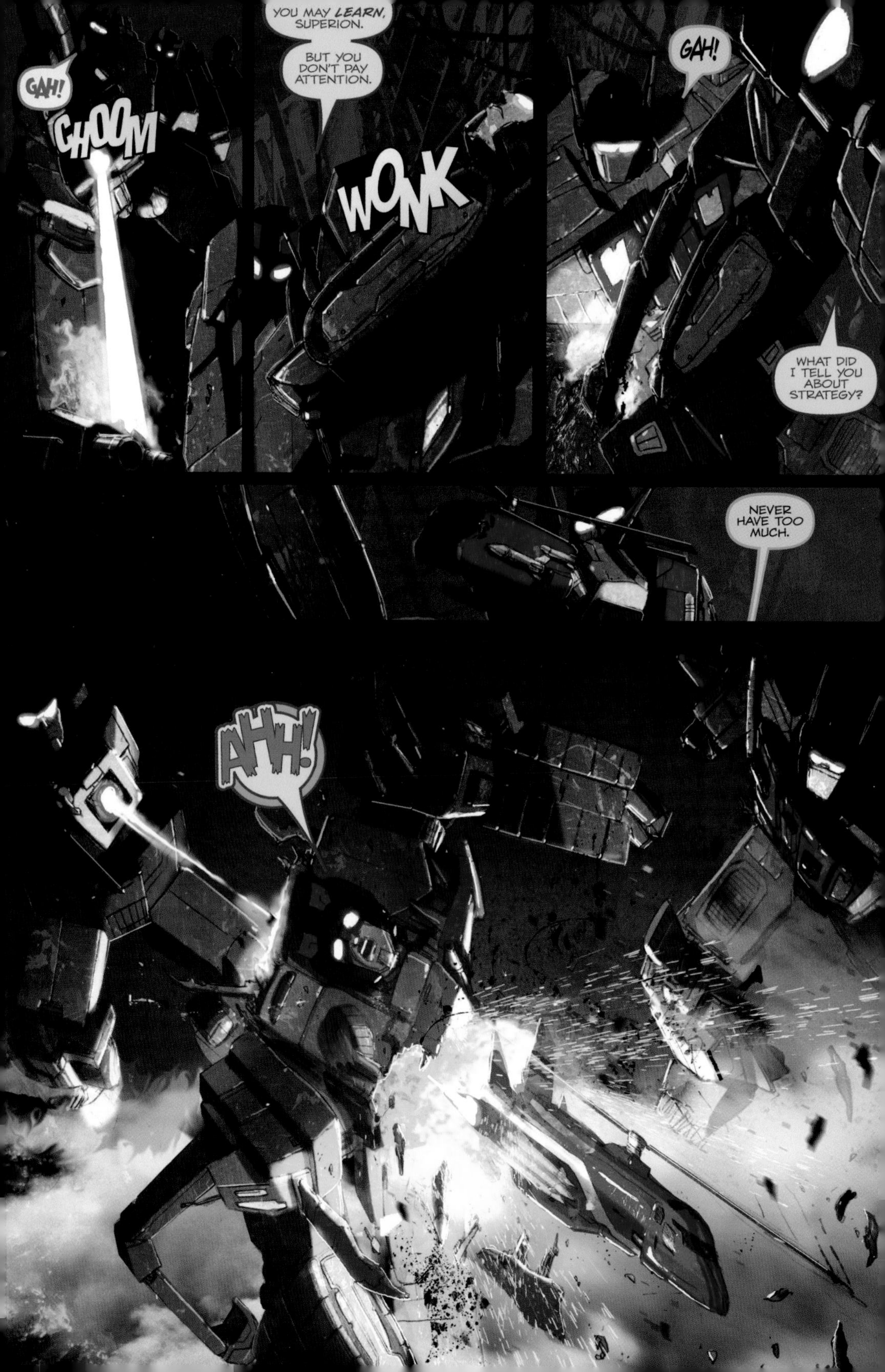
GAH!
CHOOM
YOU MAY *LEARN*, SUPERION.
BUT YOU DON'T PAY ATTENTION.
WONK
GAH!
WHAT DID I TELL YOU ABOUT STRATEGY?
NEVER HAVE TOO MUCH.
AHH!

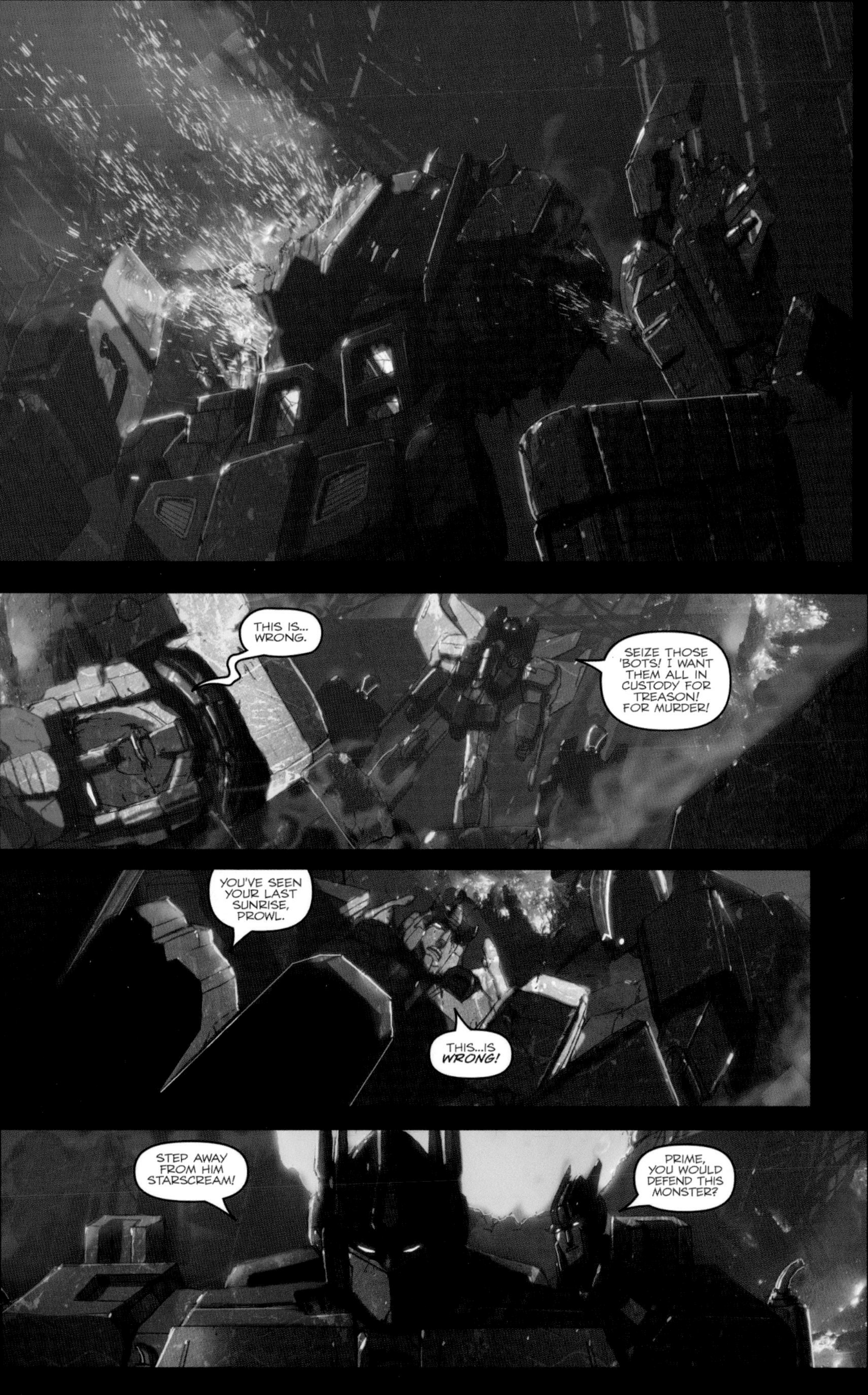
THIS IS... WRONG.
SEIZE THOSE 'BOTS! I WANT THEM ALL IN CUSTODY FOR TREASON! FOR MURDER!
YOU'VE SEEN YOUR LAST SUNRISE, PROWL.
THIS...IS *WRONG!*
STEP AWAY FROM HIM STARSCREAM!
PRIME, YOU WOULD DEFEND THIS MONSTER?

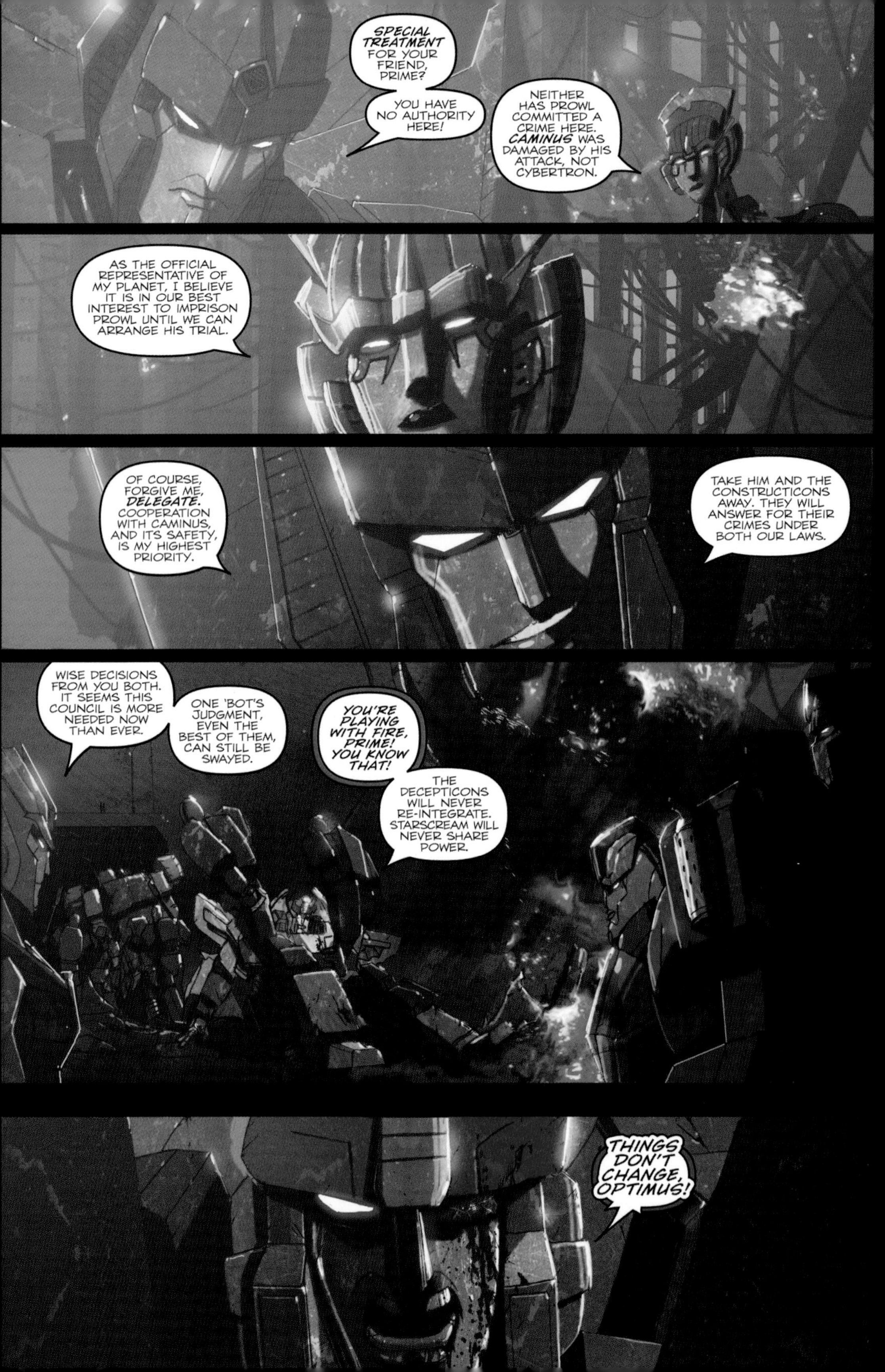
SPECIAL TREATMENT FOR YOUR FRIEND, PRIME?
YOU HAVE NO AUTHORITY HERE!
NEITHER HAS PROWL COMMITTED A CRIME HERE. CAMINUS WAS DAMAGED BY HIS ATTACK, NOT CYBERTRON.
AS THE OFFICIAL REPRESENTATIVE OF MY PLANET, I BELIEVE IT IS IN OUR BEST INTEREST TO IMPRISON PROWL UNTIL WE CAN ARRANGE HIS TRIAL.
OF COURSE, FORGIVE ME, DELEGATE. COOPERATION WITH CAMINUS, AND ITS SAFETY, IS MY HIGHEST PRIORITY.
TAKE HIM AND THE CONSTRUCTICONS AWAY. THEY WILL ANSWER FOR THEIR CRIMES UNDER BOTH OUR LAWS.
WISE DECISIONS FROM YOU BOTH. IT SEEMS THIS COUNCIL IS MORE NEEDED NOW THAN EVER.
ONE 'BOT'S JUDGMENT, EVEN THE BEST OF THEM, CAN STILL BE SWAYED.
YOU'RE PLAYING WITH FIRE, PRIME! YOU KNOW THAT!
THE DECEPTICONS WILL NEVER RE-INTEGRATE. STARSCREAM WILL NEVER SHARE POWER.
THINGS DON'T CHANGE, OPTIMUS!

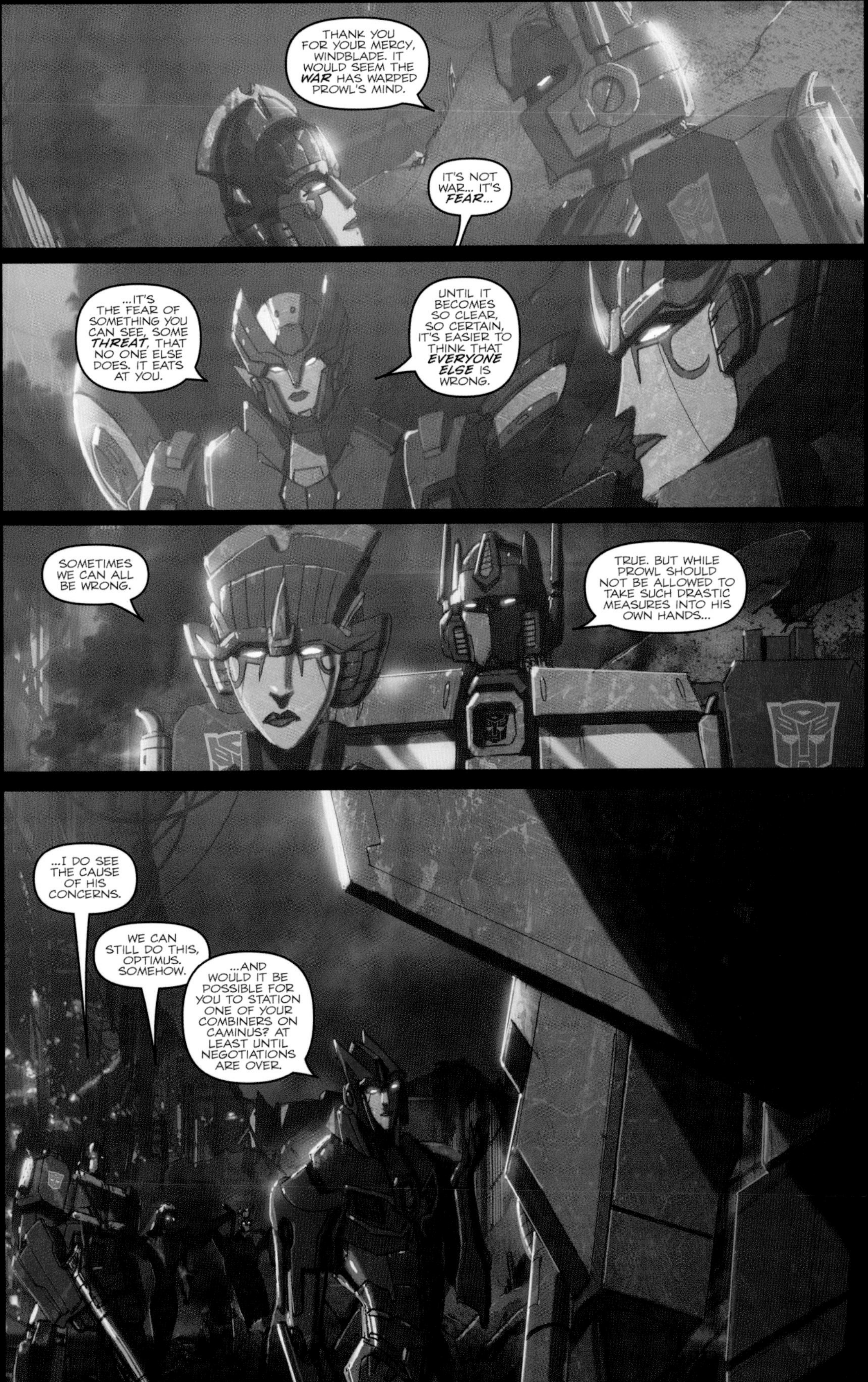
THANK YOU FOR YOUR MERCY, WINDBLADE. IT WOULD SEEM THE WAR HAS WARPED PROWL'S MIND.
IT'S NOT WAR... IT'S FEAR...
...IT'S THE FEAR OF SOMETHING YOU CAN SEE, SOME THREAT, THAT NO ONE ELSE DOES. IT EATS AT YOU.
UNTIL IT BECOMES SO CLEAR, SO CERTAIN, IT'S EASIER TO THINK THAT EVERYONE ELSE IS WRONG.
SOMETIMES WE CAN ALL BE WRONG.
TRUE. BUT WHILE PROWL SHOULD NOT BE ALLOWED TO TAKE SUCH DRASTIC MEASURES INTO HIS OWN HANDS...
...I DO SEE THE CAUSE OF HIS CONCERNS.
WE CAN STILL DO THIS, OPTIMUS. SOMEHOW.
...AND WOULD IT BE POSSIBLE FOR YOU TO STATION ONE OF YOUR COMBINERS ON CAMINUS? AT LEAST UNTIL NEGOTIATIONS ARE OVER.

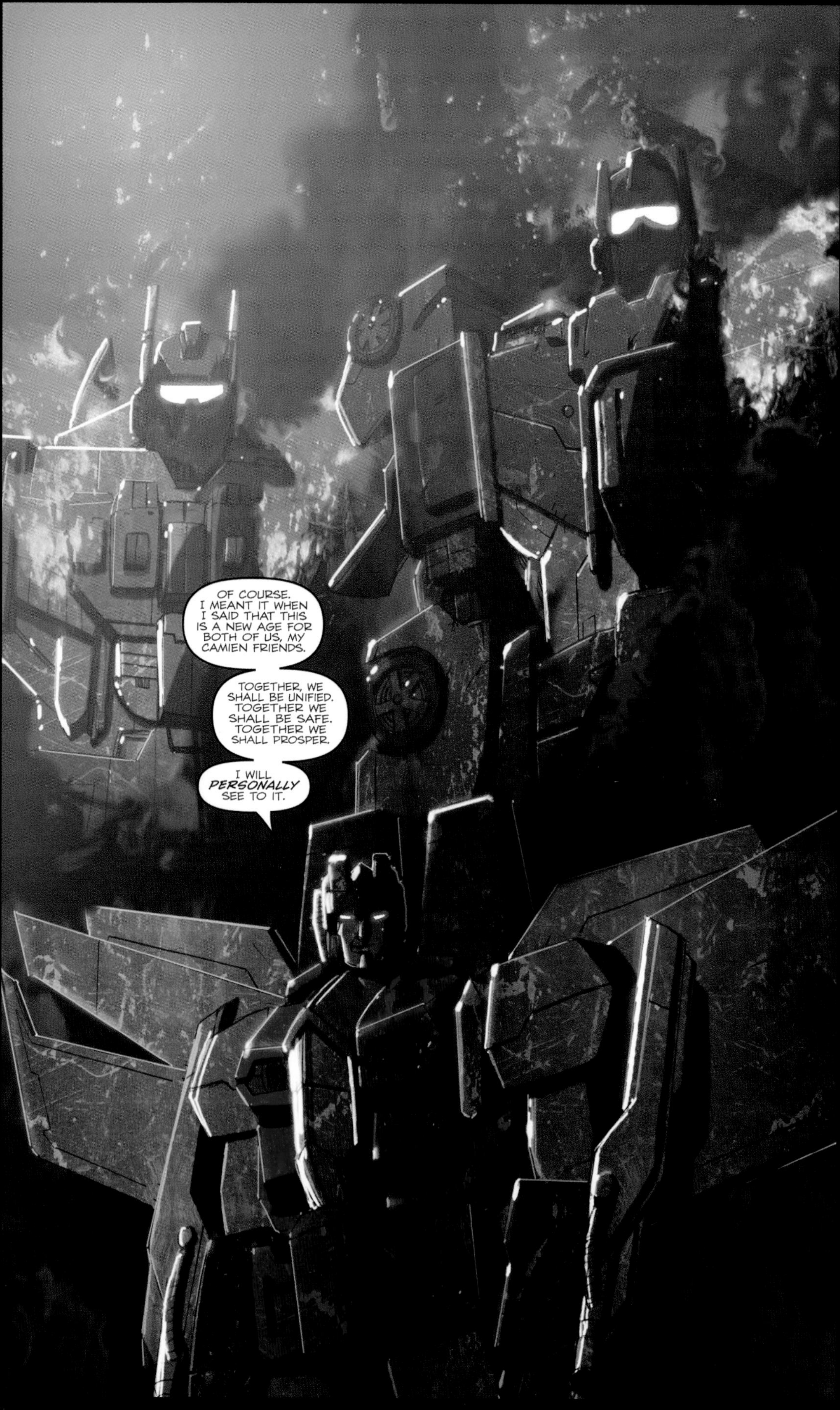
OF COURSE. I MEANT IT WHEN I SAID THAT THIS IS A NEW AGE FOR BOTH OF US, MY CAMIEN FRIENDS.
TOGETHER, WE SHALL BE UNIFIED. TOGETHER WE SHALL BE SAFE. TOGETHER WE SHALL PROSPER.
I WILL *PERSONALLY* SEE TO IT.

ART BY **LIVIO RAMONDELLI**

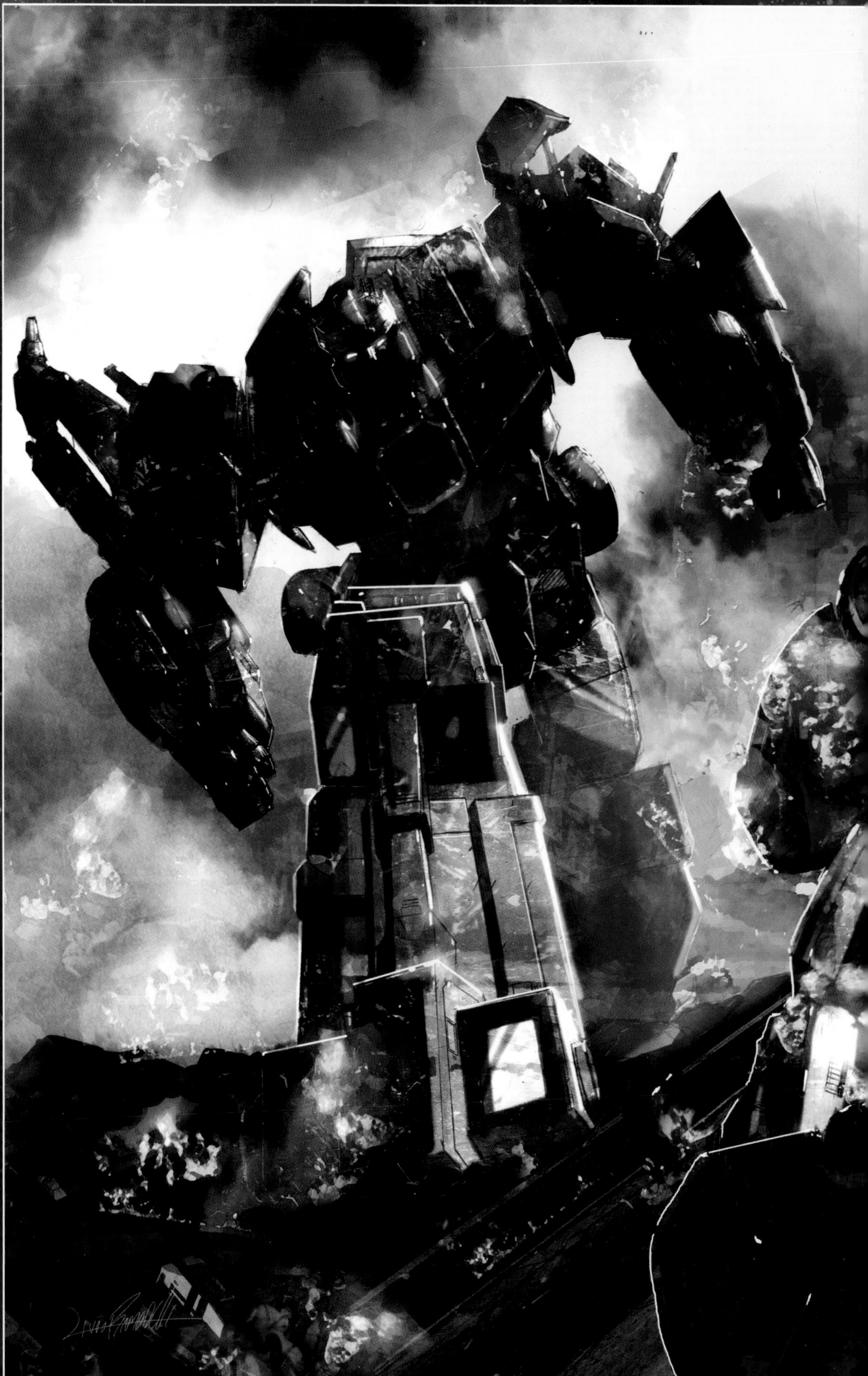

ART BY **CASEY W. COLLER**
COLORS BY **JOANA LAFUENTE**

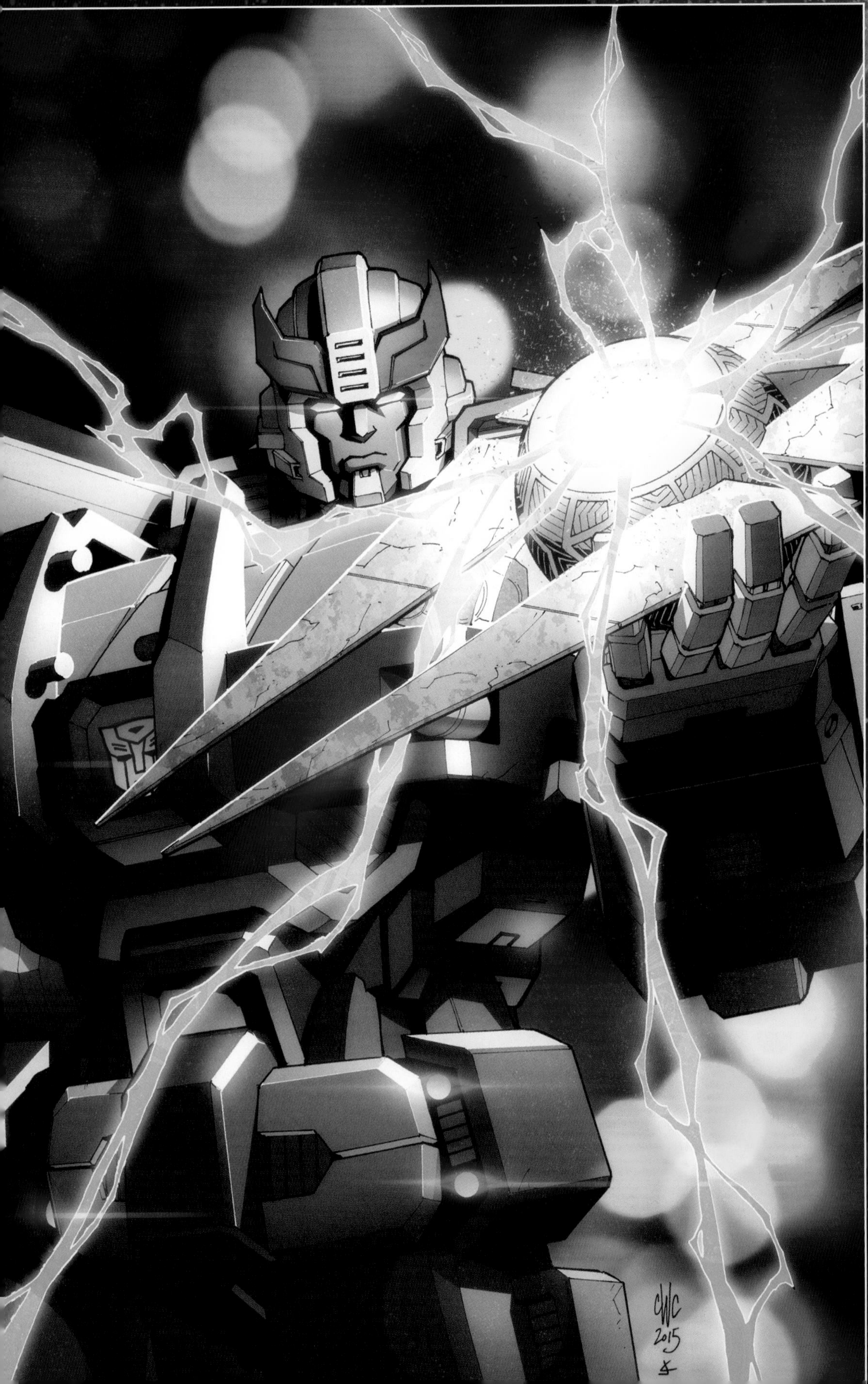

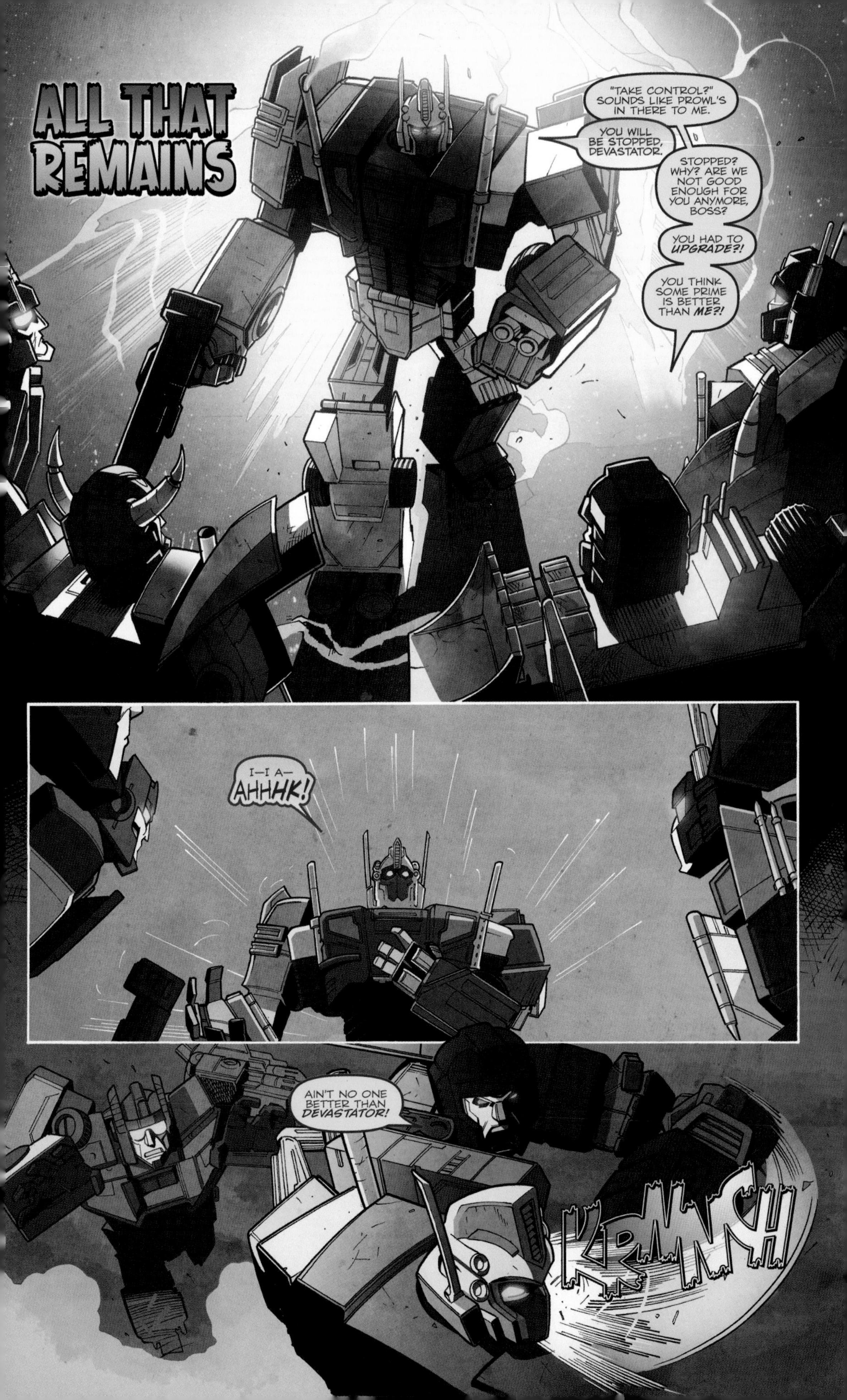
ALL THAT REMAINS
"TAKE CONTROL?" SOUNDS LIKE PROWL'S IN THERE TO ME.
YOU WILL BE STOPPED, DEVASTATOR.
STOPPED? WHY? ARE WE NOT GOOD ENOUGH FOR YOU ANYMORE, BOSS?
YOU HAD TO UPGRADE?!
YOU THINK SOME PRIME IS BETTER THAN ME?!
I—I A— AHHHK!
AIN'T NO ONE BETTER THAN DEVASTATOR!
KRUNCH

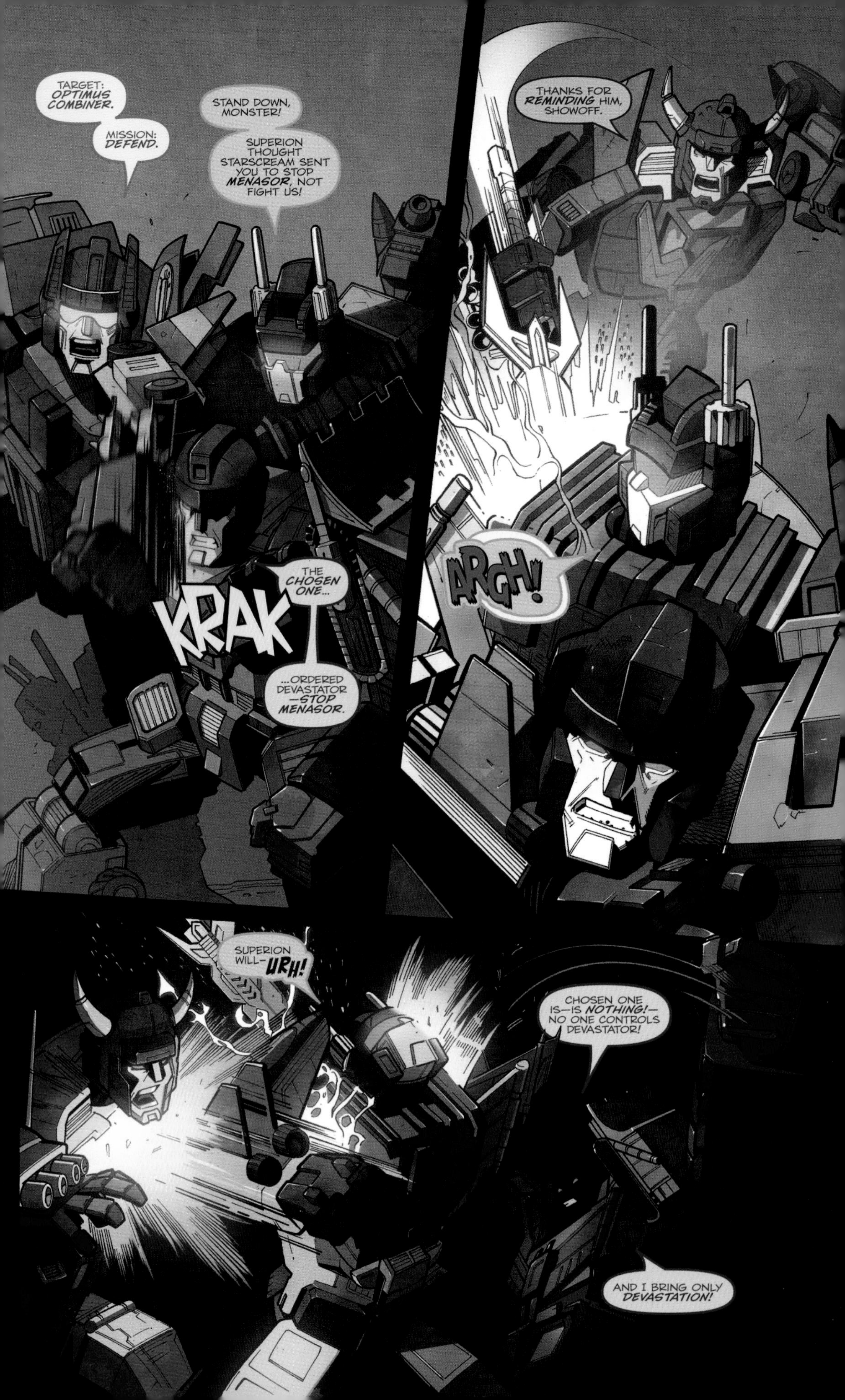
TARGET: OPTIMUS COMBINER.
MISSION: DEFEND.
STAND DOWN, MONSTER!
SUPERION THOUGHT STARSCREAM SENT YOU TO STOP MENASOR, NOT FIGHT US!
KRAK
THE CHOSEN ONE...
...ORDERED DEVASTATOR —STOP MENASOR.
THANKS FOR REMINDING HIM, SHOWOFF.
ARGH!
SUPERION WILL—URH!
CHOSEN ONE IS—IS NOTHING!— NO ONE CONTROLS DEVASTATOR!
AND I BRING ONLY DEVASTATION!

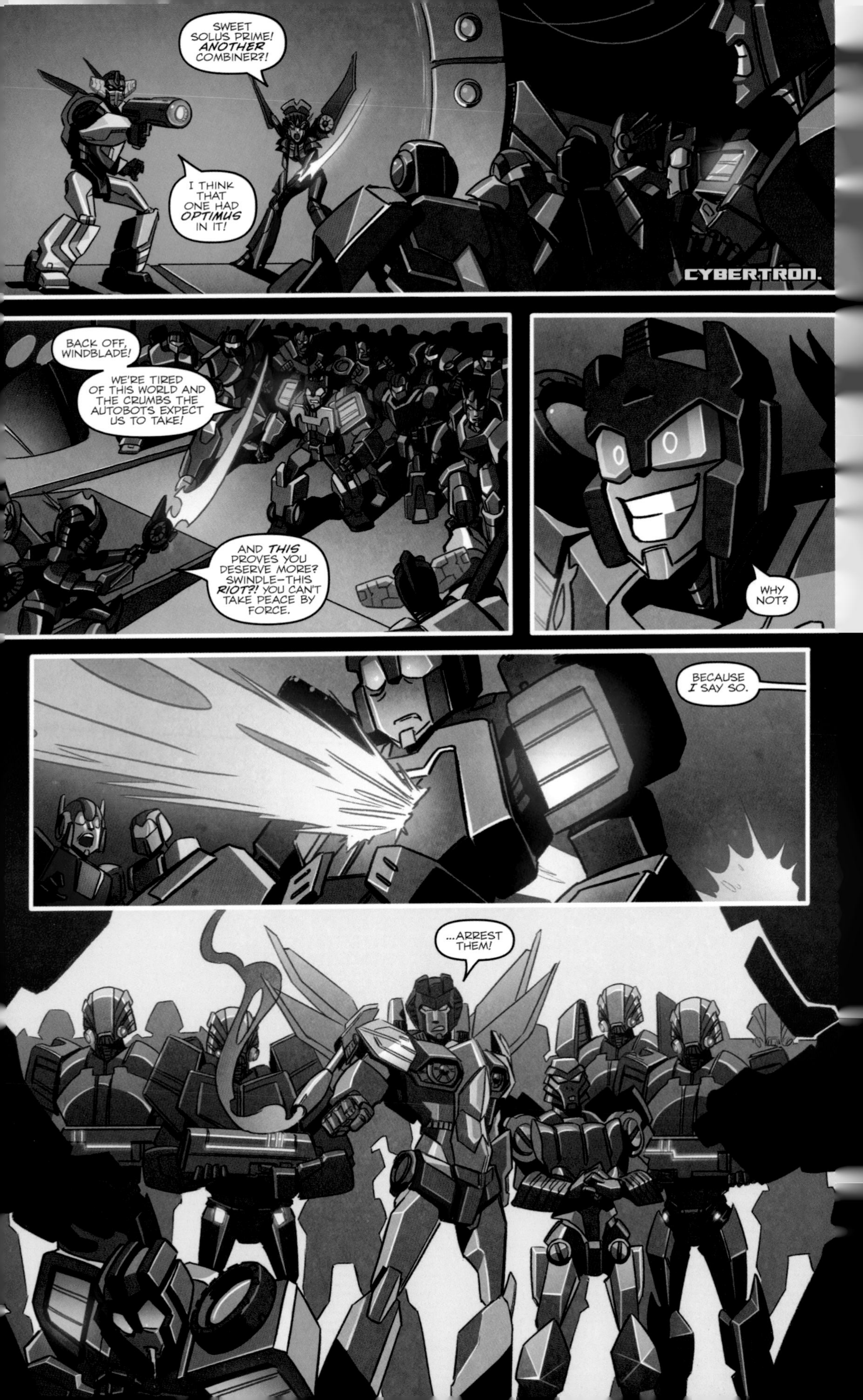
SWEET SOLUS PRIME! ANOTHER COMBINER?!
I THINK THAT ONE HAD OPTIMUS IN IT!
CYBERTRON.
BACK OFF, WINDBLADE!
WE'RE TIRED OF THIS WORLD AND THE CRUMBS THE AUTOBOTS EXPECT US TO TAKE!
AND THIS PROVES YOU DESERVE MORE? SWINDLE—THIS RIOT?! YOU CAN'T TAKE PEACE BY FORCE.
WHY NOT?
BECAUSE I SAY SO.
...ARREST THEM!

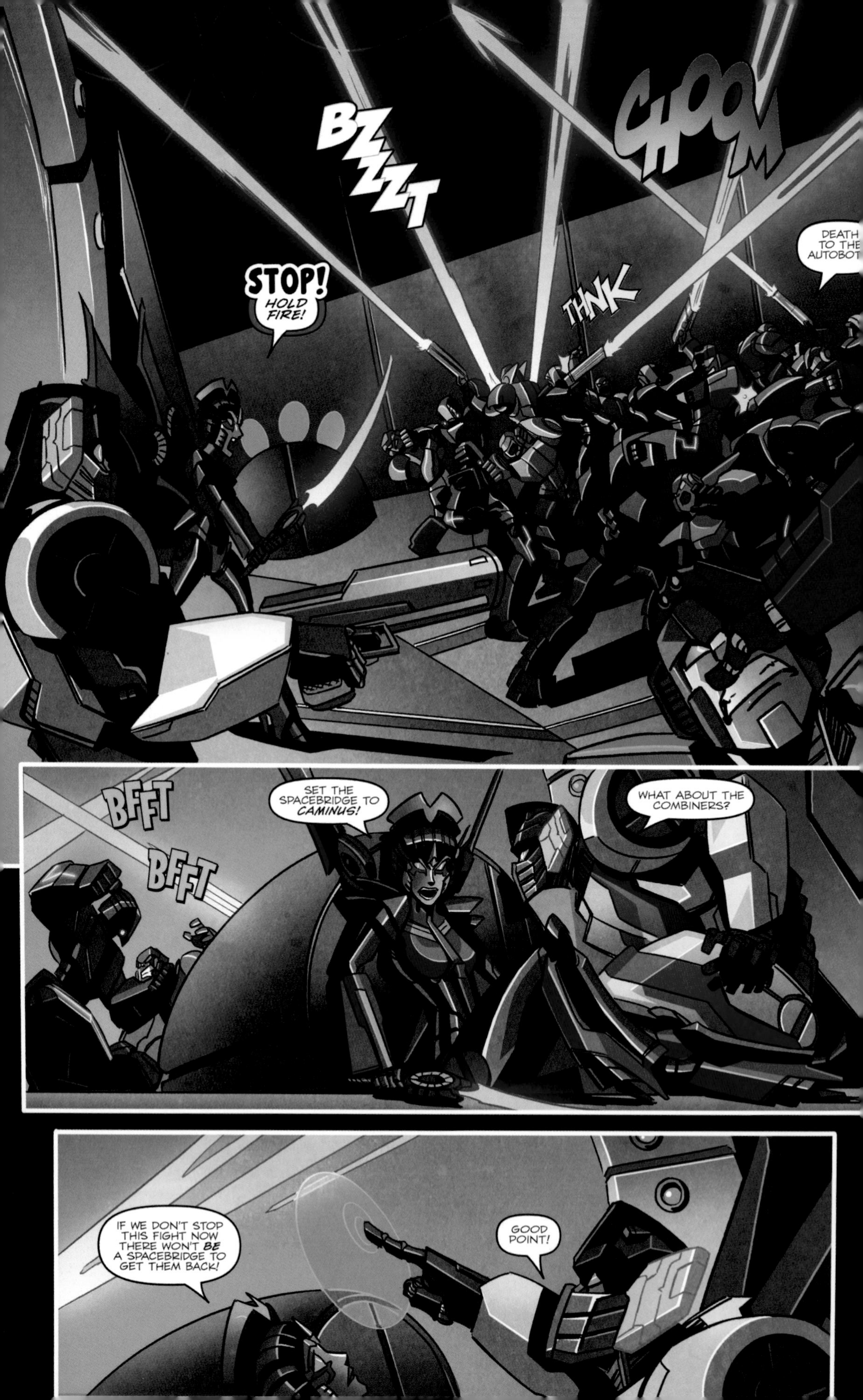
BZZZZT
CHOOM
STOP! HOLD FIRE!
THNK
DEATH TO THE AUTOBOT
BFFT
BFFT
SET THE SPACEBRIDGE TO *CAMINUS!*
WHAT ABOUT THE COMBINERS?
IF WE DON'T STOP THIS FIGHT NOW THERE WON'T *BE* A SPACEBRIDGE TO GET THEM BACK!
GOOD POINT!

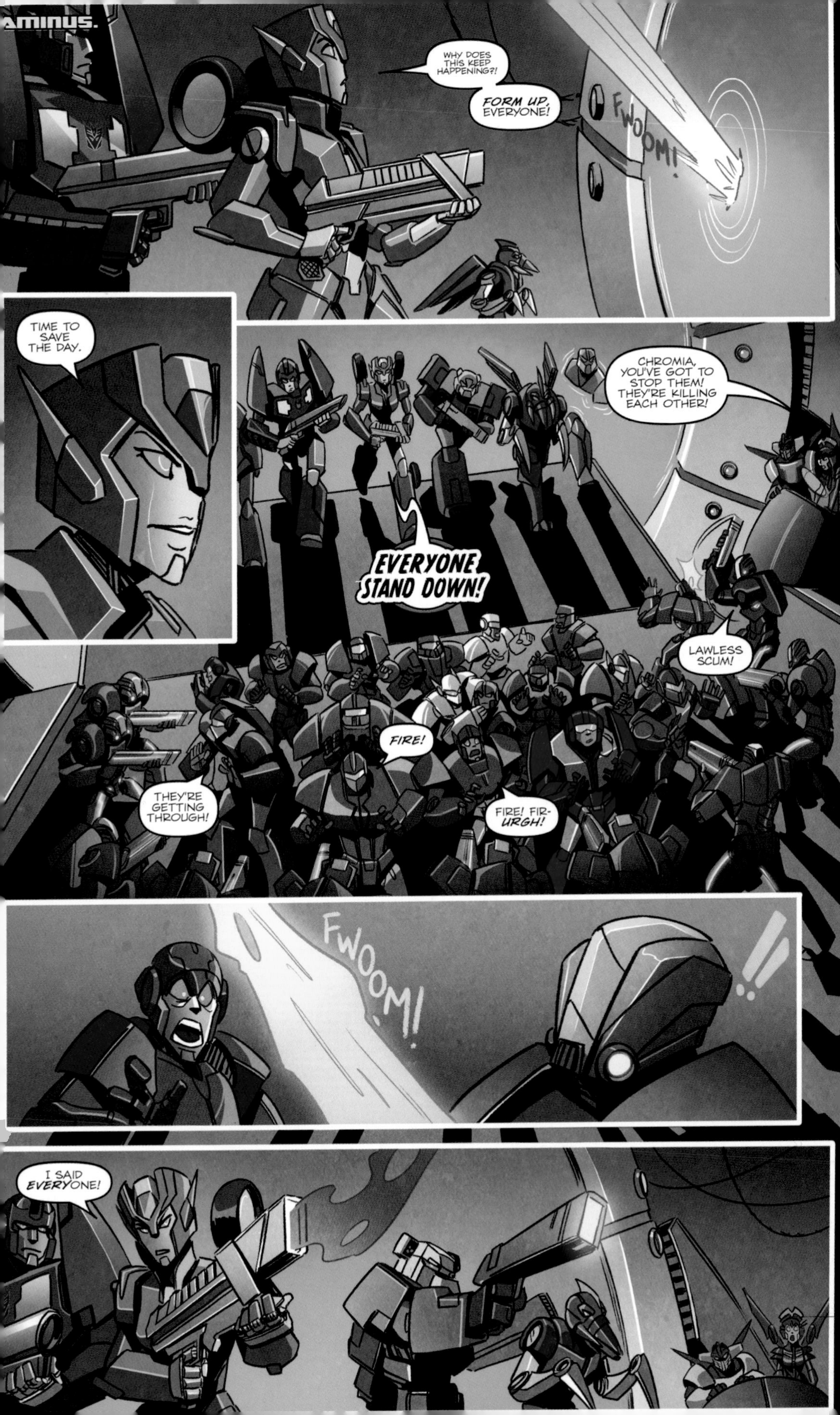
WHY DOES THIS KEEP HAPPENING?!
FORM UP, EVERYONE!
FWOOM!
TIME TO SAVE THE DAY.
CHROMIA, YOU'VE GOT TO STOP THEM! THEY'RE KILLING EACH OTHER!
EVERYONE STAND DOWN!
LAWLESS SCUM!
FIRE!
THEY'RE GETTING THROUGH!
FIRE! FIR-URGH!
FWOOM!
I SAID EVERYONE!

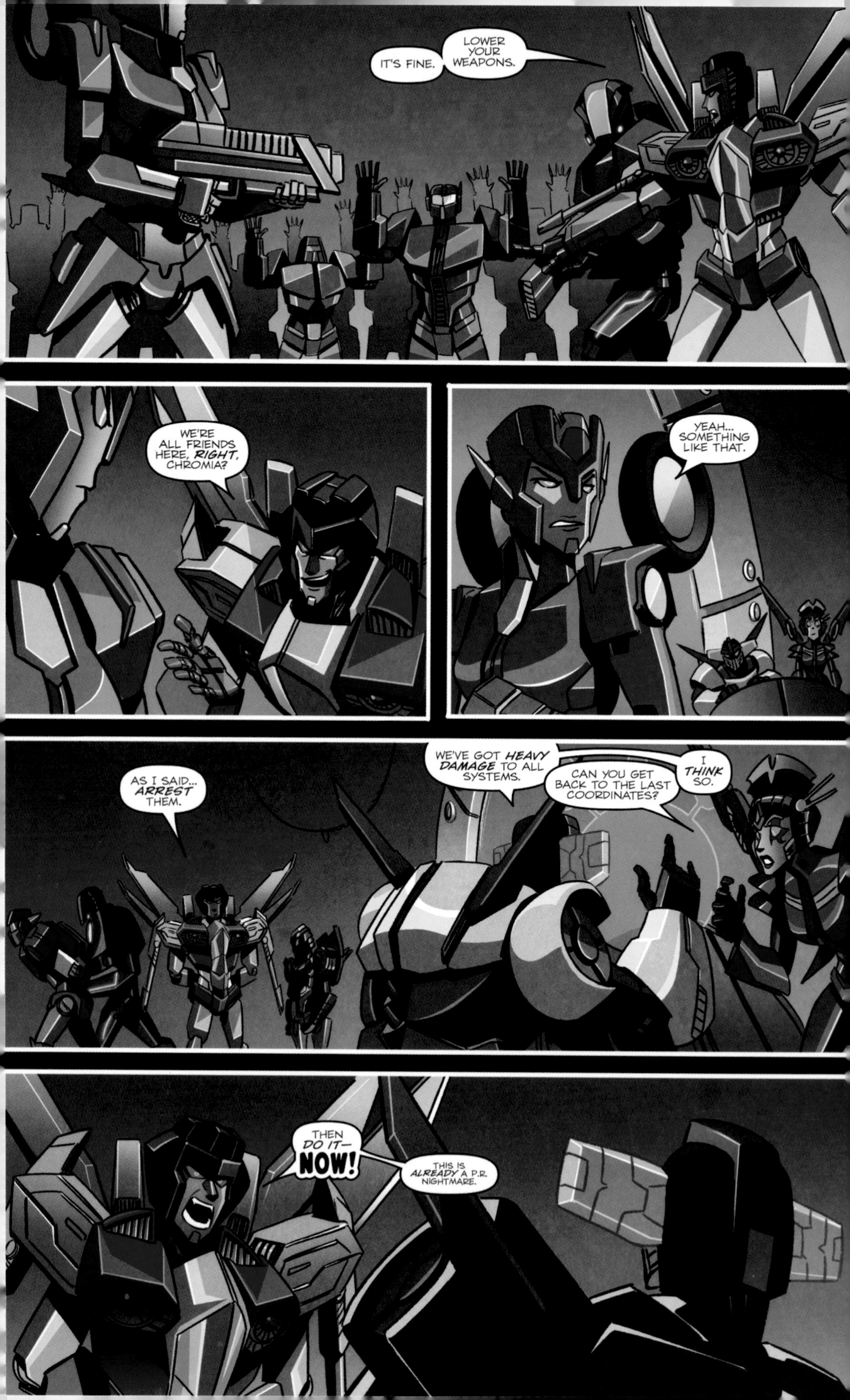
IT'S FINE.
LOWER YOUR WEAPONS.
WE'RE ALL FRIENDS HERE, RIGHT, CHROMIA?
YEAH... SOMETHING LIKE THAT.
AS I SAID... ARREST THEM.
WE'VE GOT HEAVY DAMAGE TO ALL SYSTEMS.
CAN YOU GET BACK TO THE LAST COORDINATES?
I THINK SO.
THEN DO IT— NOW!
THIS IS ALREADY A P.R. NIGHTMARE.

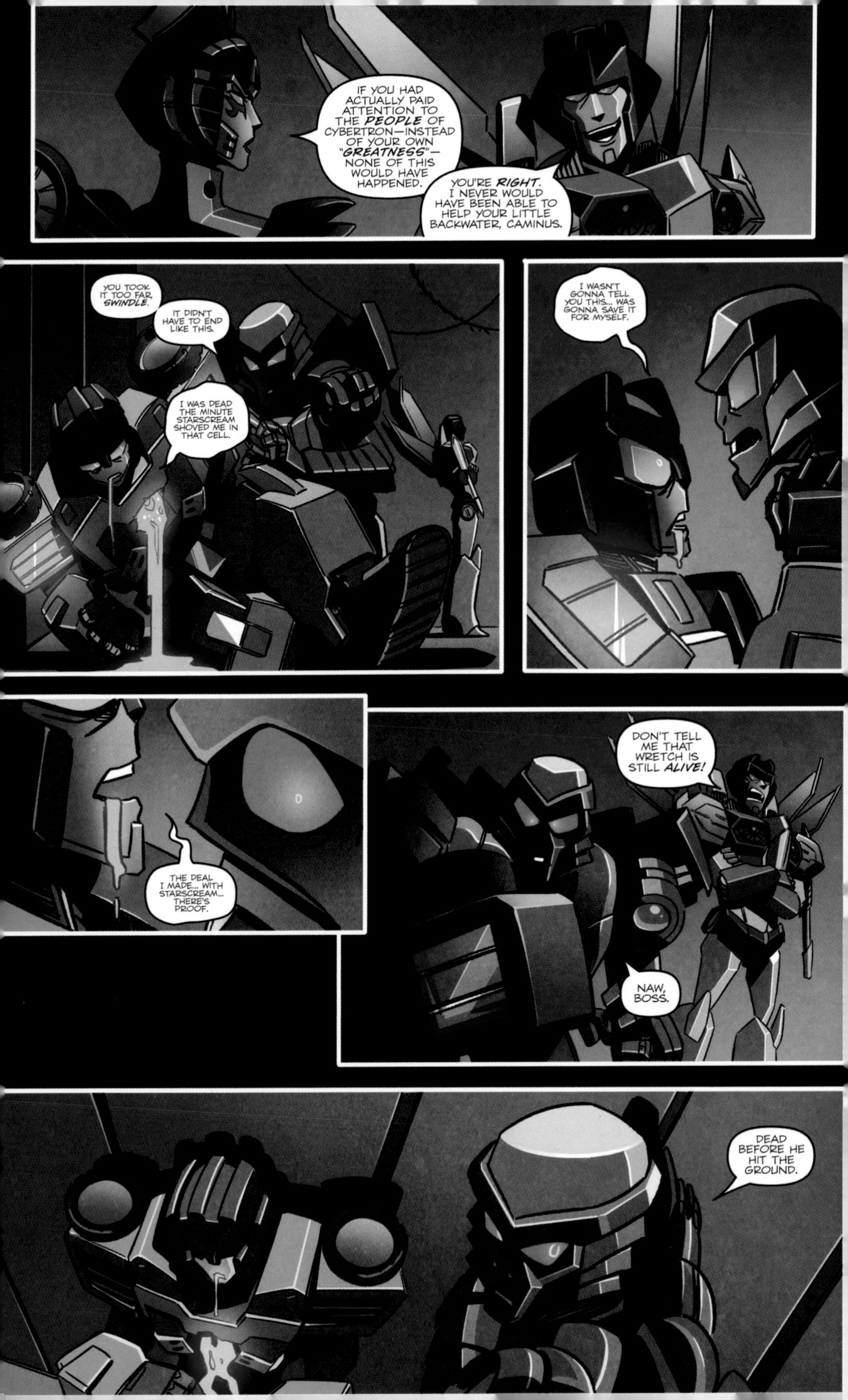
IF YOU HAD ACTUALLY PAID ATTENTION TO THE PEOPLE OF CYBERTRON—INSTEAD OF YOUR OWN "GREATNESS"—NONE OF THIS WOULD HAVE HAPPENED.
YOU'RE RIGHT. I NEVER WOULD HAVE BEEN ABLE TO HELP YOUR LITTLE BACKWATER, CAMINUS.
YOU TOOK IT TOO FAR, SWINDLE.
IT DIDN'T HAVE TO END LIKE THIS.
I WAS DEAD THE MINUTE STARSCREAM SHOVED ME IN THAT CELL.
I WASN'T GONNA TELL YOU THIS... WAS GONNA SAVE IT FOR MYSELF.
THE DEAL I MADE... WITH STARSCREAM... THERE'S PROOF.
DON'T TELL ME THAT WRETCH IS STILL ALIVE!
NAW, BOSS.
DEAD BEFORE HE HIT THE GROUND.

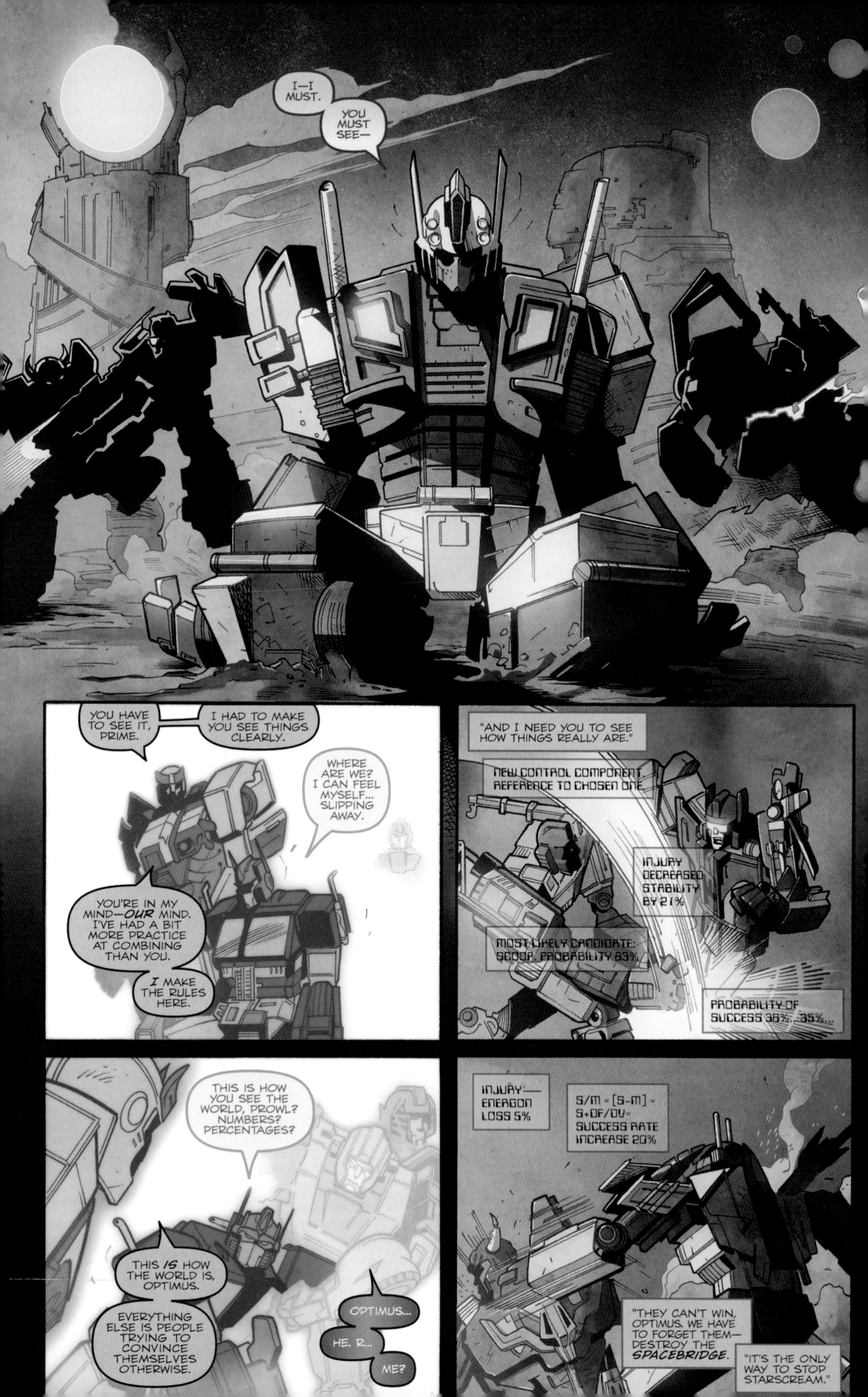
I—I MUST.
YOU MUST SEE—
YOU HAVE TO SEE IT, PRIME.
I HAD TO MAKE YOU SEE THINGS CLEARLY.
WHERE ARE WE? I CAN FEEL MYSELF... SLIPPING AWAY.
YOU'RE IN MY MIND—*OUR* MIND. I'VE HAD A BIT MORE PRACTICE AT COMBINING THAN YOU.
I MAKE THE RULES HERE.
"AND I NEED YOU TO SEE HOW THINGS REALLY ARE."
NEW CONTROL COMPONENT. REFERENCE TO CHOSEN ONE.
INJURY DECREASED STABILITY BY 21%
MOST LIKELY CANDIDATE: SCOOP. PROBABILITY 63%
PROBABILITY OF SUCCESS 36%...35%...
THIS IS HOW YOU SEE THE WORLD, PROWL? NUMBERS? PERCENTAGES?
THIS *IS* HOW THE WORLD IS, OPTIMUS.
EVERYTHING ELSE IS PEOPLE TRYING TO CONVINCE THEMSELVES OTHERWISE.
OPTIMUS...
HE. R...
ME?
INJURY— ENERGON LOSS 5%
S/M = [S-M] = S+DF/DV= SUCCESS RATE INCREASE 20%
"THEY CAN'T WIN, OPTIMUS. WE HAVE TO FORGET THEM— DESTROY THE *SPACEBRIDGE*.
"IT'S THE ONLY WAY TO STOP STARSCREAM."

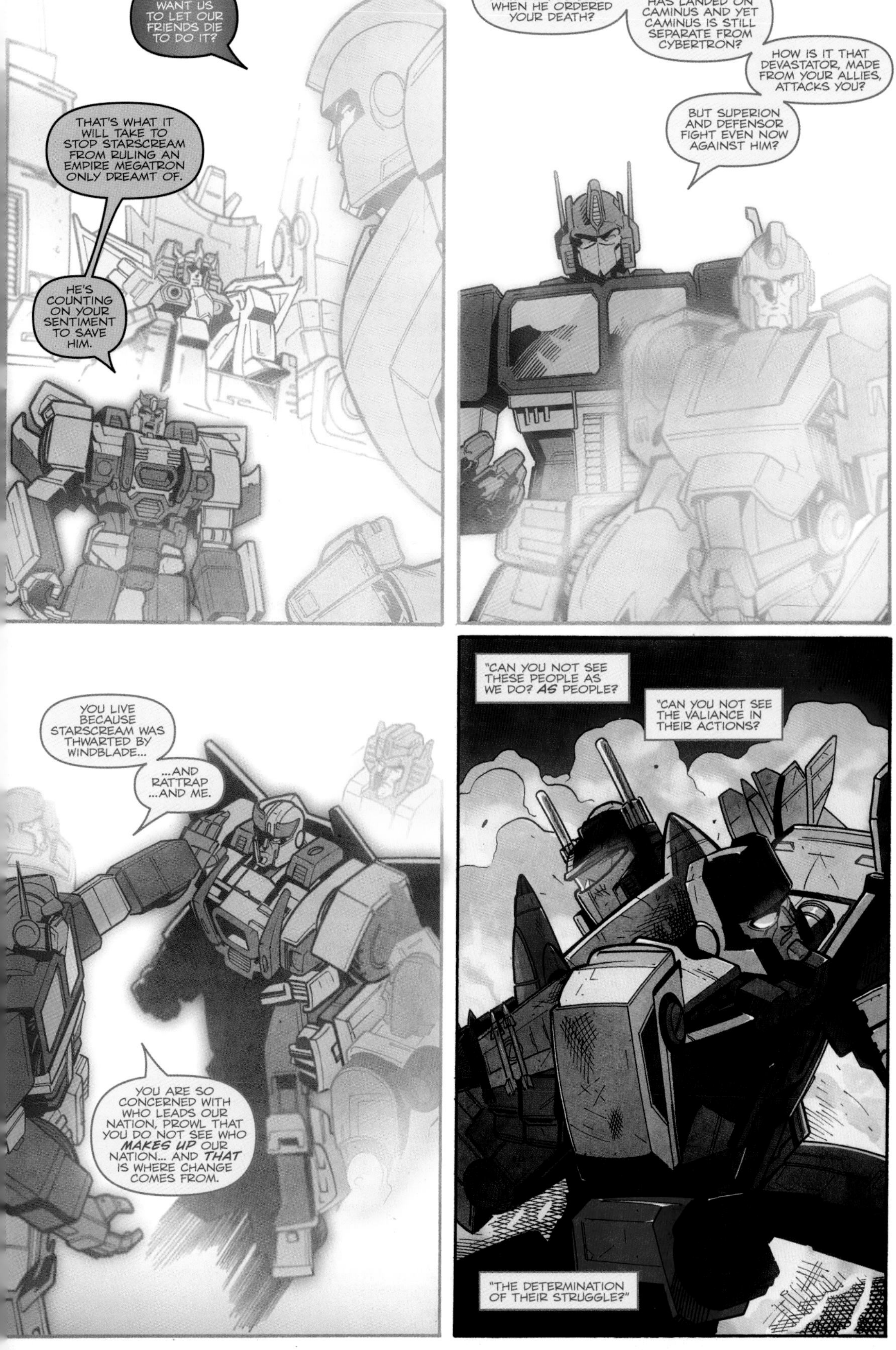
AND YOU WANT US TO LET OUR FRIENDS DIE TO DO IT?
THAT'S WHAT IT WILL TAKE TO STOP STARSCREAM FROM RULING AN EMPIRE MEGATRON ONLY DREAMT OF.
HE'S COUNTING ON YOUR SENTIMENT TO SAVE HIM.
IF STARSCREAM HAS SUCH AN IRON GRIP ON CYBERTRON HOW DO YOU LIVE— WHEN HE ORDERED YOUR DEATH?
HOW IS THAT HE HAS LANDED ON CAMINUS AND YET CAMINUS IS STILL SEPARATE FROM CYBERTRON?
HOW IS IT THAT DEVASTATOR, MADE FROM YOUR ALLIES, ATTACKS YOU?
BUT SUPERION AND DEFENSOR FIGHT EVEN NOW AGAINST HIM?
YOU LIVE BECAUSE STARSCREAM WAS THWARTED BY WINDBLADE...
...AND RATTRAP ...AND ME.
YOU ARE SO CONCERNED WITH WHO LEADS OUR NATION, PROWL THAT YOU DO NOT SEE WHO MAKES UP OUR NATION... AND THAT IS WHERE CHANGE COMES FROM.
"CAN YOU NOT SEE THESE PEOPLE AS WE DO? AS PEOPLE?
"CAN YOU NOT SEE THE VALIANCE IN THEIR ACTIONS?
"THE DETERMINATION OF THEIR STRUGGLE?"

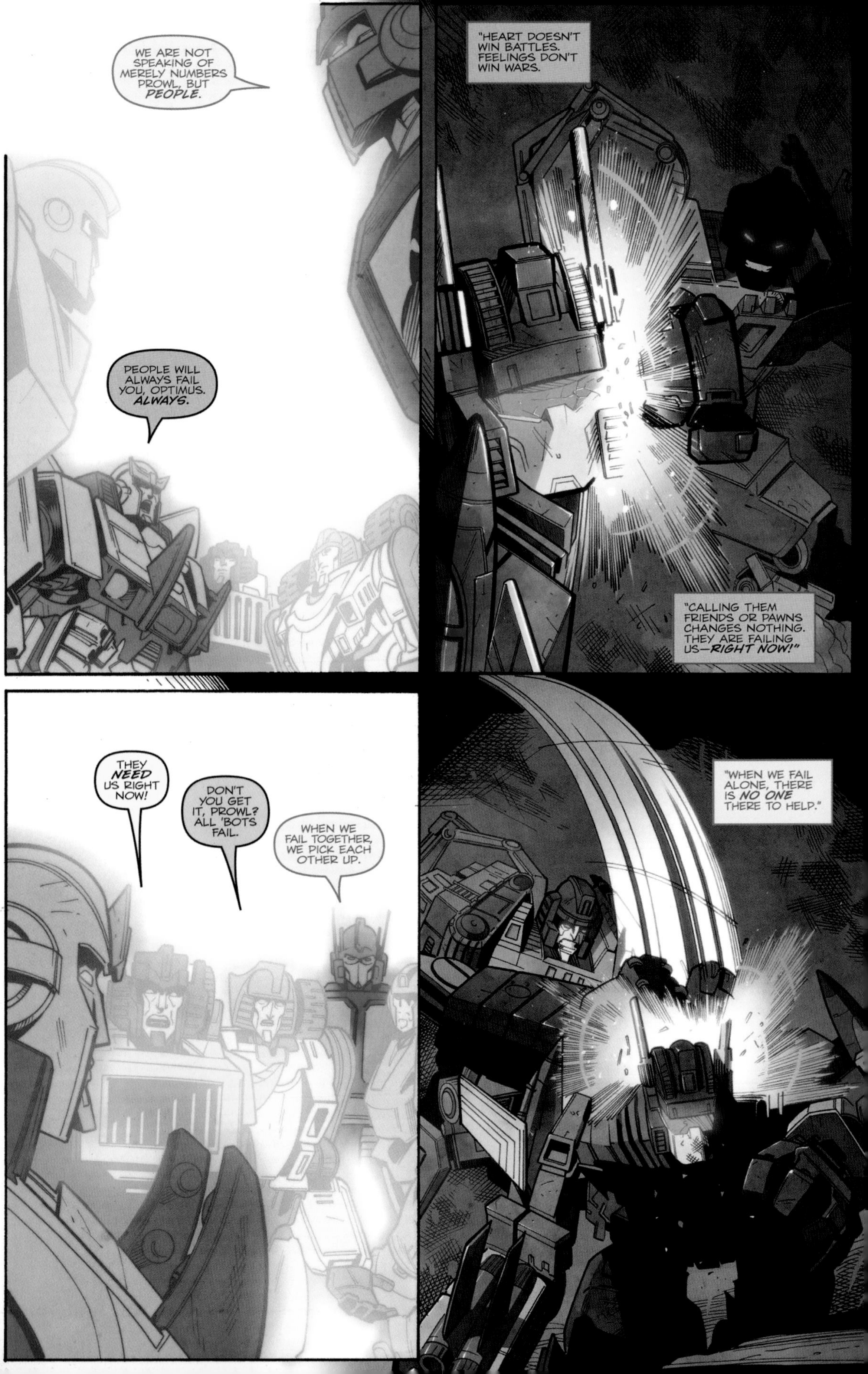
WE ARE NOT SPEAKING OF MERELY NUMBERS PROWL, BUT *PEOPLE*.
"HEART DOESN'T WIN BATTLES. FEELINGS DON'T WIN WARS.
PEOPLE WILL ALWAYS FAIL YOU, OPTIMUS. *ALWAYS*.
"CALLING THEM FRIENDS OR PAWNS CHANGES NOTHING. THEY ARE FAILING US—*RIGHT NOW!*"
THEY *NEED* US RIGHT NOW!
DON'T YOU GET IT, PROWL? ALL 'BOTS FAIL.
WHEN WE FAIL TOGETHER, WE PICK EACH OTHER UP.
"WHEN WE FAIL ALONE, THERE IS *NO ONE* THERE TO HELP."

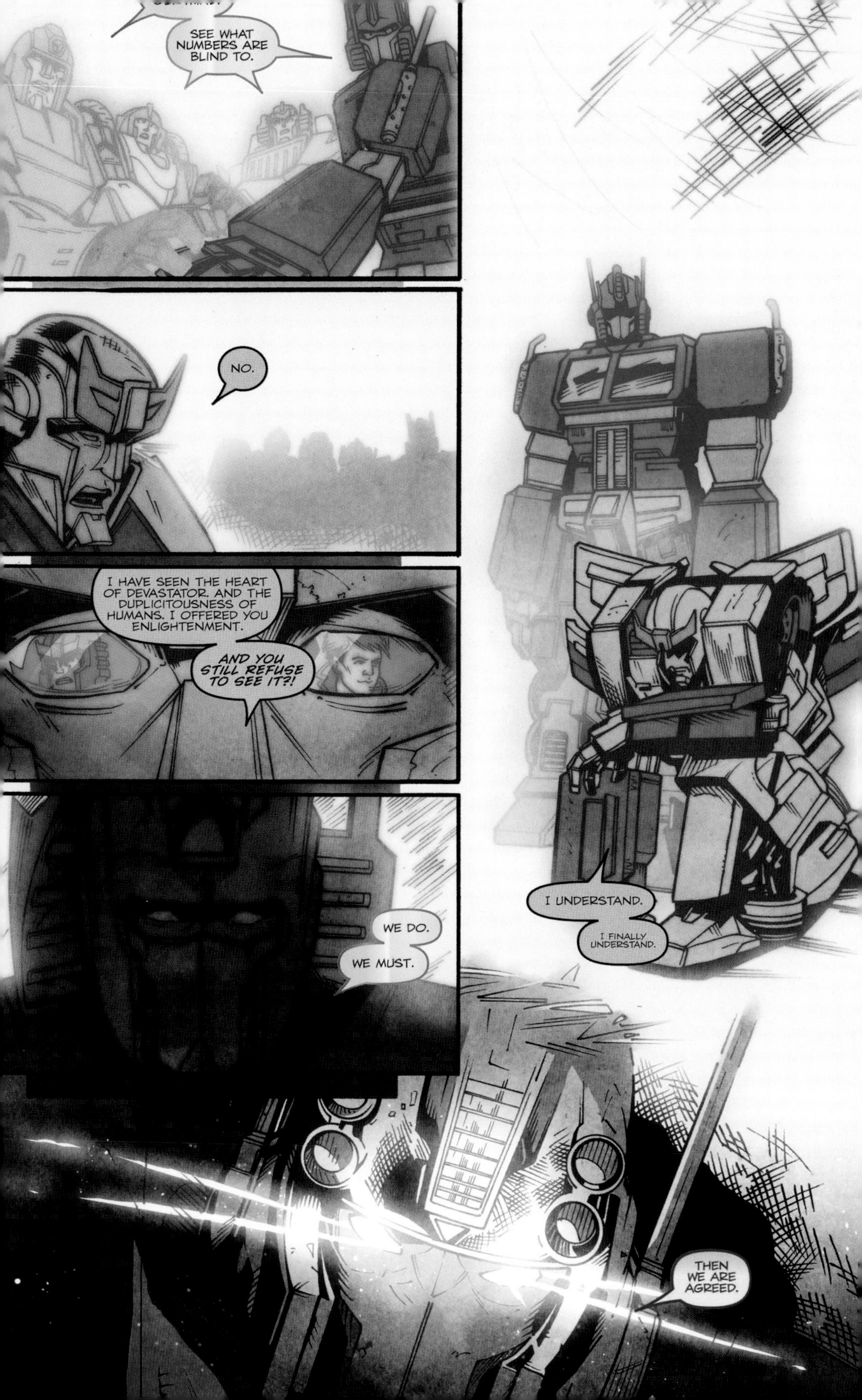
SEE WHAT NUMBERS ARE BLIND TO.
NO.
I HAVE SEEN THE HEART OF DEVASTATOR. AND THE DUPLICITOUSNESS OF HUMANS. I OFFERED YOU ENLIGHTENMENT.
AND YOU STILL REFUSE TO SEE IT?!
WE DO.
WE MUST.
I UNDERSTAND.
I FINALLY UNDERSTAND.
THEN WE ARE AGREED.

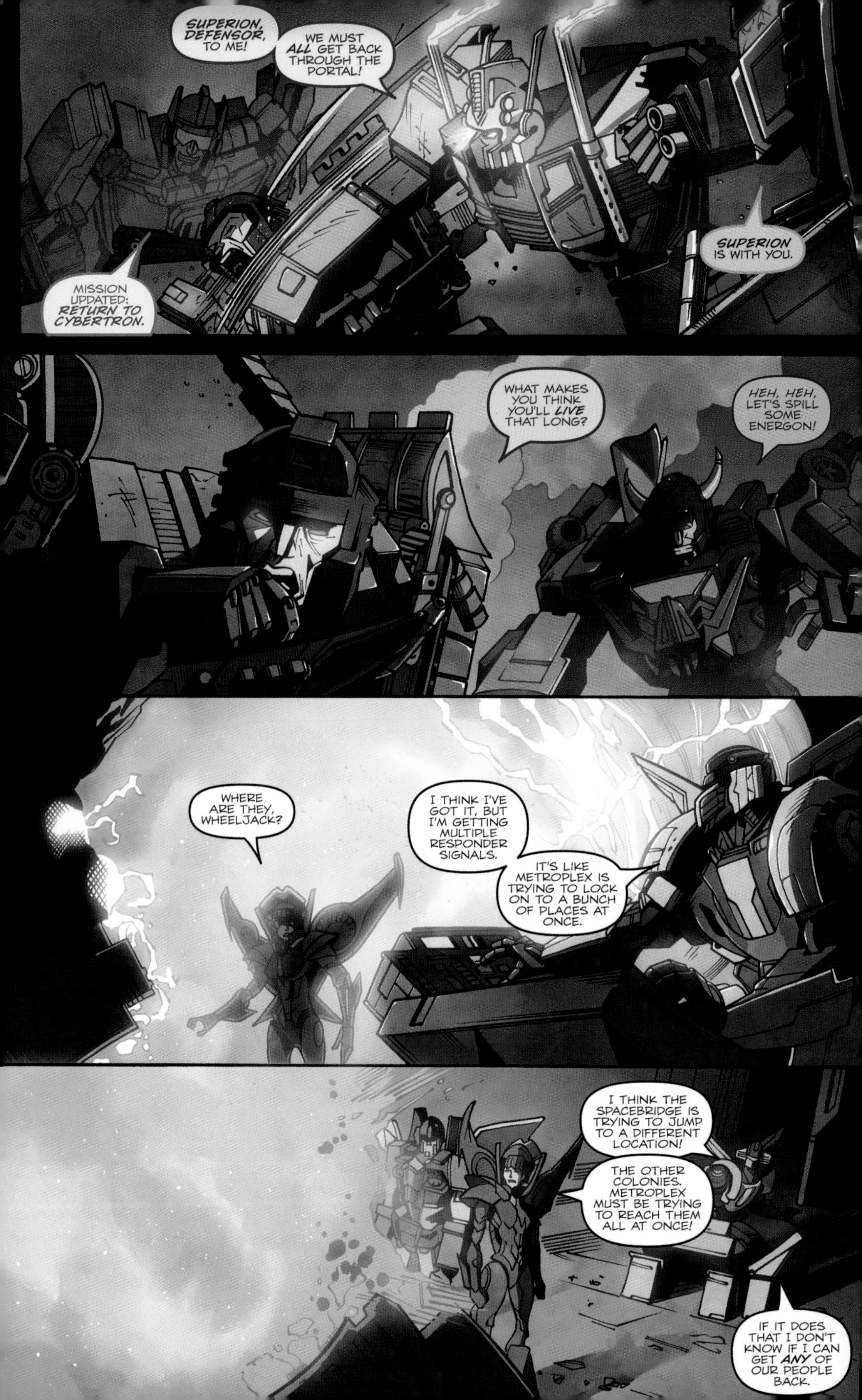
SUPERION, DEFENSOR, TO ME!
WE MUST ALL GET BACK THROUGH THE PORTAL!
SUPERION IS WITH YOU.
MISSION UPDATED: RETURN TO CYBERTRON.
WHAT MAKES YOU THINK YOU'LL LIVE THAT LONG?
HEH, HEH, LET'S SPILL SOME ENERGON!
WHERE ARE THEY, WHEELJACK?
I THINK I'VE GOT IT, BUT I'M GETTING MULTIPLE RESPONDER SIGNALS.
IT'S LIKE METROPLEX IS TRYING TO LOCK ON TO A BUNCH OF PLACES AT ONCE.
I THINK THE SPACEBRIDGE IS TRYING TO JUMP TO A DIFFERENT LOCATION!
THE OTHER COLONIES. METROPLEX MUST BE TRYING TO REACH THEM ALL AT ONCE!
IF IT DOES THAT I DON'T KNOW IF I CAN GET ANY OF OUR PEOPLE BACK.

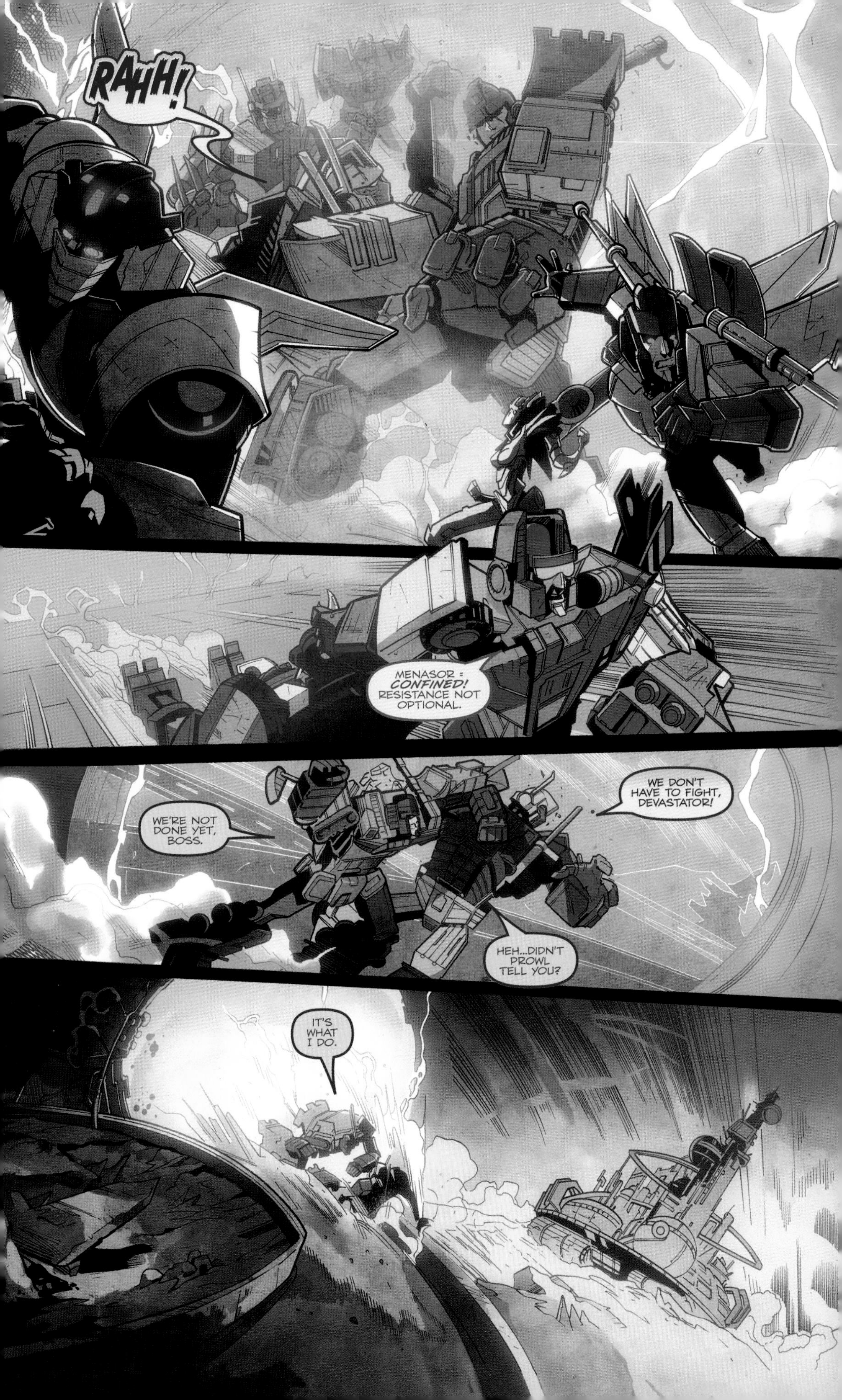
RAHH!
MENASOR : CONFINED! RESISTANCE NOT OPTIONAL.
WE'RE NOT DONE YET, BOSS.
WE DON'T HAVE TO FIGHT, DEVASTATOR!
HEH...DIDN'T PROWL TELL YOU?
IT'S WHAT I DO.

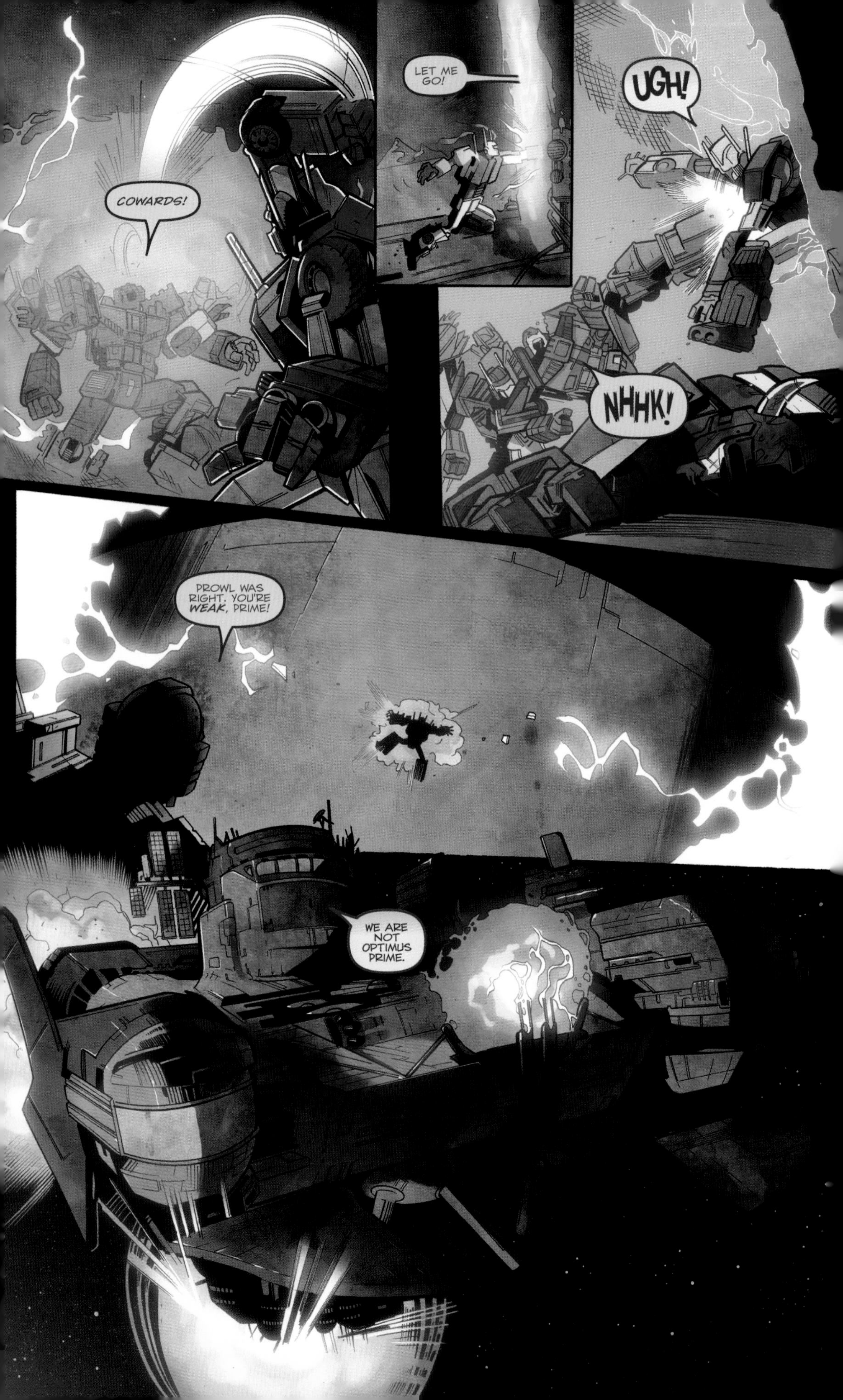

COWARDS!
LET ME GO!
UGH!
NHHK!
PROWL WAS RIGHT. YOU'RE *WEAK*, PRIME!
WE ARE NOT OPTIMUS PRIME.

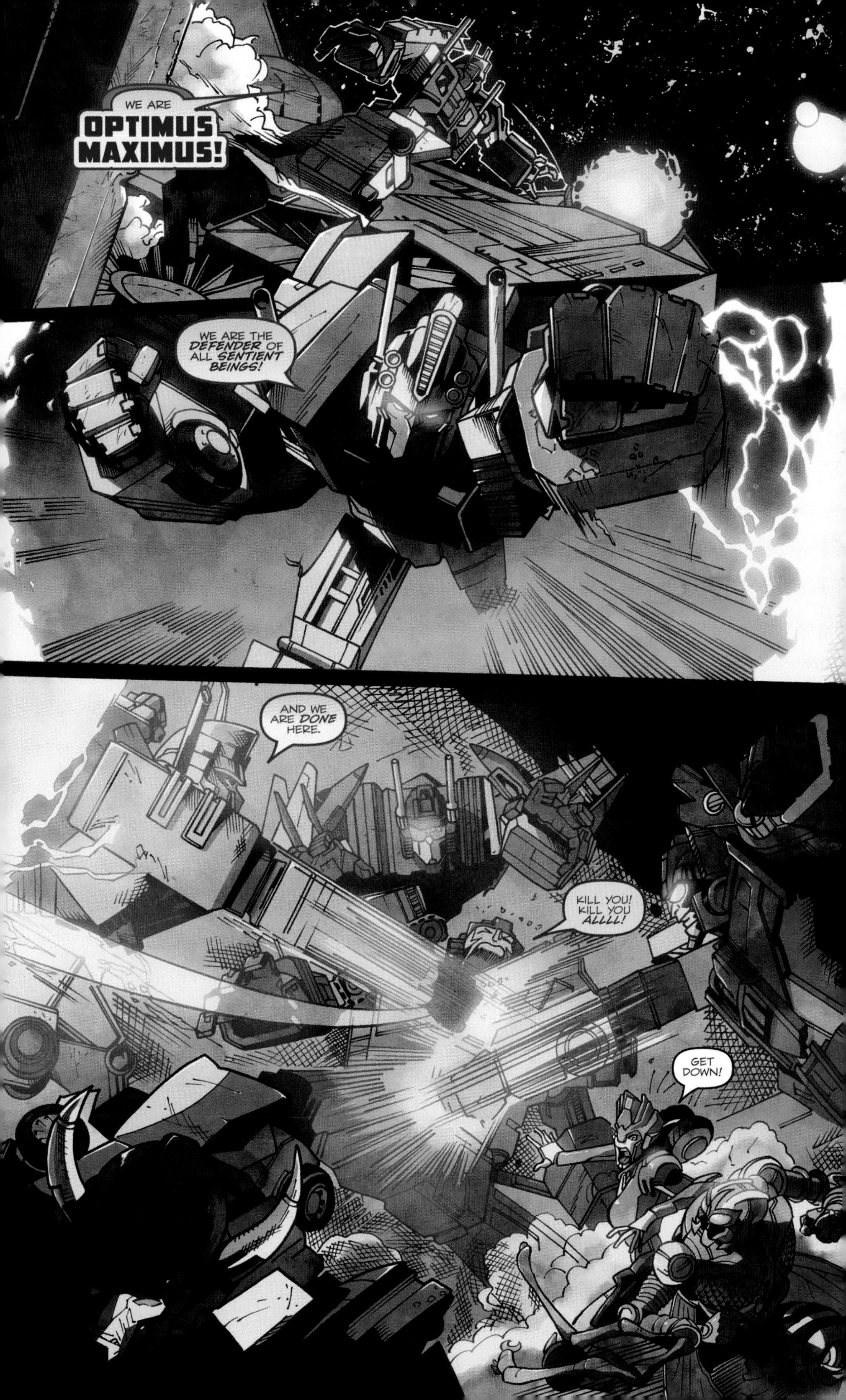
WE ARE
OPTIMUS MAXIMUS!
WE ARE THE DEFENDER OF ALL SENTIENT BEINGS!
AND WE ARE DONE HERE.
KILL YOU! KILL YOU ALLLL!
GET DOWN!

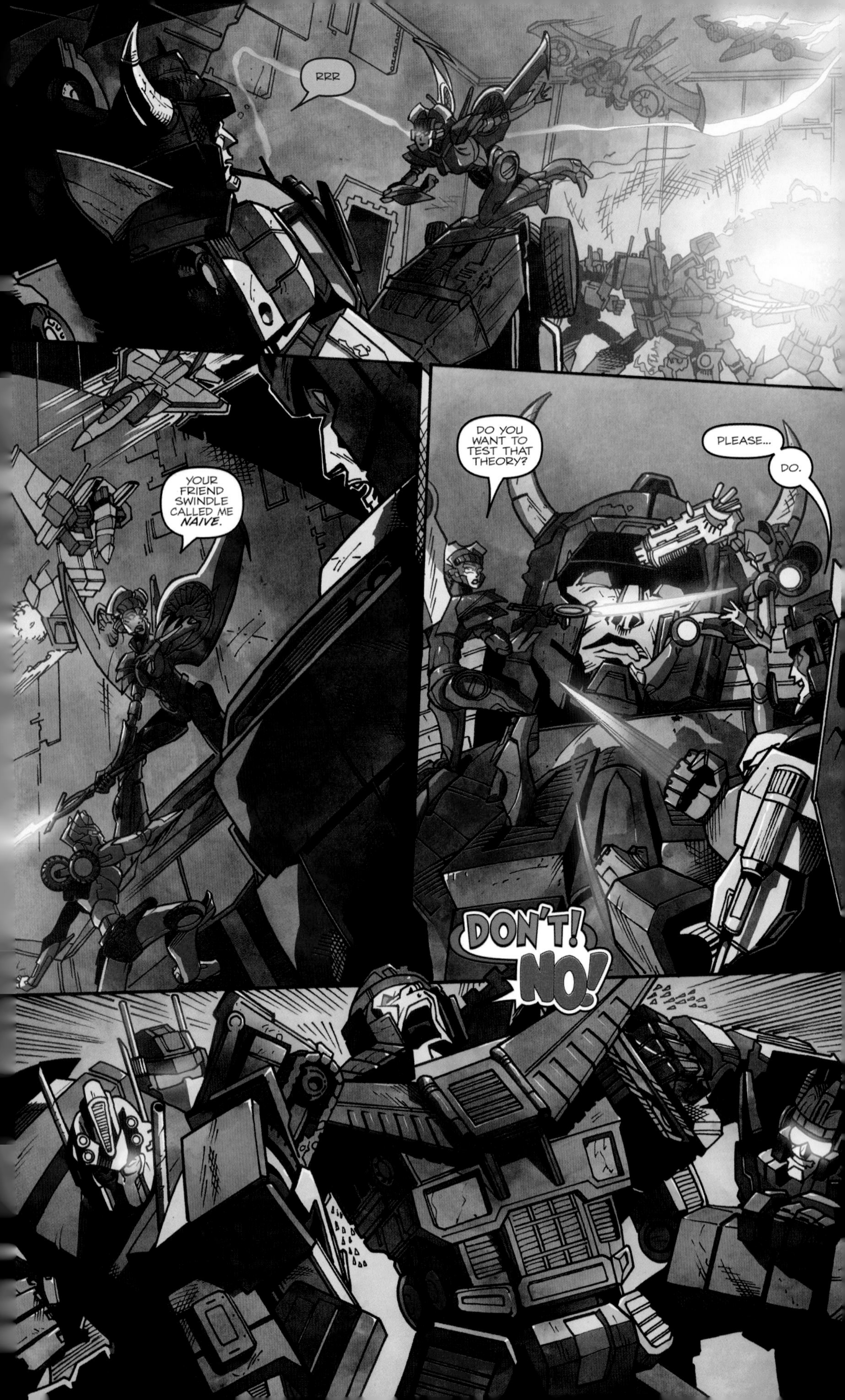
RRR
YOUR FRIEND SWINDLE CALLED ME *NAIVE*.
DO YOU WANT TO TEST THAT THEORY?
PLEASE...
DO.
DON'T!
NO!

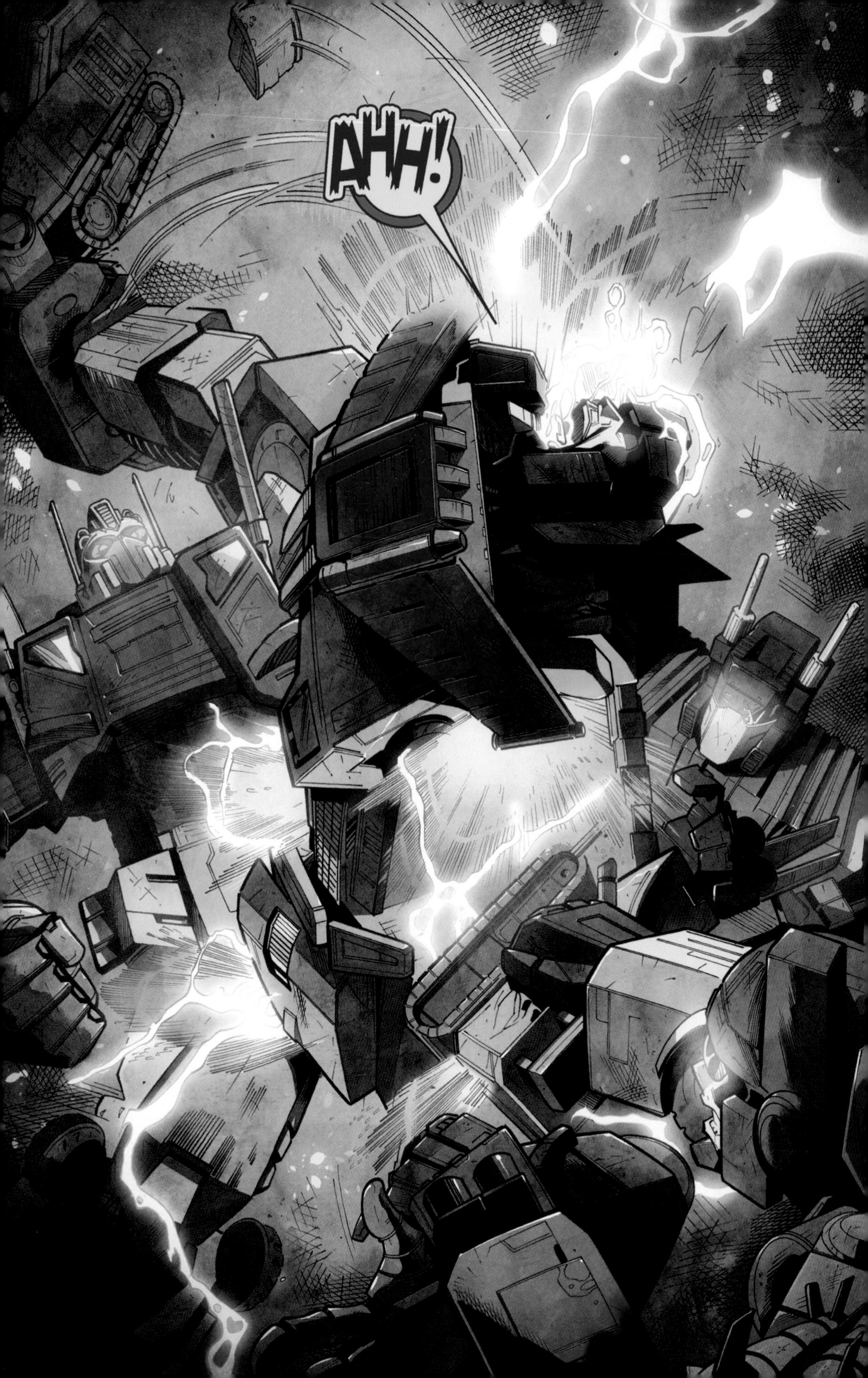
AHH!

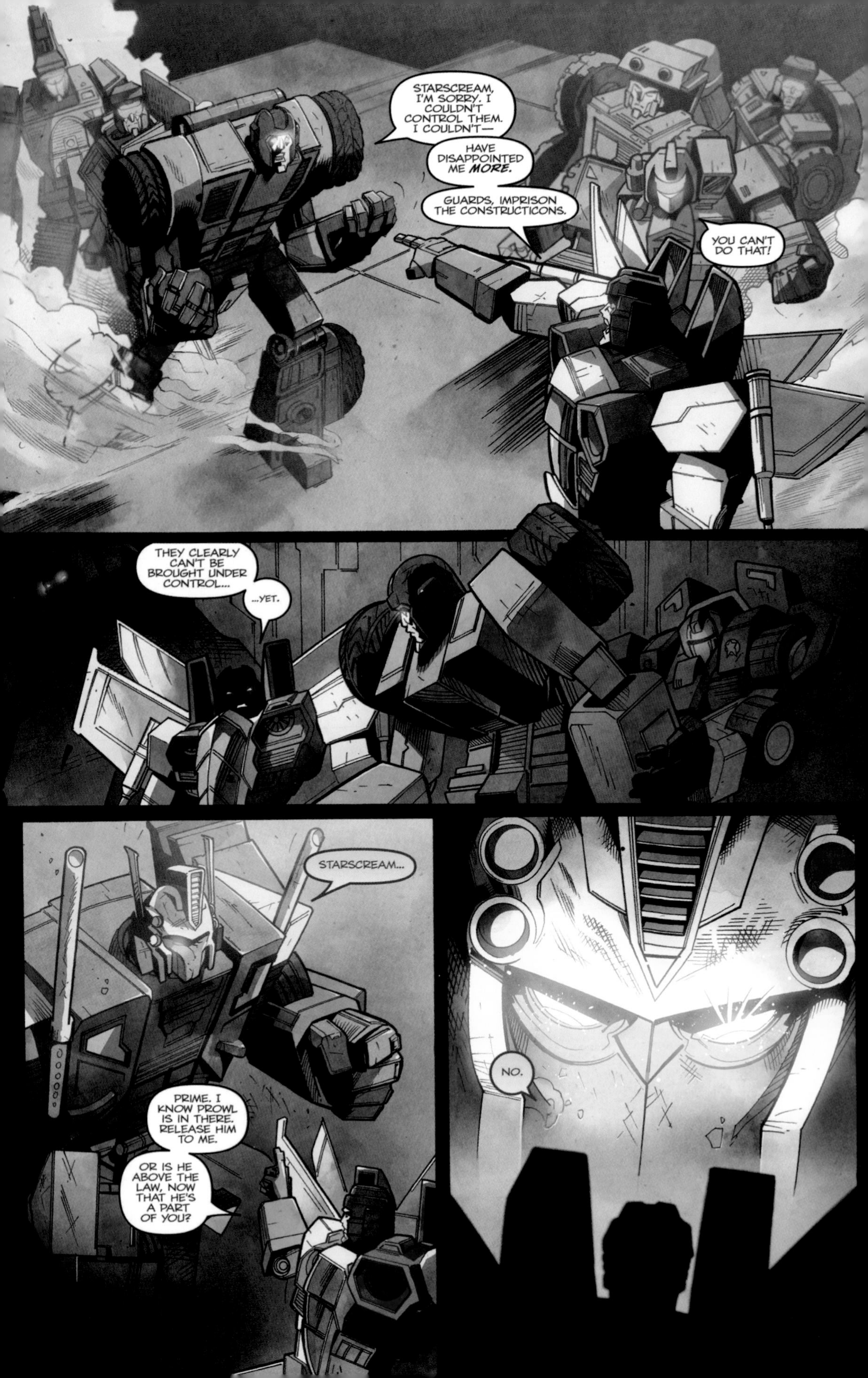
STARSCREAM, I'M SORRY. I COULDN'T CONTROL THEM. I COULDN'T—
HAVE DISAPPOINTED ME *MORE.*
GUARDS, IMPRISON THE CONSTRUCTICONS.
YOU CAN'T DO THAT!
THEY CLEARLY CAN'T BE BROUGHT UNDER CONTROL...
...YET.
STARSCREAM...
PRIME. I KNOW PROWL IS IN THERE. RELEASE HIM TO ME.
OR IS HE ABOVE THE LAW, NOW THAT HE'S A PART OF YOU?
NO.

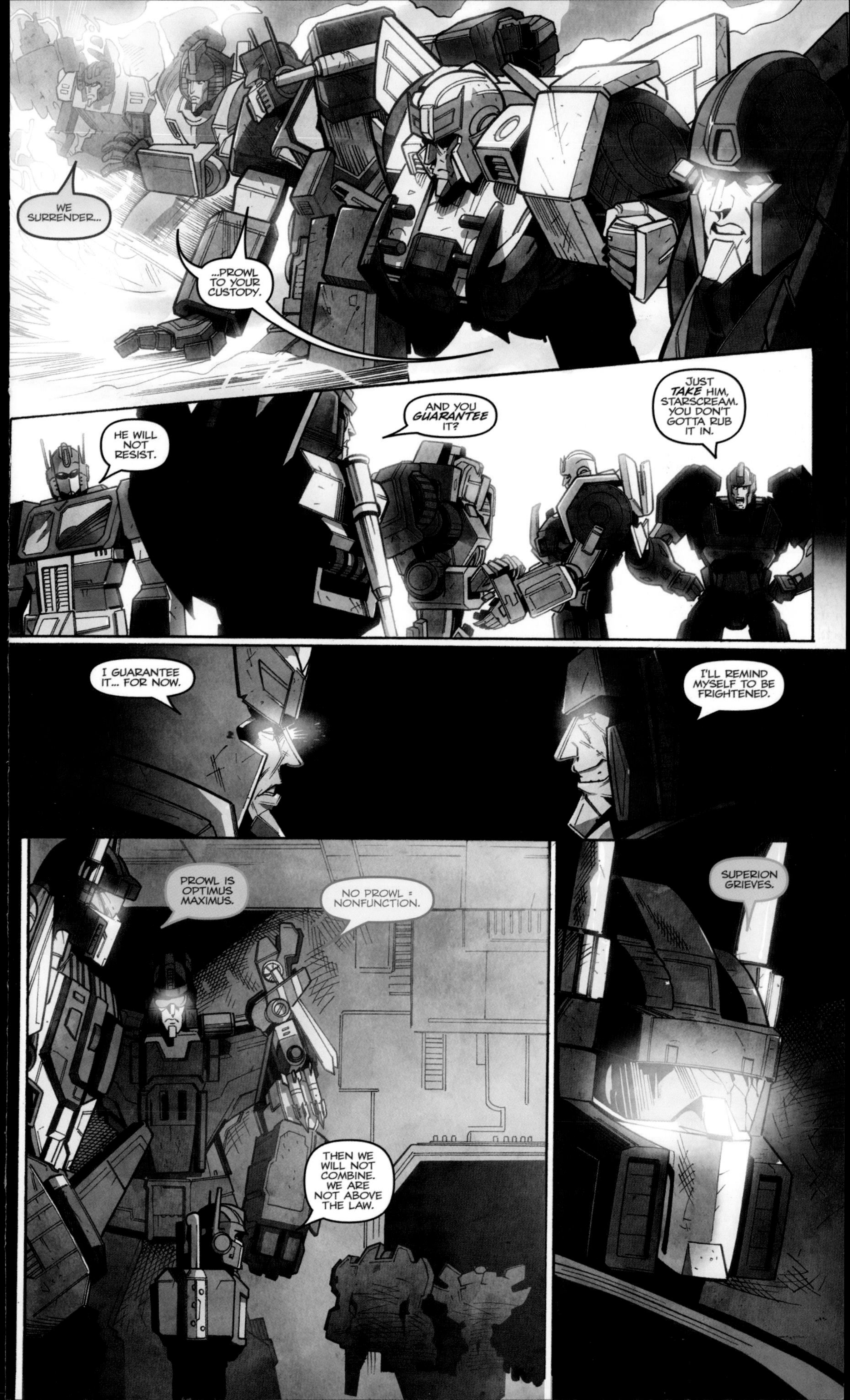
WE SURRENDER...
...PROWL TO YOUR CUSTODY.
HE WILL NOT RESIST.
AND YOU GUARANTEE IT?
JUST TAKE HIM, STARSCREAM. YOU DON'T GOTTA RUB IT IN.
I GUARANTEE IT... FOR NOW.
I'LL REMIND MYSELF TO BE FRIGHTENED.
PROWL IS OPTIMUS MAXIMUS.
NO PROWL = NONFUNCTION.
THEN WE WILL NOT COMBINE. WE ARE NOT ABOVE THE LAW.
SUPERION GRIEVES.

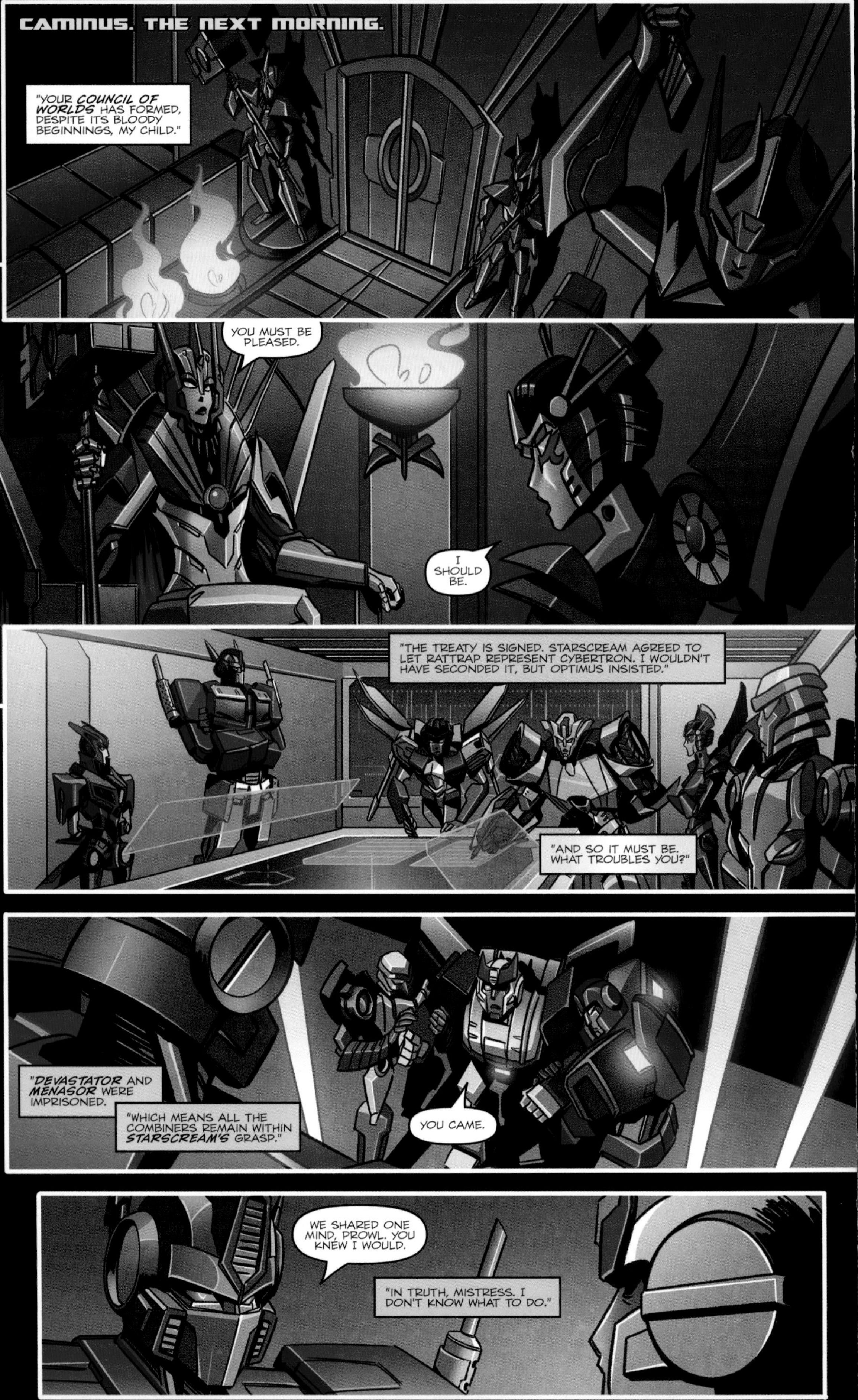
CAMINUS. THE NEXT MORNING.
"YOUR COUNCIL OF WORLDS HAS FORMED, DESPITE ITS BLOODY BEGINNINGS, MY CHILD."
YOU MUST BE PLEASED.
I SHOULD BE.
"THE TREATY IS SIGNED. STARSCREAM AGREED TO LET RATTRAP REPRESENT CYBERTRON. I WOULDN'T HAVE SECONDED IT, BUT OPTIMUS INSISTED."
"AND SO IT MUST BE. WHAT TROUBLES YOU?"
"DEVASTATOR AND MENASOR WERE IMPRISONED.
"WHICH MEANS ALL THE COMBINERS REMAIN WITHIN STARSCREAM'S GRASP."
YOU CAME.
WE SHARED ONE MIND, PROWL. YOU KNEW I WOULD.
"IN TRUTH, MISTRESS. I DON'T KNOW WHAT TO DO."

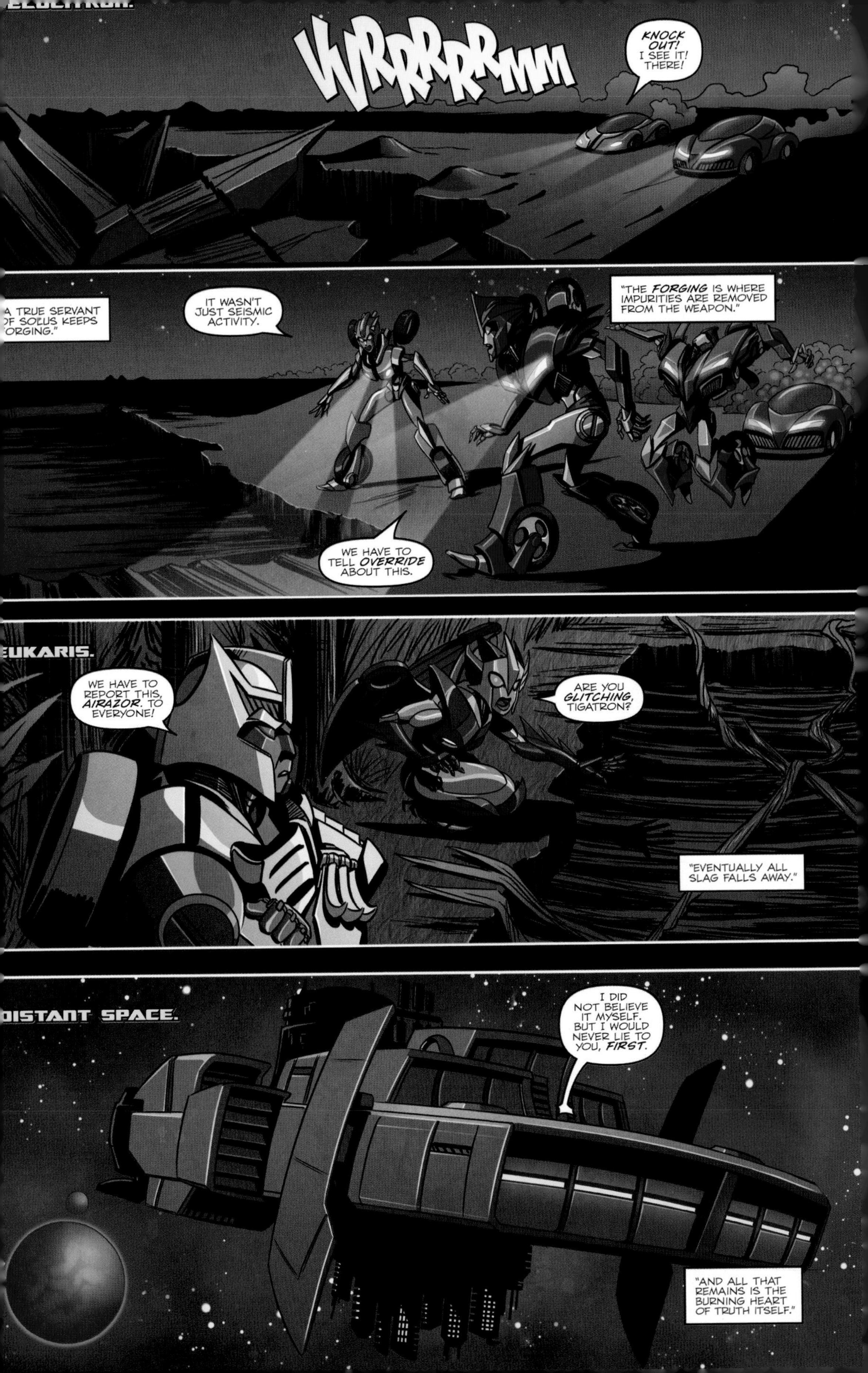
VVRRRRRMMM
KNOCK OUT! I SEE IT! THERE!
"A TRUE SERVANT OF SOLUS KEEPS FORGING."
IT WASN'T JUST SEISMIC ACTIVITY.
"THE FORGING IS WHERE IMPURITIES ARE REMOVED FROM THE WEAPON."
WE HAVE TO TELL OVERRIDE ABOUT THIS.
EUKARIS.
WE HAVE TO REPORT THIS, AIRAZOR. TO EVERYONE!
ARE YOU GLITCHING, TIGATRON?
"EVENTUALLY ALL SLAG FALLS AWAY."
DISTANT SPACE.
I DID NOT BELIEVE IT MYSELF. BUT I WOULD NEVER LIE TO YOU, FIRST.
"AND ALL THAT REMAINS IS THE BURNING HEART OF TRUTH ITSELF."

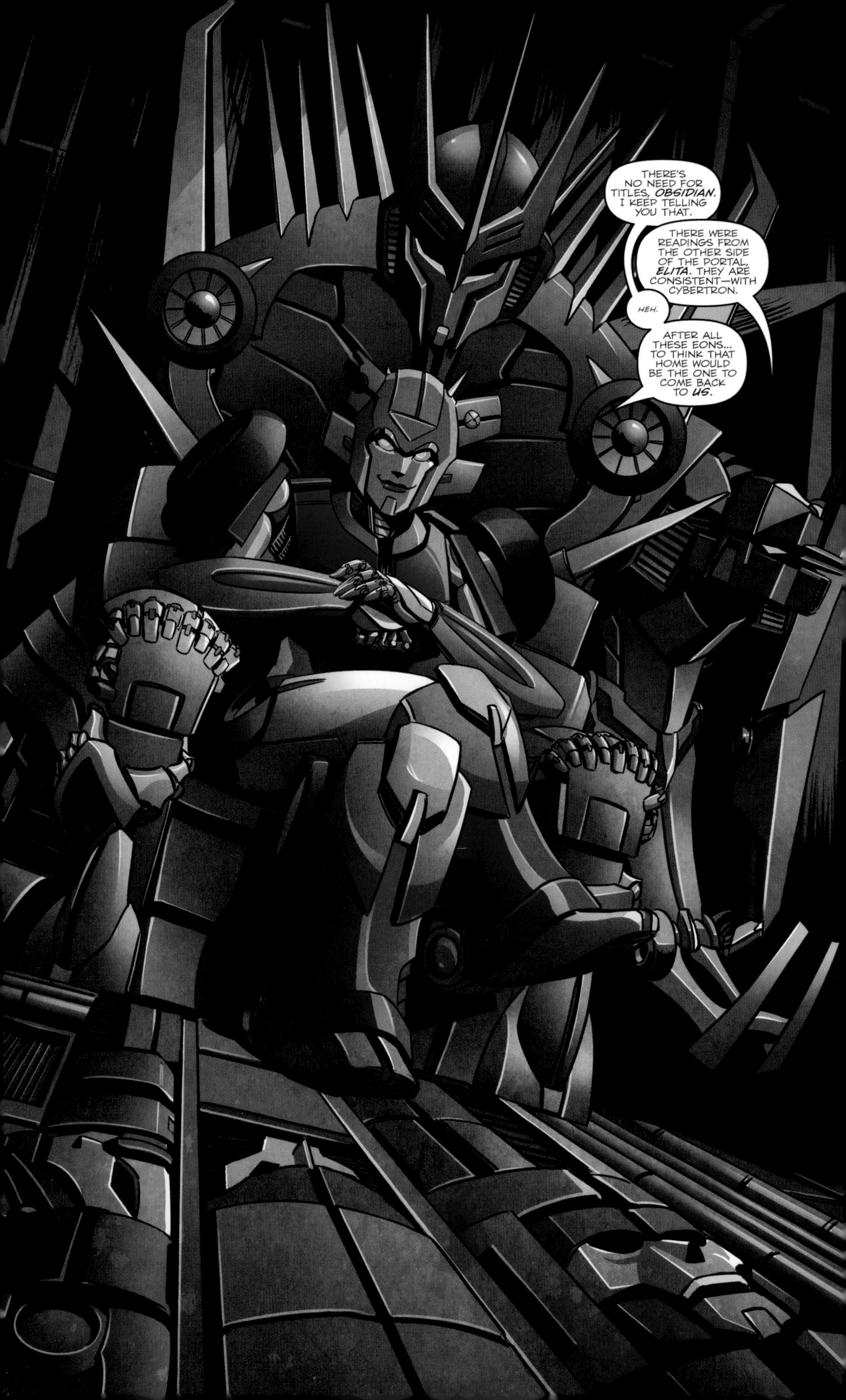
THERE'S NO NEED FOR TITLES, OBSIDIAN. I KEEP TELLING YOU THAT.
THERE WERE READINGS FROM THE OTHER SIDE OF THE PORTAL, ELITA. THEY ARE CONSISTENT—WITH CYBERTRON.
HEH.
AFTER ALL THESE EONS... TO THINK THAT HOME WOULD BE THE ONE TO COME BACK TO US.

ART BY **LIVIO RAMONDELLI**

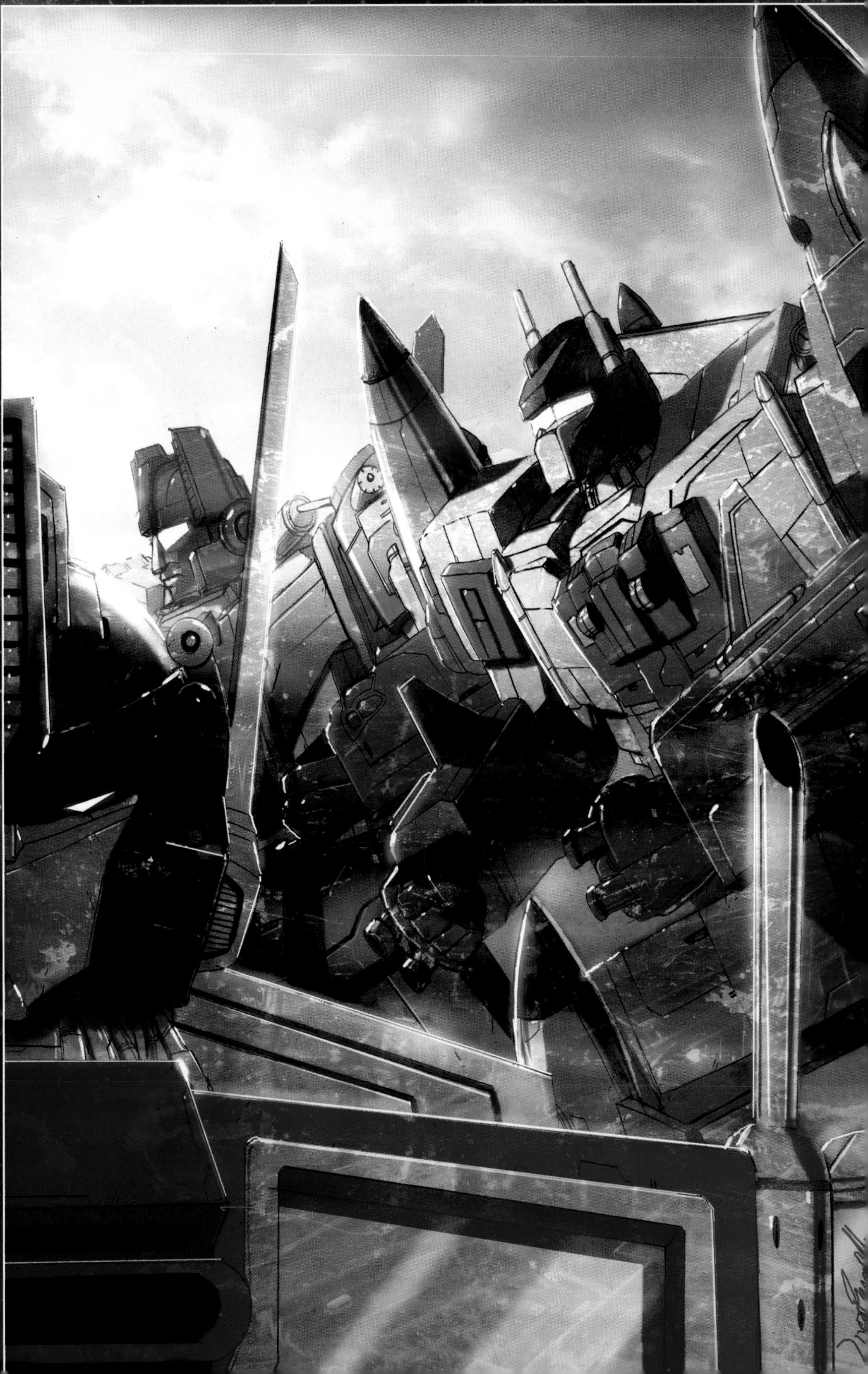

ART BY **PRISCILLA TRAMONTANO**

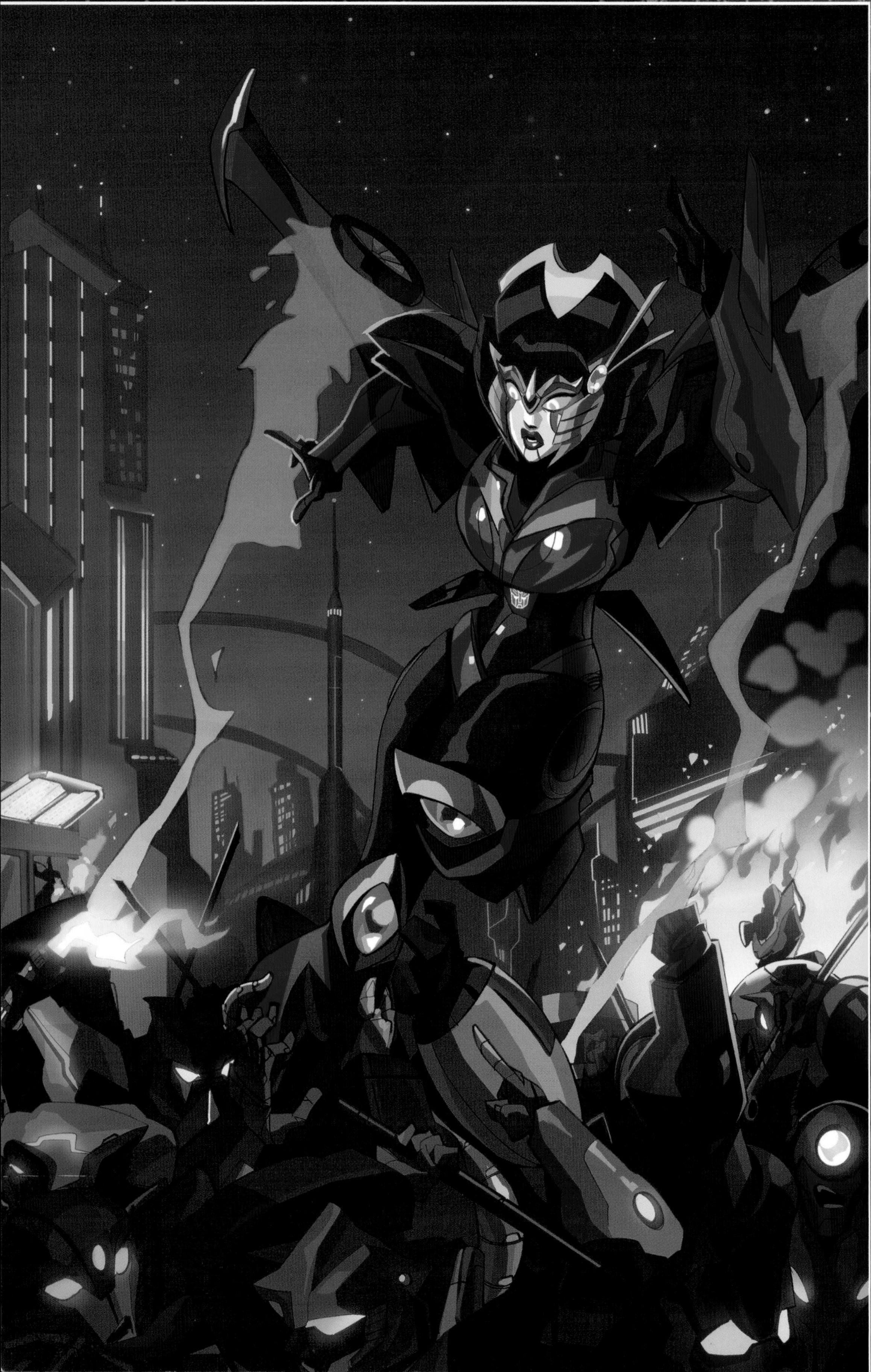

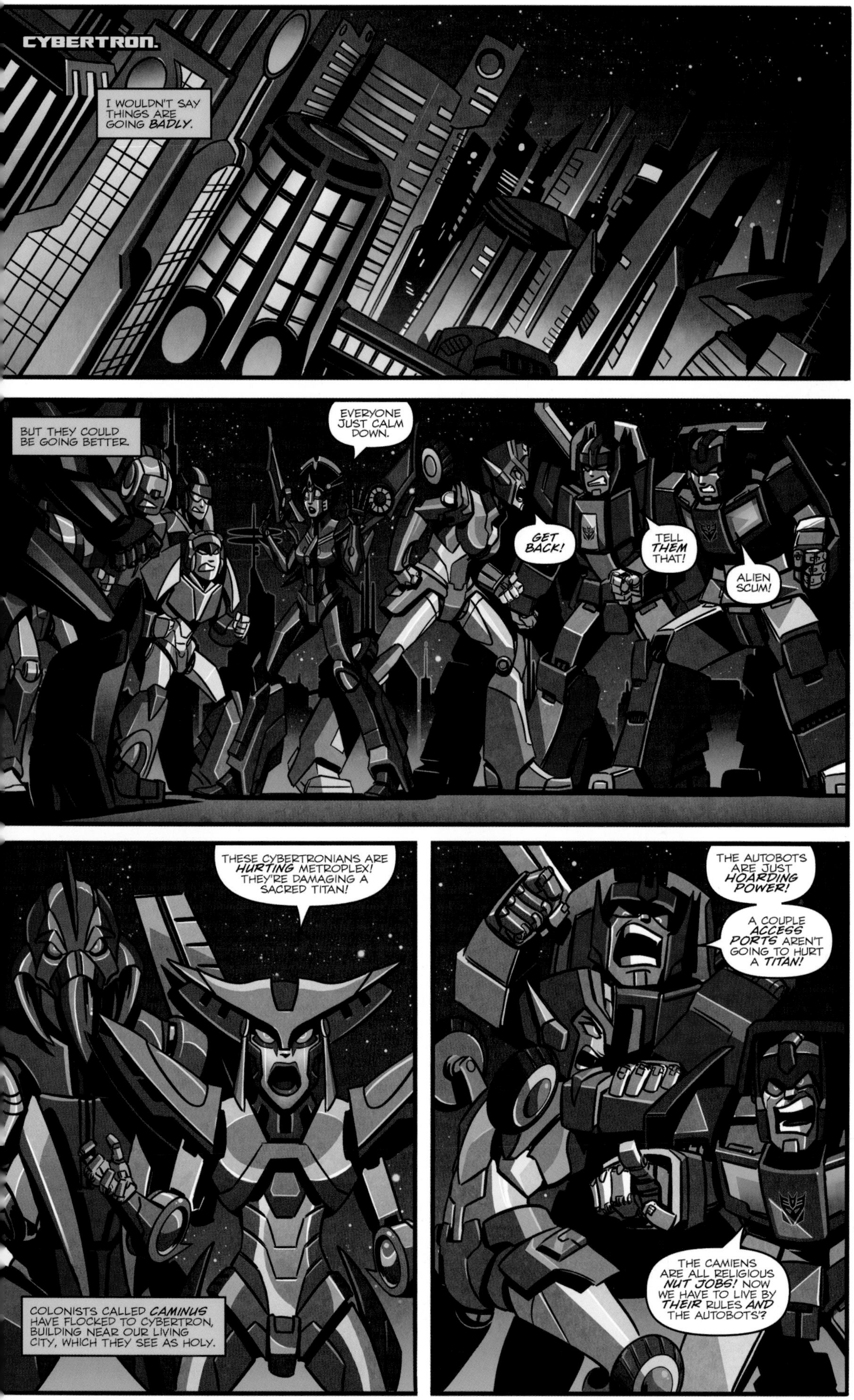
CYBERTRON.
I WOULDN'T SAY THINGS ARE GOING BADLY.
BUT THEY COULD BE GOING BETTER.
EVERYONE JUST CALM DOWN.
GET BACK!
TELL THEM THAT!
ALIEN SCUM!
THESE CYBERTRONIANS ARE HURTING METROPLEX! THEY'RE DAMAGING A SACRED TITAN!
COLONISTS CALLED CAMINUS HAVE FLOCKED TO CYBERTRON, BUILDING NEAR OUR LIVING CITY, WHICH THEY SEE AS HOLY.
THE AUTOBOTS ARE JUST HOARDING POWER!
A COUPLE ACCESS PORTS AREN'T GOING TO HURT A TITAN!
THE CAMIENS ARE ALL RELIGIOUS NUT JOBS! NOW WE HAVE TO LIVE BY THEIR RULES AND THE AUTOBOTS'?

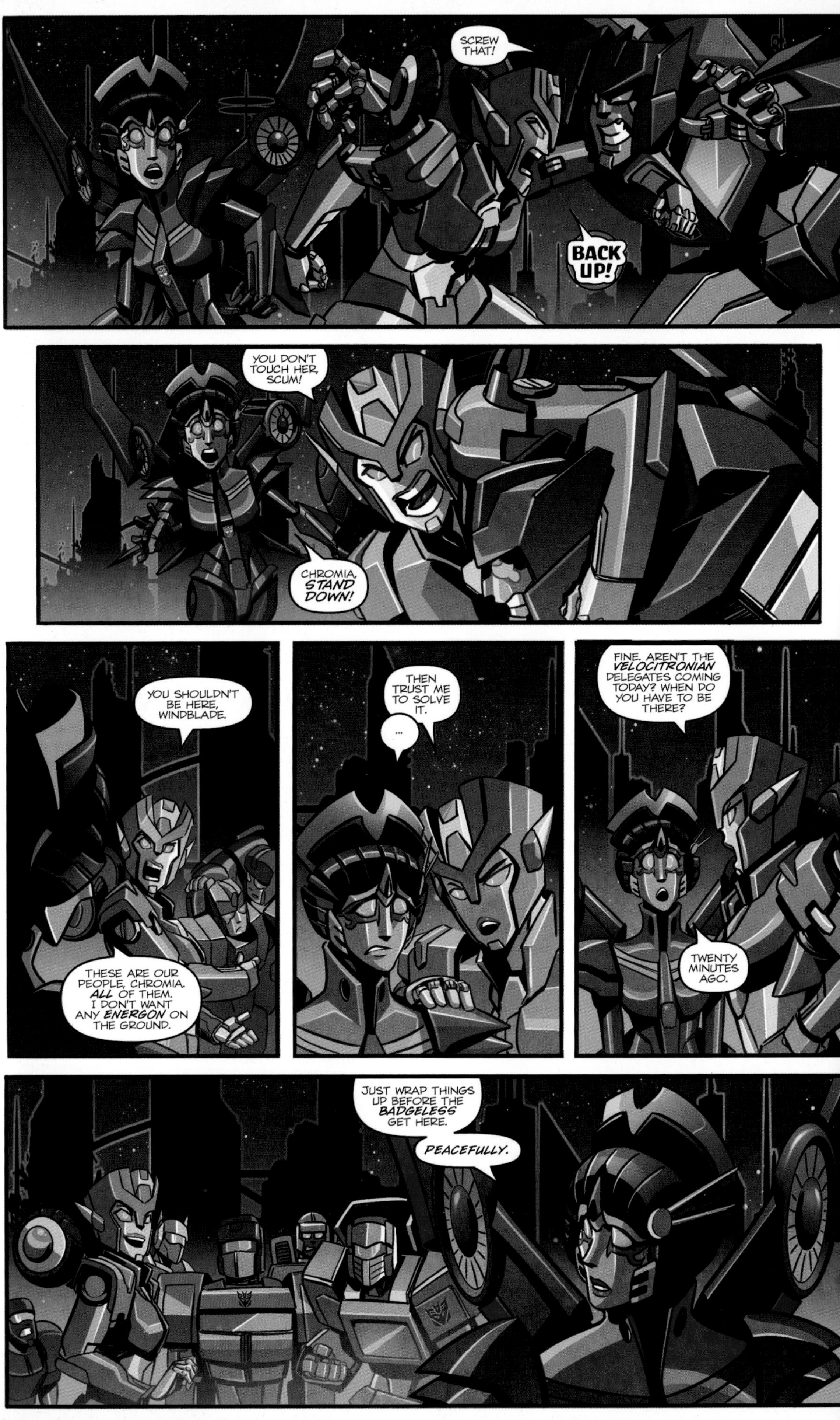
SCREW THAT!
BACK UP!
YOU DON'T TOUCH HER, SCUM!
CHROMIA, STAND DOWN!
YOU SHOULDN'T BE HERE, WINDBLADE.
THESE ARE OUR PEOPLE, CHROMIA. ALL OF THEM. I DON'T WANT ANY ENERGON ON THE GROUND.
THEN TRUST ME TO SOLVE IT.
...
FINE. AREN'T THE VELOCITRONIAN DELEGATES COMING TODAY? WHEN DO YOU HAVE TO BE THERE?
TWENTY MINUTES AGO.
JUST WRAP THINGS UP BEFORE THE BADGELESS GET HERE.
PEACEFULLY.

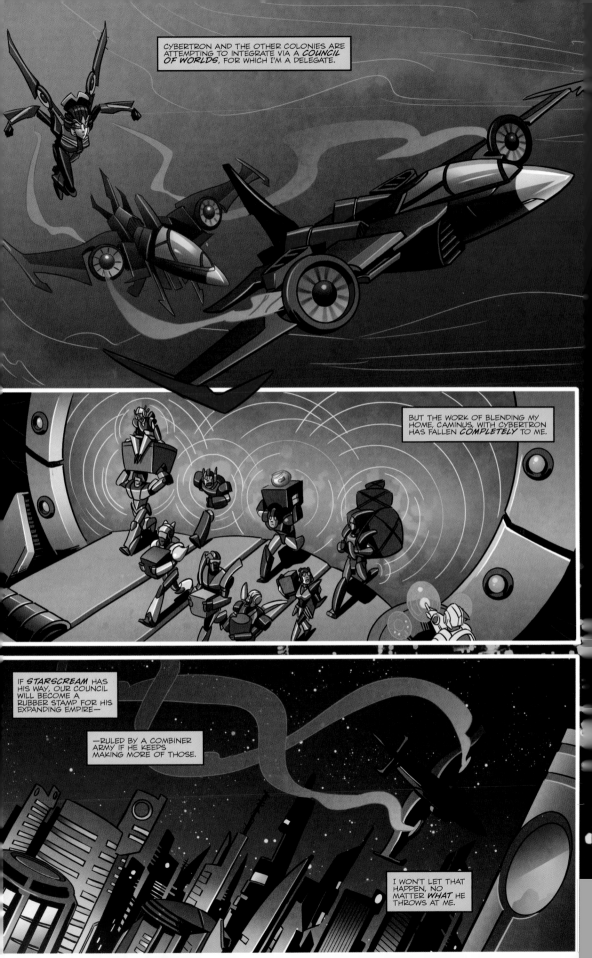

CYBERTRON AND THE OTHER COLONIES ARE ATTEMPTING TO INTEGRATE VIA A *COUNCIL OF WORLDS*, FOR WHICH I'M A DELEGATE.

BUT THE WORK OF BLENDING MY HOME, CAMINUS, WITH CYBERTRON HAS FALLEN *COMPLETELY* TO ME.

IF *STARSCREAM* HAS HIS WAY, OUR COUNCIL WILL BECOME A RUBBER STAMP FOR HIS EXPANDING EMPIRE—

—RULED BY A COMBINER ARMY IF HE KEEPS MAKING MORE OF THOSE.

I WON'T LET THAT HAPPEN, NO MATTER *WHAT* HE THROWS AT ME.

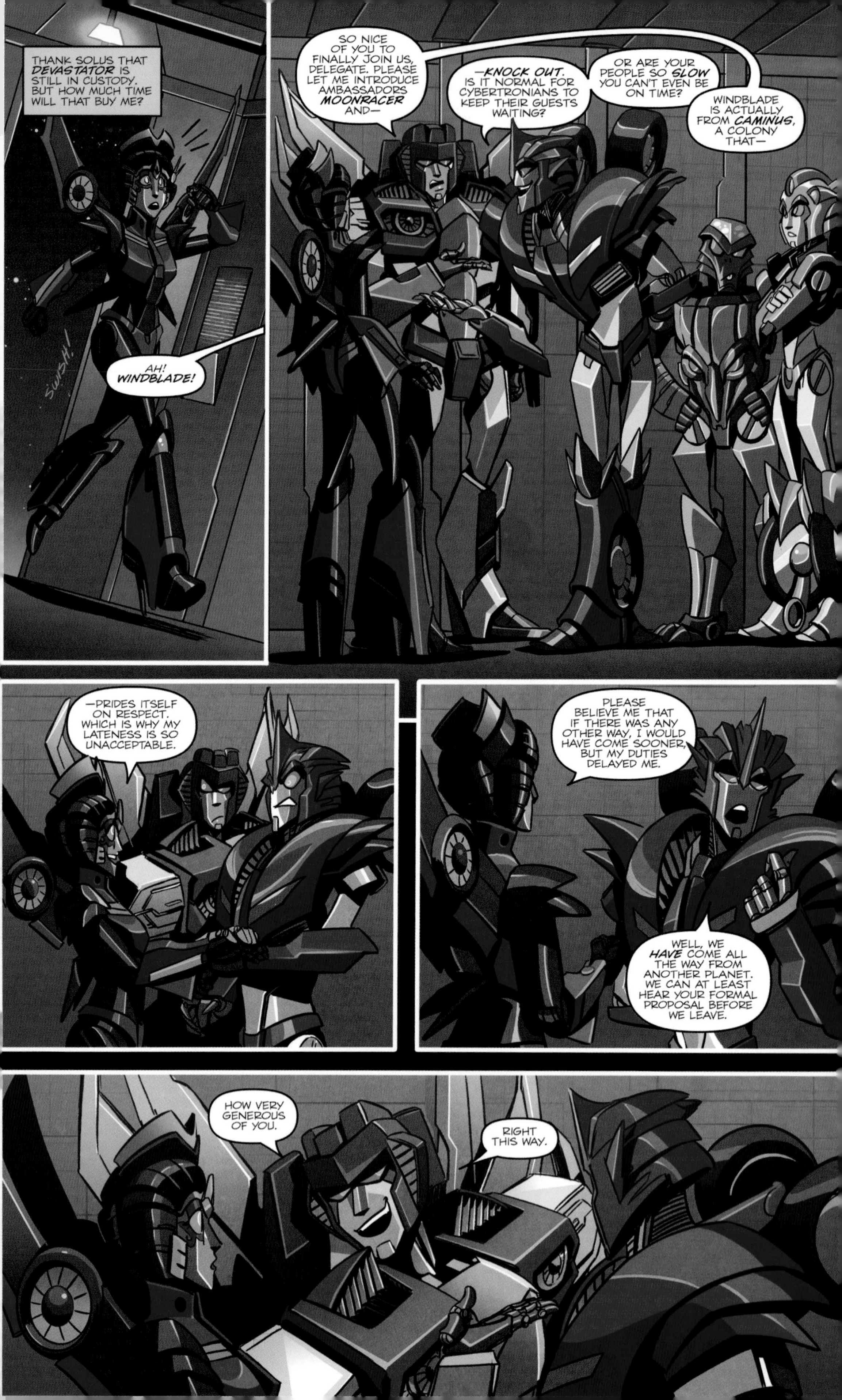
THANK SOLUS THAT DEVASTATOR IS STILL IN CUSTODY. BUT HOW MUCH TIME WILL THAT BUY ME?
SWISH!
AH! WINDBLADE!
SO NICE OF YOU TO FINALLY JOIN US, DELEGATE. PLEASE LET ME INTRODUCE AMBASSADORS MOONRACER AND—
—KNOCK OUT. IS IT NORMAL FOR CYBERTRONIANS TO KEEP THEIR GUESTS WAITING?
OR ARE YOUR PEOPLE SO SLOW YOU CAN'T EVEN BE ON TIME?
WINDBLADE IS ACTUALLY FROM CAMINUS, A COLONY THAT—
—PRIDES ITSELF ON RESPECT. WHICH IS WHY MY LATENESS IS SO UNACCEPTABLE.
PLEASE BELIEVE ME THAT IF THERE WAS ANY OTHER WAY, I WOULD HAVE COME SOONER, BUT MY DUTIES DELAYED ME.
WELL, WE HAVE COME ALL THE WAY FROM ANOTHER PLANET. WE CAN AT LEAST HEAR YOUR FORMAL PROPOSAL BEFORE WE LEAVE.
HOW VERY GENEROUS OF YOU.
RIGHT THIS WAY.

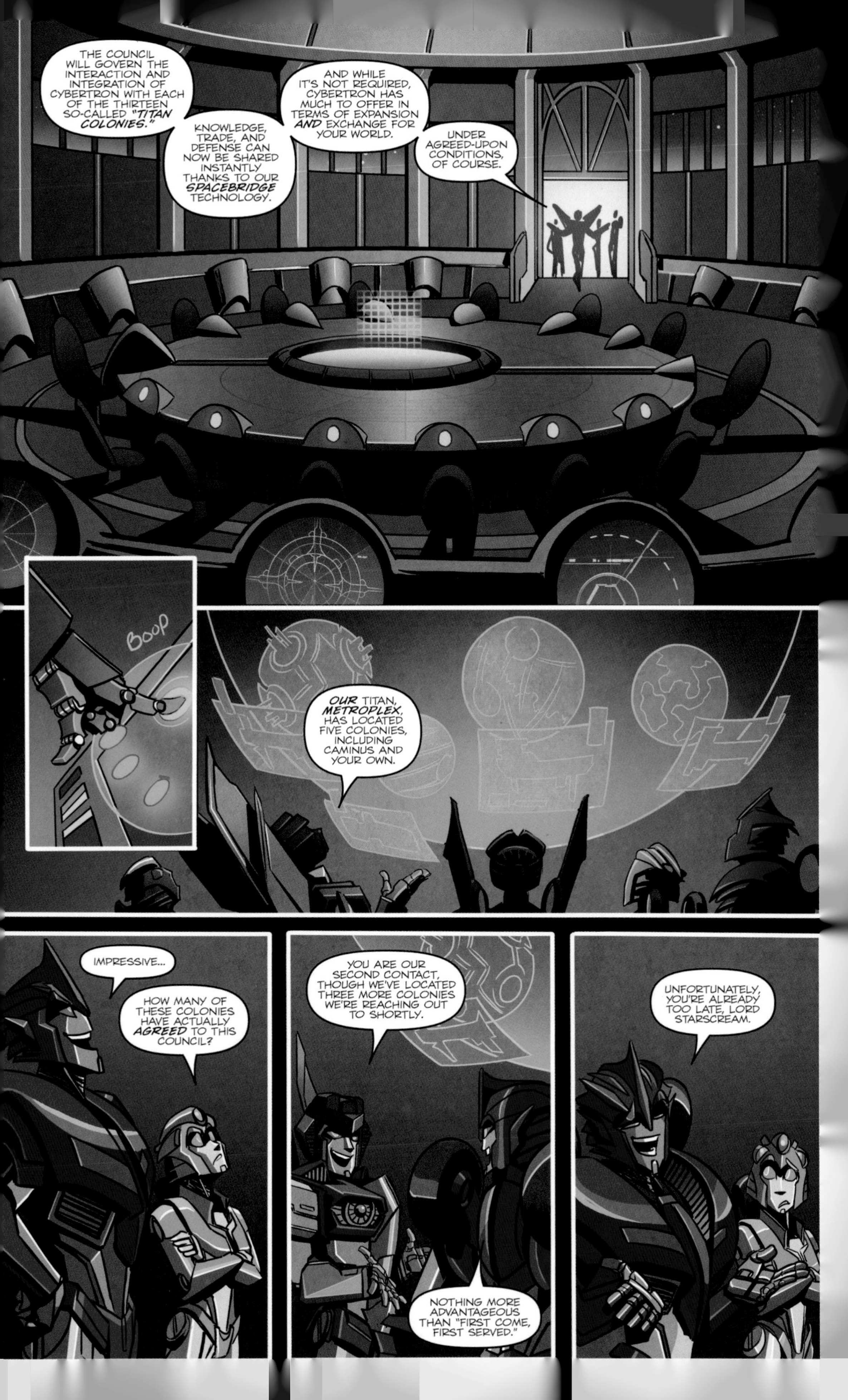

THE COUNCIL WILL GOVERN THE INTERACTION AND INTEGRATION OF CYBERTRON WITH EACH OF THE THIRTEEN SO-CALLED "TITAN COLONIES."
KNOWLEDGE, TRADE, AND DEFENSE CAN NOW BE SHARED INSTANTLY THANKS TO OUR SPACEBRIDGE TECHNOLOGY.
AND WHILE IT'S NOT REQUIRED, CYBERTRON HAS MUCH TO OFFER IN TERMS OF EXPANSION AND EXCHANGE FOR YOUR WORLD.
UNDER AGREED-UPON CONDITIONS, OF COURSE.
BOOP
OUR TITAN, METROPLEX, HAS LOCATED FIVE COLONIES, INCLUDING CAMINUS AND YOUR OWN.
IMPRESSIVE...
HOW MANY OF THESE COLONIES HAVE ACTUALLY AGREED TO THIS COUNCIL?
YOU ARE OUR SECOND CONTACT, THOUGH WE'VE LOCATED THREE MORE COLONIES WE'RE REACHING OUT TO SHORTLY.
NOTHING MORE ADVANTAGEOUS THAN "FIRST COME, FIRST SERVED."
UNFORTUNATELY, YOU'RE ALREADY TOO LATE, LORD STARSCREAM.

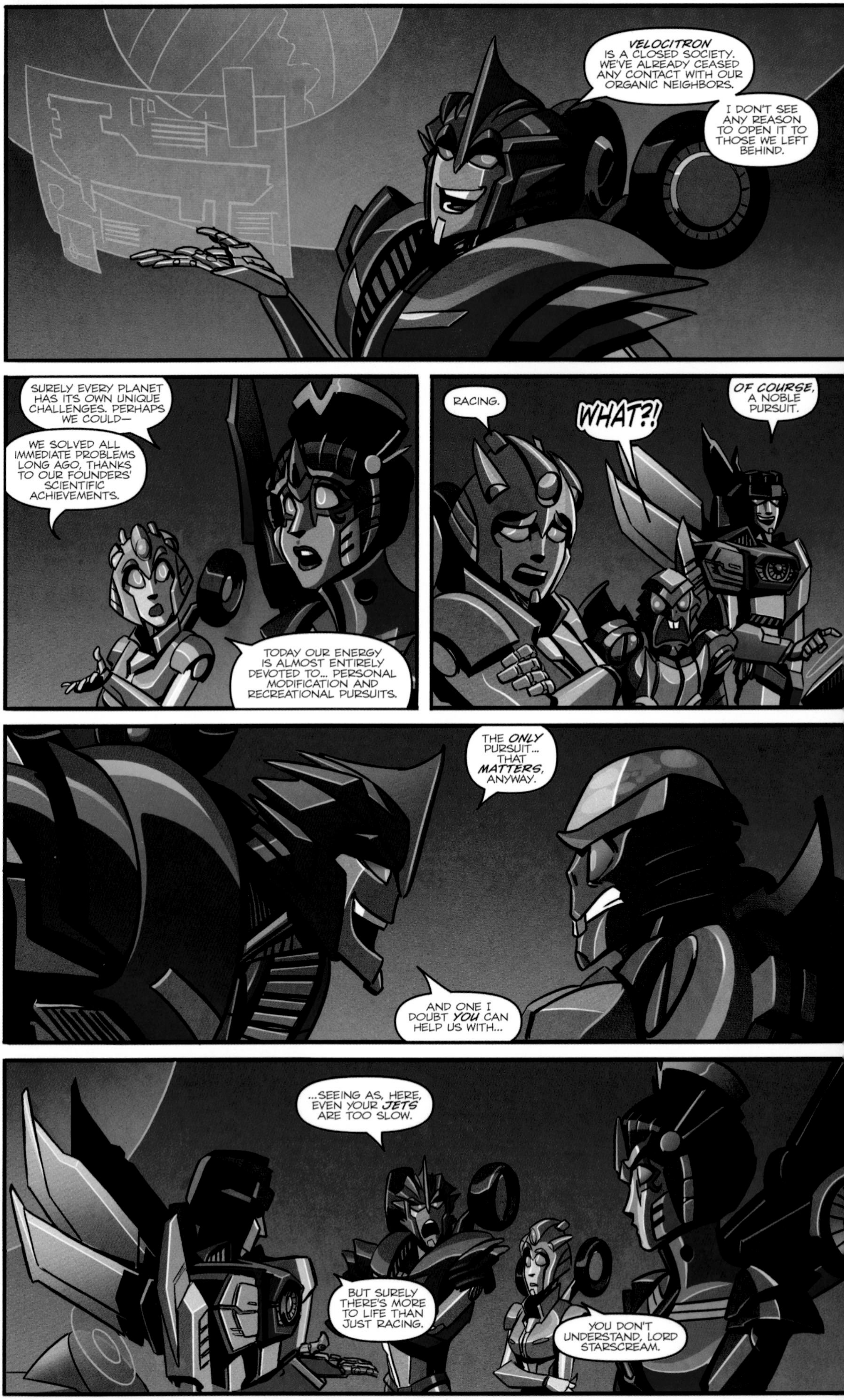
VELOCITRON IS A CLOSED SOCIETY. WE'VE ALREADY CEASED ANY CONTACT WITH OUR ORGANIC NEIGHBORS.
I DON'T SEE ANY REASON TO OPEN IT TO THOSE WE LEFT BEHIND.
SURELY EVERY PLANET HAS ITS OWN UNIQUE CHALLENGES. PERHAPS WE COULD—
WE SOLVED ALL IMMEDIATE PROBLEMS LONG AGO, THANKS TO OUR FOUNDERS' SCIENTIFIC ACHIEVEMENTS.
TODAY OUR ENERGY IS ALMOST ENTIRELY DEVOTED TO... PERSONAL MODIFICATION AND RECREATIONAL PURSUITS.
RACING.
WHAT?!
OF COURSE, A NOBLE PURSUIT.
THE ONLY PURSUIT... THAT MATTERS, ANYWAY.
AND ONE I DOUBT YOU CAN HELP US WITH...
...SEEING AS, HERE, EVEN YOUR JETS ARE TOO SLOW.
BUT SURELY THERE'S MORE TO LIFE THAN JUST RACING.
YOU DON'T UNDERSTAND, LORD STARSCREAM.

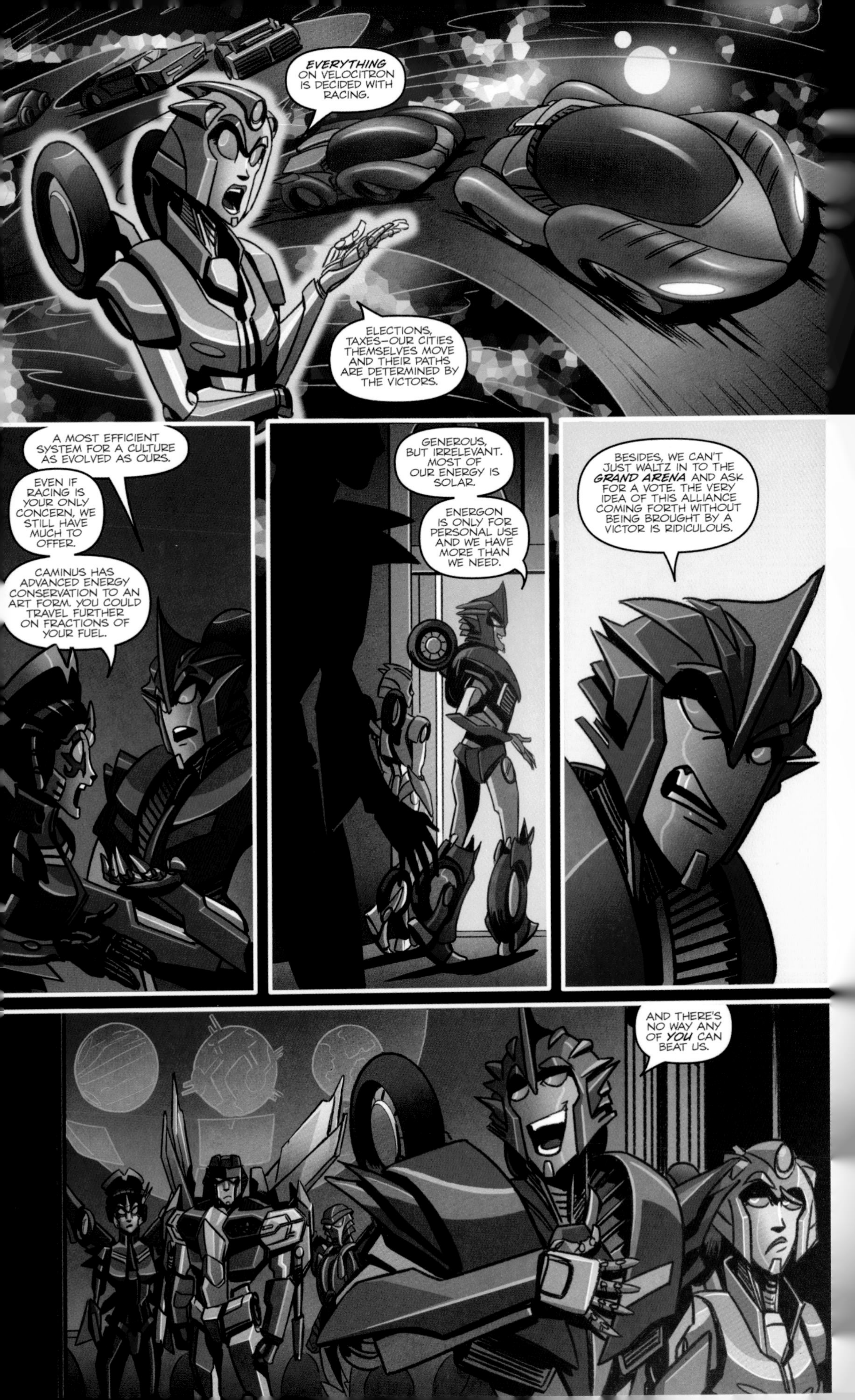
EVERYTHING ON VELOCITRON IS DECIDED WITH RACING.
ELECTIONS, TAXES—OUR CITIES THEMSELVES MOVE AND THEIR PATHS ARE DETERMINED BY THE VICTORS.
A MOST EFFICIENT SYSTEM FOR A CULTURE AS EVOLVED AS OURS.
EVEN IF RACING IS YOUR ONLY CONCERN, WE STILL HAVE MUCH TO OFFER.
CAMINUS HAS ADVANCED ENERGY CONSERVATION TO AN ART FORM. YOU COULD TRAVEL FURTHER ON FRACTIONS OF YOUR FUEL.
GENEROUS, BUT IRRELEVANT. MOST OF OUR ENERGY IS SOLAR.
ENERGON IS ONLY FOR PERSONAL USE AND WE HAVE MORE THAN WE NEED.
BESIDES, WE CAN'T JUST WALTZ IN TO THE GRAND ARENA AND ASK FOR A VOTE. THE VERY IDEA OF THIS ALLIANCE COMING FORTH WITHOUT BEING BROUGHT BY A VICTOR IS RIDICULOUS.
AND THERE'S NO WAY ANY OF YOU CAN BEAT US.

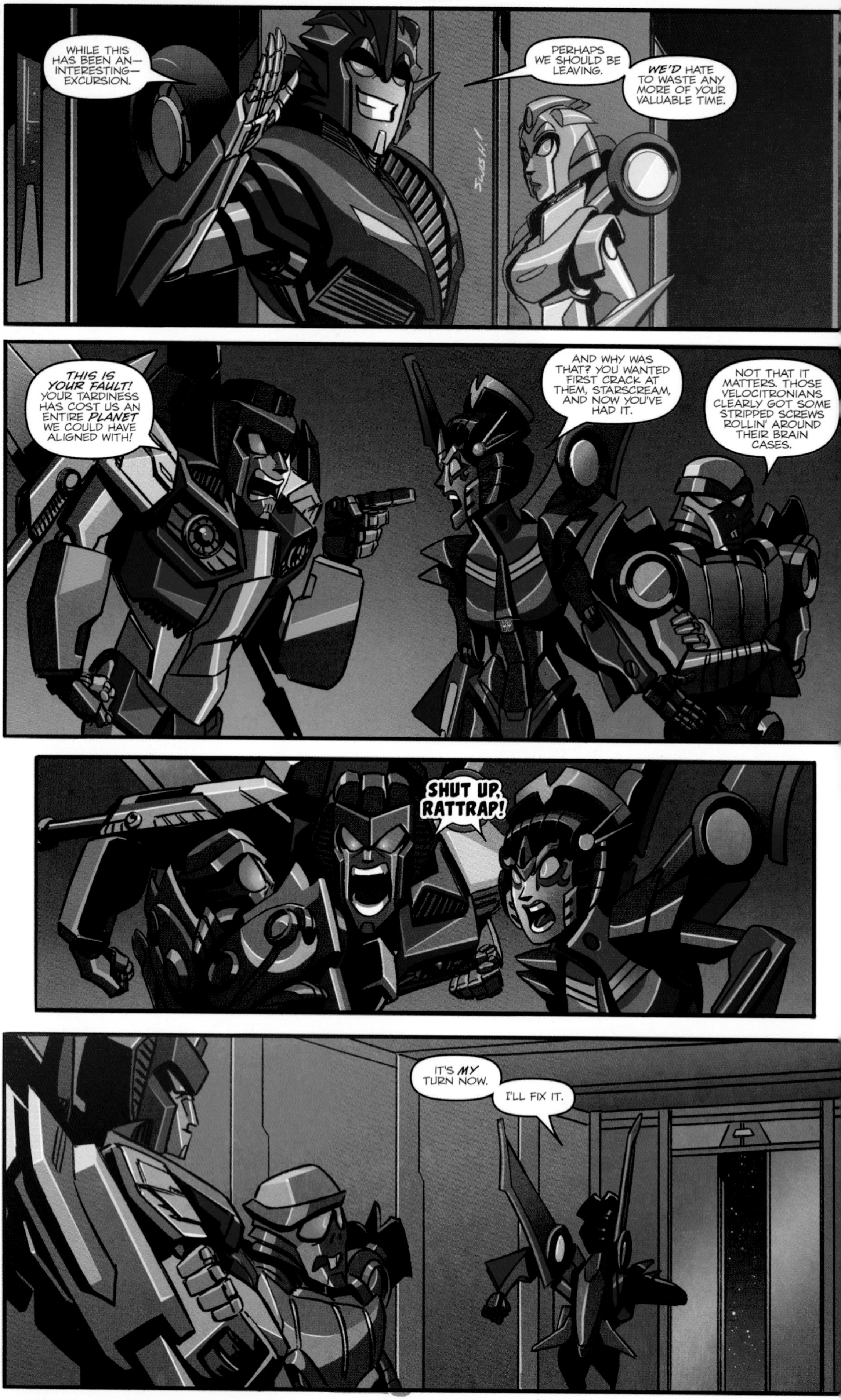

WHILE THIS HAS BEEN AN—INTERESTING—EXCURSION.
PERHAPS WE SHOULD BE LEAVING.
WE'D HATE TO WASTE ANY MORE OF YOUR VALUABLE TIME.
SWISH!
THIS IS YOUR FAULT! YOUR TARDINESS HAS COST US AN ENTIRE PLANET WE COULD HAVE ALIGNED WITH!
AND WHY WAS THAT? YOU WANTED FIRST CRACK AT THEM, STARSCREAM, AND NOW YOU'VE HAD IT.
NOT THAT IT MATTERS. THOSE VELOCITRONIANS CLEARLY GOT SOME STRIPPED SCREWS ROLLIN' AROUND THEIR BRAIN CASES.
SHUT UP, RATTRAP!
IT'S MY TURN NOW.
I'LL FIX IT.

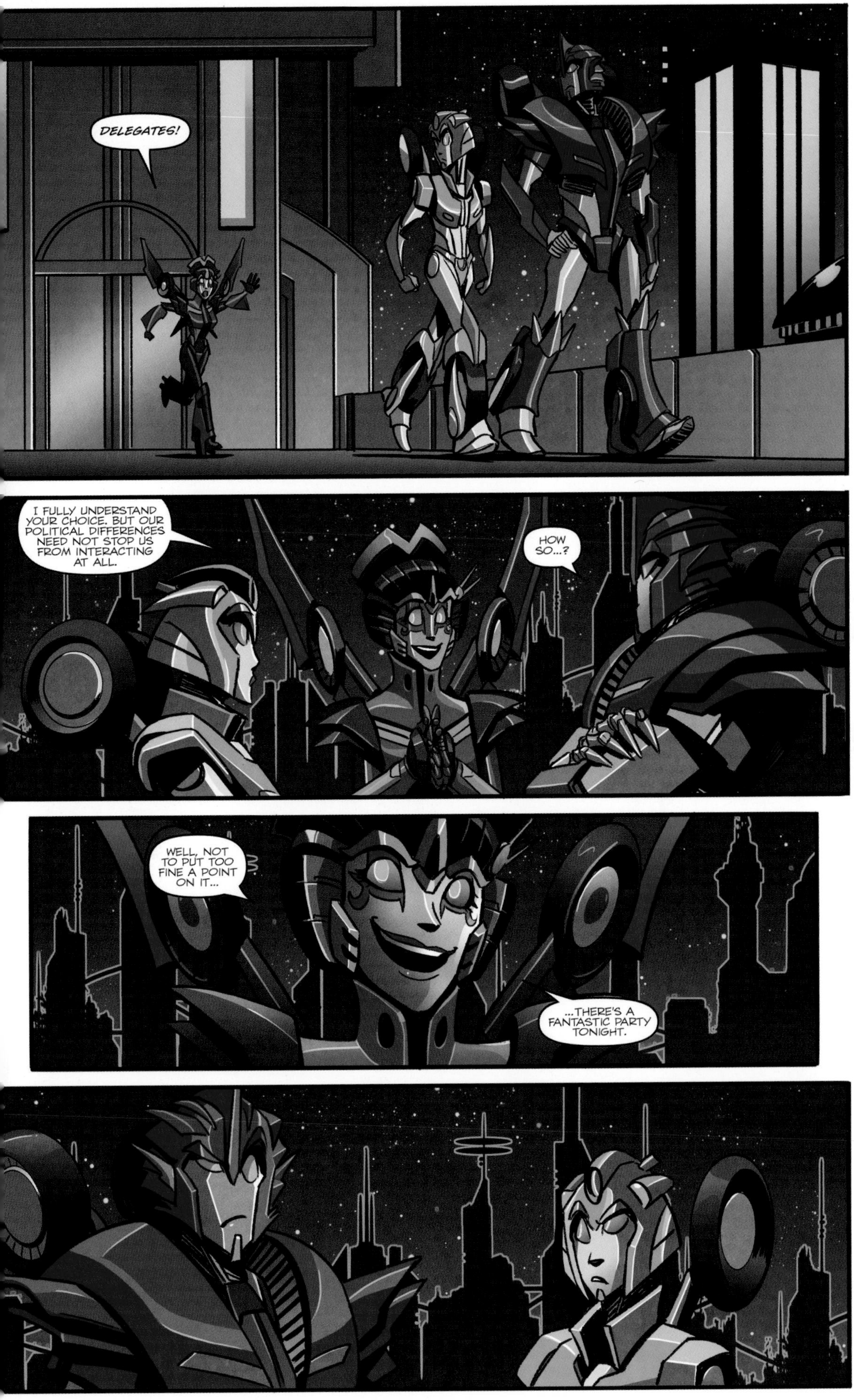
DELEGATES!
I FULLY UNDERSTAND YOUR CHOICE. BUT OUR POLITICAL DIFFERENCES NEED NOT STOP US FROM INTERACTING AT ALL.
HOW SO...?
WELL, NOT TO PUT TOO FINE A POINT ON IT...
...THERE'S A FANTASTIC PARTY TONIGHT.

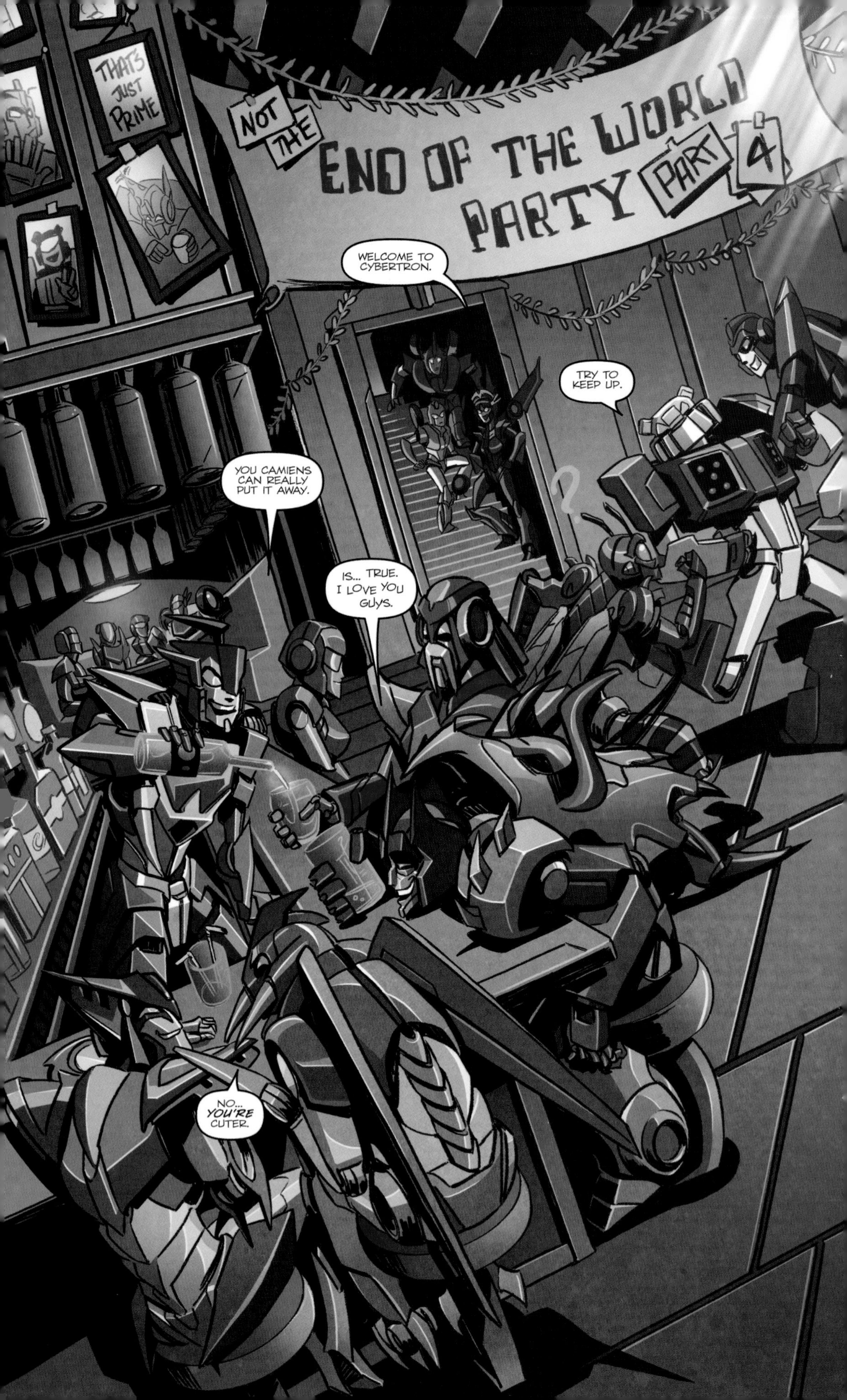
THAT'S JUST PRIME
NOT THE END OF THE WORLD PARTY PART 4
WELCOME TO CYBERTRON.
TRY TO KEEP UP.
YOU CAMIENS CAN REALLY PUT IT AWAY.
IS... TRUE. I LOVE YOU GUYS.
NO... YOU'RE CUTER.

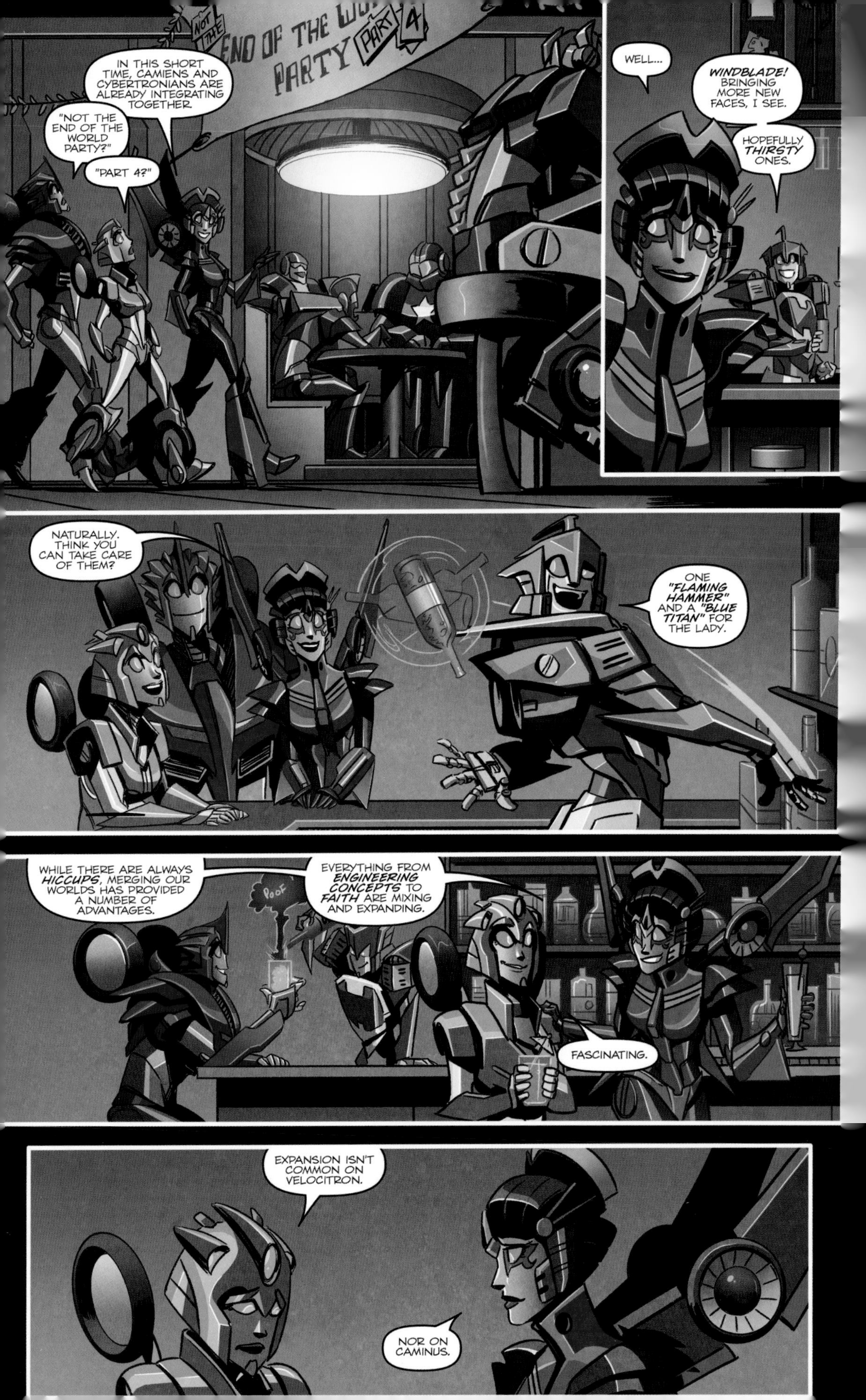
NOT THE END OF THE WORLD PARTY PART 4
IN THIS SHORT TIME, CAMIENS AND CYBERTRONIANS ARE ALREADY INTEGRATING TOGETHER
"NOT THE END OF THE WORLD PARTY?"
"PART 4?"
WELL...
WINDBLADE! BRINGING MORE NEW FACES, I SEE.
HOPEFULLY THIRSTY ONES.
NATURALLY. THINK YOU CAN TAKE CARE OF THEM?
ONE "FLAMING HAMMER" AND A "BLUE TITAN" FOR THE LADY.
WHILE THERE ARE ALWAYS HICCUPS, MERGING OUR WORLDS HAS PROVIDED A NUMBER OF ADVANTAGES.
POOF
EVERYTHING FROM ENGINEERING CONCEPTS TO FAITH ARE MIXING AND EXPANDING.
FASCINATING.
EXPANSION ISN'T COMMON ON VELOCITRON.
NOR ON CAMINUS.

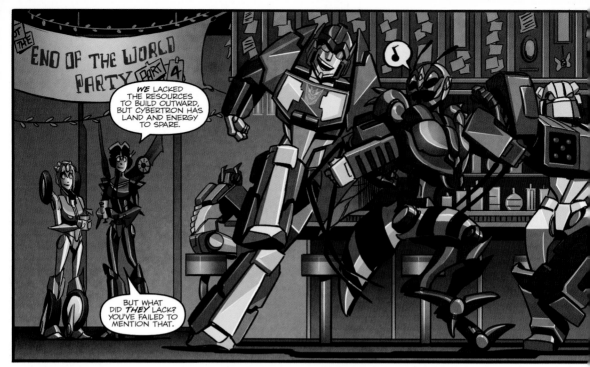

END OF THE WORLD PARTY PART 4

WE LACKED THE RESOURCES TO BUILD OUTWARD, BUT CYBERTRON HAS LAND AND ENERGY TO SPARE.

BUT WHAT DID *THEY* LACK? YOU'VE FAILED TO MENTION THAT.

THEY ARE STILL RECOVERING FROM A CIVIL WAR. THEY ARE TIRED AND THE TENSION BETWEEN FACTIONS STILL EXISTS.

VIOLENCE?

YES. BUT THE INFLUX OF NEW PEOPLE HAS HELPED.

CYBERTRON NEEDS PEOPLE HUNGRY TO MOVE FORWARD, WHO AREN'T HELD BACK BY OLD FACTIONS.

INTERESTING.

HA!

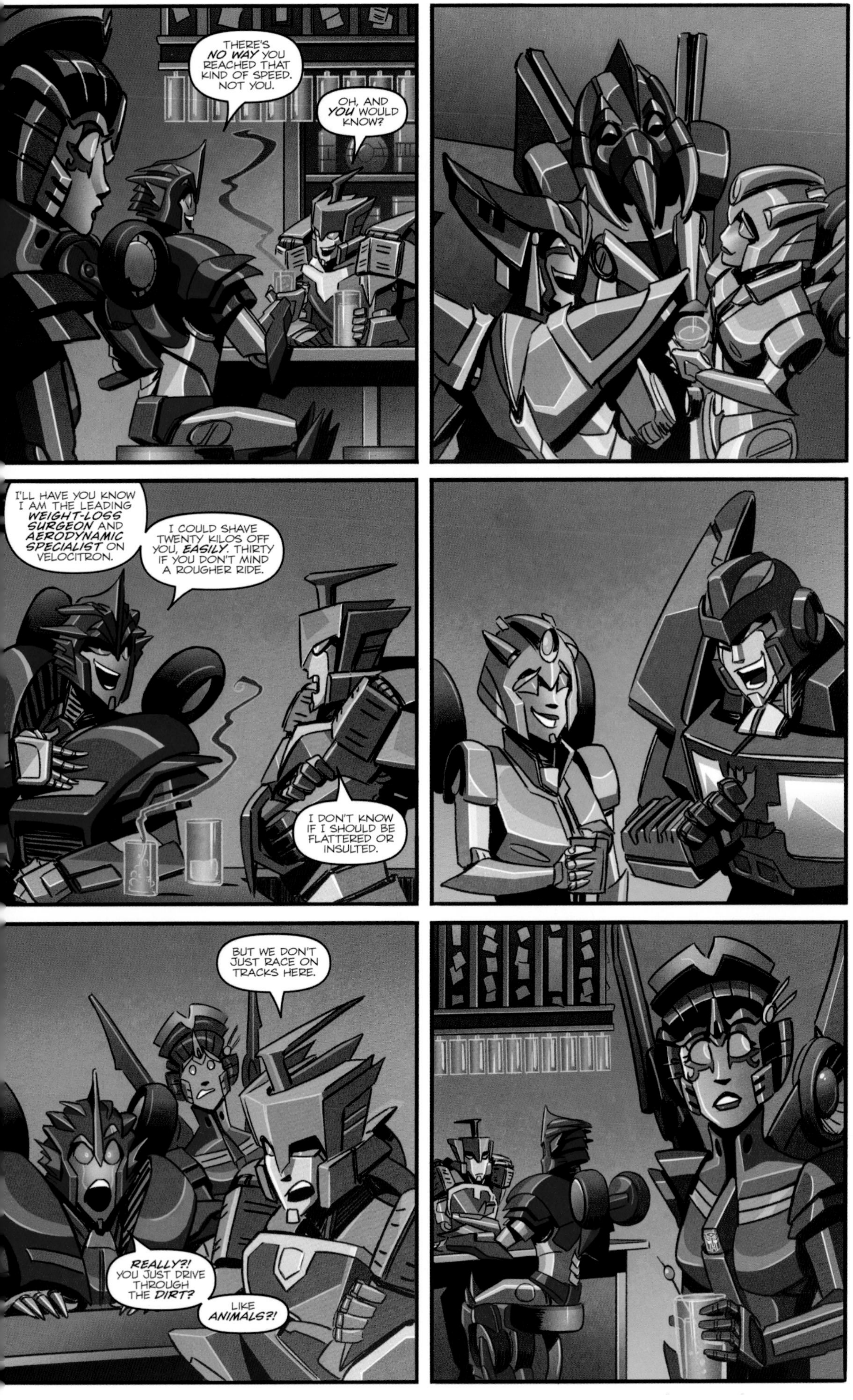
THERE'S NO WAY YOU REACHED THAT KIND OF SPEED. NOT YOU.
OH, AND YOU WOULD KNOW?
I'LL HAVE YOU KNOW I AM THE LEADING WEIGHT-LOSS SURGEON AND AERODYNAMIC SPECIALIST ON VELOCITRON.
I COULD SHAVE TWENTY KILOS OFF YOU, EASILY. THIRTY IF YOU DON'T MIND A ROUGHER RIDE.
I DON'T KNOW IF I SHOULD BE FLATTERED OR INSULTED.
BUT WE DON'T JUST RACE ON TRACKS HERE.
REALLY?! YOU JUST DRIVE THROUGH THE DIRT?
LIKE ANIMALS?!

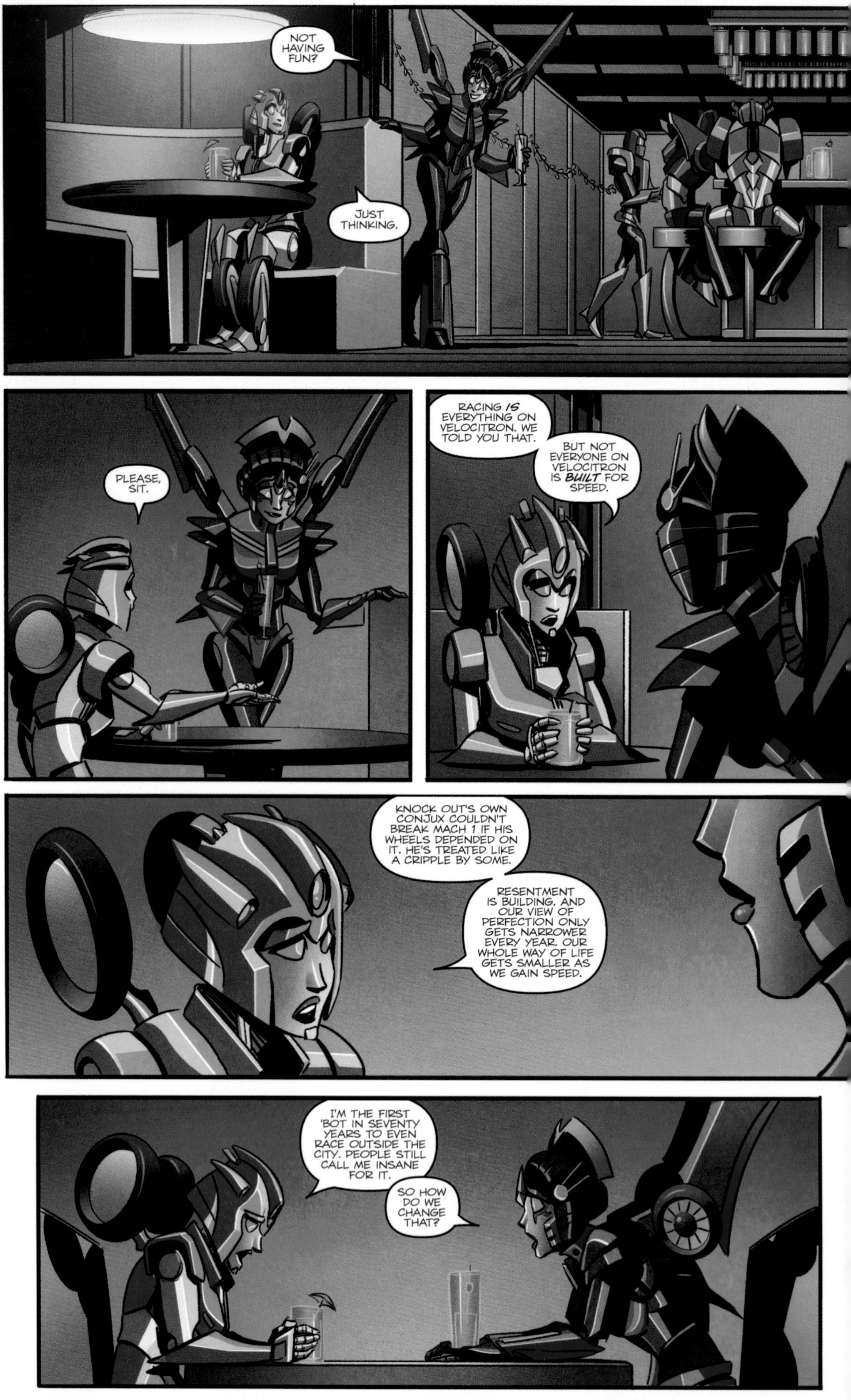
NOT HAVING FUN?
JUST THINKING.
PLEASE, SIT.
RACING IS EVERYTHING ON VELOCITRON. WE TOLD YOU THAT.
BUT NOT EVERYONE ON VELOCITRON IS BUILT FOR SPEED.
KNOCK OUT'S OWN CONJUX COULDN'T BREAK MACH 1 IF HIS WHEELS DEPENDED ON IT. HE'S TREATED LIKE A CRIPPLE BY SOME.
RESENTMENT IS BUILDING. AND OUR VIEW OF PERFECTION ONLY GETS NARROWER EVERY YEAR. OUR WHOLE WAY OF LIFE GETS SMALLER AS WE GAIN SPEED.
I'M THE FIRST 'BOT IN SEVENTY YEARS TO EVEN RACE OUTSIDE THE CITY. PEOPLE STILL CALL ME INSANE FOR IT.
SO HOW DO WE CHANGE THAT?

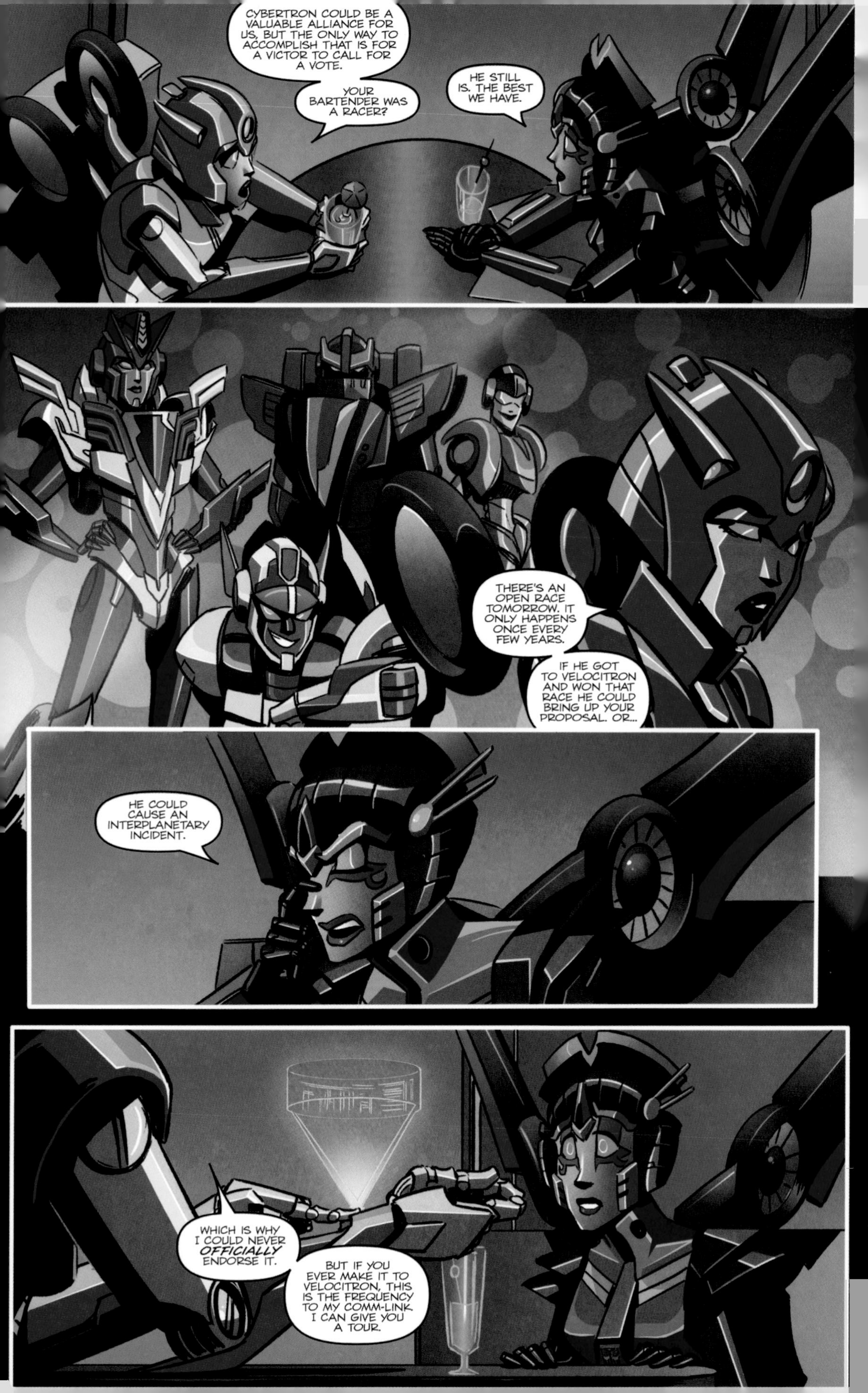
CYBERTRON COULD BE A VALUABLE ALLIANCE FOR US, BUT THE ONLY WAY TO ACCOMPLISH THAT IS FOR A VICTOR TO CALL FOR A VOTE.
YOUR BARTENDER WAS A RACER?
HE STILL IS. THE BEST WE HAVE.
THERE'S AN OPEN RACE TOMORROW. IT ONLY HAPPENS ONCE EVERY FEW YEARS.
IF HE GOT TO VELOCITRON AND WON THAT RACE HE COULD BRING UP YOUR PROPOSAL. OR...
HE COULD CAUSE AN INTERPLANETARY INCIDENT.
WHICH IS WHY I COULD NEVER *OFFICIALLY* ENDORSE IT.
BUT IF YOU EVER MAKE IT TO VELOCITRON, THIS IS THE FREQUENCY TO MY COMM-LINK. I CAN GIVE YOU A TOUR.

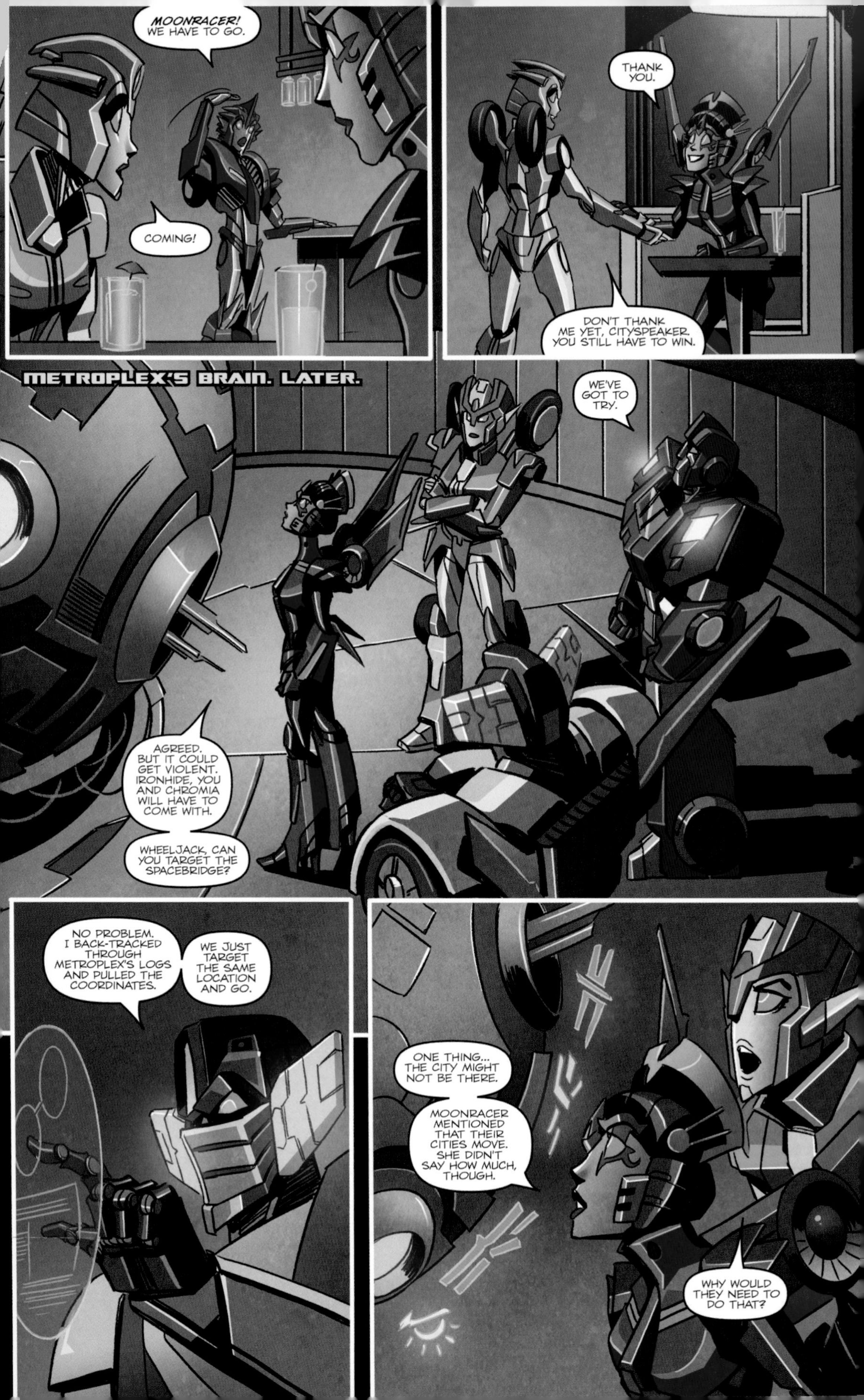
MOONRACER! WE HAVE TO GO.
COMING!
THANK YOU.
DON'T THANK ME YET, CITYSPEAKER. YOU STILL HAVE TO WIN.
METROPLEX'S BRAIN. LATER.
WE'VE GOT TO TRY.
AGREED. BUT IT COULD GET VIOLENT. IRONHIDE, YOU AND CHROMIA WILL HAVE TO COME WITH.
WHEELJACK, CAN YOU TARGET THE SPACEBRIDGE?
NO PROBLEM. I BACK-TRACKED THROUGH METROPLEX'S LOGS AND PULLED THE COORDINATES.
WE JUST TARGET THE SAME LOCATION AND GO.
ONE THING... THE CITY MIGHT NOT BE THERE.
MOONRACER MENTIONED THAT THEIR CITIES MOVE. SHE DIDN'T SAY HOW MUCH, THOUGH.
WHY WOULD THEY NEED TO DO THAT?

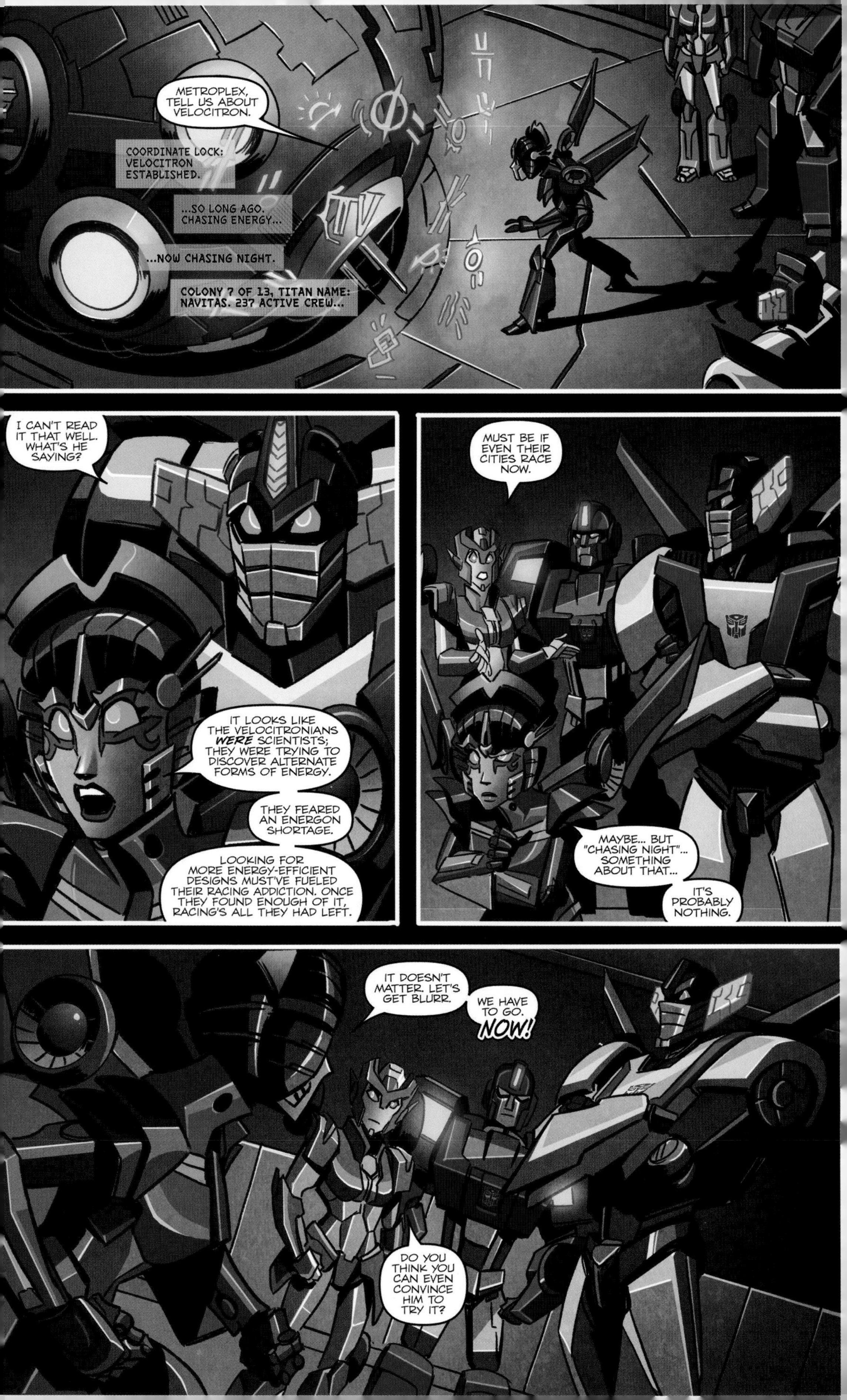
METROPLEX, TELL US ABOUT VELOCITRON.
COORDINATE LOCK: VELOCITRON ESTABLISHED.
...SO LONG AGO. CHASING ENERGY...
...NOW CHASING NIGHT.
COLONY 7 OF 13, TITAN NAME: NAVITAS. 237 ACTIVE CREW...
I CAN'T READ IT THAT WELL. WHAT'S HE SAYING?
IT LOOKS LIKE THE VELOCITRONIANS *WERE* SCIENTISTS; THEY WERE TRYING TO DISCOVER ALTERNATE FORMS OF ENERGY.
THEY FEARED AN ENERGON SHORTAGE.
LOOKING FOR MORE ENERGY-EFFICIENT DESIGNS MUST'VE FUELED THEIR RACING ADDICTION. ONCE THEY FOUND ENOUGH OF IT, RACING'S ALL THEY HAD LEFT.
MUST BE IF EVEN THEIR CITIES RACE NOW.
MAYBE... BUT "CHASING NIGHT"... SOMETHING ABOUT THAT...
IT'S PROBABLY NOTHING.
IT DOESN'T MATTER. LET'S GET BLURR.
WE HAVE TO GO. **NOW!**
DO YOU THINK YOU CAN EVEN CONVINCE HIM TO TRY IT?

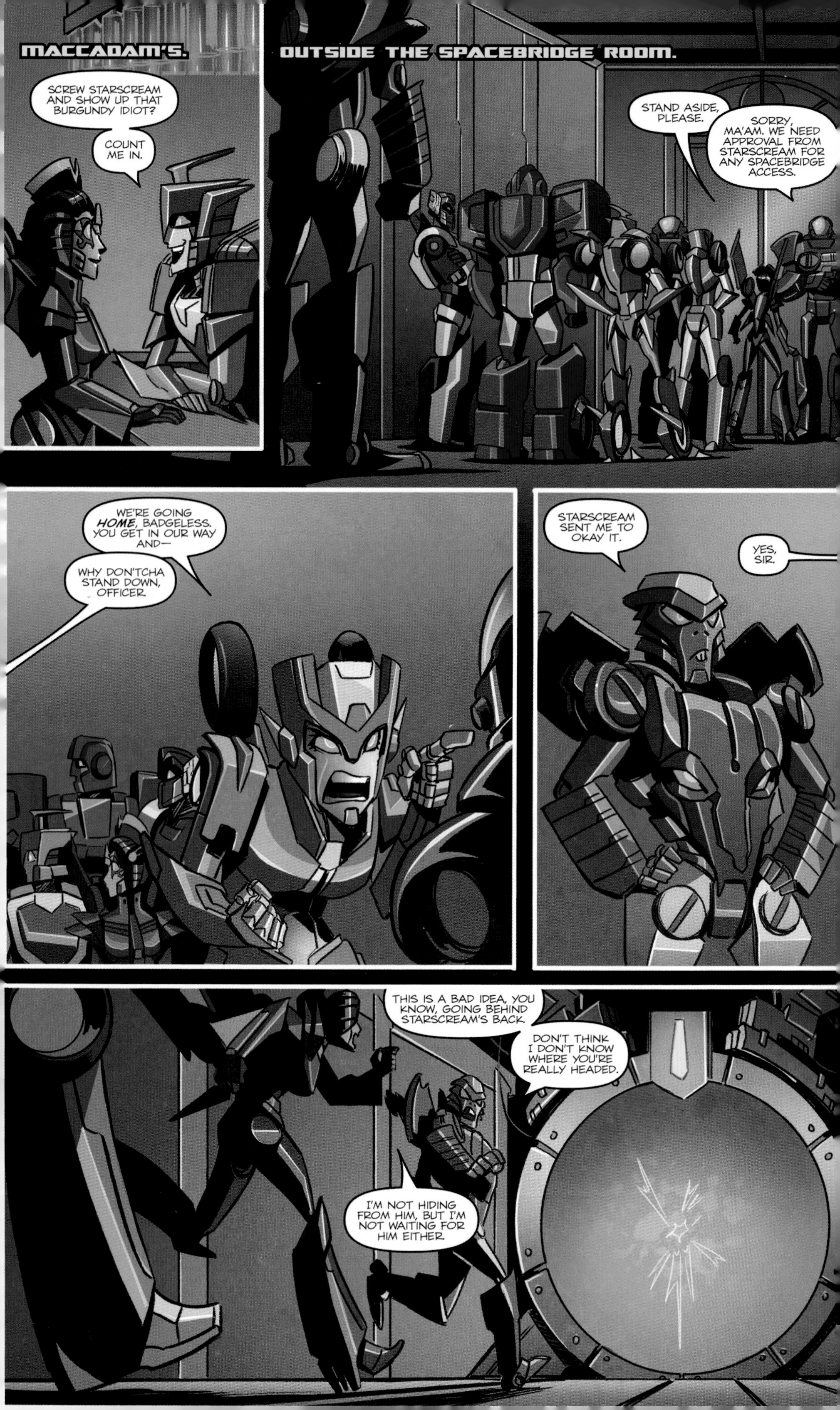
MACCADAM'S.
SCREW STARSCREAM AND SHOW UP THAT BURGUNDY IDIOT?
COUNT ME IN.
OUTSIDE THE SPACEBRIDGE ROOM.
STAND ASIDE, PLEASE.
SORRY, MA'AM. WE NEED APPROVAL FROM STARSCREAM FOR ANY SPACEBRIDGE ACCESS.
WE'RE GOING HOME, BADGELESS. YOU GET IN OUR WAY AND—
WHY DON'TCHA STAND DOWN, OFFICER
STARSCREAM SENT ME TO OKAY IT.
YES, SIR.
THIS IS A BAD IDEA, YOU KNOW, GOING BEHIND STARSCREAM'S BACK.
DON'T THINK I DON'T KNOW WHERE YOU'RE REALLY HEADED.
I'M NOT HIDING FROM HIM, BUT I'M NOT WAITING FOR HIM EITHER

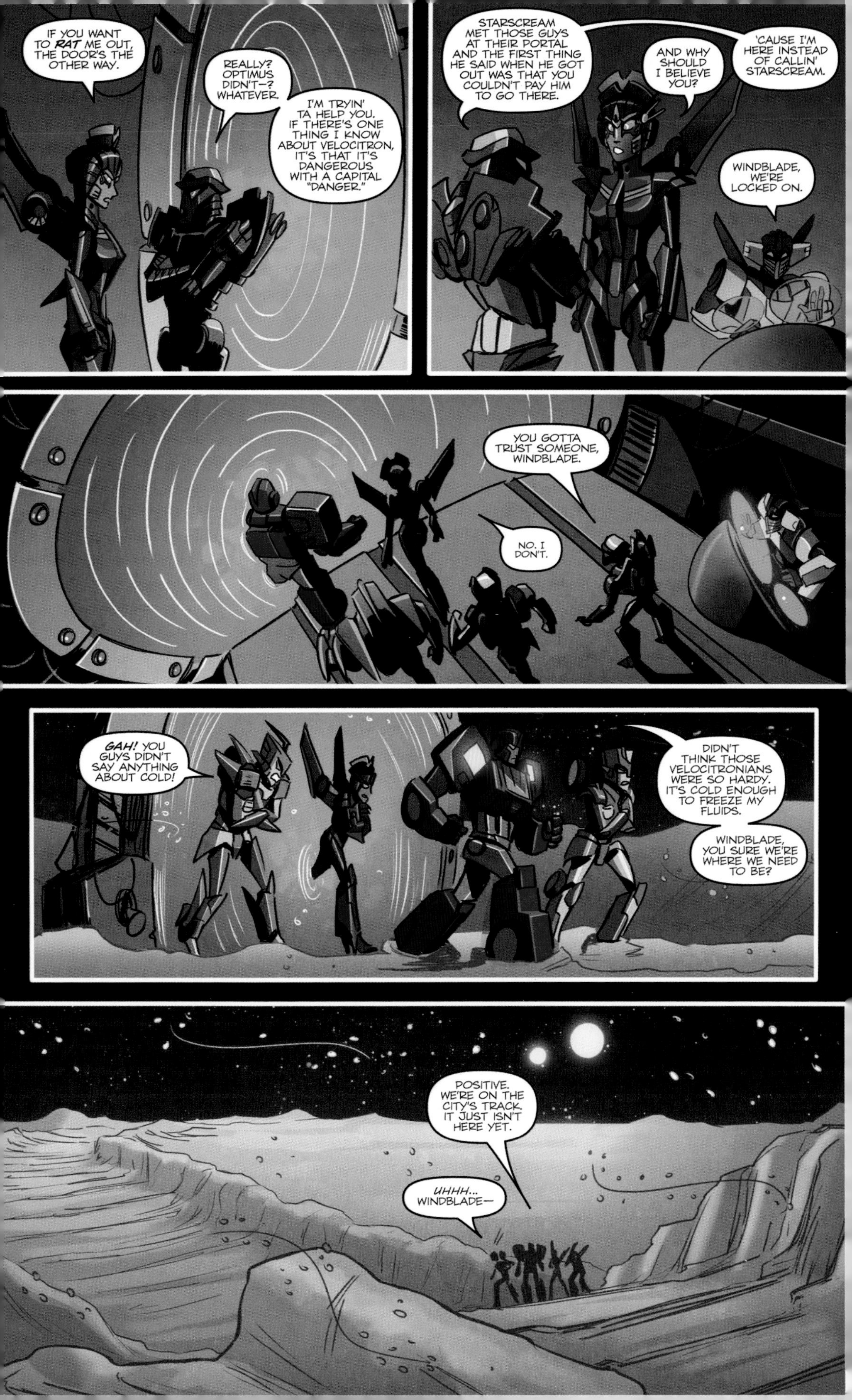
IF YOU WANT TO RAT ME OUT, THE DOOR'S THE OTHER WAY.
REALLY? OPTIMUS DIDN'T—? WHATEVER.
I'M TRYIN' TA HELP YOU. IF THERE'S ONE THING I KNOW ABOUT VELOCITRON, IT'S THAT IT'S DANGEROUS WITH A CAPITAL "DANGER."
STARSCREAM MET THOSE GUYS AT THEIR PORTAL AND THE FIRST THING HE SAID WHEN HE GOT OUT WAS THAT YOU COULDN'T PAY HIM TO GO THERE.
AND WHY SHOULD I BELIEVE YOU?
'CAUSE I'M HERE INSTEAD OF CALLIN' STARSCREAM.
WINDBLADE, WE'RE LOCKED ON.
YOU GOTTA TRUST SOMEONE, WINDBLADE.
NO. I DON'T.
GAH! YOU GUYS DIDN'T SAY ANYTHING ABOUT COLD!
DIDN'T THINK THOSE VELOCITRONIANS WERE SO HARDY. IT'S COLD ENOUGH TO FREEZE MY FLUIDS.
WINDBLADE, YOU SURE WE'RE WHERE WE NEED TO BE?
POSITIVE. WE'RE ON THE CITY'S TRACK. IT JUST ISN'T HERE YET.
UHHH... WINDBLADE—

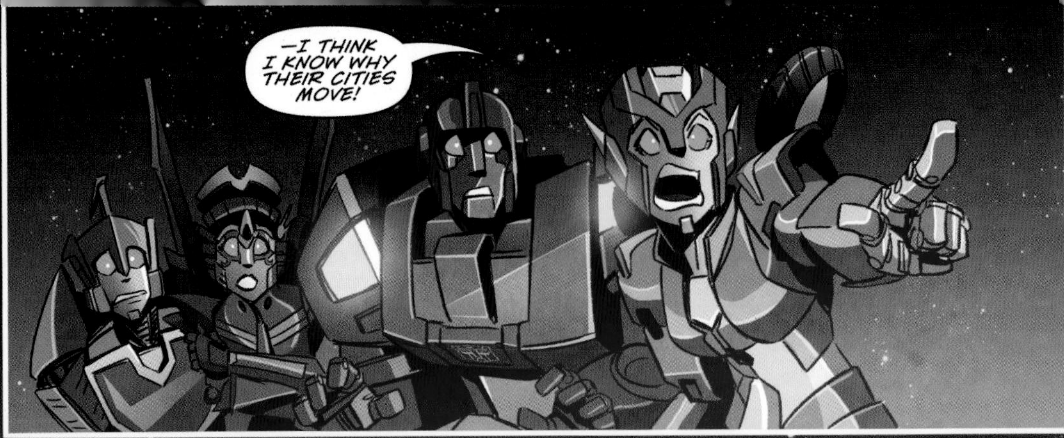
—I THINK I KNOW WHY THEIR CITIES MOVE!

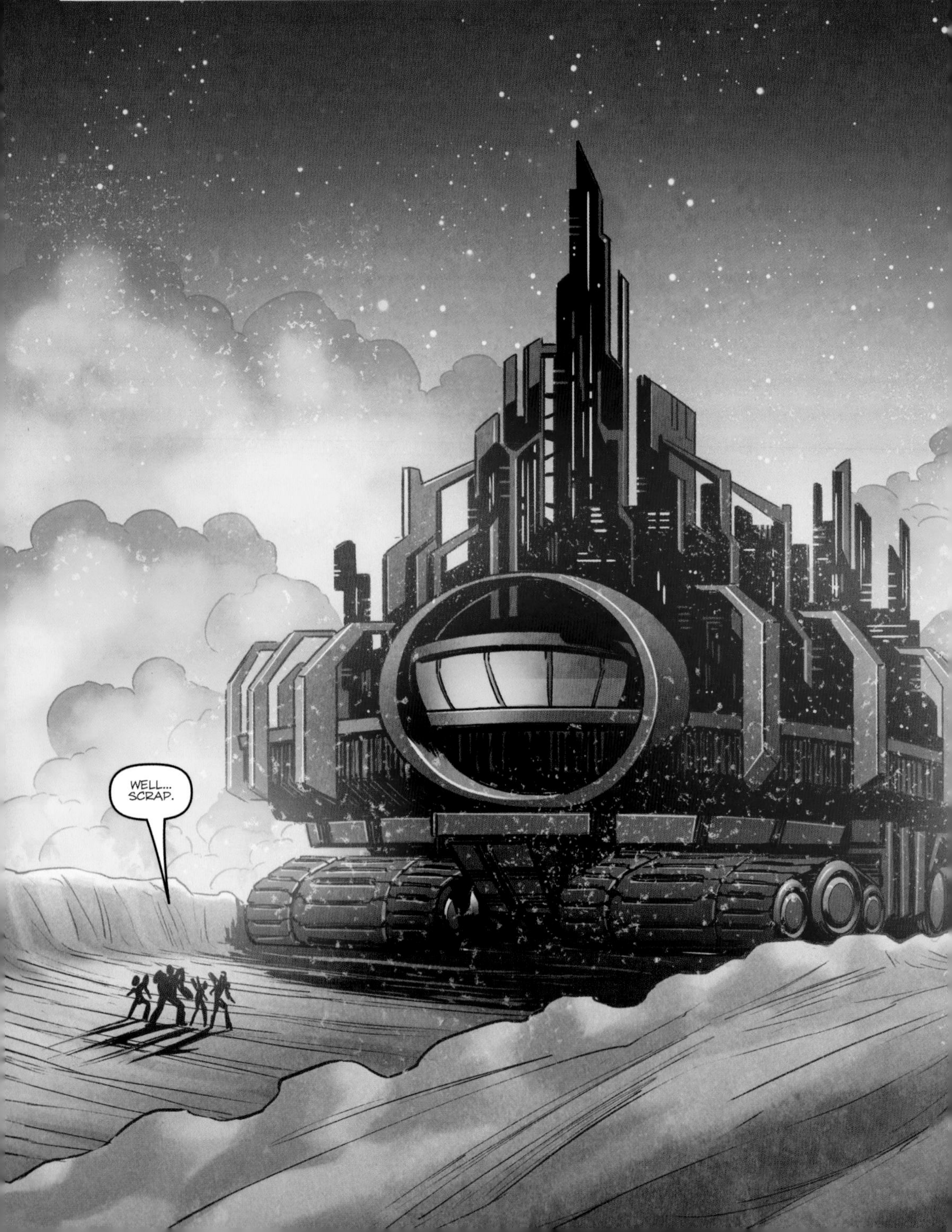
WELL... SCRAP.

ART BY **CASEY W. COLLER**
COLORS BY **JOANA LAFUENTE**

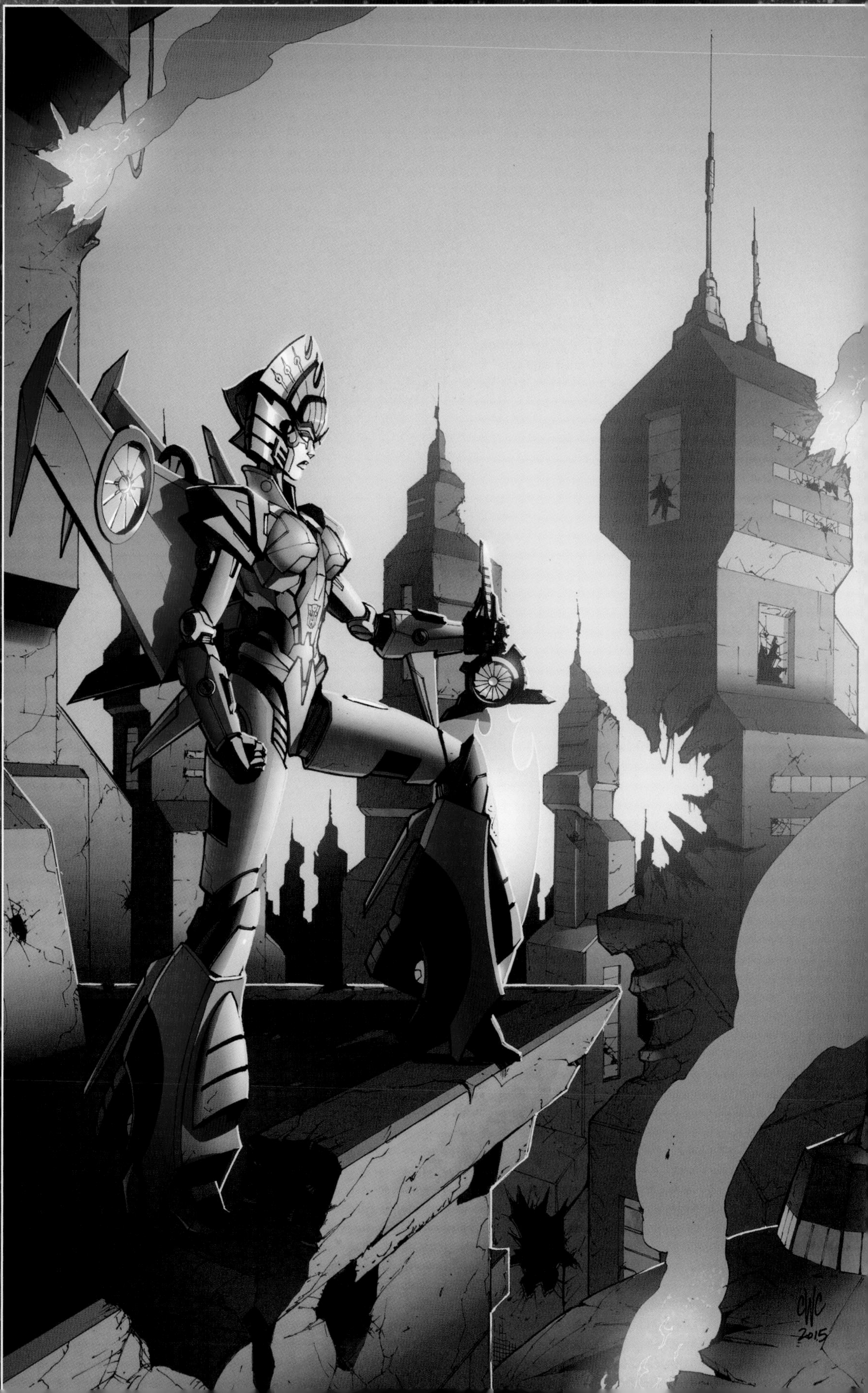

CWC
2015

ART BY **PRISCILLA TRAMONTANO**

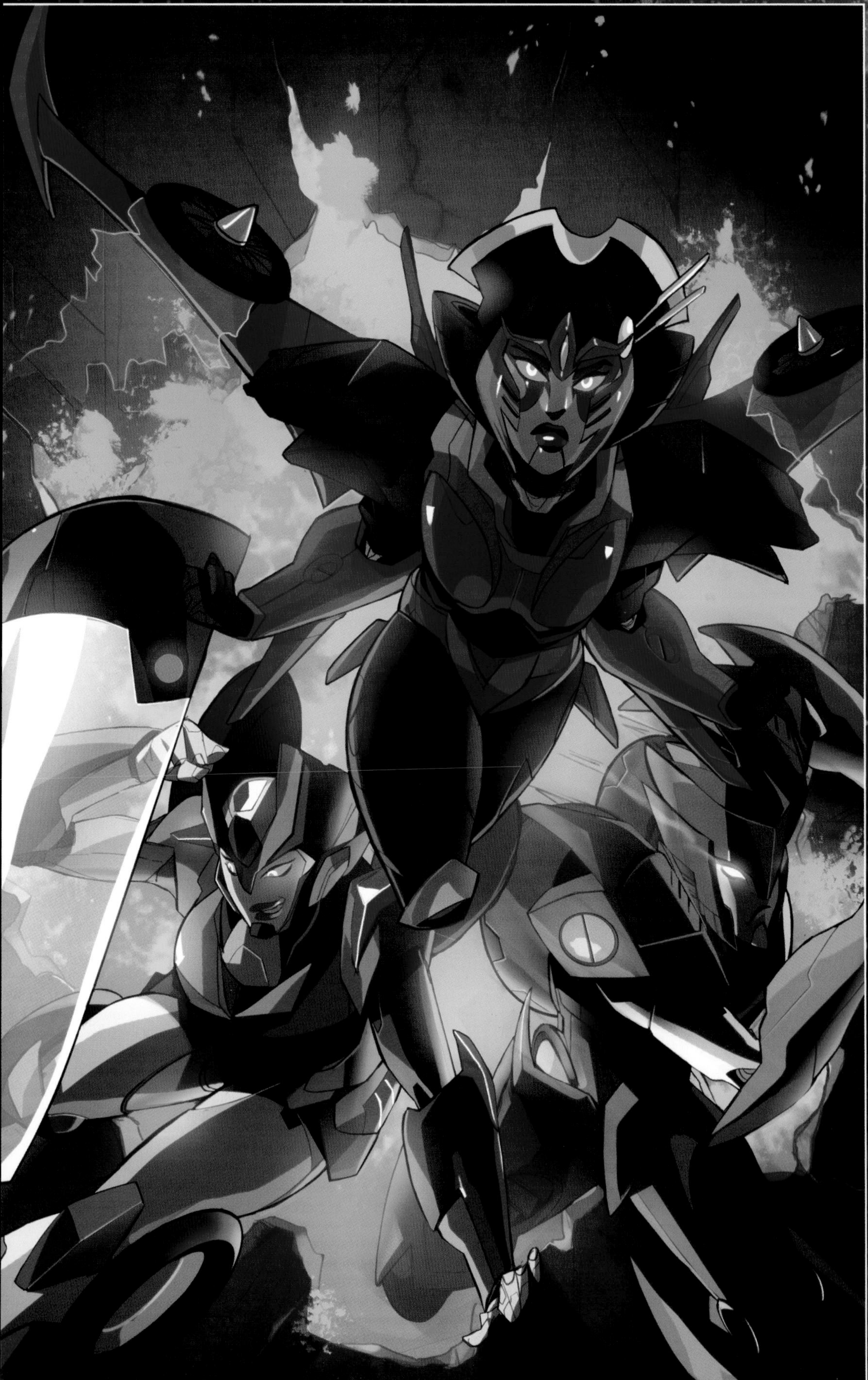

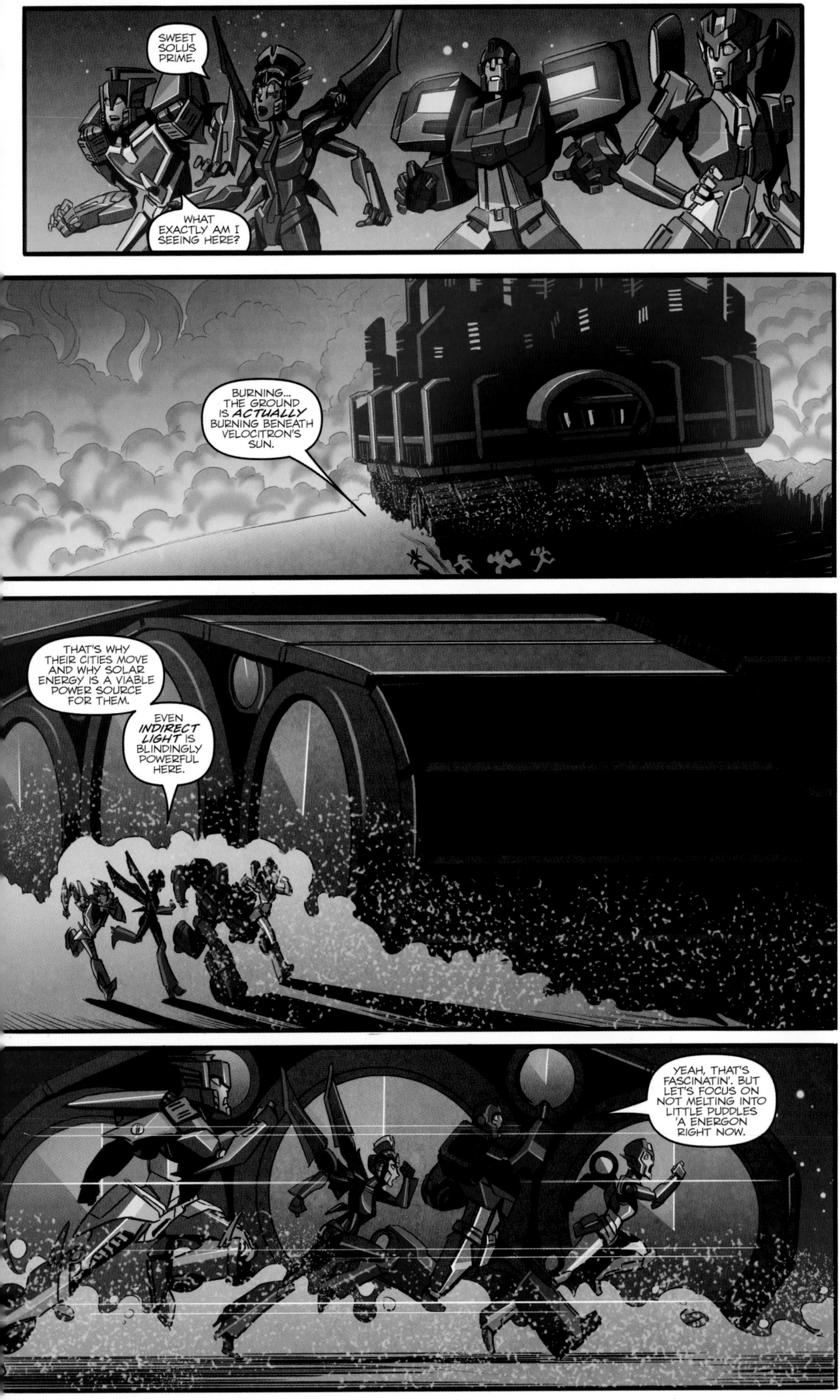
SWEET SOLUS PRIME.
WHAT EXACTLY AM I SEEING HERE?
BURNING... THE GROUND IS ACTUALLY BURNING BENEATH VELOCITRON'S SUN.
THAT'S WHY THEIR CITIES MOVE AND WHY SOLAR ENERGY IS A VIABLE POWER SOURCE FOR THEM.
EVEN INDIRECT LIGHT IS BLINDINGLY POWERFUL HERE.
YEAH, THAT'S FASCINATIN'. BUT LET'S FOCUS ON NOT MELTING INTO LITTLE PUDDLES 'A ENERGON RIGHT NOW.

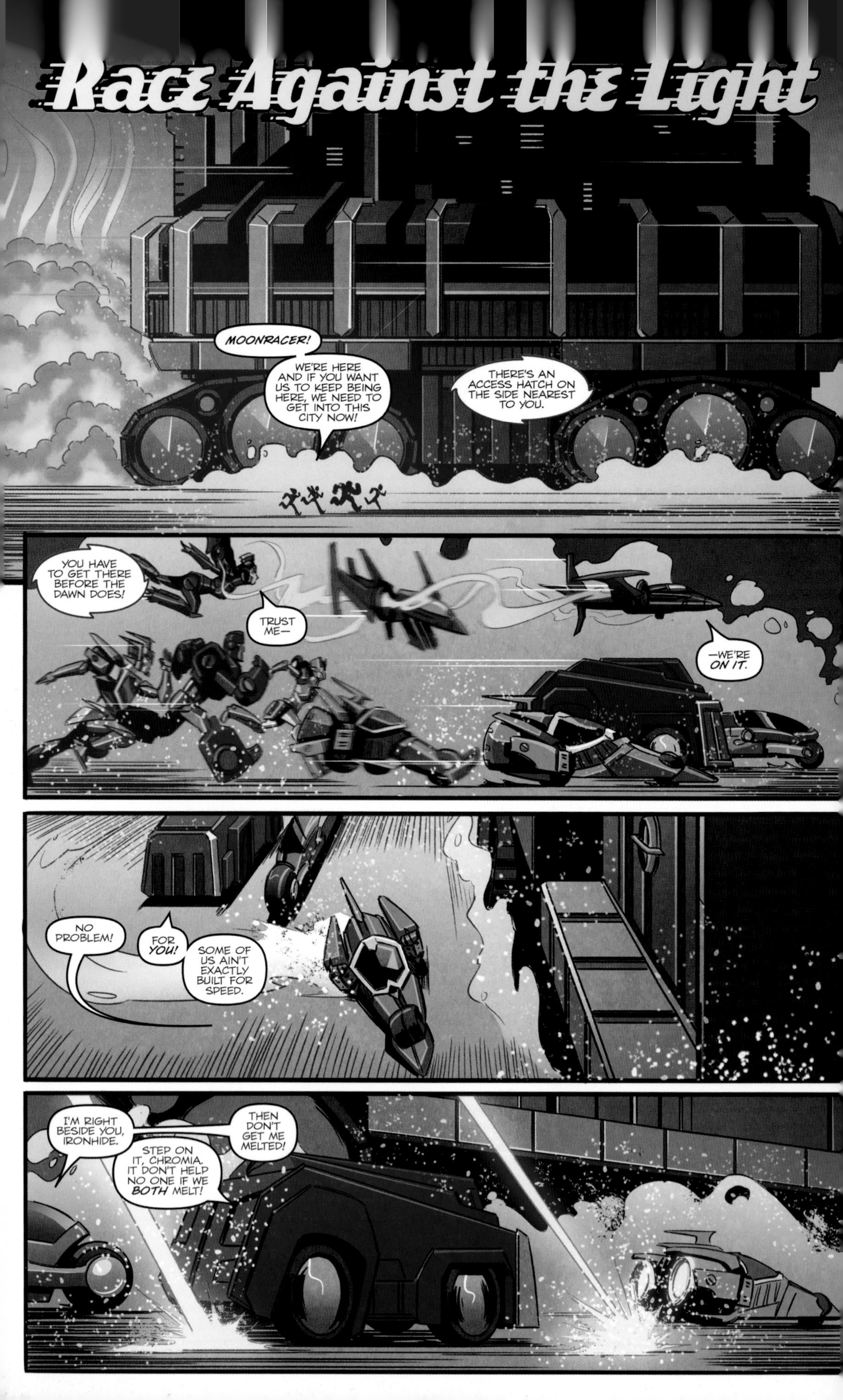
Race Against the Light
MOONRACER!
WE'RE HERE AND IF YOU WANT US TO KEEP BEING HERE, WE NEED TO GET INTO THIS CITY NOW!
THERE'S AN ACCESS HATCH ON THE SIDE NEAREST TO YOU.
YOU HAVE TO GET THERE BEFORE THE DAWN DOES!
TRUST ME—
—WE'RE ON IT.
NO PROBLEM!
FOR YOU!
SOME OF US AIN'T EXACTLY BUILT FOR SPEED.
I'M RIGHT BESIDE YOU, IRONHIDE.
THEN DON'T GET ME MELTED!
STEP ON IT, CHROMIA. IT DON'T HELP NO ONE IF WE BOTH MELT!

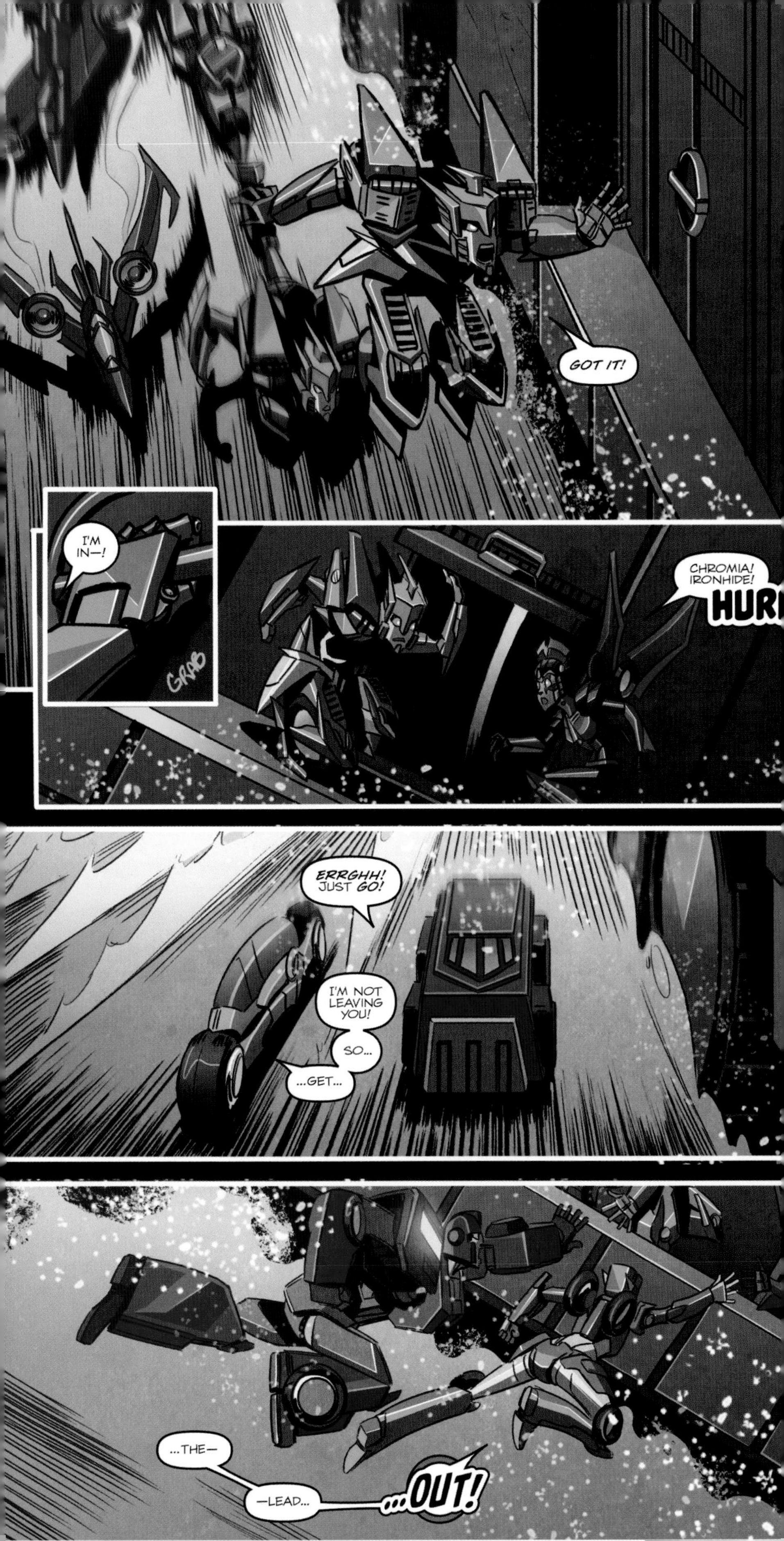
GOT IT!
I'M IN—!
GRAB
CHROMIA! IRONHIDE!
HUR
ERRGHH! JUST GO!
I'M NOT LEAVING YOU!
SO...
...GET...
...THE—
—LEAD...
...OUT!

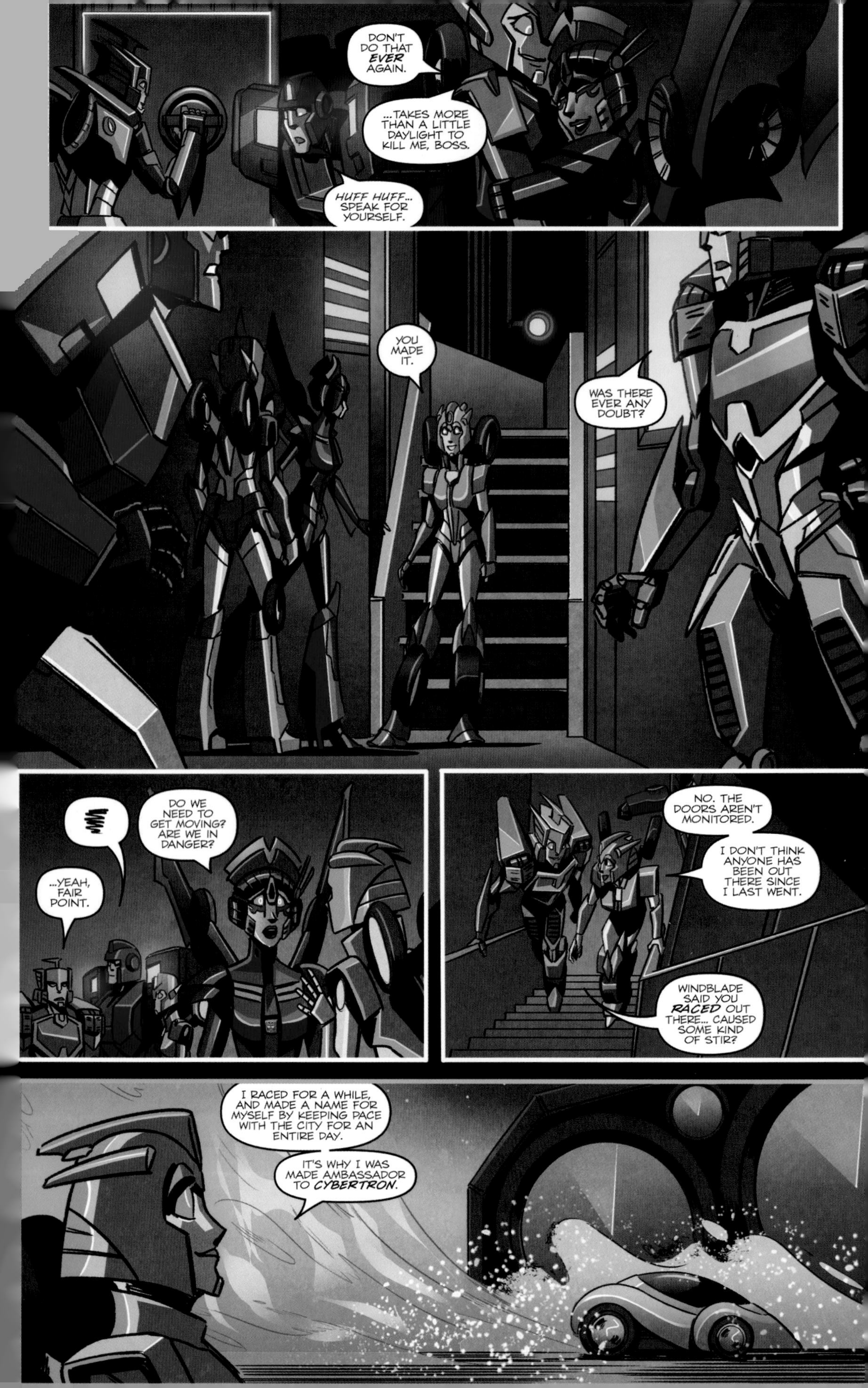
DON'T DO THAT EVER AGAIN.
...TAKES MORE THAN A LITTLE DAYLIGHT TO KILL ME, BOSS.
HUFF HUFF... SPEAK FOR YOURSELF.
YOU MADE IT.
WAS THERE EVER ANY DOUBT?
DO WE NEED TO GET MOVING? ARE WE IN DANGER?
...YEAH, FAIR POINT.
NO. THE DOORS AREN'T MONITORED.
I DON'T THINK ANYONE HAS BEEN OUT THERE SINCE I LAST WENT.
WINDBLADE SAID YOU RACED OUT THERE... CAUSED SOME KIND OF STIR?
I RACED FOR A WHILE, AND MADE A NAME FOR MYSELF BY KEEPING PACE WITH THE CITY FOR AN ENTIRE DAY.
IT'S WHY I WAS MADE AMBASSADOR TO CYBERTRON.

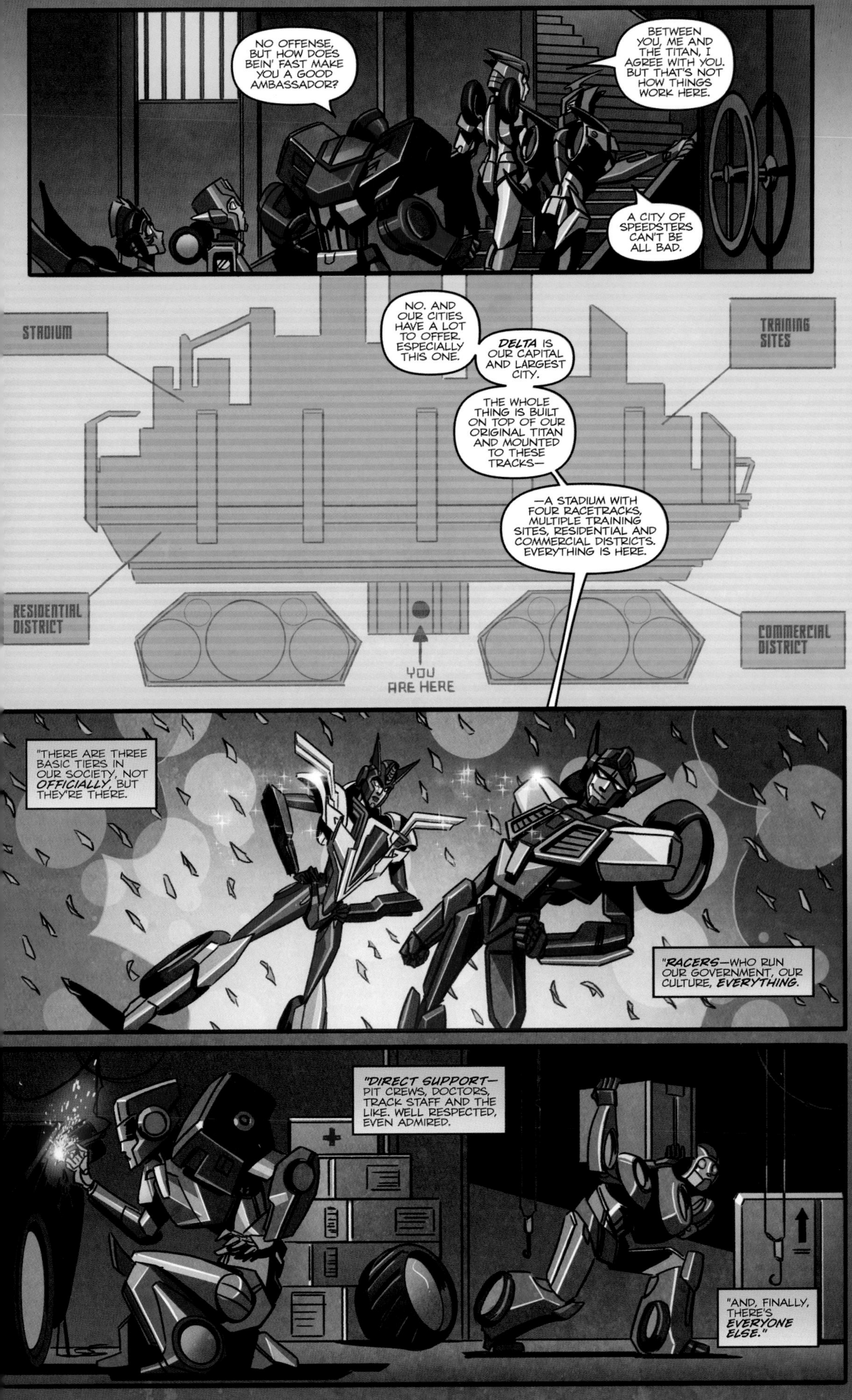

NO OFFENSE, BUT HOW DOES BEIN' FAST MAKE YOU A GOOD AMBASSADOR?
BETWEEN YOU, ME AND THE TITAN, I AGREE WITH YOU. BUT THAT'S NOT HOW THINGS WORK HERE.
A CITY OF SPEEDSTERS CAN'T BE ALL BAD.
STADIUM
TRAINING SITES
RESIDENTIAL DISTRICT
COMMERCIAL DISTRICT
YOU ARE HERE
NO. AND OUR CITIES HAVE A LOT TO OFFER. ESPECIALLY THIS ONE.
DELTA IS OUR CAPITAL AND LARGEST CITY.
THE WHOLE THING IS BUILT ON TOP OF OUR ORIGINAL TITAN AND MOUNTED TO THESE TRACKS—
—A STADIUM WITH FOUR RACETRACKS, MULTIPLE TRAINING SITES, RESIDENTIAL AND COMMERCIAL DISTRICTS. EVERYTHING IS HERE.
"THERE ARE THREE BASIC TIERS IN OUR SOCIETY, NOT OFFICIALLY, BUT THEY'RE THERE.
"RACERS—WHO RUN OUR GOVERNMENT, OUR CULTURE, EVERYTHING.
"DIRECT SUPPORT—PIT CREWS, DOCTORS, TRACK STAFF AND THE LIKE. WELL RESPECTED, EVEN ADMIRED.
"AND, FINALLY, THERE'S EVERYONE ELSE."

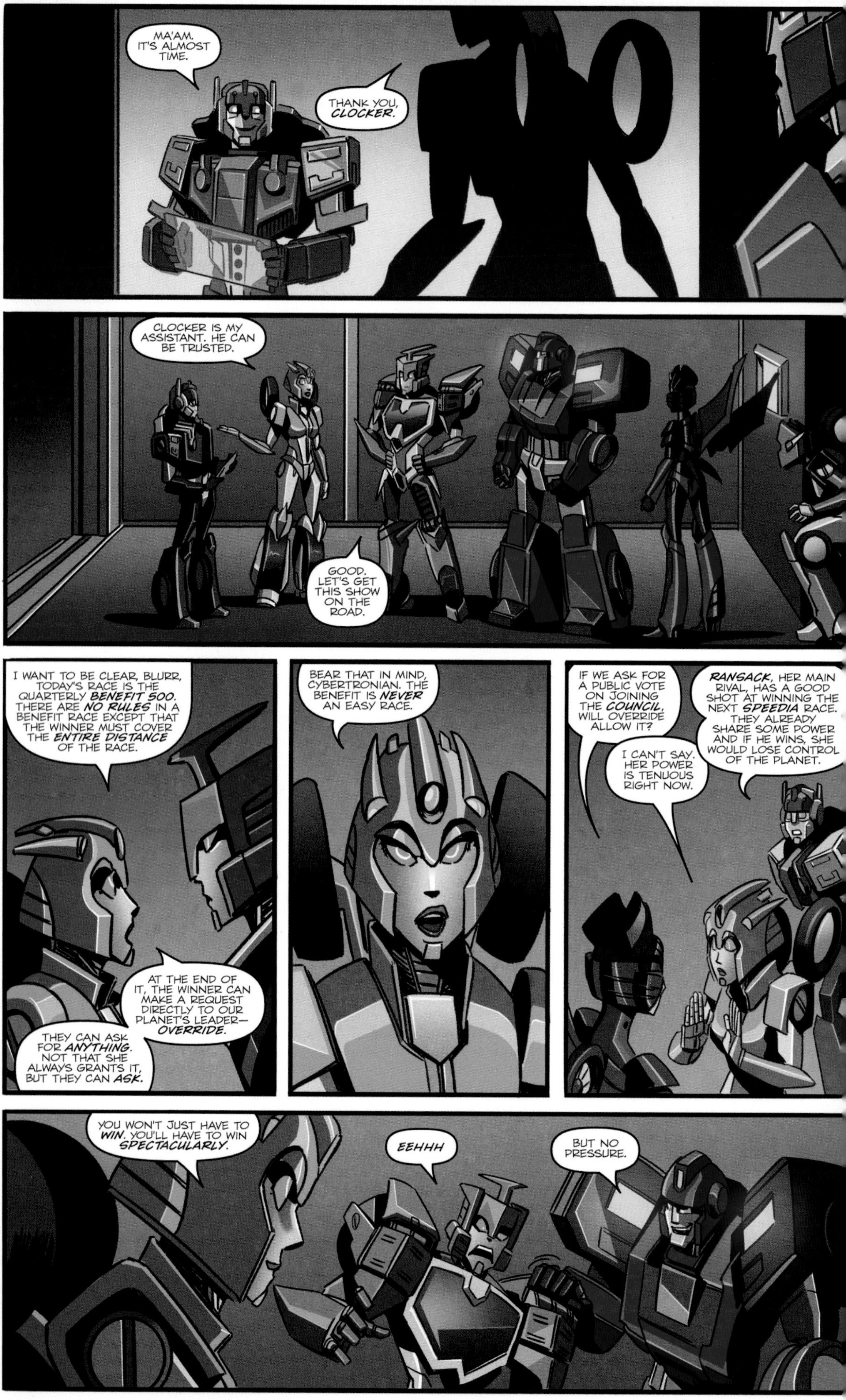
MA'AM. IT'S ALMOST TIME.
THANK YOU, CLOCKER.
CLOCKER IS MY ASSISTANT. HE CAN BE TRUSTED.
GOOD. LET'S GET THIS SHOW ON THE ROAD.
I WANT TO BE CLEAR, BLURR, TODAY'S RACE IS THE QUARTERLY BENEFIT 500. THERE ARE NO RULES IN A BENEFIT RACE EXCEPT THAT THE WINNER MUST COVER THE ENTIRE DISTANCE OF THE RACE.
AT THE END OF IT, THE WINNER CAN MAKE A REQUEST DIRECTLY TO OUR PLANET'S LEADER— OVERRIDE.
THEY CAN ASK FOR ANYTHING. NOT THAT SHE ALWAYS GRANTS IT, BUT THEY CAN ASK.
BEAR THAT IN MIND, CYBERTRONIAN. THE BENEFIT IS NEVER AN EASY RACE.
IF WE ASK FOR A PUBLIC VOTE ON JOINING THE COUNCIL, WILL OVERRIDE ALLOW IT?
I CAN'T SAY. HER POWER IS TENUOUS RIGHT NOW.
RANSACK, HER MAIN RIVAL, HAS A GOOD SHOT AT WINNING THE NEXT SPEEDIA RACE. THEY ALREADY SHARE SOME POWER AND IF HE WINS, SHE WOULD LOSE CONTROL OF THE PLANET.
YOU WON'T JUST HAVE TO WIN. YOU'LL HAVE TO WIN SPECTACULARLY.
EEHHH
BUT NO PRESSURE.

THEN WE HAVE TO MAKE SURE THAT HAPPENS. YOU SAID THIS CITY IS BUILT ON A *TITAN.* DOES IT STILL FUNCTION?

AS FAR AS I KNOW. IT'S THE BASE OF THE ENTIRE CITY, BUT AS LONG AS THE CITY MOVES, NO ONE CARES WHY.

AT THIS POINT, NO ONE REALLY CHECKS ON IT.

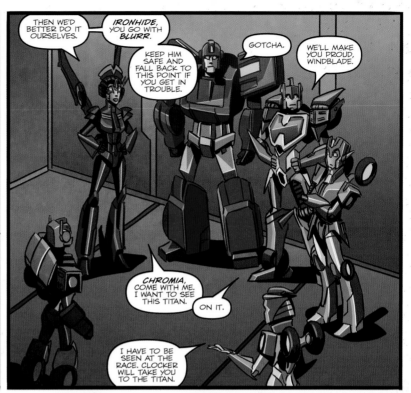

THEN WE'D BETTER DO IT OURSELVES.

IRONHIDE, YOU GO WITH *BLURR.*

KEEP HIM SAFE AND FALL BACK TO THIS POINT IF YOU GET IN TROUBLE.

GOTCHA.

WE'LL MAKE YOU PROUD, WINDBLADE.

CHROMIA, COME WITH ME. I WANT TO SEE THIS TITAN.

ON IT.

I HAVE TO BE SEEN AT THE RACE. CLOCKER WILL TAKE YOU TO THE TITAN.

THIS ENTIRE PLACE UNNERVES ME, BUT THAT'S NOT A VERY DIPLOMATIC THING TO SAY.

THE DECADENCE, THE THOUGHTLESSNESS, THE FACT THAT THIS ENTIRE CITY IS BUILT ON THE BACK OF AN ABANDONED TITAN.

THE *MISTRESS OF FLAME* WOULD SPIT TACKS IF SHE KNEW OF THIS.

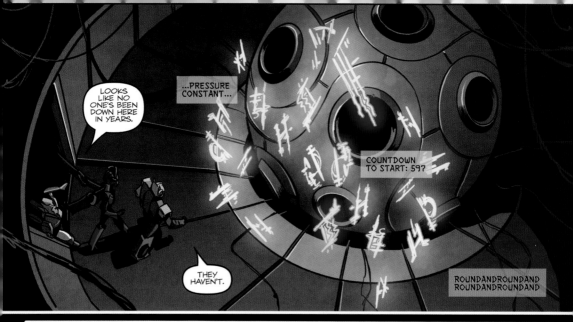

...PRESSURE CONSTANT...

LOOKS LIKE NO ONE'S BEEN DOWN HERE IN YEARS.

COUNTDOWN TO START: 597

THEY HAVEN'T.

ROUNDANDROUNDAND ROUNDANDROUNDAND

HOW SAD. HE'S WORKING SO HARD FOR YOU. NO ONE'S EVEN COME DOWN TO THANK HIM?

WE DON'T REALLY THINK OF IT THAT WAY. NAVITAS JUST... IS.

ROUNDANDROUND ANDROUNDAND

WELL, YOU *SHOULD*.

NAVITAS, CAN YOU HEAR ME?

MY NAME IS WINDBLADE AND I AM FROM ANOTHER WORLD.

ROUNDANDROUNDAND... WIND... BLADE?

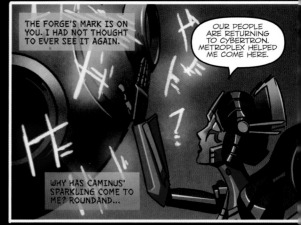

THE FORGE'S MARK IS ON YOU. I HAD NOT THOUGHT TO EVER SEE IT AGAIN.

OUR PEOPLE ARE RETURNING TO CYBERTRON. METROPLEX HELPED ME COME HERE.

WHY HAS CAMINUS' SPARKLING COME TO ME? ROUNDAND...

WE HOPE YOUR PEOPLE WILL RETURN AS WELL.

THOSE TWO... ROUNDAND... GLAD THEY'RE BACK... ROUNDAND...

BUT VELOCITRONIANS NO LONGER CARE WHAT I HAVE TO SAY.

RACE COUNTDOWN: 563...

VALVE 427. PRESSURE LOSS 5%. POWER DIVERTED.

HOW CAN THAT BE? HOW DID YOU COME TO BE OUT HERE?
CAMIENS AND CYBERTRONIANS... WE HAVE NO MEMORY OF WHAT BECAME OF YOU.
YOU WOULD... ROUNDANDROUNDAND...NOT.
WE KNOW NOTHING OF THE OTHERS' FATE. WE SAW CYBERTRON'S DESCENT INTO SUPERSTITION. WE THOUGHT IF WE COULD BREAK OUR...
...ROUNDANDROUND... DEPENDENCE ON...
NAVITAS, CAN YOU HEAR ME? ARE YOU WELL?
...WHO ARE YOU?
NAVITAS? I'M WINDBLADE, THE CAMIEN. REMEMBER?
I HAD NOT... THOUGHT... ROUNDANDROUNDAND... YOU WOULD COME.
...ROUNDANDROUND... TOO LATE FOR RE-ENFORCEMENTS
WINDBLADE, ARE YOU OKAY?
WHAT HAPPENED TO HIM?!
THIS IS HOW HE'S ALWAYS BEEN.
NO, IT ISN'T.
CHROMIA, HELP ME WITH THIS.

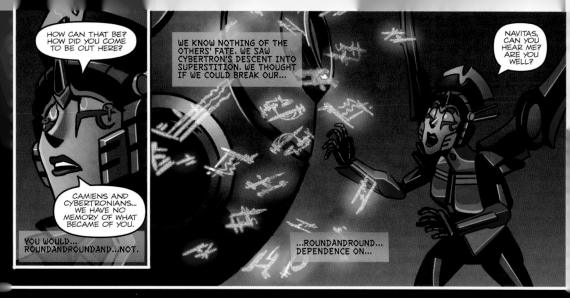

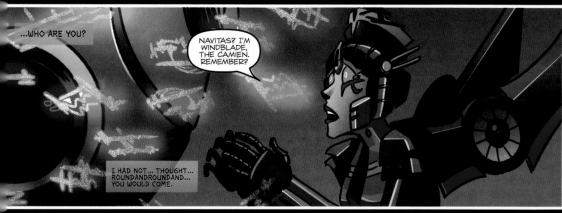

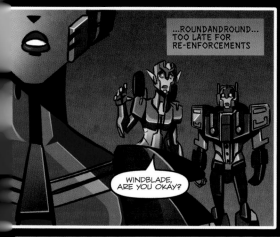

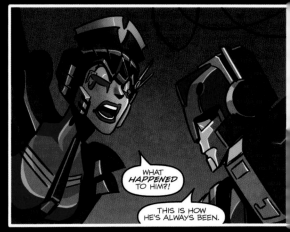

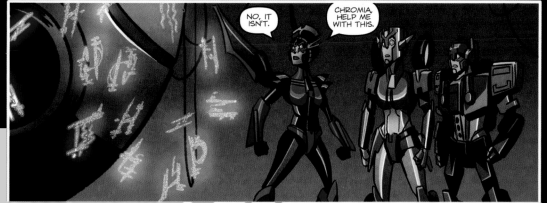

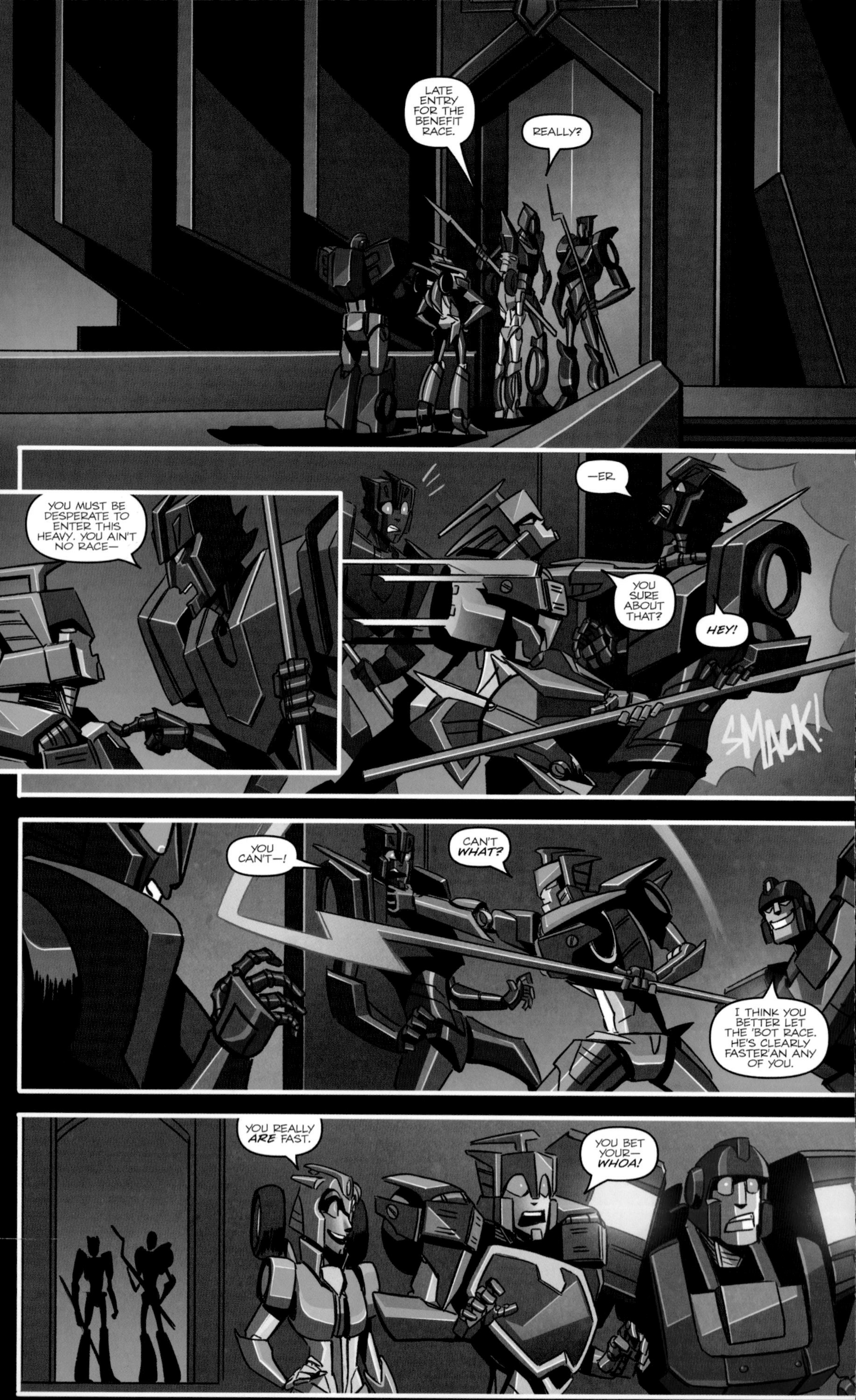
LATE ENTRY FOR THE BENEFIT RACE.
REALLY?
YOU MUST BE DESPERATE TO ENTER THIS HEAVY. YOU AIN'T NO RACE—
—ER.
YOU SURE ABOUT THAT?
HEY!
SMACK!
YOU CAN'T—!
CAN'T *WHAT?*
I THINK YOU BETTER LET THE 'BOT RACE. HE'S CLEARLY FASTER'AN ANY OF YOU.
YOU REALLY *ARE* FAST.
YOU BET YOUR— *WHOA!*

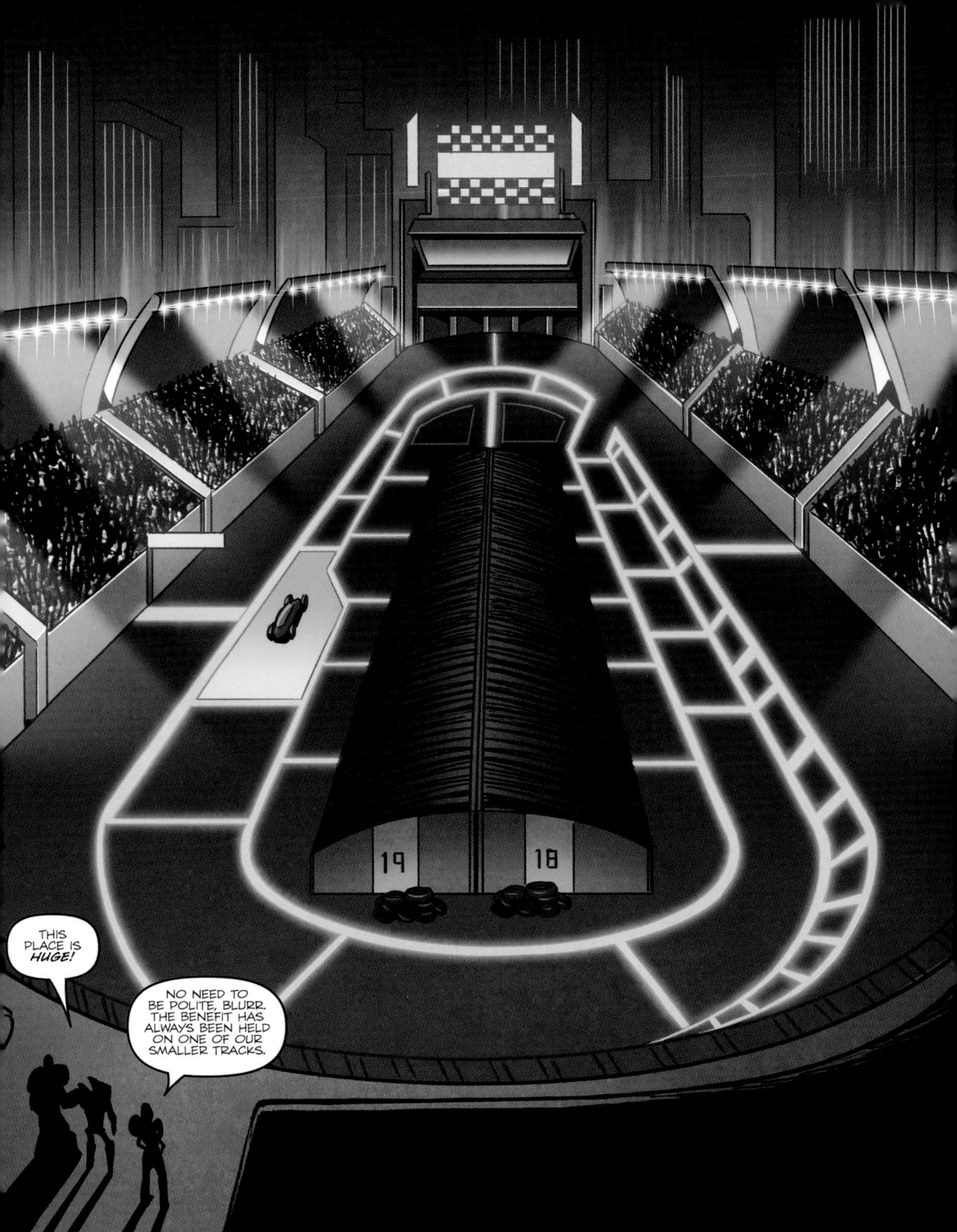
19
18
THIS PLACE IS *HUGE!*
NO NEED TO BE POLITE, BLURR. THE BENEFIT HAS ALWAYS BEEN HELD ON ONE OF OUR SMALLER TRACKS.

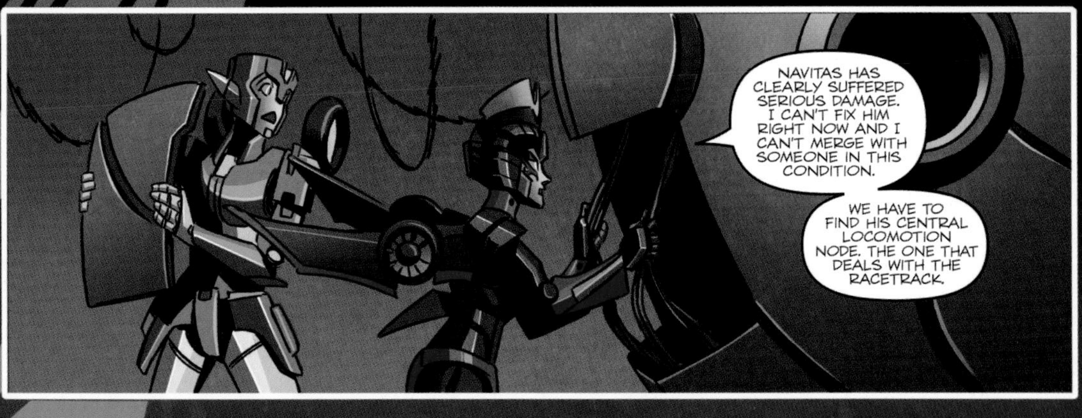
NAVITAS HAS CLEARLY SUFFERED SERIOUS DAMAGE. I CAN'T FIX HIM RIGHT NOW AND I CAN'T MERGE WITH SOMEONE IN THIS CONDITION.
WE HAVE TO FIND HIS CENTRAL LOCOMOTION NODE. THE ONE THAT DEALS WITH THE RACETRACK.

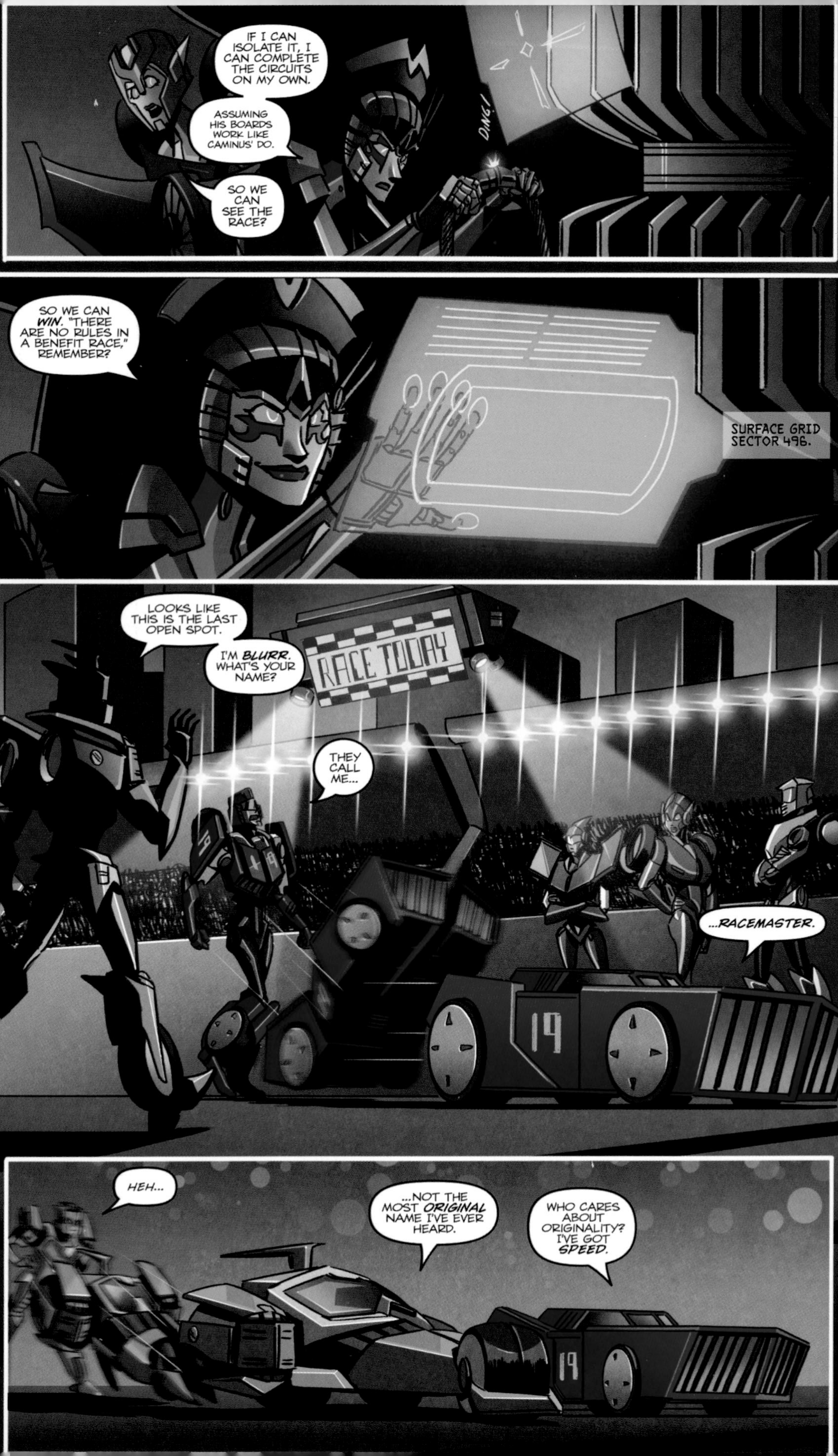
IF I CAN ISOLATE IT, I CAN COMPLETE THE CIRCUITS ON MY OWN.
ASSUMING HIS BOARDS WORK LIKE CAMINUS' DO.
DING!
SO WE CAN SEE THE RACE?
SO WE CAN *WIN*. "THERE ARE NO RULES IN A BENEFIT RACE," REMEMBER?
SURFACE GRID SECTOR 496.
LOOKS LIKE THIS IS THE LAST OPEN SPOT.
I'M ***BLURR***. WHAT'S YOUR NAME?
RACE TODAY
THEY CALL ME...
...***RACEMASTER***.
HEH...
...NOT THE MOST ***ORIGINAL*** NAME I'VE EVER HEARD.
WHO CARES ABOUT ORIGINALITY? I'VE GOT ***SPEED***.

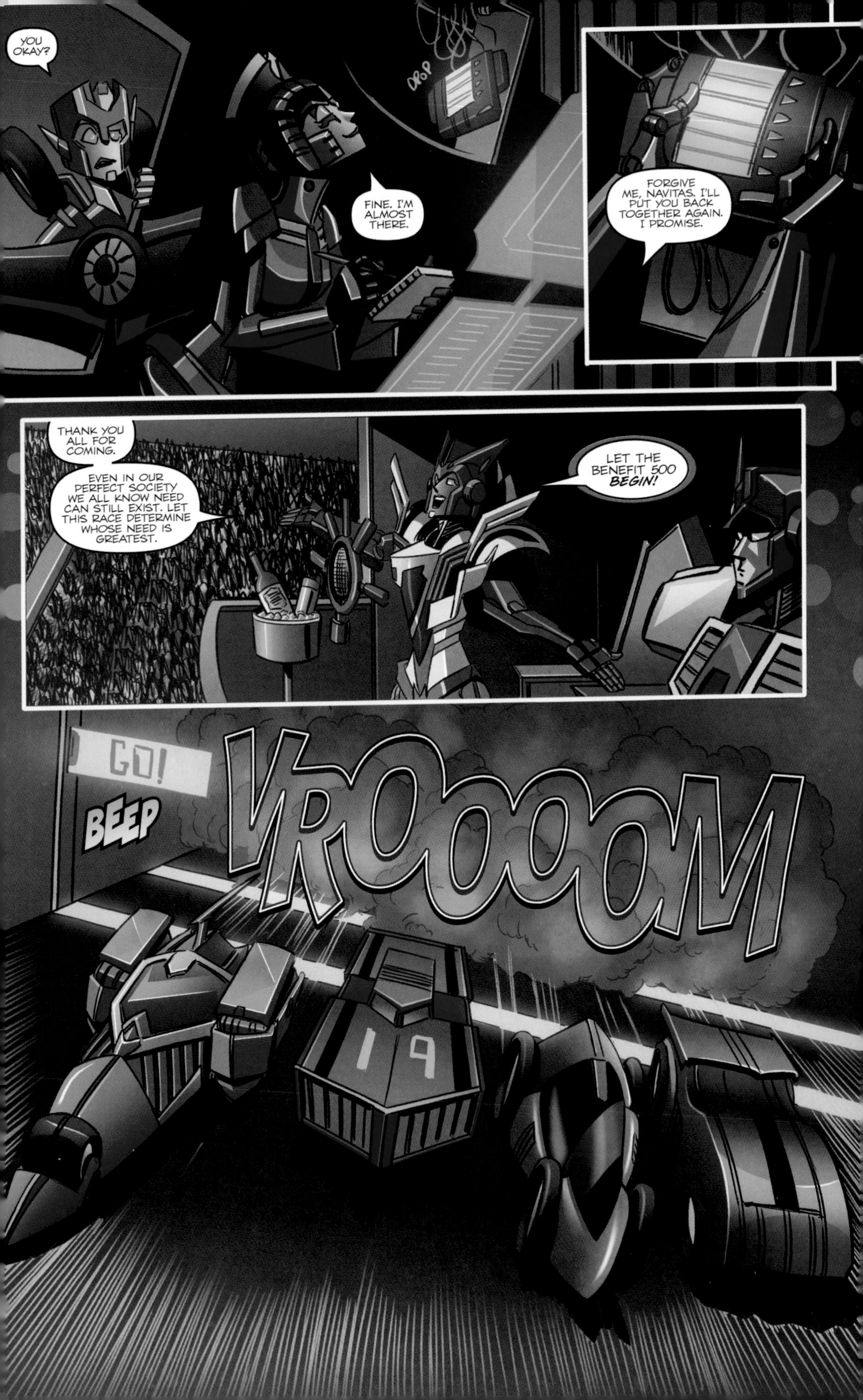
YOU OKAY?
DROP
FINE. I'M ALMOST THERE.
FORGIVE ME, NAVITAS. I'LL PUT YOU BACK TOGETHER AGAIN. I PROMISE.
THANK YOU ALL FOR COMING.
EVEN IN OUR PERFECT SOCIETY WE ALL KNOW NEED CAN STILL EXIST. LET THIS RACE DETERMINE WHOSE NEED IS GREATEST.
LET THE BENEFIT 500 BEGIN!
GO!
BEEP
VROOOOM
19

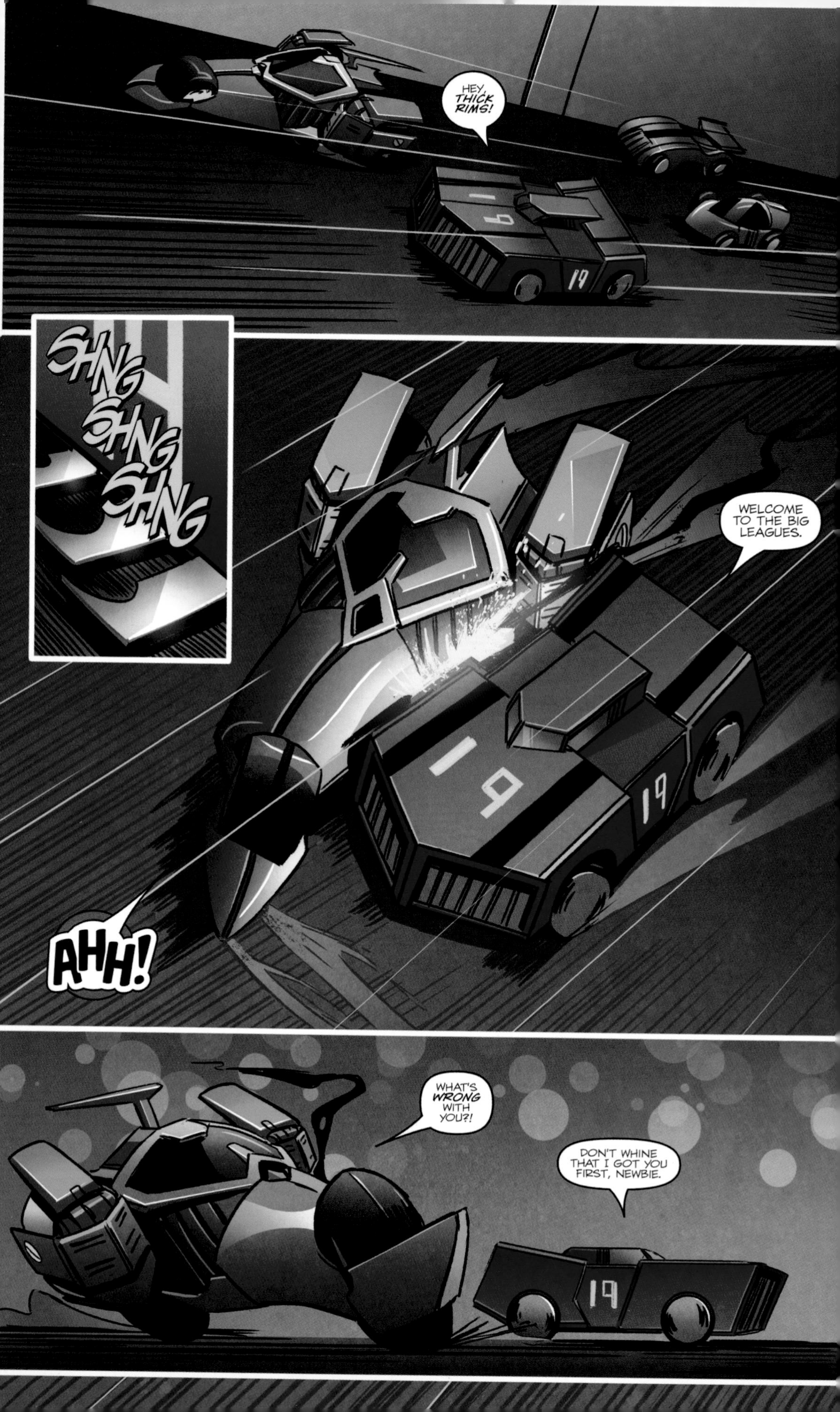
HEY, THICK RIMS!
19
SHNG SHNG SHNG
WELCOME TO THE BIG LEAGUES.
AHH!
WHAT'S WRONG WITH YOU?!
DON'T WHINE THAT I GOT YOU FIRST, NEWBIE.

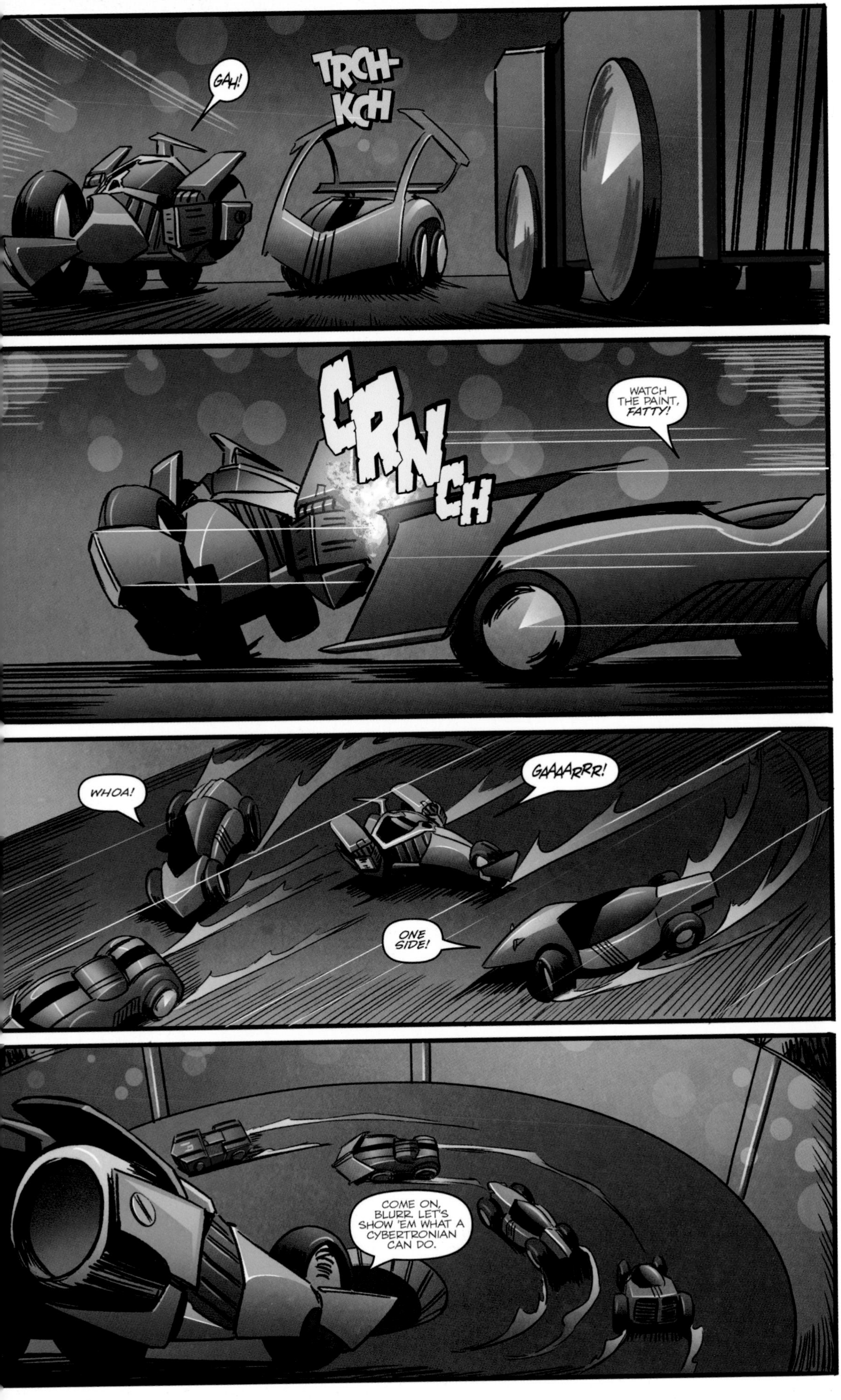
GAH!
TRCH-KCH
CRNCH
WATCH THE PAINT, FATTY!
WHOA!
GAAAARRR!
ONE SIDE!
COME ON, BLURR. LET'S SHOW 'EM WHAT A CYBERTRONIAN CAN DO.

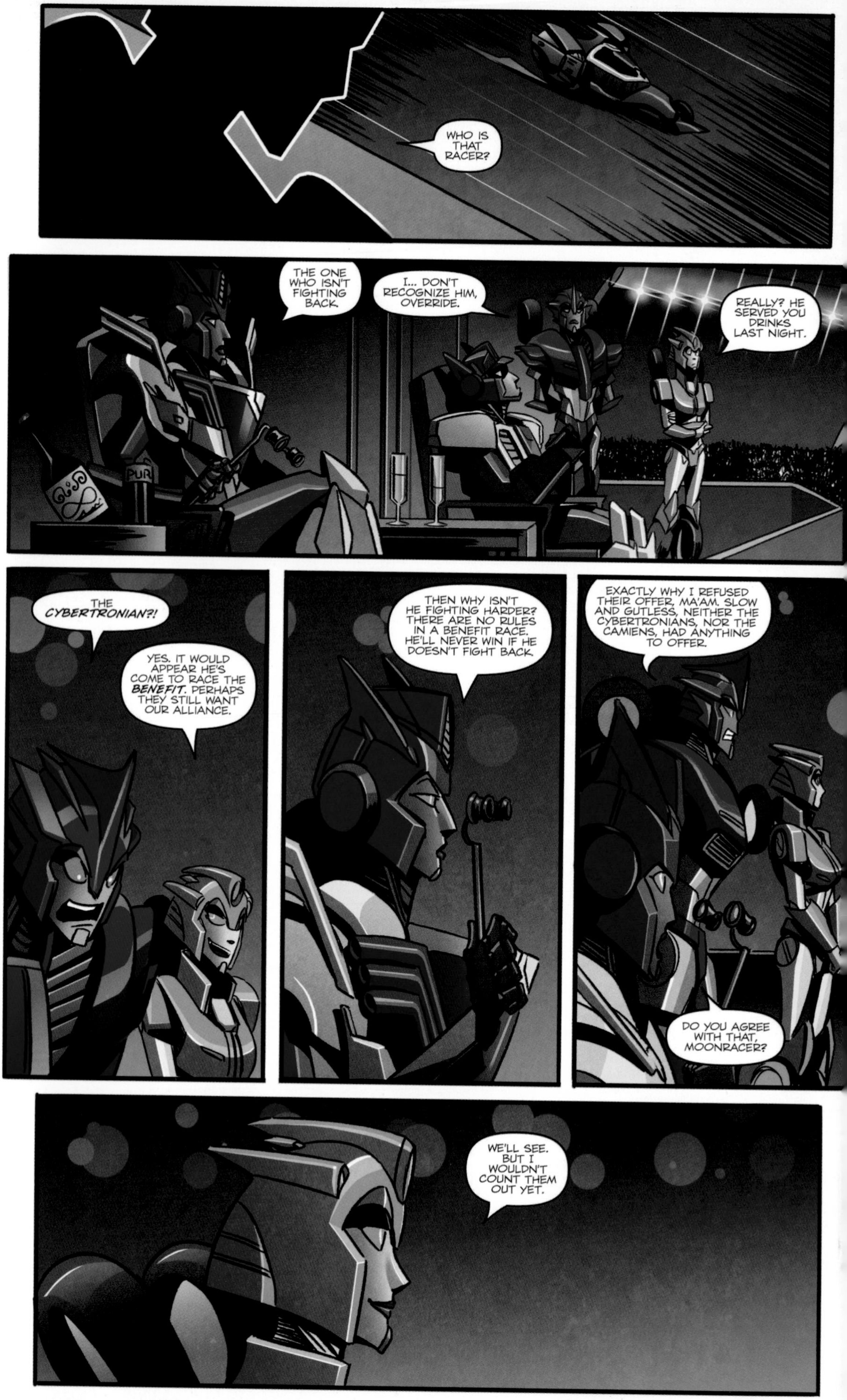
WHO IS THAT RACER?
THE ONE WHO ISN'T FIGHTING BACK.
I... DON'T RECOGNIZE HIM, OVERRIDE.
REALLY? HE SERVED YOU DRINKS LAST NIGHT.
PUR
THE CYBERTRONIAN?!
YES. IT WOULD APPEAR HE'S COME TO RACE THE BENEFIT. PERHAPS THEY STILL WANT OUR ALLIANCE.
THEN WHY ISN'T HE FIGHTING HARDER? THERE ARE NO RULES IN A BENEFIT RACE. HE'LL NEVER WIN IF HE DOESN'T FIGHT BACK.
EXACTLY WHY I REFUSED THEIR OFFER, MA'AM. SLOW AND GUTLESS, NEITHER THE CYBERTRONIANS, NOR THE CAMIENS, HAD ANYTHING TO OFFER.
DO YOU AGREE WITH THAT, MOONRACER?
WE'LL SEE. BUT I WOULDN'T COUNT THEM OUT YET.

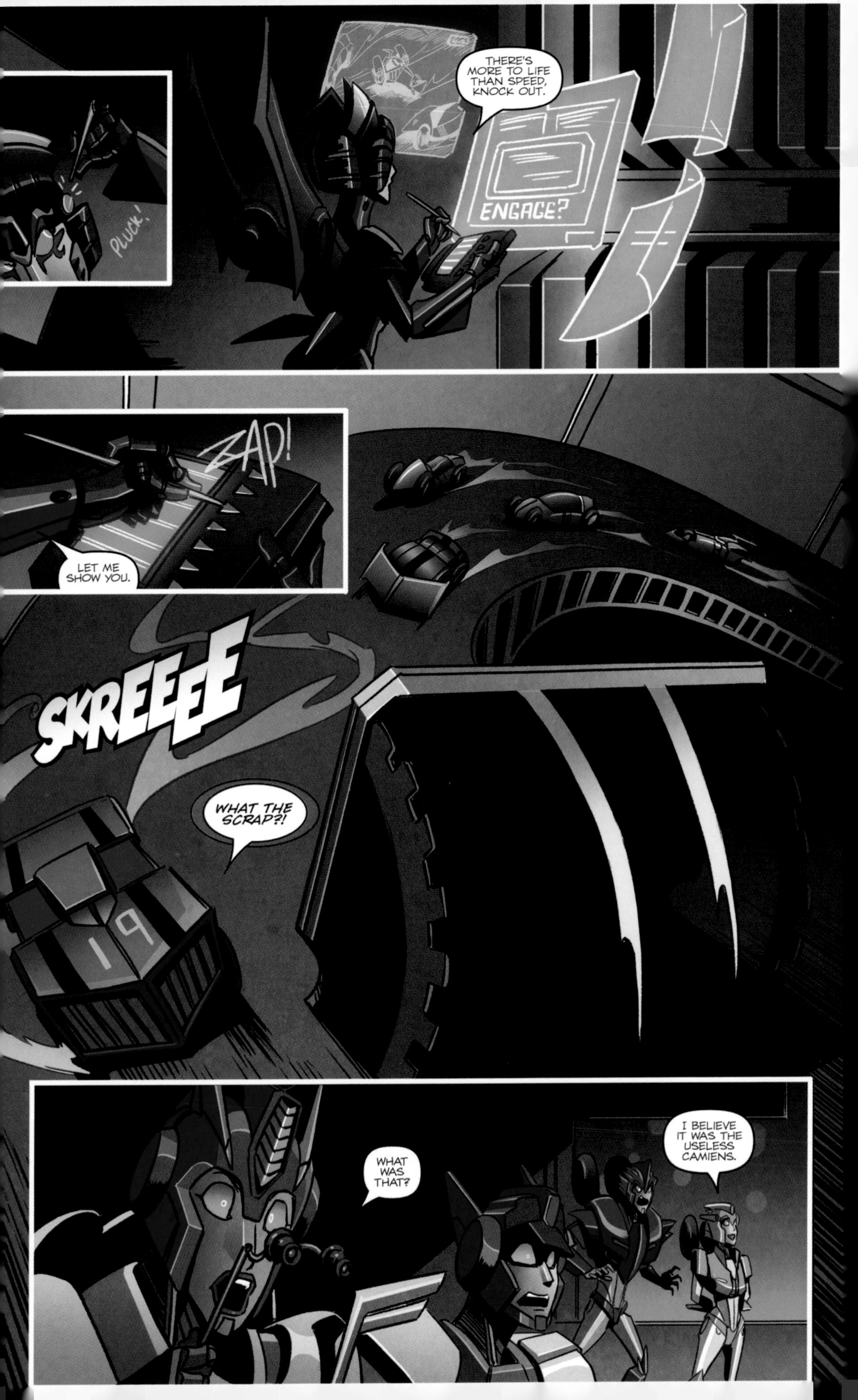
PLUCK!
THERE'S MORE TO LIFE THAN SPEED, KNOCK OUT.
ENGAGE?
ZAP!
LET ME SHOW YOU.
SKREEEEE
WHAT THE SCRAP?!
19
WHAT WAS THAT?
I BELIEVE IT WAS THE USELESS CAMIENS.

SMACK!
TCH
TCH
YES YES YES
KCH
WOOO-HOOO!

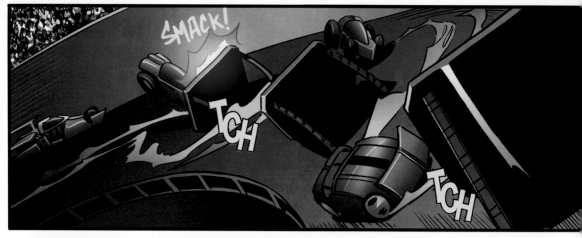

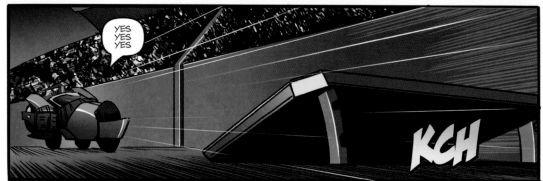

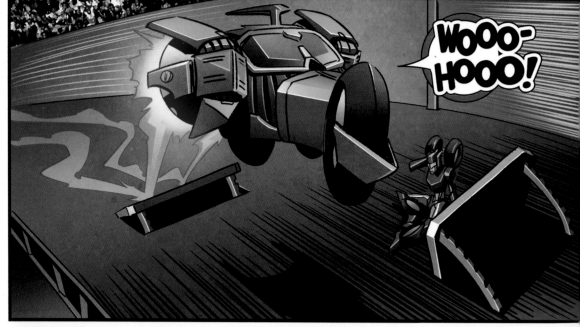

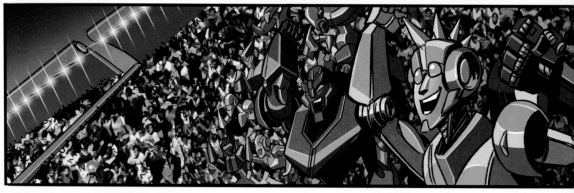

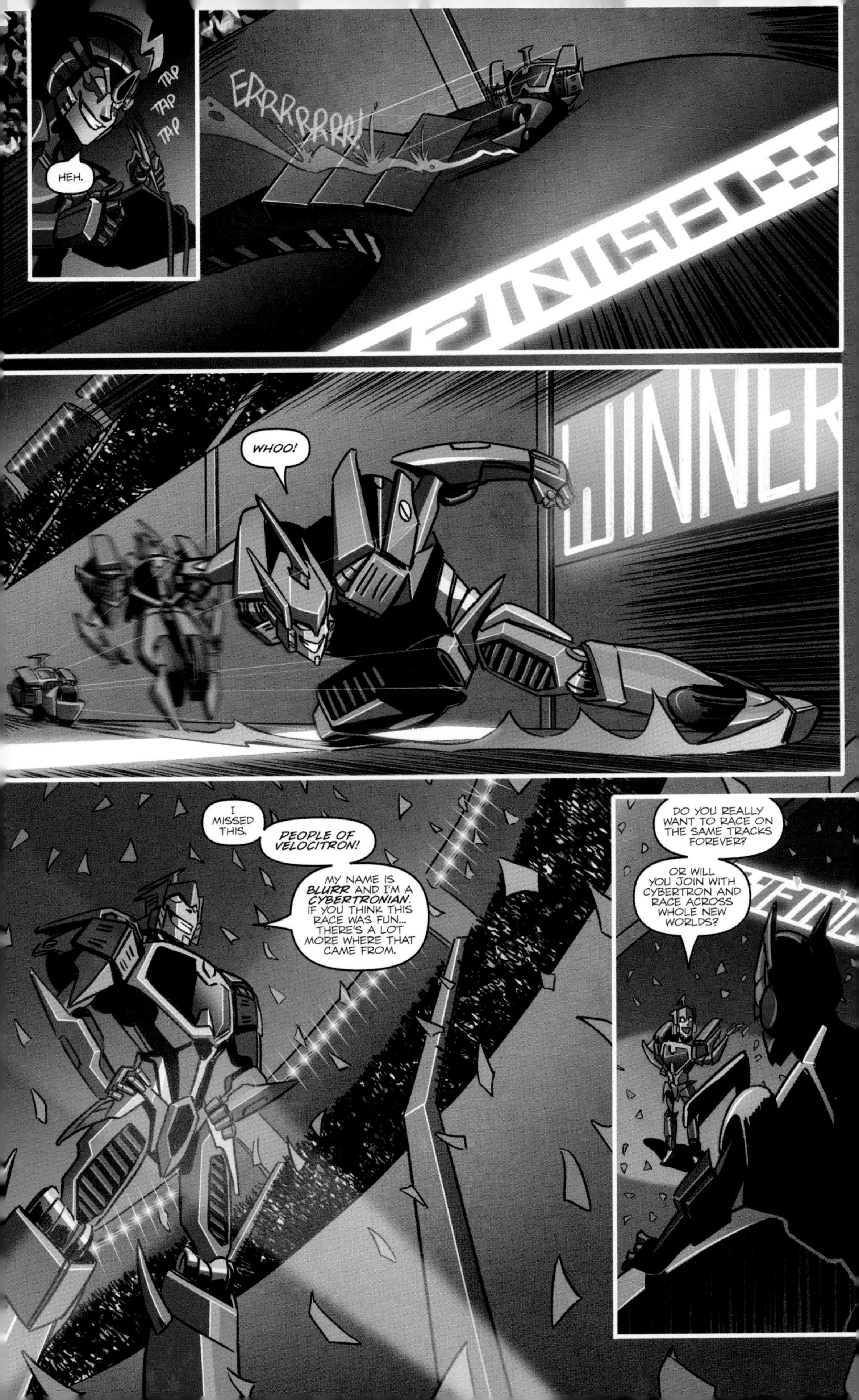
HEH.
TAP TAP TAP
ERRRRRRRR!
FINISH
WINNER
WHOO!
I MISSED THIS.
PEOPLE OF VELOCITRON!
MY NAME IS BLURR AND I'M A CYBERTRONIAN. IF YOU THINK THIS RACE WAS FUN... THERE'S A LOT MORE WHERE THAT CAME FROM.
DO YOU REALLY WANT TO RACE ON THE SAME TRACKS FOREVER?
OR WILL YOU JOIN WITH CYBERTRON AND RACE ACROSS WHOLE NEW WORLDS?

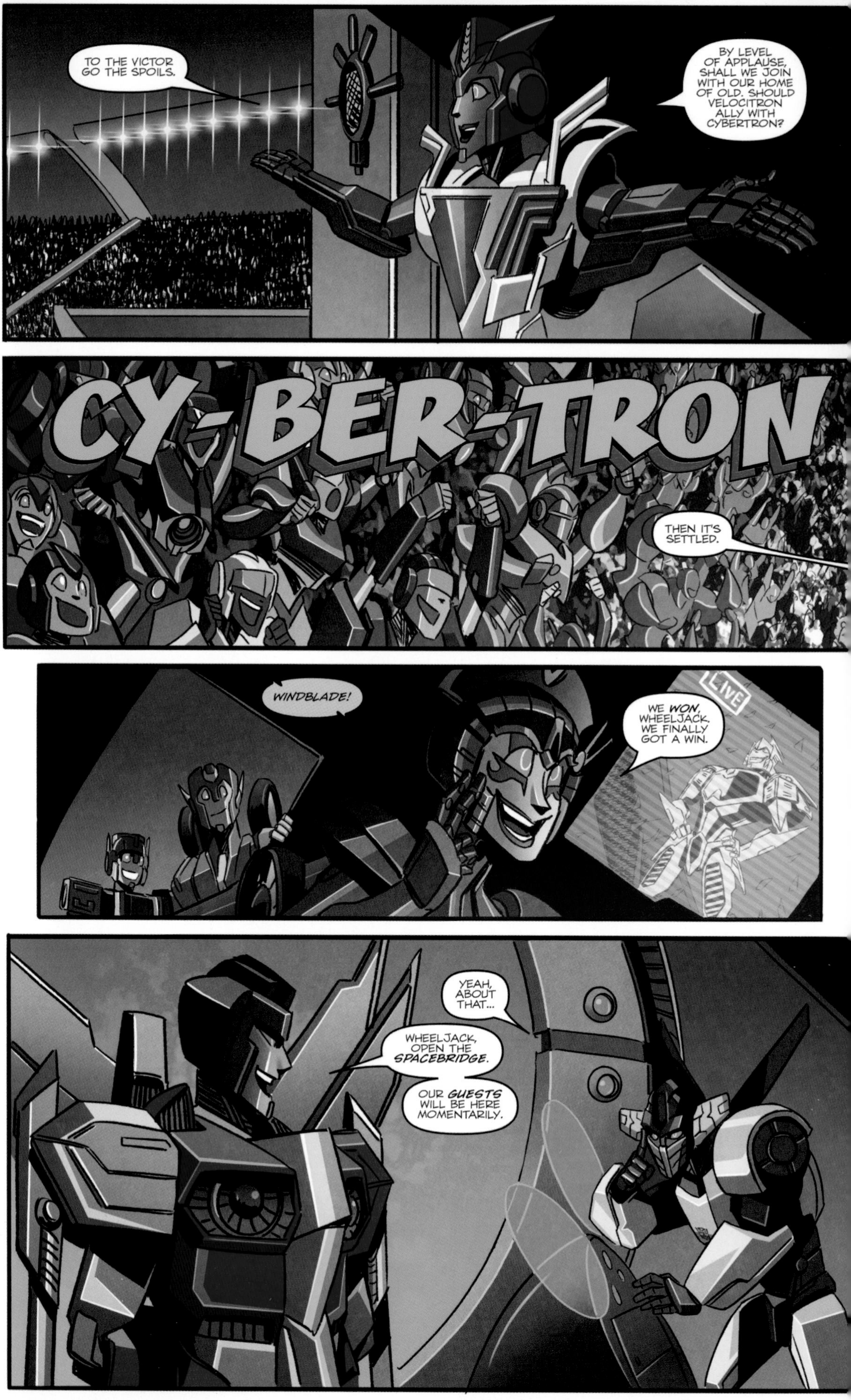
TO THE VICTOR GO THE SPOILS.
BY LEVEL OF APPLAUSE, SHALL WE JOIN WITH OUR HOME OF OLD. SHOULD VELOCITRON ALLY WITH CYBERTRON?
CY-BER-TRON
THEN IT'S SETTLED.
WINDBLADE!
LIVE
WE WON, WHEELJACK. WE FINALLY GOT A WIN.
YEAH, ABOUT THAT...
WHEELJACK, OPEN THE SPACEBRIDGE.
OUR GUESTS WILL BE HERE MOMENTARILY.

ART BY **CASEY W. COLLER**
COLORS BY **JOANA LAFUENTE**

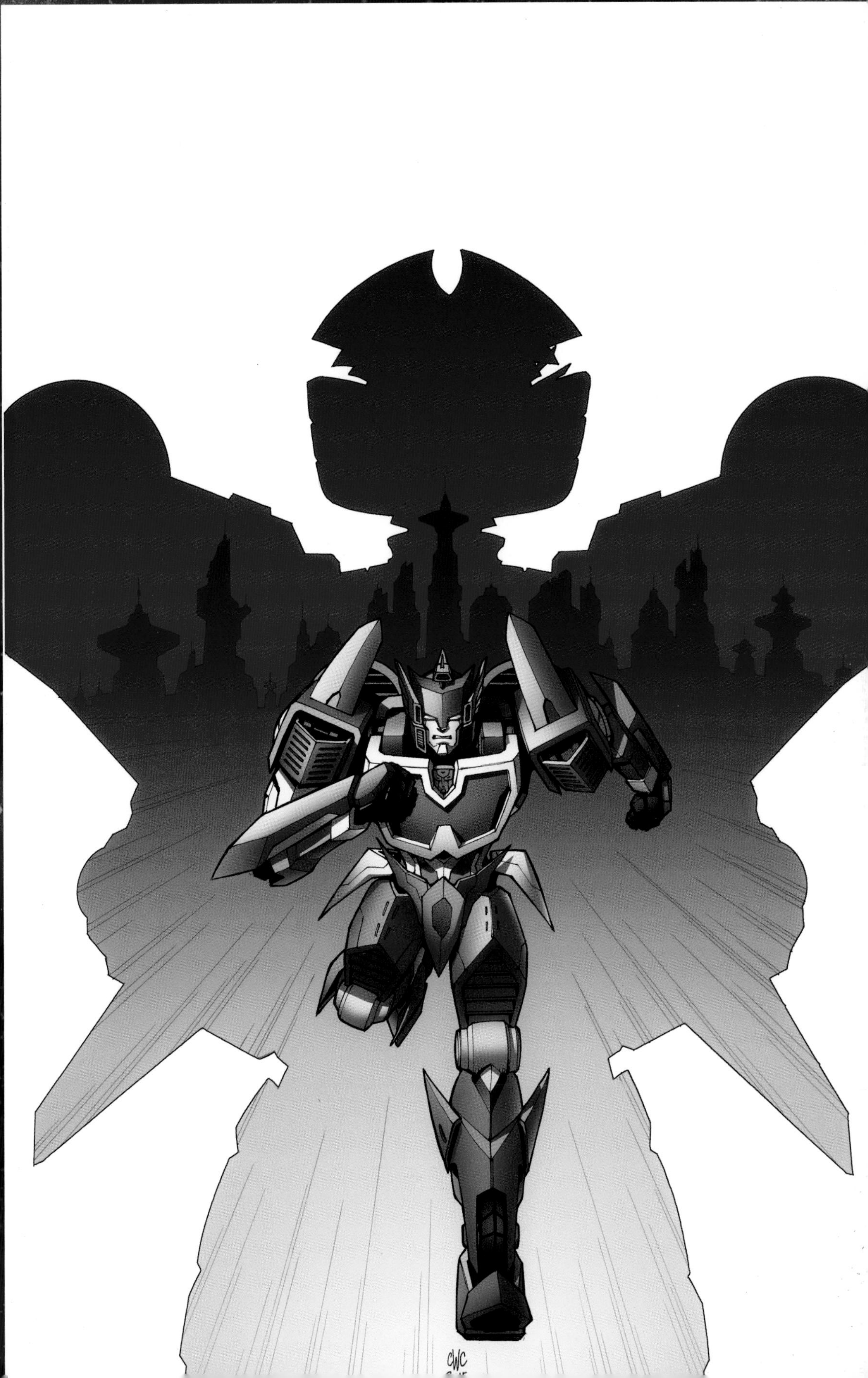

ART BY **PRISCILLA TRAMONTANO**

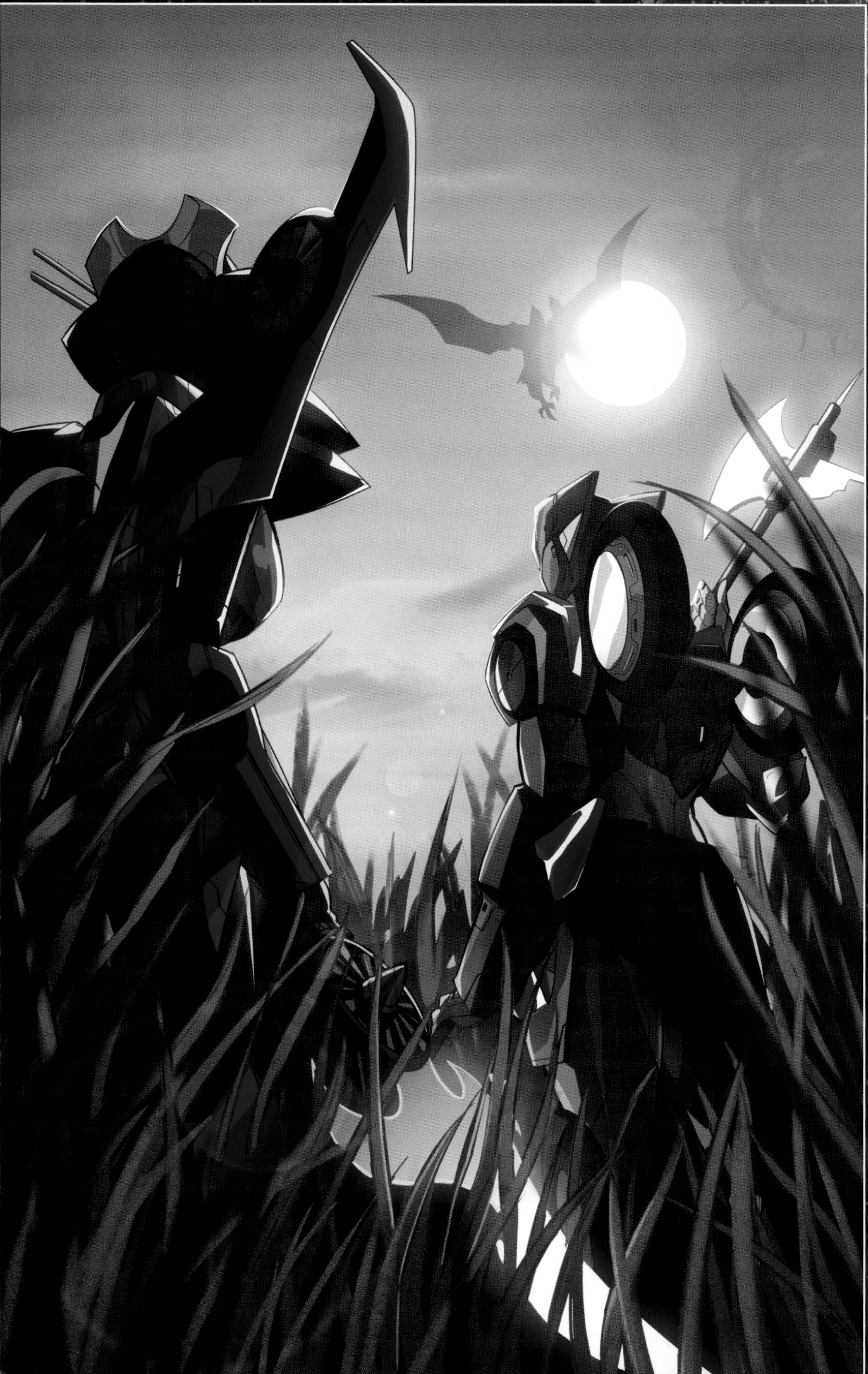

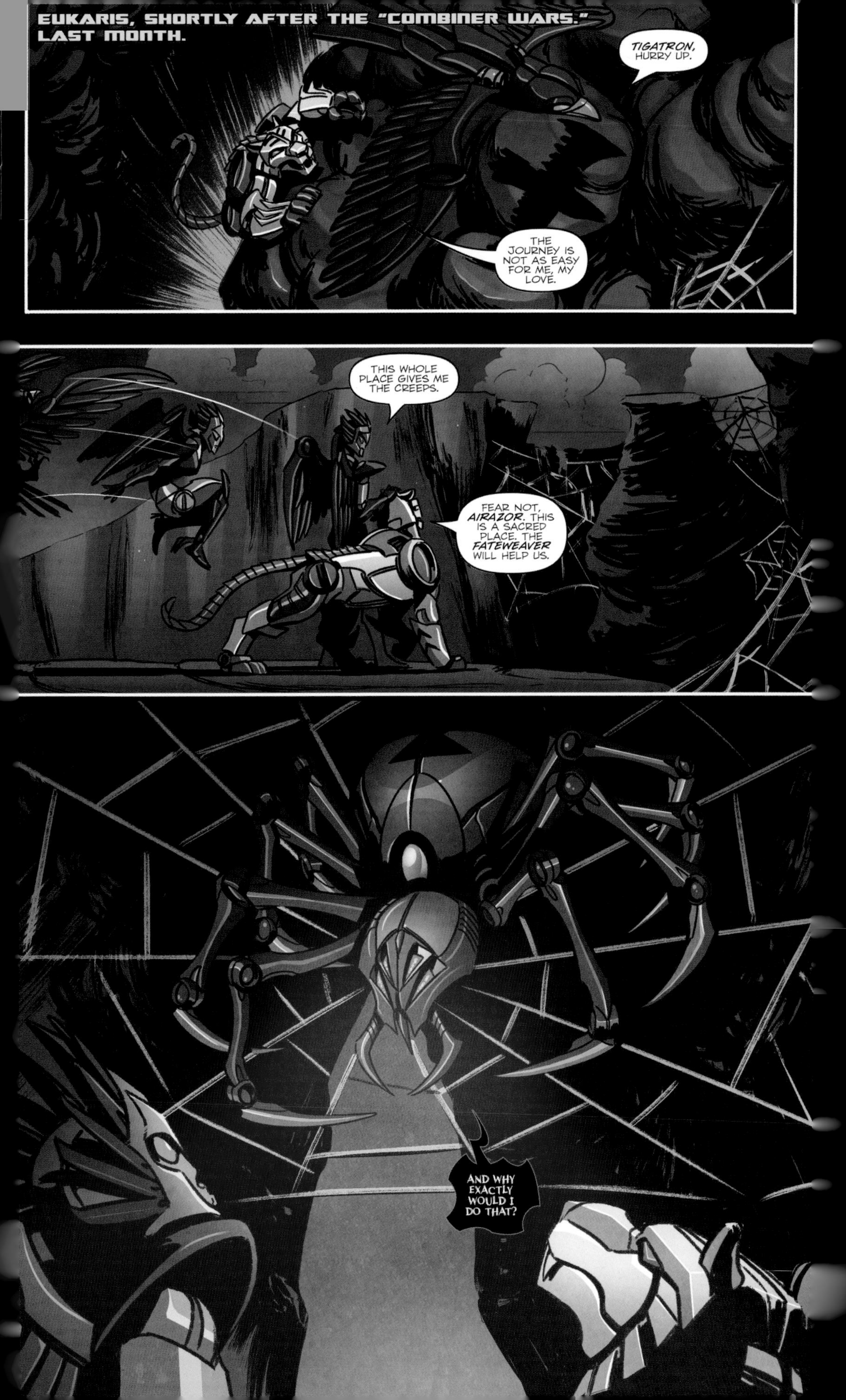
EUKARIS, SHORTLY AFTER THE "COMBINER WARS." LAST MONTH.
TIGATRON, HURRY UP.
THE JOURNEY IS NOT AS EASY FOR ME, MY LOVE.
THIS WHOLE PLACE GIVES ME THE CREEPS.
FEAR NOT, AIRAZOR. THIS IS A SACRED PLACE. THE FATEWEAVER WILL HELP US.
AND WHY EXACTLY WOULD I DO THAT?

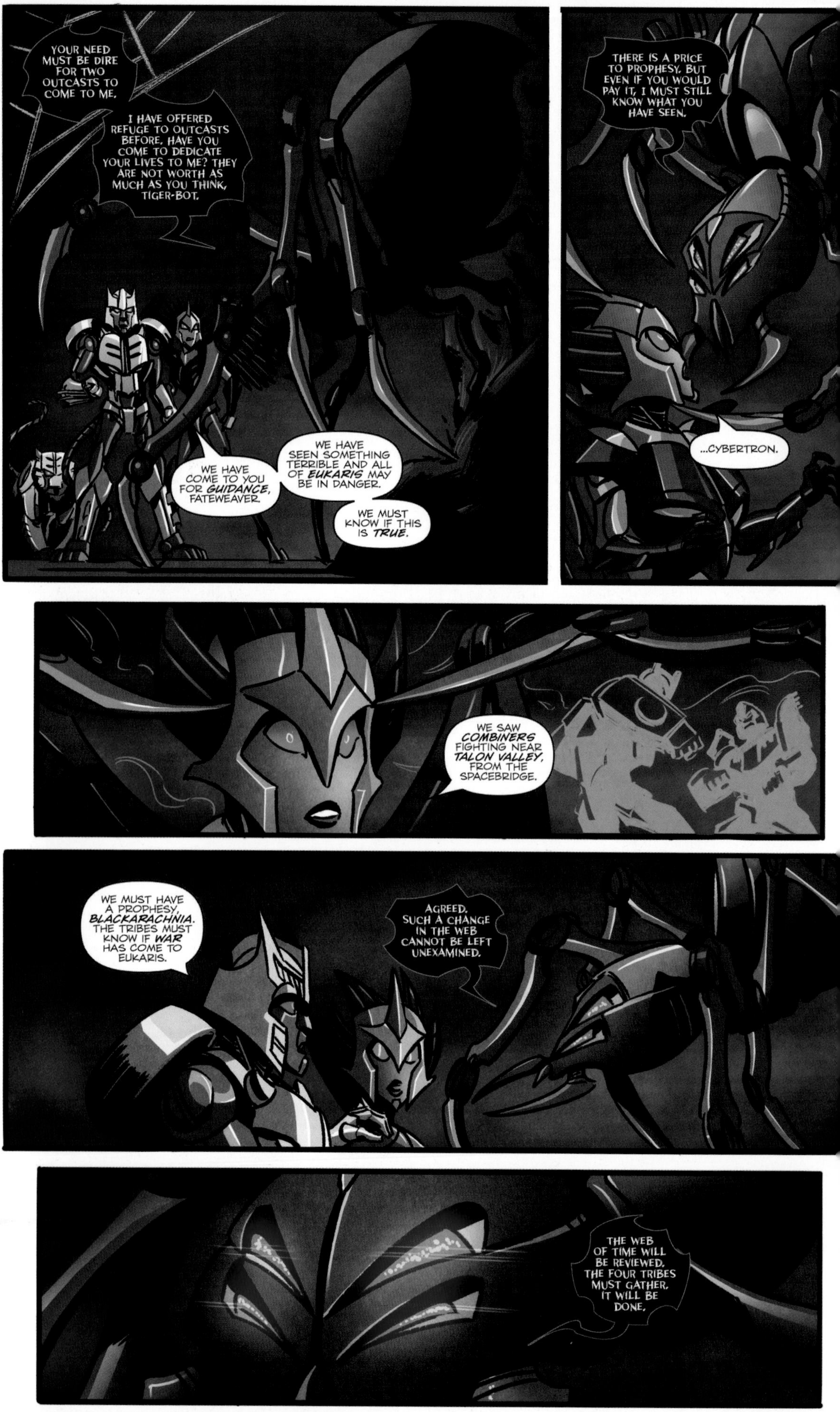

YOUR NEED MUST BE DIRE FOR TWO OUTCASTS TO COME TO ME.
I HAVE OFFERED REFUGE TO OUTCASTS BEFORE. HAVE YOU COME TO DEDICATE YOUR LIVES TO ME? THEY ARE NOT WORTH AS MUCH AS YOU THINK, TIGER-BOT.
WE HAVE COME TO YOU FOR GUIDANCE, FATEWEAVER.
WE HAVE SEEN SOMETHING TERRIBLE AND ALL OF EUKARIS MAY BE IN DANGER.
WE MUST KNOW IF THIS IS TRUE.
THERE IS A PRICE TO PROPHESY. BUT EVEN IF YOU WOULD PAY IT, I MUST STILL KNOW WHAT YOU HAVE SEEN.
...CYBERTRON.
WE SAW COMBINERS FIGHTING NEAR TALON VALLEY, FROM THE SPACEBRIDGE.
WE MUST HAVE A PROPHESY, BLACKARACHNIA. THE TRIBES MUST KNOW IF WAR HAS COME TO EUKARIS.
AGREED. SUCH A CHANGE IN THE WEB CANNOT BE LEFT UNEXAMINED.
THE WEB OF TIME WILL BE REVIEWED. THE FOUR TRIBES MUST GATHER. IT WILL BE DONE.

EUKARIS, TALON VALLEY:
A WEEK AGO.

WELL, ISN'T *THIS* JUST ONE BIG SLAGHEAP.

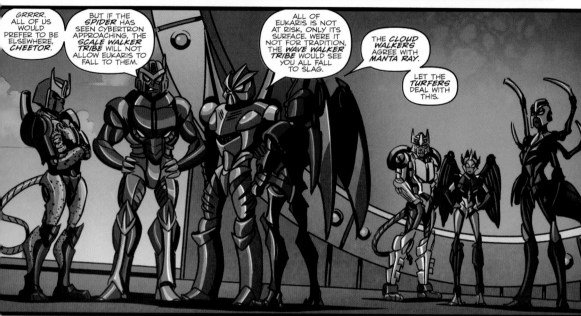

GRRRR. ALL OF US WOULD PREFER TO BE ELSEWHERE, *CHEETOR*.

BUT IF THE *SPIDER* HAS SEEN CYBERTRON APPROACHING, THE *SCALE WALKER TRIBE* WILL NOT ALLOW EUKARIS TO FALL TO THEM.

ALL OF EUKARIS IS NOT AT RISK, ONLY ITS SURFACE. WERE IT NOT FOR TRADITION, THE *WAVE WALKER TRIBE* WOULD SEE YOU ALL FALL TO SLAG.

THE *CLOUD WALKERS* AGREE WITH *MANTA RAY*.

LET THE *TURFERS* DEAL WITH THIS.

THINK, SONAR! IF CYBERTRON TAKES EUKARIS' LAND, THEY WON'T LEAVE FLIERS ALONE FOR LONG.

WE MUST—

DON'T PRESUME TO TELL ME WHAT I *MUST* AND *MUST NOT* DO, TIGATRON.

A TRIBE OF *TWO* IS NO TRIBE AT ALL.

POOF!

SILENCE...

...CYBERTRON APPROACHES.

LET IT COME— MY PEOPLE WILL DEFEND EUKARIS TO THE LAST 'BOT.

THE SPIDER SAW DANGER, BUT NOT THE CERTAINTY OF WAR. WE CANNOT STRIKE THE *FIRST* BLOW!

YEAH, BUT I'M NOT ABOUT TO LET THOSE *STANDARD-FORMERS* THINK FUR WALKERS ARE *DECLAWED,* EITHER.

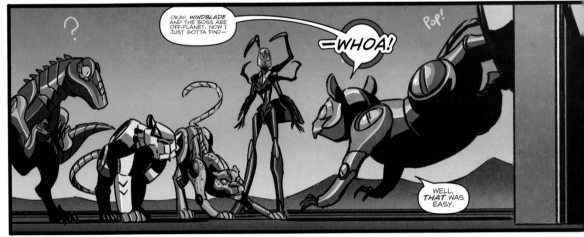

OKAY, *WINDBLADE* AND THE BOSS ARE OFF-PLANET. NOW I JUST GOTTA FIND—

=WHOA!

Pop!

WELL, *THAT* WAS EASY.

A... *BEASTFORMER?* WHO THE SLAG ARE YOU?

IT'S SOME KIND OF TRICK. *SHRED HIM!*

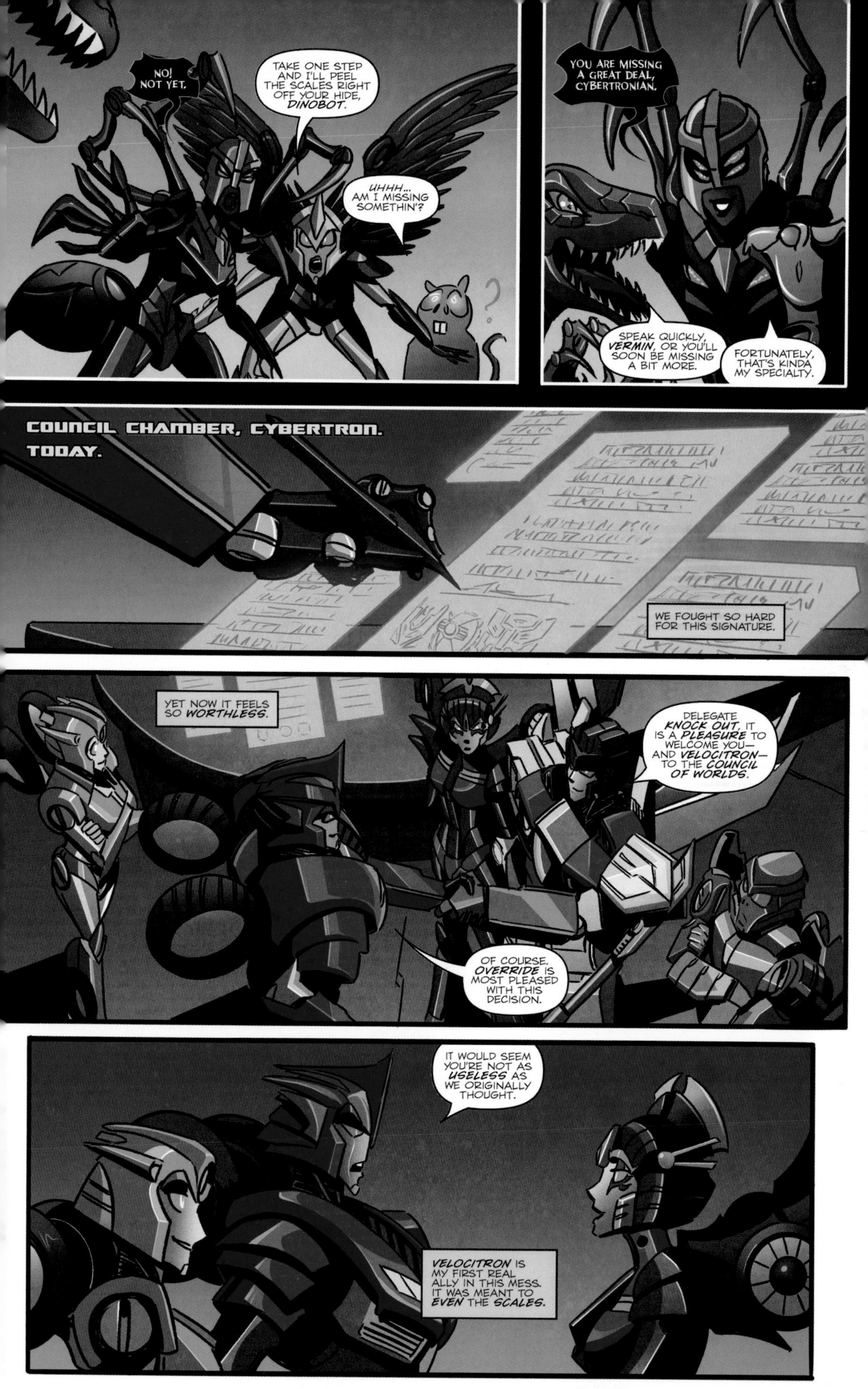
NO! NOT YET.
TAKE ONE STEP AND I'LL PEEL THE SCALES RIGHT OFF YOUR HIDE, DINOBOT.
UHHH... AM I MISSING SOMETHIN'?
?
YOU ARE MISSING A GREAT DEAL, CYBERTRONIAN.
SPEAK QUICKLY, VERMIN, OR YOU'LL SOON BE MISSING A BIT MORE.
FORTUNATELY, THAT'S KINDA MY SPECIALTY.
COUNCIL CHAMBER, CYBERTRON. TODAY.
WE FOUGHT SO HARD FOR THIS SIGNATURE.
YET NOW IT FEELS SO WORTHLESS.
DELEGATE KNOCK OUT, IT IS A PLEASURE TO WELCOME YOU— AND VELOCITRON— TO THE COUNCIL OF WORLDS.
OF COURSE. OVERRIDE IS MOST PLEASED WITH THIS DECISION.
IT WOULD SEEM YOU'RE NOT AS USELESS AS WE ORIGINALLY THOUGHT.
VELOCITRON IS MY FIRST REAL ALLY IN THIS MESS. IT WAS MEANT TO EVEN THE SCALES.

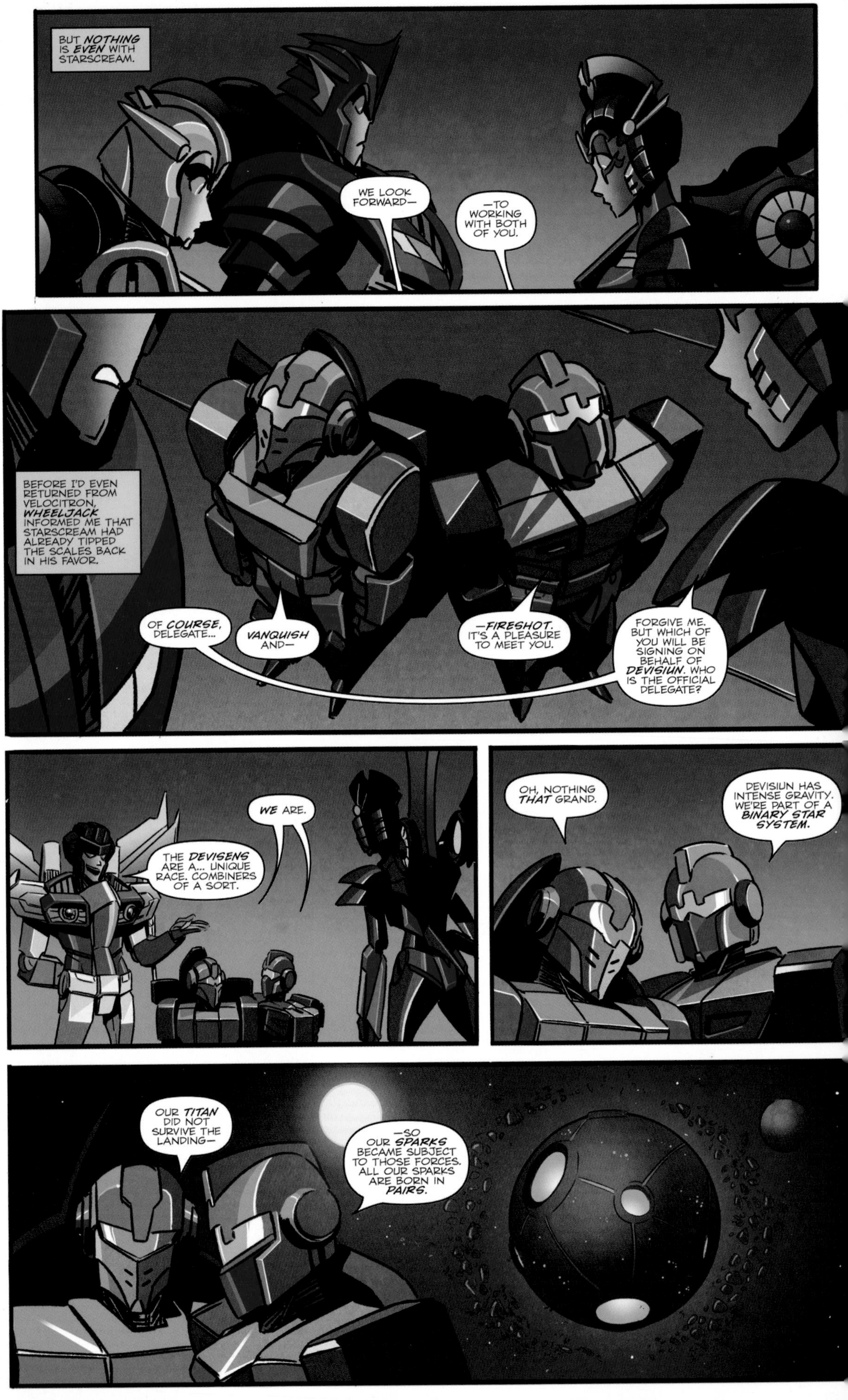
BUT NOTHING IS EVEN WITH STARSCREAM.
WE LOOK FORWARD—
—TO WORKING WITH BOTH OF YOU.
BEFORE I'D EVEN RETURNED FROM VELOCITRON, WHEELJACK INFORMED ME THAT STARSCREAM HAD ALREADY TIPPED THE SCALES BACK IN HIS FAVOR.
OF COURSE, DELEGATE...
VANQUISH AND—
—FIRESHOT. IT'S A PLEASURE TO MEET YOU.
FORGIVE ME. BUT WHICH OF YOU WILL BE SIGNING ON BEHALF OF DEVISIUN. WHO IS THE OFFICIAL DELEGATE?
WE ARE.
THE DEVISENS ARE A... UNIQUE RACE. COMBINERS OF A SORT.
OH, NOTHING THAT GRAND.
DEVISIUN HAS INTENSE GRAVITY. WE'RE PART OF A BINARY STAR SYSTEM.
OUR TITAN DID NOT SURVIVE THE LANDING—
—SO OUR SPARKS BECAME SUBJECT TO THOSE FORCES. ALL OUR SPARKS ARE BORN IN PAIRS.

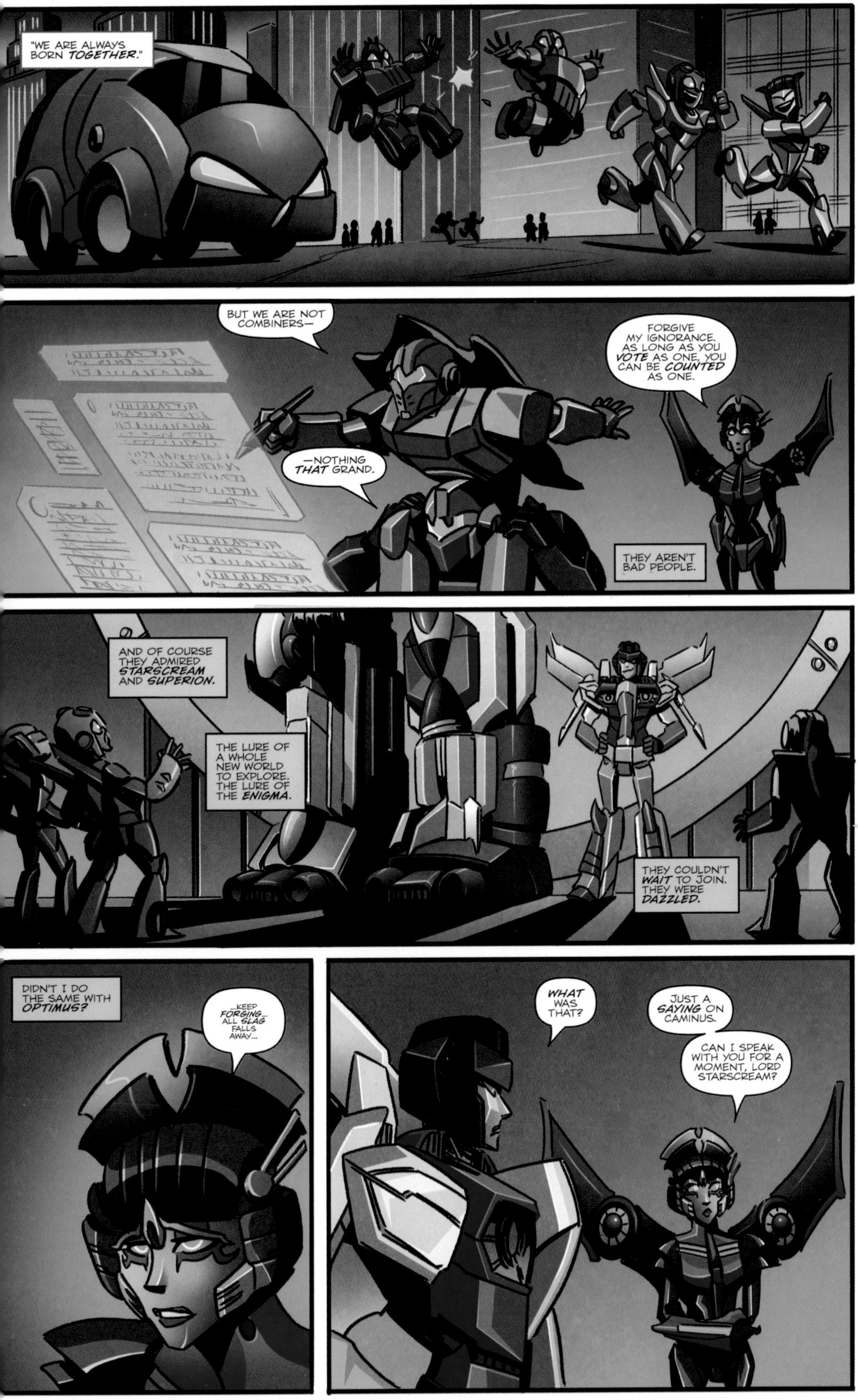
"WE ARE ALWAYS BORN TOGETHER."
BUT WE ARE NOT COMBINERS—
—NOTHING THAT GRAND.
FORGIVE MY IGNORANCE. AS LONG AS YOU VOTE AS ONE, YOU CAN BE COUNTED AS ONE.
THEY AREN'T BAD PEOPLE.
AND OF COURSE THEY ADMIRED STARSCREAM AND SUPERION.
THE LURE OF A WHOLE NEW WORLD TO EXPLORE. THE LURE OF THE ENIGMA.
THEY COULDN'T WAIT TO JOIN. THEY WERE DAZZLED.
DIDN'T I DO THE SAME WITH OPTIMUS?
...KEEP FORGING... ALL SLAG FALLS AWAY...
WHAT WAS THAT?
JUST A SAYING ON CAMINUS.
CAN I SPEAK WITH YOU FOR A MOMENT, LORD STARSCREAM?

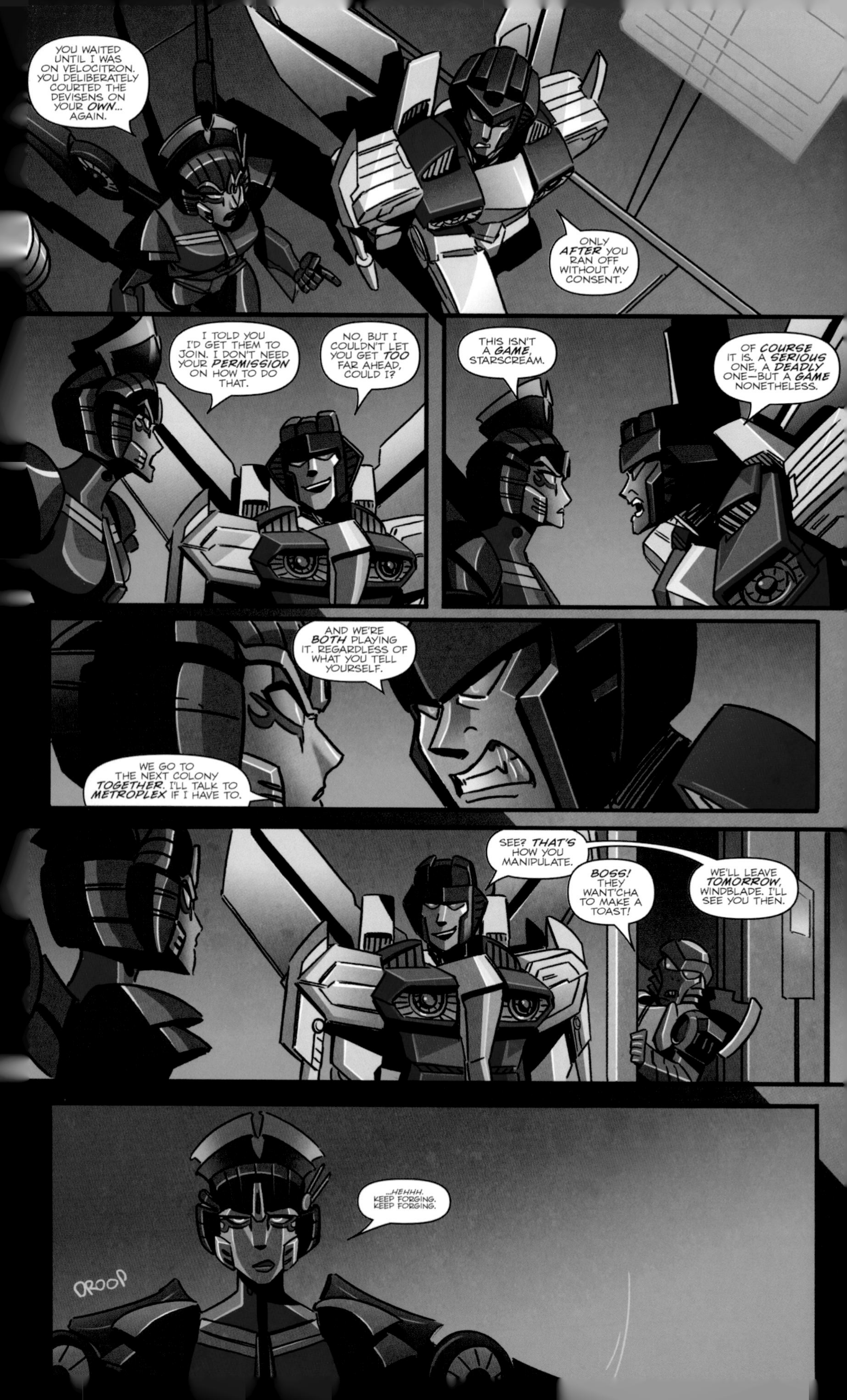
YOU WAITED UNTIL I WAS ON VELOCITRON. YOU DELIBERATELY COURTED THE DEVISENS ON YOUR *OWN*... AGAIN.
ONLY *AFTER* YOU RAN OFF WITHOUT MY CONSENT.
I TOLD YOU I'D GET THEM TO JOIN. I DON'T NEED YOUR *PERMISSION* ON HOW TO DO THAT.
NO, BUT I COULDN'T LET YOU GET *TOO* FAR AHEAD, COULD I?
THIS ISN'T A *GAME*, STARSCREAM.
OF *COURSE* IT IS. A *SERIOUS* ONE, A *DEADLY* ONE—BUT A *GAME* NONETHELESS.
AND WE'RE *BOTH* PLAYING IT. REGARDLESS OF WHAT YOU TELL YOURSELF.
WE GO TO THE NEXT COLONY *TOGETHER*. I'LL TALK TO *METROPLEX* IF I HAVE TO.
SEE? *THAT'S* HOW YOU MANIPULATE.
WE'LL LEAVE *TOMORROW*, WINDBLADE. I'LL SEE YOU THEN.
BOSS! THEY WANT'CHA TO MAKE A TOAST!
...HEHHH. KEEP FORGING. KEEP FORGING.
DROOP

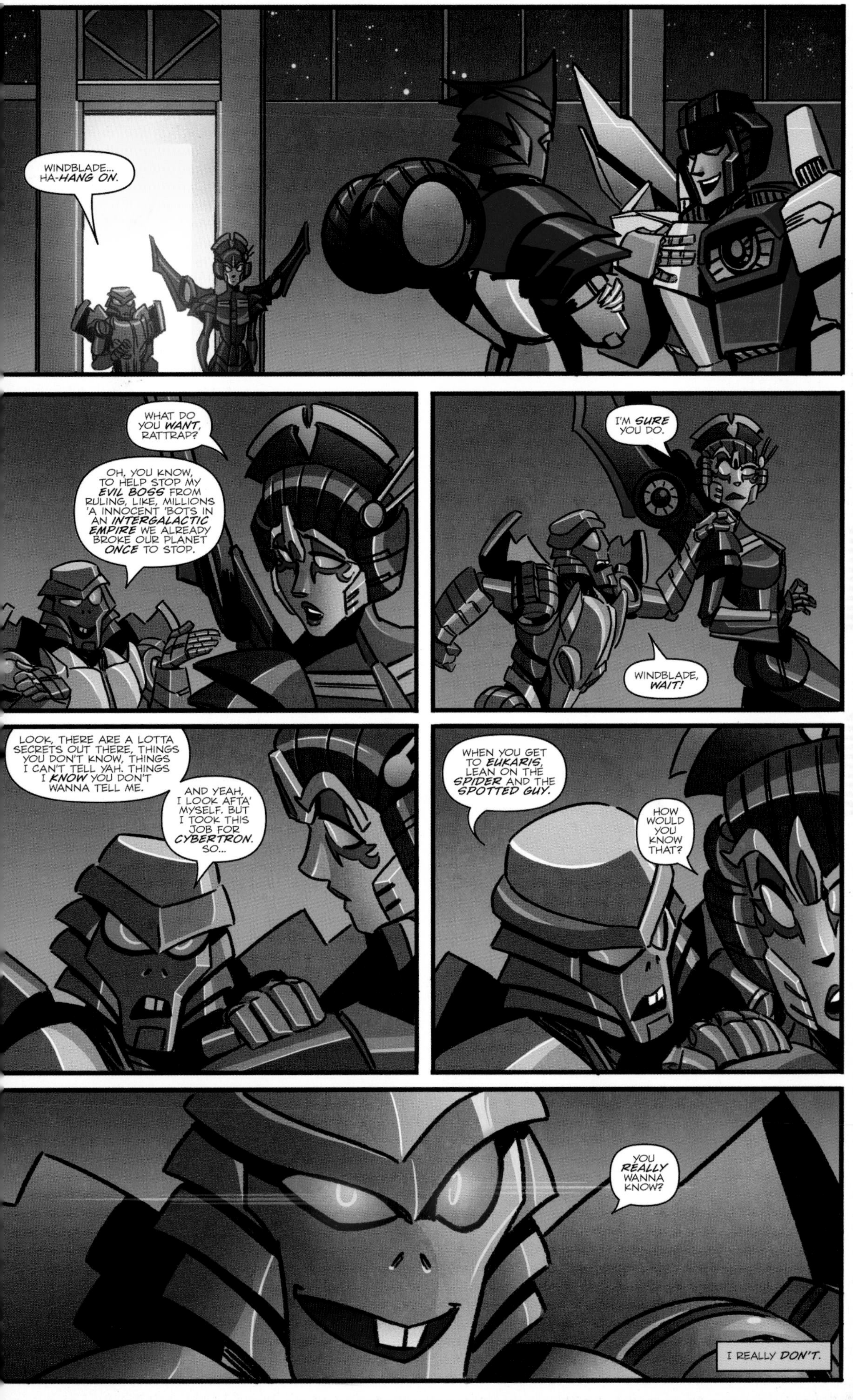
WINDBLADE... HA-*HANG ON*.
WHAT DO YOU *WANT*, RATTRAP?
OH, YOU KNOW, TO HELP STOP MY *EVIL BOSS* FROM RULING, LIKE, MILLIONS 'A INNOCENT 'BOTS IN AN *INTERGALACTIC EMPIRE* WE ALREADY BROKE OUR PLANET *ONCE* TO STOP.
I'M *SURE* YOU DO.
WINDBLADE, *WAIT!*
LOOK, THERE ARE A LOTTA SECRETS OUT THERE, THINGS YOU DON'T KNOW, THINGS I CAN'T TELL YAH. THINGS I *KNOW* YOU DON'T WANNA TELL ME.
AND YEAH, I LOOK AFTA' MYSELF. BUT I TOOK THIS JOB FOR *CYBERTRON*. SO...
WHEN YOU GET TO *EUKARIS*, LEAN ON THE *SPIDER* AND THE *SPOTTED GUY*.
HOW WOULD YOU KNOW THAT?
YOU *REALLY* WANNA KNOW?
I REALLY *DON'T*.

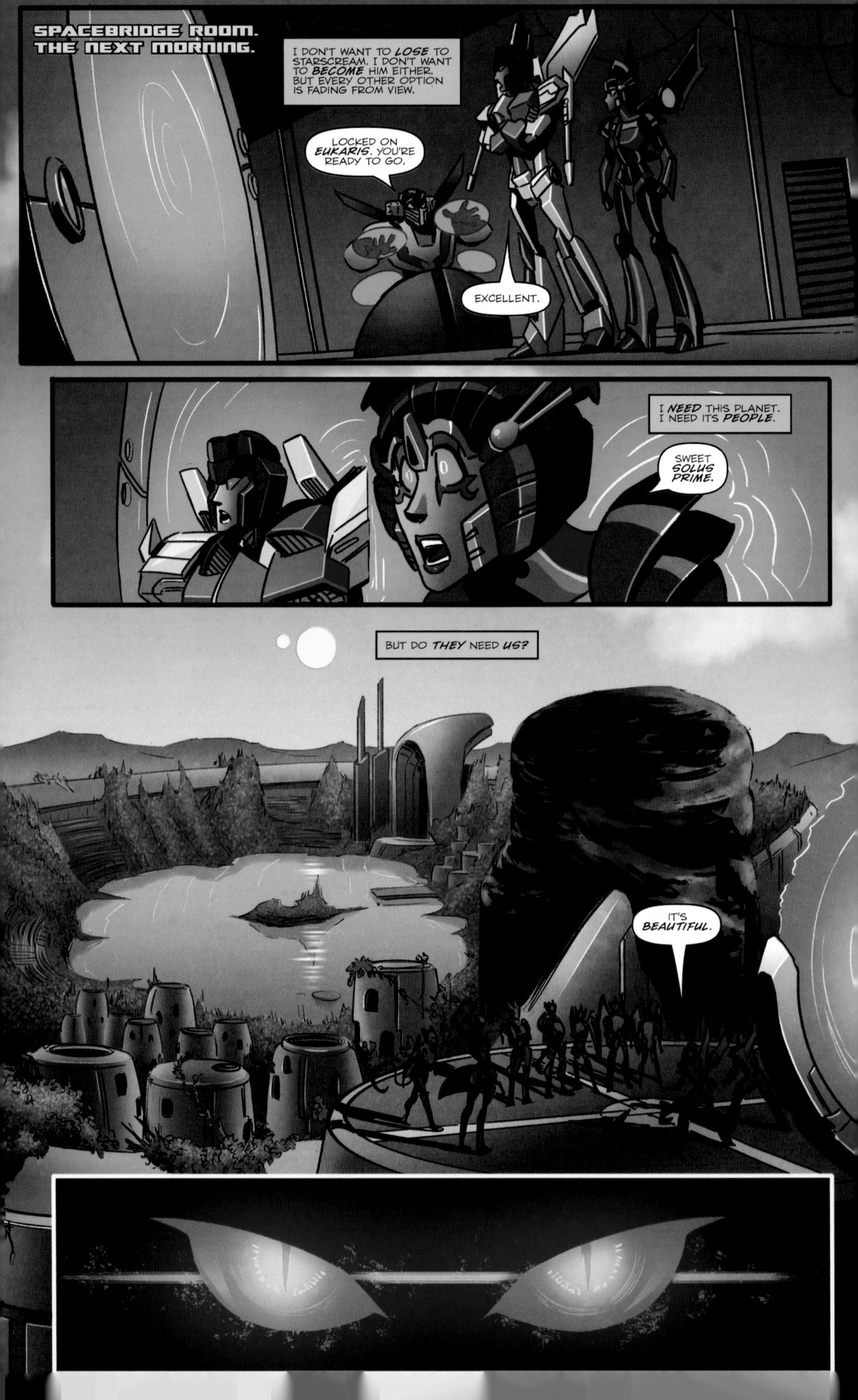

SPACEBRIDGE ROOM. THE NEXT MORNING.
I DON'T WANT TO LOSE TO STARSCREAM. I DON'T WANT TO BECOME HIM EITHER. BUT EVERY OTHER OPTION IS FADING FROM VIEW.
LOCKED ON EUKARIS. YOU'RE READY TO GO.
EXCELLENT.
I NEED THIS PLANET. I NEED ITS PEOPLE.
SWEET SOLUS PRIME.
BUT DO THEY NEED US?
IT'S BEAUTIFUL.

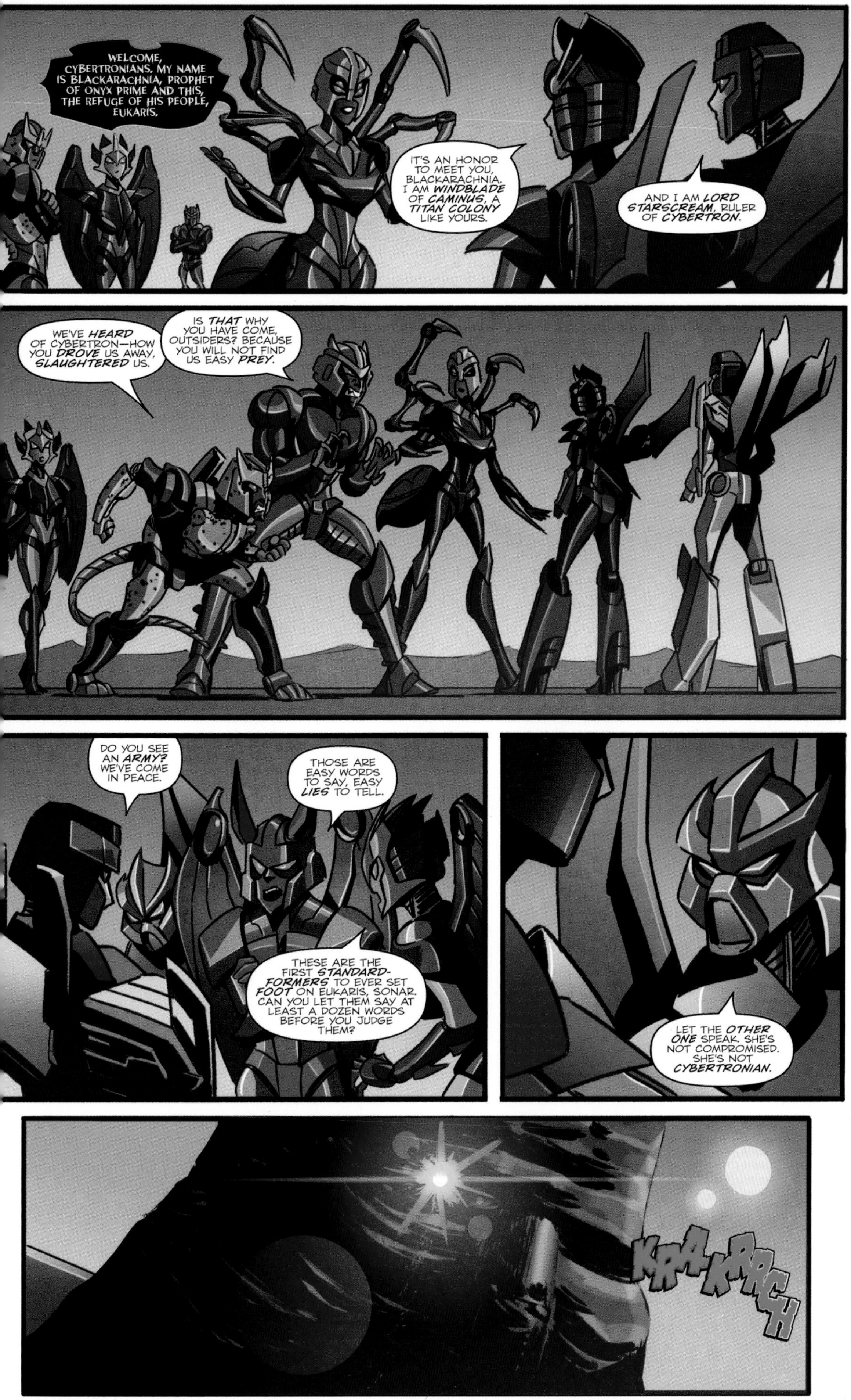

WELCOME, CYBERTRONIANS. MY NAME IS BLACKARACHNIA, PROPHET OF ONYX PRIME AND THIS, THE REFUGE OF HIS PEOPLE, EUKARIS.
IT'S AN HONOR TO MEET YOU, BLACKARACHNIA. I AM WINDBLADE OF CAMINUS, A TITAN COLONY LIKE YOURS.
AND I AM LORD STARSCREAM, RULER OF CYBERTRON.
WE'VE HEARD OF CYBERTRON—HOW YOU DROVE US AWAY, SLAUGHTERED US.
IS THAT WHY YOU HAVE COME, OUTSIDERS? BECAUSE YOU WILL NOT FIND US EASY PREY.
DO YOU SEE AN ARMY? WE'VE COME IN PEACE.
THOSE ARE EASY WORDS TO SAY, EASY LIES TO TELL.
THESE ARE THE FIRST STANDARD-FORMERS TO EVER SET FOOT ON EUKARIS, SONAR. CAN YOU LET THEM SAY AT LEAST A DOZEN WORDS BEFORE YOU JUDGE THEM?
LET THE OTHER ONE SPEAK. SHE'S NOT COMPROMISED. SHE'S NOT CYBERTRONIAN.
KRAKRRCH

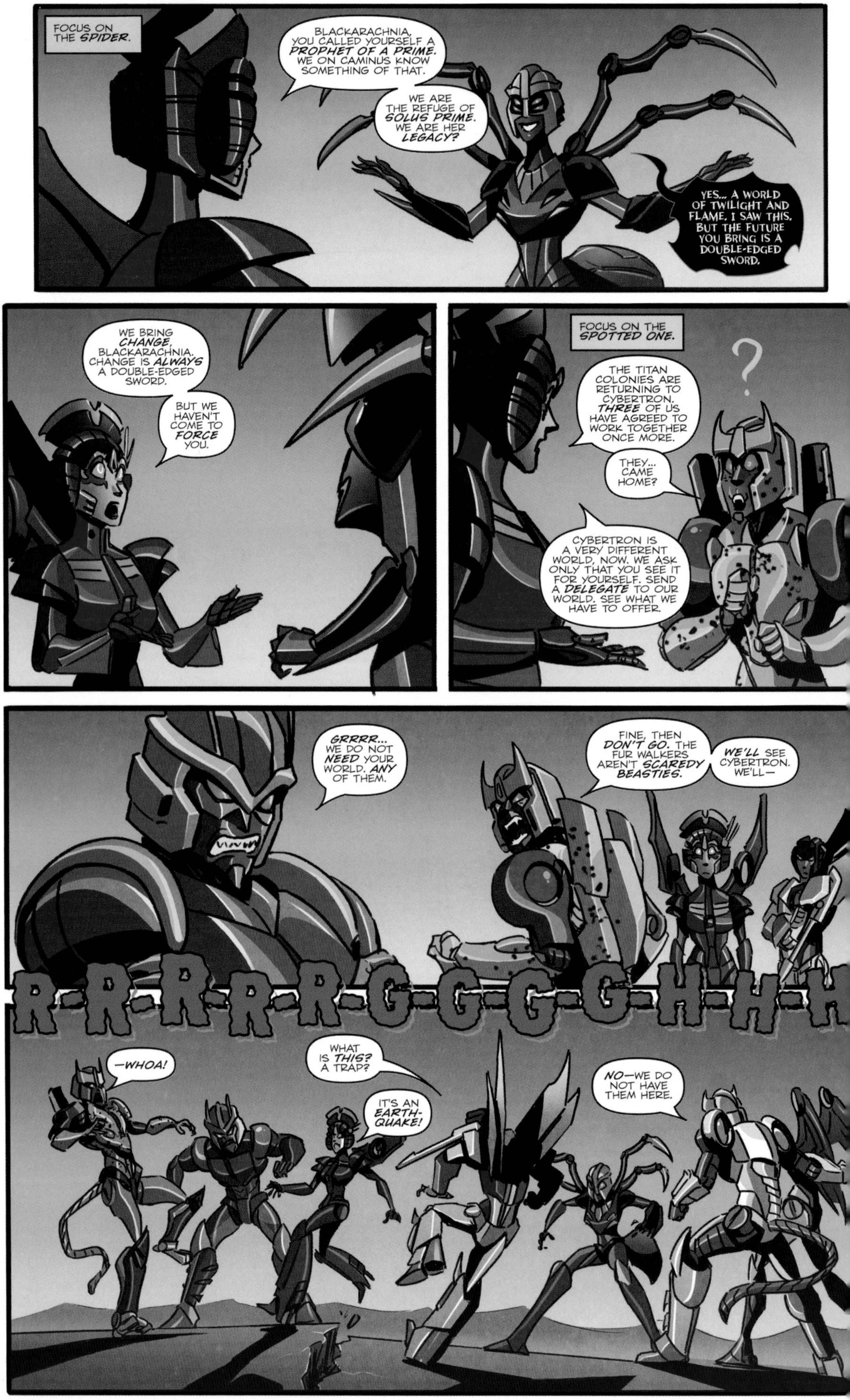
FOCUS ON THE SPIDER.
BLACKARACHNIA, YOU CALLED YOURSELF A PROPHET OF A PRIME. WE ON CAMINUS KNOW SOMETHING OF THAT.
WE ARE THE REFUGE OF SOLUS PRIME. WE ARE HER LEGACY?
YES... A WORLD OF TWILIGHT AND FLAME. I SAW THIS. BUT THE FUTURE YOU BRING IS A DOUBLE-EDGED SWORD.
WE BRING CHANGE, BLACKARACHNIA. CHANGE IS ALWAYS A DOUBLE-EDGED SWORD.
BUT WE HAVEN'T COME TO FORCE YOU.
FOCUS ON THE SPOTTED ONE.
?
THE TITAN COLONIES ARE RETURNING TO CYBERTRON. THREE OF US HAVE AGREED TO WORK TOGETHER ONCE MORE.
THEY... CAME HOME?
CYBERTRON IS A VERY DIFFERENT WORLD, NOW. WE ASK ONLY THAT YOU SEE IT FOR YOURSELF. SEND A DELEGATE TO OUR WORLD. SEE WHAT WE HAVE TO OFFER.
GRRRR... WE DO NOT NEED YOUR WORLD. ANY OF THEM.
FINE, THEN DON'T GO. THE FUR WALKERS AREN'T SCAREDY BEASTIES.
WE'LL SEE CYBERTRON. WE'LL—
R-R-R-R-R-G-G-G-G-H-H-H
—WHOA!
WHAT IS THIS? A TRAP?
IT'S AN EARTH-QUAKE!
NO—WE DO NOT HAVE THEM HERE.

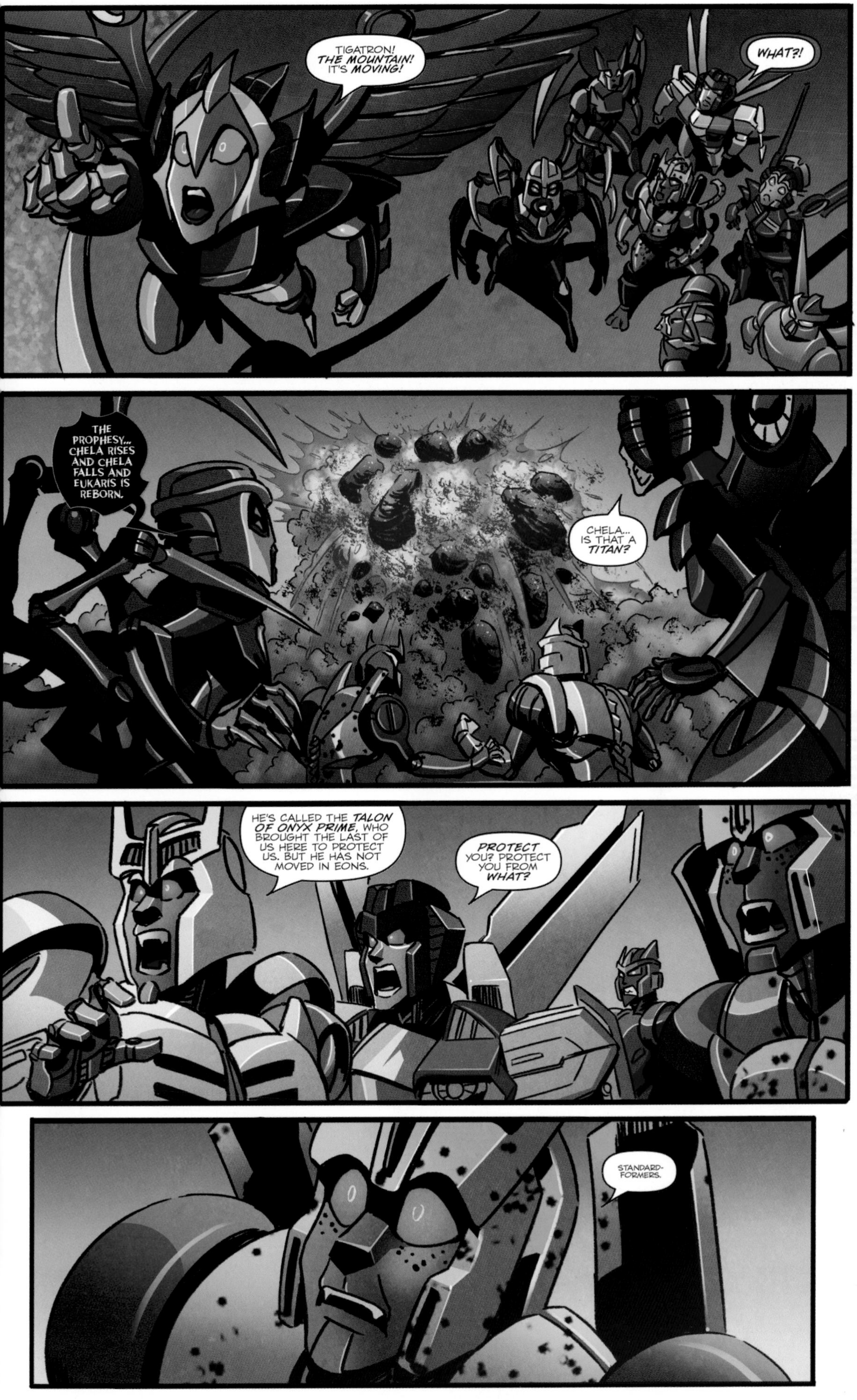
TIGATRON! THE MOUNTAIN! IT'S MOVING!
WHAT?!
THE PROPHESY... CHELA RISES AND CHELA FALLS AND EUKARIS IS REBORN.
CHELA... IS THAT A TITAN?
HE'S CALLED THE TALON OF ONYX PRIME, WHO BROUGHT THE LAST OF US HERE TO PROTECT US. BUT HE HAS NOT MOVED IN EONS.
PROTECT YOU? PROTECT YOU FROM WHAT?
STANDARD-FORMERS.

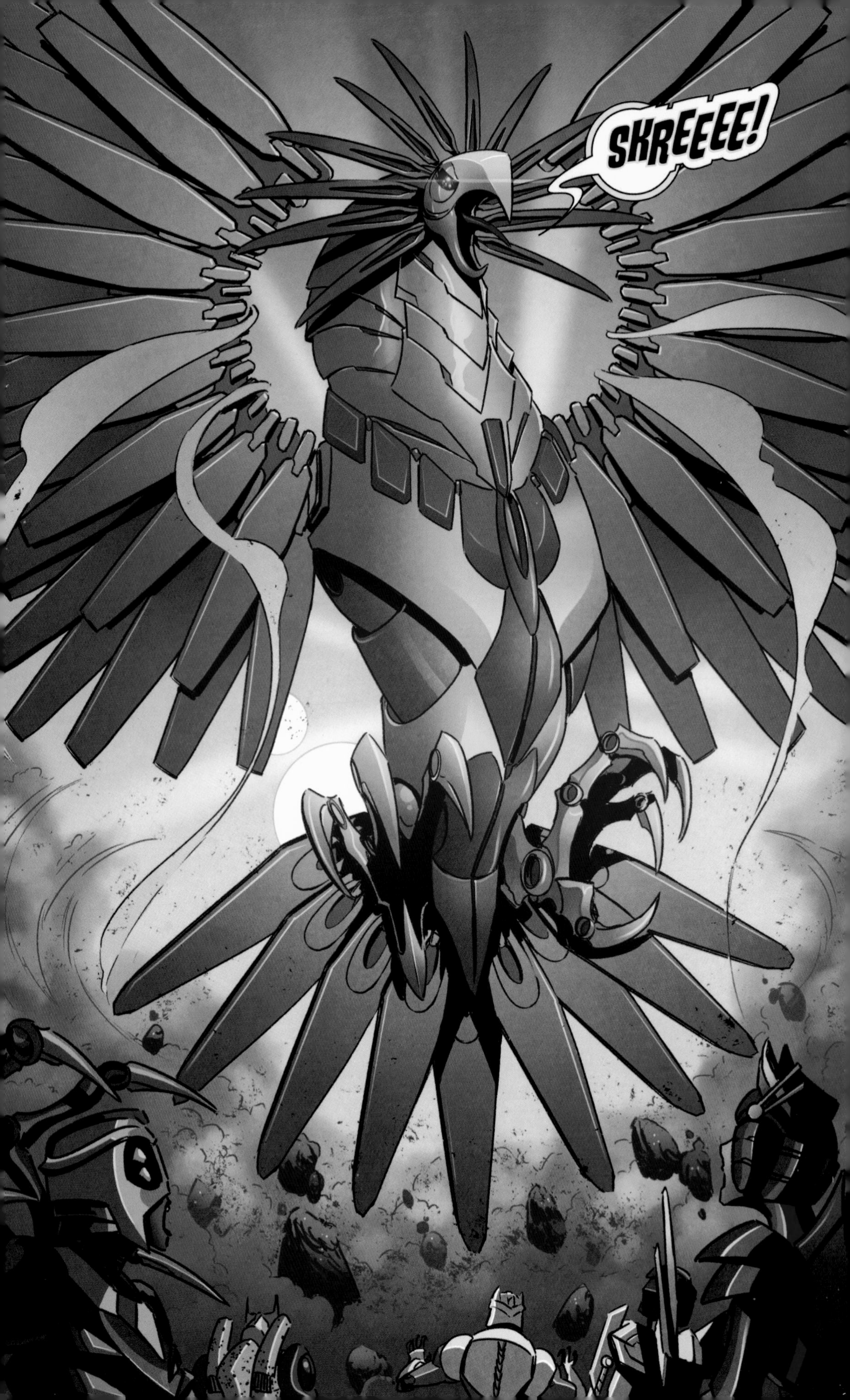
SKREEEE!

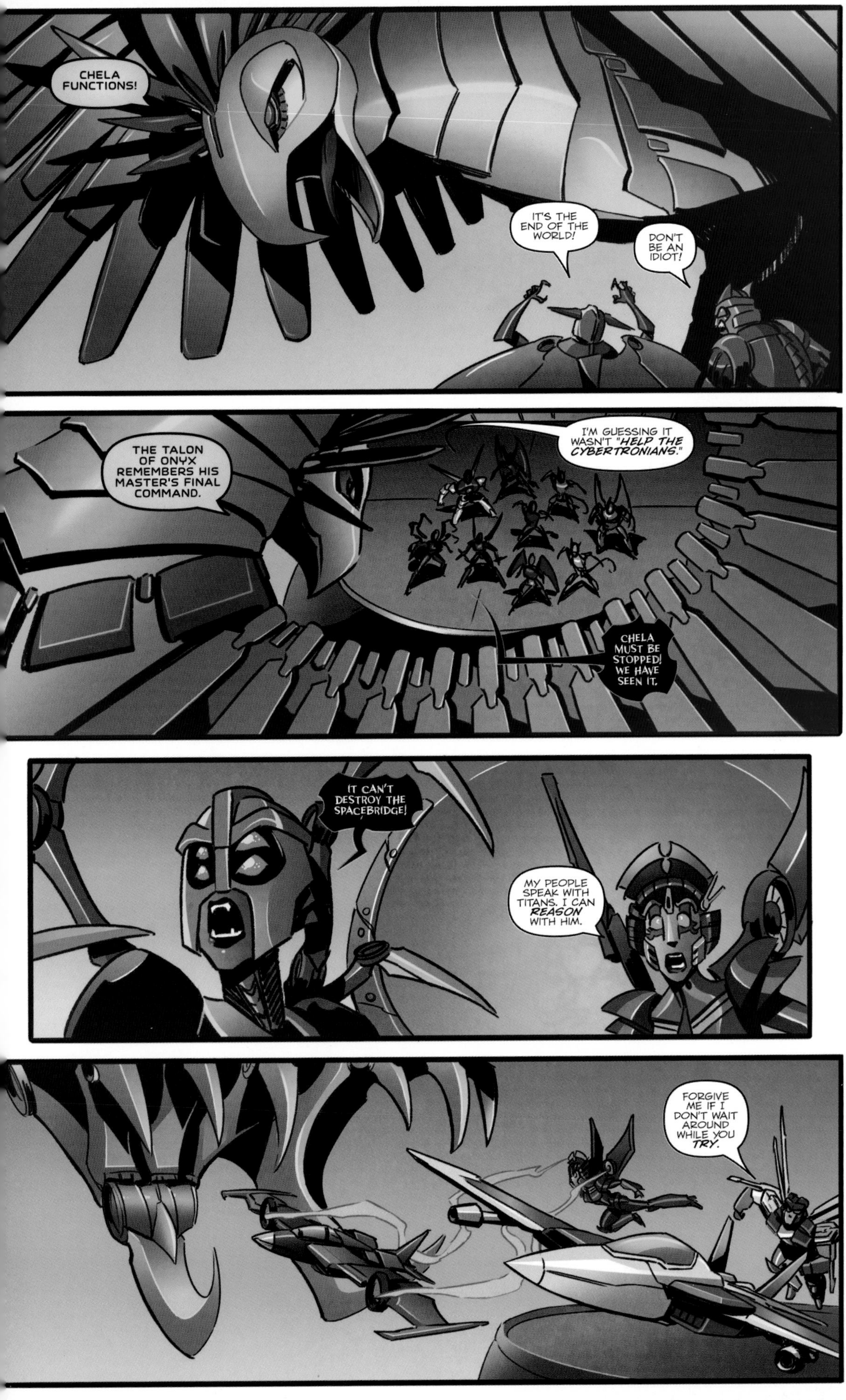
CHELA FUNCTIONS!
IT'S THE END OF THE WORLD!
DON'T BE AN IDIOT!
THE TALON OF ONYX REMEMBERS HIS MASTER'S FINAL COMMAND.
I'M GUESSING IT WASN'T "*HELP THE CYBERTRONIANS*."
CHELA MUST BE STOPPED! WE HAVE SEEN IT.
IT CAN'T DESTROY THE SPACEBRIDGE!
MY PEOPLE SPEAK WITH TITANS. I CAN *REASON* WITH HIM.
FORGIVE ME IF I DON'T WAIT AROUND WHILE YOU *TRY*.

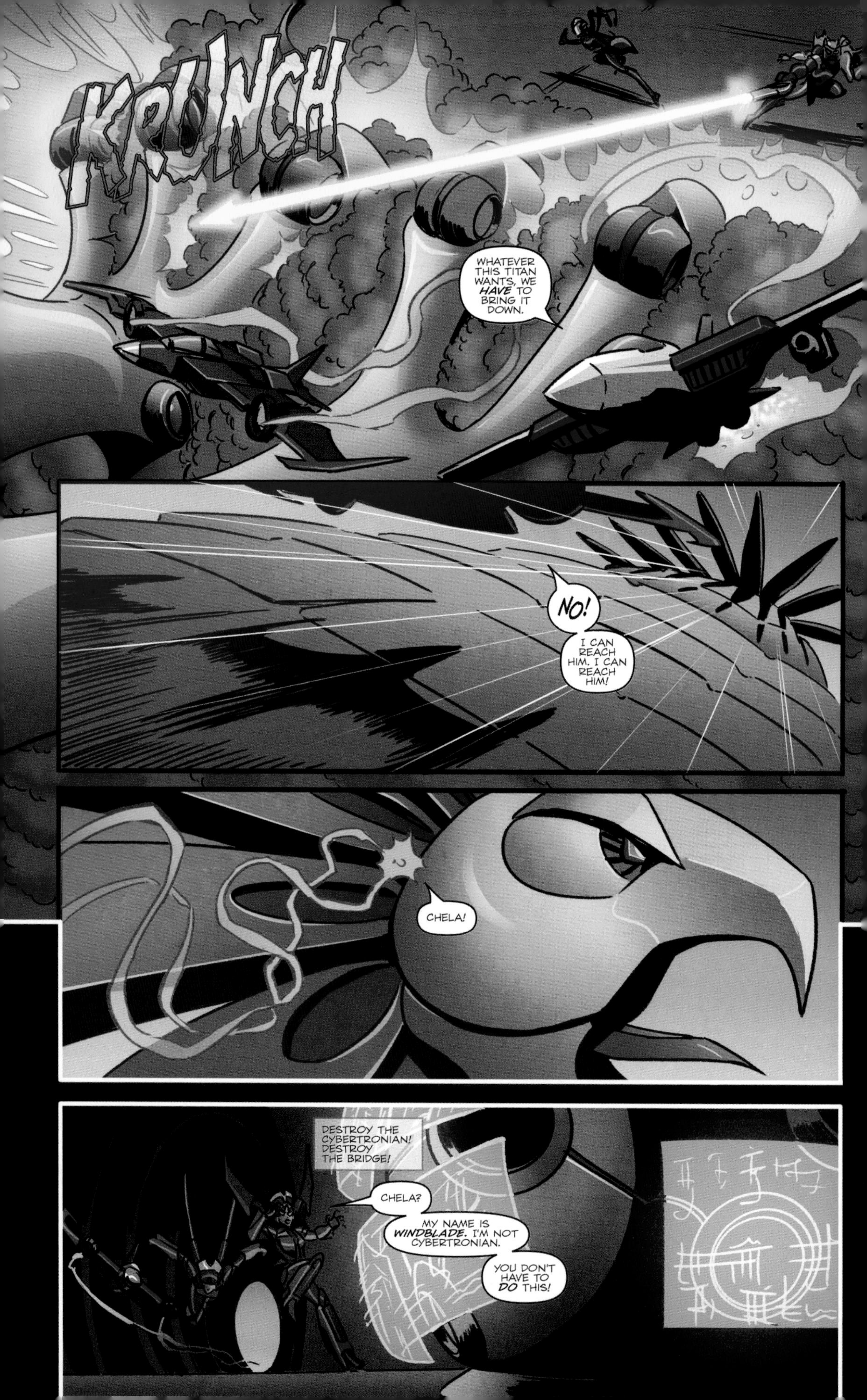
KRUNCH
WHATEVER THIS TITAN WANTS, WE *HAVE* TO BRING IT DOWN.
NO!
I CAN REACH HIM. I CAN REACH HIM!
CHELA!
DESTROY THE CYBERTRONIAN! DESTROY THE BRIDGE!
CHELA?
MY NAME IS *WINDBLADE.* I'M NOT CYBERTRONIAN.
YOU DON'T HAVE TO *DO* THIS!

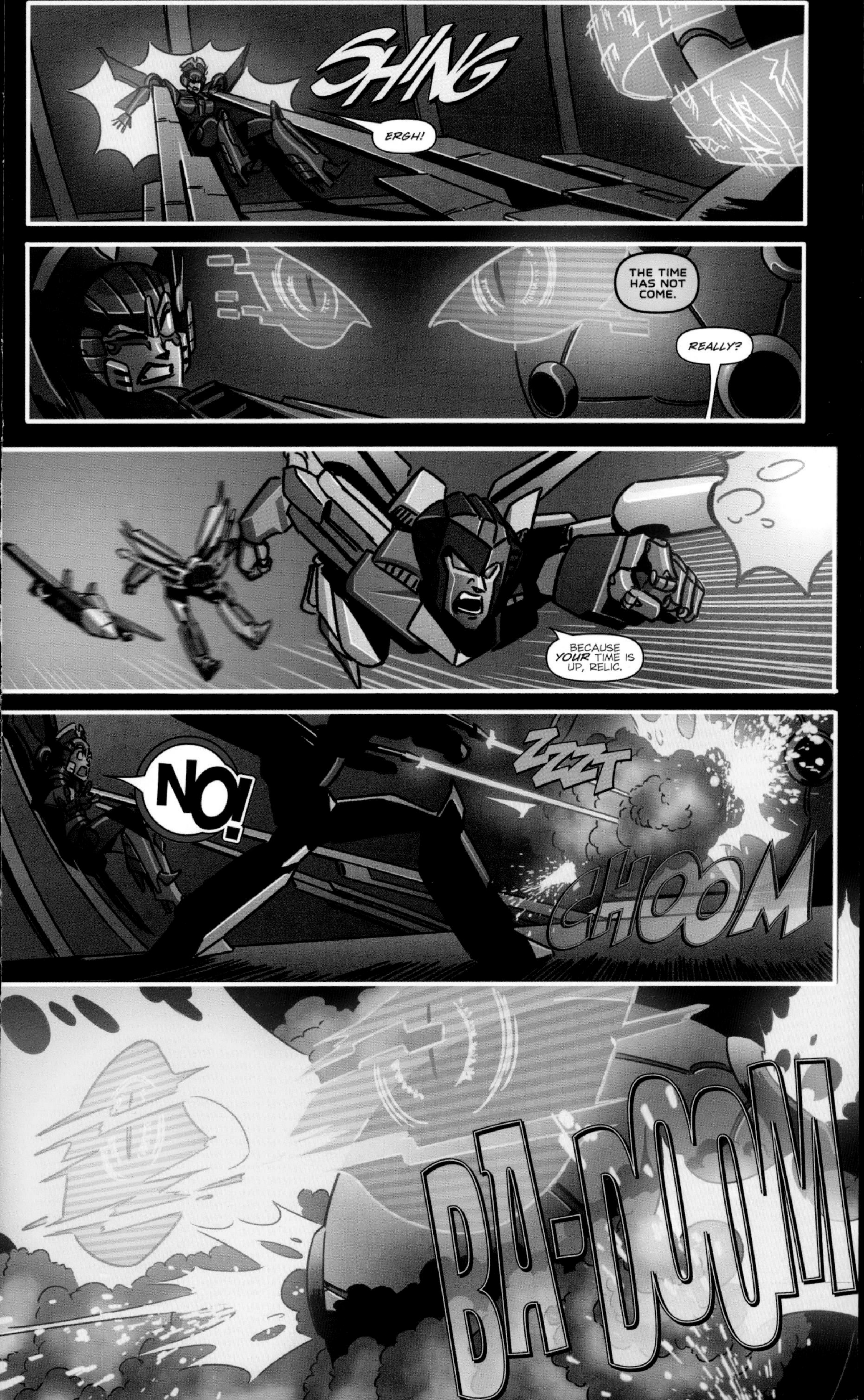
SHING
ERGH!
THE TIME HAS NOT COME.
REALLY?
BECAUSE YOUR TIME IS UP, RELIC.
NO!
ZZZZT
CHOOM
BA-DOOOM

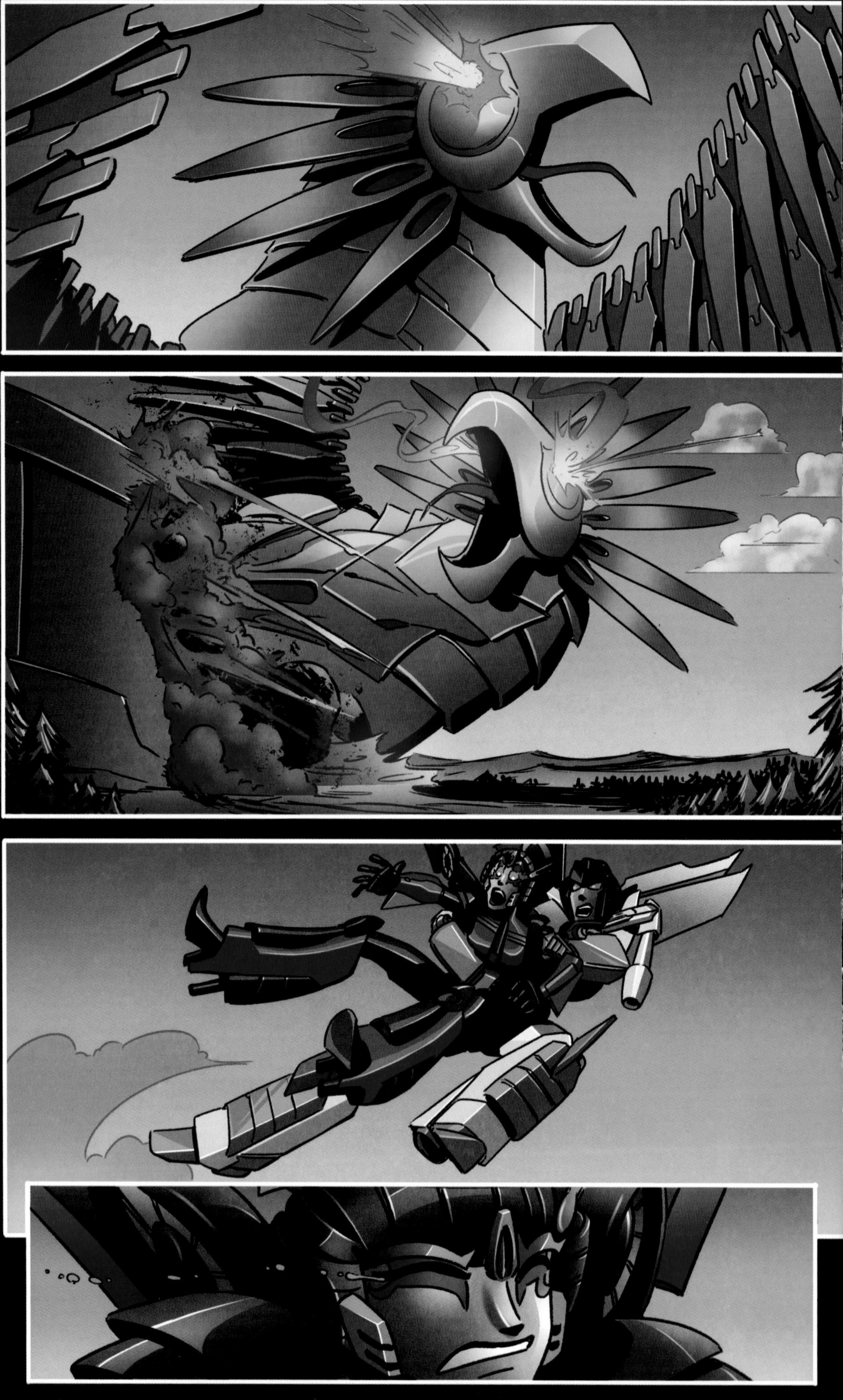

I'M SORRY.

I'M **SO** SORRY.

IT **HAD** TO BE DONE.

AGREED, YOU BROUGHT US A DOUBLE-EDGED SWORD, OUTSIDERS.

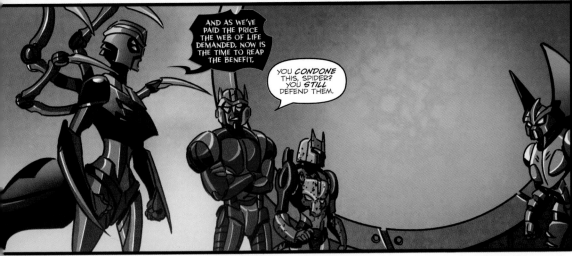

AND AS WE'VE PAID THE PRICE THE WEB OF LIFE DEMANDED, NOW IS THE TIME TO REAP THE BENEFIT.

YOU **CONDONE** THIS, SPIDER? YOU **STILL** DEFEND THEM.

I DO.

WE SHALL SEND A DELEGATE TO YOUR WORLD. WE SHALL SEE WHAT MAY BE GAINED THERE.

THE WEB HAS REVEALED IT.

AND WHICH OF US WOULD THE WEB **SEND?** WHICHEVER TRIBE GOES GAINS A CLEAR **ADVANTAGE** OVER THE OTHERS.

WHICH IS WHY NO TRIBE WILL GO.

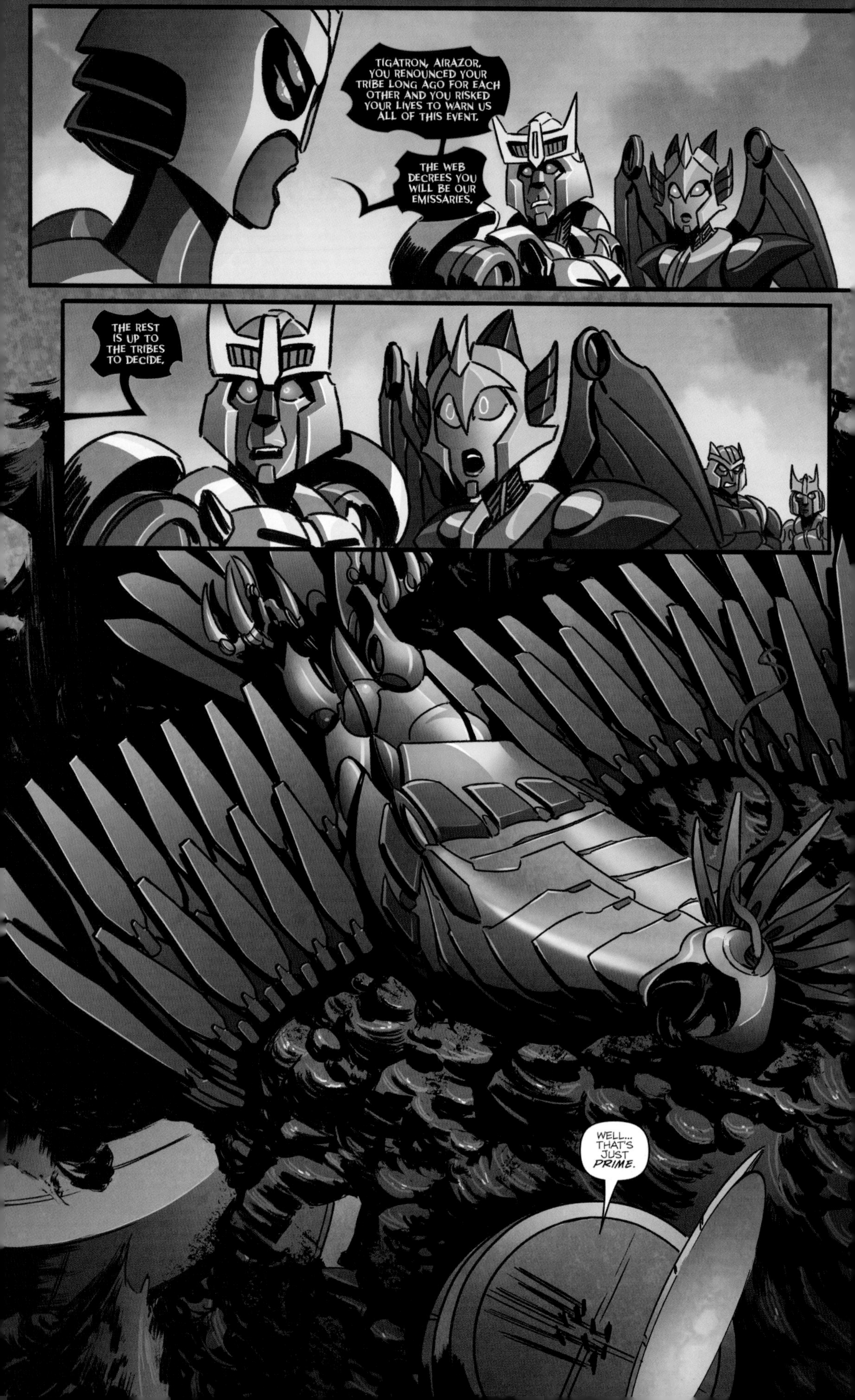
TIGATRON, AIRAZOR, YOU RENOUNCED YOUR TRIBE LONG AGO FOR EACH OTHER AND YOU RISKED YOUR LIVES TO WARN US ALL OF THIS EVENT.
THE WEB DECREES YOU WILL BE OUR EMISSARIES.
THE REST IS UP TO THE TRIBES TO DECIDE.
WELL... THAT'S JUST PRIME.

ART BY **CASEY W. COLLER**
COLORS BY **JOANA LAFUENTE**

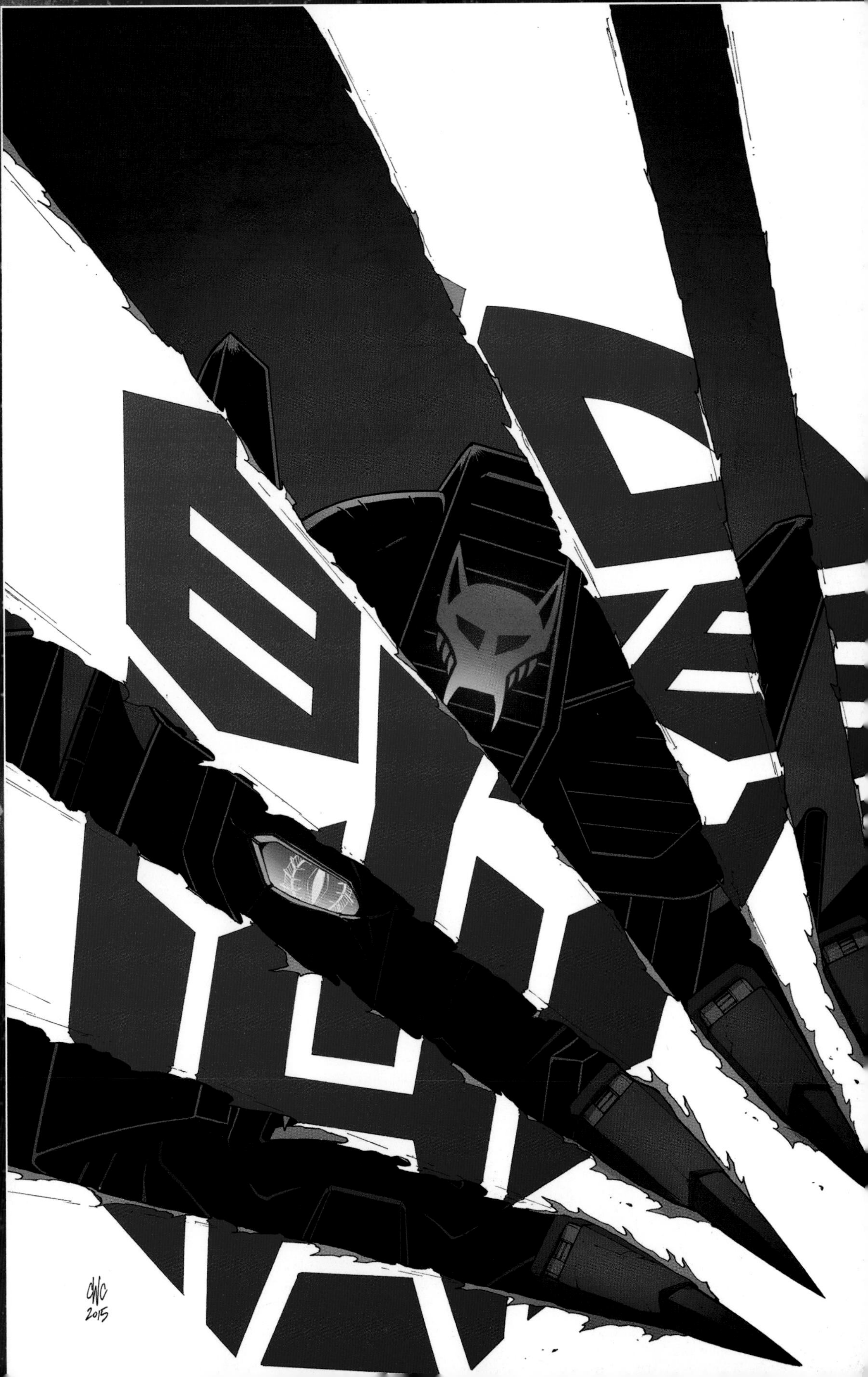

CWC
2015

ART BY **PRISCILLA TRAMONTANO**

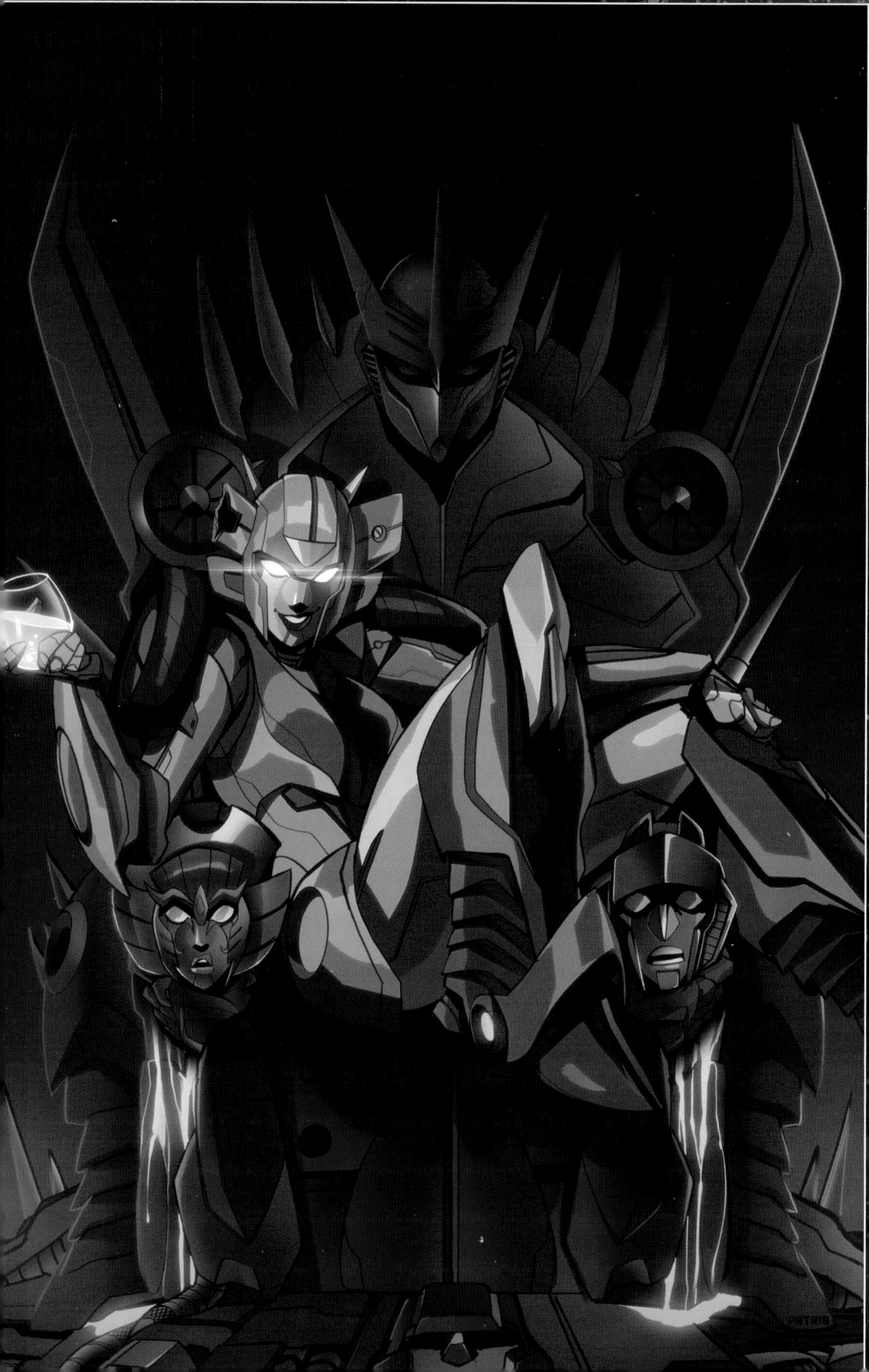

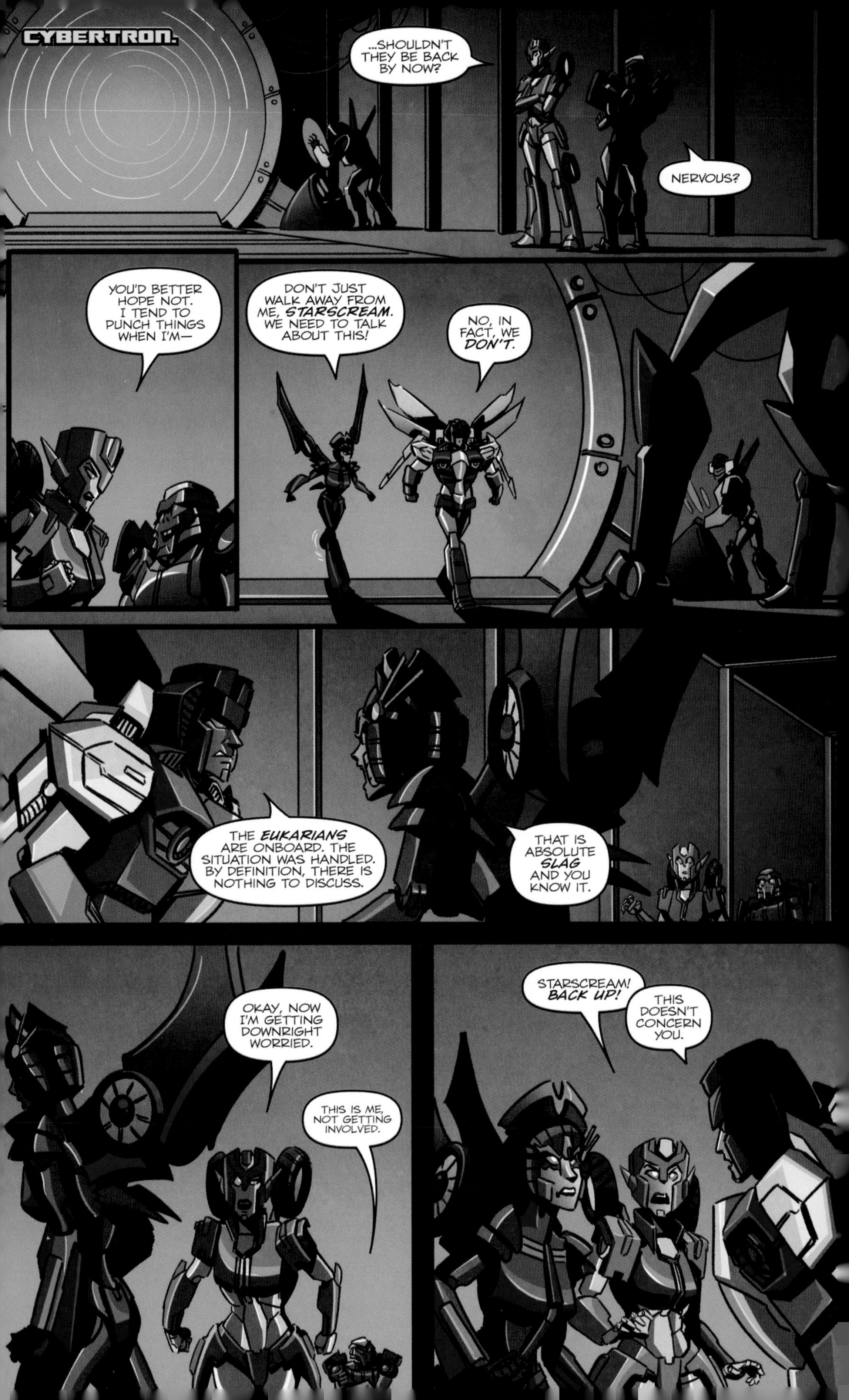
CYBERTRON.
...SHOULDN'T THEY BE BACK BY NOW?
NERVOUS?
YOU'D BETTER HOPE NOT. I TEND TO PUNCH THINGS WHEN I'M—
DON'T JUST WALK AWAY FROM ME, STARSCREAM. WE NEED TO TALK ABOUT THIS!
NO, IN FACT, WE DON'T.
THE EUKARIANS ARE ONBOARD. THE SITUATION WAS HANDLED. BY DEFINITION, THERE IS NOTHING TO DISCUSS.
THAT IS ABSOLUTE SLAG AND YOU KNOW IT.
OKAY, NOW I'M GETTING DOWNRIGHT WORRIED.
THIS IS ME, NOT GETTING INVOLVED.
STARSCREAM! BACK UP!
THIS DOESN'T CONCERN YOU.

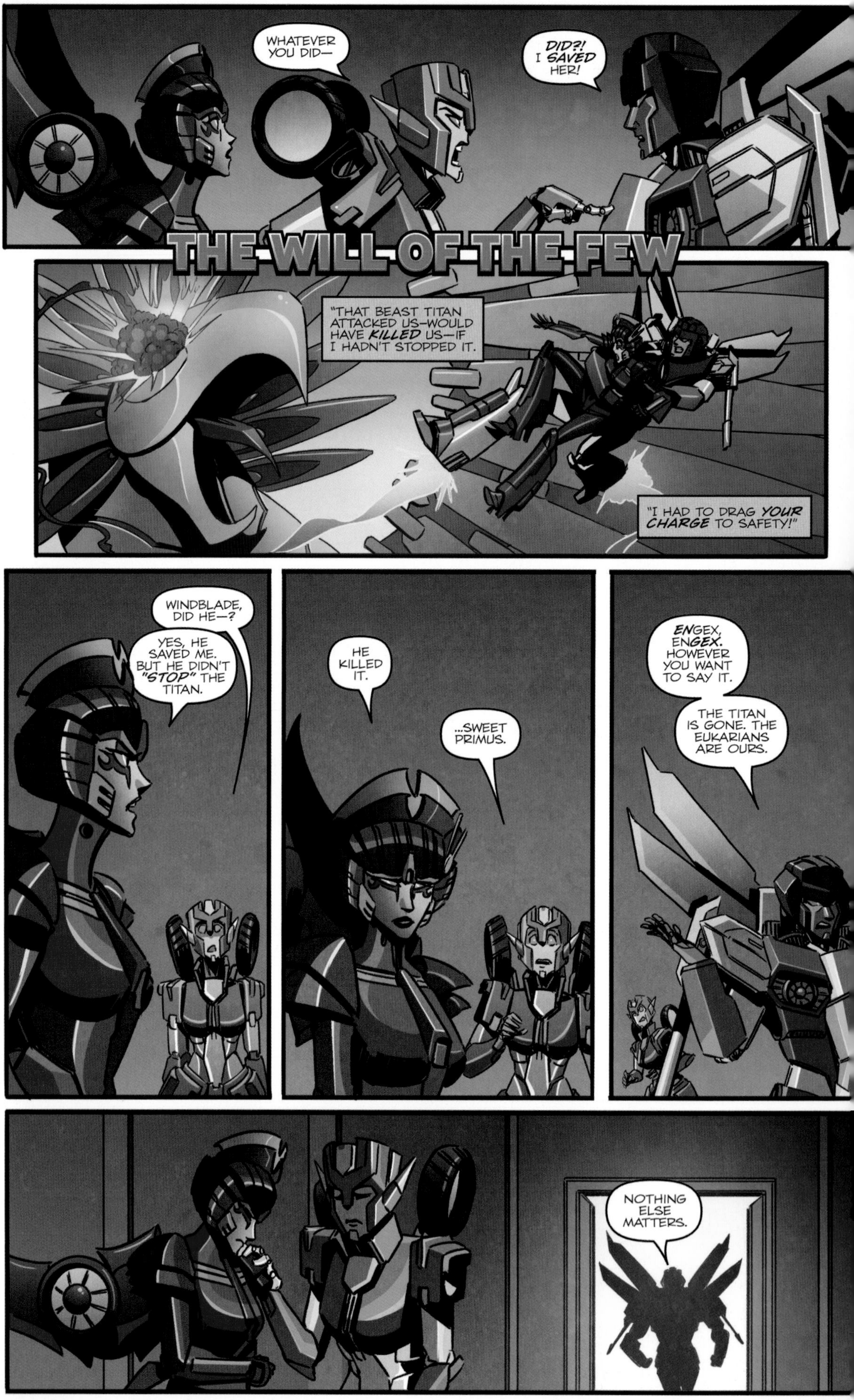
WHATEVER YOU DID—
DID?! I SAVED HER!
THE WILL OF THE FEW
"THAT BEAST TITAN ATTACKED US—WOULD HAVE KILLED US—IF I HADN'T STOPPED IT.
"I HAD TO DRAG YOUR CHARGE TO SAFETY!"
WINDBLADE, DID HE—?
YES, HE SAVED ME. BUT HE DIDN'T "STOP" THE TITAN.
HE KILLED IT.
...SWEET PRIMUS.
ENGEX, ENGEX. HOWEVER YOU WANT TO SAY IT.
THE TITAN IS GONE. THE EUKARIANS ARE OURS.
NOTHING ELSE MATTERS.

I'M... I'M SO SORRY.

IT WAS *MY* FAULT, CHROMIA.

I WAS THERE... I— I TRIED TO STOP HIM, BUT—

—I *COULDN'T*.

I'VE DEVOTED MY LIFE TO *HELPING* TITANS. AND I'VE USED THEM, I HELPED *KILL* THEM. I—

I BELIEVE IN YOU.

WHAT?

CYBERTRON ISN'T CAMINUS. THINGS AREN'T SIMPLE HERE AND I'VE SEEN YOU MAKE *TOUGH CALLS* AND *HARD CHOICES* OVER AND OVER AGAIN.

DEEP DOWN, YOU *KNOW* IF YOU DID EVERYTHING YOU COULD OR NOT. IF YOU DID, YOU HAVE TO KEEP MOVING. IF YOU DIDN'T, YOU HAVE TO LEARN FROM IT. JUST LIKE ALL OF US.

CHROMIA, I'M SO—

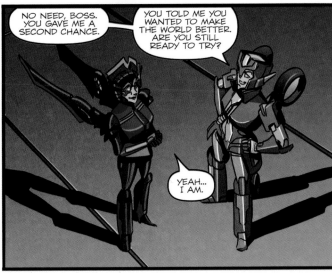

NO NEED, BOSS. YOU GAVE ME A SECOND CHANCE.

YOU TOLD ME YOU WANTED TO MAKE THE WORLD BETTER. ARE YOU STILL READY TO TRY?

YEAH... I AM.

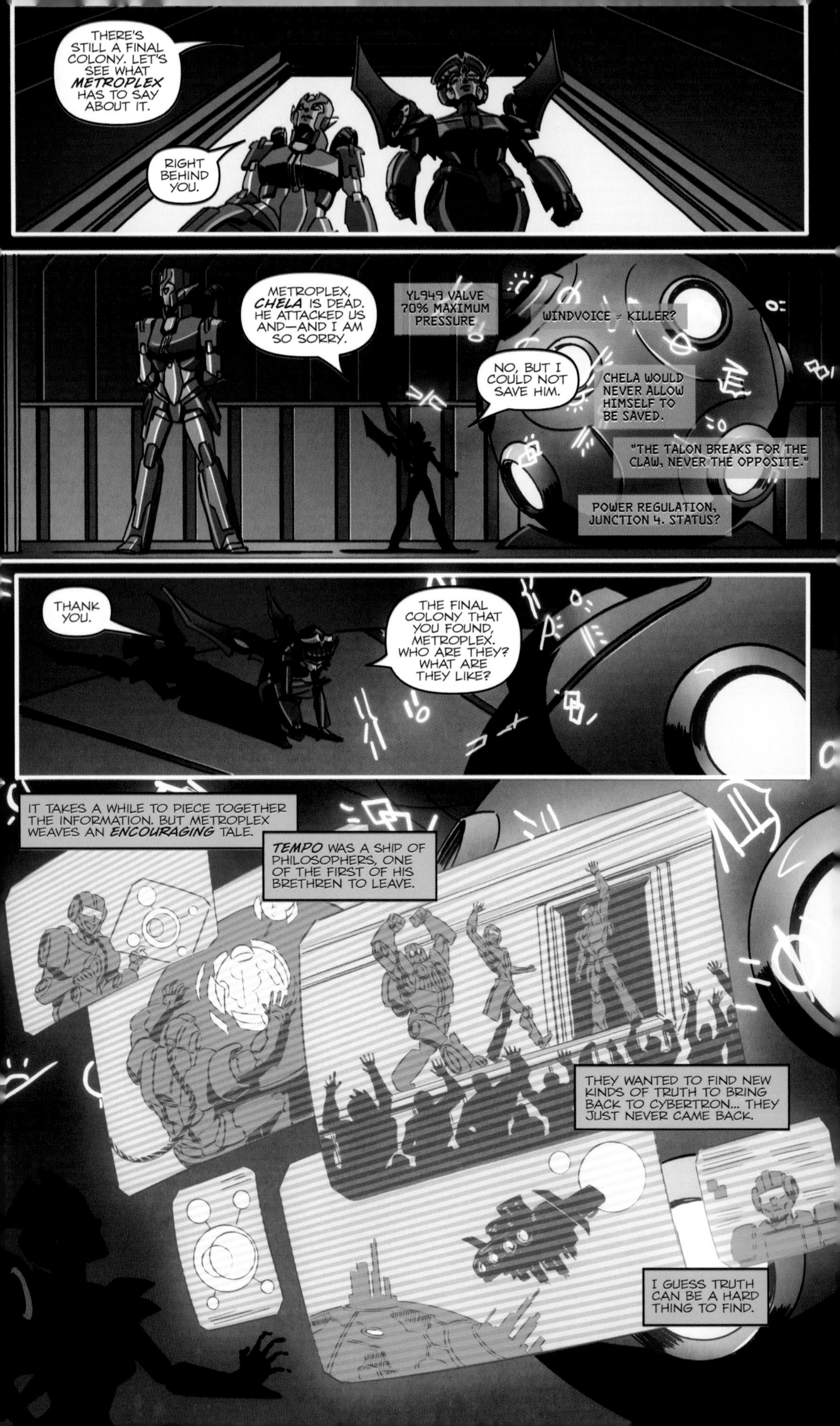
THERE'S STILL A FINAL COLONY. LET'S SEE WHAT METROPLEX HAS TO SAY ABOUT IT.
RIGHT BEHIND YOU.
METROPLEX, CHELA IS DEAD. HE ATTACKED US AND—AND I AM SO SORRY.
YL949 VALVE 70% MAXIMUM PRESSURE
WINDVOICE ≠ KILLER?
NO, BUT I COULD NOT SAVE HIM.
CHELA WOULD NEVER ALLOW HIMSELF TO BE SAVED.
"THE TALON BREAKS FOR THE CLAW, NEVER THE OPPOSITE."
POWER REGULATION, JUNCTION 4. STATUS?
THANK YOU.
THE FINAL COLONY THAT YOU FOUND, METROPLEX. WHO ARE THEY? WHAT ARE THEY LIKE?
IT TAKES A WHILE TO PIECE TOGETHER THE INFORMATION. BUT METROPLEX WEAVES AN ENCOURAGING TALE.
TEMPO WAS A SHIP OF PHILOSOPHERS, ONE OF THE FIRST OF HIS BRETHREN TO LEAVE.
THEY WANTED TO FIND NEW KINDS OF TRUTH TO BRING BACK TO CYBERTRON... THEY JUST NEVER CAME BACK.
I GUESS TRUTH CAN BE A HARD THING TO FIND.

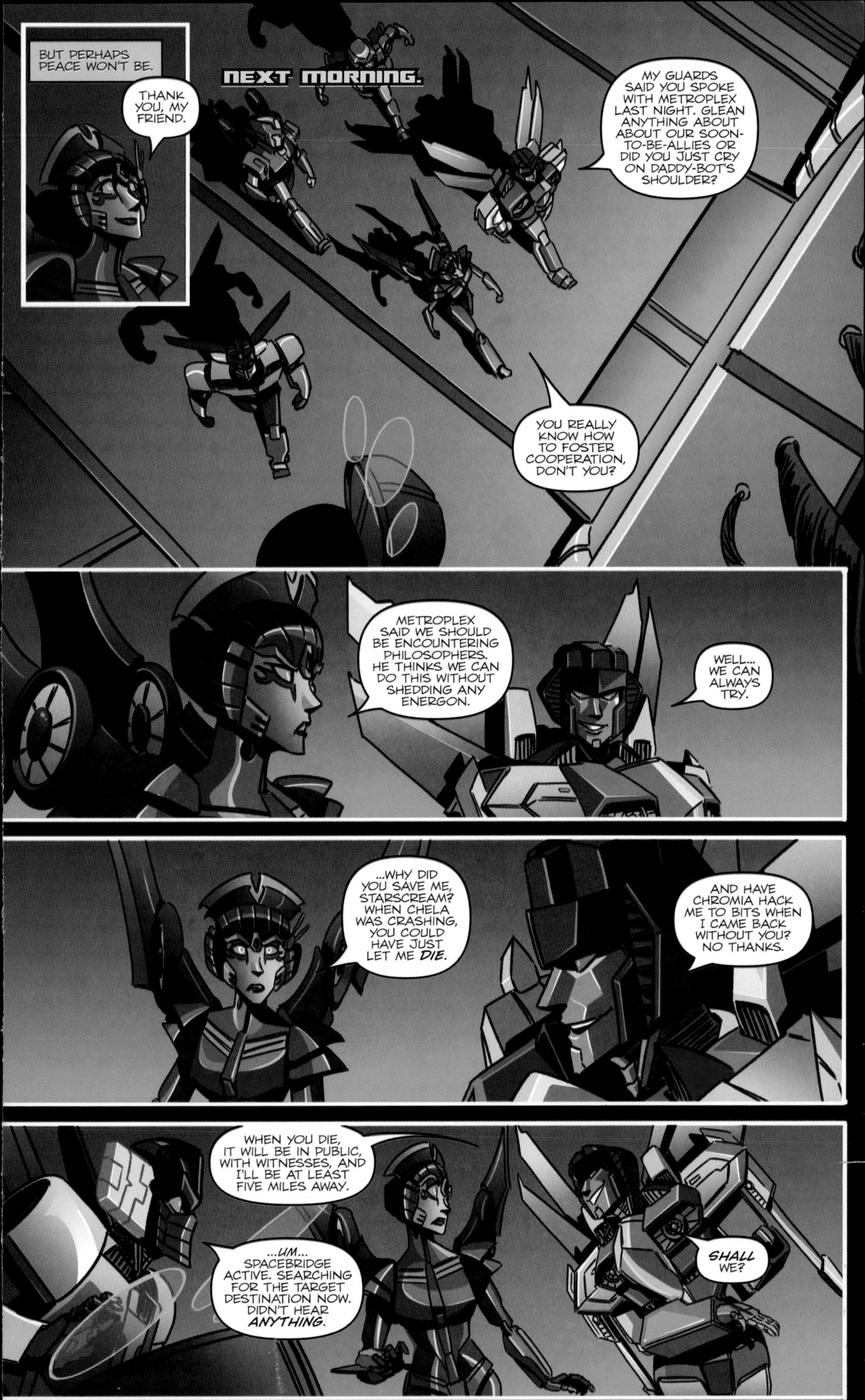
BUT PERHAPS PEACE WON'T BE.
THANK YOU, MY FRIEND.
NEXT MORNING.
MY GUARDS SAID YOU SPOKE WITH METROPLEX LAST NIGHT. GLEAN ANYTHING ABOUT ABOUT OUR SOON-TO-BE-ALLIES OR DID YOU JUST CRY ON DADDY-BOT'S SHOULDER?
YOU REALLY KNOW HOW TO FOSTER COOPERATION, DON'T YOU?
METROPLEX SAID WE SHOULD BE ENCOUNTERING PHILOSOPHERS. HE THINKS WE CAN DO THIS WITHOUT SHEDDING ANY ENERGON.
WELL... WE CAN ALWAYS TRY.
...WHY DID YOU SAVE ME, STARSCREAM? WHEN CHELA WAS CRASHING, YOU COULD HAVE JUST LET ME *DIE*.
AND HAVE CHROMIA HACK ME TO BITS WHEN I CAME BACK WITHOUT YOU? NO THANKS.
WHEN YOU DIE, IT WILL BE IN PUBLIC, WITH WITNESSES, AND I'LL BE AT LEAST FIVE MILES AWAY.
SHALL WE?
...*UM*... SPACEBRIDGE ACTIVE. SEARCHING FOR THE TARGET DESTINATION NOW. DIDN'T HEAR ***ANYTHING***.

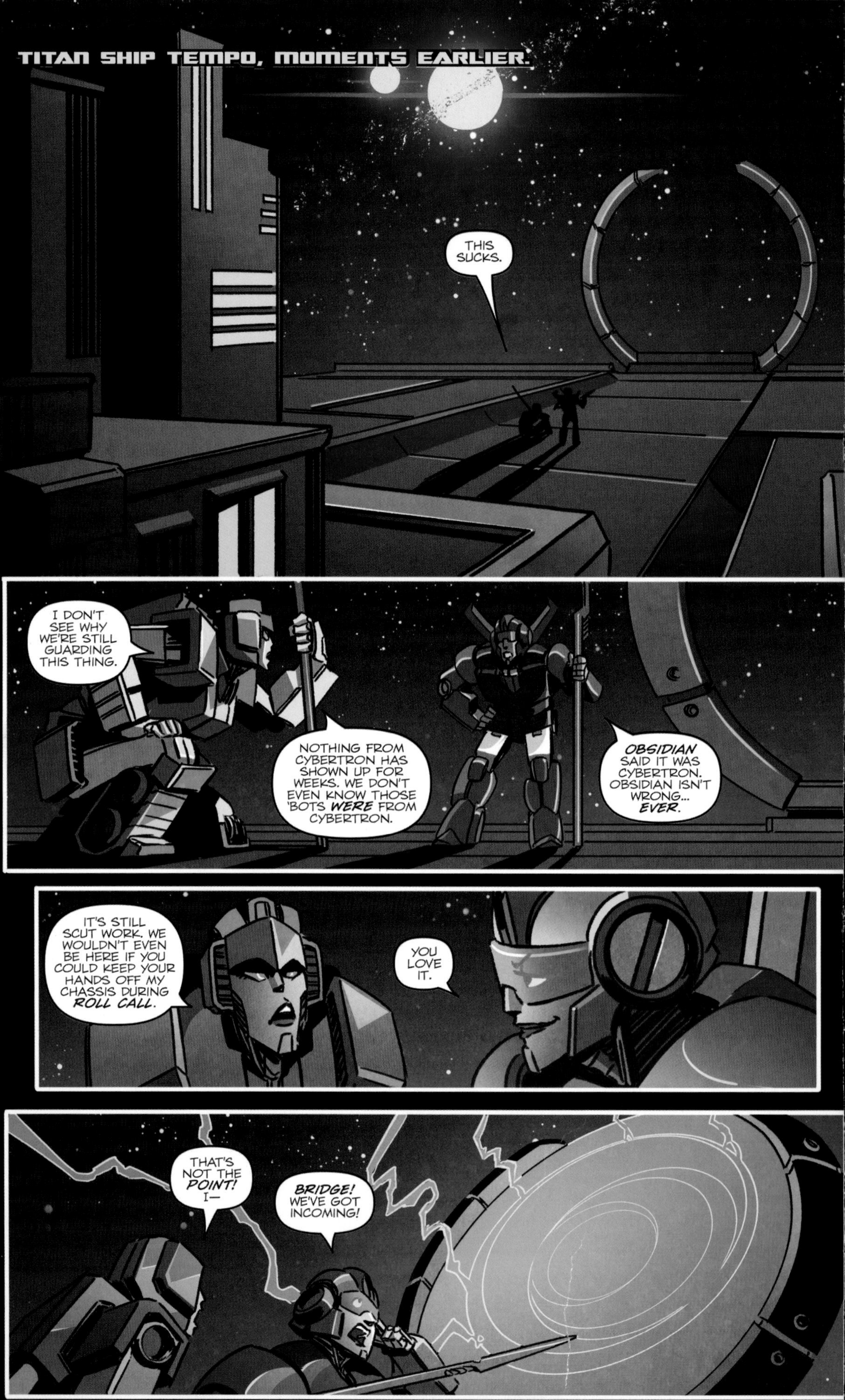
TITAN SHIP TEMPO, MOMENTS EARLIER.
THIS SUCKS.
I DON'T SEE WHY WE'RE STILL GUARDING THIS THING.
NOTHING FROM CYBERTRON HAS SHOWN UP FOR WEEKS. WE DON'T EVEN KNOW THOSE 'BOTS WERE FROM CYBERTRON.
OBSIDIAN SAID IT WAS CYBERTRON. OBSIDIAN ISN'T WRONG... EVER.
IT'S STILL SCUT WORK. WE WOULDN'T EVEN BE HERE IF YOU COULD KEEP YOUR HANDS OFF MY CHASSIS DURING ROLL CALL.
YOU LOVE IT.
THAT'S NOT THE POINT! I—
BRIDGE! WE'VE GOT INCOMING!

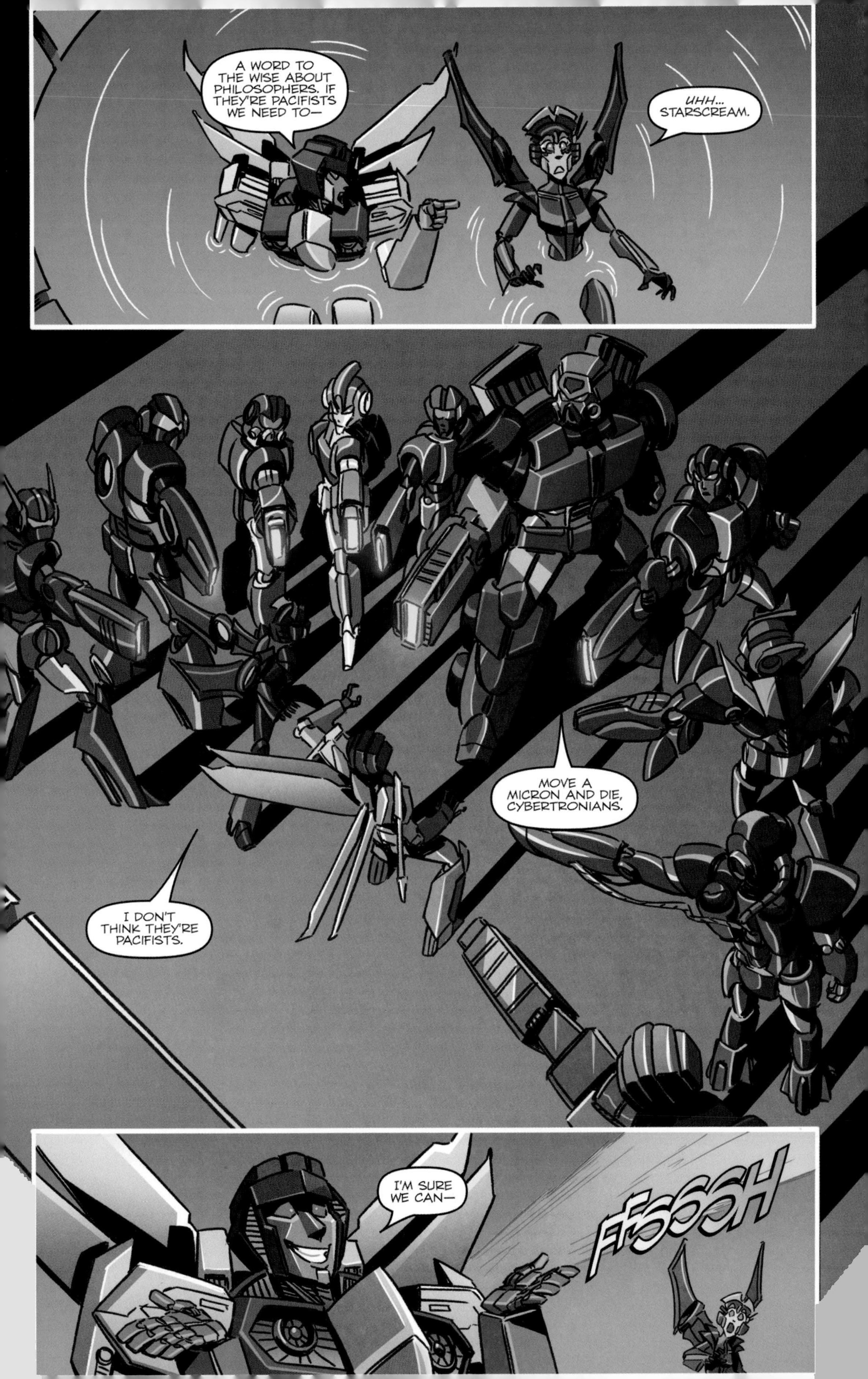
A WORD TO THE WISE ABOUT PHILOSOPHERS. IF THEY'RE PACIFISTS WE NEED TO—
UHH... STARSCREAM.
MOVE A MICRON AND DIE, CYBERTRONIANS.
I DON'T THINK THEY'RE PACIFISTS.
I'M SURE WE CAN—
FFSSSH

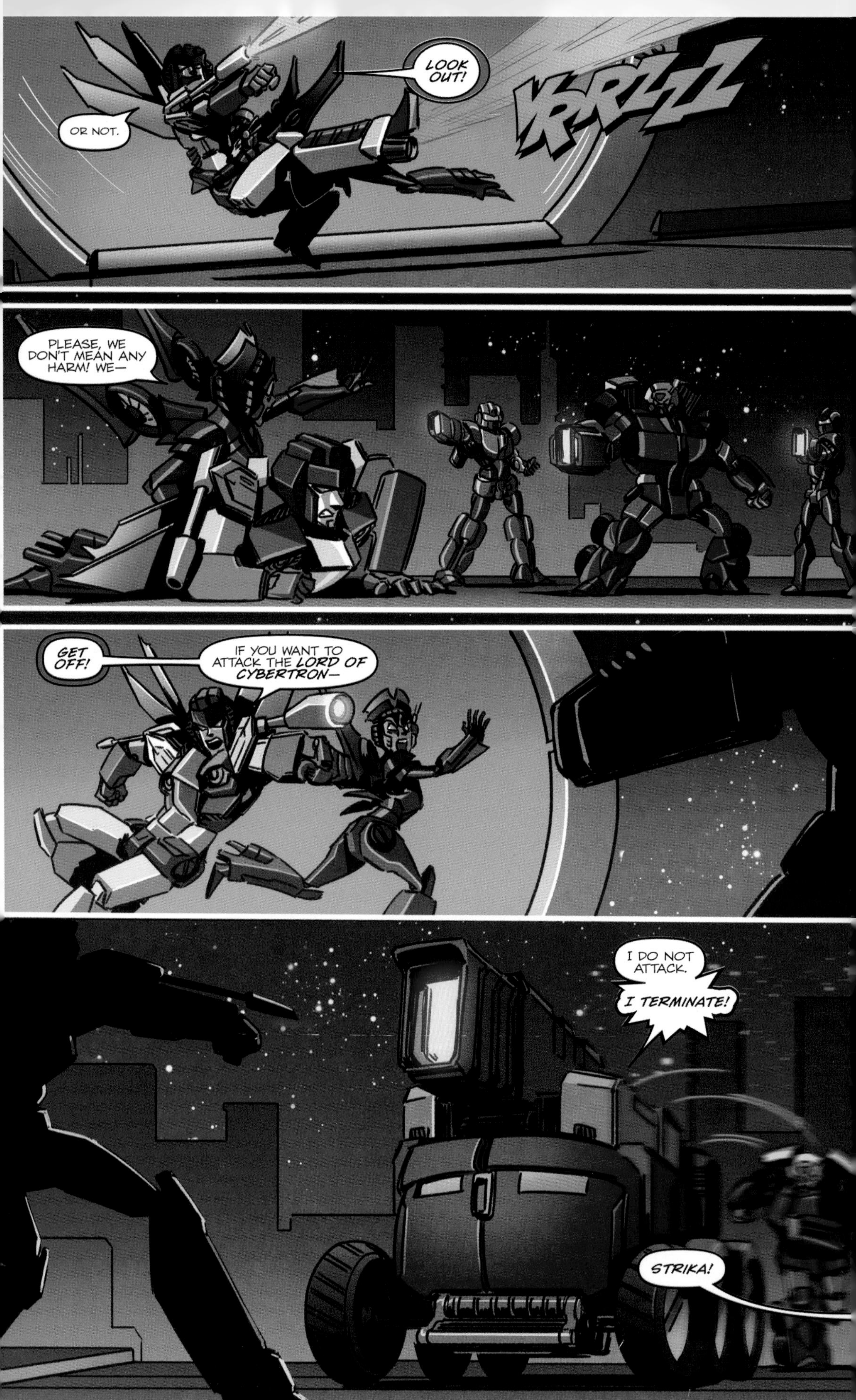
OR NOT.
LOOK OUT!
VRRZZZ
PLEASE, WE DON'T MEAN ANY HARM! WE—
GET OFF!
IF YOU WANT TO ATTACK THE LORD OF CYBERTRON—
I DO NOT ATTACK.
I TERMINATE!
STRIKA!

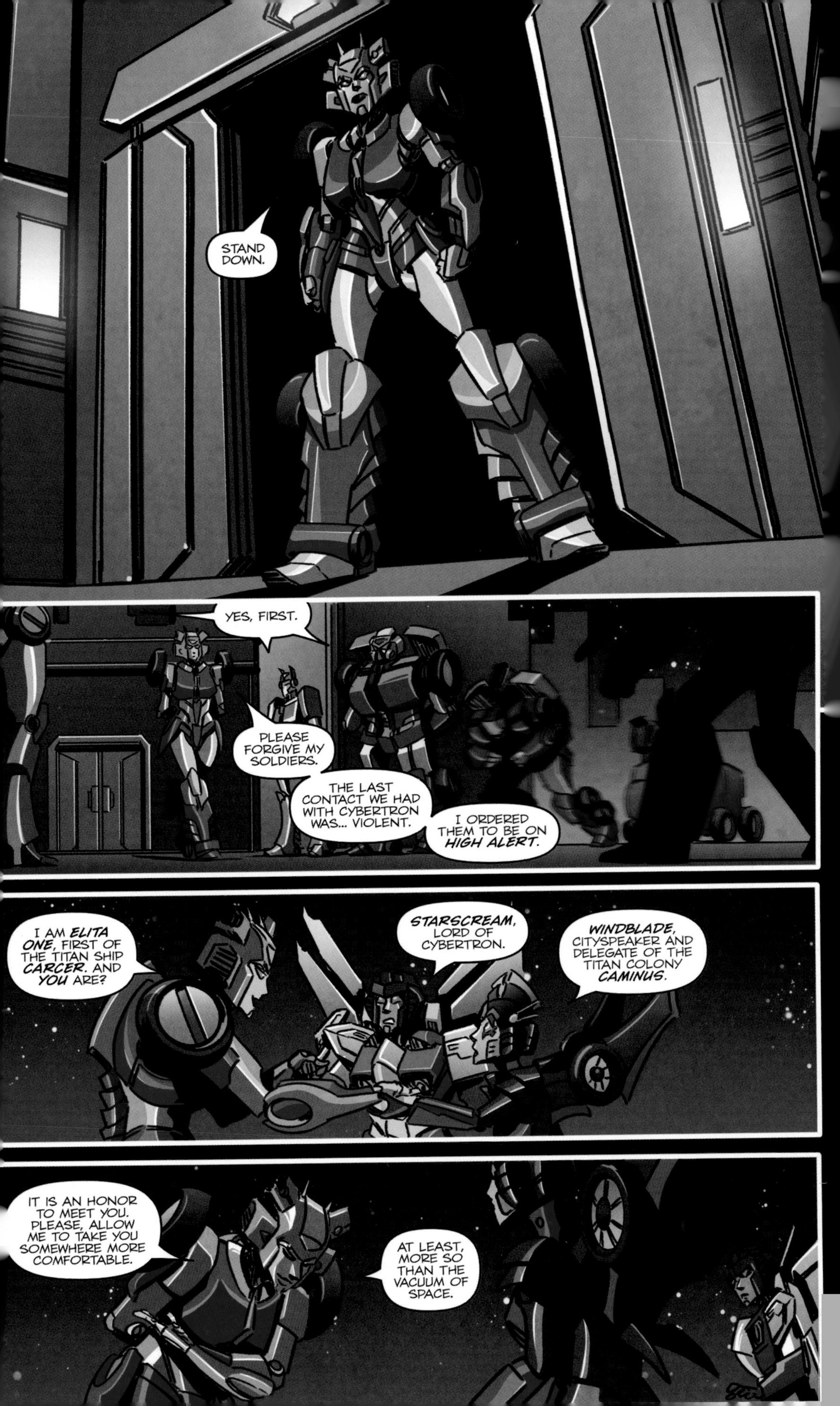

STAND DOWN.
YES, FIRST.
PLEASE FORGIVE MY SOLDIERS.
THE LAST CONTACT WE HAD WITH CYBERTRON WAS... VIOLENT.
I ORDERED THEM TO BE ON HIGH ALERT.
I AM ELITA ONE, FIRST OF THE TITAN SHIP CARCER. AND YOU ARE?
STARSCREAM, LORD OF CYBERTRON.
WINDBLADE, CITYSPEAKER AND DELEGATE OF THE TITAN COLONY CAMINUS.
IT IS AN HONOR TO MEET YOU. PLEASE, ALLOW ME TO TAKE YOU SOMEWHERE MORE COMFORTABLE.
AT LEAST, MORE SO THAN THE VACUUM OF SPACE.

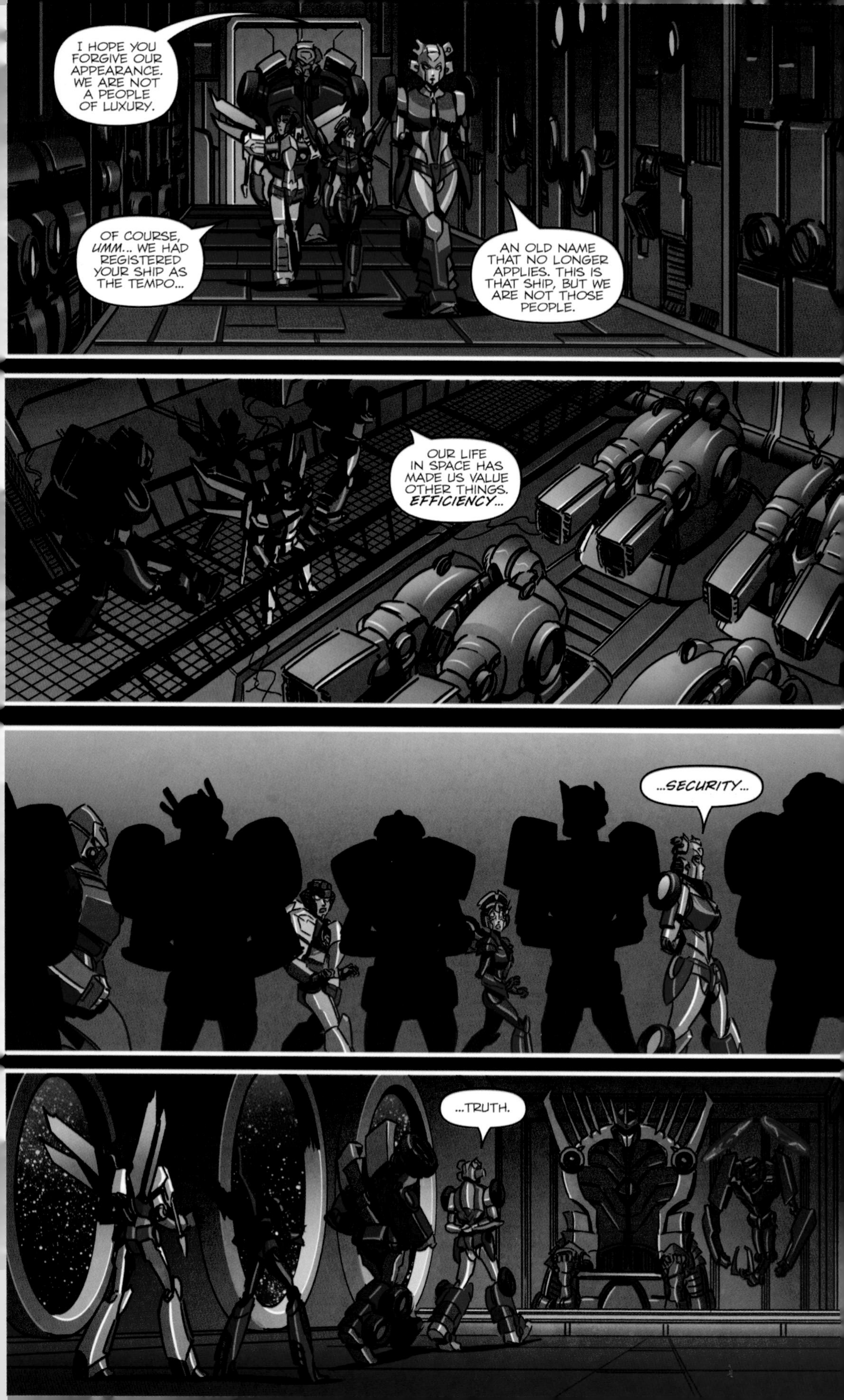

I HOPE YOU FORGIVE OUR APPEARANCE. WE ARE NOT A PEOPLE OF LUXURY.
OF COURSE, UMM... WE HAD REGISTERED YOUR SHIP AS THE TEMPO...
AN OLD NAME THAT NO LONGER APPLIES. THIS IS THAT SHIP, BUT WE ARE NOT THOSE PEOPLE.
OUR LIFE IN SPACE HAS MADE US VALUE OTHER THINGS. EFFICIENCY...
...SECURITY...
...TRUTH.

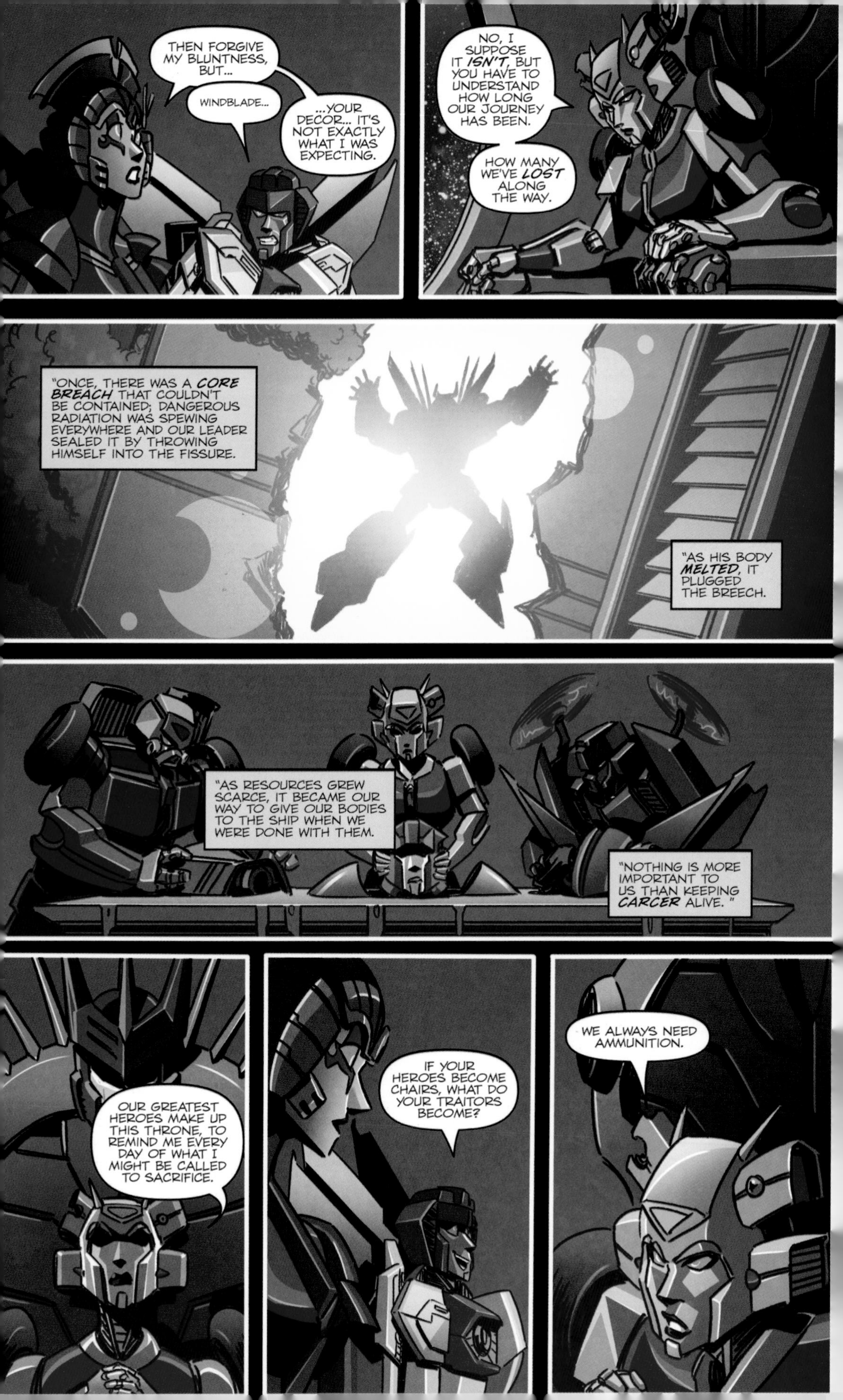

THEN FORGIVE MY BLUNTNESS, BUT...
WINDBLADE...
...YOUR DECOR... IT'S NOT EXACTLY WHAT I WAS EXPECTING.
NO, I SUPPOSE IT *ISN'T*, BUT YOU HAVE TO UNDERSTAND HOW LONG OUR JOURNEY HAS BEEN.
HOW MANY WE'VE *LOST* ALONG THE WAY.
"ONCE, THERE WAS A *CORE BREACH* THAT COULDN'T BE CONTAINED; DANGEROUS RADIATION WAS SPEWING EVERYWHERE AND OUR LEADER SEALED IT BY THROWING HIMSELF INTO THE FISSURE.
"AS HIS BODY *MELTED*, IT PLUGGED THE BREECH.
"AS RESOURCES GREW SCARCE, IT BECAME OUR WAY TO GIVE OUR BODIES TO THE SHIP WHEN WE WERE DONE WITH THEM.
"NOTHING IS MORE IMPORTANT TO US THAN KEEPING *CARCER* ALIVE."
OUR GREATEST HEROES MAKE UP THIS THRONE, TO REMIND ME EVERY DAY OF WHAT I MIGHT BE CALLED TO SACRIFICE.
IF YOUR HEROES BECOME CHAIRS, WHAT DO YOUR TRAITORS BECOME?
WE ALWAYS NEED AMMUNITION.

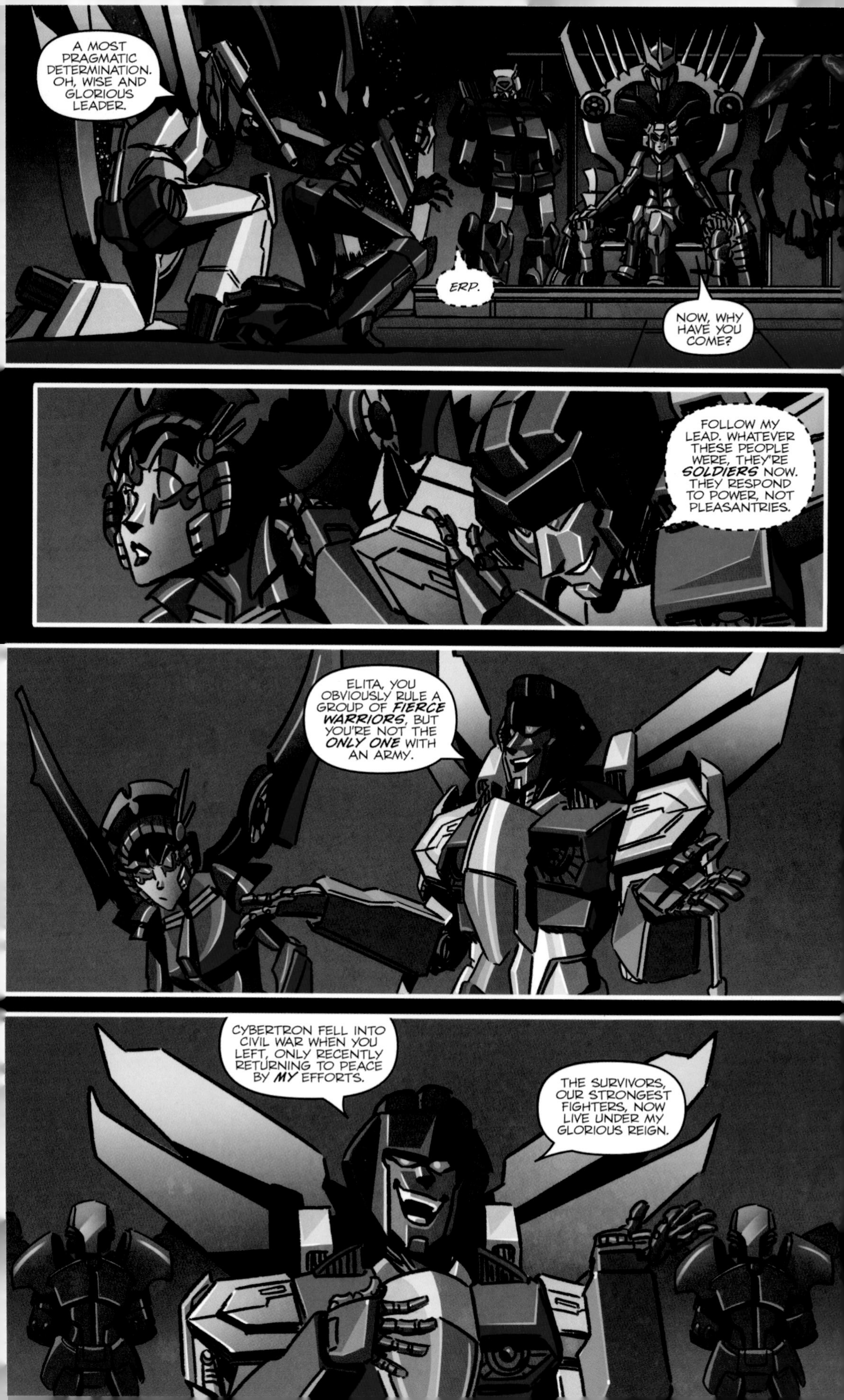
A MOST PRAGMATIC DETERMINATION. OH, WISE AND GLORIOUS LEADER.
ERP.
NOW, WHY HAVE YOU COME?
FOLLOW MY LEAD. WHATEVER THESE PEOPLE WERE, THEY'RE SOLDIERS NOW. THEY RESPOND TO POWER, NOT PLEASANTRIES.
ELITA, YOU OBVIOUSLY RULE A GROUP OF FIERCE WARRIORS, BUT YOU'RE NOT THE ONLY ONE WITH AN ARMY.
CYBERTRON FELL INTO CIVIL WAR WHEN YOU LEFT, ONLY RECENTLY RETURNING TO PEACE BY MY EFFORTS.
THE SURVIVORS, OUR STRONGEST FIGHTERS, NOW LIVE UNDER MY GLORIOUS REIGN.

WE HAVE VAST TRACKS OF OPEN TERRITORY, RESOURCES JUST WAITING TO BE CLAIMED.

AND OTHER COLONIES, LIKE DELEGATE WINDBLADE'S HOME, ARE CLAMORING TO EXPLOIT THEM.

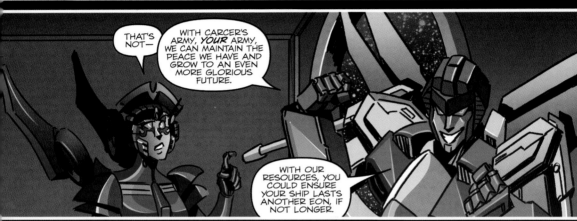

THAT'S NOT—

WITH CARCER'S ARMY, *YOUR* ARMY, WE CAN MAINTAIN THE PEACE WE HAVE AND GROW TO AN EVEN MORE GLORIOUS FUTURE.

WITH OUR RESOURCES, YOU COULD ENSURE YOUR SHIP LASTS ANOTHER EON, IF NOT LONGER.

CYBERTRON IS FORMING A *COUNCIL OF WORLDS* AND WE WOULD LIKE YOU TO BE PART OF IT.

IF THAT'S WHAT YOU WANT.

A PEACEFUL WORLD OFFERING US SAFE HAVEN.

WHAT DO YOU THINK, OBSIDIAN?

I THINK HE IS *LYING*, FIRST.

AS DO I.

STRIKA! SEIZE HIM!

WHAT?! YOU CAN'T—!

YOU CLAIM YOU HAVE A GREAT ARMY AND MAYBE THAT'S TRUE, BUT THIS "PEACE" YOU TALK OF CERTAINLY ISN'T.

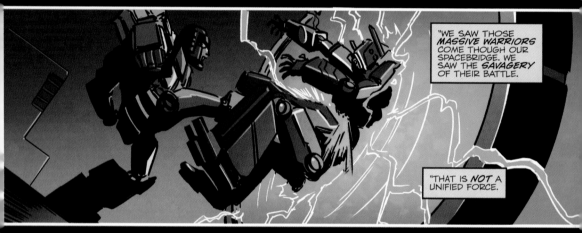

"WE SAW THOSE *MASSIVE WARRIORS* COME THOUGH OUR SPACEBRIDGE. WE SAW THE *SAVAGERY* OF THEIR BATTLE.

"THAT IS *NOT* A UNIFIED FORCE.

"AND IN ALL THE WORLDS I'VE VISITED, I'VE NOT *ONCE* SEEN A RESOURCE-RICH PLANET ASK FOR OTHERS TO EXPLOIT IT. THEY LOOK FOR LABORERS TO *ENSLAVE* TO IT."

WE MAY BE WEARY, BUT WE ARE NOT *STUPID.*

I TOLD YOU WE VALUED TRUTH IN ALL THINGS AND YOU HAVE LIED TO ME, *LORD* STARSCREAM.

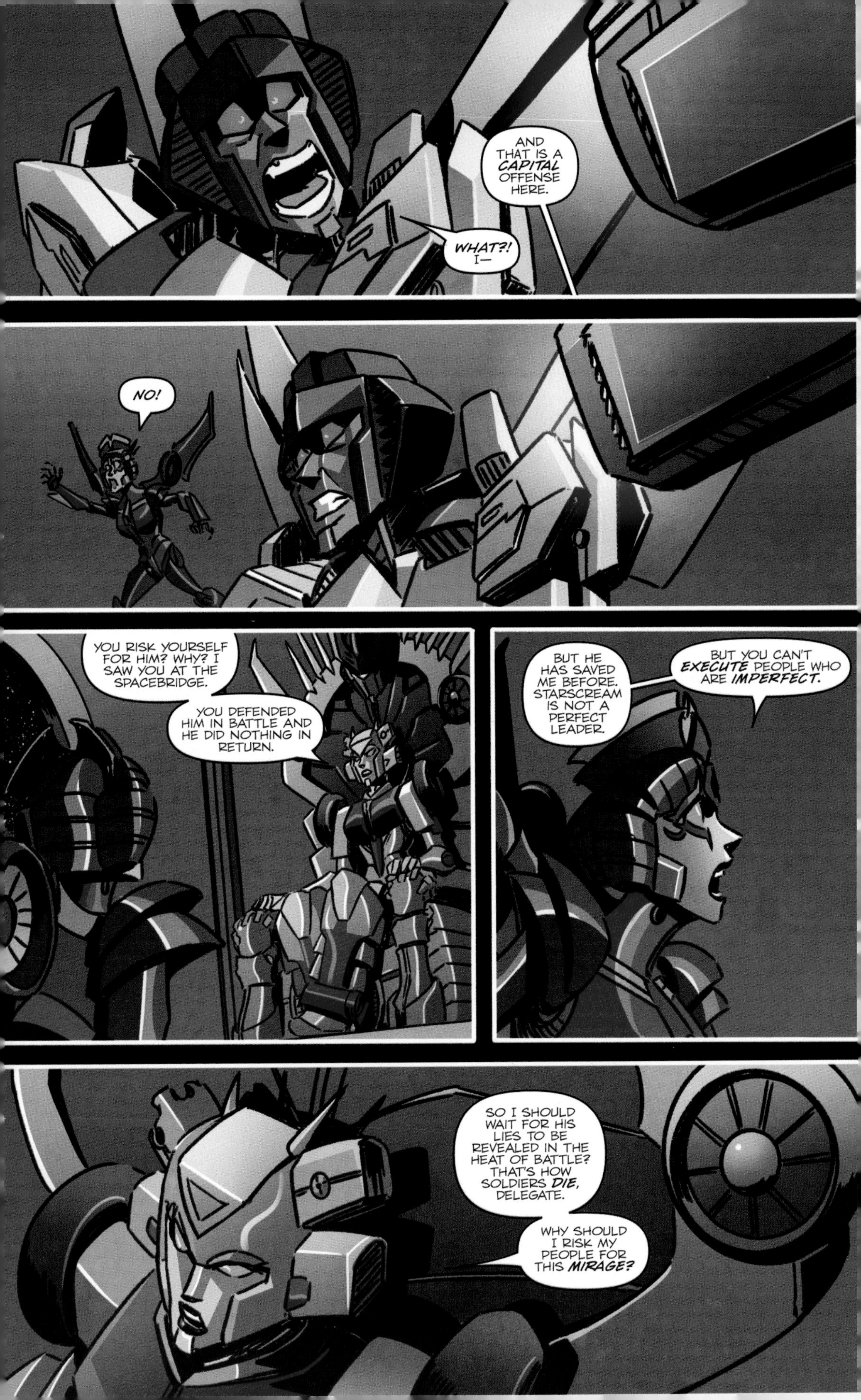
AND THAT IS A CAPITAL OFFENSE HERE.
WHAT?! I—
NO!
YOU RISK YOURSELF FOR HIM? WHY? I SAW YOU AT THE SPACEBRIDGE.
YOU DEFENDED HIM IN BATTLE AND HE DID NOTHING IN RETURN.
BUT HE HAS SAVED ME BEFORE. STARSCREAM IS NOT A PERFECT LEADER.
BUT YOU CAN'T EXECUTE PEOPLE WHO ARE IMPERFECT.
SO I SHOULD WAIT FOR HIS LIES TO BE REVEALED IN THE HEAT OF BATTLE? THAT'S HOW SOLDIERS DIE, DELEGATE.
WHY SHOULD I RISK MY PEOPLE FOR THIS MIRAGE?

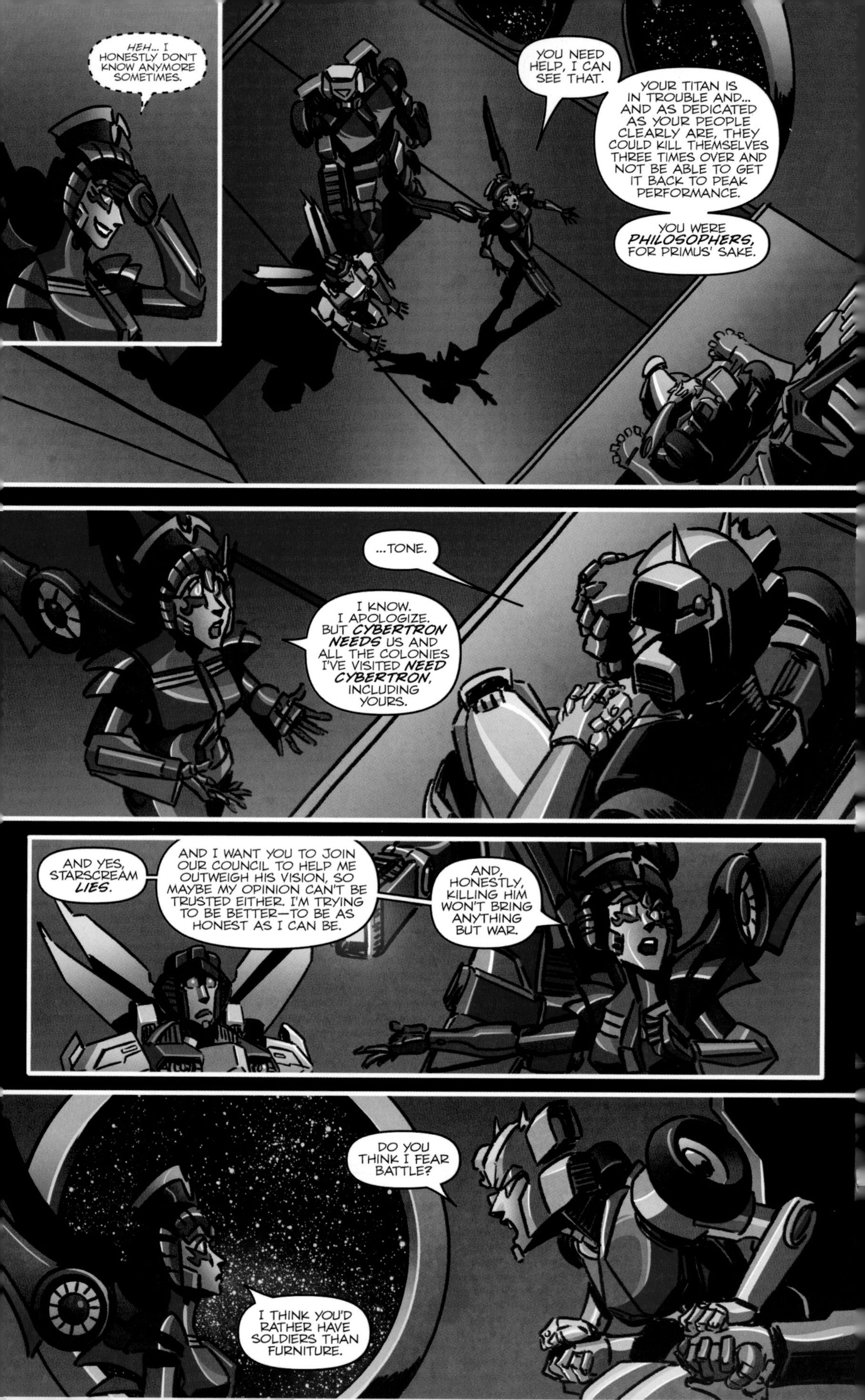
HEH... I HONESTLY DON'T KNOW ANYMORE SOMETIMES.
YOU NEED HELP, I CAN SEE THAT.
YOUR TITAN IS IN TROUBLE AND... AND AS DEDICATED AS YOUR PEOPLE CLEARLY ARE, THEY COULD KILL THEMSELVES THREE TIMES OVER AND NOT BE ABLE TO GET IT BACK TO PEAK PERFORMANCE.
YOU WERE PHILOSOPHERS, FOR PRIMUS' SAKE.
...TONE.
I KNOW. I APOLOGIZE. BUT CYBERTRON NEEDS US AND ALL THE COLONIES I'VE VISITED NEED CYBERTRON, INCLUDING YOURS.
AND YES, STARSCREAM LIES.
AND I WANT YOU TO JOIN OUR COUNCIL TO HELP ME OUTWEIGH HIS VISION, SO MAYBE MY OPINION CAN'T BE TRUSTED EITHER. I'M TRYING TO BE BETTER—TO BE AS HONEST AS I CAN BE.
AND, HONESTLY, KILLING HIM WON'T BRING ANYTHING BUT WAR.
DO YOU THINK I FEAR BATTLE?
I THINK YOU'D RATHER HAVE SOLDIERS THAN FURNITURE.

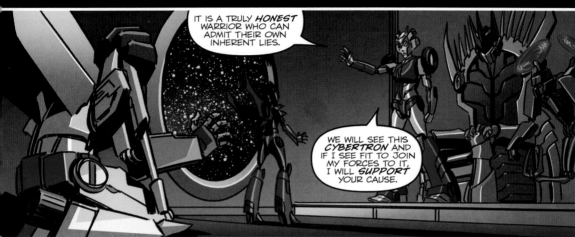

IT IS A TRULY *HONEST* WARRIOR WHO CAN ADMIT THEIR OWN INHERENT LIES.

WE WILL SEE THIS *CYBERTRON* AND IF I SEE FIT TO JOIN MY FORCES TO IT, I WILL *SUPPORT* YOUR CAUSE.

JUST BECAUSE WE DO NOT LIE DOES NOT MEAN WE ARE FREE OF... *RIVALRIES,* EITHER.

WE HAVE A SAYING HERE, STARSCREAM. *BETTER DEATH THAN LIES.*

DEATH YOU CAN SEE COMING; LIES WILL ALWAYS SURPRISE YOU.

LIE TO ME AGAIN, ON MY SHIP, AND I WILL *KILL* YOU.

RELEASE HIM.

LEAVE US. OUR REPRESENTATIVE WILL BE READY IN 48 CYBERTRONIAN HOURS.

YOU WILL RETURN FOR THEM THEN.

YOU WILL *NOT* RETURN SOONER.

...YOU COULD'VE LET ME DIE.

WHEN YOU DIE, IT'LL BE FOR SOMETHING YOU DESERVE AND ALL OF CYBERTRON WILL KNOW IT.

KEEP WALKING.

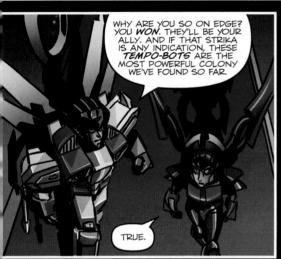

WHY ARE YOU SO ON EDGE? YOU *WON*. THEY'LL BE YOUR ALLY. AND IF THAT STRIKA IS ANY INDICATION, THESE *TEMPO-BOTS* ARE THE MOST POWERFUL COLONY WE'VE FOUND SO FAR.

TRUE.

BUT I DON'T TELL HIM WHAT I REMEMBER.

I DON'T TELL HIM WHAT METROPLEX REMEMBERED.

CARCER ISN'T A NICKNAME FOR THE TITAN TEMPO.

CARCER WAS THE NAME OF A COMPLETELY *DIFFERENT* TITAN.

ELITA MAY BE TELLING US THE TRUTH, BUT SHE'S NOT TELLING US *ALL* OF IT.

NOT YET.

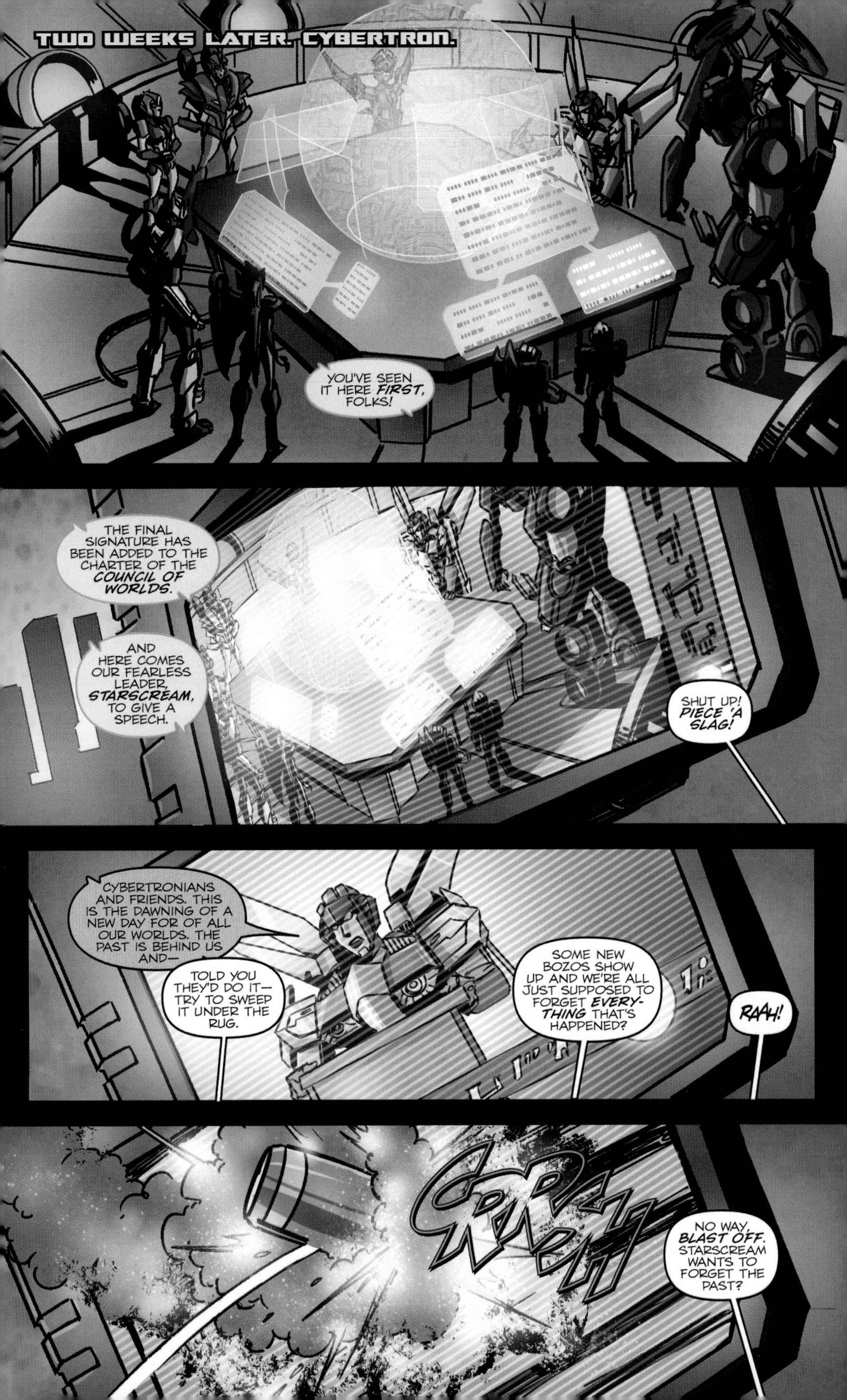
TWO WEEKS LATER. CYBERTRON.
YOU'VE SEEN IT HERE *FIRST*, FOLKS!
THE FINAL SIGNATURE HAS BEEN ADDED TO THE CHARTER OF THE *COUNCIL OF WORLDS*.
AND HERE COMES OUR FEARLESS LEADER, *STARSCREAM*, TO GIVE A SPEECH.
SHUT UP! *PIECE 'A SLAG!*
CYBERTRONIANS AND FRIENDS. THIS IS THE DAWNING OF A NEW DAY FOR OF ALL OUR WORLDS. THE PAST IS BEHIND US AND—
TOLD YOU THEY'D DO IT—TRY TO SWEEP IT UNDER THE RUG.
SOME NEW BOZOS SHOW UP AND WE'RE ALL JUST SUPPOSED TO FORGET *EVERY-THING* THAT'S HAPPENED?
RAAH!
CRASH
NO WAY, *BLAST OFF*. STARSCREAM WANTS TO FORGET THE PAST?

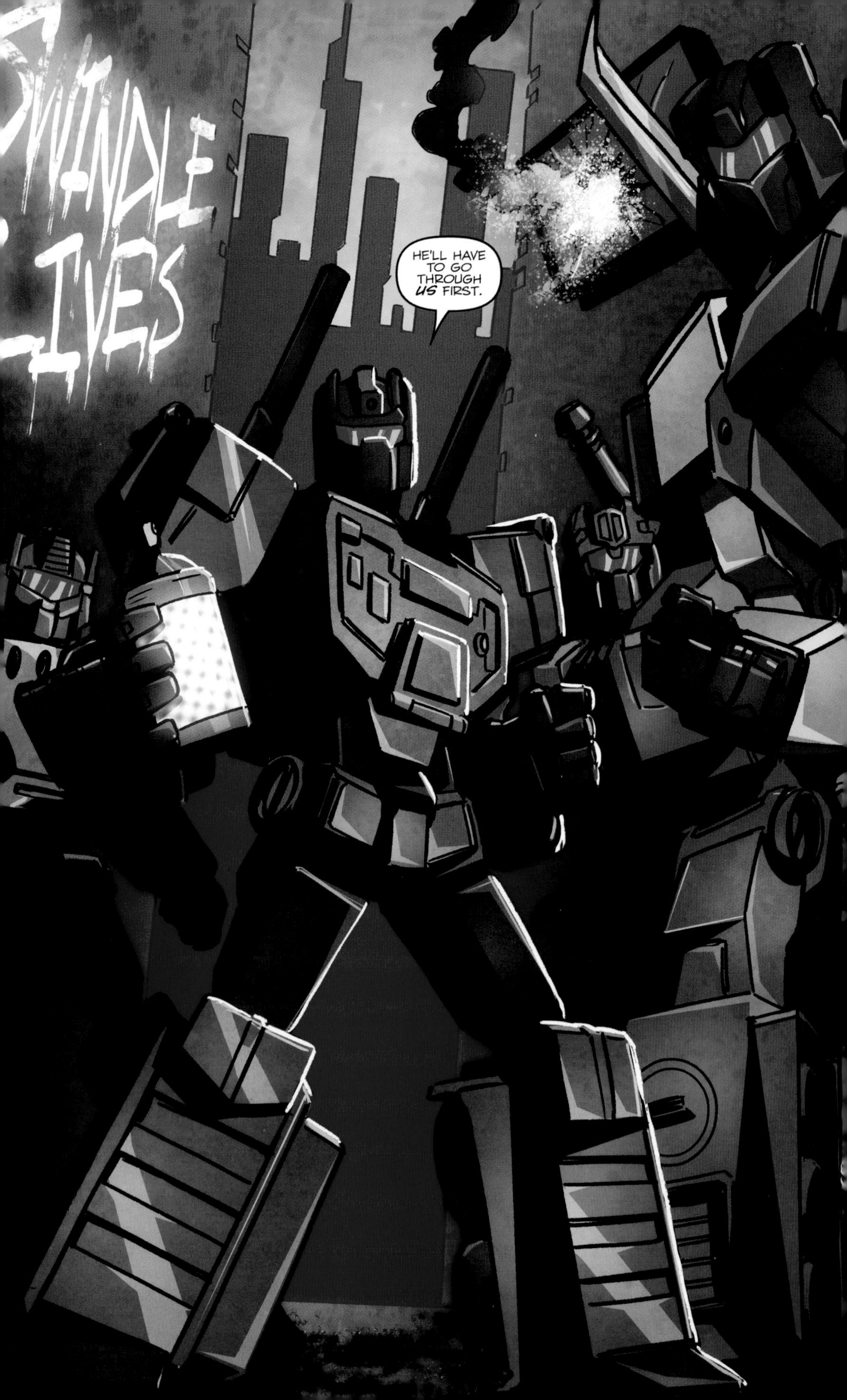
HE'LL HAVE TO GO THROUGH *US* FIRST.

ART BY **CASEY W. COLLER**
COLORS BY **JOANA LAFUENTE**

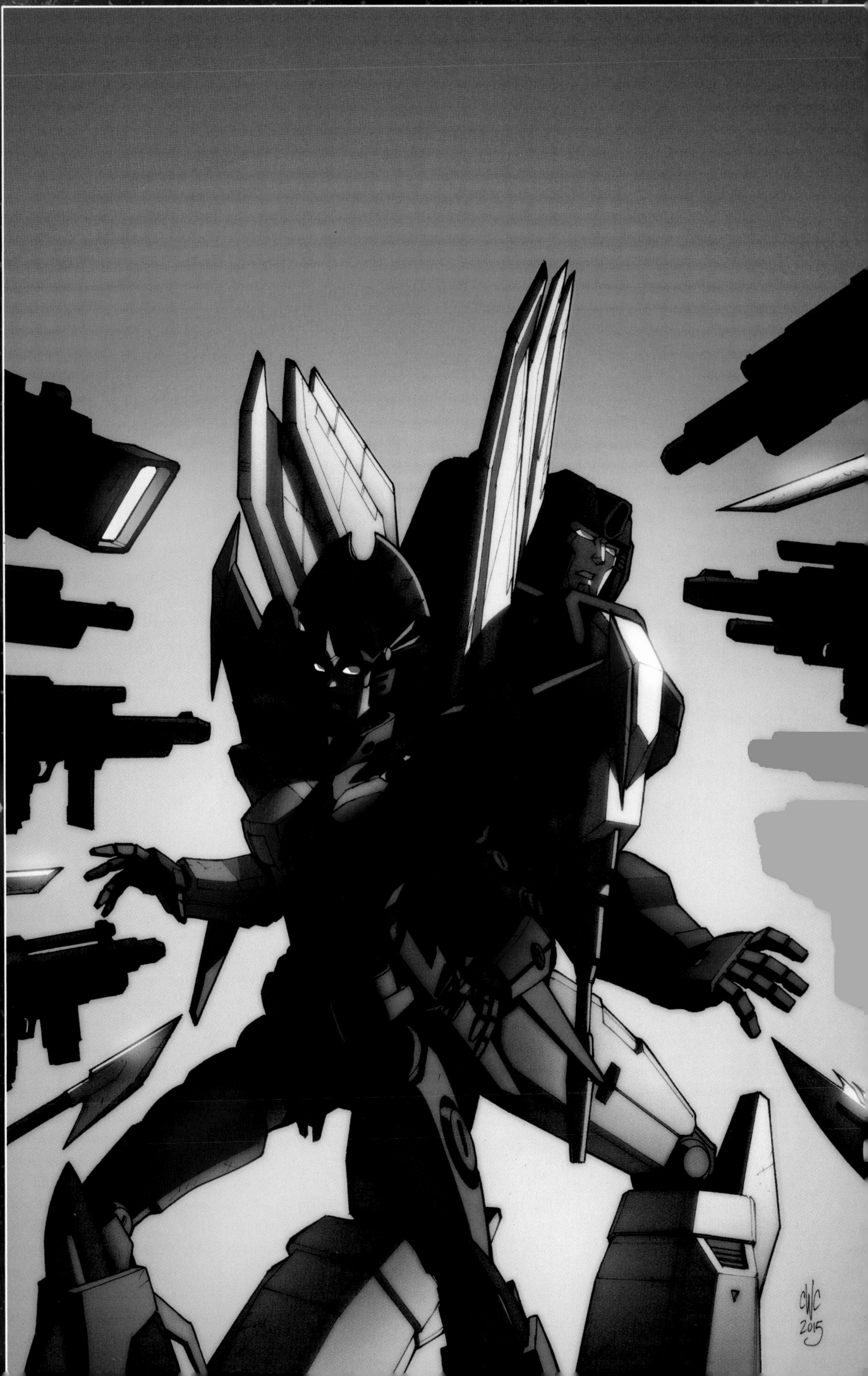
CWC
2015

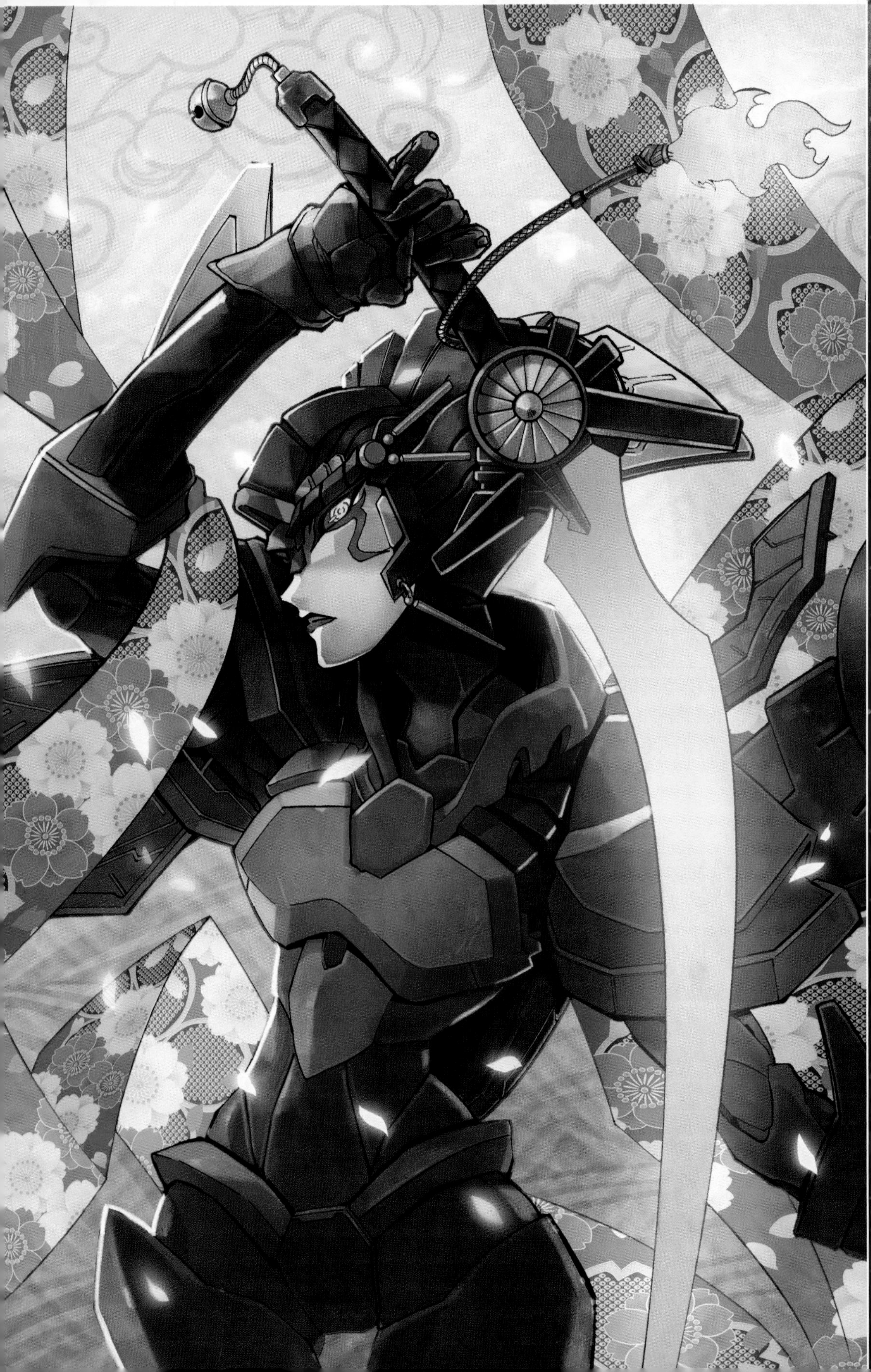

ART BY KEI ZAMA
COLORS BY JOSH BURCHAM

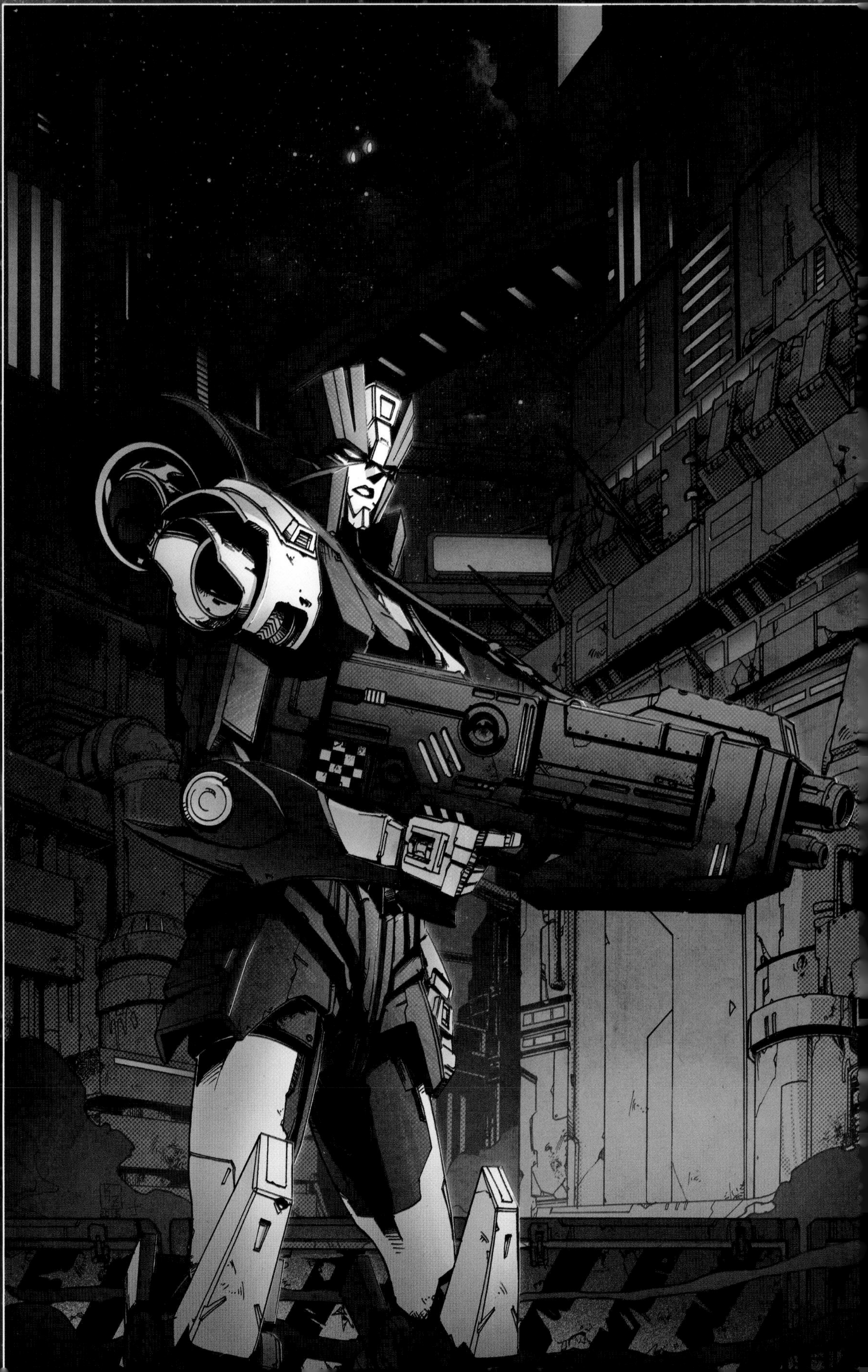

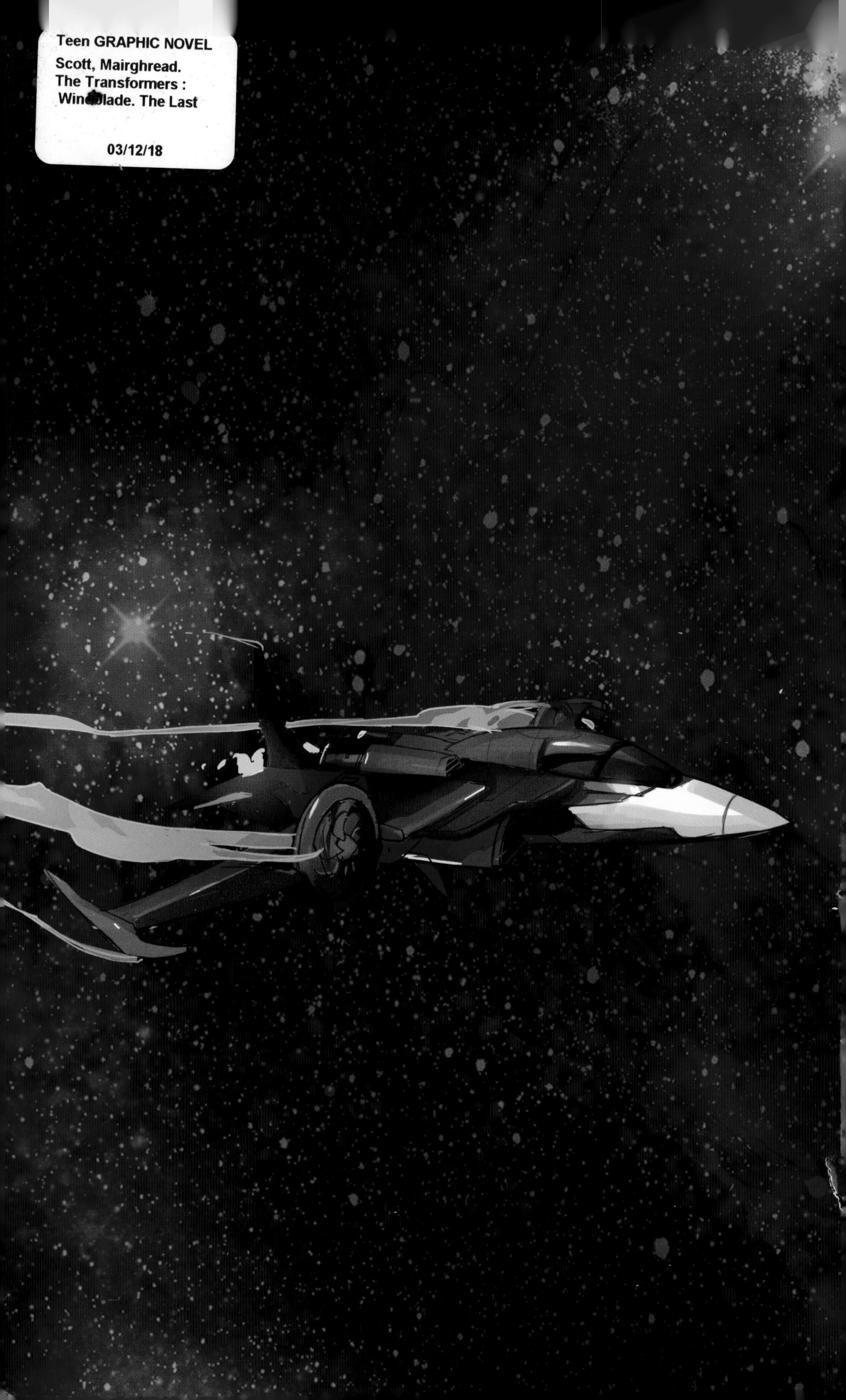